CROSSING THE FLOOR

CROSSING THE FLOOR

The Story of Tariana Turia

HELEN LEAHY

First published in 2015 by Huia Publishers
39 Pipitea Street, PO Box 12280
Wellington, Aotearoa New Zealand
www.huia.co.nz

ISBN 978-1-77550-163-3

Copyright © Helen Leahy 2015

Cover image: Courtesy of Woolf Photography

This book is copyright. Apart from fair dealing for the purpose of private study, research, criticism or review, as permitted under the Copyright Act, no part may be reproduced by any process without the prior permission of the publisher.

Printed in China by Everbest Printing Co Ltd

A catalogue record for this book is available from the National Library of New Zealand.

The assistance of the Māori Purposes Fund Board is gratefully acknowledged.

Cowardice asks the question, 'Is it safe?'

Expediency asks the question, 'Is it politic?'

And Vanity comes along and asks the question, 'Is it popular?'

But Conscience asks the question, 'Is it right?'

And there comes a time when one must take a position that is neither safe, nor politic, nor popular; but he must do it because Conscience tells him that it is right.

REV. DR MARTIN LUTHER KING
'THE OTHER AMERICA'
GROSSE POINT HIGH SCHOOL
14 MARCH 1968

CONTENTS

Foreword	ix
One Foot on the Water, One Foot on the Land	1
Whakapapa: The Binding Strands of Uru	15
Whānau: The Early Years	23
Aunty Wai	39
Together with George	55
Children – The Footsteps to our Future	73
Rebuilding Rangitāhuahua	89
A Refuge: The Te Awa Youth Trust	109
The Path to Self-determination	121
Te Oranganui – Taking Control of Our Health	147
Pākaitore: Taking a Stand	165
Walking Sovereign	195
The Pathway to Parliament	203

The Realities of Parliament	225
Institutional Racism	253
Māori Priorities in Policy	267
Nation-building and Local Solutions	299
The Foreshore and Seabed Debate	307
The Emergence of the Māori Party	343
Building the Māori Party	375
Last Cab off the Rank: 2005–2008	397
Revolution Depends on What is Done: 2008–2014	417
The Personal is Political	439
Moving Forward	453
A Mother's Legacy	493
Last Words	499
The Still Small Voice of Courage: The Honourable Dame	521
The Author's Story	539
References	545
Index	563

FOREWORD

Ko te pae tawhiti, whāia kia tata

Ko te pae tata, whakamaua, kia tina

Few people are able to deal with pressing problems in the present, and at the same time build platforms that will be relevant to the future. Tariana Turia has shown how both are possible. Well before entering Parliament she fostered community cohesion and community responsiveness to adversity and disadvantage. She did so in a manner that was to lead strong sustainable leadership within her own whānau, hapū and iwi and that helped generate greater awareness for health and the positive roles communities might play.

Then, as a Minister of the Crown she was able to introduce policies and programmes that focused on building for the future. Importantly, she saw whānau as key vehicles for Māori well-being in the decades ahead. Moreover, she recognised that focusing only on adversity and disadvantage ran the risk of creating an attitude of despair and a perception of incapacity when what was needed was confidence and a determination to succeed.

Whānau Ora will remain synonymous with Minister Turia. The development, implementation and progression of Whānau Ora would not have occurred without her advocacy, diplomacy, and determination. She was able to persuade parliamentary colleagues that change was needed, and was able to offer a model for change that has the potential to influence the whole society. But in addition to Whānau Ora her contribution to social policy across a range of policies has been groundbreaking. Her support for people with disabilities, her concern for children and her efforts to ensure health gains for Māori speak for themselves. Shortly before her retirement from Parliament, as Associate Minister of Health she also launched a refreshed Māori health strategy – Pae Ora – which set out a tripartite approach to health encompassing individuals, whānau and both natural and built environments.

This book recognises the efforts of Tariana Turia to create a society where Māori potential can be realised and where whānau can flourish. Her down-to-earth approach, coupled with her extraordinary ability to relate to all sections of society in ways that are frank and at the same time inspiring, have provided a style of leadership that can serve as a model for future generations.

The nation is indebted to her skill, courage, determination and foresight.

Kia māia

Professor Sir Mason Durie KNZM

-CHAPTER ONE-
ONE FOOT ON THE WATER, ONE FOOT ON THE LAND

We are stroking, caressing the spine
of the land.

We are massaging the ricked
back of the land

with our sore but ever-loving feet:
hell, she loves it!

Squirming, the land wriggles
in delight.

We love her.[1]

It is sometimes said that tangata whenua walk backwards into the future. Nowhere is that more obvious than in the way Tariana Turia has lived her life, her aspirations for a better world driven by her intimate associations to her whenua, her birthright, the very essence of who she is.

Tariana Woon was born to Te Aroha Uru Te Angina in a private maternity hospital in Whanganui on 8 April 1944. Te Aroha (Dorsey) was twenty-six years old, and single; the father was an unnamed American marine. It was not considered right for Tariana to be left with her mother, because she was single. The whānau made a decision, and from that point on, she was theirs.

Tariana is proud of the genealogy she was born into; a whakapapa that she takes every opportunity to connect to others. But she is also shaped by the relationship she has with the land and the river, forces that define her and gave her life. Those connections, relayed to her by the aunts and uncles that she grew up among, gave her an innate security. The features of the natural geography all around her became intrinsic to her sense of self. The place in which she lived gave meaning to her life; Whanganui is her home.

The contribution that Tariana Turia would make to our political history would be forever influenced by the phenomenon of the hīkoi that took place on 5 May 2004, on the eve of the first reading of the Foreshore and Seabed Bill introduced by the Labour Government of the day. The subsequent mobilisation of the masses which led to the formation of the Māori Party is a crucial chapter in the story of Māori political representation. The momentum generated by the hīkoi led to an unprecedented by-election result, with Tariana re-elected to Parliament on the basis of a 92 percent support at the ballot box.

Fourteen months after being sworn in as the first Māori Party MP, Tariana was joined by three others, all leaders in their own right: Dr Pita Sharples, Te Ururoa Flavell and Hone Harawira. Over the next nine years the party attracted intense interest, for good and bad, as they sought to consolidate their position as the strong and independent voice of Māori in Parliament.

This book is being written in Tariana's last days of a remarkable parliamentary career spanning over eighteen years. Throughout it all she has been consistent in her advocacy and love of the people, expressed specifically through her signature approach, Whānau Ora, but also evident in numerous developments she has led in the spheres of health, social services, housing, family violence, disabilities and the broader justice sector.

This story, is, however, more than a mere political hagiography, a tribute to a political leader who has contributed to the parliamentary debates and the policy speak of the last two decades. Tariana's life is a story of a woman who has succeeded through the powerful influence of a whānau who saw greatness in her. It is a love story of a loyal and devoted wife, a proud mother, a besotted nanny to many. No tale of Tariana would be complete without reference to the seventy-nine-day reoccupation of Pākaitore as the people of Whanganui rose up to reclaim their tribal space; or to the longest litigation in New Zealand history leading up to the Whanganui River Settlement.

Tariana refuses to accept that her leadership is exceptional; her mantra has always been that leadership resides in the people. And so it is that her story is situated in the stories of others. It is a story of the Te Awa Youth Trust – a ten-year programme of transformation for young people, for her beloved marae at Whangaehu, for community development centred around employment and skills. It is a story of Te Oranganui – the oldest and largest Māori health service provider in the Central Region. And there are children, whānau, hapū and iwi, intimately connected, at every step of her journey.

The journey taken in writing this book is one of capturing stories. Inevitably, the question of voice is complicated. Tariana and the author share a love of Maeve Binchy, swapping books and savouring her stories with great satisfaction. They also admired the approach taken by Canadian writer Calvin Helin in *Dances with Dependency*, which shares stories and strategies to reduce the dependency mindset by reframing the discourse into one of indigenous self-reliance, rangatiratanga in action.

This book combines these two genres, a tale told mostly in Tariana's voice, but also the author's, and held together with the insights of family, friends, politicians, activists and colleagues. Tariana's voice has been woven into this text from a rich collection of newspaper articles, opinion editorials, speeches, magazine features, radio and television interviews, oral recordings preserved in Archives New Zealand, submissions retrieved from the Waitangi Tribunal, Hansard debates and multiple conversations with the author. To distinguish the unique voice of Tariana, her words are in a different typeface.

Tariana describes her story this way:

The imprint of tūpuna no longer with us in the living flesh is a constant in my life. I firmly believe that the spiritual presence of those who have walked before us is fundamental in helping to guide our way forward.

For many years in my office a single photograph took pride of place. At first glance it was a photo of an old man standing in a river. But like the river in which he stood, that single photo opened up so many stories, of a deep and all abiding connection between our people and our awa; our history, our identity, our very being connected to the ebb and flow of our waterways.

It was an awe-inspiring photograph of him, arms outstretching, breathing, drinking, embracing every aspect of the river. I love that photo for all it represented of our love for our awa; the sheer fight and determination of all those who have sacrificed so much to protect and safeguard the mauri, the life essence that flows from the mountains to the sea.

That haunting image of our koroua, Titi Tihu, with his hands outstretched, positioned at the joining of the Ōngarue and Whanganui Rivers at Cherry Grove in the summer of 1984, is in stark contrast to another photograph of that same man, taken at the Dominion Museum in 1945.

Koro Titi was instrumental in the campaign to confront the injustice and restore our ancestral rights to our awa tupua, the Whanganui River. The second photograph featured riverbed claimants all adorned in the most distinguished korowai: twelve men and one woman, Kahukiwi Whakarake. In the middle of the photograph two men are exchanging a handshake: D. L. B. Morison, Chief Judge of the Māori Land Court, and Koro Titi. Two hands, white and black, Morison's hand on top; the other strong, firm, palms out and open.

Those two images tell a story of dedication, determination and devout faith in our sacred connection to te awa tupua. Titi Tihu led the Whanganui River Māori claim from 1936 until his death in 1988 at the age of 103. During the course of his life he guided the riverbed litigation through the Native Land Court in 1938, the Native Appellate Court in 1944 to the Supreme Court five years later, a Royal Commission in 1950, the Court of Appeal 1953–4; the Maori Appellate Court in 1958; the Court of Appeal in 1960 and finally a decision in 1962.

In all of these proceedings, seven Native Land Court judges, three Court of Appeal judges and a Supreme Court judge all agreed that as a matter of law Māori owned the riverbed.

It was a finding that they might well have come to earlier, if they had listened to the old man in the first place. In his beautiful book, *Woven By Water*, author David Young reflected on intimate conversations he shared with Tihu.

> 'I can read the river – I can tell you how deep, where the channel is, everything in the water, when I am travelling on the river' he once said to me. 'Wahi tapu is there all right, you can feel it by the water ... he went on breaking into a chant of emphatic beat: Nga toa pohe e ngari to hoe (You champions of rough water, keep up your chant').[2]

The source of my being, the very essence of who we are, is represented in the swirling waters of te awa tupua; the land I was born into, and that cherished bond between whenua as placenta and whenua as land.

With every pregnancy and birth, our placenta and umbilical cord, the pito, are returned to the bosom of Papatūānuku. It is a simple yet profound reminder as mana whenua, that our life-source is interwoven.

One foot in the water, one foot on the land; this is who I am.

Ko au te awa, ko te awa ko au.

My Aunty Wai used to talk to me, as a young teenager, about the loss of land and how our people were moved off it. She would talk late into the night about the impact of laws and regulations. There was one story that never left me. A story that touched me deeply.

When Aunty Wai was a small girl her father lost their land out in Turakina to Pākehā farmers. It had started with a loan of money; a loan they eventually called up. When my koro couldn't pay it, he had to sell the land to repay the debt.

Aunty Wai told me how her grandmother took them by the hand – her and Aunty Pae and Uncle Frosty – and walked the boundaries of their land doing the karanga to the old people to forgive him. It's a stark picture. All the mokopuna holding each other's hands in a line, their kuia doing the karanga, crying, crying, asking forgiveness for what her son had done.

My dad, too, used to talk to me and tell me that this was our land, and that's why I wanted to come home. He would talk about the land and who it belonged to and how it had been lost. He would talk about things that Rātana did and the importance of the Treaty and the land. He would drive us to Whangaehu from Whanganui and tell us about the land and the boundaries, whose land was there, the majority of lands having been a part of our Ngā Wairiki/Ngāti Apa history. Even though I don't think we ever fully realised what he was doing with us, as we got older and we saw the land in the hands of others we could look at that land and understand what it was all about.

Then when we got home he would put me on his shoulders and he would walk the road at Whangaehu and he would say, 'all this land belonged to your family. This was all your grandfather's land. It doesn't matter who's living on it now. This land, you were born out of this land.'

I used to say things a bit similar, to my kids, to try and make them have that same sense of place and belonging, because it gave me that. Even though I came to live in town, Whangaehu was always in my heart. When I'm coming home from Wellington and I hit the Foxton Straight, I'm home. I can't explain the feeling. It's not that the land belongs to me – it's that I belong to the land.

There were other stories that Dad told me about family who leased land to farmers, who got into debt through non-payment of rates, because the rates weren't often included in that arrangement. In the end they were borrowing money from those farmers and couldn't pay it back, and they lost their land. Māori could not get bank loans using their land as collateral. A lot of our land was also lost in the sales.

Years later, when I was Associate Minister of Housing and brought in the Kāinga Whenua housing policy,[3] I remembered back to my dad, to Aunty Wai, to my grandmother, and hoped that at long last we had done right by them. That we had secured a way for the land of our hapū and iwi to be protected for the generations to come, by making it possible for the owners of multiply owned land to access credit to keep the land in family ownership.

There is nothing that deprives tangata whenua of our identity more than to be tangata (people) without the whenua (the land) that gives us a place to stand, our place to be. We are the valleys and the mountains. I am strongly connected to Ruapehu and Tongariro maunga; Taranaki on my grandmother's side.

I have felt so strongly about the position of tangata whenua in our own land. That our lands have been taken over by others and our place in this land has never been honoured in the way that it should. Many of our people live in abject poverty, and that's because all of their resources have been taken from them. We have suffered huge confiscations of tracts of lands right throughout New Zealand. I feel hurt for our people to see the situations that they live in. When people are colonised, almost every negative indicator tends to reside in the indigenous peoples, and we have had that. We have had politicians and others criticise our people for the position that they are in. I am intolerant of that.

My determination to fight to protect our land and preserve our whenua for our future generations probably traces back to 1975. I will never forget when Dame Whina Cooper led the Māori Land March throughout the North Island. I had helped to feed the marchers when they reached Whanganui, and stayed out at Rātana Pā. The movement of marchers – Te Roopu Matakite – rallied behind the call, 'Not one more acre of land'. It stirred something in me: a restless unease that lingered long after the marchers left the pā.

When we gather at home to hui, there is one particular pātere that links us to the foundation we are born of.

It starts: 'Kia uiuia mā, nā wai koe? Māu e kī atu, e tirohia atu ngā ngaru e aki ana ki Waipuna ki te Matapihi, Pūtiki-Wharanui ...' ('Should you be asked, 'to whom do you belong?' you should say 'well, look yonder at the waves surging towards Waipuna and Te Matapihi, at Pūtiki-Wharanui ...')

The pātere travels over hills and waters, passes the long sands at Matahiwi, wanders through the battlefields of Rānana and Moutoa. The words follow the river as it flows at Paraweka, Pīpīriki, Parinui, landing upon Ruapehu and acknowledging the original fire of Paerangi-i-te-whare-toka. As our people stand and give voice to the naming of our awa, our maunga, our whenua, our whakapapa, it represents survival. It is, if you like, a powerful anthem of belonging, a tribute to resilience, to the enduring legacy of whakapapa that gives all of us our place in the world.[4]

Almost three decades after the Māori Land March, as part of the Address in Reply debate following the 2002 elections, I spoke in Parliament about what it means to be tangata whenua, born of this land. While my speaking slot was allocated to me as a member of the Labour Party, I chose to speak from the heart about what it is to be Māori, rather than as a member of a political clan:

> We of Ngā Wairiki, Ngā Paerangi and Ngāti Rangi claim to originate with the rivers and the mountains. We do not see ourselves or other hapū as being migrants from another land. We do not justify our presence in Aotearoa, or the occupation of another's tribal lands, on the basis of all of us being migrants. Our histories do receive the arrival of migrants from time to time, whom we embraced and whose descendants became part of our tangata whenua communities. The tangata whenua of Aotearoa have always been outward-looking people, willing to embrace new people, new knowledge and new skills.[5]

This view – that our people were literally born *of* the land, tracing our source back to the rivers, the mountains, the valleys and peaks, rather than land being merely a physical foundation to build a house or structure on – was not a view universally understood. On that occasion, Hon Tony Ryall, who followed on directly from me in the debate, quickly retorted, 'that speech was an example of why the Labour Party suffered such a disastrous drop in the public opinion polls during the election campaign'.

I have never been someone who looks to others for approval of what I should or shouldn't say; a value that has been of great help in a debating chamber in which individuals thrive on being able to mock or minimise the views of their colleagues. Whether other MPs understood me was not my primary purpose for speaking; what was always important to me was to be true to who I am.

This comes through the lessons of one of our leaders of the Rātana and Māramatanga movements, Mere Rikiriki – 'E ringa kaha, e ringa poto, kaore e whakahoa'. In this she always reminded us to hold true to ourselves, to be self-controlled without friend or favour.

The influence of Mere Rikiriki has been significant in the forging of Tariana's own sense of self-identity. She lived from 1866 to 1926 and was an aunt of the great prophet Tahupōtiki Wiremu Rātana. Oral history holds that she predicted that Rātana would be born and take on unheralded leadership of the people.

Mere Rikiriki named Rātana's twin sons, calling them Ārepa and Ōmeka, representing the beginning and the end. Te Ārepa (Alpha) signified the beginning of the spiritual work (te ture wairua). Te Ōmeka (Omega) signified the end of the physical work (te ture tangata); the pursuit of Piri Wiri Tua in the laws of the people and the honouring of Te Tiriti o Waitangi. Spiritual and physical pathways alike have been associated with the contribution that T. W. Rātana has made to the nation.

Mere Rikiriki also identified another leader of people, Hori Enoka Mareikura. While Rātana took up pathways of healing and political discovery, Mareikura followed a spiritual mission, including through the establishment of the Māramatanga.

There is no stronger connection to Mere Rikiriki than at the banks of the Rangitīkei River, in the heartland of Ngāti Apa/Ngā Wairiki, the place that Tariana considers her tribal home. One day, possibly as early as 1890, Mere Rikiriki experienced a spiritual awakening, and jumped forty times into the Rangitīkei River. The significance of this was explained by Tariana's cousin, the late Joan Akapita, as being about the relationship between the land and the water, the old and the new. Karen Sinclair, in her history of the Māramatanga movement, records the explanation as follows:

> Hoana explained this relationship to me thus. Mere Rikiriki had a mission to accomplish: a job whose terms she had to fulfill. It was important for her to jump into the river and thereby bring God to the people. In the process she ended one era and allowed another to begin. This would be a new life, signified by the saying, kotahi waewae kei roto i te wai, kotahi waewae kei tua i te whenua (one foot in the water, one foot on the land).[6]

Tariana has often referred to those words – taking from them a call to transformation while she still stays grounded in her identity, appreciating the past. The words spoke to her of forging a clear pathway to the future, while at the same time building on that which is tapu, and sacred: all that she inherited as whānau, hapū and iwi and that she would pass on to her mokopuna.

The influence of Mere Rikiriki was widespread during her lifetime. People came to Parewanui, her marae on the banks of the Rangitīkei, for spiritual healing, guidance, hui and prayer. Across from the marae stands a church, Te Wheriki (Jericho), built and consecrated by Rev. Richard Taylor in 1862. In Tariana's view, we should know these places as part of our history; we should know her name and her story.

Karen Sinclair notes further of Mere Rikiriki:

> On a practical level she was a healer of considerable skill (successfully treating a sick child and thereby saving an important descent line from extinction). On her marae and under her guidance, the family learned of their guardian, who has continued to serve as protector and source of revelation. She named a new generation of young Māori, including Mareikura's infant son. She gave the Māramatanga a flag, the time for prayers, and a rā, a commemorative day that enshrines the shared history of Mareikura and the prophetess of the Rangitikei. Like other prophets she found herself looking in two directions simultaneously. And like other prophets, she was fiercely protective of her people and their destiny.[7]

One of the aspects most central to the leadership of Mere Rikiriki was her power to define. Mere Rikiriki named people and places, and in doing so her messages are interwoven through lines of whakapapa and the tribal landscape that Tariana grew up in.

Mere Rikiriki gifted the names of four children from whānau across the central region: Ringapoto, Whakarongo, Kawai Tika and Tikaraina. Tikaraina (literally 'the straight line') was originally the name of a whare at Parewanui. When the families moved to Rātana Pā in the 1920s, that house moved with them. The meeting house at Maungārongo Marae in Ohakune is also named Tikaraina. In one name, therefore, the leadership and prophecies of Rātana, Mere Rikiriki and Mareikura remain closely linked to this day with those three places – Parewanui, Rātana Pā and Ohakune. It is a powerful link for both Tariana and George: the land and the people within remain central in their lives.

Pokarekare ana nga tahataha o nga wai o Whanganui
Tika rere mai i waenganui e
Ko au tenei te ao-rere-rangi nei i runga i te kapua
E titiro nei ki te Tira Hoe Waka
Pokarekare ana nga wai o Whanganui, korikori ana te mouri tipua
Ko au tenei, ko koe tena, e nga mokopuna
E rukuruku nei i nga wai te puenga ake he tipua
Ko te taurahere ki te rangi.[8]

My cousin Joan was not only a great historian – someone who placed special value on the history and location of events across our tribal environment – she was also a prolific writer of waiata and pātere. This waiata was written on the very first Tira Hoe Waka, the journey our whānau take every year, to reconnect as family while paddling the waters of the Whanganui River. The first three lines of the waiata were inspired as the composers saw their mokopuna arriving at Pīpīriki, aboard the waka, travelling their ancestral river.

Throughout the waiata there are references to our mauri tipua, our kaitiaki who continue to live in our river, to guide and protect us in our way forward.

It is a waiata which often brings me to tears, as I reflect on all that our river has meant to us as a people; to those who have gone before me who fought so passionately for our river claim to be heard. My cousins Archie[9], Tahu[10], the old man Koro Titi Tihu[11], Hikaia Amohia[12], Matiu[13], Joan[14] and Nanny Nui[15].

We are a river people. We belong to the river and the waters of our rivers flow through all our veins as a people. We have always been very strongly connected to the river.

I remember, as a child, one of our uncles, Uncle Hikaia, used to come to every hui there was, and he would talk about all the wrongs that had happened to our people through the river. As teenagers we used to get hōhā. We didn't want to hear those stories; we would wish he didn't stand up and talk. It wasn't until I was a little bit older that I began to realise the story he was telling was a story of alienation, disconnection; a story about our losses. In all of my generation, not one of us has the language.

So it has been a painful journey to where we are today, but also a journey of hope.

In every aspect of my life, I have turned to te awa tupua, for guidance, for solace, for inspiration, for a moment of calm. I treasure the times when Aunty Julie Ranginui has turned up at my door, to take me down to the river, to restore and cleanse me, to feel renewed.

There was no more vivid demonstration of this than in the heady days of May 2004, as the foreshore and seabed battle raged. By day, the Labour Party was encouraging me to abstain or to stay away from Parliament when the vote would be taken. At night my moemoeā (dreams) were telling me that I had to be true to myself; to honour the legacy of my tūpuna.

Finally, as the days came closer to the Bill taking its first reading in the House, my restless spirit led me home to Whanganui. And in the very early dawn one morning, my kuia came and fetched me and took me to the river.

There was nothing more to be said; my kuia had led me to the truth.

Ko au te awa, ko te awa ko au. I am the river and the river is me.

NOTES

[1] Hone Tuwhare, 'Papa-tu-a-nuku (Earth Mother)'. This poem refers to the Awakening; the Māori Land March that began at Te Hapua on 14 September and ended at Parliament on 17 October 1975. Te Roopu Matakite (those with foresight) started with just fifty marchers on the 1000-kilometre walk to Wellington. By the time the hīkoi reached Parliament, they held a petition with over 60,000 signatures.

'Papa-tu-a-nuku (Earth Mother)' is published with the permission of the Estate of Hone Tuwhare. Hone Tuwhare's poetry is now available in *Small Holes in the Silence: Collected Works*, Godwit Press, Random House NZ, 2011. Publishing rights for the poem are held by the Estate of Hone Tuwhare. All inquiries to honetuwharepoetry@gmail.com

[2] David Young, *Woven by Water: Histories from the Whanganui River*, 1998, p. 9.

[3] Under this policy, Māori wishing to live on their own multiply owned land may qualify for a Kāinga Whenua loan, which allows them to build on, purchase or relocate a house on that land. The scheme was introduced by Tariana Turia in April 2010; it is administered by Kiwibank and Housing New Zealand.

[4] Tariana Turia, speech to Inaugural Māori and Indigenous Suicide Prevention Symposium, 10 February 2014.

[5] *Hansard*, 4 September 2002, p. 293.

6 Karen Sinclair, *Prophetic Histories: The People of the Māramatanga*, 2002, p. 42.

7 Sinclair, *The People of the Māramatanga*, p. 39.

8 Waiata written by Hoana Akapita and Raana Mareikura, January 1988.

9 Sir Archie John Te Atawhai Taiaroa (1937–2010) was a much loved and respected leader of the Whanganui people. He took on a leadership role in the long-running battle of the iwi to reclaim their ownership of the river.

10 Rangitihi Rangiwaiata Tahuparae, MNZM, (1939–2008); New Zealand's first officially appointed Kaumatua O Te Whare Paremata; a cultural advisor, member of the Waitangi Tribunal; tohunga.

11 Titi Tihu (1885–1988) led the Whanganui River claim from 1936–1988.

12 Hikaia Amohia (1918–1991); principal claimant for Te Iwi o Whanganui (WAI 167);

13 Matiu Marino Mareikura (1942–1998) was a Ngāti Rangi elder, tohunga, actor and claimant for Wai 151 and 277.

14 Hoana Maria Joan Akapita (1930–1994) was one of the claimants for WAI 167. The principal claimant was Hikaia Amohia. Other claimants were Archie Te Atawhai Taiaroa, Raumatiki Linda Henry, Kevin Amohia, Te Turi Julie Ranginui, Brendon Puketapu, Michael Potaka, John Maihi and Rangipo Metekingi.

15 Te Manawanui a Tohu Kakahi Pauro (1907–2010). When Nanny Nui passed away in her 103rd year, Tariana referred to her as being a 'window to the old world'. 'Nanny Nui epitomised our whakatauaki – ko au te awa, ko te awa ko au. She was there at the launching of Awa FM – alongside Nanny Sophie Albert and Nanny Grace Taiaroa – knowing our strength lay in the revitalisation of the reo.' (Māori Party, 'Te Manawanui a Tohu Kakahi Pauro', 8 September 2010).

-CHAPTER TWO-

WHAKAPAPA: THE BINDING STRANDS OF URU

Though the families she lived with changed several times while she was growing up, Tariana was always surrounded by the same network of kin. 'Despite my disjointed childhood, I have still had a very privileged upbringing', she says.[1]

To unpack the sophisticated web of connections that defined Tariana's upbringing is no easy task. Each strand of her genealogy, has been influential in helping to create the leader she became.

In Labour Weekend of 2008, the descendants of Hamiora Tukotahi Uru Te Angina (Sam Woon) came together for the Woon whānau reunion at Whangaehu Marae. During the reunion a sculpture was presented, which consisted of nine pieces. The taonga had been designed by Manu Bennett from the Ngā Ariki hapū of Turakina. The main body of the sculpture represents Tariana's grandfather, Sam Woon, and his two wives, Moetu and Hokiwaewae. The remaining eight pieces represent their collective children.

The taonga serves as a living means of keeping the connections strong. A member from each of the whānau generating out was given one of the eight pieces to care for and bring back home during times of tangihanga, reunions and hui.

The name of the sculpture is Te Taurawhiri o Uru – the binding rope of Uru.

The maternal whakapapa of Tariana (Woon) Turia is as follows:

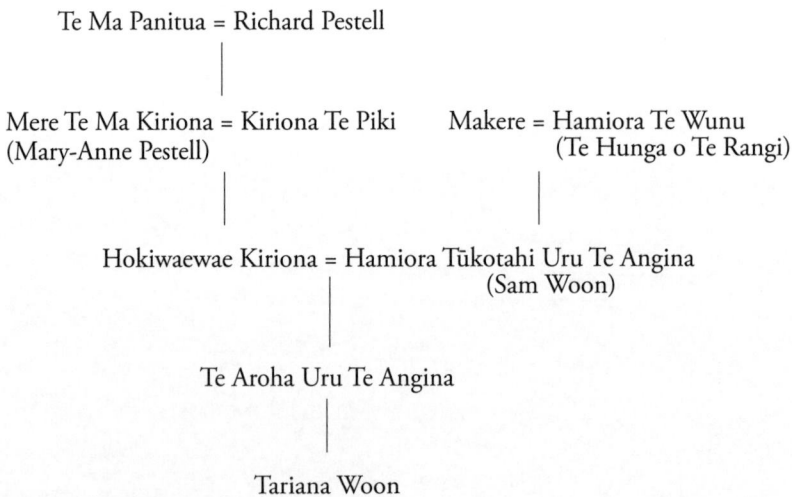

Te Ma Panitua = Richard Pestell
|
Mere Te Ma Kiriona = Kiriona Te Piki   Makere = Hamiora Te Wunu
(Mary-Anne Pestell)   (Te Hunga o Te Rangi)
| |
Hokiwaewae Kiriona = Hamiora Tūkotahi Uru Te Angina
                                        (Sam Woon)
|
Te Aroha Uru Te Angina
|
Tariana Woon

I was raised by my grandmother, Hokiwaewae Uru Te Angina (Kiriona), and later my dad and his wife Mihiterina.

When I was born my grandmother took me, and my mother virtually had no say in the matter. They were not happy that my mother had me to someone from other shores, an American marine; they were worried about that. It was a whānau decision to raise me; a decision which was made in my best interests, and to ensure I had a good upbringing.

Hokiwaewae was a daughter of Mere Te Ma Kiriona (Mary-Anne Pestell): the daughter of Te Ma Panitua of Karatia and Richard Pestell, a flour mill owner.

Hokiwaewae was, however, my grandfather's second wife. He had firstly married our great-grandmother's sister, Te Po Moetu (Elizabeth Pestell). Some of the family called her Hurihuri.

My grandfather's name was Hamiora Tūkotahi Uru Te Angina Wunu. Because of the difficulty in pronouncing his name by his Pākehā friends it was shortened to Sam Woon: a name that was to stick and become well known in the district.

My grandfather fell off the wharf in Whanganui when my mother was six; he had a heart attack and died. My mother's memories of him were quite romanticised. I don't think she would have had a lot to do with him, because he had gone overseas twice with Tahupōtiki Wiremu Rātana as well during that period, so he had long periods of time away.

Our grandmother had been made to marry him. She was young; possibly about sixteen. We have a photo at the marae which shows the two wives and some of the children. I used to look at it through my mother's eyes, because she always said such nice things about the situation. Whenever my mother talked about it, it sounded so lovely that her mother, who was a niece to his first wife, would become his second wife and then have children to him so that his whakapapa line could continue. When my grandmother married Sam, his oldest daughter, Ripeka, would have been older than she was.

I was at a tangi at the marae one day and one of my aunties of my mother's generation was there. I was talking to my cousin Retihiamatikei (Cribb). Reti's grandfather and my grandmother were brother and sister on the Kiriona line. We were talking about whakapapa, and I showed Reti the photo and Aunty Ava overheard me talking about it. She told me that my grandmother had never wanted to marry my grandfather; that he was an old man and that she had been forced to marry him, that she had run away, been thrashed and brought back.

It was amazing the impact that little story had on me actually, because I could never look at the photo again without feeling really sorry for my grandmother.

She never married again, and my mother took that to mean it was because it was a good relationship, but once my aunty told me that story, I took it to mean that it was because she had been so unhappy with him. She was quite young when he died ... and she was such a beautiful looking woman.

Tariana's maternal grandfather, Hamiora Uru Te Angina Wunu, was born in 1863 to Hamiora Te Wunu (Te Hunga o Te Rangi) and Makere. Through Makere, Uru Te Angina was closely related to Ngāti Tūwharetoa and Ngāti Poutama of the Whanganui River. Te Hunga O Te Rangi, Tariana's great-grandfather, was the son of Te Wunu Rangiwerohia (Te Ahuru o te Rangi). Te Ahuru o te Rangi had been given by his father Maiawhea to Maiawhea's first cousin, Aperahama Tipae, who had no offspring of his own.

The death of Tariana's grandfather was recorded in the *Wanganui Chronicle* on 10 July 1925:

> The late Mr Woon who was 62 years of age, leaves a family of sons and daughters, one of the latter being Mrs Toko Ratana. He was probably one of the best known natives on the coast, his genial spirit and good nature making him beloved by both Maori and Pakeha alike ... Uru Te Angina was respected in every circle he moved in as a man of the strictest integrity. No deserving cause, no matter what its limitations or magnitude went by without a practical expression of his appreciation.

Through the binding strands of whakapapa, many taonga of Tipae were passed down to Tariana's grandfather, including his taiaha and a mere pounamu taken by Ngāti Apa at the fall of the pā Tuke-a-maui on the Whanganui River.

Kawana Kerei

The heritage of Tariana's grandmother, Hokiwaewae, and her great-grandparents, Richard Pestell and Te Ma Panitua, takes us to England.

Richard Swepson Pestell had been born in England in 1826, and married Te Ma Panitua in New Zealand on 26 December 1856. He later moved to Turakina with his family of six children: Te Po Moetu (Elizabeth), Taho, Hoanna Te Pohoitahi (Joan), Rihari (Richard), Koroneho (Edwin) and Mere Te Ma. As discussed above, Sam Woon eventually married their daughter, Te Po Moetu, and later the daughter of Mere Te Ma, Tariana's grandmother Hokiwaewae.[2] And so began the Woon connections to the Pestell family of Kawana. Tariana's nephew, Che, speaks of this connection as an important link between their family and his aunty Tari.

> Our Pestell family reunion was held at Whangaehu. Aunty Joan (Akapita) and Koro Paul (Mareikura) were giving all the kōrero – this was in the seventies.
>
> Richard Swepson and his brother, Thomas Pestell, came from the United Kingdom to Australia to start wheat mills. Richard moved here to the North Island, originally to Taranaki, and then he met Te Ma Panitua and had his own mill at Turakina and set up all the other mills up the river. He was a millwright.

The Kawana Mill at Matahiwi dates back to 1854; it was used until 1913. The mill was originally named Kawana Kerei, in honour of Governor Grey, who donated millstones. Millwright Peter McWilliam built it for Ngā Poutama, to take advantage of salvageable tōtara logs lying in the riverbed. It was built by Waipahihi Stream (sprinkling waters) because the stream had a good flow and the current was very strong.

In 1865, Aperahama Tipae asked Richard Pestell, a miller from Bristol, England, who was at that time operating the Kawana Flour Mill at Matahiwi, to build him a flour mill on the Makirikiri stream. Part of the Government's expectation of Pestell in appointing him to the role of miller was that he would train Māori in his trade.

The *Whanganui River Annual* records the reflections of Raina Pine, who lived opposite the flour mill, through conversations with Arthur Bates. Her story included vivid memories of 'Pestell of Kawana':

Richard Pestell, who was born in Bedford England in 1825, was our miller for Matahiwi. We called him William but his proper name was Richard Swepson Pestell. We all called him Wiremu Petara.

He came to settle in Matahiwi in the 1850s and soon adapted to our way of living. He married a girl from Ranana. Her name was Te Ma Panitua and they had two daughters, Pomare who became Mrs Sam Woon and Mere, the other daughter, became Mrs Kiriona. They also had one son named Richard who stayed with his dad. He was highly respected among the old as well as the young people and everybody thought a lot of him. Mr Pestell spoke beautiful Maori.

In spring, Mr Pestell gave each family a certain amount of wheat depending upon the size of the family. The wheat which he gave had to last for that particular year. We never paid for our wheat in those days so money was not a necessity. The wheat was given to people as far as the Ratana area. The wheat always grew well. Mr Pestell would send each family a message, to let us know when he would grind our wheat and on what day we have to be there. He had everything planned. His word was his bond. On the day of preparation we would find Mr Pestell, who had been working for weeks, would have the water dammed up in the creek well up from the mill. He had a lot of water saved up and the mill was ready to run.[3]

Richard Pestell died in April 1912, and was buried at Karatia. His son Richard (Billy) took over the operations of the mill until it closed.

Over sixty years later, work parties led by Norm Hubbard, Whanganui Chair of the New Zealand Historic Places Trust, started to spend weekends at Matahiwi rebuilding the Kawana Mill. On 20 September 1980 the Governor-General, Sir Keith Holyoake, and Dame Norma Holyoake were accompanied on to Matahiwi marae by Dr Rangi and Mrs Wiri Mete Kingi and Mr Athol Kirk. The *Whanganui River Annual* recorded the event for posterity:

> The powhiri was led by Wai Waitere (Aunty Wai) and a spirited haka completed that part of the proceedings. Biddy Mareikura led the party

on with welcoming gestures. Then came the speeches of welcome. The senior elder on the river, Rangimotuhia Katene, spoke on behalf of the tribes on the upper part of the river and he expressed regret that so many of the elders had gone. He was followed by Taika Nikorima of the Nga Poutama who spoke for the tribes on the central part of the river. He greeted the governor with a waiata that had last been used to welcome Governor-General Lord Bledisloe in the 1930s when he visited the marae. The final speaker was Hori Hipango who spoke for the tribes on the lower part of the river. The speeches were backed by the Maori group performing the Aotea Poi waiata which relates to the river and is only sung to royalty. To them, their distinguished visitors represented their Queen whom they wished to honour.

The proceedings were concluded when Sir Keith was greeted by Paul Mareikura at the mill site, the ribbon was cut and the mill was declared open.

The 'tauiwi' (non-Māori) connection to the Pestell clan was something that Tariana recalls as being drilled into her as a young girl, as she told the *Sunday Star-Times* in 1997:

> Ms Turia recalls that when she used to speak critically about non-Maori, 'my mother always used to say "you're only talking about yourself"'…. 'I don't dislike my tauiwi side. I kind of feel that gives me the right to be critical', she explains. If in some sense she belongs to the tauiwi tribe, she has a tribal right to criticize. 'Who are the fiercest critics? The members of your own family'. … 'I've spoken to my old people about the word "tauiwi" – we see it as a much more inclusive word, a word used for settlers'.[4]

All these genealogical lines – the Kiriona, Pestell, Uru Te Angina Wunu/Woon families – formed the DNA which gave rise to Tariana Woon. The rich breadth of Tariana's genealogy, combined with the importance her ancestors attributed to maintaining these connections, laid the foundation for a strong and enduring belief in the power of whānau.

From the union of Sam Woon and Te Po Moetu came six children, including twins who died at a young age. This first family of my grandfather's went under the name of Uru Te Angina. There was Mohi Toahiko and Rangimatapu, and the eldest daughter was Ripeka. Ripeka married Rangipouri Marumaru, had two children with him, and then came back home and married Tokouru Rātana – Tahupōtiki Wiremu Rātana's son. Haami Tokouru Rātana later became a Member of Parliament for Western Māori. The youngest daughter, Lizzie, was Rangipouri Marumaru's first wife. She died during childbirth; her child died with her. The descendants from the Uru Te Angina whānau therefore spring from the children of Mohi, Rangimatapu and Ripeka.

In my grandfather's second family with Hokiwaewae, Sam would have a further five children – a son and four daughters – and a whangai daughter, Makere. This family went by the surname Uru. The descendants of Sam and Hoki from the Uru line are Mihiterina (Lena) Larkin Te Awe Awe, Mere Panitua Thompson, Patu Woon, Tangiwai Bishop, Te Aroha Wilson and Makere Haitana, their whāngai.

I remember our great-grandmother, Mere Panitua, because she lived with our Aunty Mem; she died not that much more before our grandmother. She was over 100 when she died. They all lived together; it was an accepted thing. The other whānau that I can think of who lived in very similar circumstances was Aunty Iriaka Rātana; Tahupōtiki was still with his first wife, and she was given to him. She was only very young too. It was a very similar story.

NOTES

[1] Laurel Stowell, 'A life of service to Maori', *Wanganui Chronicle*, 31 August 2005, p. 4.

[2] Mere Te Ma (Mary-Anne Pestell) married Kiriona Te Piki and had seven children: Hokiwaewae, Takiau Kiriona Williams, Kopeke Te Wiki, Kararaina Karatau, Amo Rangaihi Te Rauhi Rennie, Wanihi Waitere and Rukuwai Kiriona.

[3] A. Bates, 'Raina Pine in conversation with Arthur Bates', in *Whanganui River Annual*, November 1980, pp. 48–9.

[4] Anthony Hubbard, 'Foreign tag also fits Māori radical', *Sunday Star-Times*, 22 June 1997.

-CHAPTER THREE-
WHĀNAU: THE EARLY YEARS

Tariuha and Aunty Waiharakeke Waitere were major influences in her life; they were wise storytellers, who taught Tariana about her people. Like most children, Tariana wasn't interested in the stories, but as she grew up she came to realise that they contained sensible advice for the future. Tariana the iwi advocate and politician were born out of these stories.[1]

To the unitiated, the early family life of Tariana Woon is far from simple. Her story is not to be found in a single household with a mother, father and siblings all accounted for.

Parenting was a shared responsibility; Tariana's home spread across many physical locations. The cousins she grew up with were regarded as her sisters and brothers; an invincible line of aunts and uncles nurtured her as their own, for she was, in every sense of the word.

I knew that our household was different. I would never want to talk about our household at school. Because we were brought up by our nanny; we didn't have a mum and a dad per se in the house; we had an aunt and an uncle. But I have been blessed to have had people who have loved me, guided me and invested in me; nurturing in me dreams for myself and my future.

I don't remember much of the years before I started school. Apparently when I was a baby I had to wear a mask in the pram because my eczema was so bad – a piece of gauze with holes for eyes. My grandmother used to put netting over the pram so that people wouldn't look. Taking pride in our appearance is clearly a family trait.

I was never spoken to in the reo. English was regarded as the pathway to success. My father taught me to read before I went to school. I was the generation that was pushed the Pākehā way; my whānau always believed a time would come when these taonga (te reo Maori) would come to me. It was never to be.

Prior to starting school you could come to school for visits. Nan used to come with me and sit at the back of the room, never allowing me to be on my own. Even at that age, I used to watch out for her. Te reo was her first language. I used to be terrified that someone would laugh at her, or giggle and make callous comments. Luckily for us both my nan was a very generous benefactor of baking at the school fair, and my grandfather had given the land on which the school was situated, so our whānau had some advantages. I remember often being in the kitchen with her; she would be baking for the school, cakes and things. She was a very good cook.

'My grandmother didn't have much, but she raised six of us in her old age. I don't ever remember going without a kai. I certainly remember having to wear my cousin's clothes. I started school in clothes far too big for me, but who cares. I don't recall having a pair of shoes until I was probably about eight. We just never had the money. But it didn't really matter. The fact is we had one another. We were well fed; we were totally loved.'[2]

I remember other things. Nan smoking a pipe. My mother coming to visit my grandmother in the big house where we stayed. Mum lived in the valley, but we never really saw her. Well, let me put it this way. I would hear people say 'here's your mother', but I couldn't work out how. She was never allowed to have anything to do with me. She married somebody who wouldn't allow her to have anything to do with me when I was young, and my grandmother wouldn't allow me to stay with them. I suppose it was about protection.

But Nan couldn't protect us from everyone. The public health nurse springs to mind. At that time we would be separated into two lines, Pākehā and Māori. The Pākehā kids could escape scrutiny, and would be free to go inside, while we would be subjected to the nurse combing our hair with a pencil, on the look-out for kutu (headlice). Once the kutu test was over she would flick up our skirts to see if we had scabies. Our point of difference was obvious from an early age. 'All the Pākehā kids would laugh because the nurse would be going through our hair and checking our bodies to see if we had sores. It was really, really embarrassing because you were the ones singled out. It was really demeaning'.[3]

The public health nurse also invaded our homes, searching for unhygienic conditions. My grandmother, my aunts and mother became utterly obsessed with cleanliness, demanding our house be spotless. Our standards of personal hygiene and cleanliness were of the highest order. This was normal in our whānau, but a fear of being found wanting remained.

When I was about five I remember we were at the 'Big House'. Nan had been ill. She would always want us kids to sleep with her, and I can remember being frightened to sleep with her. It was a little bit like knowing the inevitable and not wanting to hop into her bed. Up until then I think that's where I slept – with her or my cousins, Mary or Rebecca.

One morning, early, Rebecca told me Nan had died during the night. Nan was in her mid-seventies, and she had been sick, but the shock still took some time to register. I was frightened; unsure what was going to happen to me.

After the passing of our kuia on 1 August 1949, Dad and his wife Mihiterina, my aunty Lena, became my world. My dad is Tariuha Manawaroa Te Awe Awe, but everyone called him Charlie. Aunty Lena was the firstborn of my grandparents, Hokiwaewae and Sam Woon, the eldest sister to my mum Dorsey (Te Aroha).

Dad was a really great orator. In a way he took on my grandfather's role as head of the family. He was always a firm follower of our whānau traditions and protocols. Every New Year the table would be set, and anybody who had died in the previous year would be remembered with their own place set at the table. We held the dinner in the dining room in the Big House. That room had a huge table that went right down the centre of the room, and there were also great big carved cabinets. All the family gathered around for the New Year midnight dinner as a memorial dinner to those who had gone.

One of the things that stood out about my dad was that he was a chuckler. He loved to tell stories at tangi and hui: stories embellished with his trademark chuckle, a deep hearty belly laugh that would draw us all in. In those days, it was almost like a competition in the whare where they would stand up and tell stories and everyone would be in fits of laughter. Dad was always my hero, even if he'd be laughing at his own story before he was halfway through it.

He was a great storyteller, and he told me all the stories about my grandfather going to England with Rātana to get the ratification of the Treaty of Waitangi. Stories about their childhood, their lives, the changes they went through.

A political legacy

My grandfather (Sam Woon), my father Tariuha, and my mother's two sisters Ripeka and Mihiterina (Aunty Lena) all travelled with Tahupōtiki Wiremu Rātana to England on two separate occasions to have the Treaty ratified.[4]

Rātana took two world tours to Britain; the first from 9 April to 12 December in 1924; the second in 1925 from 17 August through to 21 December. My grandfather was part of the Roopu Kaumātua that accompanied Rātana on his first world tour with a twenty-four-piece band, Te Peene a Te Māngai – twelve young men and twelve women – who travelled to perform haka, poi and waiata at the British Empire Exhibition.

The tour culminated in a visit to Geneva to take the grievances of Te Tiriti o Waitangi to the League of Nations. Both tours were ignored and snubbed by the Crown, on the advice of the New Zealand Government. As uri or descendants of these tūpuna, I feel as if I inherited a sense of indignity and rebuke suffered by those who passed before me, and I believe that spirit of unrest will continue throughout the generations, until we have done all that we can do to truly honour Te Tiriti o Waitangi.

My pathway to politics was determined by those who went before me. It was determined also by the influence of Tokouru and Matiu Rātana from Ngati Apa, and Iriaka Ratana of Whanganui descent; all whom have served as Members of Parliament; and all with whom I share a common whakapapa. It was consolidated by my grandmother, Hokiwaewae; my Mum Dorsey, and my aunts, Waiharakeke and Paeroa, who recognised in me, a spark that they believed could be nurtured for the good of our people.

When I think of the challenges, the trials, the tests of fortitude I was exposed to, in living up to the high ideals of all those who have since passed on, the process of being nominated and selected as a parliamentary candidate many years ago was a mere technicality. And to this day, their lessons are retained; their words ring in my head, and reverberate in my heart, as I try to carry out my duties in a way which honours them.[5]

Two uncles and an aunt

Tariana's uncle Haami Tokouru Rātana was MP for Western Māori from 1935 until his death in 1944. Tokouru had been born at Parewanui on 21 July 1894. In a rather fitting synergy, 120 years after his birth, almost to the day, on 24 July 2014, his niece, Tariana, stood for her valedictory speech in Parliament.

Tokouru was the eldest of seven children from the marriage of Tahupōtiki Wiremu Rātana and his first wife, Te Urumanao Ngapaki. T. W. Ratāna had made a prophecy that one day, he would control the four winds, Ngā Hau e Whā, and that his influence would be felt through the length and breadth of Aotearoa. Tokouru represented the first step in achieving that prophecy. Tokouru was schooled at Whangaehu. He served for four years in the Pioneer Battalion at Gallipoli and in France. During his war service he was badly gassed, and suffered ill health for the rest of his life.

On 7 April 1924, at Rātana Pā, Tokouru married Tariana's aunt, Ripeka Uru Te Angina, the second child of Tariana's grandfather Sam Woon and his first wife Te Po. They both travelled with the Māngai (as Tahupōtiki Wiremu Rātana was now known) on his pilgrimage to Britain, France, Japan and other nations during 1924–25.

From the *Hansard* records it would appear that Tokouru spoke only four times during his parliamentary career. Yet the passion and political fire evident in his maiden address to the twenty-fifth Parliament demonstrates a great flair for speech-making. He addressed the National Party Opposition thus:

> I wonder if they ever gave a passing thought to the welfare of the Maori people, their questions and problems, when they were in power … What about the Ngaitahu claims as mentioned by the honourable member for Southern Maori district? What about the Whanganui River claim, the Waitara and Parihaka prayers for justice, the Taranaki grievances, the West Coast settlement reserves, the confiscated lands, the ten-year leases, Maori housing, mortgages, Wellington and Nelson Tenths, the Treaty of Waitangi and many other matters that were well known to the honourable gentlemen who comprised the Governments of the past. It is said that this is an age of wonders, and I am still wondering.[6]

He didn't leave his challenges there. In the last section of his address, Tokouru took the time to share a story about the nature of civilisation:

> We are told that this is an age of civilisation but every time I think of that word it reminds me of a book I once read in which was a picture of a negro sitting outside his hut looking at his children who were at play. Underneath the picture were the words 'Savages – uncivilised'. On the opposite page was another picture showing great nations at war and depicting all kinds of man-killing devices: guns, bayonets, bombs and so on. Underneath that picture was the caption – civilisation. Whenever I think of that picture I always wonder whether our children will be brought up to recognise that kind of civilisation.[7]

Although he was often ill, throughout the duration of World War Two Tokouru continued to speak out about his opposition to conscription. Despite months of hospitalisation and illness, he raised his concerns about the need for a home guard, believing it aligned with the Māngai's wishes for Māori to defend their own land. On 18 September 1939 the Māngai, TW Rātana, passed away and his son, Tokouru, was confirmed as his successor, taking on the title Kai-Arahi (leader). From 18 to 20 October 1944, as head of the Rātana Church, he took part in a summit in Wellington with other church leaders. Together the leaders declared their support for the future direction of the Maori War Effort Organisation, and spoke up for Māori control over Māori affairs. This ideal could be seen as his 'ohākī' – his dying wishes. Tokouru took his last breath just ten days later, on 30 October 1944, at Rātana Pā, at a mere fifty years of age.

Tokouru's younger brother, Matiu Tahupōtiki Wiremu Rātana, was quickly selected by the Labour Party to succeed him and inherit the Western Māori seat in 1945. In 1946–49, in fulfilment of T. W. Rātana's prediction concerning Ngā Hau e Whā, the four Māori seats were now held by four Rātana members.

Matiu had married Iriaka Te Rio, who had been the second wife of his father the Māngai, in 1939, following the Māngai's death on 18 September of that year. Iriaka was sometimes referred to as Te Whaeaiti (the little mother), as compared to Te Whaea o te Katoa (the mother of all), the name by which Rātana's first wife, Te Urumanao, was known. Iriaka's special role was to train all the women in the cultural groups and to travel alongside the Māngai. In 1928 she had given birth to a son, Hamuera (Samuel), who died from tuberculosis when he was only six years old. In June 1937, she gave birth to Raniera Te Aohou Rātana, who eventually became the tumuaki (president) of the Rātana Church in the 1990s.

Iriaka and Matiu took up a dairy farm at Whangaehu under one of the Māori land development schemes. In 1946 Matiu was chosen by the Rātana Church synod as tumuaki. From that date he travelled the country, leaving Iriaka to look after their young family and run the farm of over sixty cows.

On 7 October 1949, while still in his early thirties, Matiu was in a serious car accident and died, leaving Iriaka a widow with six children to raise, a dairy farm to manage and a bleak future stretching ahead. His death was announced in the House by the Prime Minister Peter Fraser:

> Sir, I regret to announce that I just received word that Mr Matiu Ratana, member for Western Maori district, passed away at half

past one o'clock this afternoon after a bone-grafting operation. The operation seemed to proceed quite satisfactorily but after Mr Ratana returned to his bed there came a sudden collapse and he passed away.[8]

The House duly used its sitting hours in the morning of Friday 14 October 1949 to express tributes to the late Matiu Rātana.[9] Speeches were delivered by Prime Minister Fraser, opposition leader Sid Holland and the Hon Eruera Tirikatene (a member of the Executive Council 'representing the Maori race'). Keith Holyoake, MP for Pahiatua, spoke, as did Joseph Cotterill of Whanganui and Tiaki Omana of Eastern Māori. The speakers made reference to Rātana's skills as a fine all-round athlete and his 'close and active interest in the welfare of the Maori people'. The Prime Minister noted:

> Notwithstanding his farming activities, Mr Ratana devoted himself assiduously to his parliamentary duties and the needs of his constituents, whose material and spiritual welfare he had so closely at heart … his utterances regarding Maori problems were always worthy of close attention and respect. As a matter of fact he was constantly in my office with the Minister from the Southern Maori Electorate, discussing matters of great importance which concerned the very foundation of Maori life.
>
> Our sympathy goes out to his widow and her family of little children who followed the coffin of the father … he passed away in the full zenith of his usefulness and in the flower of his manhood.

Holland made reference to the fact that Rātana had been a quiet man, 'a man whom any one could love'; and Cotterill noted that he had been a man who in his home town 'was probably more respected by the Europeans in that district than any other Maori'. Both Tirikatene and Omana prefaced their kōrero in te reo Māori, formulating tributes, as Tirikatene expressed them, 'sacred and sincere which we pay to those who have to travel through the trails of spirit-land'. Tirikatene shared particular insights into Rātana's activities on the land:

His tractor could be heard warming up at dawn and its lights could be seen as he continued working on into the night. He was the youngest of a team of twelve tractor-drivers who helped to open up the whole of the Ratana country. In eighteen months this team of tractor-drivers cleared 1000 acres of gorse and manuka and the whole area produced a wonderful crop of wheat.

Keith Holyoake said:

He was one of the four Maori pillars. Today his seat is empty and it will have to be filled. We live in a different period in the history of the world and one fraught with dangers and perils for us all but the Maori people have their own special problems. We all hope and feel that a man will rise to take Matiu Ratana's place to give leadership and inspiration to the Maori people.

Barely six weeks after the last tributes had been made, someone indeed stepped in to take Matiu Rātana's place, but it was not the 'man' Holyoake had predicted. On 29 November 1949 Matiu's widow, Iriaka, was elected to the Western Māori seat: the first Māori woman to ever be elected to Parliament. For close to twenty years she remained, in fact, the only Māori woman in a predominantly male Māori domain. It was not until Whetu Tirakatene-Sullivan entered politics in 1967 that another wahine Māori came into in the House. The parliamentary careers of Iriaka and Whetu overlapped for two years. Whetu in turn then shared one term with Sandra Lee, who came into Parliament in 1993 after she won Auckland Central, and Jill Pettis, who won Whanganui. These terms comprised the entirety of representation for wāhine Māori in the New Zealand Parliament until 1996.[10]

It must have been a bewildering first few months for Iriaka in her new role. She was heavily pregnant, and gave birth after only one month in the new job. And there were challenges from other quarters. Upon the selection of Iriaka, Princess Te Puea Herangi of Waikato Tainui had stood at a large hui at Tūākau and contested the notion that any woman should captain the Tainui canoe.

Iriaka served seven terms in Parliament during a time when there were only four Māori Members out of eighty: roughly five percent of the House.

It was not until 1967 that it became possible for Māori to contest European electorates, a change that introduced the potential for more Māori to enter the House. For over a century until that point, Māori representation had only been guaranteed by virtue of the 'reserved' four seats.

The young Tariana knew this history intimately; it was her family history. The pulsing rhythm of a political life flowed through her veins.

You probably don't think that those stories have much impact on you as a child, listening, but in the end they do have a great impact on your thinking. I don't think Dad ever set out in telling me stories to politicise me, but ultimately I think that's where it all began.

Dad particularly valued education. He always told me to appreciate the fact that our grandfather had given the land for the school at Whangaehu. He taught me to read really young; I remember he'd show off to our uncles, getting me to 'read the paper, read the newspaper' to demonstrate my prowess. This life of love, of laughter and learning was all I needed.

> I remember when the principal of our school strapped one of our whānau. My dad, my whāngai dad, came to the school to tell the principal that we don't hit our children. How much love can you get when your family truly believe in the essence of you as a tamaiti, and take care of you in such a way that you never want for anything, other than perhaps a pair of shoes and some flash clothes.[11]

But of all the things I remember most about my dad, it would be his values:

> When I was very young my greatest memory of you is the stories you told me that shaped your thinking, the values you upheld, the respect you had for the mana and dignity of others, and your gentleness. In everything you did there was a kaupapa and a tikanga associated. I remember how important it was that earning the respect of whanau and others was more important than whether they liked you. It is with these things in mind that you have often been in my thoughts.[12]

The year I turned eight was one that I remember for the loss we experienced in the passing of my cousin Ngana. She belonged to Dad and Aunty Mihiterina's son, Hunga, or, as we used to call him, Nig. Her full name, Rangingangana, came from Dad's Raukawa side. While Dad was of Rangitāne and Raukawa heritage, his whakapapa to Raukawa would become significant to me, particularly at the onset of the Māori Party many years later. My dad came from the union of Rangingangana Nicholson and Manawaroa Te Aweawe Larkin.

We called my cousin Ngana. In fact I didn't even know her name was Rangingangana until way, way after she died. My cousin had always been sickly; she had rheumatic fever. Sixty years later, in 2012, when I launched the 'Sore Throats Matter' campaign to address the rising crisis of rheumatic fever among Māori and Pasifika communities, Ngana was never far from my mind.

I think because of Ngana's sickness – and the complete dedication of Aunty Lena towards her – Dad kind of spoiled the rest of us. And in turn, all of us were so very close to Dad. And then Ngana died.

I think we had expected she would; she was always so ill. I remember her dying; we were at Uncle Patu's house. She must have been eleven or twelve; I was probably sevenish, going on eight. It would have only been about three months after she died that my Aunt Lena also passed on. Our aunt's life had been completely dedicated to Ngana: she was amazing. She had utterly adored her. Aunty Lena died when we were down in Khandallah.

By that time, Dad was working for Aunty Iriaka. Aunty Lena and I came down with him. We had been staying at Gogo's[13] place – and that was where my Aunty Lena died from a heart attack. I always thought Aunty's passing was more likely death from heartache. My aunt died grieving; her heart shattered for the mokopuna she had lost. Those two tangi signalled the end of my idyllic childhood.

Immediately after Aunty Lena's tangi, Aunty Wai swept in and picked me up. I was devastated. I didn't want to leave. I loved my dad, and staying with him was enough for me. But it had not been part of Nan's great plan. Long before her passing, Nan had already made plans, but had not talked about them with me. Aunty Wai and Uncle Ted were my godparents. Both were very closely related to the Woons.

Nan had already arranged when I was born that if anything should happen to her that was where I was to go. Aunty Wai used to come out to the 'Big House' almost every weekend, and so I knew them really well.

But Aunty Wai and Uncle Ted were so different, and I just couldn't adjust to the change.

Dad talked to me before they came and got me, but nothing could persuade me. I didn't want to go. It's amazing how you cry about those things. It was really hard, leaving Whangaehu and coming into town, leaving Dad and my darling cousin, Didi.

My brothers Joe, Wilson and Johnny remember the day clearly:

> We were living at 7 Konini Street in Gonville when Tari became a member of our family. It was a big house with a big back section. There were plum trees and a chicken house. Uncle Ted would fatten up the chickens and kill them for Christmas.
>
> We were all outside playing. The car pulled up, a girl got out and we were told, 'this is your new sister'. 1952. She was eight. That's when we found out that girls were tough too. It took a while to get used to her. She's very headstrong. There were no other girls in the house at the time. She was always right. If there were any arguments it was always between Joe and her. Tari could dig her toes in; she could answer back alright, and argue.

I had only been there a little while before I ran away. There was a Pākehā girl up the road, Kathryn, and she decided she'd come with me and we would run away together. Trouble was we went the wrong way; instead of heading south to Whangaehu we ended up in the opposite direction, out towards Upuk [Ūpokongaro].

We were hitch-hiking along the road, and somebody must have stopped. It was getting dark, and I was starting to get frightened. Of all things, the person who'd stopped said that they'd get us a taxi, and so next minute, we've arrived up where Dids worked, and there was a mad panic to find somebody to pay the taxi fare. I was not very popular, I can tell you – got the biggest thrashing of my life from my uncle when I got back.

Little did I know that worse was just around the corner.

The time I spent with Dad after that was precious. I used to go by my cousin, Mary, for holidays, and then I'd see Dad, because he'd come and see me. By this time, Dad was in a position of considerable trust as an advisor/private secretary to Aunty Iriaka.

It was my aunty who told me that Dad wasn't my father.

I was at their place with Mary's kids one day. There was a kuia; I don't know where this kuia was from, but her name was Moe. I remember her as clear as daylight. She had plaits over the top of her head, quite a big woman.

And I said something about my dad. Aunty Iriaka looked at me and she said to me, 'who's your dad?' And I replied, 'Dad, Dad Charlie'. That next moment sliced my heart in two with just four little words: 'he's not your dad'. I protested, but she continued on, seemingly oblivious to the dark cloud that had entered the room. 'No he's not; your dad's an American. A Yankee.'

Suddenly, when she said the Yankee bit, a faint memory resurrected itself. I remembered as a small child people saying to me 'that kid's a Yankee', but I never knew what it meant, so it never resonated with me. I didn't know what it meant, but it sounded derogatory. I always wondered about that.

It bloody devastated me. I took off, and I hid: hid in the drains. The hours drifted by as I watched Dad drive his truck up and down the road. Eventually when it got dark and I was frightened, I hopped out of the drains to flag him down. That's when Dad said to me, 'I may not be your father, but I am your dad in every sense of the word'. He was so upset. He told me, 'no one, no one can take that away from you and me'. To this day, I hear those words and I feel comfort.

I didn't forgive Aunty for years for telling me what turned out to be the truth. I was married before I ever forgave her, and then only through the passing of time. That whole time was absolutely traumatic. Right up until I was fourteen years of age I had never doubted that my dad was my dad and my grandmother was my mum. I never even questioned it. On that day, my perception of my world was suddenly abruptly redefined.

I definitely played up after I found out about Dad. He was somebody who I just had the greatest love in the world for, and still do. He taught me everything I know about unconditional love. Probably that's the reason why I never bothered about my own father.

I've always been intrigued at the interest others have shown in possible candidates who might fulfil the description of my birth father. From what I've pieced together, my birth father was an American marine of Sioux descent who called himself Bob Roberts. I was told that he died on Guadalcanal, in the southern regions of the Solomon Islands. I can't be totally convinced on the issue of identity, as I've also been told my father's real name was Robert Montijo and that he may have survived the War. I've never tried to track him down. I think my children are disappointed that I didn't pursue it, because I've always been so firm about whakapapa and the importance of it.

My daughter Lisa tried to contact him a couple of times, but to no avail. I know that as far as Lisa was concerned, she wanted him to be proud, to know what had happened to me in my life, that I had children, grandchildren, great-grandchildren who are his descendants.

Lisa and her brothers went to enormous lengths to track their grandfather:

> I probably started looking about twenty-five years ago now. By then Nan (Dorsey) had passed away, but there were still quite a number of relatives that were alive that knew or had met him; that I could talk with and find out details. One that I spoke to was Uncle Frosty. I remember him saying that he didn't smile often, but when he did he had a beautiful smile. 'That's probably the thing that I remember the most was that he had just the most beautiful smile'.

Tariana's children interviewed elderly relatives, contacted the Alexander Turnbull Library, wrote letters to the United States Military Archives and approached the support group 'War Babes' for help. Lisa advertised in a magazine in a column headed 'Find missing people', and later, her brother Mark wrote to the television series *Missing Pieces* to tell their story. Lisa says:

> When we had the first meeting with Sue Donald and David Lomas they talked about the process they would use. They had to be sure they had [Tariana's] full consent. It would expose so many things about her and her family. They asked how she felt about him. She got really, really upset, started crying terribly and had to leave the room. I went after her and she said 'I'm sorry, I can't talk'. She was sobbing, but she wouldn't talk about it. Just told me, 'I know it's really important for you kids'.

After *Missing Pieces*, the siblings approached a show called *Family Secret*, and eventually the show's researchers tracked down the family of Robert Montijo living in Dothan, Alabama. But the much anticipated reunion did not happen, leaving that vital connection still unresolved.

Lisa continues:

> David [Lomas] told me that essentially they had slammed the door in their faces and there was no possible chance of meeting them. I was gutted. Gutted knowing that he only died in 2006 and we had had so many opportunities where we could have met him.
>
> As hard as it would have been if we had gone over there, if they had been uncomfortable and [it had not been] a good reunion, if we had had the DNA tests and they were our family, even if it was bad, at least we would know. Mum plays it down. She had a father whom she loved and adored, and that's all that matters. She believed that he died, that he was killed. I don't know whether Nan said that to protect Mum because he never made contact again.

In all honesty, it doesn't matter to me. By the time my mother was ready to tell me about the man responsible for my birth, my own dad, Dad Charlie, had died. When I was fourteen my dad died in a car accident. Aunty Iriaka was badly injured in the same accident, and retired from politics. At that time they didn't take the deceased into the Manuao (at Rātana Pā). But when Dad died, and his boy with him, that was where he lay.

> We record with sorrow the tragic death of Mr Charles Tariuha Te Aweawe Larkin in a motor accident last May. He was a descendant of Peeti Te Aweawe, and a chief of Rangitane and Ngati Apa; his influence in his district was considerable and beneficial.[14]

When I went to live with her in my sixteenth year, Mum was persistent in her enthusiasm to tell me about the man who gave me the gift of life;

more often than not after she had had a few drinks. Problem was, I wasn't ready to hear her with a bottle in her hand. I've always had a thing like that. I didn't want to listen to her while she was under the influence.

Besides, I loved my dad and always will. Try as she might, I didn't want to talk to Mum about somebody who I didn't know and I had no memory of. I suppose in a way it feels a bit like a betrayal of my dad.

I loved my dad, and that was enough for me.

NOTES

1 Roihana Nuri, 'Main Protagonists of the new Māori Party', *Te Karaka Koanga*, issue 25, 2004, p. 12.

2 *Te Waonui a Manu Korihi*, Radio New Zealand, 10 August 2014.

3 Anthony Hubbard, 'Foreign tag also fits Māori radical', *Sunday Star-Times*, 22 June 1997.

4 Ripeka was the eldest daughter of the first family: the union between Hamiora and Te Po. Mihiterina was from the second family.

5 Tariana Turia, 'Being a Maori Woman in Politics', speech to Mana Wahine course, School of Māori Business Studies, Canterbury University, Christchurch, 22 September 2006, *Scoop Independent News*: www.scoop.co.nz/stories/PA0609/S00509.htm (accessed 11 February 2015).

6 *Hansard*, 21 October 1937, pp. 1014–15.

7 *Hansard*, 21 October 1937, p. 1016.

8 *Hansard*, 7 October 1949, p. 2679.

9 In those days it was quite common practice for the House to sit on a Friday. In today's Parliament, the House only sits on a Friday when a previous sitting is extended under urgency.

10 In the 126 years following the Maori Representation Act of 1867, only four Māori women served Parliament, compared to fifty-one Māori men.

11 *Te Waonui a Manu Korihi*, Radio New Zealand, 10 August 2014.

12 Tariana Turia, 'Letter to my Dad', *The Listener*, 4 September 2004, p. 21.

13 Gogo (Rangimatapu Uru Te Angina) was the second eldest boy of the first family – between my Koro Sam and Te Moetu.

14 'Haere ki o Koutou Tipuna', *Te Ao Hou*, no. 28, September 1959.

-CHAPTER FOUR-
AUNTY WAI

The best advice I have been given is to be true to yourself and the people you serve. It is something my aunts and whānau who raised me told me and it has been a guiding principle for most of my life.[1]

My grandmother and my two aunts, Waiharakeke Hunia-Waitere and Paeroa Hunia-Hawea, were definitely the people who had the most influence over my thinking. They gave me strong values and had huge expectations of me. They taught me the importance of kaupapa and tikanga, responsibility and obligation in our lives. I still think about them constantly.[2]

In 1952, at the age of eight, Tariana moved from Whangaehu to live in Whanganui with her godparents, Ted (Piripi) and Waiharakeke ('Aunty Wai') Waitere. They first lived at 7 Konini Street in Gonville, and later followed Aunty Wai's sister, Paeroa, to live close to one another in Pūtiki.

Ted had served in the Twenty-eighth Māori Battalion and the Second New Zealand Expeditionary Force in World War Two. He was wounded in Egypt.

Waiharakeke Hunia-Waitere was a strict woman; very Victorian. She was an ardent loyalist to the Queen. In pride of place above her fireplace was a big photo of King Edward and the royal family. Her influence upon Tariana would be profound.

Wai and Ted had one son, Kawana Hunia Piripi Waitere. Kawana was named after Wai's brother, Takimoana (Doug) Kawana Hunia. He later became a musician and toured the world with the Maori Hi Quins band. He left the country in 1963 when he was seventeen and didn't come back until he was well into his forties.

I was the last to be consulted, but my future had already been mapped out for me. And so when cousin Ngana and Aunty Lena died, I left Whangaehu to move into town and live with Aunty Wai and Uncle Ted.

When I came to town it was so different. It took me a long time to settle in. Uncle Ted was my mother's cousin. Truth be known I always thought of him as a grumpy old shit, but my cousins absolutely loved him. His wartime experience probably explains why he was the way he was.

My memories are, however, saturated with the influence and impact of my formidable but unforgettable Aunty Wai:

> We talk about carrying the mana of our ancestors with us – it is that sense of always being mindful of the whakapapa that you were born into; the family connections that are associated with your name. For me, it can sometimes be as simple as asking myself the question – what would aunty Wai do? If I am ever in doubt – that one question generally sets me right.[3]

Michael Payne, a family friend, remembers:

She [Wai] was pretty formidable. I don't remember ever having clashed with her but I know plenty of people who did.

Aunty Wai spoke with quite a plum in her voice, and yet she was also very strict about tikanga. She expected us to fit into both worlds, Māori and Pākehā. She mostly spoke English to us, only turning to te reo Māori when she didn't want us to understand what she was talking about, but all the concepts that she talked about were driven by an appreciation of the tikanga that governed your behaviour. Sometimes Aunty Wai used to sit in the chair and sing waiata. I was always really cheeky; I'd switch the light on and say, 'come into this century'.

It would drive you nuts, her adherence to the values that you should base your life around. You felt as if you were letting the world down if you did anything wrong; she knew how to play on the old emotions, that one.

When I first came to live with Aunty Wai, I had to bike all the way over to Gonville from Pūtiki for school. I'd started off at Whangaehu; I went to Rātana School. When I lived with my dad I went to Khandallah at some point, and then Gonville: all up about four different schools before I was eight. There were lots of Māori kids at Gonville. The Bennett family used to live in Moore Avenue, and I used to go round there on my way to school. Their daughter, Rii (now Rii Templeton), was my mate. The old lady would give me another breakfast and I'd sit up at the table. Aunty Wai used to get so embarrassed. She was so ashamed; me going round to people's places and eating their food, and especially a big family like that.

When we lived in Gonville, before we went to school we would have to shine the breakfast room floor. Kawana was away most of the time at boarding school then. Everything had to be immaculate. The kitchen and dining room had lino, so you had to polish them with Tan-ol, a cream you put on and then shined off. You'd polish everything. We even had to polish along the skirting boards; you had to clean them every week. Aunty Wai would supervise. She would come along and run her finger along, promise, to see that I had done every single one of those boards. Old bag!

I wasn't a very good cook. In fact I was a hopeless cook when I got married. Aunty Wai did all the cooking. I had to prepare veges, but I didn't cook them.

She used to do the washing too. In those days you had a copper. Aunty Wai would light it. Everything had to be boiled and put through the wringer.

The sheets had to be put into Bluo to make them 'whiter than white'. You had to make sure it was really mixed right through the water. The sheets would be rinsed and then they would be soaked and then put through the wringer again and hung out. My job was to help to put the sheets back through the wringer. You could never just make do. Nothing but immaculate was acceptable.

Aunty Wai was unequivocally dedicated to the Anglican Church: she was dyed-in-the-wool Church of England. She was the pou of the Hāhi: we always had to go to church. Even though my grandmother had seen to me being baptised in the Rātana Church, Aunty Wai took it on herself to see that I was confirmed as an Anglican.

I remember one time Bishop Vercoe came to Whanganui. One of our uncles stood up to mihi to the bishop for coming and to say goodbye. When the bishop went Aunty Wai stood up and she told our uncle off for saying goodbye without waiting for the bishop to say it first. 'You never, ever said poroporoaki to anybody until they said it to you.' She told him how embarrassed everybody was. Truth be known we were all embarrassed about her for telling our uncle off.

Afterwards, Aunty Wai and I walked up to my uncle's place in Airport Road. She was saying to me on the way, 'it hurt me to do that to Uncle but he was wrong; he was wrong what he did, and it's really important for all of us in that hui to understand the tikanga and so I had to do it; I had to'. Honestly, I was walking along the road and thinking, 'oh, you are so embarrassing'. We got up to the house and he cried, him and our kuia, she cried, and Aunty Wai cried too, but she explained to him. And he knew. He said to her, 'you were right', but he cried because she had done it in front of everybody. She felt it had to be a lesson for all of us; that was the kind of person she was.

It was not the first time she did a thing like that. She used to say to me, 'it doesn't matter if nobody likes you, so long as you know that what you are doing is the right thing'.

Aunty Wai believed in the Māramatanga, but she didn't believe in the Rātana Church as such. She would say that Tahupōtiki Wiremu Rātana never wanted a church. But her grandmother, Ruruhira Ngakuira, had totally supported the Māramatanga, so she had always taken them to Rātana: her and Aunty Pae.

Aunty Wai would tell us that everyone was Morehu (a follower of the Rātana movement). She believed Rātana's message was about faith. It was about values. There was a kaupapa and tikanga that you lived by, but it wasn't confined to the teachings of a church. With our Ngāti Apa link to

Rātana, and growing up very much as part of the Māramatanga, I never actually realised that Rātana was a faith, because everyone was Rātana – that was just the way life was.

When I was a kid and we would go out to the pā at Rātana, I loved that there were no fences. You could wander in and out of people's houses. It's a bit different now: there are fences, and dogs too. But in those days the pā was our world; we could roam as we pleased and everyone looked out for us.

Tariana's brother Wilson remembers the efforts they had to go to as a family under the leadership of Aunty Wai:

> We were all brought up very strict Anglicans. Had to go to Sunday School every Sunday. Go to church every Sunday night. Go down and mow the lawns and polish all the brass. Tari used to help Mum and Rua (sister) clean the church.

Emeritus Professor Whatarangi Winiata, a long-standing member and financial advisor to the Anglican Church, also remembers Wai's distinctive manner in an encounter he had with her when they were choosing a bishop:

> She was very articulate and very sharp in her thinking, and consistent. I remember going to Tauranga with her. We had decided down here what we were going to do up there, and I had the idea at the last moment that we should change it. She reminded me of what we had decided; bang, that was it. Oh, she was formidable, consistent. I remember writing to her, asking her if she could come to a meeting here in Raukawa, and she did and she was very helpful. She said to me, 'I came because you asked me to come'.

Aunty Wai had a style of her own. A friend and mentor to Tariana, Sister Makareta Tawaroa, described her as a very 'sedate, wonderful lady – her bun and twinset'. Kui Piki Waretini also remembered Aunty Wai for her 'prim and proper' ways:

> She never believed in the guitar being played with kapa haka. She used to teach at Turakina Girls College. She believed that the kaupapa was te reo, because in the olden days the old people never had guitars.

A thousand pairs of eyes

Sister Makareta Tawaroa recalls of the young Tariana:

> Tari had the most beautiful clothes. My early memories of her were being well dressed – white socks and patent leather shoes. Dressed like that – we'd never seen anything like it. We were in bare feet and gumboots. Had she come from another planet or somewhere? Hair all beautiful – oh this beautifully dressed girl.

Aunty Wai used to buy me really old-fashioned clothes. They were very nice, very dressy sort of things. In those days everyone wore gathered skirts with a wide belt. It would be short and lots of petticoats under them so they stuck out. But oh no, she'd buy me an oatmeal-coloured gored skirt – promise she would – a similar-coloured cardigan and a little blouse. Talk about Granny Three-Bob. I used to feel resentful that she made me do things like that and made me feel so different to the other kids. I hated that. I didn't want to be different.

Later, when I was moving into my teenage years, I'd go to the garage up from the pā at Pūtiki and I'd get changed. I'd put on these clothes that other kids had given me to wear. Talk about the village raising the child. That was exactly what they were like at Pūtiki. You couldn't do anything and they'd tell on you: 'I saw Tari up town and I know you would never have allowed her.'

> When I was growing up in Pūtiki and the Pā, I would devise a vast array of schemes to be able to change out of my home clothes and look halfway decent whenever I had the chance to get to town. No matter how hard I tried inevitably I would return home to my Aunty Wai knowing from the look on her face that my great plans had been

revealed. Unbeknown to me there were aunties all over the pā who took it upon themselves to report the state of my dress. The village would literally be abuzz with the collective concern for what I was told was 'in my best interests'. They told me then, and I have never forgotten it, that no child ever walks alone. Every child is an expression of their whanau. And that is one of the paramount principles of the Whānau Ora approach.[4]

Waicy's girl

Family friend Marilyn Payne remembers:

> We just loved Tariana's independent fiery spirit as a young woman. She used to tell me things about when she was at Girls' College; things that blew me away. I think she was quite a handful. She was a very free spirit, Tariana – original, creative, but she probably had the same fire as Wai. I mean you could see the family connection.

Referring to my similarity to Aunty Wai, my brother Kawana liked to call me 'Waicy's girl'. At the time I didn't think of myself as that way at all. Today, I proudly accept he was probably right.

Of all the resentments I held, and there were a few, the one that I felt most deeply was that Aunty Wai sent both Kawana and me off to boarding school. I could never understand why she would send me off to board at Whanganui Girls' College when we lived right in town. Frankly it brassed me off.

I guess I never really appreciated my Aunty Wai until I grew up. Truth be known I couldn't stand her when I was a teenager. I thought that she was just over the top. I resisted it in my early teenage years, but I know that much of the values and beliefs that I hold today are really from my aunts, and probably my dad. I just didn't realise how precious my aunt was until I was an adult.

I know she wanted a particular future for me. I think she saw something in me, and she thought the discipline of boarding would do me good, as well as teach me to live with other people.

I had to board at college during the term and only go home on holidays. My mother paid for me to board. As far as I knew, I was the only girl from Whanganui who lived in the boarding hostel. It was awful. Going to college was a case of total immersion into a Pākehā environment. There was only one other Māori girl at the hostel, Naomi Hapuka, and she didn't come till my second year at college. But there were Māori girls at the school who weren't boarders. We started a Māori club, and one of our kuia, Aunty Rangi Tamou Takarangi, used to come in and take us for action songs, and taught us the old Whanganui waiata.

But I didn't like the way Māori students were treated. I could never find a name for it. All I knew was that it was wrong and it was unjust, and it used to really get me going. If somebody's lunch went missing, all the Māori girls had to report after assembly and show their lunch. They made us wear sandshoes inside, and your name had to be written across the front of them. They'd check to make sure that you weren't wearing someone else's. It was just disgraceful. I knew they were picking on us; picking on the kids because they were Māori.

They'd tell all the Māori kids to go to a class because someone from Māori Affairs was coming. They didn't include me in a lot of that because I was a boarder, but I'd go anyway because I was Māori. I used to be pissed off. The Māori Affairs officers would come to make sure that we were behaving. They weren't there to tautoko you or anything; just kind of like checking up.

They had a Pommie teacher there. She would always single me out – *Tarrr-eee, Tarrr-eee*. I can hear her now. Anyway, one night this particular teacher picked on me and she just went that step too far. I was in the dormitory and she grabbed my hand and pulled me, and I can remember grabbing her and pushing her back against the wall. I got into really serious trouble over that. I think Miss Page, the principal, knew what this teacher was doing. But she still made me do all the gardens around the bloody hostel, as a punishment. I was happy to oblige – in fact I pulled *all* the plants out just to thrill her to bits. As a teenager it was probably the first time that I felt there was something not quite right for our people. I used to talk it over with my aunt. I was angry about what I believed had happened to our people to put us in the position we were in.

At the time, I think I disappointed Aunty Wai because I was so rebellious. And I thought that the teachers didn't like me because I didn't know my place.

That was everyone except Miss Robinson, our science teacher. She was the one teacher that I really liked, and because of that I really enjoyed science. She inspired me to see science as about our environment; about absolutely everything. The other thing that she let us do was to do these experiments. It was just amazing, the opportunity to find out what happened when you mixed certain chemicals together. It just really grabbed me. She gave you that belief that you could do things. She wasn't the type of teacher who sat there over the top of you like some teachers did. She encouraged you to believe that you could so you wanted to participate, to be one of the ones who understood and could make it all work.

Tariana's memories of school days are reinforced in the reflections of her best friend of that time, Helen Drew:

> At college Tari was such a shy girl, but even then she would stand up to anybody for what she thought was fair or what she thought was right. She would always defend the underdog. She was always honest and forthright in her opinions. She would say exactly what she thought. She might be the only person in the room that would think it, but she had the courage to come out and say it while most of us would keep quiet. I always admired that about her.
>
> We met when we were third form in college, and we have been very firm friends ever since. She has a great sense of mischief. We had a lot of fun over the years. I remember one time in school assembly. The girls were sitting in front of us with their girdles hanging down. She quietly snuck along and tied them to the folded chairs we were all sitting on. So when everybody stood up to sing a hymn, it was absolute havoc. As young girls we thought it was hilarious. She probably got a detention – I'm sure she did – but it was worth it for the laughter.

If Tari was getting into trouble at school, it wasn't anything that she thought worthy of talking about at home.

I didn't tell Aunty Wai any of the stuff that went on about us as Māori – it seemed pointless; she would have just expected that I would deal with things myself, and I wouldn't have expected her to interfere.

She modelled the mantra of being able to stand on your own two feet: 'learn to live with it; get over it'. That would have been her attitude.

If I talked to her about families being pōhara (poor), she would say to me, 'There's no reason for anybody to be in that situation. There is plenty of kai. You just have to go and look for it. No one needs to starve.' She always used to say that. 'No one needs to starve.' And she used to say to me, 'If you have bread and butter and jam, that's a kai, that's a kai. Nothing wrong with that'. Not that we ever had just bread, butter and jam, I can tell you.

During my boarding days, I lived for the days when I could return home for the holidays. Home was firstly based at Gonville and then later, when Aunty Pae (Paeroa) shifted to Pūtiki and built a home over there, Aunty Wai followed suit and bought a home there too. Aunty Pae and my beautiful cousins: Johnny; the twins, Maana (Takimaana) and Dan (Horo Parapera); Joe; Wilson; and ten years later baby Rua. Rua was named after Aunty Wai and Aunty Pae's mother, Ruakohatu Ropata.

My aunty Paeroa Hunia-Hawea was married to Uncle Tom Hawea. He was Rua's dad. Aunty Pae had been married first to Tihema – that's Johnny's dad – and then the twins and Joe and Wilson belong to Frank Huwyler. I so loved my Aunty Pae: she was so good to me. I could go and talk to her and tell her things that I could never tell Aunty Wai.

And I had my Uncle Frosty; I mustn't forget him. He was always loving, always caring. He was the younger brother of Aunty Wai and Aunty Pae. His real name was Pahia: that's who I named my youngest boy after. The original Pahia was Ruakohatu's brother Pahia Ropata, who died in Gallipoli in World War One.

There were four of them who survived into adulthood – Uncle Frosty (Pahia), Aunty Wai, Aunty Paeroa and Uncle Takimoana, who went on to marry Aunty Ruihi (Lucy) Arthur.

Tariana's brother Joe remembered Uncle Frosty as always biking 'with his cap on and this rag on like an Arab, so everyone called him Lawrence of Pūtiki'.

Uncle Frosty taught me to play tennis when I was quite young; bought me my first tennis racquet and tennis shoes. He was lovely, my uncle. I was a really good tennis player at school; I was always in the top three all the way through school. There was one girl I could never beat: Shirley Taylor. Even remember her name to this day. Uncle Frosty ended up putting a full-length concrete tennis court down at the homestead.

I loved it when I'd go home, because my Uncle Frosty was there, and he'd play cricket and tennis and all sorts with us. I suppose in lots of ways I was a bit of a tomboy, because the boys were all my age.

We had a koro living with us as well, Koro Wiremu Te Tauri: he used to make us run and play sport and do things together. We'd go and cut willow sticks for hockey, and cut a thick stick for a baseball bat, and play cricket.

Under the watchful gaze

No matter how much I loved my cousins and my uncles, inevitably the steely gaze of Aunty Wai was always cast over me. I can remember my first dance. I was sixteen. And there's my aunt, chaperoning me, sitting on the side of the hall:

> I didn't want her to come but I desperately wanted to go to the dance. So along she came. It was at Pūtiki Marae and the Hi Quins were playing. I begged her to let me go with my uncle who helped organise the dance, but she refused. She wanted to see whether it was all properly controlled. She embarrassed me by sitting at the end of the hall by the door, watching everyone coming through the door. My cousins were all laughing at me. They weren't surprised but they all giggled and had me on. I was too scared to go out with the others. Anyway I wouldn't have dared because I knew that would deeply upset her.[5]

At sixteen I lived with my mother for the year. Aunty Wai was so hurt. But I was obsessed with my mother, even though I didn't know her that well.

I was going into my last year at college and I got sick; ended up in hospital with appendicitis. Anyway I asked if I could go home. And that was when I got to know my brothers and my sisters: Ngahuia, Lena (or Mihiterina), Steven, Anthony, Bernard and Susan. There was another brother, Phillip, who later died of malignant hypothermia because he was allergic. He had gone into hospital for a minor ear operation; they put him under and he never came back. Years later I met another sister, Naani, who made contact with me when she discovered we might be sisters through our father, Robert Montijo.

The year with my mother wasn't a good year. One night something happened which made me know that I needed to get away. The next day I went into town, got Kelly Puohotaua, a Māori welfare officer, to write a reference for me, and with that entered the nursing hostel and a new chapter in my life.

Uncle Ted died in 1979, Aunty Wai in 1988.

I remember distinctly at Uncle Ted's funeral when we were in the Big House on the corner and we looked down the path and heard a band of angels, singing the most angelic harmonies you could ever imagine. It was truly as if the heavens had opened and provided us with a direct line. That was the sound we always associate with Ngā Paerangi, our whānau from Kaiwhaiki, who have been gifted the blessing of Hineraukatauri, the goddess of song.

Cousin Morvin was one of the ones I remember from Ngā Paerangi, serenading my uncle through song.

Morv was an amazing performer, singer, writer, historian and conductor. When he died in 2014, Tariana, on behalf of the Māori Party, said that his talent:

> … was seen in the incredible repertoire of compositions which made your heart soar, lifted your spirits and then moved you to tears. … Like te awa tupua, his waiata could move from tempestuous rapids to smooth waters that caress your every trouble away. E riporipo ana nga wai – the one comfort we can turn to is to know the river flows on, and the melodies will be taken up by all our mokopuna to lift our hearts at this time of sorrow.[6]

When Aunty Wai passed on, the heavens opened again, but true to her form, it was as if the elements had conspired with her to ensure she had the final word. My brother Joe tells the story:

> It made me aware that there's a spirit world out there at Aunty Wai's funeral. … We took her out to Whangaehu and then to Turakina to be buried with Uncle Ted, and it was a beautiful day. They bought her out of the church, put her in the hole, and then it clouded over, as if the whole storm was centred on her grave: hailstones from nothing and then five minutes after that it cleared up; it was beautiful again.

Aunty Wai had always told me that she wanted to be buried with Uncle Ted at Turakina. Even when she was dying, she said to me, 'now when I go you are to take me home because Dad lay there'. By 'home', she meant our house in Pūtiki. I said to her, 'well, you won't be, it's really thoughtless of you'. And she said, 'what on earth do you mean?' I told her, 'look, when Aunty Pae died we had Tainui come down because of her daughter-in-law'. (Dan's wife was part of the Kīngitanga,: her mother was the Queen's aunty, and so they all came when Aunty Pae died.) We couldn't host them; we had nowhere to put them. So I said, 'no, we're not going through that. Anyway, you will be dead so you will just have to do as you are told. I'm taking you home, it's easier'.

We had her out at Whangaehu. We knew it was going to be a big tangi.

At the time I had come down to Wellington for a meeting. She got septicemia when she broke her hip. It was just shocking. Poor treatment, misdiagnosis. I'd gone and seen her in the hospital the morning before I'd left. And she said to me, 'no no you go, I'm alright'. And she sounded alright, you know. I thought she would be okay.

By that stage my youngest son Pahia was at boarding school, at Te Aute. While we were in Wellington I rang up the school; he was miserable, my baby. So I said to George, 'let's go over to Te Aute on our way home, round that way'. It was a long way to go, from Wellington to Whanganui via Hastings, but George agreed. Pahia had a friend with him, and we asked if we could take them out for dinner. Without a word of a lie, we had just sat down for dinner and my stomach, it just turned. I get like that when I'm really upset about something. It's quite an amazing feeling; my stomach actually completely turns.

We had just ordered and I got this damn feeling. I said to George, 'I need to ring home; I need to find a phone'. Of course this was in the day before cell phones. And he said, 'don't be silly, we're going home straight afterwards, have a kai.' I said, 'no, I need to ring home; I think something's happening'. I rang home and nobody answered. And I thought, 'shit, where's Kawana? I mean by that stage my brother had had an accident leaving him a tetraplegic – where can he be? So I tried to ring Rua's – nobody answered; rang Joe's – nobody answered; and then I rang the hospital. And the nurse at the hospital said to me, 'are you family?'

I just about bloody died. I said, 'yes, I'm her daughter'. And she said, 'oh hold on a minute please, I think they're trying to get hold of you'. Rua was just beside herself. She said to me 'you better hurry up and get home, because she's dying'. I couldn't believe it.

I went and told George and he said, 'well, we'll just finish what we've got here'. I wanted to get up from the table right there and then. We went straight back to the hostel, and I remember we asked if Mick (Pahia) could come home with us. Te Awi Riddell, who was the principal, said, 'maybe you should wait'. I said, 'no I'm not waiting. He can come home with us now'. So we took him.

And truly we got to the hospital and Morvin was there; Morvin was doing karakia with her. I went in. She was unconscious, but I took her hands, and held them in mine ... and she sort of came to, looked at me.

I told them, 'we're going to take her home'. Rang the undertaker to come and get her; took her home. Put her on a mattress in the lounge. Aunty Moki was there with us; there was only us, me and Rua.

And the bloody cat.

She had this cat – its name was Pūtiki. The bloody cat used to rattle the doors to open them; used to jump up and grab the handles. We're sitting in the lounge with her and this bloody cat leaps up and tries to open the door. We're all sitting there looking at the door waiting for someone to walk in and we hear a noise but nobody comes in. I say to Rua, 'go and have a look down the passage'. And she said, 'you go and have a look!'

Anyway, I open the door and this bloody cat was sitting there. It was amazing. It sort of walked around her, looked at her, and then hopped on the side of the mattress, curled up beside her, this bloody cat.

Last year a waiata written by Aunty Wai came to light.

The National Library archives include a copy of *Te Ao Hou* published in July 1958. An article in this publication describes the farewell song written for Reverend Kīngi Ihaka, who had served the North Māori Pastorate in Whanganui, and was based at St Paul's Anglican Memorial Church in Pūtiki from 1952. His transfer to the Wellington Māori Pastorate in 1958 was 'deeply regretted by his parishioners', the article noted:

> There was a gathering at Te Paku-o-te-rangi, the Putiki marae, at Wanganui. There were only a few persons present to arrange and finalise a few matters. During the occasion, speeches were delivered, all of which were followed by the singing of ancient Maori songs of a somewhat sad nature. It was well after midnight, when those assembled departed for their respective homes.
>
> Amongst those present, was a woman of faith and one who took an interest in learning the ancient Maori songs of her particular tribe.

Arriving home, she was saddened by what was said and sung during the night. Eventually, she retired to bed and soon fell asleep. No sooner was she asleep however, when she had a most vivid dream. In her dream, she witnessed a vast gathering of Maoris at which a number of orations were given. Following one of the speeches, she was obliged to sing a lament, and whilst doing so, tears readily came to her eyes.

When she awoke, her face was wet with tears, but the strange feature of this true incident, is the fact that she not only remembered the words of her lament, but also the air. She had sung this as a farewell song for the Rev. K. Ihaka who was about to be transferred to Wellington.

The woman concerned is Mrs Waiharakeke Waitere, of the Ngati-Apa, Muaupoko and Whanganui tribes, and this incident is recorded in order to reveal to the public in general that Maori 'mana' still exists today. It is a beautiful song – a real Maori classic, which should find a place in future editions of *Nga Moteatea*.

The article went on to note that the composer of this song 'had never before composed a Maori song and her first has indeed surpassed all modern Maori songs; in fact it is the writer's belief that the standard is equal to a number of classical songs included in treasured volumes such as *Nga Moteatea*'.

The last word, then, in the story of Aunty Wai, is her own lament to 'my beloved one, taku piki amokura':

> Taku piki amokura, amohia te aroha;
> E kore rawa e mutu i nga tau maha e.
> Ka haere koe te takiwa, titiro iho ki nga awa
> He roimata no te iwi e tangi atu i muri nei e.
> Ko Whanganui tenei, hei putiki i te aroha;
> Tiehutia te wai ko Whangaehu tera.
> Turakina te rakau, ko Turakina te awa:
> Tikeitia te waewae, ko Rangitikei e.
> Ka tangi taku mapu i konei e taku piki amokura,
> E tuku nei te roimata i aku kamo e …

My esteemed, beloved one, uplift that which bears love;
A love that will ever flourish till eternity.
Wherever you walk, ever behold our ancient rivers;
For they are but the tears of those who mourn your loss, my loved one.
Tis Whanganui that calmly flows, to bind together charity;
Turbulent waters run close by, for tis Whangaehu
A tree once felled: the origin of Turakina;
Long steps taken: the origin of Rangitikei.
My lament flows freely, oh my esteemed, beloved one;
Freely too do tears flow from my eyes, my loved one.

NOTES

1 Tariana Turia, 'The best advice I ever got', *The Listener*, 1 January 2011.

2 M. Johnston, 'The women who shape New Zealand: Tariana Turia', *New Zealand Women's Weekly*, 27 June 2012.

3 Turia, 'The best advice I ever got'.

4 Tariana Turia, Handover of Report from the Taskforce on Whānau Centred Initiatives speech, 11 February 2010. www.beehive.govt.nz/speech/handover-report-taskforce-whanau-centred-initiatives (accessed 11 February 2015).

5 Christine Robertson, 'It's been hard', *Mana Magazine*, February–March 1999, pp. 42–3.

6 Māori Party press release, 'Poroporoaki – Morvin Te Anatipa Simon', 14 May 2014. *Scoop Independent News*. www.scoop.co.nz/stories/PA1405/S00221/poroporoaki-morvin-te-anatipa-simon.htm (accessed 11 February 2015).

Tariana's father, Tariuha Manawaroa Te Awe Awe.
Source: Personal collection (Tariana)

Tariana and George on their wedding day, 10 November 1962, at Rātana Pā.
Source: Helen Drew

Tariana and George circa 1966 with Alan (L), Lisa and Mark.
Source: Helen Drew

'Our aunties were always there – always guiding us.' Aunty Paeroa, Aunty Wai and Tariana attending a hui at Whakarongotai Marae, Waikanae in the late 1970s.
Source: Personal collection (Tariana)

The Rātana faith has had a significant influence on Tariana over the years. Here her aunt and mentor Iriaka Rātana speaks to supporters at Manukōrihi Marae, Waitara in 1966. Iriaka was the first Māori woman elected to Parliament.
Source: www.nzhistory.net.nz, *NZ Archives*

Tariana with her mokopuna in front of the tupuna whare, Rangitāhuahua, at her home marae in Whangaehu. Together, Tariana and George were one of the driving forces restoring the marae in 1985 after fires and floods had wreaked havoc.
Source: Mana magazine

On 15 August 2001, Mark's daughter, Piata, came into the world. George and Tariana took up full-time care of their mokopuna and their life was never the same.
Source: Shane Bennett

-CHAPTER FIVE-
TOGETHER WITH GEORGE

Most of what we've done, we've done together. And I think that's what bound us together. So no matter what we've gone through in our lives, it's kind of like we were bound together.

Marilyn Payne says of George Turia:

> My impression was that he was Tariana's rock, you know; that steady quiet man. I'm quite sure she sounded out a lot of her ideas on him; he was always there supporting.

In 1961 Tariana Woon entered the hostel for nurses at Whanganui Hospital. She was barely seventeen at the time. At the start of her nursing career, she met her husband-to-be, George Turia, and promptly fell in love. In those days you couldn't be married and be a nurse. Against her family's wishes, Tariana chose George over the nursing career they had wanted her to follow.

I had just started nursing when I met George. I went to a dance with one of the twins, Maana, my cousin. Dan and Maana were the same age as me, and Maana often used to take me out. It was the only way Aunty Wai could allow me out of the house. I'd never been allowed out to what they called the 'Rock Club'. When you're not allowed to go, well, you want to go. So Maana used to come and pick me up from the nurse's hostel and we'd be off.

This particular night, Aunty Moki's daughter, Mana Te Patu, was also with me. We went to this dance, and this guy started being really annoying; he was a bit creepy. I was beside myself because he was chasing me around.

Mana said to me, 'see that guy over there?' and she pointed out George. The plot was that we'd go over and pretend that we were with him, and in the process get rid of the other guy. George is sitting on his motorbike outside and my mate tells me 'go on, hop on the back'. So I do, and he takes off with me on it, and that's how I met him. I thought 'oh god, what have I done!'

We must have gone about four blocks down Glasgow Street, hadn't said a word, and then of all things the bike runs out of gas, so we have to push it back to the dance hall. George was very shy and I was very scared, so it was a long quiet walk trudging along, pushing this bike. About one block before the hall he goes, 'What's your name? Where do you work?' And that was about the extent of our conversation.

But the next week he rang me up and asked me out. I quite liked him because he was quiet, he didn't drink, and there was a sense of security about him. I think it was that that attracted me to him. Aunty Wai always used to say to me that I only wanted to marry him because I wanted a father figure. I'd say to her, 'whatever'. I didn't think it was true, but she may have been right. I was definitely looking for a particular kind of male.

Anyway, I started going out with George. We would go to dances. We would walk for miles, because we had no money. Silence was golden. George has never really been much of a chatterer.

The first date we had, we wanted to go for a picnic by the river. Aunty Wai couldn't see why we couldn't have a picnic on the bottom lawn, where she would be sitting at the window watching us! Why would I argue back about that?

The first time I was going to go away from Whanganui I was going to stay with my girlfriend Helen, and Helen's godmother in Wellington; it was a dental nurses' do. George, me and Bill Teupo Bates: we were all going down. I think secretly I knew Aunty Wai would disapprove, and I wanted her approval to go. So we stopped at her place and I told her we were going to Wellington.

Her interrogation began: 'so who are you going with?'

'With George and Bill.'

'Oh no', she said, 'that's not right'.

'Helen's meeting us down there. We're staying with Helen.'

'No, no, it's so inappropriate for you to travel with two young men. You're not going.'

George said to me, 'I knew we shouldn't have called in here. If you don't get in this car, we're finished.' Well, I went back inside the house.

We mostly went out in groups, with other nurses, and George was friendly with the Cook Island and Samoan community – played rugby for them – so we used to do a lot of things with them. George boarded with a Pākehā family, the Penningtons, and a Samoan guy lived there too: Louis.

George had told me he was Cook Island, and I believed him because that was all he mixed with, Samoan and Cook Island people. Conned alright. It was probably a good year before I found out the truth. Gloria, his sister, got osteomyelitis in her arm and I was nursing and all his family came down to support her at the hospital. That's when I discovered they were just river rats, from the bloody river, no more Cook Island than I was – trying to be all exotic.

It was a bit nerve-wracking, all the same. I'm sure his mother disliked me on sight. And we'd been going out together for over a year by that stage.

Aunty Wai liked him – well, right up until she realised that he wanted to marry me. And then it all changed, because he was interfering in all her plans. She wanted me to finish my nursing training. Marriage was frowned upon, as of course you couldn't be devoted both to a husband and a career at the same time. I recall my aunt saying to George that they had dreams for me and they didn't include him!

We married on 10 November 1962. The Samoan and Cook Island people put it on for us, and we had it in the back garden of a house that we were renting. They put a marquee up.

Aunty Wai said she wasn't going to come to the wedding. But she did come out to Rātana, to the temple where we got married. She wouldn't come to the house, and nobody else was allowed to either. I was devastated; they were my family. But Maana came, my darling cousin. He was the black sheep, so he would always do what he wanted.

And some of my cousins came: mostly the rugby ones and Wiki Phillips; she was my bridesmaid, from Whanganui. She was a bit older than me but always really good to me. She was the same family as Aunty Moki and Mana, who was my really close mate; she was that family too. Wiki insisted that I have a wedding; we weren't going to, but she insisted. She made me get a dress: pale pink, it was. You see I couldn't possibly have white. I was pregnant. Six months after we were wed, my first born, Alan, was born in April 1963.

Aunty Wai was so ashamed of me. I'd let her down. She told George, 'You can't keep her in the manner in which she's been accustomed'. After that he didn't go around there for about five years.

She hated jandals, and she'd want to buy me things because we were poor – get me shoes or a coat – and I wouldn't take it. Besides, George would be saying to me, 'you're not to take anything off her'. She used to get things for the church – clothes and shoes – and I'd go round there and my uncle Ted would say to me, 'Hey Nigger, go and have a look in there, I think there's some shoes'. Aunty would get mad at me if she saw me wearing something out of the church box. That would be so embarrassing; especially if I turned up at the church wearing them. She was a snob in a lot of ways. But as I got older, I understood that it was about wanting the best.

In the end she changed her mind. As she got older she'd be praising George, and I'd say, 'well, you didn't think that when I met him. You didn't want me to marry him then'. And she'd go, 'Oh, I course I did'. You could never win with Aunty Wai.

When I had our babies, George and I were poor. It didn't occur to me that you shouldn't have one (a baby) because you're poor. You just learn to manage better; you cope because you have to. You have a bigger garden.[1]

It wasn't an easy start to our life, all the same. We had married very young, and we struggled in those early years. We were really poor; making do on George's meagre wage as an apprentice plasterer and bricklayer.

I used to love going out to Uncle Harry Tamehana's at Whangaehu, opposite the marae, to be with my much-loved cousins Raymond and Bessie. When George and I were newly-weds, we would catch the 4am workers' bus in the morning out there and spend the day with him. We'd play cards and just enjoy being together.

Uncle Harry used to pick up one member from each household of our whānau in the Whangaehu Valley, and we would take two buckets to Waitārere Beach to gather pipi. When we returned we shared the kai with all our whānau. In those days, if anyone went hunting, there was always a sharing of the bounty. This was in the time before fridges and freezers, so kai only lasted a short time unless it was dried, smoked or preserved. Today we freeze everything and a consequence of the technology is that it limits who we share with.

Everyone grew their vegetables, and there were massive gardens always developed within the concept of sharing. Government policy has denied us the opportunity to build on family land, as we were moved into towns and cities to work in places such as factories, railways and the freezing works. It was there that we discovered the corner dairy for our daily needs, and realised that a quarter-acre section wouldn't graze a milking cow. We lost our ability to sustain ourselves. There is so much for us to restore.

In spite of everything we always managed.

One of the themes that consistently comes through Tariana's story is the practice of manaakitanga: generosity of spirit towards others. Sharing her home, her family, her life comes naturally to Tariana, and always has. Lifelong friend Helen Drew remembers the open-door policy that Tariana and George always extended to her:

> On the way home from work I would pop in and see her. Half the time I would end up having a meal. If they were having a chop she would have to cut hers in half to share with me, and George would have the other. We didn't care – we just had a lot of fun in those days.

The friendship between Helen and Tariana continued long past their school days. Helen says:

> Tari and I were as thick as thieves. We spent so much time together. When [she and George] were first married I was at their place nearly every day, after work or in weekends.
>
> One time we were pregnant at the same time. We'd go and look along the roadside for those red-leafed trees that have those red plums on. We weren't very well off, either of us, at that stage. We'd fill our laps up with plums and we'd sit down on the grass and eat them, or we'd go raid my father's tree for feijoas. We ate a whole bucket of feijoas one night when we were pregnant. We both had a craving for fruit.

Although the two were close, Helen was careful not to get in the way of the relationship George and Tariana had as young newly marrieds. She says:

> I think that's been a beautiful love story – she and George. She came and stayed with me once when I was living in Levin. She woke me up about midnight and said she had to ring George because she was too lonely. We had to ring George and he had to come and get her. She hadn't ever been apart from him, and she just couldn't stand it. By then they must have been married for probably ten years. George is amazing. He was never anything but welcoming. He always appeared to be glad to see me, but I'm sure there must have been times when he wished I would go away so that he could just be with Tari. He took both of us on there for a while in a way. He's a lovely, patient quiet man and he's been her strength and her rock really.

George, having grown up one of fifteen children in a two-bedroom house, has always upheld a very strong work ethic. His father died young and yet his mother, Mere Turia, had never gone on a benefit. She worked in the market gardens in Ohakune; their whole family did.

His cousin, Jo Maniapoto, was very clear where the source of George's strength was derived.

> George's mother was an amazing woman; she's a woman I have the highest admiration for. As a kid I saw her work in the market gardens, drive up to Auckland, with a sick husband and all these kids. She made sure every one of them had a trade; absolutely refused to let them finish school, because she wanted the best for her children.
>
> As soon as the children could pick a carrot they were out there in the gardens too. They learnt to stand on their own resources; to be completely independent.

George's ability to fend for himself comes through in a story told by his aunt, Julie Ranginui:

> George was born up the river. I used to say to [Tariana], 'you'll always have your background with you but when you go into other marae where part of your genealogy is there, then you stand on that. Never ever make yourself feel like a visitor when you are up the river, because your husband is tūrangawaewae'. And she said, 'what does that mean?' I said, 'his feet came out on the river first when he was born from his mother'. His mother always said there was panic when he was being born, because of his feet coming first. I've always kept that alive, you know – he goes in feet first. Te putanga mai o ngā waewae tuatahi.

George was self-employed by the time he was twenty-one. His resilience, his determination to succeed no matter what, and his belief in the art of possibility has been an ongoing source of inspiration for his wife. Whatever challenge she took on, he would be there, feet first, helping turn the dreams into action.

We had so much trouble finding somewhere to live. We would go and look at a flat. If George came with me they would say, 'Oh, I'm really sorry but this one's taken'. If I went by myself they could never be sure whether or not I was Māori. We had a lot of difficulty getting a decent one. The only ones available to us were quite run-down. They were quite blatant in those days; they'd actually say, 'we don't have Māori tenants'.

In the end I walked in off the street to this legal firm in town. I burst into tears and told the lawyer how we couldn't get a flat, and that if we were offered a place they were always substandard. Right there and then he offered us an estate home he was handling. In doing so, he restored my faith in people.

Helped by George's boss, we eventually bought a section in Whanganui East, where George built our home. We owned our own home by the time we were twenty-two: it was a great start in life. And then we set about creating a family.

First, in 1963, was Alan George Kawana Turia, carrying the name of his father and my loved brother, Kawana Waitere.

Two years later, along came Mark Teina Charles Turia; and two years after that Lisa Te Aroha Turia. The name Te Aroha comes from the words 'he aroha te mea nui o ngā mea katoa' – love is the greatest thing of all. It was also the name of my mum, known by everyone else as Aunty or Nanny Dorsey.

And our baby, Pahia Simon Anthony Turia, was born in 1972.

Along the way we were also blessed with three precious whāngai daughters: Ilona, Carmelle and Francie. Ilona is my god-daughter; Carmelle is the daughter of my brother, Anthony; and Francie came to stay with us when she was just a young girl and quickly became part of our family.

Our precious firstborn, Alan, was probably about six months old when it became clear that there was something not right with me. I didn't want to mix with people; I wanted just to be at home. I'd walk for miles and I'd cry. I'd be crying round the streets, and people would ring George at his job. At that time we only had a bike, and he'd have to get on his bike and look for me.

I was young, and I was terribly depressed. At that time postnatal depression was never talked about, and certainly not understood. I was like that for about eighteen months. The doctor put me on medication – it kept me in a dozy state.

I probably would have stayed in that haze had it not been for an intervention from Waimiha: the arrival of a great big woman who turned up out of the blue to stay with us. Aunty Rita was married to George's dad's brother, Uncle Vic. She said to George, 'you take a month off work and you come home with me, and I will fix this girl'. We got the impression there wasn't much room for negotiation. Needless to say, George took the month off and we traipsed up to Waimiha to stay with her.

I hated her guts.

She'd take us out for a drive and then suddenly say, 'stop here' in the middle of town, and George would have to go and pick pūhā. I would be sitting inside the car. She was huge, Aunty, and she'd be bending over, picking pūhā. I'd think, 'oh god, please don't let anybody come and see us'. She made me go out to socials and again, I'd go and sit in the car. And she'd say to George, 'leave her; if she wants to sit in the car, she can sit in there by herself'. She threw my pills away: flushed them down the loo. I remember being shattered, thinking, 'I'll go crazy. I need those pills.' I really thought I did.

She got me some knitting needles and a Fair Isle pattern – me, who couldn't even knit. It was brown and cream, that bloody jersey, and she made me knit it. I thought I was going to go crazy. She even made me look after the baby; she just made me pull myself together. And then about a week before we left, she told me 'If you don't pull yourself together I'm going to tell my nephew to leave you: he deserves better than this'.

And I'll tell you what: it did make me pull myself together.

I remember very distinctly that I would feel a panic attack coming on and I would just not allow it; I wouldn't allow it. I'd walk and I'd do everything I could. Then I got involved in netball and sport – I was very determined to never let that happen to me again. And since that time I've never allowed myself to have a panic attack. It was sheer determination to never go through that again.

She'd say to me, 'Ah, there's nothing wrong with you. Just need to pull your bloody self together. For goodness sake. I'm not going to have my nephew shacked up with some sheila like you who thinks that's she depressed.' She really was so funny, but in the end she was good for me. A long time later, I realised I loved her: loved her to bits. We used to go up and stay there and she'd say, 'fix you up, eh?'

At the time all our babies came along I took on jobs where I could take a day off and I wouldn't be missed. I worked in factories, which of course distressed my aunt, and cleaning, where I could take my boys along; waitressing or a bit of sewing. Anything where I didn't have to leave my children with someone else.

As a young parent I knew all our neighbours in our street. When I walked our tamariki to the kindergarten the neighbours would be out the front of the houses, saying good morning. I remember one of the neighbours saying to me, 'you keep your children so beautiful and you are a very quiet family'. I was nearly going to say to her, 'and why wouldn't we be?' When George came home I said to him, 'Gosh some of these people are cheeky – they think because we are Māori we are going to be a noisy family having parties all the time and our kids are going to be dirty'. And he said to me, 'oh Mum, you're defensive'. And I said, 'No, I guarantee she doesn't say that to the young Pākehā couple across the road'.

But in those days you knew everybody and you watched out for everyone. We lived in a back section, and I remember one of our elderly neighbours at the front died overnight. Well, my boy is on the way to school and he sees the ambulance outside, so he hops over the fence and knocks on the door: 'Mr Lincoln, what's the ambulance here for?' He comes running home to me: 'Mum, Mrs Lincoln has just died'. So over we went – that was how it was. Everyone was our business. I believe we have to return to those values: to restore to ourselves the importance of being everybody's business. When I was young growing up in Pūtiki, we were everybody's business. In fact we used to get hoha with our aunties: our whānau knew immediately whatever we did. But perhaps that's the kind of surveillance we actually need.

Some of our whānau have got stupid. You ring them up and they say, 'who do you think you are?' and it makes people a bit nervous about intervening. We need the community to come together; people to care for one another. We need to restore the ability to care about the people in our street, our whānau, maintaining the connections between one another. That's the biggest work.

We were really poor, and I was always trying to make ends meet. I had to make all my kids' clothes. I had to learn to sew whether I liked it or not. I wouldn't say that I loved it. My kids laugh now when they look back at pictures and they say 'Mum, did you make those out of the curtains?' You made do. You wouldn't have dreamt of spending more than you had; it wouldn't have occurred to me to not live within my income. I cut up George's shirts to make the kids clothes; cut up winter coats. It was how it was: at least they were warm.

I loved my children dearly, and there was nothing that I wouldn't have done for them, but I never thought I could look into my own culture for the answers; I was always looking elsewhere.

I took the children to kindergarten. I hated going, but my boys loved going there and playing with the other kids. I had to walk because I had no money. I used to walk them three kilometres from Whanganui East to Pūtiki, three days a week. I'd take them in a double pushchair with a rain cover over top. I walked them every day until the woman next door said, 'why don't you take them around the corner? There's a kindergarten there.' She was the chair of the kindy, and she'd ask me every time I saw her. I told her, 'the other one's got mainly Māori children, and I want to go there'. She said, 'it would be so much easier to go round the corner. Why don't you just try it?'

Much the same thing was said to me by the regional director of Māori Affairs in Whanganui, a Mr Cater, a Pākehā guy I met when he was having lunch at Aunty Wai's one day. He asked me why I went to Pūtiki instead of the one in Whanganui East. I told him, 'because I don't know anyone and I'm not sure if I would fit in'. He replied, 'I never thought I would hear you imply that you weren't as good as anyone else'. I said, 'I didn't say that. I didn't think I'd fit in – it's a bit different.' And he said to me, 'I would have thought, with the family you come from, that you could fit in anywhere if you chose to.'

He was probably right. It did make me go around there to see what it was like. So I took Alan and Mark there. There was nothing cultural there – most people were more interested in what my husband did for a job. The first time that I went to a meeting, you had to stand up and say what your husband did for a job; it blew me away. So I said, 'my husband works on the rubbish trucks'. He was a bricklayer and plasterer, but I just thought they were nosy Pākehās. Even as young as I was I knew there was all this status bullshit that used to go on about what your husband did and all that.

I wanted more for my kids. I wanted them to know the essence of what it was to be Māori. I felt really strongly about it, especially because our schools failed to provide any reo. We used to travel some distance to take our children to Māori club, just so they could participate.

It was during the sixties that Tariana started her love affair with netball. She had struck up a friendship with Aroha Henry, grandmother of Silver Fern Jolene Henry. Aroha talks about Tariana's techniques on and off the court:

> Tariana and I got married about the same time, and our children all grew up together, and we did a lot of things together. Partly because we were friends we played netball, because she wanted to play and I went along with her. She was more a tricky player than a good player. She used to be down one end and I used to be down the other. She was a centre because she was tiny, and a shooter. She used to shoot

goals: quite good too. We played with Pākehā teams for the start – I think they were called Revellers – and then she started taking a Māori team coaching.

Tariana also has very fond memories of her years of netball.

I coached netball for years – club netball, school netball. I loved it. I used to umpire. I used to take my kids with me, rain, hail or snow. My kids were brought up on the netball courts.

I was quite strict with my coaching, as well as my umpiring. I remember one of my nieces was a brilliant player, and she didn't turn up to training one week. The rule was that if you didn't come to training, you didn't get a game. It just so happened that her mother turned up that Saturday to watch her daughter play. I had to tell the girl that she couldn't play because she didn't come to training and she didn't ring me. Her mother came over and had a go at me, but I wouldn't give in; I didn't let her play. It broke my heart because I so loved my niece, but you had to be disciplined and to have high expectations of the kids. They knew how important it was for them to be there; they loved their netball. But her mother didn't speak to me for a couple of weeks.

If people had the misfortune to die on a Saturday, I would be extremely upset. So inconvenient. George would get so angry with me because I wouldn't want to leave until after the games. I was netball mad.

You used to get graded as an umpire, and I got to regionals, where you could referee inter-regional games. Then I went for my nationals.

It's funny – no matter what I've done I've always managed to offend someone. A lot of our Māori kids loved to umpire. They'd come on a Saturday morning and it would be freezing cold – they used to have to wear their little white gear or a school uniform. I had become the president of the Umpires' Association in Whanganui, and I decided they should be allowed to wear tracksuits to keep warm. Most of the tracksuits those days were Adidas: our kids couldn't afford them. I said what we should be thankful for was that they were coming out early in the morning and umpiring the primary school games, and we shouldn't make such a big deal if instead of an Adidas tracksuit they had jeans on or something.

In response, one particular woman said I'd lowered the tone of the Umpires' Association and she did everything she could to undermine me, to make it look as if I was doing something wrong. When I went for my New Zealand badge, she went round and round the court, talking to all the people who were judging me.

I asked to see the original marking sheets, and saw they had scaled me back. I told them I was really disappointed that they had scaled me back. I know I'm a good umpire; all the players think I'm a good umpire, so that's enough for me. I thought to myself, 'just be satisfied'. I had my regional certificate.

George and Tariana's life together has involved a series of projects and joint ventures on a business and personal front. Each new project has become an opportunity to forge new friendships, and to develop relationships which in some cases have become lifelong connections.

When George and Tariana's children were still young, Tariana was working as an occupational therapist and then as a recreational officer. She ran recreation groups in Pūtiki and in schools for people on low incomes. One of these groups was Haumihi: a sporting and cultural group for young people. George and Tariana's friendship with Michael and Marilyn Payne first developed through this group.

Michael, an architect, is well known in Whanganui. Michael had designed the reconstruction of the central communal space at Rātana, Te Manuao. He was also well known to Aunty Wai. In the 1970s, he had worked to Aunty Wai's instructions in reconstructing the meeting house at Pūtiki and building the kindergarten.

Michael also presided over the creation of the Quaker Settlement, where he and Marilyn have lived for over three decades. The Settlement is a place Tariana has loved to visit over the years; to hold professional development meetings, workshops and conferences or just to be part of the communal meetings. But it was not architecture that brought Michael and Marilyn into Tariana's life. They came together as young parents with young children, who enjoyed each other's company. Marilyn Payne says of Tariana:

> She always struck me as being a lovely, lovely mum with the children when they were young. Our kids adored her and kapa haka. Michael and I wanted the kids to have as much involvement [as possible]. She set it up and she ran it.

> We met through kapa haka – the Haumihi Kapa Haka club. That's probably the last place that people might think Michael or I would meet up, but it's true. And then there was the kindy. We used to have kindy in the Parish Hall to start with. Aunty Wai used to run it; she was very strong on education.
>
> We all had to fundraise to build that kindy. That kindergarten was built by our families; every month we had to give money to the kindy. You never entered her home when there wasn't a blimmin' raffle book for the church or for the kindy.

About the same time they met the Paynes, Tariana and George forged a friendship with another couple who would become lifelong friends: Jens and Karen Bukholt, who had arrived from Denmark in 1962. Jens recalls:

> When our children were in primary school, we enrolled them in the Māori club led by George and Tari. Esther, our oldest daughter, loved it, and became quite the expert in performing with two or four long pois. Karen and I attended the weekly session with our children and gained not only a deeper knowledge and understanding of the Māori culture but also a lifelong friendship with George and Tariana.

Conversations with Karen and Jens are colourful, the words flowing as freely as the fresh strong coffee bubbling in the pot. Through the ever-constant laughter emerges the sense of significance that both attributed to their earliest conversations with Tariana. Jens says:

> I absolutely loved Tari right from day one. She was such a wonderful person to debate with: she had her view, I had my view. I learnt a lot from her, and I'm sure she learnt a little bit from me too, because she respected the international type of feelings. We wanted to be part of New Zealand, and you can only be part of New Zealand if you're also part of the iwi, the Māori situation.

Karen sewed the bodice for all the uniforms for the Haumihi Kapa Haka club, using her own cross-stitch embroidery techniques. For his part, Jens brought his artistic flair to the creation of the tīpare (headbands). He says:

Tari and me were sitting there making the artwork for them – we sat out in Whangaehu. We had the honour of actually being part of helping to produce headbands. We didn't have enough of those, so I would paint it on and at a distance it looked all the same.

It was during this time that Tariana and Marilyn became particularly immersed in community development. Marilyn remembers:

> We did a lot. You do when you're young mums and the kids come with you; you're doing things in amongst them. One of the things we got involved in was the Community Volunteers [programme], and we used to do a lot of fundraising. I remember we ran some dances, and these great big Māori blokes came in looking absolutely wild. I remember Tariana and me were sitting behind the desks and she says, 'oh, they are so beautiful'. I looked at her and I thought, 'well, they are lovely, but it's not quite how I would have put it'. But she just loved them all.

The Department of Social Welfare, established in 1972, funded the establishment of the Community Volunteers programme, which supported community-based service delivery by community voluntary and not-for-profit organisations.

Community Volunteers was also closely tied to Holdsworth School, with which both George and Tariana and Marilyn and Michael had associations. Holdsworth had opened on a site in June 1971 that had formerly been the New Zealand Friends School, administered by the Quaker Society. Holdsworth was a national training institution for disturbed or disadvantaged boys aged between eight and twelve years old; it aimed to provide social, education and recreational training for such boys. Māori made up at least half the number of boys admitted to Holdsworth every year between 1972 and 1981. In 1981, 70 percent were Māori.

The boys came to Holdsworth with a history of various placements in foster and family homes, private institutions, boys' homes, health camps and residential schools for 'maladjusted children'. In the 1975 report the roll listed children who exhibited patterns of behaviour including 'chronic truancy, running away from home, petty theft over lengthy periods, markedly aggressive behaviour towards others, severe educational under-achievement, explosive behavioural outbursts, inability to relate adequately with others and acting out behaviour'.[2]

At the time that Tariana and Marilyn became involved, the principal of the school was seeking 'substitute families' with whom the boys in residence could be provided with family experiences. One of Tariana's whāngai daughters, Ilona, remembers the boys from Holdsworth who came to live with the Turia whānau:

> We already knew they had a troubled past. Things that still weren't right for them. I sort of felt like I fitted in with them. I could understand and identify. In actual fact I thought they were worse off than me, because I didn't end up getting put into a home. I thought I was lucky because I got to go into a nice home. Most of the boys that stayed with us – none of them caused any trouble when they stayed at Mum and Dad's.

Marilyn had a more active involvement in the day-to-day life of Holdsworth – she taught art at the school. She recalls:

> I taught art there for about four days a week. I had an old house and we used to have potters' wheels running. I had a couple of kids; they were little. One was sitting on the seat, the other was working the treadle, and I was really impressed with how they would work together. 'Oh,' said one of the older blokes, 'they used to convert cars – one would get down and do the pedals and the other would kneel on the seat and drive'.

As a consequence of their involvement with Holdsworth, Marilyn and Tariana started to work together in supporting young people working in community jobs. Subsequently, in 1980, Tariana and George established Te Awa Youth Trust, the country's first marae-based training programme.

NOTES

1. Oral history interview between Tariana Turia and Taina Tangaere McGregor, 25 May 2006, Oral History Political Diary project, Alexander Turnbull Library.
2. Ministry of Social Development, Social Welfare Residential Care, 1950–1994, Volume Two, National Institutions, Holdsworth Reports F000001599381, 2006, pp. 1–2.

-CHAPTER SIX-

CHILDREN – THE FOOTSTEPS TO OUR FUTURE

I remember her at really tense times cuddling her grandchildren. She was labelled all sorts of things by Pākehā newspapers and politicians, yet there was a complete disjunction between the media image and what she's like and what our people were thinking of her.[1]

My greatest triumph is being a young mother and therefore today being able to see my great grandchildren. You never imagine these little extensions of your whakapapa are going to be there running around – it gives me the greatest joy. I've been at almost every birth.[2]

Professor Whatarangi Winiata, founding president of the Māori Party, used to refer to Tariana as 'Te Whaea o te Motu'; literally 'the Mother of the Nation'. His intention was clear. Like a mother, Tariana has sacrificed so much for a better future for all her children to enjoy. In referring to her in this way, Professor Winiata attributed Tariana's initiative Whānau Ora as being the greatest legacy she would leave her children and grandchildren, for generations to come.

The term 'legacy' is apt for the contribution Tariana has made. It encapsulates notions of a gift, an inheritance, bequeathing inspiration for others to follow. The values and taonga embedded within cultural heritage were seen as a birthright. Nowhere is Tariana's legacy felt more personally than in the family tree that George and Tariana have cultivated in their own home.

George and I are the proud parents of six children – Alan, Mark, Lisa and Pahia; and two whāngai daughters, Ilona and Carmel. And then there was Francie, who died at the age of eighteen. From all these children have sprung twenty-six grandchildren and twenty-seven great-grandchildren.

If I think about it, it was really through my children that I became politicised. I always wanted something more for them. I wanted them to know the essence of what it is to be Māori. I will do whatever it takes to make that happen. To look into the faces of our children, grandchildren and great-grandchildren, and know that they are the seeds of our future is truly everything I need. Te kanohi ora o rātou mā kua whetūrangitia.

I often think about my poor kids while they were growing up. One minute I'd be kneeling besides their beds, reciting 'Jesus gentle Shepherd, hear me; Bless thy little lamb tonight; Through the darkness be thou near me; Keep me safe till morning night'. Then I went through, 'don't believe in any of that. No, look what they did to us'. I was the most confusing mother, because I did the Jesus thing with them and then I was opposed to all that: 'We're going back to our own Atua'.

When I was about twenty-eight years old I decided I would give the Church up: a decision that greatly distressed Aunty Wai. I was reading a lot – anything I could get my hands on – and meeting people who were really politically active. I read about an issue down south where the tangata whenua had given some land to the Anglican Church. Instead of using it for the purpose for which it had been gifted, the Church was using it for a vineyard and turning a nice profit. I talked to Aunty Wai about my dilemma; how could I believe in a church that behaved like this? I remember her response clearly: 'that's about individuals, not the church'. It satisfied her – but I still had questions. And I still do – but my faith in te hunga wairua has never left me.

Che Wilson says:

> I think it's too simple for people to say she's anti-'religious establishment'. It's too simple for people to say that, because she's not anti-wairuatanga. She was always very clear in differentiating the two. She knew that her cousin Ritchie might be doing a long decade of the rosary for her, but she knew that it was the wairuatanga associated with that, that was looking after her. Just like the Anglican Church at Pūtiki and Nanny Wai. We often see them as the same thing, but most of the time they aren't.

And then I got into the politics thing. I was part of the ones that went around Whanganui saying 'don't vote; you're only encouraging them'. And then I go and join the Labour Party. My kids would say to me, 'God, mum, you're just so confusing; we don't know what to believe'.

Perhaps the clearest summing up of Tariana's belief system and its influence on her children may be found in the words of son Pahia:

> I think you see in my brothers and sisters where Mum was at, at that particular time of her own development and understanding of the world. It's probably reflected in our personalities. I look at Alan; he's the rock, he's solid, he's grounded, he's got all of those real strong characteristics. And then I look at Mark and I think to myself [his birth] was when Mum really started to become aware about the shit

> that happened to us as a people. That's reflected in his character as well, you know: he doesn't like authority and all that type of stuff.
>
> Then Lisa came through a period of time when Mum understood what had happened – started to get into this, 'how do we make this the consciousness of all of our people'. And then I came through that period, so, 'ok what are we going to do about it?'
>
> I think we are a reflection of where Mum was. I can remember as a kid I'd lie there for hours and Mum would sit there with me in her arms and she'd have a *Mills and Boon* book: she'd read hundreds and hundreds of them. We always had real conversations. She'd never say to me, 'just because'. She'd always talk to me – provide me with a rationale – and I realise how much time she actually invested in kōrero and conversation.

It has been well over fifty years since Tariana and George first welcomed a newborn baby to the world. Throughout that time, their parenting practice has reflected a sense of responsibility to raise their children with values that will protect them from harm and keep them strong in life.

> When situations happen within your whānau that you may have had no control over, but you often feel very deeply that you could have done things better as a mother to prevent them from happening. There have been times where I have felt considerable pain that I have not been able to foresee certain things and have not been able to intervene.[3]

Tariana's second son, Mark, was a person of interest for the press gallery early on in her days as a Member of Parliament. One of the first issues that brought Mark into the public arena was the subject of Tariana's speech to the Psychological Society in the year 2000. The speech contrasted the impact of colonisation with the concept of home invasion. In it Tariana said:

> I can see the connections between 'home invasions' which concern many of us to the invasion of the 'home lands of indigenous people from another land'. What I have difficulty in reconciling is how 'home invasions' emits such outpourings of concern for the victims and an intense despising of the invaders while the invasion of the

'home lands' of Māori does not engender the same level of emotion and concern for the Māori victims.[4]

Psychologist Professor James Ritchie responded to the resulting media outcry as follows:

> The leap from home invasion to colonial invasion is a hell of a big leap. But Māori people suffered invasion not just of their homes but of their whole territories and the actual record of atrocities has been dropped out. For example colonial bushrangers in the Urewera campaign brought in prisoners, tied them to horses and dragged them through the bush at a gallop. These things are part of the collective memory and continue to be told.[5]

While the substance of her speech was feeding a rapid frenzy of reaction on talkback and in the chamber, Tariana was concerned about the impact of her statements upon those in her own home; particularly her son.

When I first came into Parliament the media found out that my son had been to jail and that he had committed what they call home invasion. Now I'm very creative with language, and I'd talked about the home invasion of our lands. So the media picked up on it, and they said, 'well, of course she knows all about home invasion, because her own son committed home invasion'. And they got the family whose home he had gone into to go public.

The interesting thing about it was that I hadn't been here very long, but people here in Parliament – even National Party members – immediately rang me up or came over to me in the House and said, 'that is appalling. That is just shocking to bring your family into this environment, and we want you to know that we are absolutely appalled'.

I rang my son up, and I said, 'you are not to talk to the media. Say nothing'.

The media interviewed me. Because it was about my son and I probably felt like a tiger – protective – I said, 'yes. It was seventeen years ago; he has paid the price, and none of us are proud of what he did. But I'm not going to allow your inference that I'm not good enough, or that I can't talk about these things because of what my son has done'. I did go on attack that day.

I don't think George and I ever understood addiction. That was until one day, a group from Palmerston North who have been extremely good in the smoking cessation area began doing these genograms of families involved in smoking. Four generations, all big smokers. It blew me away. It wasn't until I saw it in those genograms – of maybe about seventy people, there were only two who didn't smoke – that I realised just the impact that would have on an individual within that family setting. I remember our kids saying to George and I that we were the abnormal ones: all the cousins, all the aunties, everybody smoked. With Mark and his addictions, when I think back about it, I didn't understand it. I think that right from when he was little, you could almost see the pattern beginning.

When he was only about three he would sniff petrol: hop under the house and do it. We would go to visit relatives and he'd have a little drink of the petrol. And I just thought it was bad behaviour, naughty behaviour. I was always up at A and E. Honest. He used to even do it at school. They couldn't let him mow the lawns at school. I never connected it at all. I just thought he was really naughty.

He would climb up on the drawers, pull the drawers out, climb up on my benches, open up the cupboards, hop into the cupboards and go right up to the top where he would find the poisons and the pills; you wouldn't credit it. He got up there one day and he drank an antiseptic you used for cuts and scrapes. It would stain the skin red when it was applied. Anyway on this day, Mark had a big red stain around his mouth. I didn't know how much he'd drunk. I raced up to the hospital. In the end the doctor, Dr Wittison I think his name was, said, 'I don't think you should lock the petrol or pills or whatever away from Mark. We might have to find something to lock him in instead.'

Linda Te Ora is a mate of mine – we used to do sewing and lots of things together. One day I'm down at her place and we're sewing in the front room. We look out the window and Mark's walking down the pathway, and he looks drunk. He's probably about four, staggering everywhere. I thought he was shamming, just being silly. And then I think, 'oh god, he's not pretending'. So we both rush outside. Anyway, he'd been into the petrol that was in the shed. So again, another trip to the hospital.

I remember having a wringer machine and Mark putting his arm through it. I was out at the clothes line, and I just heard this yelling. I was just lucky I didn't have it squeezed down tight. You had to whack the release and the thing all jumped apart.

Another day, when he was only two, I was out at the clothesline, hanging out the washing. George was painting the roof of our house. And I hear George say, 'hello, what are you doing up here?' And there's Mark, sitting up on the roof. And George is saying to him, 'oh, you come up to help papa', talking all nice to him.

You know, when I think about it, I'm utterly amazed that he survived his childhood.

In gathering stories about Tariana, it was fascinating how many times the various adventures of Mark came to the surface.

It is clear that Mark's life experiences have had a huge effect on the whole whānau. Pahia remembers vividly the day that Mark first went inside:

> Mark had gone into the Army, and he was in and out of trouble. When he was eighteen he went to jail for armed robbery. I always remember the day he went for sentencing and he didn't come out. We went into this side room, me, him and Dad, and I remember Mark crying, and he goes, 'Dad, I'm scared. I don't want to go to jail'. It was the first time I'd ever seen Dad cry – ever. I was crying because Dad was crying, and when we drove back I said to Dad, 'how come you cried?' He said to me, 'when you have kids, son, you will realise that there's nothing worse than being a father and having your kids in a situation that you can't help them'. It went a little bit over my head but it was like that absolute powerlessness that existed because his son was in trouble. It had a huge impact on us as a family, and a huge impact on Mum.

Whāngai – to feed and nourish

> The Maori child is not to be viewed in isolation, or even as part of nuclear family, but as a member of a wider kin group or hapu community that has traditionally exercised responsibility for the child's care and placement. The technique, in the Committee's opinion, must be to reaffirm the hapu bonds and capitalise on the traditional strengths of the wider group.[6]

It wasn't just a case of Mum, Dad and the four kids when it came to the Turia household. First there was Ilona. Ilona came into the family's lives when she was about two years old. Tariana was still nursing at that stage. Ilona recalls:

> She [Tariana] became my godmother. I recall going and staying with her. She was a good friend of my real mum's sister, because I was also their flower girl when they got married. If you see the wedding photos and you see a snotty-nosed girl then that's me. I've been in their lives for a very long time.
>
> I think I had holidays with them, but I don't really recall until I was about ten. At that age I went and stayed with them for longer stays. I was reasonably close to Mark and Alan. I started living between the two homes. I come from a really large family of eleven brothers and sisters. I am the middle child of all those brothers and sisters.
>
> I would stay with Mum Tari and when my father demanded that I come home I would go there. To and fro. And then it became more permanent stays when I went to Girls' College. I loved it because it was like being treated very differently. I can remember having cornflakes and rice-bubbles – it was the first time I had ever eaten them – and even Honey Puffs. It felt like I was staying with the Queen and King.
>
> It was fun to be with them. I always enjoyed the music. If we drove anywhere we would have Dad's radio blaring with music and sing along to the music. Dad Turia really used to like nice cars – he had a brown Statesman – and he'd be playing Cilla. Dad used to really like Cilla Black – I still remember that song of hers in my head that we used to play a lot: 'You've lost that loving feeling'.

Then there's Carmelle. Carmelle is the daughter of Anthony Wilson, Tariana's younger brother. She recalls:

> I lived in Murupara as a young kid, but we always travelled back to Whangaehu for the building of the dining room, the whare. Our whole family would come back, and had this sense for the marae and love of it. Aunty always said to her brother, 'you should send her down here for college'. When I heard that I was like, 'yes, you know, I want to

go'. Every time we used to leave home I'd always cry or play up or take off. Me and her, Francie, were the last. Francie was there before me.

Aunty is a lovely person: a person you can always count on, to ring and talk to. You know how in our party we have all of those 'tangas[7]': she's all that. She's taught all us kids that and what it is about being whānau. I always had to cruise around with her in Whanganui, and she always spent a lot of time visiting family who were sick and who were in hospital – it's the little things. She always took food wherever she went; it's probably that rule of manaakitanga. We really focus on those things back at home. And how important your marae, whānau, hapū, iwi are.

While Ilona, Carmelle and Francie became part of the family, staying longer and remaining closely connected, there were many others who came to stay with Tariana and George over the years. Forty or so children passed through their homes over the years, as Alan recalls:

Mum and Dad would always bring boys home. Our home was always filled with people. We'd have other people's kids living with us: aunts' and uncles' kids, lots of cousins living with us. It was sweet. That sort of thing rubbed off on us, really. We've sort of followed in her footsteps in terms of opening up your home and having different ones live with us over the years.

Tariana was determined that as a family they would always make room to share with others; open their home to those who needed a warm bed, or a place to stay.

George and I used to take kids out from Holdsworth for weekends – our kids were quite small then. My kids understood. I used to say to my kids, 'you have no idea what it is like to live with other people because you have to; that's really hard to do'. We have to be a bit understanding, and we have to be supportive. We have to show a bit of love and care. And sometimes things might go wrong. But we have to try to really understand. My kids were great, actually. I was proud of them.

I knew what it was like to go around and have to adapt and fit in. I think that's what drove me to take kids – to try and give them a bit of security; a bit of love. Just so they would know that even though they couldn't live at home, they could live somewhere where people cared about them.

But it wasn't perfect. In a speech Tariana gave years later, she referred to some of the issues her family had encountered in taking on children from outside of their whānau:

> I do know the experience of bringing up children who are outside of kin – and if I was to be perfectly honest I would have to admit that despite our best intentions we were never able to give these children everything that they needed. Because although we could care for them with abundant love; clothe them, feed them, be there for them when they needed; we were unable to make the intimate connection with their own bloodlines that someone within their own kin could. And I know too, of the immense challenges of raising children who have begun life in difficulty. It takes extraordinary parenting skills to restore these children to the sense of wonder that is inherent in every child.[8]

Certain experiences in this sphere would later help form Tariana's views about how to respond to violence within the home, how to support families to support themselves, and, indeed, the framework for Whānau Ora.

> I remember one of our girls – she would have been about fifteen the last time her father beat her up. The police knew she often stayed with us, so they rang me, and George and I went and we got her. And we thought the right thing to do was to go round and tell her parents that we had her. The father asked if we could leave her there for the night so that they could talk things through. He sounded reasonable, so we thought it was okay. Well, he beat her up again. She went straight down to the police station. The police rang me up and they said to me, 'if you're just going to take her back (to her father), we will put her somewhere else'. And I said, 'no, I won't take her back'.
>
> The father rang up George, and he asked, 'who's the head of your house?' George said, 'we both are; why?' He goes, 'because she's my daughter, and you should return her back here to me'. And George said, 'I would, if you were the kind of person who would treat her right, and you're not, so she's not coming back'.

Recently one of the kids who stayed with us reflected back on the childhood she'd left behind, some forty years prior. It could have been yesterday, for the sadness, the hurt and the humiliation was still there in her voice.

> It was over a really, really little thing. I had a younger sister, and she had taken a little chain off me that belonged to me, and I'd asked for it back and she wouldn't give it back. She yelled out to Dad, 'Dad, she's going to hit me'. He came out. I remember him kicking me in the stomach; I was winded. I remember not being able to breathe, and I remember then several more blows.
>
> I remember him saying, 'give that fucken thing back to her', and that was the end of it. I remember looking up and getting another whack in the face. I went to work that day, scratch marks and bruises on my face. I didn't say anything. I just got up and walked to work. My mum tried to stop me, saying, 'don't go to work', it didn't look good. I never pressed charges. I know that I was hurting and angry, but I just never wanted my dad to go to prison because there were all my other siblings still at home.

If there was one thing that bringing so many children into our home taught me, it was that we can always do better by them. We can intervene earlier; we can hear them the first time; we can be there every step of the way.

Through my own childhood days and through the wounded eyes and broken hearts of children in our care, I formed a view of the world that eventually led to Whānau Ora. It was a view clearly shaped and moulded by the warmth of my aunts, the wisdom of the pā. I took instruction from their example; I learnt to distinguish doing the right thing from perpetuating the wrong.

But it was also a framework fashioned out of fear; a sense of knowing that comes from seeing too much; being exposed to pain and hurt; to violence exacerbated by the fuel of booze; the sheer cruelty that can torture and scar.

> We must expose and address the abusers in our midst and wrap support around families to keep children safe. Exposing a sexual predator is not an act of betrayal of the family, but an act of protection of children and young people.[9]

I had one girl who had been quite seriously sexually abused. Keeping her connected back into her family wasn't easy; her father was the perpetrator. But I knew that for her to be able to get through it and for my own daughter to stop being fearful about him, I had to allow him to come to the marae, and I did. We did.

We called his probation worker, called a social worker whom we trusted, because the Department (of Social Welfare) would never have agreed. We had a hui. Lisa and the girl were part of the hui. My boys were away at boarding school then; Pahia was still at home.

It was a good thing to do. I never supported what he did. But it was really weird; he did love her, and I think deep down she loved him too. But she hated what he had done to her. She stopped being frightened. We made it really clear in the hui: 'you keep on turning up at the school, following the bus, frightening these kids, then we will go to the police. We can do this in a good way, and everybody can feel safe, and everybody can feel that this relationship will continue – but it will only continue with George and I being present'. And so that's how it happened.

He would come out to the marae, and we would all be there. He would come out for her birthday, on her terms. Lisa stopped being frightened of him, because suddenly she saw him as a person: she got to know him a little bit. Our whāngai didn't like him, but he was her father. We all tried to be a bit forgiving about it. As I say, hated what he had done.

I think that if we know that there are issues that are impacting on our people we need to support them to address those issues within their whānau setting. I know sometimes that our issues come out of the whānau that we belong to, and for many of our people they think, 'how can we address this?' when the perpetrator is sitting within our whānau. If we want to heal we have to be able to have facilitation provided within our hapū, if necessary, or our iwi, to help us to reconnect, to restore and to actually address those issues.

I have seen it happen within my own iwi – we have had kaumātua who had been inappropriate with our tamariki who have been taken to the marae and dealt with in that setting. Very painful but really enhancing of all of our whānau, because then our kids know that they will be forever safe, because everybody will be keeping an eye on that kaumātua or whoever the perpetrator has been, to ensure that those things never happen again.

We shouldn't be afraid to restore those practices to ourselves.

Some years later, Tariana referred to this experience in more generic terms. She said she believed whānau should remove abused children to safety without police intervention, even if the parents had committed criminal offences against the children:

> 'Calling the police should be a last resort. The state should be the last point of intervention' Ms Turia said. Dealing with child abuse on marae would 'expose the wider issues' so children's extended families would know the extent of their responsibilities to provide love and support for those involved.
>
> Ms Turia said whanau stepping in to deal with child abuse was how all families, Maori and non-Maori used to handle such cases in the past. Calling in police and putting parents before the courts was 'retributive' justice. 'Restorative justice on marae could deal with many abuse situations in a family context', Ms Turia said. 'It would put right what's wrong, which is more important than seeking revenge against the parents' she said.[10]

Francie's story

If there is one story that really stands out over all the various experiences that George and Tariana had in caring for children in their home, it would be Francie's story. Pahia describes the impact Francie's death had on Tariana and the wider whānau, attributing particular leadership in the aftermath to his oldest brother, Alan:

> There have been quite significant events in Mum's life that I know have really rocked her, and losing Frances was one of them. What had happened that day was that we'd had all this internal fighting happening in our hapū at the time. It was pretty much Mum and Dad against all of her cousins. Alan was there, and he reckons this black cloud came over and just poured down, and then the phone call came through that Frances had been killed. Alan reckons as soon as that happened he walked back in and he said to them all, 'This shit's

going to stop today. We're not having this no more. I don't want my kids growing up with this'. It was huge. We put that old net aside and pretty much all of our generation took over the marae as of that day.

The year was 1986. Mark was serving time in Rangipō Prison, and his wife, Pip Thompson, with Lisa, Pahia and Frances, had gone up to visit him. Everyone remembers where they were the day that Francie died. Tariana's whāngai daughter, Carmelle, had been scheduled to travel with them. She says: 'We had something on: a marae meeting I think. I was meant to go on that trip to see Mark at the prison, but that morning me and Pahia were fighting, so Uncle said, "nah, you stay home"'.

On the way back from visiting Mark, the car the group was travelling in was involved in an accident, at Horopito, and Francie was killed.

The tangi was fraught with tension and grief. Pahia remembers the challenges the family faced in considering Francie's final resting place:

> After she died we brought her out to our marae. I know that when her family came down to ask for her, Mum didn't want to let her go. We sat down as a family because they were asking for her. I think Mum knew regardless of what had happened that at the end of the day that was her whānau, and they wanted to take her back to her ūkaipō. As hard as it was to let her go, Mum knew that it was the right thing to do. I think that all of these events that have happened in her life have really sort of created the person that she is.

For Tariana, that tangi was a turning point; a time in which she reflected on the whole concept of out-of-kin care, and the crucial role that whānau play in every decision affecting their own.

> It was terrible; that was a very hard time for all of us. You know, you worry about your kids seeing something like that and being there with her while she was dying. I didn't think they would ever get over it. I didn't handle it very well: her getting killed after she had gone through so much in life. She had just left school in the August holidays; she wanted to go nursing. She was going to go on to a reo course, she wanted to do the reo. And we thought it would be quite good for her to have between August and the end of year off school.

They went up to visit Mark. The car tyre blew out and went over the bank, so it was terrible. And that's probably when I first saw the strength of my son, Pahia, because he was only about thirteen then. Even the police couldn't get over him, how he looked after Lisa and Pip and also Frances. Pip ended up in hospital. She was pregnant; a month off having Teina. Pahia: the long bone in his knee had separated. Lise wasn't hurt. Francie and Pahia were in the back of the car: she had pushed him down on to the floor and she went through the back window. It was the weirdest, weirdest accident.

We took her back up to Parikino: that broke my kids' hearts. We had a meeting all night – George had to go up and identify her – poor thing, him and Alan – that was so hard for them. They got back to the marae (at Whangaehu) and we stayed up all night, and we knew.

Uncle Ned Tapa was still alive then. We knew they'd come. Anyway, about 4.30 in the morning they came onto the marae, and God it was awful.

Alan was saying to them they had no right to come and ask for her. I said to the kids that she was going to go; it didn't matter what anyone else said, she had to go back to Parikino because that's who she was. I said I didn't want anyone to walk into our urupā and look at her headstone and say, 'who is this girl? What's she doing here?' So she went home. We had her for one night at home and then took her back.

I did something that afterwards I just so regretted. I told Dennis Rātana – he was her close family – I told him that they would have to go into the undertakers to see her, because I wasn't going to allow them to open her. And I didn't allow them to. I felt really terrible afterwards – but Pahia didn't want to look at her again, and I just thought it would be too much for my children. Den said she looked lovely. He tried to talk to me but I couldn't cope; it was just too much. It took me a long, long time to get over it, and my kids too. That was a hard time.

We found this waiata in among her things when she died. A kid from the pā had written the song; Frances must have helped her write it. Ivor, from the Blacks (Black Power), put music to it, and they sang it at her tangi. That waiata – it was beautiful.

Song for Frances – a child only lent to us

> I cried and cried my heart out
> Feeling all alone
> Nobody wanted me; nobody cared for me
> Until I finally found a home

He took me out of my despair
He gave me love that I could share
I'm glad he didn't pass me by
For I finally found a home

Oh Lord don't hold your mercy back from me
You're always in my life
fears and pain will be no more
Oh Lord don't hold your mercy back from me

NOTES

1 Moana Jackson, cited in N. Shepheard, 'Fierce Kuia: profile of New Zealand Member of Parliament Tariana Turia', *North and South*, February 2004.

2 M. Johnston, 'The women who shape New Zealand: Tariana Turia', *New Zealand Women's Weekly*, 27 June 2012.

3 Johnston, 'The women who shape New Zealand'.

4 Tariana Turia, speech to New Zealand Psychological Society, 29 August 2000.

5 B. Ansley, 'Tariana Turia does not talk to Bruce Ansley', *The Listener*, 16 September 2000, pp. 12–13.

6 Ministerial Advisory Committee on a Maori perspective for the Department of Social Welfare, *Puao-te-ata-tu (Day Break)*, 1988, Wellington.

7 Manaakitanga, kotahitanga, wairuatanga, rangatiratanga, kaitiakitanga, whanaungatanga.

8 Tariana Turia, speech to New Zealand Family and Foster Care Federation, 18 June 2010.

9 Māori Party press release, '"The abusers have to be outed" says Turia', 24 October 2007. http://maoriparty.org/panui/the-abusers-have-to-be-outed-says-turia/ (accessed 11 February 2015).

10 'Whanau way worked for me', *Northern Advocate*, 11 November 2000.

CHAPTER SEVEN
REBUILDING RANGITĀHUAHUA

Titiro iho ki ngā awa kei uta ko Mangawhero

Tīehutia te wai ko Whangaehu Ka hinga te rākau ko Turakina

Tīkeitia te waewae ko Rangitīkei Ka whakamau ki Oroua[1]

One of the most significant achievements for Tariana and George was their rebuilding and restoring their marae to be a vibrant centre of activity for all of their whānau, hapū and iwi to value.

The contribution that marae can make towards revitalising the spirit of a people is aptly described in the words of Māori language champion and the founder of the kōhanga reo movement, Dame Iritana Tāwhiwhirangi:

> There are roughly 1200 marae in this country. The marae have endured for generations without government funding, and if there has been government funding it has been minimal. Now, why have marae endured and still hold a place of absolute key significance in Māoridom? Marae have sustained because of the extended families. They are investors, they are shareholders and they are obliged. You have a group of trustees who look after marae, but they are caretakers of all that interest for whānau.

The one place on earth that Tariana calls home, Whangaehu marae, has a distinctive place in her story: particularly the tupuna whare, Rangitāhuahua. Usually whare are named after a particular ancestor, but 'Rangitāhuahua' refers to a significant place in the tribal history of Ngā Wairiki/Ngāti Apa. Rangitāhuahua is more commonly known as Sunday Island, and is located in the Kermadec Islands. It was at Rangitāhuahua that the Kurahaupō waka took refuge after becoming wrecked by a storm while on its journey from Hawaiiki to Aotearoa.

The old tupuna whare stood on Whangaehu marae from around the turn of the century until the fateful day of 10 April 1968. On that day, the lower North Island was ravaged by treacherous storms: some of the worst ever recorded in New Zealand. Two storms came together at the time that the Lyttleton–Wellington ferry, the *Wahine*, was approaching the harbour entrance. The ship was wrecked, and fifty-one people lost their lives.

In Whanganui, the Aerodrome recorded a peak wind gust of 83 knots (154 km/hr) on that day. The Castlecliff Town Hall lost some roofing iron. Two huge pine trees fell across a house. Windows were broken and television aerials twisted. At the airport, about half of the hangar roof was stripped by the wind. The grandstand at Whanganui Racecourse lost its roof. Toll and telegraph communications were cut for over ten hours. Powerlines were cut by fallen trees. Orchards were stripped of apples, and fruit trees smashed.

It was on that same day that the sacred tribal buildings of Whangaehu, the marae and church house, were swept away, consigned to a pile of memories. What does it do to the soul of a people, to see their tribal home decimated; their place of sanctuary taken from them by the cruel force of nature? Tariana recalls the impact of the storm and the way it mobilised them into action.

It probably took me five years to truly appreciate what we had lost. During that time, we had lived in town. And then, in 1973, I learnt that my mother, Dorsey, was selling her land. Aunty Wai told me to go and get a loan and buy the land, so of course we did.

George and I saw it as a new start. We had bought the farm, and started getting involved in regenerating life back into our marae. Our urupā was overgrown. I got a real sense at last of what my Aunty Wai had raised me to do: to take up the challenge of restoring a marae for us at Whangaehu.

I have always tried to work hard with our kids, to get them to love their place. I remember when Pahia was little, he'd say, 'why is it that we're the ones who always have to be here? Why do Dad and you have to work? Why can't everyone come and do the work?' And I'd say to him, 'we're just lucky that we live out here on our wee farm so we can be here.'

It was never easy, though. We worked all the hours of daylight and more; determined to run the farm while at the same time pour our heart and soul into the marae. Some of the happiest days in my life date back to that time when we were on the farm at Whangaehu. We were raising our tamariki in a safe rural environment. They were being taught to be independent, to be self-determining; they learnt the value of hard work. It couldn't get any better.

George and I were now trained artificial inseminators. There was one stage when George contracted leptospirosis from the animals on the farm. It's not a nice disease – he was stricken with profound fatigue, headaches, aching muscles and vomiting. But eventually it passed, and we both kept working: working at the marae, on the farm, at my job.

At that stage Alan and Mark were at boarding school at Feilding Agriculture. Alan recalls:

> Mum and Dad were leasing the Bishop whānau[2] farm down the road and they were milking. Once they had bought the farm they got settled here and they started to look at rebuilding the marae and starting to generate interest with the aunties and uncles.

Years passed, and eventually we purchased the old Salvation Hall in Whanganui, which we relocated to our lands, to gather together as whānau and hapu. Once more we had a place to gather: a tribal sanctuary of our own. But our joy was short-lived. Twelve years after the *Wahine* storms took our marae, a blaze of fire leapt from the rafters of the old hall, and reduced our new home to ashes.

I think that was probably the first time that I saw upfront what it meant for our hapū to lose something that we had come to treasure so deeply. It was 1980. The night our marae burnt down our whānau came from everywhere, within the shortest space of time. There were about a hundred of us standing there, just watching it burn.

The shock of that moment is associated with another event, equally traumatic in my memory. The week before our marae burnt down, one of Mum's first cousins, Aunty Roka (Kiriona-Marsh) from Taranaki, had come to the tangi of one of our uncles from Turakina. He was a Karatau. Mum had gone and asked for him to be brought home to our marae, and so we had him in the big tent.

Aunty Roka stood at the gate and cried. I'll never forget that sight of her all hunched over, her whole body consumed by grief. We didn't know her; I couldn't even remember having seen her before. Later she told us this story that as she had stood at the gate, she saw flames leaping out of the windows and our marae burning down. I remember feeling terrified that we had done something wrong.

After our whare burnt down, that same kuia wrote to Mum, enclosing some money and encouraging us all to think about a new beginning, to be strong and committed enough to start again. She didn't want our families to be disillusioned by all that had happened. She told us it was a new time, and the fire was a way of helping us all to move forward.

When all our families gathered round the night of the fire, it sparked something in us: an urge to come close, to bring a sense of purpose back into our lives. It made us realise that we didn't want our children to go through a period again where we had nothing. It brought us together, making us stronger. It put the heart back into all of us that night – we knew what we'd had and we knew what we wanted for our future.

And so we picked ourselves up, dusted ourselves off, and started again. George took two years off to help rebuild the marae, while me and the kids managed the farm. We had been fleeced by the insurance company: we got about a quarter of what we should have. But what was wonderful was that most of our marae on our Whanganui side sent us money. On top of that my cousins started fundraising every week. They used to run housie. I hated housie, and wouldn't go. I'd tell them, 'you go and do your housie thing and I'll work at the marae'. By that stage, George was laying the foundations for our dining room.

Māku anō e hanga i tōku nei whare – I will build my own house[3]

In 1984, George and Tariana embarked on a new project: a wharenui to be built using an ancient technique of rammed-earth construction. Before doing so, they consulted with local writer and builder David Jones to discuss the process. David had built his own rammed-earth home thirty years prior, and was very familiar with various aspects of the craft. He later wrote about his experience at Whangaehu with the first rammed-earth wharenui in New Zealand:

> I worked with the Whangaehu people in the building of the wharepuni and it was a beautiful experience. Most of the members of the tribe were used to hard physical work, we had builders, plasterers, contractors, railway track workers, and many people who had worked in useful building projects. The marae committee knew what they wanted and without a great deal of discussion got cracking. In a few days the foundation was laid, the earth was on the spot, the shuttering made, the permit to build granted and away we went.

> We used blocks and tackles secured to overhead beams, had one person on the rope and one on the rammer and the job got underway. In five days we rammed forty cubic metres of material.

During this time the ladies of the marae cooked up large feeds to keep our strength up and it was an extremely successful combined effort. Members of the families came from as far away as Australia and Singapore. Some from Auckland, Wellington, Levin, Otaki and the operation was used as a Christmas holiday and get together and everybody had a great time.[4]

When we were building our marae, our aunties were always there, guiding us. I remember when we finished we were so proud; our marae was so flash. Aunty Wai and Aunty Pae came out there and looked around with so much pride. And then they got us all together in the dining room, in their characteristic way gently bringing us back to earth. They said, 'Our marae is really beautiful, but it will only be as good as your ability to manaaki people. So don't get carried away thinking how flash you are; with this comes huge commitment, and you need to prepare. It's one thing to have a marae, another to be the kaikaranga, another to be the one out the back doing the cooking.'

When I was growing up, Aunty Wai would always be out the front and Aunty Pae would be running the storeroom. Aunty Moki Te Patu taught us to work in the dining room so that right from when we were young we were taught how to manaaki people; how to look after people. You went into the dining room first thing in the morning and you never left till after the last dishes were done at night.

We had to wait on the tables and set the tables. Aunty Wai was like the quality control person. She would stand at the door and she would go, 'Yes, that looks nice, no, don't do that, don't put that over there, that looks untidy'. Everything had to be just nice. I think I am like that at the marae now, although not as bad as she was. My kids and nieces would probably beg to differ, but I do like things simple and I like them nice. She wouldn't have ever put a great big bunch of flowers anywhere!

Our aunties were encouraging us to prepare properly for the opening, including taking on the role of kaikaranga. We'd get terrified when they talked like that. I was probably mid-thirties when we began. At the time none of us had the reo, and so even the thought of having to do a karanga made us nervous. We knew we'd have to step up at some point. We would run our little training sessions – we would send some of us out to the gate and some of us would stay inside, and we'd have to karanga to one another. And of course we'd get the giggles. I mean, when I think back, I see how stupid we were, but we would be in fits of laughter because we were so nervous and scared. Aunty Wai would say to us, 'That's all right for you to do this while there's just us here, but don't you ever do that around others'.

Rangitāhuahua II was officially opened by Matiu Rata,[5] leader of the political party Mana Motuhake, on 31 August 1985. Tariana's whāngai, Carmelle Wilson, was the puhi at the opening of the whare. Tai Te Kawa was performed by Ruka Broughton, and the opening honoured with the presence of the toki 'Te Āwhiorangi', a sacred adze said to have been carved from the Aotea canoe. Ruka had been schooled in the history, waiata, whakapapa and karakia of Ngā Rauru, Taranaki and Whanganui, as well as the use of the taiaha. This knowledge led him to become guardian over Te Āwhiorangi.

Tariana explains why Matiu Rata was invited to open Rangitāhuahua.

I really liked Matt and his wife Nelly; we knew them through the Rātana Church, and that was why we'd asked him to open our wharenui. I'd actually been approached by Matiu to stand for Parliament. I had a lot of respect for him. I admired him for leaving the Labour Party because he didn't agree with what they were doing. Matiu had left Labour in 1979 saying that he believed Labour paid too little attention to Māori matters. He resigned from Parliament in 1980 and came to my marae, asking me to run in the Western Māori seat. He contested the 1981 election on the Mana Motuhake ticket. It was a purpose that many of us agreed with: to retain Māori land; to focus on self-determination. But the timing just wasn't right for me.

Matt was the first one to talk to me about politics and standing. I told him that I wasn't even slightly interested in politics; I had too much work to do at home. I just didn't think I was ready to leave my home and family at that time. Besides, it wasn't anything that I had ever aspired to – I really didn't think that I would ever go into national politics. I thought being politically active at home was what mattered. At that point in my journey, I was probably more interested in throwing stones at the Government than being part of it.

Robert Reid, a friend and colleague of George and Tariana shares a vivid memory of the opening of Rangitāhuahua II:

> I remember the horror when the hangi was opened and it was cold and not cooked. Found out later that one of the little lads had seen a hose and poked it down into the covered-over hāngi pit and turned the water on. I think it got reheated, second course became first course and it got solved. In some ways it was the story of their lives that nothing would ever go according to plan.

Tariana and George had moved back to the marae with the kids – Lisa, Pahia and Carmelle – when Tariana's mother became terminally ill.

> We built the flat for her, and George and I lived up the road in our farmhouse. When our mother died, she always worried about leaving the marae with nobody here. George and I shifted down here with our kids. My kids grew up sleeping in the wharepuni. We were here right until three months after I entered Parliament. I came home one day and George told me that he was moving into town; that it wasn't right for him to be here without me on my marae, when he wasn't from here. It was hugely painful, I have to say. If I'd known he was going to do that I probably wouldn't have gone to Parliament![6]

Both Carmelle and Pahia have memories to share of their sleeping space at the marae. Carmelle says:

> The mattress room used to be Nan's flat. It was really small upstairs; there was just a lounge and a very small kitchen, and you'd use the marae toilets. Aunty stayed over there every night with her. Once Nan passed away, Aunty and Uncle stayed on. We stayed down at the marae and that was our bedroom, the whare. We'd say, 'we've got the biggest bedroom out' but then it had a security light, this little red light that used to beep, and all of our mates used to get scared of that, like, 'oh, someone's moving around', because of the photos and everything. But even with me and Pā [Pahia], when we didn't have mates over, we'd try and sneak back in to the flat and just sleep downstairs. Uncle would always be like, 'You kids, get back in to the whare!'

The fear factor of the whare is also something that Pahia recalls:

> We had those little metal basket drawers so if there was a hui on we'd have to pack our bedroom up and shift it into the lounge in the flat. We lived there from when I was twelve or thirteen until I was twenty. Mum and Dad would live there for about another three years after that just before Mum shifted into Parliament.
>
> My Nan had lived there in a caravan, and then they built the flat on the back specifically for her. I can remember taking my mates out for the weekend and I'd make them a bed in the whare and they're like, 'oh, is this your bedroom bro?' And I'd go, 'yeah'. 'And all those people up there are dead, bro?' 'Yeah, bro', and they'd be like – 'oh, this is out of it bro'. And then I'd go and sneak out and sleep with Mum and Dad. I caught up with one of my Pākehā mates over in Sydney Airport and he goes, 'I can remember that first time I came out, bro – you made my bed – then you went to sleep with your mother!'

It would be satisfying to say that Tariana's house of heaven, Rangitāhuahua, was erected in 1985 and since then has withstood the perils of earth, wind, fire and water. But that wouldn't be true. There were more torrential rains; floods upon floods. Tariana is quite matter-of-fact in recalling the various twists of nature that have occurred over the years.

> I remember the first flood. Lisa was living back home, and I remember going to the top of the hill and seeing the water raging through the valley – it was devastating. And we were badly flooded at the marae. Each new event pushed up the costs of insurance and took its toll on our whānau.

Twenty years after Rangitāhuahua II was opened, two massive floods, one on 16 February 2004 and the second on 7 July 2006, forced the community to take drastic action to protect the marae from further harm. When the first flood struck, there was up to four inches of mud in the buildings. Quiet creeks had risen up and swallowed whole houses, lashing winds had felled giant trees, hillsides had fallen away, and floodwaters had swirled across the face of the land, invading farms and streets and homes. In the hours of crisis, people turned out in the face of the storm to warn neighbours, to rescue children and old people, to secure property, to offer shelter and warmth. Ratana Pā literally opened its arms wide, picking up people off the roadside, and hosting them on the marae until the waters receded. There were huge economic losses: stock swept away, land eroded, cars and equipment damaged by floodwaters. Destruction of or damage to houses, marae and community halls had a devastating emotional impact.

The Great Wall of Apa

After the floods receded, for a six-month period George, Mark, mokopuna Arena and Robert Young came together to build a flood wall that now surrounds the marae at Whangaehu. We were lucky to get some support from Te Puni Kōkiri and the Whanganui Community Foundation. We needed it. It was a massive investment of time and resource. Ten thousand concrete blocks were lovingly plastered in place in a wall reaching over 420 metres in length.

So now as we stand resilient in our whare made from the powerful foundation of Papatūānuku and nestled within what we call the Great Wall of Apa, I have come to know another meaning to our name. Rangitāhuahua also refers to 'our sky father taking care of us.' Our whānau have become adept at crisis management. We clung to each other in our grief, and when the tears subsided, we leant on each other for strength. We began to practise waiata that had previously slipped away. Our reo became a priority. We grew more fascinated with our tribal histories.

I never realised the reo was all around me until one day I was at a hui in Whanganui and they sang this old waiata and I knew all the words. When it started I was tentatively picking up words, and by the time we got to the end I thought, 'God, I knew almost all of that waiata'. It lit a spark in me, a desire to learn.

We started to think about ways of building our knowledge – we began holding wānanga. We cherished the photographs that we had retained.

One of my most cherished paintings is of our kuia, Te Rangi Pikinga. A couple of years ago I was asked to speak about this photograph, at the launch of Whakamīharo Lindauer online.[7] The exhibition featured over sixty portraits of Māori as painted by artist Gottfried Lindauer, catalogued together as the Partridge Collection. Our tupuna was found among them.

The story of Te Rangi Pikinga is a story of great sadness and loss for Ngā Wairiki/Ngāti Apa. In 1819, at the age of sixteen, Te Rangi Pikanga was taken by Te Rauparaha and given to his nephew, Te Rangihaeata, to live in the rohe of Ngāti Toa Rangatira. She never returned. Her story is one we relive in our tribal histories; her name had been recited, her life retold but I had never seen the physical representation of her face. And so when I first looked into those sorrowful eyes, I wept. I wept for her life; I wept for our loss; I wept that in the midst of Auckland I would finally gaze upon the sight of our tupuna.

As a whānau, we have been blessed now, with three further images of this amazing photograph.

The first was when my cousin found a decoupage of her at a garage sale. The second was gifted to us by a Māori person coming across her picture in the estate of a recently deceased, finding her name on the back and tracking us down. And the third was when a Māori man found her portrait in the basement of the Hastings District Council; contacted us, and we took a tira over to Hastings to bring her home.

Some may wonder why a mere photograph can assume so much importance in our lives. I remember some years ago, our whānau were embroiled in considerable controversy over the possession of some other Lindauer portraits – the paintings of Te Ahuru o te Rangi and Aperehama Tipai – the brother of Te Rangi Pikinga. These portraits of our tūpuna had been in my mother's care.

When she was approached by one of the former curators of the Whanganui Art Gallery, she agreed to let the two portraits be shared with the gallery, out of respect for him. Time passed, and that curator left. When the new curator arrived, he sent a receipt to my mother for the paintings that he described as being on 'permanent loan'. At that time my mother thought nothing of it – that was until our brother died, and she wanted to bring those two portraits of our tūpuna out to our home, to lie with him, to connect him to the whakapapa that unites us all.

Suddenly there was a problem. Supposedly the receipt represented a transaction in which the museum now owned our ancestors.

Eventually we received the paintings back into our care. After the tangi, as a whānau, we decided we wanted to avoid going through that distress ever again, and that we would protect and respect those tūpuna best by keeping them in our care, in our tupuna whare.

One by one, the curator, the mayor, the board members, and eventually the Member of Parliament at that time, Hon Russell Marshall, came out to the marae and attempted to persuade us to give them the paintings, and thereby avoid legal action. We were not persuaded, and the battle continued. Finally, one day when I was away down South, my mother and my uncle Hop were confronted with a television crew coming on to the marae, to broadcast the story of the Lindaeur paintings.

The whānau from all around our rohe came to discuss what we should do – and eventually we agreed that if these two paintings were not able to remain in our care, then all of our whānau would fight to return all of the paintings in our art gallery back to whānau care. Suffice to say, if you were to go to Whangaehu Marae today, you will gaze upon the Lindaeur paintings of Te Ahuru o te Rangi and Aperehama Tipai.

I remember at the time when all this erupted, I asked my mother, 'why are these paintings so important?'. She said, simply, 'These whakaahua are who we are; we are who they are'.[8]

In essence, during the process of rebuilding our marae, we came to rebuild our whānau. We reminded ourselves that whakapapa tells us that we are what our tūpuna were. We were comforted by the fact that building a strong base for our survival was also about protecting and extending our whakapapa.

For our greatest discovery in finding Rangitāhuahua was that we found ourselves. We were able to talk about our issues in the open; we knew where to go for help. We supported each other; we lifted each other through the hard times and we made more effort to celebrate the good.

My mother was raised to know te reo Māori as her first and principal language. It was the language of the home; the language of the pā; the language of her world. That is until she entered school. From that day on, things were never the same. My mother was part of the generation who was hit and spoken sharply to, every time they uttered a Māori word. And yet it was the only language she knew.

As time passed, her voice was silenced and replaced with a new persona – a quieter, more restricted one. To the end of her days, I never heard her using te reo Māori. Yet sometimes I would watch her intent in conversation with fluent Maori speakers. They would speak to her exclusively in te reo and she would reply exclusively in English – but it appeared that there was perfect and mutual understanding.

There was only one time that I recall her coming close to sharing what it must have been like to have your true voice beaten out of you. We were sitting with a group of others who were talking about having been hit at school for speaking te reo Māori. My tiny mother said nothing but hung her head in her knees and sat there, huddled in her own quiet distress.

As I think of her experience, it reminds me of my uncles who returned from war, never to speak of that experience again. They returned damaged, shell-shocked and in too many cases destroyed by the trauma they had endured. Just as there was a huge vacuum in our understanding of what they saw and lived through, I believe there is a similar void in trying to comprehend the level of trauma experienced when your tongue is silenced forever; when you are denied your voice. In te reo we might say 'kua ngaro', one interpretation of which is 'something which is gone'. But a fuller interpretation of kua ngaro is 'to be unseen or unheard'.

And so it was on my own marae, probably not more than twenty-five years ago – we thought that our language was indeed 'kua ngaro'.

When my Uncle Hop passed away there was no one of the next generation who had the reo, and so we went through a period in which were relying on people from other iwi to take on the role and responsibilities of taking care of our paepae. And so those who would welcome on manuhiri to our marae, who would put down the kōrero for the day, came not from Ngā Wairiki/Ngāti Apa but from Tainui, Hokianga, Raukawa, Tūwharetoa.

That was until one day a kaumātua arrived at our marae to dine with us at New Year. The old fella, Paringatai Rauhina, was from Tūwharetoa and Raukawa. His mokopuna, Andrea, eventually married my eldest son, Alan.

When our hākari was over, the old man stood to mihi to us, and we were so embarrassed because we didn't have anyone in our whānau who could mihi back to him. I remember Pahia, just thirteen years old, standing up, and he attempted to mihi back to the old man. Although his language was still developing, Pahia's commitment was intense, and the significance of him standing on our behalf stays with me till this day.

This kaumātua took my boy aside and told him that the korowai of the hapū had landed on him, and that he would do everything he could to support him in developing his voice. He said to us that the mantle of our tūpuna had fallen upon Pahia. My son took that message really seriously, as young as he was.

True to his word, that kaumātua took my son home, and invested his time and energy in him, and by the time he was sixteen, Pahia was fluent in te reo rangatira, and was ready and able to take on his responsibilities on the pae.

From then on he was determined to learn the reo. We had people from the pā, Dave James and Tapihana Shelford (Dobby), who would come out to the marae, stand Pahia on a chair in the dining room and get him to kōrero. Quite amazing stuff really. Up until then we had always relied on those from other iwi – Bob Penetito from Waikato, Dave and Dobby from the North. I used to feel sorry for Pahia, because he'd be playing rugby or other things that kids get into, and if we had tangihanga I'd say to him, 'you can't go. Your job is here. We need you at home'. I can remember he'd cry. He'd tell us, 'Mum, I wanna play rugby; I wanna play'. And I'd have to say, 'well you can, but today, you can't'.

Pahia himself remembers those times as clearly as if they were yesterday:

> I can remember times where I said to Mum, 'look, I've got rugby this afternoon', and we had a hui at the marae or tangi, and Mum just said, 'you can't go'. And she would always take me into the whare, look at our photographs of our tūpuna, and she'd go, 'who would maintain the mana of the marae?' She still does it to this day: shocking guilt trips! They were real strong reminders, because we'd always had other people looking after our pae.
>
> I know, probably more so from my dad, there was this real pride in seeing me doing those things that he has never been able to do. We'd go away to family hui– and Dad would go, 'oh no, no, my boy can speak Māori'. I knew for him it was something that he had always wanted for himself, so to have one of his own kids that could kōrero – I just know that it meant so much to Dad.

The other memory that dominates this period of Tariana's life was the loss of her mother Dorsey. Tariana and George moved home to the marae to support Dorsey in her last days. It became a cherished period of Tariana's life: she treasured the moments of closeness she had with her mother; moments she had been wanting since a child.

Tariana once said of her mother, 'She was the sun in the morning and the moon at night'.[9]

Growing up, I always yearned to be with my mum. I had it all, but I wanted more.

My mother was a big smoker. She smoked in the dining room, she smoked in the bedroom, and I picked on her constantly all my life. I picked on her and all my cousins who smoked, who I just loved so much. Very few of them lived beyond fifty. I know how addictive cigarettes are; I know how difficult it is to give up.

I remember my mother when she was dying. I gave up work and had gone home to look after her. My husband had bought her a waterbed when she was on her way out. She was so tiny, and he was worried that if she was in bed for such a long time she might get bedsores. I'd have to say she didn't really like it, but the thought was there.

I used to go and sleep on the couch by her. I'd pull the couch up next to the waterbed and next to her, and she and I would talk almost all night. The Commonwealth Games were on, so Mum and I would watch the television all night. She would say to me, 'you know Daughter, when people come out here to see me and they bend down to kiss me and they've been smoking, do you know, they smell'. I'd say, 'yes Mum, I know'. And she'd go, 'but why didn't you tell me? I'd have given up if I'd known.' And I thought, 'yeah right'.

I was with Mum when we got the diagnosis that her cancer had progressed to such a stage that she might have only six months left to live. I remember vividly the doctor telling her she'd been a heavy smoker for forty years, and she should be happy that she had lived so long. But we didn't take into account my mother's incredible will to live. Six months turned into six years; the gardens at Whangaehu flourished, and our whānau cherished her and each other.

Mum responded to the challenge of cancer with an incredible attitude that we must live each day as if it is our last, and by thriving in the support of our whanau. Her will was clearly evident when she completed a series of chemotherapy, paralysed on her right side. Never one to worry about mere technicalities like paralysis, Mum got to work in the vege garden, her left hand dragging her right hand back, as she tilled the soil with all the energy she could muster. And while we were all blown away, Mum just took it in her stride when a couple of months later her paralysis disappeared.

Mum spent her final six years in splendid health – in fact so independent and so proud was she that it was only the night before she passed away that she finally let me wash her.

One of her great loves was her garden. Our marae was flush with vegetables; the flower beds overflowing with blooms of all variety. All our families were nourished with her generosity. I know that she took great comfort in the fact that our land was the source of our food; no artificial sprays or contaminants had polluted her vegetables. Her habit of preparing and feasting on a home-grown meal was another factor in her well-being.

In her last six months, I moved in to her flat at the marae to see how I could support her on a daily basis, as well as to be there to support our wider whānau in coming to terms with the inevitable. It was an incredible time that I will forever cherish. At first she didn't need me in the way I thought she would. Instead, a lot of the need was mine.

My need of Mum was to talk through many issues of my own, and that time was precious. The privilege of being able to assist my mother on to her journey to the wairua has stayed with me.

When her time came, I found myself so much more resolved to the transition between life and death. We had been able to celebrate the wondrous; grieve for the loss; share our differences; and cherish every day we had with one another. I was able to hear her expectations, and could truly appreciate the depth and dignity of that time. It will never leave me.

There were many things that happened afterwards that made me know Mum was lingering. We'd hear a door bang in our dining room, and George would go, 'There's Dorsey, checking to see we've cleaned the sinks till they shine'.

And at one hui my sister was looking extremely jittery, and she took me aside and whispered, 'Mum's here – I can smell her presence'. I was a bit iffy, but said I'd go back in the whare and see for myself. We used to rub Mum down with frangipani oil, and because she would walk barefeet through the whare, weeks after she passed on I could often smell the sweet fragrance of frangipani and think of Mum. But this hui was many, many months later. I sat by my cousin Joan, and whispered in her ear, 'Cousin, you smell just like Mum'. She turned to me, laughed and said, 'Oh cousin –

that's so beautiful – but just before I got out of the car I spilled a bottle of frangipani oil right through my bag'. We had to laugh.

And that's really important too. That our loved ones live on in us – in our laughter, our tears, our quirky gestures, our memories, our early waking moments and our moemoeā.

In contemplating the nearness of death we learnt more fully how to live life to its absolute abundance. Our well-being as a whānau became all-important, as we remembered how to treasure the very essence of who we are.

The sad thing is, Mum could have still been with me had she known and understood what tobacco would do to her life.

I feel really sad that some of my mokopuna still smoke. None of my kids do, thankfully. But I have a few mokopuna who hide away from me, and they are swallowing gum, or gargling mouthwash, as if I won't guess what they've been up to. I can always tell when they've had a smoke because I smell that smell.

When the Māori Party later went into coalition with National, I never thought we'd get tobacco on the agenda. In fact I always secretly thought that they were getting money from the tobacco industry. So when there was an agreement that they would move on this issue I just couldn't believe it. I couldn't believe that at last we had a little window to achieve some change. And of course I always try to push the window up to achieve as much as we can.

I'm very proud of what we've achieved with tobacco reform. I'm pleased that we have made a difference.

Tariana took on tobacco reform as part of her delegations as Associate Minister of Health; over her time in office, tobacco consumption plummeted, dropping from 961 cigarettes per person in 2009 to 683 in 2013: a decrease of about 29 percent.

There is no doubt that raising the price of tobacco products through taxation increases has been the most important contributor to this drop, particularly in the context of youth smoking. On 28 April 2010, the Government increased tax on tobacco products by 10 percent, and brought in further 10 percent increases on 1 January 2011 and 1 January 2012. In October 2012, Tariana convinced Parliament to legislate a further four tobacco tax increases of 10 percent, to come into effect on 1 January each year from 2013 to 2016.[10]

After the Māori Affairs Select Committee reported back on their inquiry into the tobacco industry in November 2010, Tariana was able to draw on the strength of their recommendations, to mobilise support for a longer-term vision, to make Aotearoa a smokefree nation by 2025. Their first recommendation provided Tariana with all the fuel she needed to drive the reform process; *'That the Government aim for tobacco consumption and smoking prevalence to be halved by 2015 across all demographics, followed by a longer-term goal of making New Zealand a smoke-free nation by 2025'.*[11]

Prevention can't work in isolation of health promotion and education. In 2012 Tariana established the Pathway to Smokefree New Zealand 2025 Innovation Fund to support innovative approaches to reduce the smoking prevalence amongst Māori, Pasifika, pregnant women and young people. The fund distributes up to $5 million per annum.

Tariana was able to reduce tobacco advertising by persuading Parliament to introduce a measure banning the display of tobacco products in retail outlets in July 2011. In Budget 2014, she announced that from November 2014 the duty-free cigarette allowance would fall from 200 to fifty.

Just when Tariana was preparing to leave Parliament, the Health Committee reported back on a plain packaging regime for tobacco products and put forward the Smokefree Environments (Tobacco Plain Packaging) Amendment Bill. In the words of journalist Patrick Gower:

> Stand up Tariana Turia, you have done what few other politicians can claim – beaten Big Tobacco, beaten the multi-nationals, beaten the industry, beaten the lobbyists. …
>
> Turia has shown she has the power here.
> The Government listened to her – not to Big Tobacco.

> Many people ask what the Maori Party achieves in Government – often rightfully so.
>
> Well, getting plain packaging past a Cabinet of cautious National ministers is quite frankly an incredible achievement. …
>
> Turia already has a huge legacy.
>
> Plain packaging looks set to become a big part of it.
>
> In her retirement Turia will be able to look at plain packaging and say 'I did that'.[12]

On 'World No Tobacco Day' on 31 May 2014, Tariana became the recipient of one of six international awards in the Western Region awarded by the World Health Organization for her accomplishments in the area of tobacco control.

And on the day that the fiftieth Parliament dissolved, the New Zealand tobacco control sector formally honoured her at an event held in Pipitea Marae. The Heart Foundation's newsletter recorded:

> August 14th was a day full of heart felt tributes and thanks for the parliamentary champion on tobacco change in New Zealand, Tariana Turia. When asked what she is most proud of in her time in parliament she said she was 'proud that the whole parliament supported various aspects of the tobacco reform strategy she had actively pursued over the last six years.'…
>
> The Heart Foundation thanked the Minister for all her support around rheumatic fever while Tala Pasifika highlighted the achievement of Smokefree Aotearoa 2025 as the stand out direct legacy of her work.[13]

The last word comes from a tribute made on that same day from Dr Jan Pearson, acting chief executive of the Cancer Society of New Zealand:

> I salute you and your passion, vision and commitment to the health of the children of Aotearoa and the generations of children to come.
>
> The sector will miss you very much. However your ongoing influence will be strong and the champions you have mentored will continue your work. Haere ra.[14]

NOTES

1 www.ngatiapa.iwi.nz

2 Dorsey's sister, Tangiwai, married Allan Bishop.

3 Kīngi Tawhiao. Rahui Papa and Paul Meredith, 'Kīngitanga – the Māori King movement – Tāwhiao, 1860–1894', Te Ara – the Encyclopedia of New Zealand, updated 4 June 2013, http://www.TeAra.govt.nz/en/kingitanga-the-maori-king-movement/page-3

4 David Jones, *Nga Whare Uku: houses of earth and how to build them*, 1996, pp. 11–12.

5 Matiu was MP for Northern Māori from 1963 through to 1980 and the first Māori to have been appointed Native Affairs Minister for almost fifty years – since Sir Apirana Ngata.

6 Tariana Turia, interview with Dr Maarire Goodall, *Te Ahi Kaa*, Radio New Zealand, 28 September 2014.

7 Whakamīharo Lindauer online is a website run by the Auckland Art Gallery Toi o Tāmaki and dedicated to the portraits of Gottfried Lindauer: see www.lindaueronline.co.nz.

8 Tariana Turia, speech to Whakamīharo Lindauer Online launch, Awataha Marae, Northcote, Auckland, 3 July 2010.

9 Tariana Turia, speech to the Central Cancer Network Hui, 27 February 2009.

10 See the Customs and Excise (Tobacco Products – Budget Measures) Amendment Act 2012.

11 Inquiry into the tobacco industry in Aotearoa and the consequences of tobacco use for Māori, report of the Māori Affairs Committee, Hon. Tau Henare, November 2010, p. 5.

12 Patrick Gower, 'Opinion: Turia has absolutely smashed Big Tobacco', 19 February 2013. *3news.co.nz*: www.3news.co.nz/opinion/patrick-gower/opinion-turia-has-absolutely-smashed-big-tobacco-2013021909#axzz3YmfH5ShK (accessed 30 April 2015).

13 Heart Foundation, 'Heartfelt Tributes for our Smokefree Champion', 21 August 2014: www.heartfoundation.org.nz/news-blogs-stories/blogs/heartfelt-tributes-for-our-smokefree-champion (accessed 1 May 2015).

14 Dr Jan Pearson, acting chief executive of the Cancer Society, tribute on behalf of the Cancer Society, at the Tobacco Control Sector's farewell for Hon Tariana Turia, 14 August 2014, Pipitea Marae.

-CHAPTER EIGHT-

A REFUGE: THE TE AWA YOUTH TRUST

While the loss of her mother affected Tariana deeply, she received many gifts out of the time the two women spent at the end of her mother's life, not the least of which was the whānau becoming so linked in to life revolving around their marae. And so it was that Rangitāhuahua became the perfect place for the Te Awa Youth Trust to take root, and provide young people with a refuge from the world; a place to grow and to develop a future for themselves.

Tariana and George managed the Te Awa Youth Trust for over ten years, from 1980 through to 1990. In its heyday, over ninety students went out to Whangaehu every day. Tariana had taken on the role of a detached youth worker, under a scheme funded by the Department of Internal Affairs, which began in 1977. The scheme provided a grant of up to $16,000 towards the salary of a detached youth worker for up to three years. In its first five years, the scheme funded forty-seven projects, thirty-eight organisations and fifty-five workers. The workers funded by the scheme supported young people under twenty-five whose needs were not being met by existing programmes. It enabled 'detached youth workers to work with, not for, young people and encourage them to develop their own personal strengths, resources and self-reliance'.[1]

Te Awa became a safety net for rangatahi who had dropped out of school; who were looking for a new direction, or drifting. Over the ten years that it ran, it provided a shelter for hundreds of youth. The courses at Te Awa included peer-tutored literacy programmes, engineering, welding, catering, weaving and organic gardening using Māori rotational planting methods. Mechanics was taught on the marae, there was a health and recreation programme, and there were courses designed to teach students to be self-sufficient. An apotoro from Rātana Pā, Sam Paki, supported by master carver Dean Flavell, ran a carving module. Over four years some twenty-four young men went through the programme. Dean lived on the marae, in a caravan next to Dorsey's. He thought of George and Tari as his second mum and dad.

With such large numbers of students, some of whom had young families themselves, Tariana decided they also needed to provide childcare facilities.

And so Tīehutia Te Waka Te Kōhanga Reo was established in the early 1980s. Aunty Bobbie James from Rātana Pā was the first kaiako of the kōhanga, and many of the children who attended were also from the pā.

Te Awa was in all respects a bustling village, bringing life back into the marae and creating opportunities for the young people who came. One of the tutors of that time, Te Reo Hemi, explains that Te Awa was more than just the activities based at Whangaehu:

> I used to drive a fifty-four-seater bus and pick up people in Whanganui. We had our own bus. One of the ladies that was doing the administration at the marae, her husband worked for the local bus company, Greyhounds, and they were getting rid of some buses. So I went and picked one out and the Trust grabbed it. We had the bus and two twelve-seater Bedford vans that used to come into Whanganui every day and we had a couple of smaller vans that were bringing people from Rātana down.
>
> We opened up a satellite in Marton, and we ran that at the Te Kotahitanga Hall. We had a garden there; it was more educational than what they were doing down the marae. It was teaching them life skills and also how to budget, and how to live on the land – that there was a bit more to life than McDonalds and all that other stuff.

On one of those early courses in the eighties was present-day toihau/chief executive of Te Oranganui Iwi Health Authority Nancy Tuaine. Her time at Te Awa Youth Trust was formative in guiding her towards a plan for her future, she says:

> I first met [Tariana] when I was in Taihape and we were part of a rōpū rangatahi with Aunty Mihi [Rurawhe]. There was a group of wahine in Taihape and they supported our rangatahi rōpū and they brought us down to Whangaehu one weekend to meet up with some other rangatahi, and that's when I first met up with Aunty Tariana. She leaves an impression with you; doesn't matter who you are.

High school was too much of a culture shock for me. I came down to Whanganui in the sixth form and I lasted to the May holidays. Then I persuaded my very good friend Melody Te Patu, who left not long after me, to leave, and we found our way to Te Awa Trust. That was the MACCESS courses done at Whangaehu that Aunty Tariana and Uncle George used to run. It was a village: they had created such an environment down there, with all of us coming from either town or Rātana. We had our own bus, a big forty-seater that travelled from town to Whangaehu, and if you played up Uncle George would kick you off the bus and then Aunty Tariana would blow him up. Me and Melody were on a business administration course, and they had a really good programme, with a hot lunch every day because they had a catering course. We loved our time there, and after that they had a really good person who would put you into work placement.

Tariana also remembers the days of the Te Awa Youth Trust with great fondness.

I look at those kids today who had been part of Te Awa Trust and I just feel so proud of them, because they've grown and developed just from having been given that opportunity that we believed in them.

We were under the leadership of the old man, Paringatai Rauhina, my daughter-in-law's koro. He was our kaiārahi, a beautiful man who made sure that everything was about the young people.

Aunty Girlie (Te Oranga Hemi) ran the catering course, which at one stage had about thirty to forty tauira. The course provided morning tea, lunch and afternoon tea for all the tauira, and when there was any hui at the marae they did the catering. The catering had to fit into the marae concept. The catering group would cook, they would make jams and preserves, and the goods would be shared out to our kuia and koroua. The kids could take some home but more importantly, each week they would take something out to the old people.

We had the most exquisite, lush organic gardens at the back with more tauira there, supervised by Ginny Rātana, Pikiora Girlie Tunua (née Tamou) and Tracey Hemi. The garden supplied vegetables for the marae. Our tauira would pay $5 a week and get hot lunch every day – pretty good value! Ginny was a beautiful weaver, so not only was she helping the kids to help themselves by growing kai but she was also teaching them to weave. Maggie Kaiwai was working on the tukutuku panels for the marae. Then there was te reo Māori run by my good friends, Tapihana Shelford and Rewi James.

We had an administration module going, and some of the girls used to go into different offices in town and work. Harete Hipango was also on the Youth Trust. She came there as a tauira and ended up tutoring the administration course, and now she's a barrister and solicitor.

The tauira were aged from fifteen years up. Some of the students weren't accepted at school – some of them couldn't read when they came in.

I became really involved in doing work with all the young people. We'd look around and there would be twenty or so young people who had all been kicked out of school. I'd be looking at these kids and I'd be thinking, 'what is it about them that they have been turfed out by so many schools? For fighting or swearing? Really?' Then I realised they all had one thing in common: they were dark, really dark. Not milk chocolate; I'm talking dark chocolate. I said to George, 'you know what, I bet if we sat down with these kids and really explored the issues with them, I guarantee it would be about colour'. He said, 'we don't know that', and I said, 'yes, we do know'.

I sat down with these kids, and sure enough not only did they have Pākehā kids calling them black, they had our own kids doing the same. They didn't fit anywhere, and they were really isolated in the school environment. All of those things were stirring me up, making me wild. You could go from one end of Whanganui to the other and you'd be hard pushed to find a Māori person working behind a counter. We filled all the factories, all the other places.

The anger that Tariana was experiencing at Whangaehu – her resentment at the injustice of different treatment on the basis of race – was becoming increasingly focused through her experience as a detached youth worker.

While the objectives of the scheme were forward-thinking for their time, rising unemployment and crime rates created an almost insurmountable challenge to its likelihood of success. As Nancy Tuaine identified, the Te Awa Youth Trust had a dedicated employment officer looking for employment opportunities for its students – but times were still very hard: only 25 percent of those who trained went on to get jobs. At times Tariana and George felt like it was an uphill battle.

An evaluation of the scheme in 1984 found that deepening economic and social problems, coupled with growing political activism and the drive of many rangatahi Māori to assert their cultural identity, lead to detached youth workers being asked to address issues far beyond the reach of the resources. Tariana saw this as providing a great opportunity for social change.

Te Reo Hemi also recalls that the detached youth worker role set up the platform for many other developments:

> Dickson Chapman was involved; he was a detached youth worker as well. Tari tried to steer us into all these different committees around the country, like the National Youth Council. We ran this youth work training, and we called it Ka Hao te Rangatahi. Our job was to administer this fund from Internal Affairs for youth workers in the central North Island, which was from Gisborne across to Waitara and down to Wellington. We used to have national youth worker hui at Whangaehu.

Another detached youth worker was Pati Umaga – someone Tariana would meet up with again years later, when she was Minister of Disability Issues. Pati's memory of that time is particularly vivid:

> There was a national youth workers conference, detached youth workers conference, held at her marae. For me, youth work was all about just working with street kids – you're just there at the coalface and trying to stick up for kids' rights. The first time I heard her talk I was trying to look around, saying, 'who's this woman talking?' 'cause what she was saying was to me quite radical. I looked at her and I thought, 'she must be a kuia that just works here as part of the marae'.

> And then I heard her talk, and I think it was the first time that I'd ever had the idea that you could be a visionary within youth work. Because I could never connect to the whole kind of political movement, the social change that you could try and capture within youth work. To me that was a Dr Martin Luther King moment, 'cause it felt like that, 'I have a dream'.

As well as the younger tauira at Te Awa, there were long-term inmates, some of whom had been lifers. Tariana has always thought that chances of employment provide much more positive prospects of a future. Her cousin Reti reflects on the difference that the Te Awa courses made to Reti's brother:

> He always proved to be quite stable when he had work after coming out of jail, and so [Tariana] and George provided [programmes to find work for prisoners coming out of jail] out at Whangaehu. If he didn't have work he got into more trouble and ended up back in jail. Tariana took him, and I know Tariana took care of a lot of people like that – and you know she's still taking care, fighting hard for her people.

The success of the experience we were having at Whangaehu led me to see if we could take the learning further by attracting government support.

During that decade (1980s) I spent two years as a regional co-ordinator for the MACCESS programmes[2] with the Department of Māori Affairs. I belonged to the National Employment Network after the Hui Taumata in 1984[3]. We felt that certain Māori males were working against the interests of what people were wanting and instead being driven by a Government direction. And then Māori Affairs hired me, basically as a change agent with MANA (an enterprises business startup project providing low-interest loans for Māori-owned businesses) and MACCESS. I worked from New Plymouth across to Gisborne and all of the South Island as well: me and John Coutts. I don't think the Government thought it would work.

I had an ulterior motive at that time. It was always on the cards that the Department would be devolved back to the people and the central bureaucracy disestablished. So I was keen to be on the inside for a while, to make for a smooth transition when the time came, to move governance back to where it belonged in whānau, hapū and iwi. Devolution was on everyone's lips, and I wanted to be part of the action.

Labour was in at the time, and I recall a document that Richard Prebble had written became a focus for Head Office concern. I was working at Head Office and was summonsed to the Chief Executive on the charge that I had supposedly leaked the Prebble document. I said to the Chief Executive, Wira Gardiner, 'You've got more leaks in here than a sieve'. And I told him, 'it was nothing to do with me, I can promise you. Ask the men in here who go drinking at the club, the Dragon (the Dungeon)'. They used to go down there and booze. 'They're more likely to be the leaks than I ever will be'.

The trouble was that the people I was mixing with were the ones that had got access to this document. So the boss had made the great big leap in connecting me to the crime. Well, I wasn't going to have that!

This is how Sir Wira Gardiner describes the situation:

> I first came into contact with Tariana Turia at Putiki Marae in 1986. In 1986 I had been appointed by Dr Tamati Reedy, the Secretary for the Department of Māori Affairs, to head the training and economic development unit. This was a new unit in the Department, and was established as part of the follow-on from Hui Taumata in 1984, where Māori leaders gathered from around the country and held a major symposium to develop a strategy for lifting Māori achievement across all sectors.
>
> I led the development of MANA and MACCESS under the general direction of Uncle Bert Mackie, who was chair of the sub-committee of the Board of Māori Affairs. I had a small staff including Ripeka Evans and Harete Hipango (whose family was a notable family from the Whanganui area). Ria Earp joined us later. Once we had developed the policies we had to take the programmes around the country.

Our purpose for going to Pūtiki was twofold. Firstly to apologise for some slight that my unit had created – and I can't remember what it was, but it was of sufficient seriousness for us to be summonsed to Pūtiki. The second purpose of our visit was to brief iwi and providers on what we were doing in the areas of MANA and MACCESS.

I recall the warmth of the pōwhiri, and felt good about the meeting we were about to enter with the key people involved with training and economic development. Well, my antenna sure was wrong, because as we settled comfortably in the meeting house we were confronted with this short, robust Māori woman with a steely gaze. She did not shout at us, but she eviscerated us with clinical logic. I have personally been in many tight situations in my life, including leading soldiers in combat in Vietnam, so I fancied myself as a tough customer! But all my military training and bravado went out the only door in the building under the unassailable attack from this woman. This was Tariana Turia! And this was our first meeting. And I never forgot it!

So over the years that first experience taught me a number of things about her, the principal one of which was, 'cross this lady at your peril'. The other abiding lesson I learned about Tariana even in those early days was how principled she was. I had got used to meeting many Māori leaders who enforced their positions by cultural dominance through the reo and tikanga. When they ventured off this cultural pathway they often got lost. But with Tariana I learned very quickly that she came off a logic base rooted in an ideology of care and attention, especially for those whānau who were deprived or impoverished. When dealing with a person with an ideological foundation it is very hard to shift them from their position, as they have arrived at that position from deep thought, maturity and profound experiences amongst those most in need. In a word she was 'formidable'!

> After I left the MANA/MACCESS unit in 1987 and as I moved around the place I would catch a flutter of her activities out of the corner of my eye, giving a thankful prayer to myself that I would not have to deal with her again.

Towards the end of the eighties, Tariana became disillusioned about the impact of government funding on the Te Awa Trust programmes; she believed that being tied to the state stifled their capacity to be innovative. The students were now receiving only a limited income; they had started on $350 per week, and then the Government reduced this amount to $50. Tariana felt that essentially all that the Government was doing was imposing a form of social control.

George wasn't happy with me – he told me I was being too political. 'Just think about the kids and think about what we're doing here', he said. But I've never been good with just settling for second best. 'No,' I said, 'because we're helping the Government out by running this here on the marae. We are assisting the Government to keep our families poor'.

Basically I felt our kids were being used in a way that wasn't going to help them to develop fully, and so we just stopped. It blew everyone away. They never thought we would actually do it.

Te Reo Hemi recalls:

> We got to a stage where Tariana and George had the thing pumping that well that the funder, Government, was saying, 'well, seeing you are doing so well, why do you need government funding to do it?' What they were forgetting was that it was because of the government funding that it was happening.

In 1990 then, we just handed back everything to the marae. It was no longer viable to continue.

Over and above all the various outcomes our tauira had achieved over the years, there was, however, one achievement that outshone all others. In locating Te Awa Youth Trust at our marae, we had injected new life into our tribal home, and there was no looking back.

Te Reo Hemi says:

> It was awesome for the marae, having that sort of integration, people that belonged to the marae, people who had no connection with it whatsoever. We even had Pākehās there as well; it wasn't just for Māori. There were a couple of Pākehā as tauira and supervisors as well. That was home for her – tōna tūrangawaewae.

There is nothing quite like the buzz of a thriving village to give you confidence that you can run things on your own, without needing the hand of the state pulling all the strings.

NOTES

1 Bruce MacKie, *An Evaluation of the Detached Youth Worker Funding Scheme*, Department of Internal Affairs, 1984, p. 10.

2 The ACCESS programme was established in 1987, and targeted people who were disadvantaged in the labour market. ACCESS offered funding for each trainee based on the level of disadvantage they faced. Māori ACCESS (MACCESS) ran alongside it , was separately administered by Māori authorities, and was largely delivered through Māori providers.

3 The Hui Taumata (Māori Economic Summit Conference) was held at Parliament in 1984. The summit emphasised that the economic wellbeing of Māori is inextricably linked to the health of the New Zealand economy.

-CHAPTER NINE-
THE PATH TO SELF-DETERMINATION

We have to believe in our own right to do whatever we need to do. The barrier that we constantly have in front of us is the tauiwi telling us that we cannot do this and that. They have created the structures for us to fit into. We must exercise that legitimacy that we never gave up. There is a desperate need for us to get this relationship right. No nations that are divided against themselves can stand.[1]

The experience that Tariana and George had had with the boys from Holdsworth and the youth attending Te Awa Youth Trust; her role as a detached youth worker; and the experiences she and George were immersed in through fostering so many children from difficult circumstances eventually led Tariana down a political road in the late eighties. It was around this time that Tariana and George, with others, established the Whanganui Regional Development Board.

The establishment of the Board grew out of the experience with Te Awa Youth Trust, and also the wider political context evolving out of the 1984 economic development conference, Hui Taumata. That hui had produced a charter, 'He Kawenata', calling for a decade of development to assist Māori in participating in the economy. Sister Makareta Tawaroa, from the Congregation of the Sisters of St Joseph of Nazareth, articulates the impact that the Hui Taumata had on the river people:

> The Treaty workshops were beginning; we were flexing our muscles. We were thinking, 'well, we've got to be the decision-makers around all this new thinking'. Hui Taumata had a profound effect on us; it pinpointed that jobs were a priority.

The MANA and MACCESS schemes had emerged as a direct result of the Hui Taumata. Funding for both was provided directly to tribal and regional providers from Vote: Māori Affairs[2]. Government required all providers to be incorporated bodies, to ensure transparency and accountability.

The Whanganui Regional Development Board was established to act as a conduit for these funds, but more importantly to seed local projects. Jo Maniapoto, George's cousin, who was also involved, explains:

> We set up the Whanganui Regional Development Board, which George headed at the time, that was a combination of the key people who were part of this whole push for employment – and [there was also a feeling] that we couldn't do any worse than Rogernomics. Really it was saying, 'hey, we don't care what you do; we're going to do this.' There were people like Michael Bowler, who was a Rarotongan and the only businessperson; and there was George, and of course he had abilities in terms of Te Awa Youth Trust. It was really saying to the

Government, 'we can't do any worse than you do now.' Our people gave koha so that we could set up our own businesses.

At around the same time that she was setting up the Board, Tariana was moving from her Mills and Boon library to a new literature, including New Zealand history and politics and Donna Awatere's classic manual for activism, *Māori Sovereignty*.

> I'd sit in front of the stove reading while dinner was cooking and it would burn. George went through a stage of burning my books – I almost left him for that.[3]

It was during this time that the process of conscientisation as defined by Freire[4] emerged as a key influence upon Tariana's developing commitment to social action.

For a period of fifty-six days in the winter of 1981, husbands and wives, parents and children, employers and employers, entire neighbourhoods found themselves opposed in a massive civil disturbance around a game of two sides. More than 150,000 people took part in over 200 demonstrations in twenty-eight centres, and 1500 were charged with offences stemming from these protests.

Historians would later show that the Springbok Tour of 1981 was merely one of a string of tours that had pitted New Zealanders against each other in a bitter context of race versus rugby. Jo Maniapoto remembers the 'No Māori, No Tour' campaign that eventually led to the 1967 All Black tour to South Africa being cancelled, in which Tariana's own Aunty Wai had played a key part. Until then, because of the racial segregation policy operating in South Africa, the New Zealand Rugby Football Union chose not to select Māori players for tours to South Africa.[5] This provoked Aunty Wai to set up a petition in protest.

Jo Maniapoto says:

> Before I even understood about the whole apartheid thing I remember her with a table in the main street with a petition and making people sign. So she (Tari) was brought up around that

kind of thing, you know. I personally didn't know what the hell Aunty Wai was on about at that time, because I was probably not politicised then and I hadn't realised how colonised I was; I don't think any of us did at the time.

By 25 July 1981, the stage was set for the ultimate play-off at Rugby Park in Hamilton. Tariana was planning to go to the match with Cathy Penetito and their friend Chris Church.

George just about left me during that winter. He'd get so mad with me. He would be down the pub and they would be all watching, and I would go along with a cue and whack the TV and switch it off. He'd tell me, 'you're bloody nuts'. Anyway, on this day, I was getting ready to go and George comes in from the farm. I'm all dressed to go. He looked at me and said, 'where are you going?'

'Stop the game,' I replied. And he said to me, 'well, have you stopped to think about the kids, and what if you get hurt?'

I said, 'oh no, no, I'll be right, and I'm going'.

He said to me, 'well, I don't very often ask you to not do something, but I'm telling you I don't want you to go'.

I couldn't bloody believe it. I was packed; I was all ready to hop in the car. I had to go out and say to them, 'I can't come'. They were so mad with me. But I just couldn't. It was just the way he said it to me: 'I don't ask you not to do things. No – I don't want you to go'.

Pahia remembers that particular incident:

That Springbok tour was a real defining moment for Mum. I can remember my Aunty Cath Penetito and her were going to the game. Her and Dad – they had the hooliest argument. Dad's going, 'you're not going down' – he just hit the roof. I thought to myself, 'she's going to leave'. In fact she told him – 'I'll leave you, I'm asking you to stand beside me on this, support me'. And Dad said, 'no, it's unsafe, you've seen what's happened, protesters getting beaten up'. I don't know whether it was a safety issue for Dad or whether it was making a bloody storm in a teacup over nothing.

The tour made an even more dramatic impact upon Pahia later that winter:

> I can always remember in 1981 when the Springbok tour came. I was nine. Dad's taking me to rugby practice and Mum comes out. She goes, 'get out of the car'. Dad goes, 'sit in the car', and then Mum goes, 'get out of the car' – so I'm like, 'what's going on here?' Anyway, this conversation/argument comes about with Mum and Dad. Mum said to me, 'you can't play rugby any more', and I was like, 'what! – What did I do?' And that was her stance – 'this is a principled stand that I'm taking'.
>
> Dad's going, 'Stop being so ridiculous Tari –he's only a kid, it's not his fault about the black people', And I'm sitting there – like, 'what black people?' I can remember going inside and crying and just saying to Mum, 'But I love rugby; I just want to play'. So she sat there for ages and explained to me why I couldn't play. I said, 'but I don't care about the black people'. At a very young age Mum took the time to explain, and I can remember going to school the next day and saying to everybody – 'you shouldn't be playing rugby'.
>
> Mum, she brought all of us up that if you feel that an injustice is taking place – don't you sit there and say nothing. As a result of that I was a real prick of a kid at school because if I questioned or didn't feel right about what I was doing, I'd say, 'well, why are we doing that?' If there wasn't a good rationale, then why would I do it? She instilled that in us, and I could always remember Mum saying that she regretted doing that in some ways because you ended up being this kid at school that the teacher goes, 'you're doing it because I told you to' – and I'd go, 'But that's not a good enough reason!' As a result you're always stuck in the principal's office.

Pahia wasn't the only kid at school who was influenced by actions Tariana was taking. There were other students, and teachers as well, who became a focus of Tariana's action.

The other day at home, this man came up to me on the street and made a point of stopping me. He told me that the one thing that really struck him was that during my political career I have never been any different to when I was at home. If people had issues they would bring them to me, and I would take them up.

He shared with me a memory of a particular incident up at the High School. Dennis Rātana, Sister Makareta, myself and a couple of others had paid a visit to the principal and told him clearly what we thought of him for standing down this young Māori girl. Our parting shot had been to tell him how childish we thought he had been. Apparently the man on the street had had a good friend at the school at the time, and he had told him how terrified the principal had been – after all, he had a school to run; he had to maintain discipline.

As soon as he started talking, I could remember that girl like it was yesterday. She had had a terrible life, and her heinous crime that led to suspension had been some stupid graffiti on the toilet walls. Basically we told the principal he was petty; all he'd done was judge her on an isolated incident. We asked him to reinstate her. After we left the school I went straight round to see the parents. I was really furious with them for not standing up for her.

We were Joe Nobodies really, but we never let the lack of a job title or an ID card stop us when there was business to be done. If our kids were getting kicked out of school we'd go as a group to the schools and have them on.

We used to attack issues as we saw them. Our thinking was always that we couldn't just sit back and let things happen. We should speak out. It was because of actions like this that we became known as the 'Māori mafia'. We met together as Māori women, probably every two or three months, plotting how we would change the world.

In an article in *North and South* headlined 'Fierce Kuia', Tariana recounts that time in her life:

> At 35 I was quite militant in my thinking – I was a raging lunatic. The police hated me. We'd bring them on to the marae and show them a video about police attitudes to Māori children and they'd get really mad. I think we polarized people to start with because they weren't used to being confronted. We never did it nicely, we were fairly in-your-face. My mother would ring up and say, 'people I've grown up with are really mad with you and you've got to stop doing this'. But it just made me worse, to think people were personalising

what I was saying and not seeing these systemic issues that in lots of ways they'd benefitted from the system. I thought, I'm here picking up the pieces, having to look after kids damaged in the school system, by the behavior of others towards your families and yet you judge them, you make all these assumptions but you know nothing of what's happened to their families historically. You don't know what they've been through. I'd get on my little rampage.[6]

During her years with the Whanganui Regional Development Board, Tariana worked out of a unit attached to the Board's office called Whai Oranga that worked on a range of issues. There were three in the unit: Tariana as manager and Mihi Rurawhe and Marie Moses as social workers. Part of the purpose of the unit was to help to make the Department of Social Welfare more responsive to Māori needs.

We worked together for probably a good two or three years. Establishing the unit really came out of us challenging the Department of Social Welfare about hiring a French Canadian woman as a cultural advisor. It was about this time that my friendship with Ken Mair started to develop a stronger connection.

Through Whai Oranga, Tariana and Ken Mair started to come together, motivated by a mutual desire to make a positive difference for families coming into contact with the welfare agencies. Ken says:

There was major disappointment in regard to the social statistics and all the negative data, and we'd lined up a couple of people who we thought would have been much more appropriate [for the position of cultural advisor at the Department of Social Welfare] and then they go and appoint someone external to us. Tari was very much involved in that; I think she was probably at the centre of it, if I recall. She was extremely articulate – what was good about Tari and still is, of course, is her ability to analyse off the cuff; it is quite a skill, you know; to be able to quickly pick up the question, to be able to answer it, analyse with some in-depthness – very few people have that.

Tariana remembers the incident with great gusto.

We went around and told all of our organisations to pull out and to not take any money from the Department; to have nothing to do with them. Needless to say they didn't appoint her. John Grant was the Deputy Secretary in those times. It was after the action we took to challenge the appointment that we were able to set up Whai Oranga, funded by the Department. This was the period in which the police were still using dogs to bite our kids. We'd arrange for someone up at the hospital to photograph the kids when they came in and then use that as evidence to have them on.

Dennis Rātana and I were particularly close partners in arms. We had worked in Mātua Whāngai[7] together as volunteers, but in fact we'd almost got had up for fraud for using the money in a particular way for families. What we would do was that if families had a whole heap of bills, we'd pay their bills, and we would make them pay it back. But we would save literally thousands of dollars on the interest that they would have had to pay, because of course in those days you didn't get two years interest-free.

Back in the eighties, budget-holding was definitely what the people called for. The budget being held on to look after beneficiaries: making sure they were fed, housed, clothed. Once they had a strong base the social service agency would start dealing with all the other issues by bringing in other interventions: Parents as First Teachers, Family Start, parenting programmes. And you know, we've been very concerned for years about our people being on benefits as such, because we can see that it's killed their spirit; it's killed their soul. When you've got poverty of spirit, how can people think about transforming their lives?

But what Dennis and I were doing was a bit different. We would get all their bills together: if it was someone with a family or kids, we'd look into it. And then we'd make them take control of their own circumstances. I remember one woman that we did it for – she had never been home (to her tribal base). She had never had a holiday, so we paid all her bills, and the second year she was able to go and have a holiday with the kids. We taught her to budget so that she could live on the money she had coming in, and she could pay off this loan. We collapsed all her loans into one, and she paid it off over a two-year period. But she had money in the bank. We told her she had to pay in for two years, and she did, and there was money left in there for her to go home. We did that deliberately so that she would have money.

Anyway, we just about got had up for what we saw as simply being constructive. In many ways it was a little bit like Whānau Ora. We wouldn't just automatically give people things. We always made sure they paid it back. If they needed clothes or different things, we would always go round the families first. We would have the odd whānau – very odd I would have to say – who would say no, they wanted new stuff. Please! Their view was why should they have second-hand? And I'd say, 'because you can't afford to buy it new, and we're not going to spend the kind of money you want us to'. Wanting us to buy label shoes! They were related to us too, cheeky buggers.

One of the ringleaders of the self described Māori maha was Sister Makareta Tawaroa from the Sisters of St Joseph.

The Sisters trace their beginnings back to 1880, when pioneering Sisters Terehia and Arawirihana arrived at the mouth of the Whanganui River in the steamboat *Whakatu*. In 1883 they moved to Hiruharama, where they forged a relationship with the people of Ngāti Hau in collaboration with Suzanne Aubert, founder of the Sisters of the Home of Compassion. To this day the Sisters maintain a very close association to the whānau along the river: particularly Ngā Paerangi at Kaiwhaiki. It is there that Sister Makareta Tawaroa still tends her enormous garden, cares for her mokopuna and plots the revolution.

In the late eighties, in between planting the kamokamo, teaching at local schools and supporting rangatahi Māori who were appearing in court on various charges, Sister brought together the Whanganui Māori Women's Group, including Maria Moses, Jo Maniapoto, Hilda Renee and Te Kuia Peeti. The group was guided by the leadership and radical ministry of Father John Curnow. A Marxist and liberation theologian, Father John literally wore his heart on his chest. He had a badge that said 'there will be no peace without justice'; a mantra that he lived by. The Sisters' mission with Father John was clear: to learn how to use the system to effect change.

Sister Makareta explains:

> He was teaching Paulo Freire's theory of liberation education: 'by the work of your own hands will you liberate yourself'. Nobody gives it to you; you have to take it, you see. All this wonderful kōrero. It makes sense.

Through Sister Makareta and her friendship with Father John, Tariana came to know the writings of Mauritian Catholic priest Phillipe Fanchette, who asked the questions: 'Who are the poor? Why are they poor? Who benefits? Who loses? Who owns? Who controls? Whose interests are served?'

These are the questions of conscientisation, the stuff of the social activism that became Tariana's platform for transformation. Father Curnow trained the women in structural analysis, encouraging them to look at how systems worked and how they operated against the people. Father Curnow had a theory based on action: 'see, judge and act'. His seminars in Marxist structural analysis were designed to open Catholic eyes to the inequalities in society; particularly those impacting on tangata whenua.

And so they began, the sisterhood for solidarity, making structural analysis of the economy, and of the organisations they were part of. The group would look at the interlocking power structures between corporations, multinationals, and the different companies with which various politicians were associated. It was an eye-opener for Tariana, and shaped the way for her political career to follow.

Sister Makareta talks about a virtual network of wāhine Māori throughout the country: the Solomon sisters of Kaikōura, Terehia Stafford in Te Tau Ihu, Irihapeti Ramsden and Linda Erihi (Thompson) in Wellington, Barbara Ball in Otaihape, Ani Mikaere – networks upon networks. She says:

> We got together with them, and it was the days when we'd be singing, 'people of Aotearoa'. We'd go through streets, all these Māori women; we'd go to hui in Waikato, and travel through Taumarunui singing songs: 'we'll fight on forever'. You know we loved those words.

The process of politicisation started to take hold in Tariana's life.

George remembers two particular hui that I went to where someone asked the question, 'would we die for the movement?' It provoked a great deal of soul-searching – how strong was my commitment? What would be my tipping point?

The following year the question changed a little – 'would we be prepared to kill for the movement?' At this point George said I was bloody stupid!

Funnily enough a few years later, I got almost the same reaction from John Maihi[8], when I posed a similar question in the context of the reoccupation of Pākaitore.

John Maihi says of that occasion:

> This particular day we were all sitting on the paepae; she got up and made this big speech, and she went, 'you, you, you, you: we're all dying for the cause'. I went back to her, 'I don't remember talking about that'. And the look on her face – it was like she could kill the lot of us, like, 'oh, you mongrels; you're all supposed to agree!'

Some key moments in Tariana's politicisation process were promoted by Sister Makareta, and later by Tariana's good friend, Rob Cooper, who was pioneering change through decolonisation workshops. Both were involved, through the Catholic Church, in a series of hui raising consciousness around Catholic social teaching.

> Around 1981 Manuka Henare led a symposium in Wellington to discuss the place of the Treaty in New Zealand Church life. The question that came out of this was, 'What does the Treaty mean for us?' Up until then the understanding about the Treaty was often expressed as 'the Treaty is a fraud,' but there was a new understanding that the Treaty needed to be honoured.[9]

Tariana was reading Freire and finding wisdom in the path to emancipation that was being preached. Freire held that 'No pedagogy which is truly liberating can remain distant from the oppressed by treating them as unfortunates and by presenting for their emulation models from among the oppressors. The oppressed must be their own example in the struggle for their redemption'[10]. In Tariana's eyes, it was time for the theory to be tested; for liberation to be enacted. Tariana was primed and ready for the revolution to begin. In 2014, she articulated views that she had begun to formulate with her reading of Freire:

> Inequality began at the signing of the Treaty of Waitangi. When somebody takes all of your resources, they take the language away from you, they take away the essence of who you are, deny your language, that's the beginning of inequality.[11]

My reading of the activist library and of Freire; my passion for my kids; and that sense of social justice I'd inherited from Aunty Wai came together over our right to our own education. All we wanted was for te reo Māori to be introduced into the school. We called for a hui at Te Kura o Kokohuia; in those days it was Kokohuia School. It was to be a big hui involving all the whānau, but when we arrived we found we had been blocked out.

Ninety-five percent of that school were Māori. So next thing we all turned up to their board meeting. Aunty Huia Hipango was so dramatic; she was a bit like Aunty Wai. She stands up in the hui and she goes to the principal, 'I am leaving here immediately – who do you think you are? As for you sitting around this board table: I am ashamed of you. I am ashamed of you'.

I had to get the board on our side. I said to the hui, 'I'm really disappointed that you are standing up talking against what we are saying. I want this school to meet the needs of your kids in the way that you are telling us tonight, but I never expected that you would go against us for what we want'. Nowadays years 1–8 students at Kokohuia are taught in total immersion te reo Māori and year 9–13 is a bilingual unit. We got there in the end, but not without a fight.

Our next mission was to establish a kura kaupapa Māori in Whanganui. This meant raising $47,000 from iwi contributions for the first year before the kura was approved to receive funds from the Crown.

We opened the doors of Te Kura Kaupapa Māori o te Āti Haunui-a-Pāpārangi in 1989. It sounds easy. It wasn't.

The Whanganui Regional Development Board gave us some initial funding, and a couple of us contracted our services out and paid the funds earned straight back to the Board, who gave it to the kura. We couldn't get resources up front. That was when we called on all our families and asked them for koha to support us. We had enough to pay a principal for a whole year, and then with that money we went back to our people and asked them to support us: 'Can you contribute to an educational opportunity for our kids?' And lots of families gave.

The Path to Self-determination

Sister Makareta says of this initiative:

> We all promoted it: $1, $2 a week, you know. The unemployed, the beneficiaries – what we found was those that had very little give far more, are more generous than those that have a lot.

We knew that with the money we'd got from the contracts and then the koha contributions mostly from whānau and supporters we would have enough money for two years. We thought that would be how long it would take to get off the ground. Eventually most of us paid in for five years, so that our kura had some fairly strong backing behind it.

We started off in a converted garage belonging to Sister Makareta.

Sister Makareta remembers:

> I said, 'well, I've got a double garage outside Glasgow Street; you could use that'. So we got it carpeted and cleaned, and they used it, and I think no more than eleven children were allowed to come. They'd been everywhere: they'd been to an education board, to offices next to KFC, and then they were in the old Saint Joseph Hall for a while, the most moved school in the world.

I'd call in every day to make morning tea; hot soup in winter. It took us two years, five different moves to other premises and sustained pressure on the powers that be before we finally got a council-approved site in Pūtiki and state funding. That in itself was interesting. Our whānau were interested in a prime site in Whanganui. However, when we approached the Whanganui District Council their response was that the site was out of the question, as it was designated for housing. Fair enough. Well, it would be, if all other educational institutions were given the same fob-off. That was precisely the point. When the Japanese-owned Asia-Pacific International University made similar inquiries about a site for their institution, that same site we had expressed interest in was offered to them.

One of the great lessons that Sister Makareta would impress upon Tariana was the importance of being principled about the way the money was used, and more importantly that the source of any funding should be transparent, and consistent with the integrity of their work. A classic example of this came in the production of the paper *Mana Tangata*.

> During the eighties we set up a local newspaper, Mana Tangata. The Development Board funded us for three years, but we were always struggling. Families would buy it, but they would only buy one paper and then they'd share that one copy around. We started off charging $2 and then raised it to $3 when we realised what everyone was doing, but it was still really difficult. We even changed our focus a bit, trying to be more whānau-orientated. We would have all the political stuff upfront, and then in the middle of it, we'd promote all of these whānau events. Sister thought the middle section a bit of wasted space, but I said to her, 'Sister, we have to get them to buy our paper, and are they really interested in something that happened in 1870? No.'
>
> When it came to the crunch, we were looking for sponsorship, and the only people that wanted to advertise with us were the tobacco companies and alcohol outlets. I remember meeting with Sister Makareta and she was so funny: 'I don't even know why we're meeting to discuss this. Waste of our time'.
>
> The interesting thing was that the first lot of investment we received from the state for our kura kaupapa Māori followed an embarrassing situation at a pōwhiri, in which I'd challenged a breach of kawa that had occurred; another instance for Sister Makareta about holding fast to our principles no matter what was at stake. It was at an education and training hui in Wainuiomata. Russell Marshall, then Minister of Education, was there. There was a big crowd – I can remember Richard Brooking, Alec Wilson from Te Arawa, Grant Knuckey from Taranaki – all seeking to secure the funding for training purposes.
>
> During the pōwhiri one of the kaumātua spoke. When he finished, up from the ranks came a Department of Education officer. He side-stepped in front of the old man and put down the koha.

Sister Makareta, who was also at the hui, recalls this moment:

> He had the audacity to actually come up after the kaumātua had spoken and he laid down the koha. Right in the middle of the pōwhiri Tari gets up and lets him have it with all her full righteousness: 'We are here to keep the kawa of the marae. Why did he not give the koha to the kaumātua who spoke? Did he want to be seen as the beholder of the power?' Oh,

> she went on. We were beside ourselves. The poor man didn't have a leg to stand on. She wiped the floor with him. And that turned the hui into a kōrero around tikanga. She has a lot of guts; she has guts.

The others were furious with me for making a scene. I thought it was highly offensive that instead of allowing the kaumātua to complete the proceedings properly by waiting to lay down the koha after he spoke, the protocols had been breached. I remember saying to them all, once the pōwhiri was over, 'I want to know what's going on here. I think there's another little agenda going on, and that was done deliberately to make us notice you. And we have noticed you. And I am challenging you – how dare you do that to the kaumātua? That you would keep the koha and then step out with it?'

It was after that hui that we got our first contract in education. We got it directly: a $46,000 contract to do a report through the Development Board. We took that money and we gave it to the kura kaupapa to get it established. Karma, I guess.

This period of Tariana's life was characterised by her drive to take action to find solutions. She was loving all that she was learning and reading of Freire; her contact with Father Curnow; and the brilliant mind of her friend Fernando Yusingco, a Filipino community development worker. From that point on, her beliefs became a manual for how she lived her life. The momentum of the Development Board was a turning point:

> I could see the light come on in our people's eyes in terms of doing for themselves. It was a huge driver for me to make things happen. I was driven by a firm belief that our own kaupapa, tikanga could drive that. We could use our values and practices in a positive way to take us forward.[12]

Tariana's friend Robert Reid attributes her involvement in structural analysis workshops as pivotal in developing her 'self-determination tino rangatiratanga outlook':

> I guess looking at what makes up Tariana, who comes from quite a conservative rural background, it was the participation in these structural analysis courses that the late John Curnow ran for both mixed and separate audiences of Māori and Pākehā for a number of

years. Because things within Maoridom sort of moved as well. I often joke with Māori friends about when they were in demonstrations and the main slogan was 'honour the Treaty'. I said, 'I grew up in the Donna Awatere days, which held that the Treaty is a fraud'. It was a maturing of the movement, and seeing where the contradictions were and being able to drive those contradictions, and Tariana was certainly there.

The theory was never confined just to the pages of a textbook. Tariana and the other members of the Māori Mafia were living it – acting locally, thinking globally. Tariana's cousin, Retihiamatikei Cribb, reflects on the day she started putting the theory into practice, during her time as the principal of Kokohuia School:

> Years ago it was our turn to go to the Splash Centre. There was three classes going down to the pools. I'd just become the principal, and I had to go to a meeting at the Ministry. I came back past there and thought, 'I'll call in and see the kids swimming', because 1 o'clock was their swimming time. Well, it was about five past one when I went in and they're still all bloody sitting up on this seat. I'm looking in the pool and there's this woman teaching lifesaving skills in our three lanes.
>
> I went up to the office and I said, 'excuse me, we're supposed to be in the pool at 1 o'clock'. They said, 'Oh yeah, so? Whatever her name was teaching lifesaving was running a bit late'. I told them, 'Well, that's not an excuse, and that's not going to happen ever again'. I walked down to the front of the pool and called out. 'Kokohuia, in the pool'. Well, all the kids ran into the pool, and the Pākehās jumped out. I reprimanded the teachers. I said, 'don't you ever let anybody do that to our kids, because look, they accepted it, and if you don't stick up for them they're always going to be doormats. You bloody stick up for them; it's five past one, they should have been in the pool'.
>
> That's the stuff I see Tariana on about – it is about justice and making sure that we're talking about self-determination. That's not self-determination, being a doormat: hell no.

The community has work to do

vivian Hutchinson says:

> I think there is a resonance between Tari and Jo [Maniapoto] and myself and others that says, 'community has work to do'; it's not just something that's nice if you've got spare time.
>
> Community is a fundamental part of the fabric. In Māori terms I would say iwi and hapū is an essential part of the fabric; in Pākehā terms you would say community. It's always contested space, but whatever problems we've got it's going to take community to solve some of these things. Our most fundamental and complex problems are not solved by programmes and schemes.

––––––––––––––––––––

Following the success of the Te Awa Youth Trust, and the momentum growing at the Whanganui Regional Development Board, Tariana started reaching out across New Zealand to other activists working in the community space. One of those people was vivian Hutchinson, community activist, social entrepreneur and a thoroughly good person. vivian says of his relationship with Tariana:

> Our connection came through the employment projects that were held in the eighties. There was much more government investment in the community sector in those days; it was largely under a National Government too, you know. Jim Bolger and some of those people were putting far more money into the community sector and particularly into employment programmes than this generation's National Government has actually been doing. There was far more commitment to supporting people in that early time of unemployment.

vivian had been part of the Taranaki Work Trust. He says:

> We probably spent three or four years pushing the Government to make training a legitimate thing for unemployed people. Up until

that time it was mainly work schemes. You had all of these people running around in yellow vans, scrub-cutting and putting paths down and all sorts of 'make work' stuff. The community leaders were saying, 'actually, these people are quite capable of working at another level'. We pushed them to introduce training for unemployed people. The cost of that politically was that all the work schemes disappeared and were redefined as training, so it was a success on one hand and a failure on the other one, because we also realised we were dealing with a cohort of people who didn't want to get into work.

Tariana and George formed a close relationship with vivian. What he was doing in Taranaki with different work schemes was very like what they had been doing with Te Awa Youth. vivian wanted to take more local control; to create a local response, and that led to a series of innovative programmes, such as the skills for enterprise training course, which Tariana and George had also run at Whangaehu. vivian says:

> Part of our connection was the fact that we had a local entrepreneurial response to a common question of economic decline and unemployment, particularly as it was affecting young people. There was a commonality in our analysis. There was a whole bunch of people who would say, 'what is the government going to pay for? That's what we're going to do'. We were saying, 'what do our people need, and how can communities get around that to make that happen?' You come up with different answers. The Government preferred to fund people who started with that first question, 'what's the contract and how do I deliver it?', so you end up farming for people rather than solving problems.

The mid-eighties were a hotbed for fertile discussion about fundamental questions of nationhood, the role of communities, relationships between people, and of course the fundamental underpinning of national identity, Te Tiriti o Waitangi. vivian makes a very clear analysis of how discussions about employment had to intersect politically, culturally and strategically with the burgeoning interest in nation-building and the crucial Treaty relationship between tangata whenua and tangata tiriti: the people who came to Aotearoa by virtue of the Treaty of Waitangi:

Most of my Pākehā colleagues in the eighties who were working on employment issues hadn't had much contact with Māori people, so Jo [Maniapoto] and Tariana were a very important bridge for a whole generation of activists and a bit of a wake-up call. In terms of land rights issues, there was fundamental historical amnesia as to the theft of assets and the trans-generational trauma that would happen. You can trace many of the issues that we are talking about back to the loss of community and loss of assets and theft of Māori land, which in the seventies was continuing to happen – it wasn't a historic thing. One of the reasons for the Māori Land March was unemployment –the first group to be pushed off were Māori people.

For a lot of Pakeha – you know, seventies liberal community people – it was a huge wake-up call as to what was going on in their own country. Many of them had no real authentic friendships with Māori people or were willing to step up for that challenge. They had superficial friendships – 'we all know so and so' – but certainly there was a deep challenge in reconciling the historical stuff that came into it, at that time, late seventies early eighties, and no real conversation about the Treaty of Waitangi.

Another important contact for Tariana during the eighties was Robert Reid. Robert always had a strong interest in employment solutions. He recalls how, one day, he went to meet his old friend Paul Swain:

And he said there was a group coming together to hold a conference of people around the country who had been or who were involved in employment solutions and trying to create jobs at a community level. They were work trusts; co-operatives; community organisations trying to create work for people in them. As can be imagined, a large number of them were Māori.

I attended that conference; the group of attendees came to call itself the Employment Network. At that conference a couple who stood out for me very much were these two women from Whanganui: one being Tari, and the other being Sister Makareta.

> I was interested in the kaupapa of the Network. It was an interesting organisation in that it was a bicultural one; it was Pākehā and Māori working together. They needed a co-ordinator – they had got money from the then Labour Government to do work co-ordination work, which was in order to prepare for an employment summit. I put my hand up and was appointed to that position.
>
> The first Māori and Tauiwi chairs of the Employment Network were Paul Swain on one hand and Tariana on the other. Essentially I worked to Paul and Tariana, trying to link up around the country many of those initiatives which had been created possibly ten years before, around 1984, in the last period of Muldoon, where unemployment started rising.

Paul and Tariana were appointed as community representatives to a Government advisory panel on training and employment policy. They helped to argue for regional training councils that would administer schemes but also have a broader employment focus.

And so began an era in which the Whanganui Regional Development Board started to take on prominence as a means of backing local initiative, seeding a collective interest in creating opportunities for work. The process was problematic, as Jo Maniapoto remembers:

> One thing that we didn't do was make sure that our people who got loans from us had the business skills, but we didn't know it at the time. The only one of us who really had those business skills was Michael (Bowler). At one time the Board were getting something like $9,000 a month in koha, you know. It didn't come from those that could afford it; it came from those that couldn't, the low paid.

One of the limiting factors was a lack of people with appropriate business skills to manage the successful implementation of projects.

Many marae and local Māori organisations were putting at the top of their agenda that they needed to do something to get their people back to work.

If you meet Tariana, you meet George, and seeing them working together, you couldn't help but be impressed with the absolute commitment beginning at Whangaehu Marae and then spreading out almost in concentric circles from there: picking up on the needs of local people, local Māori, and trying to do something about that. There was an employment resource centre set up at the back of the old *Wanganui Chronicle* office. It was there that the planning was done with Tari and George and others in the community, to set up their health centre, which was their next project.

Robert Reid says:

> I remember after the Employment Network days, I was driving from Wellington to Auckland and stopped in at Waiouru for a burger, and lo and behold, behind the counter were George and Tari. The Trust had decided as an economic unit to provide work for people by buying that burger bar. As often happened, things didn't quite go to plan: the other people didn't work out, so George and Tariana ended up running it. That was typical of them. It was all done without acrimony or judgment of people who had let them down and not necessarily responded to their vision. They just keep on going and keep doing it.

In a speech Tariana later gave to the Community Economic Development Conference in her capacity as Minister for the Community and Voluntary Sector, she reflected on the significance of this period for helping her to develop a sense of community awareness:

> I have always been an advocate for communities long before I was given the warrant of the Minister for the Community and Voluntary Sector. It is a sector I came from myself. I remember in the 70s and 80s, two community champions who had a profound influence on my thinking – the late Father John Curnow, from the Catholic Commission for Evangelisation, Justice and Peace, and Fernando Yusingco who was a Filipino community development worker. They worked with a group of women in Whanganui, training us in structural analysis, helping us to understand how the system worked or more to the point didn't work in the interests of the people.

Our conversations of that time were rich and passionate. We talked about the power of the people; we debated how to move from aid to development; we plotted a course of organising for liberation.

But most importantly of us, we changed the paradigm from asking 'what is wrong' to instead creating the context for developing a vision for our future.

In all of these discussions we realized, powerfully, that community was the fundamental framework for our own empowerment. We moved from environments where communities were seen as incidental to our real life, to a journey where the community was essential.

We would go to our own people and ask them for their money to empower us to get going. We called it the Whanganui Regional Development Trust and before long our people were giving anything between two dollars to twenty dollars a week – whatever they could afford – and miraculously they expected nothing in return.

They were making an investment in optimism; a down-payment in the prosperity of their own futures.

When I think back to those times it was one of the most exciting periods in my own history – being part of a group of people who had the self-belief that we could do for ourselves, that we didn't need the State to do for us.

We set up the board, we established a number of small businesses, we founded a kura kaupapa Māori and then in 1993 established our first health centre – employing our own doctors, nurses and midwives. We got all of our young people together to paint the buildings for nothing; the Trust bought three buildings and allowed us to use them for free for two years.

And best of all we were collectively owned; the community had invested in our own development.

We made it happen – from possibility to profitability – and we never looked back.

I truly believe that the agenda for building strong, resilient communities is a journey in which we must reflect the power of the people at its very core.

This is not a journey which can be run via remote control from an office in Lambton Quay.

This is about the community ownership of assets, it is about collaborative action, communities having the wherewithal to solve their own local issues and challenges.

And crucially, Government cannot be the only investor. ...

I think the fatal mistake we made, was that in our heyday the Government was promoting what was known as the Mana loans and they offered us money to the Development Board in this context. It completely changed the whole philosophical base upon which we'd established ourselves. ...

If there is one thing I learnt from our experience in Whanganui, social lenders also need to be ready to say no to a loan and to be ready to foreclose. We need to respect the discipline required for a stable cashflow; to embrace better and stronger collaboration and to insist on a focus on outcomes and robust business practice.

And on that note, I saw vivian Hutchinson here tonight who played a very important role in our Whanganui community. I have never had the opportunity to thank you publicly for all the good you have done in our community teaching others social enterprise skills.[13]

While vivian had certainly played an important role in promoting the value of communities coming together, he also worked hard to facilitate a

Treaty-based partnership between Māori and Pākehā. He remembers one of the more contentious gatherings tackling this issue, a hui held at Whangaehu in the early eighties, at which Tariana was very much involved:

> Hundreds of people turned up to Whangaehu who were involved in employment schemes. A lot of these people were paid by the Government to be on these schemes: this was for many of them their first time on a marae. When they got to Whangaehu, in a very controversial move, right at the very beginning, they were welcomed onto the marae and they were told, 'Māori please go to the dining room and Pākehā to the marquee outside'. You can imagine that was the only workshop that took place. People spent ages processing that whole sort of thing.

During the eighties and nineties then, Tariana and others were trying many different approaches to delivering services that were of the people, by the people, for the people. On 1 September 1997, Tariana announced one such initiative: the opening of the Iwi Community Law Centre. Like previously established health and education services, the Whanganui Development Board had wanted the service to be iwi-driven but this was not part of the vision of the Legal Services Board, which was to fund the project.

We had been discussing the concept of establishing an iwi law centre for several years without success. The Legal Services Board eventually went ahead with a Community Law Centre instead. In my local column in the *Wanganui Chronicle* at the time, I summarised progress: 'In the final analysis the board didn't trust our committee. They saw us as an uppity group who needed to be put in their place'.

The Iwi Committee decided that 'it was better to proceed on our own terms rather than compromise our own values and visions as the board's criteria was very restrictive'.[14]

And so, just as the kura kaupapa had established itself, funded by the community for a year before it became eligible for government funding, the Iwi Community Law Centre set up shop, driven by a group of people who were prepared to work on a voluntary basis.

NOTES

1 Tariana's maiden speech: see *Hansard*, 26 February 1997.

2 The appropriation for funding to specific Ministers is channelled through a Vote administered by a specified department. From 1947 to 2014 funding was appropriated to Vote Maori Affairs. From 2015, the vote was renamed Maori Development.

3 N. Shepheard, 'Fierce Kuia: profile of New Zealand Member of Parliament Tariana Turia', *North and South*, February 2004, p. 57.

4 The process of developing a critical awareness of one's social reality through reflection and action. Action is fundamental because it is the process of changing the reality. http://www.freire.org/component/easytagcloud/118-module/conscientization/

5 In the 1970 tour, Sid Going (Māori) and Bryan Williams (Samoan) participated as 'honorary whites'. This was a term applied by the South Africans to certain ethnicities to enable them to have most of the rights of white citizens.

6 Shepheard, 'Fierce Kuia', 2004, p. 57.

7 Mātua Whāngai was a strategy to strengthen whānau, hapū and iwi links. It is based on nurturing Māori children within the context of whānau as the principal means of child placement.

8 John Maihi, MNZM, kaumātua and leader for Whanganui; a member of the Whanganui Māori Trust Board since 1988, and Chair of Ngā Tai o Te Awa, a broker for Māori health services.

9 Council for International Development, *Treaty Journeys: International Development Agencies Respond to the Treaty of Waitangi*, 2007.

10 Paulo Freire (1970), *Pedagogy of the Oppressed*, p. 54.

11 Tariana Turia, interview with Colin Peacock, Radio New Zealand, 6 February 2014.

12 Laurel Stowell, 'A life of service to Maori', *Whanganui Chronicle*, 31 August 2005, p. 4.

13 Tariana Turia, speech to the Community Economic Development Conference, 20 April 2011.

14 Tariana Turia, 'Pushing on with project but under our terms', *Whanganui Chronicle*, 1 September 1997.

-CHAPTER TEN-

TE ORANGANUI – TAKING CONTROL OF OUR HEALTH

It's very clear to me that until we encourage doctors, GPs and others to work with families and encourage families to understand their roles and their responsibilities in assisting and keeping their family member well but more importantly realising that they can be afflicted with these diseases too then we will never be successful. Nothing will change until we start to think more broadly about health and social issues and start including family.[1]

Tariana's approach to health was shaped by her experiences growing up as a child in Pūtiki in the 1950s and informed by her nursing days in the 1960s, but gathered impetus through her experiences in setting up Te Oranganui in the 1980s. Her interest in the structure of the health system started to crystallise in a particular hui held in July 1986: the first and most significant hui of the National Council of Māori Nurses, hosted by the Whanganui Regional Development Board.

Rātana Pā was chosen as the ideal location for the hui. The political and spiritual leader, Tahupōtiki Wiremu Rātana, had also been a Māori healer. About 2000 participants attended the hui. Education officials John Tapiata and Whare Te Moana had worked with the Development Board to fund nursing students from outside Whanganui to attend the conference.

The hui recommended moves to recruit Māori into nursing, to encourage Māori nurses to complete their training and return to the profession, to encourage qualified Māori nurses to return to the profession and to ensure Māori nurses maintained optimum standards. While the recommendations were predominantly based on nursing as a profession, what also emerged was a stronger emphasis on the role of whānau as health champions; leading positive change within the home.

A report commissioned in 1989 by then Minister of Māori Affairs Hon Koro Wetere took up the challenge. Koro established a review team headed by Professor Eru Pomare and including Irihapeti Ramsden, Vera Ormsby, Hohua Tutengaehe, Makere Hight and Neil Pearse to critically review the systems in place for Māori asthma management. The team's comments in their final report are still relevant:

> There needs to be a buffer between existing health services and Maori people – a person who can liaise with each camp – a Maori person. In many places the review team visited this person is already there, formally or informally. The strength of Maori society is the positive support system and the framework which is already often in place to conduct health education. Within each whanau people are respected for their life experiences, including the kuia and kaumātua, who show common sense, understanding compassion, and sincerity.

> These people take time to talk, can be contacted readily, are accessible at night or in the weekends and demand no fees.
>
> No matter how much knowledge the Pakeha caregiver holds, if they are not an acceptable messenger, the attempt at health improvement will fail. In the far North the review team heard of a good team in existence, Te Ringa Atawhai. This group has 61 health workers operating with little funding on the exact basis we recommend. In Wanganui there is a similar group, Te Korimako Maori Health Committee, also enormously successful using these same methods.[2]

Te Korimako Health had been established in 1986 and serviced the Rangitīkei, Otaihape and Ohakune areas; the area around Ruapehu; Ngāti Uenuku; Raetihi; Whanganui; and Ngā Rauru. Establishment of the committee that ran it was the start of an important new development in Tariana's career: one that would influence the roles she later had as Associate Minister of Health in both Labour and National Governments.

We had been planning for some time to set up our own health centre. There was a group of us involved with Te Korimako – my cousin Linda Thompson, Huia Hipango, Rii Green and Matt Huirua from Ngā Rauru. We had been meeting at the Development Board rooms at the back of the old *Wanganui Chronicle* office. We had set up an employment resource centre to create work for the Te Awa Youth Trust, and out of the relationships we'd built we started thinking about taking our health into our own hands.

We found out that the District Health Board had some money that they wanted to put into the community, but that they weren't prepared to resource anything independent of the DHB. We had a number of hui and then we called an inter-iwi hui with Whanganui, Ngā Rauru, Ngāti Apa, Otaihape and Ngāti Rangi.

It was during these hui that I reconnected with my cousin, Linda Thompson. My grandmother, Hokiwaewae, was the older sister to Linda's grandfather, Kopeke Kiriona. I had nursed the old man when he was dying of lung cancer in Whanganui Hospital. I didn't know him, but someone had told me to go and make myself known to him, because that old man was my koro.

It has been wonderful to reconnect, and to work so closely together in areas we are both so passionate about.

Linda always had a way with words. She says:

> I've never had any other working relationship with anybody else like that I have with Tariana. We just clicked when we knew what our connection was as whānau. We finished one another's sentences. We'd be in with the DHB, we'd work out our strategy first – there were the three of us: Sister (Makareta), Tariana and me. We'd do all this strategising together. At the meetings I'd be scribbling away and muttering and while I'm muttering Tari's right in, giving it to them. She'd say the same thing but say it in another way, and as only she could.

We all came together and decided that we would challenge the Area Health Board, because they had the resources. We basically put it to them that they had been given $100,000 for community health work. We wanted that contract, but we wanted it independently of the DHB. We saw it as really testing the waters, extracting funds from the state.

I always remember that hui because of the key role played by one of our kaumātua, Uncle Taitoko Tawhiri from the river. At that time I had been working at the Department of Māori Affairs as Coordinator of Mana/ Maccess. My mate and co-worker at the time, Matt Huirua, used to have all the kaumātua in town come into the office on Monday morning. Matt was the director then. Every Monday morning we'd sit with the kaumātua. It got bigger and bigger, because the townfolk realised they would never get an issue mandated unless those kaumātua had heard about it. The DHB used to come, the City Council, the Museum; it was exhilarating, and our kaumātua used to conduct the whole show. We would listen to them, learn from them, take everyone's opinion on board and end up with a direction.

Linda remembers how the hui to develop health services came about:

> Our mates, Loretta and Elaine rang me up to say, 'get over to the kaumātua hui; we're going to tell them about that hundred grand that the DHB has got and that they're not talking to us about what they're going to do with it'. It was tagged for the community, and that was our in, to say, 'we're the community; we've got the most needs'. So we went to the kaumātua and they said, 'oh well, you better go and get it' – that's the direction.

We set the meeting up with the District Health Board. Betty Bourke was the chair – she was an Australian who would say things where angels fear to tread. Betty was the head of the Board for some years.

We used a strategy that we used in other groups when we were up against anything – we'd say, 'Oh we need to caucus separately, to talk'. Essentially we get them out of their own room. There were about fifty or sixty of us at that hui. We always planned our approach well in advance.

Linda says:

> We wouldn't have got anywhere without her mind – Tari, Sister and I. We used to label ourselves – the good, the bad and the ugly. I was always given the goodie role. Tari and Sister used to say, 'you know what these Pākehās are like: you're a nurse, you trained in that system'. And I said, 'what about you? You were a nun'. What could be worse? Tari if she needed to be would just be the ugly, and the ugly was just sitting there and squinting at them. Tari said to me, 'that nursing stuff doesn't really mean anything to our people. What we want out of you is what you've got in your head about that system that's got all of our resources, so chuck the bloody stethoscope and the thermometer away and start thinking about what drives that system that you came out of'.

Linda explains the importance they realized of agreeing to a strategy to run the meeting:

> Our structural analysis was teaching us about negotiations, and when you do Treaty-based negotiations you're facing each other: one's the Treaty side and the other side is the side that's got all our money, so you have to learn how to trade with people who have got what you want. We said that we would like the hospital board to consider handing over that $100,000 to our community. Of course they all reeled back and thought, 'who the hell are you lot to tell us what to do with our money?'

> It was Tari's way of talking again that put the case to them: 'Yes, you are responsible, responsible for our health, and we're not doing very

well here at all, are we? If you can't do it, we've got a few ideas about how to help you do it better, but more importantly how we can do it better for ourselves.' It was very exciting to hear it the way she put it: those first thoughts of 'we can do this by ourselves'.

Betty Bourke goes, 'we have to think about this: you have no track record'. And up goes our kaumātua, Uncle Taitoko, and he goes, 'well, we're not children, and don't you start talking to us as though we are. You don't know what we are doing'. It was seriously powerful. In the end they had to excuse themselves from our meeting and Tari said, 'if you have to go and discuss this without us, we will sit here and wait – we can wait'. So we sat, and waited and waited and waited – and we started singing. All the songs, Whanganui songs. And we sang and sang, and they still didn't come back. We were all jubilant to start with – all iwitanga – and then we ended up singing, 'why are we waiting'! What should have been only a half-hour meeting ended up being most of the day.

They finally came back and decided to give us $100,000. We said, 'Don't you expect us to change the whole world in Whanganui with $100,000 when you've had a hundred million dollars – and you're only giving it to us for one year, so don't expect a lot.

The contract was the first in the country between a health authority, a hospital board, and an iwi to deliver services for iwi. The headline in the paper was 'Iwi gets first community contract with a hospital board'.

I'll never forget that hui. We got the money, and we were able to employ two people. My sister Rua was one: she was our first treasurer. We asked for a little house on the grounds of the DHB: we told them we wanted that whare. It meant we could save rent, power and all of those things. But it would also give us access to the people in the District Health Board. The second person we hired was my amazing mate, Dennis Rātana. I loved him so much.

Then we decided we'd try and maximise our money, and employ Bumpsy (Kataraina) Raurangi from Rātana. We employed her to do the cervical screening; she became one of the first lay cervical smear-takers in the region. Linda was the one who worked most closely with her.

Linda recalls:

> It was the first job Bumpsy ever got. She was a community health worker – she was over the moon to get the job, and she was a bloody hard worker. She'd be down on her hands and knees scrubbing the floor in Mauriora, our little house, and cussing and cursing. Her and I were great pals, because we swore like troopers.
>
> We said, 'we're going to interview Dennis Rātana for the job of the psychologist'. I'd already checked the psychologist register for his name, and he wasn't on that bloody register. So we whipped him over the head with the facts – and he said, 'ok ok, no, I'm not a psychologist'. We'd go and moan to Tari, but with any of that sort of stuff, she'd always look at the good work that people were doing. She'd say, 'Don't forget, you know, he can get into our families in ways that you can't'. Everybody always had their good points.

We had the kuia Waireti Walters from up North involved. She was really inspirational: she did all of the early cervical screening promotion in those days.

Linda put in an application for a national programme. She says:

> Tari would say, 'it's got to look like this, and it's got to do this, and it's got to say this', and I wrote it up. The Ministry were setting up some pilots around the country to see how well it would go if they gave the funds to community groups to recruit women to have cervical smears. About that time it was $90k a year for three years. Tari was thinking, probably before any of us had seen the potential, that some of us would win an opportunity for development. The Development Board was on about all of that: probably her and George were instrumental in seeing that big picture way ahead.

That's how we became involved in the very first national evaluation of the cervical screening programme. We were getting very ambitious by this time – we wanted more. We wanted the Central Regional Health Authority! We had already established Whai Oranga, the social services arm of the

Board. Working in that unit we could see we needed to expand our health services. So in 1993 we established Te Oranganui.

Linda and I had gone to Wellington for a conference. At that conference was Dr Laurence Malcolm, professor of community health at Wellington School of Medicine. Linda and I stood up. We talked about our rights and what we should be doing for ourselves. Laurence appeared to be captivated by what we had said. He told us, 'I will help you in any way that you need help. I will provide you with statistical data. If there are any issues about getting your medical centre started, I will come to Whanganui; I will meet with the GPs'.

Also at the conference were Dr Don Matheson and his wife, Dr Julia Carr, who worked for Newtown Union Health Service in Wellington. Don remembers his first meeting with Tariana:

> I distinctly remember going to meet her in a hotel at the top of the Terrace – it was her and George – and we had this incredibly intense discussion about how primary health care is funded – you know, the funding mechanism, the forms about capitation and ACC and all that sort of thing – her and George were very much into trying to develop more of a primary medical care model. I had been working with Newtown Union and putting together different groups of providers. We had this discussion which was basically a technical discussion. Tariana and George were both seriously on the case. Just the sheer mechanics was what I remember about that first discussion, rather than the broader philosophical approach, which was all taken for granted I think.

During the establishment phase we had amazing support from the union health centres[3] and in particular Peter Glensor, the manager of the Pōmare Health Centre. They were amazing. They gave us access to information that nobody would give us in Whanganui. They opened up their books: 'this is how much it would cost; this is what you need to get it up and running'. Peter was a huge help to us in those early days.

Peter Glensor says:

> About 1991 or 1992 I had helped start a primary health service for low-income families in Pōmare, just north of Taita in the Hutt Valley: it's the poorest little community in the whole of the Wellington

region. I'd been a community worker for several years, and health was a presenting issue. After lots of false starts, we decided that a full general practice was what was needed, so we began Hutt Union Community Health Service. I had a phone call from Tariana to say that she and her husband George were working with Te Oranganui in Whanganui and were wanting to start a GP service as part of that, and would they be able to come and spend a bit of time with me.

So they came and spent nearly a week with me in the community house in Farmer Crescent. I spent those days with them going over what's involved in setting up and running a GP. At that stage George was the CEO of Te Oranganui. Tariana was working for Māori Affairs but was clearly a leading light in the development. They went back to Whanganui with that information and set up what is now Te Waipuna, the GP clinic.

I remember vividly our first visit to Farmer Crescent. It was hilarious. This Pākehā lady from their community centre stood outside the house. There's Ripeka Green and all of us, walking in ... and she throws out her arms, and calls out 'welcome, welcome, thrice welcome'. Honestly, Ripeka looked at me: we didn't know what to do – to karanga or what. But it was actually lovely, blimmin' lovely. We loved going there. It just meant everything to us.

I was working fulltime at Te Puni Kōkiri as the Kaiwhakarite, and working at the health centre at night. Linda and I, with Huia Hipango, Rii Green and Lil Smith, were working towards a new and larger Māori health organisation, Te Oranganui.

Tariana later said of this period, 'We were very determined. We worked day and night. We would still be going at 3am and Auntie Huia would be up all night cooking for us'.[4]

Linda was the ideas person; I was the 'do it' person. We also had Nancy and Piri Cribb come away with us and type all weekend.

Nancy says:

> Piri and I were there at the time with her and Linda when they started to write up the first service spec for Whānau Ora. We would type to

early hours of the God knows when, because she thinks best at night time. That's when she starts to do all her work, and you got to be just working there with her – and as much as you might say, 'ok, I want to go home', it just never happens. I put in a lot of hours with her over the years, and she is very demanding as a boss but it teaches you good work ethics too, and discipline, and a whole lot of things about how you can manage your work with expectations of people.

Linda and I knew that the central point would be the development of the GP service – that would be the catalyst for bringing all of it together.

Linda says:

> I said to Tari, 'you need money for a GP: where the hell are we going to get money from?' We needed $100,000. Tariana said, 'well, there's the Development Board, and we've saved $30,000. And there's the Trust Board, $30,000 from cousin Archie (Taiaroa). Iwi needs to be involved, plus board members. Then there's $30,000 from our policy development stuff – $90,000. Would $90,000 do it?' I said, 'that's a bloody good start'. And the other ten came in from the Community Employment Group, from Geoff Mariu.

Geoff was another good mate of mine. We used to be so close that a weekend wouldn't go by without Geoff ringing me up at all hours of the night, pouring his heart out. Geoff was with the Community Employment Group headed by Parekura Horomia.[5] That was how Parekura and I became good friends. I loved Parekura as a special friend; he was my special mate through thick and thin. But we started off on a bad note – he was being bureaucratic. I'd asked him for some funding to help employ some people, and he'd replied, 'you're a health service'. I said, 'no, we're an economic development unit, and we are developing our people, so you need to give us some money'. Anyway, he kept on saying no. So one Friday we went down late in the afternoon, parked outside his office and said that we weren't going home until he could help us. He gave us a miserable $36,000 to hire someone. And he told us that he expected us to be able to grow that and grow our workforce.

The thing is, we needed Te Waipuna, the GP clinic, for Te Oranganui to be a true umbrella service: everything under one roof. John Maihi and others around him had already started Te Waipuna o te Awa. They wanted to keep it, but Archie (Taiaroa) as both iwi leader, and Chairperson of the Whanganui River Maori Trust Board, managed to persuade them to come under Te Oranganui.

We eventually established the first health centre, employing our own doctors, nurses and midwives. The Development Board owned three buildings in Drews Avenue. I'd gone to George in his capacity as chief executive and told him we had to help the iwi; I said, 'you need to give us those buildings for two years, and you need to also give us some money to help us get established'. We got all our young people in – our kids, our relatives – to paint the buildings and tidy it all up for free. It was a really exciting time. Our first two doctors were both specialists at the hospital. They were both really brave women, because all of the GPs in town came out against us: wouldn't give us after-hours coverage because we weren't individually owned.

We threatened to take them to the Commerce Commission, and we called on our new friend, Professor Malcolm. He and Don Matheson came up to Whanganui and met with all the doctors, and essentially told them that we had a case to take them to court if they didn't give us services. So the debate moved up a notch. Then they wanted us to pay for any after-hours services they gave to our patients. It was pure outright racism.

At that time we decided to change our name to Te Oranganui to represent the coming together of Te Korimako and Te Waipuna o Te Awa. Our kuia asked us to: Nanny Nui Manawanui Pauro. She gave us the korero: 'Korowaitia te puna waiora hei oranga motuhake mō te iwi'. It translates into our vision of 'Absolute wellness crossing generations'. But it was also, powerfully, about the concept of being self-determining. It was just wonderful to watch that grow – where people became really confident about what they were doing, and realised there was no reason why they couldn't run their own business, establish their own services.

We developed a reputation for speaking our truth. I remember the day when we invited the District Health Board to come to our structural analysis workshop being run by our friend Fernando Yusingco. He was sitting in the middle of the floor, and Sister Makareta, who used to help with organising these groups, was sitting there too. The head of the District Health Board said to Fernando, 'You are one of the most dangerous men that I have ever met', and he turned to us and said, 'What he is doing with you women is dangerous'. Sister Makareta looked at him and said, 'No, I think you are talking to the wrong person. I think we are in more danger from you than we are from Fernando'.

> That reputation drew people to come to visit us.

Those who visited included Minister of Health at the time, Hon Bill English. He says:

> I first met her when she was running Te Oranganui. At the time I was keen to see the development of alternative health providers, and they had built up a reputation as one of the more innovative, and well-run early Māori providers. When I met her she seemed to me to have a unique combination of intensity, a clear philosophy and more importantly the courage to turn it into something. She was a strong believer in whānau taking control of their destiny and rangatiratanga. But had the courage to follow through into action and take enough people along with her, despite a reputation for being combative.

> Where we got combative, I suppose, was around the relationship between Te Oranganui and Taumata Hauora. Taumata Hauora, a Māori development organisation, held a significant number of contracts with Māori health service providers across the region, from Pipiriki to Nukumaru and Waiouru to Bulls. We were trying for the whole rohe. At the time, to go against an iwi group was just not good form, but we were determined that it had to work. We said to them, 'you either come on board with us or you can stand outside; it's your choice'. John Maihi, who was a trustee and then Chair for Taumata Hauora, took years to forgive us.

John recalls:

> I held onto Taumata Hauora. They did everything to close that down. Oh crikey, she [Tariana] stood in the Pūtiki whare and gave me the biggest lecture in town, and her and that son Pahia were going flat tack: 'you got to do this, you got to do that'. I rang Marty Davis[6]: 'you fellas coming to the hui?' They said, 'nah'; they said, 'it's not worth coming, John will be gone by lunch'. So I went into the hui and I looked at the time: quarter to twelve. They said, 'the decisions are made', and I stood my ground; I wanted to talk, so I went, 'kia

ora mai koutou, kua mutu tēnei hui, he hōnore, he kororia, he maungārongo,' and I went past Ken and Nancy and said to them, 'gone by lunch eh, we'll see about that.'

At that stage, suffice to say, we didn't have the rūnanga on board.

While Tariana, Linda and others were frantically preparing the paperwork to set up Te Oranganui, similar developments in Māori health provider collectives were occurring right across Aotearoa. Eventually a meeting of minds occurred, and Te Oranganui joined in the newly formed Health Care Aotearoa. Peter Glensor took on the role as national co-ordinator of this new entity. He says of its establishment:

> In 1993, a group of us came together. The eight union health services around the country had always worked very closely together; we came together with people from Hokianga Health Enterprise Trust, with people from Waiheke, where there was a community health trust, and with George and Tariana from Whanganui, and we began to talk about the possibility of working in a collective way together to support each other, to protect each other, to share good ideas and, where possible, to try and work collectively rather than individually trying to battle for this new model of general practise that we were embarked on.
>
> Health Care Aotearoa was established as a national network of community-owned and -controlled primary health services, and we had a vision of promoting that model of community ownership, of building health professional teams, of focusing on population health rather than just individual people's issues, of having a holistic view of health which took into account public health issues, social justice issues, poverty, education and so on.
>
> At one of those very very early meetings when we could see we were going to form this national organisation I distinctly remember Tariana

saying that Te Oranganui was a Māori organisation; that it had an inflexible, unyielding permanent commitment to Whanganuitanga; that that would always be their top priority; and that if we were willing to accept that then Te Oranganui would like to be part of this national organisation. We were delighted to agree to that. Te Oranganui became a founding member of Health Care Aotearoa and Tariana became the vice-chair of the organisation.

Te Oranganui was chaired by Niko Tangaroa, and Tariana was its chief executive. From the outset, Te Oranganui proved to be influential in guiding Health Care Aotearoa towards Treaty-based practice. Pat Snedden, who had taken on the role of business advisor to the organisation, later said that its Māori partners 'though initially smaller in numbers, appeared substantially more competent in an all-round fully integrated sense than their Pākehā counterparts':

> Tariana Turia was invited to present her perspective on health from the standpoint of leading a kaupapa Māori health service. She responded by providing a simple, eloquent and clear account of the elements that constituted good health for Maori. This traversed her personal experience and that of her husband, George. She covered the tribal history of her hapū and the life experience of being Māori in that small community. It was a spell-binding first hand account of the world as seen through the eyes of Maori, not as victim, nor as a social drain on the State, but as one person's story that was representative of a people determined not to relinquish their own authenticity as tangata whenua. It was about health, but not as we knew it.
>
> Pivotal to her explanation were two inescapable truths. There would be no health for Māori without recovery of their whenua and recognition of their rangatiratanga. This was such a different philosophical approach from that of the mainstream health providers that it provided a profound challenge to network members. In Tariana's world, health meant a commitment to the Treaty because

inherent in this process was an affirmation of Māori recovery of self- in short control over their own affairs. 'Give us what is due to us and we will deliver the service to our own people'.[7]

The inaugural hui of Health Care Aotearoa, held at Whangaehu Marae in 1994, left strong impressions upon others who attended, including Don Matheson. He says:

> I remember very distinctly a meeting in Whangaehu with HCA at which Tariana was the main speaker. She spoke in that meeting almost entirely about the Treaty. It was quite significant in terms of where the organisation then went. It gave a bit of a reality check to the organisation's attempt to be bicultural; and the organisation started to have quite a strong Māori presence – it had been very weak prior to that.

Peter Glensor too has strong memories of the importance of that first hui in setting an agenda:

> Tariana was the vice chair, and she stayed in that role until 1996, when she left to go into Parliament. Tariana was a key player in articulating the vision of social justice, an effective understanding of health, of new models of funding from day one. At the first national gathering of Health Care Aotearoa, we agreed that we would work as hard as we could to incorporate a bicultural focus in the way we ran the organisation. Every national meeting of Health Care Aotearoa has been held on a marae or it's become more and more comfortable about working in a Māori context and adopting elements of Māori tikanga in the way we did our business, and that was helped hugely because of the first annual hui at Whangaehu.

> It was just a small gathering – maybe fifty or sixty people – and George and Tariana acted as hosts of course. I remember we spent time hearing from George about how they built the marae and the commitment to using mud bricks as a basis for it, and we had a wonderful time in the first evening where we heard about the famous

story of the painting of the tupuna that was on the wall of the marae and how it had got there from the museum.

Over the decades the provider organisations affiliated to Health Care Aotearoa returned to Whangaehu for hui many times.

Peter Glensor shares a story about the establishment of quality standards for Health Care Aotearoa:

> Tariana went on to offer a lead in a number of ways. Quality was an important issue; Tariana offered Whangaehu as a base for a gathering to talk about quality standards. We identified the standards programme that was most appropriate for our understanding of quality accreditation; it was based in Australia. As a result of that conversation a few years later, we managed to get a significant grant from Bill English to bring the Community and Health Accreditation and Standards Programme (CHAS) to New Zealand, to create a strongly Aotearoa-based context for it and to weave through elements of Treaty and Māoritanga issues, creating a new programme called Te Wana, which is still operating. We behaved and felt like pioneers trying new ways of working; we had a very robust spirit of dialogue and challenge, mutual challenge.

In 1996 everything took on a new perspective, as Tariana was elected to Parliament. Her cousin Linda stepped up to the chief executive role of Te Oranganui. For Linda, Tariana's voice continued to ring in her ears.

> That was one thing that she used to come back and say: we just don't believe in ourselves; we don't think we're ready. How come when we've done all this work and we've got all that stuff – how can we still believe that we're not ready, when we've already been doing it? It was that kōrero about self-belief. How come we're not believing in ourselves, that we can do this? Any little setback would have such a huge impact, and a domino effect right throughout the iwi. That used to drive her nuts.

But before Tariana entered Parliament, an event occurred that would place Whanganui on the map, and bring Tariana Turia to the living rooms of the nation – Pākaitore.

NOTES

1. Tariana Turia, speech to the New Zealand Business and Parliament Trust, 18 June 2014.

2. *He mate huango: Maori asthma review: Report to the Minister of Maori Affairs from the review team to consider asthma among Maori people*, 1991.

3. The Hutt Union and Community Health Service opened its first Hutt Valley clinic in the Pōmare Community House in 1991, following similar services in Porirua in 1990 and Newtown in 1987, with support from local trade union and community activists. The aim of the union health centres was to provide low cost primary health care services to low income residents.

4. Laurel Stowell, 'A life of service to Maori', *Wanganui Chronicle*, 31 August 2005, p. 4.

5. The Community Employment Group was set up in 1991 to maximise employment opportunities and move unemployed people towards self-sufficiency. Parekura Tureia Horomia (1950–2013) was a Labour Party politician and Minister of Māori Affairs from 2000 until 2008.

6. Te Pahunga (Marty) Davis has been both Te Tumu Whakarae of Te Kaahui o Rauru and Chief Executive of Ngā Rauru.

7. Pat Snedden, *Pakeha and the Treaty: Why it's our Treaty too*, 2005, pp. 124–5.

-CHAPTER ELEVEN-
PĀKAITORE: TAKING A STAND

Great minds discuss ideas, average minds discuss events and small minds discuss personalities. The challenges that came from the Council and the media in particular focused on individuals like characters like myself, and that's very dangerous because it takes away from the actual kaupapa of why were we there – around the 1848 land purchase, our river claims and just how the Crown had treated us.[1]

She was a really strong presence in that place, eh. I think it was good for everybody to know that, that that calmness was in the camp. She wasn't there all of the time but when she was there you knew she was there.[2]

In 1995 the people gathered at Pākaitore in Whanganui to reassert their rangatiratanga, their Whanganuitanga, over the land, claiming that the area was the site of a pā and a traditional place for trade and that it had been set aside for them since the purchase of Whanganui. They drew up a covenant of sorts, 'Te Tikanga tūturu o Whanganui', to protect their lands, their waters and their peoples.

The covenant stated that 'the relationship of the iwi with their lands is a spiritual bond with Papatuanuku and a cultural kinship with the source of life – it is no coincidence that the word for the sustainer of life within the womb and the source of nourishment after birth, the earth itself, is in each case, whenua'. These words had a very personal meaning for Tariana: during the reoccupation of Pākaitore, her mokopuna of the same name was born.

The covenant spelt out the obligations of the iwi with respect to the land and the people of the land:

> This sovereign power exercised by each iwi and hapū is a political authority and obligation to care not just for the land, but to care also for the people of the land. One cannot sell forever the land, for that is to deprive future generations of their mother: parts may be gifted for others to nurture, but the iwi always retains the authority of ultimate tangata tiaki. One cannot give one's mother permanently into the care of another. It is an idea that is spiritually incomprehensible and legally impossible. To maintain that such authority can be ceded or given away misreads the political reality that no rangatiratanga ever has or had the right and authority to do so.

The reoccupation of Pākaitore demonstrated to the Crown that Whanganui believed they had sovereign rights as descendants of Whanganuitanga. At the end of 1994, Prime Minister Jim Bolger had launched a package of proposals to help 'Maori and the wider community shift their focus away from grievances towards the growth and development of Maori potential'.[3]

The bureau-speak of Māori potential was a smokescreen for the intention to impose a fiscal cap on Treaty settlements. In the detailed proposals, principle 7 set out the expectation that 'settlements will take into account fiscal and economic constraints and the ability of the Crown to pay compensation'. This was code for the contentious proposition of a billion-dollar cap on funding available for the settlement of all Treaty claims within a ten-year period; that is, by 2004. Other elements to the Crown proposals were equally controversial. The proposals failed to recognise tangata whenua ownership interests in natural resources. Māori interests in the conservation estate and natural resources were to be treated the same as those of any other group, with no acknowledgment of the Treaty's Article Two guarantees of tino rangatiratanga.

The billion-dollar fiscal envelope fiasco occurred in the wake of Waitangi Tribunal hearings for the Whanganui River claim, WAI 167. From March to July 1994 the Waitangi Tribunal had heard the claim, which had been originally filed by Tariana's uncle, Hikaia Amohia, and the Whanganui River Māori Trust Board on 14 October 1990, on behalf of all who affiliated to Whanganui iwi.

The spirit of the claim has never wavered. The people of Whanganui originally possessed and controlled the Whanganui river and all things that gave the river essential life, and such possession and control has never been willingly relinquished. That is how it has always been. Whanganui have had the longest litigation in the history of this country over their ancestral river – te awa tupua. The first petitions made to Parliament on behalf of the iwi date back to 1873, against the Timber Floating Bill, a statute that authorised the use of the river for transportation of timber. Later petitions date from 1887, in response to the destruction of pā tuna (eel weirs) by the actions of steamers on the river. By the time the Tribunal came to town, Whanganui had been making petitions, claims and other submissions and attending hearings for well over 120 years without receiving an adequate response from the Crown. Patience was wearing thin.

Tariana explained to *North and South* in 2004:

> We were sick of the way the government was drawing the process out; the millions of dollars it had cost over the years; our people who'd died over the struggle for the river who would never see it come to fruition. Our losses were too great and too many of our kids had gone down the tubes.[4]

The beheading of Ballance

Less than a fortnight after Bolger announced the Fiscal Cap policy, my son Mark and his friend Dennis August strolled into Moutoa Gardens and beheaded the statue of 1890s prime minister John Ballance.

When the case was eventually heard before the Whanganui District Court, the pair explained their actions within the context of a book by James Belich, *I Shall Not Die: Titokowaru's War, 1868–1869*. The *Dominion* reported:

> August's counsel, Graham Takarangi, said when Belich's view of Ballance in his book *I Shall Not Die* was analysed, it was clear Ballance was anti-Maori – he reportedly regarded the only good Māori to be a dead Māori and even looked with disdain on Maoris friendly to Europeans. He was also alleged to have taken part in the killing of a respected elderly Māori woman. 'This is the man this community in the early 1900s regarded somewhat as a great son',[5] Mr Takarangi said.[6]

Our close friend John Rowan had defended Mark. John told the court that Mark had been distressed by passages in the book relating to the loss of Māori land and to the indignities offered to Māori in what were described as military skirmishes. He had also made reference to kōrero he had heard at a hui at Pākaitore just three days before the incident when the role that Ballance had played in Māori land policies had been discussed. Mark and Dennis had discussed the book, and had decided to knock Ballance's head off the statue, to symbolise taking away his mana. To be fair, Mark was not acting in isolation. In my submission to the Tribunal on the Whanganui River claim, it is fairly clear that I also had strong views about the statues:

> We are a people with a history of protecting the Pākehā settlers against our own who were protecting our whenua and our awa. It is a painful history for some of us and we still weep. In Moutoa today stands a racist monument dedicated to this battle. It tells our mokopuna that they are the descendants of kupapa and barbarians. Who has the right to tell that story to our children without the full facts of the time? This and other monuments must go.[7]

Long before Pākaitore, I remember the kuia Eva Rickard standing outside the town's courthouse, talking to our rangatahi and describing those same monuments as racist.

Pākaitore: Taking a Stand

In 1998, in her tribute to Eva, who had passed away the previous year, Tariana said:

> For years a group of Whanganui women had been talking about these same monuments but to no effect. Eva did not tell our rangatahi to take this action, but she did challenge us as to what we intended to do about our land and those monuments. You can only talk for so long, she said.[8]

In his summing up of the case, Judge John Hole concluded that he could understand the deep-seated feeling that the two men had about Ballance, but that anyone going outside the law should be held accountable for their actions.

Mark was given five months periodic detention for willful damage, but he chose not to do that, and to go to jail instead. His younger brother Pahia explains why:

> Why did he knock the head off the statue? Why did he go to jail instead of doing community service? All of that can be attributed to Mum; she politicised us. I always remember when I went to court and the judge told him, 'you're going to get community service'. Mark said, 'I'm not doing it. Why would I do community service – that's a way of me admitting that I've done something wrong, and I've done nothing wrong'. I knew he didn't want to go to jail, but I thought to myself, 'well, it's the first time you've really stood and backed yourself.'

For the remainder of the occupation, the head of Ballance was replaced by a pumpkin jack-o'-lantern.

Our lands are not for sale

The site of Pākaitore – Moutoa Gardens – was deliberately chosen for reoccupation because of its historical significance: it was where the Treaty and a subsequent deed of sale for Whanganui had been signed. The gardens themselves were part of a historical fishing village that had never been up for sale; a view that the Whanganui City Council contested. Pākaitore had also been a sanctuary for the river people in earlier days. Originally it was a safe place – a place from which the people would go out to sea, and come back with fish to trade.

Negotiations for the purchase of Whanganui were initiated in 1839 by the New Zealand Company. A year later E. J. Wakefield of the Company arrived in Whanganui flush with gifts: the equivalent of about £700 worth of trade goods. All that he required in exchange was the first sale of 40,000 acres. Historians have latterly criticised the haphazard way in which Wakefield distributed gifts among the Māori gathered at a small village in the vicinity of Pākaitore:

> It is questionable if in point of law such a bargain could be accepted as a legal transaction even in those days as the Maoris did not understand the European system of land tenure. This sale ... marks the beginning of all the land troubles which were soon to follow.[9]

In 1841, Governor Hobson allowed 50,000 acres to be surveyed, and offered the land to new settlers. Two years later William Spain, Government Land Commissioner, travelled to Whanganui to look into irregularities around these land acquisitions. Despite this, the 'sale' of a total of 86,200 acres was finally completed in May 1848; Māori were granted reserves equal to a tenth of the land surveyed. No additional payment was made to compensate for the additional 36,200 acres that had been acquired by the Crown.

Building up the momentum

Tariana was actively involved in the occupation of Pakaitore for the entire seventy-nine days. When Tariana speaks about the time in which the iwi lived again at Pākaitore, she speaks about it as a time of storytelling; a restoration period in which the people lived as whānau, within the protection of the village. Inevitably those stories come back to the surface.

Te Ururoa Flavell, Tariana's future Māori Party co-leader, was there at the dawn karakia that signalled the beginning of the seventy-nine day occupation. He recalls:

> I was working in Taranaki and involved with Te Korimako Taranaki (iwi radio); I was pretty much the station manager. We had organised, me with Te Miringa Hohaia, and his son, to travel down to be with the group before they went on, and that was because we had the link to Ken [Mair]. Ones like Tahuparae;[10] Piripi Haami and Ken of course. We stayed the night. I remember Tahuparae saying 'nō kai'. We went to bed late, at about 12, and we were up before 4am. We went down to the river and Niko did a karakia and on we went, and the rest of that is history. I was ringing back to the station, giving them direct input about what was happening for the whole day. It was a huge day.

Tariana has a vivid memory of what happened next.

> We went down to the river, about 300 of us, had karakia, and then we went up on to the whenua. The first thing we decided we would do was to dig a hole and put a pou whenua in the ground. Well, of course you're not allowed to break the soil on what is categorised as parks and reserves, but we did it anyway. The Mayor, Chas Poynter, then came down, wagging his finger and telling us it was against regulations. The fact that those regulations went against our Whanganuitanga didn't seem to enter his head. The Council could have acted differently. They could have filled the hole with dirt, planted a tree; it surely wasn't such a federal offence. In other circumstances, such a reprimand might have been tolerated, or at best little made of it. But in the context of a century-long delay in a response to our river claim, the sheer numbers of us gathering that day, and the way in which he talked to us and wagged that finger, that one action instead triggered something in us all.

Ken Mair also remembers the 'wagging finger' as pivotal to the subsequent action:

> We decided that we would go in, hit hard in the sense of making our statement and ensuring people understood the frustration, some might say the anger, in regard to how we'd been treated as a people, and to highlight the fact that we weren't going to take it any longer. What turned it of course was the reaction by the local council.

> We'd had a wānanga that morning with a whole lot of young people down there, and we talked about colonisation and how Governor Grey had treated our people – seen us as third-class citizens. Ironically, two hours later council came down with Chas Poynter as the mayor and basically, just about word for word, his actions were a classic example of a Pākehā leader speaking down, putting us in our place. And that really set it off in regard to – 'well, we're not moving'.

What started as a one-day event turned quickly into the seventy-nine-day reoccupation. The Council initially presented the 'protestors' with a five-point plan that they wanted them to abide by. Once they realised the iwi weren't prepared to sign on the dotted line, they ordered an eviction notice, giving them seven days to pack up and leave the site. It was what you might call a perfect storm – a range of factors coming together.

Tariana said of the reoccupation in 2001:

> I was really angry about how long our river claim had taken, our land issues, the way we were always recipients rather than determining, the way the Crown did not seem to be acting in our best interests. It was never about that piece of land. It was about everything that had happened to us. It was really to affirm our right to be self-determining. My husband is really conservative. For him to go there and stay there, it was really something.[11]

In many ways, the lessons of Father Curnow were falling into place. Sister Makareta Tawaroa remembers of that time:

> We don't only want to be riding in the bus; we want to own the bus. We don't just want to be a passenger; we want to change direction. We were saying quite radical things for a place like here, because Pākaitore gave us a whole new perspective. It was a lot of things: it was the fiscal envelope, our claims were so slow, there was a whole lot of dissatisfaction.

Ken Mair remembers the sense of build-up to the twenty-eighth of February 1995, when about 150–200 Māori walked on to Pākaitore.

> There was quite a bit of lead-up. In 1994 you had the fiscal envelope, all that nonsense happening; Mark and Dennis had bowled the head of Ballance off the statue down at Pākaitore, so there was all of this momentum. He [Ballance] was part of the army of the time, the cavalry, and he was responsible for the pillage, the injury, murder of a group of people. It was about the cavalry army impacting upon us as a people. Much of that did come about because of the history and the background knowledge that was being given to us by some of the olds, so we decided that we'd sit down and plan and work out how we were going to do all of this.
>
> She [Tariana] was once again very central. In regard to the leadership of Pākaitore, you could see there was a woman, a very strong woman, namely herself, articulate, a fighter; Niko Tangaroa with an older type head, with a lot of wisdom; and all the olds that came with us, the kaumātua; and a younger head, myself. We were getting a lot of knowledge from some of our kaumātua around land, Pākaitore, river etc, important knowledge in regard to how we got shafted, genuinely shafted, by the Crown.

Kaumātua and kuia played a significant role in the lead-up to and the duration of the stay at Pākaitore. Nancy Tuaine, who was also present, recalls their influence:

> There were other kuia, like our Kui Nui, there; many of our kuia from the river. There are photos of them outside the whare at Pākaitore, so it had the support of our old people. They could remember Pākaitore being the fishing village that our people used to come down and occupy when they were going out to sea. Aunty Tari was the active part of that, and she in her leadership with the boys, with the men, was critical to ensuring that whole thing had balance and a female role to it, and she was pretty much it, her and Aunty Julie. Aunty Julie was critical in that time for making some of the decisions and working with the other kuia to make decisions about how we would come off there (at the end of the occupation) and those kind of things.

An outside observer, fifth-generation Pākehā Pat Snedden, appreciated the difference that the elders brought into the camp. Pat came on to Pākaitore on a cold Wednesday night as part of a 'continuous series of pōwhiri that go on right through the night', as he described it. He marvelled at the enormity of the organisation required to feed hundreds of people for ten weeks, three times a day, on a piece of land 'where running water comes from a couple of taps and a public toilet'. As he feasted on 'mince, mutton and tea', he noticed something else:

> There's a difference here. A sense of peace and calm, so completely at odds with the news reports on the way down. The editor of the *Whanganui Chronicle* is quoted as saying 'the town is sitting on a powder keg'. That may be the case in the town; it's no description of the marae, where there is a complete absence of tension. The reason for the calm becomes clear. It is the presence of so many elderly people, grandmothers, great-grandmothers, all the kuia out in support. Not just one or two but twenty or more. Here not just for a passing visit but living here, sleeping in the makeshift wharenui on mattresses spread out on wooden pallets that in turn rest on dirt floors, their only cover a tarpaulin that during the night springs many leaks. The privations suffered by these old people are so obvious that their commitment needs explaining. If your grandmother or mine were to make such a sacrifice on the basis of principle, would we not want to know why?[12]

Ken Mair fully understood the power of the elders in terms of their strategy:

> Chas Poynter, the mayor of the time, was trying to bring about division among us by saying when we first went in, 'this is just a small group led by two or three radicals' – he was aiming towards me and Tari and even Niko – 'and this will fall over in a couple of days so don't worry about it'. He realised a week or so later that actually this was getting bigger, and he played the old divide and rule game: 'their kaumātua don't support'. As part of our plan we had made sure that we had spoken to our kaumātua and worked it through. A large majority were extremely supportive.

Ken was closely associated with the strategic preparation for the reoccupation. At the start of 1995, Ken, Piripi Haami and a small team of protestors took over the TVNZ studio in Auckland, delaying the nationwide news bulletin by about ten minutes. The protest was in response to the state broadcaster's decision to suspend *Te Karere*, the Māori language news programme, during the summer holiday period. Sporting a cheerful red cap, and a lime-green sweatshirt tied around his waist, Ken hardly looked the 'veteran activist' he was described as, but his point was well made. In the line of sight of a national audience, the group was escorted by police from the set, but not before Ken had spoken to the cameras, declaring that Māori and Pākehā news should be treated in the same way.

The Ballance statue was decapitated in December, the TVNZ studios were held up in January, and Pakaitore was occupied the following month. On 3 February 1995 Ballance's monument was embellished with red paint; at the same time, the highway north of Whanganui was barricaded with a pile of refrigerators. This latter protest, strategically scheduled for three days before Waitangi Day, was intended to provoke people to think about the meaning of that day and to draw conscious attention to the settlement of Whanganui claims. The events were attributed to Te Ahi Kaa, a Māori rights group of the time, of which Ken was a key member. He says of the period:

> Most of the things we entered into were thought through and well planned – a lot of people don't believe and understand that, but the mere fact we've been able to get away with a lot of stuff, in my opinion whether it was the TV raid, or Pākaitore – obviously proves that it was well planned. We knew exactly what we had to do there.

The iwi went on to Pākaitore on the same day that the Crown came into the rohe to present the fiscal envelope proposals. It wasn't about the gardens; about Pākaitore. It was about the river.

> We went there quite deliberately. We wanted to draw attention to the fiscal envelope. It was very planned and quite deliberate: taking a political opportunity to draw the country's attention to the longest litigation in the

history of this country over this river. Unfortunately the media got the idea that we were occupying it because we wanted those two and a half acres, which wasn't quite right.

The Crown hui went on to Kaiwhaiki marae on 1 March. During the pōwhiri, Tariana's cousin Rangitihi Tahuparae addressed the Crown, in:

> ... what could only be described as a harangue against the Government and all the preceding administrations that had been responsible for the plight of the people of the river. He talked of the efforts by colonial troops and administrators to deliberately poison Māori along the Whanganui River.[13]

Other speakers put forward the case with comparable power and passion. Gray Matthews stood on behalf of Ngāti Apa, and said:

> We have dissected your proposals and what did we see, Sir? I'll tell you what we can see. We can see here a deliberate effort to put together a grandiose rip-off. You have drawn up your proposals without any consultation with iwi ... What right has the thief got to determine restitution?

Ngā Paerangi were represented by the kōrero of Ina Whanaruru:

> Thank you for your offer, but we are not for sale. Our lands are not for sale. We want full control and power over our own lands, the resources and the right to control our own destiny.

Chairperson for the day, Morvin Simon, rounded off the kōrero in characteristic Whanganui style:

> We argue that the Crown is required to redress the full extent of its indiscretions. We, as the iwi of this region, owe it to our people to ensure that their sacrifices were not made in vain ... Our presentation has been cool, calm and collected because we too believe that anger and belligerence in the throat is the death rattle of reason in the mind.

It was a message that Tariana had great empathy for; it emphasised a lesson in life she had learnt early on from her own Uncle Frosty.

His guidance to me in times of turmoil has been invaluable. The view that he pursued was that when faced with situations of conflict and stress the natural reaction tends to be that we respond in a like manner, with elevated emotions and raised voices. He taught us when we were quite young that if you lose your temper, you lose your cool; if you don't remain calm then you lose perspective. Uncle Frosty used to say to my aunty who was a bit feisty, 'now Pae, when you get heated up you lose control and you lose the argument'. He would say it to her in front of us, and we would watch it play out. Without realising it he had a huge influence on me. His advice to me was that in such times the key is to deliberately keep your voice quiet and to focus on expressing your views in the calmest way possible. It was a skill I practiced at Pākaitore and have tried to maintain throughout my life.

With the exception of a number of placards to 'reject the fiscal envelope' and a haka executed by a small boatload of people on the river, Wira Gardiner observed that the Kaiwhaiki hui was somewhat unusual for the absence of protesters. It was an observation shared by John Maihi, who spoke at the hui about the people's desire to follow 'our own pathway, that of Whanganuitanga':

I was up at Kaiwhaiki at the time because the fiscal envelope was out and we wondered where all our young people have gone from the marae. There weren't many there – and I thought, 'shit, where's all our people?' And then Tahu got up and made a big announcement that they were all down here at Pakaitore.

Following the fiscal envelope hui at Kaiwhaiki, the people from the hui came down to Pākaitore. Twenty years on, John can reflect on their time at Pākaitore, and laugh off the arguments that he and Tariana had along the way. He recalls what he learnt while they camped out, placing particular value on the educative role that the wānanga took on:

Every night she [Tariana] played a leading part in setting the theme I suppose for the kōrero for the night: 'what are we going to do about this? What are we going to do about that?' You know, those seventy-nine nights, for me really set the pathway for us about how we were going to develop, and she lad most of that, or Uncle Niko would bring something out in deliberation with Ken.

Pākaitore became a fundamental platform for long-term planning as an iwi. Ken Mair says:

> Every day down there, every night, 7 o'clock, we had karakia and hui. We talked about the previous day and about the next day, how we're going to plan it, what had happened during that day; we talked through all those issues. We always sat down with our people; that's where the decision-making was made. We didn't have any preconceived ideas thought up by us three. Tari was very strong about making sure that the people decided at the end of the day – it was their lives at stake.

The foundation that Pākaitore laid for iwi development within Whanganui is beyond question. Tariana's son Pahia sees it as having had a lasting effect on the way in which they now tackle iwi and Treaty justice:

> I look at our kids and our mokopuna. These things are talked about on an everyday basis now. Our kids are really aware about injustice, whereas we weren't having those conversations before then. I was so proud of Mum; that my mum was there and she was fighting for something she believed in. It meant that we needed to come together and it was seizing the opportunity to politicise our people, to educate our people on why we're here and what we need to do to move forward.

Ken Mair always understood the impact that the events of those three months would have on the development of whānau, hapū and iwi of Whanganui:

> I think it had a massive influence upon us as an iwi in bringing us together, highlighting the issues, bringing about an awareness internally and the need to work together in moving forward as an iwi and hapū. There's no doubt in my mind that it posed some major challenges to our own internal leadership. There was concern by some of us as younger ones that our leadership had tended to err on the side of the Crown and Council, and we were no longer going to

accept that as that being an appropriate way in regard to setting the aspirations of our iwi.

Nancy Tuaine also credits Pākaitore with facilitating the conscientisation of the people:

> It rose up a whole lot of fire inside some of our people. That whole decolonisation process happened during that time, because it was some people's first time to really understand these issues and get a sense of loss of what had been taken away from them; to get an understanding that actually all these statues in this park are symbols of assimilation. That did make some of our young men angry, and there were times if they were pressured that that would come out, but the majority of the time Uncle Niko and Ken were able to control that. That kind of sense of grievance was very much alive in our people at that time. We had a lot of young ones who came through that process of decolonisation, and it hit home. It was very cool and the mauri down there, the spirit down there during that time was cool; just the people coming and sharing their music and kōrero over those days was awesome.

Nancy highlights an aspect of the occupation that was central to its organisation – discipline. Alcohol and drugs were not allowed on site; some of the young people from the occupation who went to the pub across the road were sent home. You didn't get another chance; it was that strict. This was a particular concern for Tariana, who had actively involved so many young people in the reoccupation. Marilyn Payne remembers this as being a deliberate approach to keep a sense of calm among the rangatahi in light of the opposition to the fiscal envelope hui:

> Tariana told us she was taking the young people. We knew there were a lot of plain-clothes police, and she didn't want them arrested. They had been reading all the river claims going on and they were really angry, the young ones; she didn't want them to get caught.

Tariana remembers a time when the tensions seemed precariously high.

At one point, those bloody kids were going to go and burn down Whanganui – burn the old town down. They were so angry. One of the kids told me, so I turned up at their hui. I said to them, 'well, if that's what you want to do, you do it. But you just remember this: you do that, and they will probably burn down every marae on our river. Are you ready for that? Because that's what will happen'. We knew that members of the town community would retaliate; they had already cut down the pole at Hipango Park. I told our kids, 'it's up to you, if that's what's going to happen, and you make sure you are prepared to accept the consequences of it'. They didn't do it. Then they were blaming me: 'oh, it was Aunty's fault; she wouldn't let us do it'.

Marilyn Payne also remembers when various gangs were welcomed on to the site:

> I remember being on there with her and all these gang members coming up from Wellington, and she said to them, 'you don't wear any patches on here', and she'd have them picking up cigarette butts; Tariana had an enormous love of all these young people.

The 'protest' action was influenced by the model of passive resistance that had been established at Parihaka more than a century ago by the prophets of peace, Tohu and Te Whiti. Ken Mair says:

> It was deliberate, and if you knew Niko Tangaroa of course you couldn't get a finer, more passive type of person. Tari was the same. Our family has connections with Parihaka, so we try and uphold that quite strongly. There was never any doubt in my mind that we were looking at it from a passive resistance point of view. When we left, the only ones that were being violent towards us was the state themselves, who couldn't wait to lock us all up, beat us all up and cause general mayhem.

> The kaupapa of Pākaitore around our land and our river was miles, miles, much more important than it being remembered for the big stash up with the police. To this day I think our integrity has always been intact because of the mere fact that we've kept that philosophy – peaceful resistance permeated throughout the whole occupation. Of

course there were moments ... I mean you were dealing with some of our people who had been marginalised by the system.

The importance of discipline, and of retaining a peaceful stand, was especially important the day the police came to evict the occupiers. The police turned up in riot gear at 5.30am, in response to a suggestion that there were stolen building materials on the site – an allegation that proved to be unfounded. Nancy reflects on the way in which the camp was organised that day:

> My brother and sister lived at Pākaitore, and the day the police came to take them off, the wharepuni was here, the children were inside, the women were outside, the men were in front of them, the police were in front of them. Dad would go down every day and sit and listen to the kōrero in support, but when the police were there my dad sent me in to get the kids out. I came down to the police blockade and they wouldn't let me through, so I demanded that they go and get our children, and we got our children out of there.

During the seventy-nine days at Pākaitore, the iwi were always conscious of the tensions evident throughout the town. Nowhere was this brought home more clearly to Tariana than with her own brothers.

> Joe used to get on my nerves. He'd say things. When I went to Pākaitore, he rang me up one day and he said, 'I hope you're satisfied now. None of my Pākehā friends will talk to me again'. I said, 'that's because you've got the wrong ones. All of my Pākehā friends are down here, supporting us'.
>
> Dan was the one. He asked me, 'what do you think Aunty Wai would have thought about this?' I told him, 'I don't think she would have been happy at the way we did it, but she would have been proud that we stood up for what we believed in'. She may not have liked how we did it because it was so divisive, but I know she would have been proud. When you take a leadership role, and you are asked to do that, which I was with Niko Tangaroa, you know that what will come with it is the downside. And it did have a significant impact; definitely our families felt it.

Tariana's in-laws were probably just as nervous about the impacts that the negative media portrayal would have on the Turia name. Pahia saw first-hand how the publicity affected some of the wider family:

> Our family was totally opposed to what was happening down there; all Mum's generation, her cousins, some of their kids, they wanted to distance themselves from us. There was a lot of sacrifice there for Mum – what she had to sacrifice to do what was right. Dad's family were really concerned: 'my God, our name is all over the TV. It was a really big thing. My cousin's got a business in Auckland, and people rang him and said, 'oh look, you're not related to Tariana Turia are you?' My cousin Jason told me years later that he'd say, 'I'm not related to her' because that'd cripple his business. I laughed; I could totally understand that – Pākaitore definitely had an impact.

Nancy was conscious of the tensions reverberating through the town. She says:

> Whanganui is a very white middle-class city. The city itself had very little regard for iwi Māori matters or even interest. It was highly, highly negative in town and was really a critical tension point in our history.

Tariana reflects on the power of perception created at Pākaitore:

We had been 140 years negotiating with the Crown over our river. It was a huge issue for us at home. We tried to be constructive, I thought; even with the media. But there was a particular way in which we were portrayed, and I think that it wasn't so much me who made people afraid; I think there were actions that took place there that made people fearful, even our community. People doing the haka on the streets, a mass march through the town by Taranaki when they came down; all of that was quite intimidating. Maybe because I was one of the leaders down there, that image might have been sheeted back to me and Ken and Niko.[14]

Tariana's good friends, the Quakers Michael and Marilyn Payne, were conscious of the tension. Tariana was deeply moved by their support.

Mihi Rurawhe (L), Marie Moses, Angela Wilks and kaiwhakahaere Tariana Turia at Whai Oranga in 1990. The success of Whai Oranga led Tariana to believe the recipe for Māori success in general was for Māori to be given resources to do things for themselves; this belief is reflected in Whānau Ora.
Source: Wanganui Chronicle

Niko Tangaroa (Te Oranganui Iwi Health Authority chairman) with Tariana, Jill Pettis (Wanganui MP) and Labour Party spokesperson on health Lianne Dalziel on 15 July 1996, discussing the success of the initiative, which to this day provides, among other services, a primary medical service for rural Whanganui people.
Source: Wanganui Chronicle

Tariana and lawyer (and fellow political activist) Moana Jackson share a joke at the opening of the Whanganui Iwi Law Centre in 1997. Tariana was a Labour MP at the time, and had been instrumental in setting up the Centre, which was based at her office in Whanganui.
Source: Wanganui Chronicle

Tariana as Associate Minister of Māori Affairs, speaking in February 2000 to a public meeting in Whanganui about the need to provide Māori with resources to help themselves, as part of a free seminar series entitled 'Getting On, Moving On'. As an example of a successful Māori initiative to provide health resources, Tariana spoke of the establishment in 1984 of Te Oranganui Iwi Health Authority. She stressed that the best way to help Māori was 'from the bottom up', so that Māori were empowered to help themselves.
Source: Wanganui Regional Museum

George (second from left) and Tariana (partly obscured) are welcomed on to the new Pākaitore marae in 1995, to support the occupation on the Whanganui river bank.
Source: Wanganui Chronicle

Pākaitore 1995. Ken Mair, Dardanella Metekingi-Mato, Niko Tangaroa, Rosie Rātana and Tariana. The cliff in the background of the photo is known as the lair of Tūtaeporoporo (see 'Aokehu strategy' in chapter 13)
Source: Shane Bennett

The Quakers all came down to the camp. I remember the night of the vigil – it was such an amazing sight. The community, three rows deep, surrounded Pākaitore one evening to show their support and to provide some protection to the people there from the police and others. The Quakers held hands all the way around Pākaitore, each person holding a candle. It was incredibly moving. There were some beautiful things – it reminded us about our relationships and how important it was that no matter what happened we mustn't destroy those relationships.

Marilyn Payne was instrumental in bringing women from across Whanganui to demonstrate their active support. She says:

> We were really concerned with what was happening. Tari supported me in getting the women's network going, and she said that I could organise that and she would welcome them on to Pākaitore. We rang all our friends and said, 'please all ring six other women', then each of them phoned six more, and when we took them on it was just lovely, because we went into the big tent and a lot of these women with prams and babies had never been on a marae before, and they were welcomed.

> I remember this big tent where they were feeding people with fresh flowers on all the tables and Tari gave the most magnificent talk, and I remember thinking she had the gift of making things very personal. She spoke from the heart and I think touched a lot of those women. Some said, 'I don't want my husband to know, because I've never been here and experienced this before'. I think people were deeply touched. Tariana had a wonderful way with large groups of people; I was so full of admiration for her.

About 150 women came to Pākaitore on that day; mainly Pākehā. Marilyn remembers asking a reporter whether she was going on as a reporter or as a woman, and telling her that if it was the former, she couldn't come in – that was the condition. She says, 'When she stormed off, she was so cross, but we had to respect that we were going on just as women and nothing else.'

Michael Payne also remembers the clear conditions that had been set up around media reporting:

> The thing that absolutely appalls me is the way that the media actually stirred up racism. I was appalled at the influence that the media had; they set the agenda – the way they interviewed people. Paul Holmes should have been locked up for the kind of stirring that went on.

As Quakers, Michael and Marilyn helped in practical ways. Marilyn says:

> We were very supportive. We had a huge canvas tent that could sleep about ten or so, and we used to take pumpkins and food down every day. Most of it was our connection with Tari and really admiring what she was doing.

The generosity of people who supported Pākaitore profoundly moved Tariana.

We got $72,000 in koha from Pākehā and Māori all over the country. I remember we'd only been there a few days and this young Māori farm-worker came across the marae with a sheep slung across his shoulder. He said he didn't understand all of the issues but wanted to contribute. Another day a Tongan group came from Auckland, they'd cooked a hāngi and came across the marae with these huge nets of kai. For those who spent time there and listened to the issues, it made a really big difference about how they felt about it and stopped them from being fearful.[15]

For the eleven weeks of the reoccupation, the iwi was sustained by support of a much wider network of New Zealanders who came to Whanganui to find out for themselves what it was all about, including those involved with Health Care Aotearoa. Peter Glensor says:

> We used to hold regular teleconference meetings of our National Executive, and Tariana raised this issue and asked for the formal support of Health Care Aotearoa. Immediately people were saying, 'look, we are not a political group; we're a support network for our members, so to what extent is this going to create a whole precedent?' And then other voices were saying, 'yes, but this is one of our members saying this is an important issue for us, and what are we going to do?' The result was a clear and strong and positive decision by the

organisation that it would give its formal support to Te Oranganui and to the Whanganui people in this process.

> [When we visited Pākaitore, we saw that] the camp was in full establishment; Tariana was clearly the leader. We spent the afternoon there, and the entire afternoon she spent with us. I couldn't believe it. We walked around and she explained the history of the place, the history of the occupation, the issues they were dealing with. And all the time she was being interrupted as Ken and other people were coming in saying, 'this is happening, and that's happening', and she was giving instructions about what to do. It was quite a remarkable afternoon, and I went away feeling tremendously privileged. That was an amazing experience for me, to watch her in operation as a leader but also to watch the way that she put so much aside of her time to host Joan and me.

One of the most enduring aspects of Pākaitore was its contribution to starting a conversation between Māori and Pākehā about nationhood. Michael Payne initiated a series of lectures involving speakers such as Sir Paul Reeves and Dr Manuka Henare to inspire constitutional debate. Another idea of his was to promote conversation through a dinner series. He says:

> With Pākaitore, because there were such negative things, we got this idea of having a dinner together. We put on a really nice dinner for them with a couple of people who are extreme, but with the idea of getting conversations going. I just admired Tari and Ken; their generosity and their willingness to be open despite our other guests being just so rigid and fixed in their positions.

The dinner series was inspired by a group Michael and Marilyn established, Citizens Concerned for a Peaceful Protest. As part of their campaign, they took out a page advertisement in the local paper. 150 people signed up to their call for peaceful dialogue.

The reoccupation was also a powerful means by which the iwi were able to express their Whanganuitanga, and to stand strong on their own whenua. From all across the land people came to share the journey, to affirm iwi rights; to make sure constitutional reform began at home. At no point was this more obvious than on 30 March 1995, the eve of eviction day. Eva Rickard was one of about 3000 others who had come to tautoko. Tariana remembers:

> I recall as the time approached for the Police to move on, the music, singing and dancing continued as if nothing would happen. In the midst of all the rangatahi dancing and singing was Eva, dancing up a storm, encouraging our youth and our iwi to celebrate who we were and our inherent right to be on this land of our tūpuna.[16]

Every aspect of the seventy-nine days had been carefully planned to ensure maximum impact with minimum conflict. And so, just as they had thoroughly planned their entrance, the iwi took meticulous care with their exit. Tariana told *North and South*:

> We made a conscious decision we'd go but with the knowledge that if claims for our river weren't resolved we'd go back and continue to use that piece of land whether the council liked it or not. Our young people were angry with us for wanting to move off. They wanted to fight to the end. But I believe in any political struggle you don't take on the might of others unless you know you are going to win, otherwise people lose their spirit and we wanted to retain our spirit and our dignity.[17]

Nancy reflects that the way in which they left Pākaitore paved the way for an ongoing conversation about how to make the progress Whanganui iwi needed to make:

> It has changed a whole lot of attitudes and fostered acceptance of Whanganui iwi in the role that we play. That whole landscape changed because they made a stand, so how we would come off there was critical, and Tariana played a critical role in shaping that. And then of course representing us when they went to conversations with the Crown and the local council over it. She would go with the men off to those hui, so her leadership became apparent, her ability to mobilise people became apparent. And then she was, ironically, headhunted to become a politician.

Pākaitore gave new life to our old people, and an amazing sense of revitalisation for our young. We had kids involved who had never participated in anything Māori, let alone been on a marae. They all turned up in their droves, and I think it was the first time that they'd ever had a strong sense of the essence of who they were.

George, who's never been an activist of any description, slept with me under the tarpaulin on the ground the first night we were there. That in itself was revolutionary. He said to me that it just felt right. Had I stayed there on my own I think some of our relations would have thought, 'oh, that's just Tubs; she's up to no good again!'

I think the wonderful thing about it was that from one end of the river to the other, even though there were no doubt some who were unhappy about the way in which we went about doing it, they never spoke publicly against us. No marae, no hapū spoke out, which was hugely uplifting. It felt to me as if the kaupapa of Whanganuitanga was uniting everyone, upholding our right to be who we are, celebrating our nationhood. It wasn't about being Māori. It was about being of Whanganui; being a descendant of te awa tupua. It was a wairua thing that affected all of us there. The extent of our action was never anticipated. We had started off with about 200 people and ended up at times with over 2000 people here. Other iwi came and joined us; kura from across the rohe, international delegations, activists and individuals just curious to learn.

At Pākaitore, the iwi started plotting out their future development, assigning different people specific roles. John Maihi was one of the first. He says:

> They gave us tasks. I became the karere, and I said, 'so what's the karere do?' 'Keep out of trouble and go and meet with the police, the Council and the Crown, the Government – you do that job'. I hadn't done anything like that before, so I went back up to the old people of Ōtoko. My grand-uncle says, 'what's wrong with you, boy; we taught you all that you should know. Do you know the history of the house?' 'Which house?' I go. 'This bloody house', they said. 'What did we teach you about the house?' I realised what they had been doing all these years. 'Yeah, well, don't ask us any dumb questions again; you've been fully taught'. It wasn't long after, they were all dead, about eleven of them, and that's when I got put on the front.

> So when I came back down [to Pākaitore] I put this whole scenario in my head. This became the tupuna whare and I was able to then work it out, who was going to do this, who was inside, and I said, 'well, Tariana, I guess you are the rangatira, girl'; I had to admit it. This was me figuring the house out. I didn't talk to her about it; hell, I would never say that to her; I'd get a hard time. I figured it out who was all sitting in the house, who was all there; that's when I realised I had a task.

John set about meeting with all the local authorities:

> I started to really get what she was talking about, you know. They really broke it out of me; what I should have known when I was born. But as the old people said, 'you've already been taught; don't come back again'.

John's responsibilities extended to travelling to Wellington on 12 April 1995, to urge the Speaker, Peter Tapsell,[18] to persuade then Prime Minister Jim Bolger to negotiate with the Whanganui iwi. At first he appeared to have succeeded; Tapsell promised to approach the prime minister to see if a compromise could be reached on the dispute. 'I'm hopeful that I can assist to overcome the present impasse,' he told the press.[19]

All sides of the political spectrum were now involved. Sandra Lee, on behalf of Mana Motuhake, had expressed support for the occupants of Pākaitore Marae. Meanwhile Ross Meurant, leader of the Right of Centre Party, issued a challenge to the Government to move the people:

> Let's not kid ourselves, this group is challenging the sovereignty of our nation. They are a group of nationalists seeking to cloak their actions under the mantle of legitimate grievances.[20]

Persuaded by John Luxton, then Minister of Māori Affairs, and his call for a 'calm, reasoned approach', the Whanganui District Council pulled back on their original threat to evict the iwi at 5pm on 30 March. The reoccupation had escalated through the courts; an urgent hearing was scheduled at the High Court to make a ruling on who owned the land. Tariana was named as one of three defendants, with Niko Tangaroa and Henry Bennett[21]. The three appointed John Rowan as their representative.

On 16 May 1995 Justice Heron ruled that the Moutoa Gardens belonged to the Whanganui District Council, and any protesters were trespassing. The next day the iwi resolved to leave the site at dawn on 18 May. The *Herald* quoted Tariana as stating:

> We know that we can't battle the system if we are forcibly removed. We are going out the way we want to go out and the way our people came in … with integrity and under our own tikanga.[22]

It was a temporary departure, executed in the knowledge they would return. Ken Mair says:

> We deliberately decided and planned that we'd leave at 4 – 4.30am, and we would leave in a dignified manner, never refusing to give up the fight for Pākaitore, our lands and river. And of course we've been back there every time.

Since that time, the people of Whanganui return to Pākaitore every year on the twenty-eighth of February, to kōrero, to reflect and to celebrate Whanganuitanga.

For Tariana, however, there were immediate consequences for the seventy-nine days of action.

Taking the consequences

The fact that I was so closely involved in Pākaitore eventually came to the attention of my employer, Te Puni Kōkiri (Ministry of Māori Development). There had been a lot of pressure on me not to engage, not to be seen to be a leader, because of my role with a government department. Wira Gardiner was faced with sitting me down, and discussing the consequences of my choice.

Wira Gardiner explains:

> In a series of anecdotal reports it seemed that all was not as it seemed in the leadership of the protest and occupation of Pākaitore. It would appear that Tariana Turia, an employee of mine, was knee-deep in the

action and decision-making, albeit not appearing on TV. Now why should I be surprised!

After some reflection I called Tariana to Wellington, and she and I had a cup of tea. I said to her that I thought that she was more involved in the protest and occupation than was appropriate for a public servant, and that if it continued I would have no option but to terminate her employment with the Department. She disagreed with my assessment and told me that she was not involved to the extent that I suggested. Stalemate. So I suggested a course of action: if I thought that her actions came close to breaching her duties as a public servant I would call her up and we would have another meeting. If she thought she was coming close to that line she could also exercise her right to call me up for a discussion.

The upshot of this was Tariana went back to Whanganui and no doubt continued her involvement where she had left off. But she was much cleverer at not leaving her fingerprints on any action! I suspect we were each pleased with our respective positions. I was pleased, as I had laid down the law firmly and reminded her who was the boss. She had made her position clear, and seemingly accepted my position. So, importantly, there was no loss of face on either side. But we watched each other carefully. My learnings from that time: Tariana's influence and networks were growing, and she had become more sophisticated in the development of her thinking. Most importantly she was firmly grounded in the people who she represented.

On the basis of this initial meeting with Wira, I thought it would be relatively simple once the reoccupation had dissolved to return to work. I walked to work, came in and sat down at my desk. Poor old Brendon (Puketapu), my manager at that time, told me, 'I don't think you should be here. You better wait until they get in touch with you'.

He said, 'I gave you leave? I didn't give you seventy-nine days leave!' After all, he had been distracted because of the Fiscal Envelope.

Haami Piripi at that time worked in Head Office. He might have been regional manager. The media went to him, and he implied that I would be sacked. So when Brendon asked, I said to him 'if Haami is thinking of sacking me I might as well tell you that I've gone to a lawyer'. I hadn't really; I had sought a bit of advice around it. Probably my lawyer was Ken.

Anyway, I went and saw Niko Tangaroa, and then Wira said for us to come down and have another talk. He asked me what I wanted: did I really want to go back and work at TPK? I said no. He asked me what side of the fence I was sitting on; was I a public servant or was I iwi? And I said, 'don't make me choose, because I will always choose whānau, hapū and iwi'. So he gave me my salary for a year to go and start up Te Oranganui. A win-win all around.

Six years after the iwi left Pākaitore, an agreement was signed by Whanganui District Council, Whanganui iwi and the Prime Minister, Helen Clark, on behalf of the Crown in February 2001. Under the terms of that agreement, the land would be established as a historic reserve and run by a reserves board with three District Council representatives, three Whanganui iwi representatives and one Crown representative. The Ballance statue would be repaired and relocated.

It was, as Ken Mair suggests, a solution of sorts that the people could live with:

> The deal, the tripartite deal, with Helen Clark: [Tariana] was obviously part of that, trying to get that through. One thing about Tari, she's very solution-focused. It's just a matter of what level, what the solution is.

It would be gratifying to say that the 2001 agreement achieved enduring peace at Pākaitore. But it was less than a year later, in 2002, that the iwi planned to return again, in protest at Genesis Energy seeking a resource consent to use the Whanganui River for thirty-five years.

However, relative progress had been made towards resolution of the issue through the 2001 agreement.

It was almost two decades after Pākaitore that a Deed of Settlement, Ruruku Whakatupua, was signed on 5 August 2014. The signing took place at Rānana Marae, and gave birth to a new legal framework for management of the Whanganui River, Te Pā Auroa nā Te Awa Tupua. At the core of this framework is a recognition of Te Awa Tupua as a legal entity with legal standing, rights and an independent voice. The deed is a powerful legislative mandate of the life force of Te Awa Tupua, and the relationship that the people have to the river.

There is one more and extremely significant reason why Pākaitore will always hold a very special hold on Tariana's heart. Pahia should have that story.

> I can remember the occupation for the twenty-eighth in 1995. My partner Tam (Tamala Davis) was pregnant. And I can remember our son was born on March the eighth. Mum said, 'I'll get a caravan and she can have him down at Pākaitore,' and Tam was like, 'I don't want to be in a caravan'. We'd decided we'd have a home birth you know. Mum was saying, 'I think it would be great; the kuia have said that they will look after us, blah, blah, blah'. So anyway, we decided. He was born at the marae, at Whangaehu; we had him there.
>
> Dad had never got to name any of our kids, so I said to him, 'Dad, we want you to name this baby'. Baby pops out at 6 o'clock. Dad then goes straight back to Pākaitore to the 7 o'clocks when they have all their karakia and wānanga. He comes back and at half past nine tells us, 'I've got a name'. And I go, 'oh yeah?'
>
> He goes, 'I went into the meeting and talked to all the kaumātua that were there, and I told them that our mokopuna had been born, and they've given the name.' And I said, 'what is it?' And he goes, 'Pākaitore'. And I can remember I looked at Tam and the first thing I thought was, 'well, he won't get a job in Whanganui'.
>
> So I go, 'do they have any other names?' I really did. I thought it was in the media that every Pākehā hated us, and I'm like, 'I don't want

him to have that name'. But then Mum comes in – big bright Nan – going, 'isn't it awesome they've given that name!' And I'm like, 'I'm not excited about it'.

The next day we took him into Pākaitore as a one-day-old baby, and he got passed around by a whole bunch of nannies. One of them asked where his whenua was, and they said, 'you bring it and we'll bury it here at Pākaitore'.

And then Nanny Nui said if we bury his whenua here we can't leave here. If we get evicted from here, we can't let you bury that boy's whenua here. That means we have to stay, and we will take whatever has to come with that. And I was sitting there thinking, 'holy shit', you know, 'do I even have a say in any of this?' I was thinking 'far out, this is pretty hard out', you know – sort of freaking out. Anyway, they sat there and they had this big long-as wānanga about it, and I said 'no, no, we won't – we are going to bury it back at home, by his sister's'. But I can always remember Mum – 'I think you should consider it – I think you should consider burying his pito here'. As I think back now, I know that we were privileged to have this name bestowed upon our whānau. It is a name that we, as a whānau, hold in the greatest of respect for all that comes with it.

And there it was: Pākaitore the mokopuna and Pākaitore the pā became one and the same – the heartbeat of the iwi. The reoccupation represented a new spirit of vitality that would provide a foundation for their future.

NOTES

[1] Interview with Ken Mair, 10 June 2014.

[2] Interview with Hone Harawira, 12 June 2014.

[3] Office of Treaty Settlements, *Crown Proposals for the Settlement of Treaty of Waitangi claims*, 1994, p. 50.

4 N. Shepheard, 'Fierce Kuia: profile of New Zealand Member of Parliament Tariana Turia', *North and South*, February 2004, p. 58.

5 It should be noted that when a new solid bronze statue of Ballance was eventually unveiled outside the Whanganui District Council Chambers on 29 October 2009, TV One's news persisted with such a view, under the title, 'Wanganui's favourite son returns'.

6 'Lawyer blames history for statue's beheading', *Dominion*, 29 July 1995.

7 Tariana Turia, Submission to WAI 167, 1995; A055 Waitangi Tribunal.

8 'He maumaharatanga ki a Tuaiwa', in 'Tuaiwa Hautai Kereopa Rickard 1925–1997', in *Nga Puna Roimata; He maumaharatanga ki a Tuaiwa*, 1998.

9 Maxwell J. G. Smart and Arthur P. Bates, *The Wanganui Story*, 1972.

10 Rangitihi Rangiwaiata Tahuparae, New Zealand's first officially appointed Kaumatua O Te Whare Paremata; a cultural advisor, member of the Waitangi Tribunal; and tohunga.

11 E. Wellwood, 'Closing the gaps in a different guise', *The Press*, 20 August 2001.

12 Pat Snedden, *Pakeha and the Treaty: Why it's our Treaty too*, 2005, pp. 102–3.

13 Wira Gardiner, *Return to Sender: What Really Happened at the Fiscal Envelope Hui*, 1996, pp. 134–5.

14 Notes from an interview with Audrey Young, 25 September 2014.

15 Shepheard, 'Fierce Kuia', p. 59.

16 'He maumaharatanga ki a Tuaiwa', p. 100

17 Shepheard, 'Fierce Kuia', p. 59.

18 Sir Pita Tapsell served as MP for Eastern Māori from 1981 to 1996. He was New Zealand's first Māori Speaker.

19 David Barber, 'Maoris appeal to the Crown', *Sydney Morning Herald*, 12 April 1995.

20 'MP critical of "pussy-footing" over Moutoa', *New Zealand Herald*, 28 March 1995.

21 Tariana's cousin, Henry D Bennett, QSM, was a prominent Whanganui leader. He instigated the bilingual teacher training programme, Te Rangakura, and was Head of Department of Rangahaua, the Maori Studies Department at Whanganui Polytechnic.

22 'Occupiers say they will quit Moutoa', *New Zealand Herald*, 16 May 1995.

-CHAPTER TWELVE-
WALKING SOVEREIGN

If you think you're sovereign, walk sovereign.[1]

Māori are no longer content to react to government proposals which have been unilaterally formulated by Cabinet. Until the country has a constitution that allows Māori to determine policies for Māori, there will be continuing disquiet and an ongoing sense of injustice.[2]

In January 1995, at Hīrangi Marae, over a thousand Māori from across New Zealand met for the first of a series of hui to discuss the Government's proposals for the settlement of Treaty Claims: the $1 billion fiscal envelope. The hui canvassed response to the process adopted in developing the proposals, the principles on which they were based, the assumptions made to justify the proposals and the framework in which they had been drafted.

The hui had been called by Tūwharetoa chief Sir Hepi te Heuheu. In doing so, he expressed his grave concerns, making it clear that he also wanted at the hui to resurrect the issue of the constitutional significance of the Treaty of Waitangi; to provide a forum for iwi, organisations and groups to come together on the marae to express their views.

In his commentary, Mason Durie noted:

> A climate of secrecy and unilateral declarations has surrounded the proposal, suggesting a lack of good faith by the Crown and undisclosed motivation for developing a proposal of this nature.[3]

Along with comprehensive representation from iwi, major Māori organisations attended the hui, including the New Zealand Māori Council, the Māori Women's Welfare League and the Māori Congress. There was universal rejection of the Crown's proposals and a call for an alternative process of constitutional review jointly undertaken by Māori and the Crown.

Nine months later, a second Hīrangi hui attracted approximately 1500 representatives of iwi and Māori organisations. Among them were Tariana and Ken, attending just months after their reoccupation of Pākaitore.

The strength and the growth of our Whanganuitanga had inspired in us the hope in our eyes and the fire in our belly that we had the power to take on the world, if we did it together. It was through that collective force that we decided we would indeed step out and enter local and national politics. By now I had been freed of the constraints of working for the Crown, a freedom I cherished. I was always aware of the challenge of living out our tribal politics when we are employed under the auspices of the state.

When you are a Crown agent it's pretty difficult to speak out publicly and be highly critical of the Crown. But when you come from here it's even harder to say nothing.

It was with renewed energy that I became a member of a working party to review the submissions from the Hīrangi hui held earlier in 1995. With me on the working party were lawyers Moana Jackson and Annette Sykes and academic Professor Margaret Mutu. When we met up in September, our proposals fleshed out the types of goals with which we were seeking to expand upon the 'Hīrangi recommendations'. Uppermost in our list was to educate tangata whenua around decolonisation and the recognition of rangatiratanga for hapū and iwi. We also sought to achieve constitutional change acceptable to Māori in a process which reflected the relationship between Māori and the Crown.

Stripping away the unwanted layers

The second hui called for a series of working parties to develop analysis and strategy to present to a third hui, which eventually took place in April 2006. It was a significant hui by any estimation, and resulted in unanimity about the goal of Māori playing a bigger role in the future of our country.

Our working party defined decolonisation as 'the stripping away of the unwanted layers of another people's culture accumulated over generations to expose and rediscover the vivid colours of one's own cultural heritage and the political power and sovereignty which can give effective expression to that heritage'.

The basic premise of decolonisation is that tangata whenua have been adversely affected by tauiwi values, processes and institutions. It is aimed at rediscovering and restoring tangata whenua philosophies of life. The layers of colonisation have been all-pervasive, resulting in loss of land, language and resources; the theft of ideas; and the denigration of indigenous spirituality.

'Decol', then, is about a process to reclaim tangata whenua values as a basis for life today. It is not about a return to the past, and acting in traditional ways. Rather, it is about a recovering of those values which have been life-enhancing in the past and pressing them into service in meaningful ways today. I firmly believe that one of the binding strands of strength and unity that we must continue is a deep belief in ourselves. We must pursue these with vigour if our mokopuna of the future are to have a sense of their own worth, their own authority and their own power as tangata whenua.

My role at Pākaitore appeared to have created a profile that followed me to Hīrangi. One newspaper featured a headline, 'Wanganui woman had key role at hui', and proceeded to describe me as a 'key figure'; an 'outspoken supporter' of the Moutoa Gardens occupation.

We left the hui in a jubilant mood. Te Kuru Waaka from Te Arawa concluded the Government would have to take notice of the hui's resolution because nearly all of Maoridom was represented. However, almost immediately, Parliament's first Speaker of tangata whenua descent, Hon Sir Peter Tapsell, dismissed the Hirangi hui as a waste of time, stating publicly that what we wanted was totally unrealistic.

If anything, Mr Speaker's reaction inspired us towards a greater expression of the desire for tino rangatiratanga. I was proud that one of Māoridom's most respected leaders, Sir Hepi te Heuheu, had taken such a bold stand in calling the people together to reject the Crown's proposals as being contrary to the Treaty of Waitangi. The three Hīrangi hui provided a significant challenge to the Crown; that governments could no longer expect to act unilaterally on issues of importance to Māori.

Tragically, just over fifteen months after the third hui, Sir Hepi passed away, on 31 July 1997. I reflected, at that time, on the impact of Sir Hepi's life:

> Sir Hepi was a chief amongst all chiefs, a man of great dignity and humility. He was a true ariki in that he took his lead from his people. ... Only a man of such mana could gather 3000 people from all tribes and from all persuasions. He believed in iwi self-determination. He knew that we could not remain subservient to systems and structures that were not ours and were not working in our interests. He supported the drive for constitutional change. Sir Hepi wanted us to move from dependency to interdependence as iwi collectives. In establishing Māori Congress he was looking for a means to bring about unity between our tribal nations.[4]

Back to fight another day

We returned from the second hui in Tūrangi to take on the Whanganui local body elections. This was all part of the plan prepared at Pākaitore.

John Maihi says:

> When we all left here every one of us had a job to do; we needed to go into the boards, the councils, Parliament – and of course we thought Tariana was going with Mana Motuhake. Ken and all the others went for the District Health Board, and I think only Uncle Hemi got into the District Council. And so we can't get into the DHB, we can't get into the Council, and so we went into the prisons, and I'm still there today doing voluntary work.

The strategy John refers to perhaps explained what our local paper described as 'exceptionally big fields of nominated candidates' for the 1995 local body elections: seven for the mayoralty; thirty for the Whanganui District Council's nine-seat urban ward; five for the three-seat rural ward; and seven for the six-seat rural community board.

I contested the mayoralty with Randhir Daahya, Stephen Palmer, Terry O'Connor, Bruce Lochure, incumbent Chas Poynter and Ray Stevens. An article in the *Dominion* at the time described me as the only candidate to refer directly to the Gardens, 'which she calls Pakaitore':

> 'I have respect for and an understanding of the diverse nature of our society, an ability to articulate the issues clearly and concisely and a commitment to using full consultation processes to all community sectors on issues that impact on them' Mrs Turia says. 'I want to see a council that is balanced and able to be representative of all views, because in the past Maori views have not been articulated fully on all issues in council, with Pakaitore being, in fact, a wake up call to Wanganui.[5]

When the results came to pass, however, it was clear that the community that turned up to vote didn't share my view about the value of a balanced council. I received a dismal 529 votes for the mayoralty; ninety less than Ken's share of the Council vote, much to his great delight.[6]

Chas Poynter couldn't help but gloat:

> Wanganui has been a barometer for the whole country. We have people like Tari and Ken who on the one hand say they don't recognise the laws of New Zealand and on the other say they want

to stand for local government. I find that ironic. They've been well
and truly given the message by the community.[7]

I wasn't having that, and responded to what Chas had described as a
convincing win:

> More people didn't vote for him than did, there were eight or nine
> thousand who voted against him and 32% of the electorate didn't
> bother to vote at all. He's under some grand illusion that the polls
> say that what he did was right but it wasn't right because it hasn't
> been resolved. The issue hasn't gone away and we'll be back to
> fight another day.[8]

Our strategy to make sure the issues stayed alive underscored our approach
in standing for Council.

Ken says of the campaign:

> I managed to convince her that she'd be the ideal candidate for mayor.
> It was deliberate in the sense of highlighting the issue, informing the
> community that the issues hadn't gone away: 'we're here and we want
> to deal with them in a proactive and positive way'. The result showed
> a different outcome, which wasn't unexpected.

Nevertheless, the outcome was disappointing. Although we accepted we
were dealing with a conservative community, the Māori turnout was a
worry. At that time, in 1995, there were about 4000 Māori registered on
the Whanganui District Council roll, and the same amount again that
would be eligible to be registered. A number of Māori candidates put
themselves forward, but not one of us was elected. The last time a Māori
had been elected to council was in 1983, when Henry Bennett had become
a councillor.

Each of the new councillors elected came up with a reason for our
lack of success. Councillor Daahya had no doubt the Māori reoccupation
of Moutoa had adversely affected the Māori candidates' chances. Former
Councillor Paul Mitchell shared his view, saying that the 'instigators of
the Moutoa Gardens occupation should take a clear message: the public
did not support what they did and they showed it by the way they voted'[9].
We were not deterred. By now there was another forum for our issues to be
aired: the 1996 general election.

NOTES

1. Tuaiwa Eva Rickard, cited in a speech by Tariana Turia to the International Council of Thirteen Indigenous Grandmothers Conference, Te Wānanga o Aotearoa, Gisborne, 5 December 2013.
2. Sir Hepi te Heuheu, opening Address to Hirangi hui, 29 January 1995.
3. M. H. Durie, 'Proceedings of a hui held at Hirangi Marae, Turangi' (1995) 25 VUWLR 109.
4. *Hansard*, 5 August 1997.
5. 'Poynter faces six challengers in Wanganui's mayoralty contest', *Dominion*, 14 September 1995.
6. 'Moutoa helped in win, says Poynter', *Dominion*, 16 October 1995.
7. Ibid.
8. Ibid.
9. 'Poor Poll no surprise to Maori themselves', *Wanganui Chronicle Extra*, a special election supplement, 16 October 1995, p. 2.

-CHAPTER THIRTEEN-
THE PATHWAY TO PARLIAMENT

I was of the view that governments came and went but advanced the interests of our people very little, and operated under an assumed authority.[1]

The 1996 general election turned out to be a showcase for the new mixed member proportional (MMP) regime, for which a national referendum had obtained universal support in 1993. A significant feature of the 1993 general election had been the election of the first MP to represent Mana Motuhake, Sandra Lee. Sandra was also the first Māori woman to win a general electorate seat.

Mana Motuhake had been established by Matiu Rata, for whom Tariana had profound respect. Matiu had been the key architect of the Waitangi Tribunal. His foresight had provided the nation with a vital mechanism to examine injustices that had created long-standing grievances. Matiu also played a key role in establishing Waitangi Day, promoting 6 February as a day to publicly recognise the signing of Te Tiriti o Waitangi.

I believe that without Matiu's commitment, foresight and dedication we would not have reached the level of engagement we have. Matiu planted the seed that formally acknowledged the Treaty of Waitangi as our founding document and gave Māori a channel for claims for the return of their land or compensation. We should not forget that, or his vision to ensure Māori would get a fair and just settlement.

In many ways, I always saw myself walking the same pathway that Matiu had taken, particularly after he left Labour to set up his own party. I placed him firmly along the trajectory of indigenous representation, from the Young Maori Party in the late 1800s through to the establishment of the Māori Party in 2004.

In a speech in 2010, Tariana noted:

> Around the closing of the 19th century, the Young Māori Party was established, ostensibly to increase Māori political participation and representation in Parliament. That it was successful in achieving this goal is without question when we recall the impact of some of that party's members, including Sir Maui Pomare, Sir James Carroll and Sir Apirana Ngata. But it would not be for another eighty years with the birth of the Mana Motuhake political party, before a Māori Party

in its own right would emerge to seriously contest parliament. In 1960 the Independent Māori Group had formed, which paved the way for independent Māori representation.

The late Matiu Rata extended the call for independence even further and founded Mana Motuhake to protect and represent Māori interests. As history shows, however, Mana Motuhake was unable to win any seats in its own name, and so in 1991 it was decided to form a strategic alliance with the Alliance Party. In that same year, Eva Rickard founded Mana Māori and in the decade to follow a rush of new Māori parties came on to the scene – Te Tawharau, Mana Wahine, Te Ira Tangata, Mauri Pacific, Nga Iwi Morehu, Aroha Ngai Tatou and the Derek Fox party.[2]

Mana Motuhake put forward candidates in every election from 1981 through to 1990, but was singularly unsuccessful on every occasion. In 1991 the party formed the Alliance Party with the New Labour Party, the Green Party and the Democratic Party. It was on that banner that Sandra Lee was elected to Parliament in 1993, and she was joined by Alamein Kopu in 1996. The scaffolding for MMP was gradually being erected.

In 1996, however, while Mana Motuhake merged into the Alliance, a new breakaway Māori political party entered the fray – the Mana Māori Movement, founded by Tuaiwa Hautai Kereopa (Eva) Rickard.

Eva was someone whom I had long admired since I first watched a video taken when she was welcoming the Crown on to Raglan, the Independent State of Whaingaroa. Eva knew that if our people were to free themselves from the oppressive situation we found ourselves in, words, negotiation and advocacy were futile, and instead we needed strategies of action. The stand that she had taken over Raglan Golf Course was one; entering Parliament was another.

I remember when she came to our marae to speak alongside Matiu. Unlike me, Eva had accepted Matiu's invitation to stand for Parliament, and she stood for Mana Motuhake for Western Māori for every election between 1981 and 1990. I can recall some of our whanaunga being blown away with her kōrero.

> Many of them did not want to believe that things are quite as bad as Eva was portraying. It meant that they would have to challenge their own thinking and learn the truth about our country's history. Everything she uttered was a political testament of who she was. What she believed was that we needed to act collectively to change the situation we were in as a people. I was inspired by her korero, although I did not believe in my heart that Mana Motuhake was on about our haputanga. Their regional focus required the establishment of new social structures instead of acknowledging the existing hapu structures and strengthening those.[3]

Eva herself lost faith in Mana Motuhake when they chose to come under the umbrella of the Alliance. Sandra Lee summarised her challenge to the Alliance: 'Dead fish flow with the current', a sound message for anyone in leadership.[4]

And so in 1996, the Mana Māori Movement was born. The new party put up eighteen candidates on the list. Eva's daughter Angeline was first (standing for Te Tai Hauāuru), Tame Iti second (Te Tai Rāwhiti), Hone Harawira fourth and Mereana Pitman fifth. Ken Mair, eighth on the list, stood against me for Te Puku o te Whenua.[5]

After setting up Mana Māori, Eva returned to Whangaehu to ask me to join with her in creating political change.

Tariana has written about this request elsewhere:

> In January 1996, following the death of Rino Tirakatene Senior, Eva and her two mokopuna came to our marae at Whangaehu. She asked me to withdraw from Labour and join Mana Maori as it was clear that my philosophical base was more in line with that of Mana Maori. Morally I could not. I felt it would appear that I was only joining Mana Māori because I had missed out on the Labour Electorate nomination for Te Puku o te Whenua. Eva questioned what she saw as my 'misguided loyalty' to Labour. I knew that Eva left the marae disappointed and disillusioned with my decision and I felt as it I had let her down.[6]

I'd never really thought about national politics, but people from Labour had come and talked to me. They're probably sorry now they ever did. I didn't have any desire to go. I wasn't sure if anyone could effect change in that environment. But I had tried everything else to get change for our people, and maybe Parliament was one last hope. Relatives and friends had said we needed to look at fighting on all fronts; that it was important to have a voice there that would open the doors to information. And so Labour it was.

By this time I had already been approached by Robert Pouwhare to put my name forward for Labour, for Te Puku o te Whenua. I said no, right up until the day nominations closed. But they kept on at me, ringing me, asking, 'why don't you give it a go?' A lot of our iwi were also saying to me, 'we've got a fight on our hands; we think you should go into politics'. On the last day I decided I would. They then had to find six people to nominate me. Jill Pettis ran around and got six members. I think she might regret that now. My cousin Reti remembers one of the selection hui:

> We put her in Labour, my sister and I. Jill Pettis came to Kawhaiki looking for someone to nominate her for Labour. I put my hand up and my sister, Sharon McKenzie, seconded my motion, and we have never seen Jill since then. I said, 'I'll nominate Tariana'. She was our cousin; why not?

I stood for the seat but I never got it. It went to Rino Tirikatene Senior. Then on the campaign trail for the 1996 elections, Rino suddenly died at the age of fifty-five. Our iwi went to the tangi and they told Whetu Tirikatene-Sullivan, who was by now a veteran of ten terms as the Member for Southern Māori, that she should let that seat go to me. However, they put up Rino's son, and I wouldn't stand against him. I found the process really demeaning. It was just awful. I went home and decided that I would just go on the list, spurred on by the faith placed in me by Labour leader, Helen Clark, and then president, Maryan Street.

Maryan Street says:

> I first met Tariana in 1995 when she had been persuaded by supportive whānau and people of importance to her to run for Parliament under the Labour banner. I had heard of her, but did not know her. I was president of the Labour Party at the time, and had had for a while a lingering feeling that the Labour Party had not moved sufficiently with the Māori renaissance of the seventies and eighties. I knew the Māori firebrand women of the eighties like Hilda

Halkyard-Harawira, Donna Awatere and Ripeka Evans, and older mentors such as Mira Szazy, and was disturbed that they did not find in Labour the automatic home for their broader politics that I did, given Labour's long-standing and traditional connection with Māori through Rātana and other leaders over many years.

I presided over the selection contest for Te Tai Hauāuru in 1995, which Tariana did not win. However, I encouraged her to run for the Labour Party list because I thought she would bring a deep connectedness with Māori whānau struggling to realise their deeply held aspirations for their land, their language and their families.

When we met to discuss her possible entry into Parliament, I was struck by the deep humility and burning ambition for others which shone out of this diminutive woman. She was a person of real stature, if not height! She was also passionate about her people's health, welfare and dignity. She had a reputation as something of a radical. I thought the Labour Party needed to win back Māori imagination and trust and that she was the person to do it, along with Nanaia Mahuta. She and I wrote a carefully crafted media release together after she agreed to contest for a list position. Some saw the Labour Party as taking a risk by putting her on our list; others saw the risk as all hers.

I never expected to get in on the list. I knew that Helen Clark was telling people that were nervous about me getting in that I wouldn't get in because I was too far down the list. I had been at twenty-one and then, on 27 May 1996, five months out from the election, deputy leader David Caygill stood down, letting Dr Michael Cullen take over his position. David subsequently left. That made me one step closer to the Beehive.

The *Dominion* reported in June 1997:

Her inclusion at number 20 on Labour's list sparked fury by Labour MPs Geoff Braybrooke, Jack Elder and George Hawkins, who called for her removal. But their disapproval was mild compared to that of her family. 'They were disappointed – they thought I was selling out. All those years I had been telling them "Don't vote, it will only encourage them", and now I wanted to go into Parliament'.[7]

Years later Shane Jones suggested to the *New Zealand Herald* that supposedly senior Māori had also opposed my inclusion on the list:

> Never, ever overlook the fact that Tariana only became a parliamentarian because of the Labour Party. Helen Clark, against advice from senior kaumatua, decided to take a punt with Tariana.[8]

I publicly challenged Mr Jones to name the kaumātua, but their identity remains unknown, if indeed they ever existed.

I was definitely hesitant about standing for Parliament. I was absolutely committed to constitutional change, and I wasn't convinced a mainstream party would allow me to continue to hold those views. *Mana* magazine reported my views at that time:

> But she decided the political arena was one place where you can use the system to make changes. If she doesn't make any headway, however, she won't hang around.[9]

It was probably as much a surprise to myself as many others that I didn't join up to the Mana Māori Movement list.

John Maihi describes the general reaction to that decision:

> It shocked the shit out of us that she went with Labour. We were, 'what? What the hell?' I thought they were going to go Mana Motuhake because we had Eva Rickard here and all that; I thought they'd all agree with each other.

I was determined that whatever vehicle I chose, I needed to maintain the capacity to name the world as I saw it; to fight for what was right.

Ken Mair says:

> Labour had already approached her; Helen had approached her. But in my head space if she can get through that system, go for it, because we need people all over the place, strategically, and she was a person that would never lose where she came from and her values and that – which has proven to be critical.

Labour told me that in an MMP environment diverse voices could be heard. I knew no one apart from Jill. I told her, 'you need to know that I'm not going to change'. She reassured me, 'you won't need to change; this is MMP – diverse views and all the rest of it'. Yeah right! It wouldn't be long before I found myself stifled, constrained, out-voted, harassed and denied a voice.

Election night 12 October 1996

The night of the election, Ken and I went to my son Pahia's house for a barbeque. At midnight I said to Ken, 'you're not in and I'm not in; we might as well go home'.

I wasn't going to sit up and see if I'd got in: I didn't think I had a shit-show of getting in. At 2 o'clock in the morning, Rua rings me up: 'you're in, you're in'. I said, 'you're in what?' (I was half asleep). And she said, 'you're in Parliament'. I said, 'you're joking' ... and she said, 'well, put your TV on'. Oh my God; I nearly died.

Honestly, I was terrified. I had allowed my name to go on the list because Labour was polling low and I didn't think I had a show. I think they were at about 16 percent – it was very low – and I was at 20 on the list. So I had worked out that by the time all the ones had won their seat I'd be out. Trouble was, three of them didn't win their seats, and they had to go for recount. And when those three lost their seats I was in. Helen insisted that I had to come down to Wellington, because they knew that those three weren't going to win. I didn't go. I was uncomfortable for ten days while they were counting. I had to watch Richard Northey and Chris Carter cry – they were two who lost their seats – and the other one was Whetu Tirakatene-Sullivan. I was scared to look at her. I felt so terrible: she lost hers, and that's how I got in.

The 1996 election represented Labour's worst result since World War Two. The three marginal results were all part of the wider story of Labour's crushing defeat.

In Maungakiekie, a substantial chunk of votes that would previously have gone to Labour were captured by the Alliance (Matt Robson) and New Zealand First (Gilbert Miles). Richard Northey, who had previously served the Onehunga electorate, was ousted by National's Belinda Vernon. The same splintering of the vote occurred with Waipareira, an electorate that only lasted that single term. Waipareira had the slimmest margin that election: National's Brian Neeson received only 107 votes more than Chris Carter. New Zealand First's Jack Elder and the Alliance's Laila Harre picked up close to 9000 votes between them.

Te Tai Tonga was swept up in the euphoria of a Māori voter landslide change of vote. In 1996 Māori voters temporarily placed their faith in New Zealand First[10], bringing in the 'tight five', as the media branded the new pack, comparing them to first five forwards pushing their way through the political scrum. Whetu Tirikatene-Sullivan, having served ten terms in office, retired from politics, ending the Tirikatene legacy of sixty-four years in parliamentary service[11].

There's one more story about Tariana's pathway to Parliament that probably should be told. Tariana's nephew Che tells that story.

The Aokehu strategy: devouring the monster from within

> We always refer to Aunty as adopting the Aokehu strategy.
>
> The Aokehu strategy can apply irrespective of what party you are in – if you call on them to help you. That's what we've always talked about on the marae – that she adopted that strategy for us. Uncle Archie, Uncle Tahu – they would say, 'Tūtaeporoporo; Tū Ariki; Tama-Āhua; Aokehu', and that's all they would need to say in their kōrero, and the people would say, 'ah yes'.
>
> The metaphor that has been placed on Aunty, that she adopted the Aokehu strategy, for us is huge. It's huge because Tūtaeporoporo was a Ngāti Apa taniwha. Tū Ariki is an ancestor from Ngāti Apa.[12] We see him now as the central pole: the tupuna inside the whare at Aunty's marae, Rangitāhuahua.
>
> Tūtaeporoporo, a shark, was the cherished pet of Tū Ariki. Tū Ariki had travelled down to Nelson to find a pet shark, and he reared that shark along the Rangitīkei and inside some of the lakes. One day, Tū Ariki had not been seen for some time, and Tūtaeporoporo went looking for him. He smelt the scent of his master and he knew that he had been killed. He started to follow that scent; got to the Whanganui River, and the scent was there. Tū Ariki had been killed by Whanganui; Tama Āhua's clan. Tūtaeporoporo's fury was so intense that he retreated to the Whanganui River, to avenge the death of his master.

The people of Whanganui started to be killed by Tūtaeporoporo. Tūtaeporoporo went right up as far as Pīpīriki; this was a big shark. He killed all the people along the river, swallowing whole waka and devouring their contents. The river relations ended up going to Ngā Rauru to ask for the help of Aokehu, who was a famous dragon slayer. Aokehu hid, concealing himself in a log. He smeared it with rotten stuff, dead fish, and before long, Tūtaeporoporo, the taniwha, swallowed the log. Aokehu then drew on the strength of his two māripi (knives), one with the name of Tai Timu, the other named Tai Paroa. With these two knives, Aokehu started to cut away at Tūtaeporoporo from within the stomach, and was eventually able to kill Tūtaeporoporo. Peace was restored to the people of the river.

Aunty adopted the Aokehu strategy. It is a strategy that is sourced from Aunty's whakapapa – Whanganui/Ngāti Apa/Ngā Rauru. But more importantly, Aokehu is at the top of the house at Pūtiki. On the pole at Pūtiki at the front of the wharepuni: the scaled taniwha – that's Tūtaeporoporo. The taniwha comes up into Aokehu's mouth. Aunty would have seen Aokehu every day when raised at Pūtiki.

That strategy is about going into the taniwha and confronting the taniwha from within. Going in the inside to represent an interest for us. Doing what has to be done when it's not always easy; when it's sometimes easier to get the popularity vote. All those old girls knew about Aokehu – Nanny Maudie, and the others. They knew she had a certain job to do, and that was Aokehu.

Aunty did an invocation on her first day. She spoke straight after her cousin Rana Waitai. He talked about his connections, and then Aunty stood up and she invoked Nanny Iriaka to give her the courage to be in that place.

And so, I was in. The day after the election, I'd organised a hui at Pūtiki to talk through some strategic work we were doing, looking at our future as an iwi and trying to develop a set of policies that would clearly demonstrate our own authority when we were working with the Government on any issue. I still had it in the diary. I rang them up and tried to get out of it; I tried to cancel the hui. They said no, I had to come back. I couldn't cancel the hui: 'everybody's already coming; you're to come'.

I went round to just sit a while with Uncle Frosty, with Kawana and Wilson, just to share the moment. Uncle Frosty was very proud.

I arrived at Pūtiki, and I hadn't told any of them that I'd got in, and I was hoping that none of them had watched the TV in the night.

When I got to the door I looked in there and I wept. I saw all the faces of all these kuia whom I had known all my life: I had grown up at their feet. Kuia who had taught me everything that I knew about working at the marae, working in the dining room, working out the back. Who had growled me, told on me when they saw me up town when I shouldn't have been. I was fifty-two, and I had known them all of my life. Everything I knew and understood – they had passed down to me. And they cried.

Our people saw it as the hunga wairua at work, believing more than anything that I was meant to go; I was meant to be there. It was the most incredible feeling, I can tell you.

They told me that from the time I was born I was prepared for this work. I didn't really want to go into Parliament, but our old people at home, when they knew I'd been approached by Helen Clark, said, 'no, you've got to do it'.

It blew me away. 'Oh no', they said, 'it didn't just happen'. I never ever saw it as about me – I saw it as about all of these people who had in their own way contributed to who I was. I realised probably more vividly than ever before how much each of them had contributed to shaping the person that I was.

They cried for Aunty Wai. They said, 'she would be so proud of you'. And I knew she would be. The challenge would be to live up to her expectations.

Starting as I mean to go on: entering Parliament

I entered Parliament as I intended to go on, respecting the traditions and the people of that place, but not feeling any particular need to be constrained over what I should say, or how I might say it. That was another thing that Aunty Wai used to say: 'Always start as you mean to go on'. Don't try to be someone that you're not. Don't take somebody else's vision. I had to set the tone for the way I was going to be, because I didn't want them to think that I was going to be something that I'm not. I wasn't going to give Jonathan Hunt licence to sanitise what I might say. I said, 'no, Jonathan, I won't be giving it to you, because it's what I want to say. It may not be what you want me to say'.

In many Westminster systems there is a convention that maiden speeches will include a tribute to previous incumbents in the seat, and be relatively uncontroversial. In the Labour Party at the time Tariana entered, there was also a convention that new members would have their maiden addresses vetted by Jonathan Hunt. Jonathan was New Zealand's longest-serving politician, having served for thirty-nine years. His unofficial title was 'Father of the House'.

On 26 February 1997, Tariana Turia delivered her maiden speech.

TARIANA TURIA (NZ Labour):

Te wehi ki tō tātou Atua. Koia te tīmatanga me te w'akaotinga o ngā mea katoa. E ngā reo, e ngā mana, e ngā mātāwaka nō ngā tōpito e w'a o te motu, e aku rangatira, e kui mā, e koro ma, tenā koutou, tenā koutou, tenā koutou katoa. E rere kau mai te awa nui mai i te kāhui maunga ki Tangaroa – ko au te awa, ko te awa, ko au. Ko Tariana Tūria toku ingoa. Nō w'angaihū ahau. Ko Ngāti Apa, ko W'anganui, Ngā Rāuru, Tūw'aretoa oku iwi –tenā koutou, tenā koutou, tenā koutou katoa.

[Subsequent authorised translation: Awe to our God – He is indeed the beginning and ending of all things. To the voices, authorities, and ethnic groups of the four extremities of the land, to my chiefs, to the elderly women and menfolk, greetings to you, greetings to you, greetings to you all. The great river flows without hindrance from the mountain (Ruapehu) to Tangaroa (god of the sea), to the sea; I am the river and the river is me. My name is Tariana Tūria. I am from W'angaihū, my people are Ngāti Apa, W'anganui, Ngā Rāuru, and Tūwharetoa – greetings to you, greetings to you, and greetings to you all.]

I acknowledge the honourable Mr Speaker and the members of the House. I also take this opportunity to acknowledge those Māori members from the different tribal peoples who have served our people over many years in very difficult circumstances. In particular I pay special tribute to Tokouru and Matiu Ratana, both of Ngati Apa iwi, and Iriaka Ratana of Whanganui, Te Ati Haunui A Paparangi descent, with all of whom I share a common ancestry. I also pay tribute to the Honourables Whetu Tirikatene-Sullivan, Ta Pita Tapsell, Koro Wetere, and Matiu Rata, all of whom made major contributions to our people.

I come from a long line of Māori political activists who, despite their efforts, died without ever seeing their vision come to fruition. My grandfather, Hamiora Uru Te Angina, my adopted father, Tariuha Manawaroa Te AweAwe, my mother's two sisters, Ripeka and Mihiterina, all travelled with Tahupotiki Wiremu Ratana to England on two occasions to have the treaty ratified. They were both snubbed and ignored by the Crown, on the advice of the New Zealand Government of the day. As mokopuna of these tupuna we continue to feel those same rebuffs and humiliations.

The Declaration of Independence is an international declaration that recognises the sovereignty of the independent tribes of Aotearoa. It was the forerunner to the Treaty of Waitangi, and it has a flag to symbolise tribal rights to trade as independent nations, which has been ignored for years by successive New Zealand Governments and never been acknowledged as an important part of our history by the education system.

The Treaty of Waitangi was a declaration of traditional Māori rights of absolute authority over Aotearoa, reaffirming the conditions set out in the Declaration of Independence. The treaty document is a statement of this concession and forms the fundamental constitutional basis of our nation. It is the document that cements our relationships by guaranteeing tauiwi rights to be in this country and to have governance over yourselves, and acknowledges tangata whenua rights to our rangatiratanga as independent tribal peoples. The Hon. Doug Graham, Minister of Treaty of Waitangi Negotiations, in 1995 made statements regarding Māori perception of the treaty and their right to sovereignty. He concluded by saying that: 'None of these arguments have any validity. The simple fact is that the British Crown's assumption of sovereignty, assisted certainly in part by the treaty, unquestionably succeeded, and it has as a matter of international law, lasted. In other words, what is, is.'

A revolution in New Zealand has occurred, and as Professor Brookfield in his recent valedictory lecture says: 'Revolution rests upon what is done, not what is legal or necessarily moral or just.' It is this statement that attempts to justify the illegal, immoral, and unjust establishment of governance in this country. It highlights the need for us to be forever vigilant in our efforts to seek redress and reaffirm our rangatiratanga. The fact that some claims have been met, albeit only partially, does not take away the immorality and injustice of the stealing of our lands. Nor does it take away the subsequent effects of the loss of our lands, language, culture, and spiritual base, which are highlighted in the negative statistics and which are an indication of how successive Government policies have failed to address the needs and aspirations of tangata whenua.

What has been delivered to us? One hundred and fifty years-plus of struggling to have the treaty recognised in law; that we have survived despite cultural extermination practices; assimilation of policies; monocultural institutions; treacherous land-stealing laws; tauiwi bureaucracies that have run our affairs; denial of our tangata whenua status; and, struggling to maintain cultural identity, integrity, tikanga, and to keep our language alive.

Every tribe is a sovereign people in its own right. Two years ago the hapū of Whanganui celebrated their Whanganuitanga at Pakaitore. It was a time to retell of our struggle, and to have our river and lands returned to us. Whanganui have made many attempts to be heard in the courts. Their claim has been heard in the Māori Land Court, the Māori Appellate Court, the Supreme Court, the royal commission, the Court of Appeal, the Planning Tribunal, and, more recently, the Waitangi Tribunal – 120 unsuccessful years: the longest litigation in the history of this country. Yet the Mayor and council of Whanganui, politicians, and the community at large continually ask why Whanganui iwi refuse to go through the right channels.

The issue was never one for the courts but was constitutional, which the Crown failed to recognise and acknowledge. Even today the mayor and his council continue to use the usual arguments of mandate and establishing legal consultation processes spelt out through the Resource Management Act, for example, to cover themselves with legal protection and authority, and to give them the power to act against certain individuals. This same council reviewed by-laws in 1996 to ensure that if the iwi went to Pakaitore this year to celebrate again their Whanganuitanga, that the council could invoke the law against us.

We celebrate our Whanganuitanga, our Ngāti Apatanga, our Ngā Raurutanga, and our Tūwharetoatanga daily, and we will mark iwi occasions when we want to. We are talking past each other. We are being listened to and not heard. The iwi is so powerless that we are forced to take a position that will surely lead us into conflict. The issue has become one of power and control, with all the power in the hands of tauiwi. Jailing us will not prevent our celebration, and the issues of our rangatiratanga will not go away. We are stripping ourselves of the shackles of colonisation. The process of decolonisation has already begun. Following three major hui at Hirangi, attended by more than 3,000 people, it was agreed that it is necessary to establish a constitutional framework based on the tikanga and tino rangatiratanga of our tupuna. The programme of decolonisation education was seen as a necessary step in the process of establishing proper constitutional arrangements.

It is timely to talk about the media and the power of this institution. The media of Aotearoa favour the interests of the dominant culture. It should be the voice of the people, not the voice of the State and its powerful friends. Our situation is different from that of tauiwi because it is often through the media that thought control is exercised. We know this because we experience the backlash from negative media all of the time. The average New Zealander continues to be influenced by the negative stories and images provided to them by mainstream media, and then act against our interests and hinder our progress and development.

The ATN [Aotearoa Television Network] saga is a classic example of how Māori are punished over the actions of one or two people. While it was agreed that all the outputs had been reached, the funding was still stopped, not in the interests of Māori staff, or ensuring the restoration of the language, or the positive programmes that would have been culturally affirming, but purely in the interests of politics. How long will we have to wait now for a Māori television company to be re-established?

Ki a koutou ngā mema Māori, kei te rerekē te wairua i roto i tēnei Whare, kāore te wairua pai. [Subsequent authorised translation: To you the Māori members – the spirit within this House is different; it is not good.

In the words of Professor Timoti Karetu, Māori Language Commissioner: 'It would be less of a victory if we emerged from the current renaissance with an economic base but no living language'. We are brainwashed into believing that our language has very limited value in everyday life and is appropriate for ceremonial occasions only. The late Sir Robert Muldoon stated: 'Maori language was not a language of diplomacy, international business or modern technology'. Only in Aotearoa is Māori the language of the land. Let Māori language flourish in all its beauty, values, and meanings, because it is the language that holds the key to the culture.

Our spirituality, our wairuatanga, is that which provides the balance, the wellness, and the wholeness to our existence as a people. We are the ones who are forced to live in two worlds. Many of us are not suitably equipped to live in either. People are shocked and surprised when we become schizophrenic and overcrowd psychiatric institutions. It is our young people who are forced to seek support together, often in frustrated violence, because of their deep sense of powerlessness. It is our young who are dying, believing that there is no future for them. Being young, Māori, and unemployed is a high occupational hazard.

For every negotiation we enter into we have to doubly justify ourselves, perform twice as well as other providers, and open our books to minute scrutiny. Everything we do must turn to magic the first time around. There is never a second chance for us. Negotiations for change normally take place on tauiwi terms. We have been conditioned into thinking that our efforts are inferior and that we need expert assistance, usually tauiwi. We are drip-fed, spoon-fed, and acted upon like imbeciles. We are under siege from all sides: from the colonised within our own culture, and from tauiwi as well. Our people are saying that enough is enough. How many of us need to die, to go mad, to underachieve, to go to jail, to be unemployed, for people to say enough is enough? We cannot do any worse than what has already been done. It is our right and our responsibility to take control of our own affairs. Only we can truly restore our dignity and integrity. We know the problem, then let us be our own solution.

The challenge for us is to believe that we have the legitimate right to do what is consistent with our tikanga, and then find the appropriate ways to do it. These ways will differ from hapū to hapu, from iwi to iwi. One iwi Māori never sought the legitimacy from another iwi Māori in order to pursue its own rangatiratanga, so why should we believe that we have to seek legitimacy from tauiwi? We have to believe in our own right to do whatever we need to do. The barrier that we constantly have in front of us is the tauiwi telling us that we cannot do this and that. They have created the structures for us to fit into. We must exercise that legitimacy that we never gave up. There is a desperate need for us to get this relationship right. No nations that are divided against themselves can stand. At every turn, Māori people are being asked to divide their loyalties upon party lines, church lines, and class lines. What is needed is not the same worn out, stereotyped, political patronage that keeps Māori locked into dependency but a new system based firmly on tino rangatiratanga, guaranteed in the Treaty of Waitangi.

I want to affirm my support and acknowledge the role of all those people who have been at the forefront of the Māori struggle towards self-determination. Without their actions, the consciousness of the people at large would never have been jolted and the Crown would never have addressed the grievances, even in the limited way that they have been addressed. To those of us of iwi descent in Parliament, it is my belief that it is our collective responsibility to advance the needs and aspirations of our people and this should transcend any party political affiliation. We need the understanding and support of our colleagues to do this.

Finally, I pay tribute to my tupuna, my kuia, koroheke, whānau, and friends who, I know, stand here alongside me today and who will stand with me during the period that I am here. Without their love and support I would not be standing here today. Nō reira; tēnā koutou; tēnā koutou; tēnā koutou katoa.

―――――――――

They say that if you put a frog into a pot of boiling water, it will leap out straight away to escape the danger. But if you put a frog in a pan that is filled with water that is nice and cool, and then you gradually heat the kettle until it reaches boiling point, the frog won't become aware of the threat until it is too late. The frog's survival instincts are geared towards detecting sudden changes.

Years later when Hone Harawira entered the House, he used my speech as a template about how to retain his voice in his own maiden address.

Hone Harawira says:

> I remember thinking, 'what am I going to do?' I went back and I got Matiu's; I got Winston's and I got Tari's. The thing I remember about Tari's maiden speech – because she had been stalked by Helen Clark pretty much to come in – was that she didn't even mention the Labour Party. I thought, 'oh shit'. So I read it again. It said actually a lot more about Tari than it did about Labour. It said about all the things that she wanted to be.

I never talked about Labour, even when I'd go out on the road. I used to say to them when they were telling me what I should be saying, 'if all those things rang true, you wouldn't need to talk about them'. Do the right thing and you don't need to talk about it – that's what Aunty Wai used to say. If you're right, you don't need to tell everybody.

I had started my maiden address by summonsing up the courage to stand from those who had walked this path before me. Che described it as an invocation: calling on the strengths of those who had passed before me for guidance and support. Their example stood before me in reminding me of the greater gain, serving the aspirations of our people.

When I entered Parliament in 1996, there were sixteen Māori out of 120 MPs: 13 percent of the House. There was the tight five in the Māori electorate seats. We had two Māori MPs in general seats (Jill Pettis in Whanganui and Winston Peters in Tauranga). The rest of us occupied list seats. In Labour there was me, Dover Samuels, Nanaia Mahuta and Joe Hawke. Donna Awatere-Huata took up an ACT seat. And there was Ron Mark (New Zealand First), Georgina te Heuheu (National), and Sandra Lee and Alamein Kopu (Alliance).

It was a vastly different world to the one that my aunt inherited when she first took up the call to serve. I often wondered how that must have been for my Aunt Iriaka and what support she felt during the long hours away from home, away from her children and the farm. One of my dearest friends, Tapihana (Dobbie) Shelford, would frequently draw comparisons between me and Aunt Iriaka. Dobbie was an astute politician; his family's association with politics over many generations gave him a unique perspective that I found invaluable. He was fascinated at the connections we had as Morehu and as MPs for Western Māori/Te Tai Hauāuru and ultimately in terms of our decisions to cross the floor in pursuit of better outcomes for our whānau, hapū and iwi.

Of all the sacrifices that Aunt Iriaka made over two decades of service, it was in her decision to cross the floor to advance the aspirations of her people of Rātana pā that I found most to admire. During the 1950s, Iriaka worked with Ernest Corbett, a National Minister of Māori Affairs, to utilise the resources of the Department of Māori Affairs to build many of the houses that now comprise the village of Rātana. I later wrote about the impact of that action:

> One of my mentors in politics is my aunt Iriaka Ratana, who courageously brought people together from across the House to provide housing at Ratana Pa. Her motivation was clear. In the 1950s the pā had no sewerage, no water reticulation, tuberculosis and other diseases were rife, but no-one was doing anything about it other than to criticise. Iriaka invited the Prime Minister to Ratana to see the conditions himself and eventually a housing programme, road development and other benefits were achieved. She was a trail-blazer and a huge motivation point for me in making practical action happen at the local level.[13]

As well as my two uncles and my aunt, I also made reference in my maiden address to four other predecessors who had taken up parliamentary office. I acknowledged firstly Whetu Tirikatene-Sullivan, who was a mentor in so many respects. Both my Aunt Iriaka and Whetu were pioneers for wāhine Māori in politics and in public service. Both of them came at a time when there were mostly males in Parliament, and yet they combined motherhood with long political careers while they were there. I learnt from them the importance of hard work ethics, loyalty to the people and the responsibilities of public office.

Like my aunt before her, Whetu paved the way for women to combine a full working life with parenting, from as early as 1970. She returned to the House two weeks after her baby's birth and looked after her child in her office. She also earned a reputation as the longest-serving woman in New Zealand's Parliament. From 1967 through to 1996, the year that I entered Parliament, she represented an electorate that covered three-quarters of the country.

I paid tribute to two other members of the 1996 Parliament, Koro Tainui Wetere and Pita Tapsell. Hon Koro Wetere gave nine terms of parliamentary service to the constituency of Western Māori on behalf of Labour. Sir Pita Tapsell had also stood for Labour, as MP for Eastern Māori. I remember being told by ministerial drivers that Sir Peter used to pick up Māori hitch-hikers and take them home for a meal and a bed for the night. I liked that. I thought this showed his interest in young people and his empathy for their situation.

The final member I paid homage to was my mentor and friend, Hon Matiu Rata. A man of principle, of dedication, of belief in doing what was right. My son Pahia shared a story with me that expressed the power of Matiu's political legacy; a story that illustrated his determination to find a way.

> This lawyer told me a story about going to see him in 1975 about the Waitangi Act and Matiu said to him 'this is an atrocity, you can't allow this to happen', because they were saying that any grievance pre-1975 couldn't be claimed. Matiu said, 'I want you to look through every piece of legislation; we need to find a way through this'. He walked back into the office three weeks later and he said, 'so what have you found?' The lawyer said, 'look, I've searched every piece of legislation; I've looked at every nook and cranny, there's nothing we can do'. Matiu Rata smashed his hand on his desk and he said 'you find a way!' That was powerful. I thought to myself, 'sometimes we are faced with different challenges and stuff but what's important is that we find a way.'
>
> That's what I've admired about Mum – it is that absolute drive – 'don't tell me we can't; tell me how we can, and find a way that we can do that'. I think that's what's inspired people as well. Mum oozes love, she oozes passion, she oozes compassion, and people have gravitated towards that because they sense the genuineness of her commitment to that. I think that when you come into a place like this, it beats the black out of you – you know the story about the frogs?

I like what Pahia said. The frog's story is a reminder that sometimes we can get ourselves into terrible trouble if we sit, noho puku, just watching the world go by without being alert to any danger that may occur just around the corner.

If there was one thing I was determined to do, as I began my parliamentary career, it was to never allow complacency to creep into my life, to distract me from the issues our people faced every day. I owed it to those who had put me there, and those who had been before me, to make sure I could be the very best servant for the people that I could be.

NOTES

1 N. Shepheard, 'Fierce Kuia: profile of New Zealand Member of Parliament Tariana Turia', *North and South*, February 2004, p. 59.

2 Tariana Turia, speech to Māori Law Students Association; Canterbury University, Christchurch, 29 September 2010.

3 Ibid.

4 'He maumaharatanga ki a Tuaiwa', p. 96.

5 Te Puku o te Whenua, literally 'the belly of the land', was one of five new electorates created in 1996.

6 Tuaiwa Hautai Kereopa Rickard, 1925–1997, 'Nga Puna Roimata', 1998, p. 100.

7 Helen Bain, 'Tariana's will', *Dominion*, 14 June 1997, Edition 2, p. 18.

8 'Tariana Turia hits out at Labour', *New Zealand Herald*, 20 April 2014.

9 *Mana* no. 14, Summer 1996/1997, p. 36.

10 Tau Henare (Te Tai Tokerau) was joined by Rana Waitai (Te Puku o te Whenua), Tukuroirangi Morgan (Te Tai Hauāuru), Tuariki Delamere (Te Tai Rāwhiti) and former All Black and first five-eighth, Tutekawa Wyllie (Te Tai Tonga).

11 Sir Eruera Tirikatene, the first Rātana Member of Parliament, was elected in 1932 and stood for Southern Māori until 1967, at which time his daughter Whetu succeeded him in the seat, which she held until 1996.

12 Tū Ariki was a direct descendant of Ruatea, who captained the Kurahaupō waka from Hawaiki. From Ruatea came Apa-tika; from Apa-tika came Apa-Hapai-taketake, Tupuahoronuku, Tawhito and Tū Ariki.

13 Tariana Turia, Beehive Chat, 3 September 2013.

-CHAPTER FOURTEEN-
THE REALITIES OF PARLIAMENT

For every negotiation we enter into we have to doubly justify ourselves, perform twice as well as other providers, and open our books to minute scrutiny. Everything we do must turn to magic the first time around. There is never a second chance for us.[1]

From the moment I took up my pew in the chamber, I knew I had to get it right first time round. I've stuck with things that people have talked about to me for years. I wanted to do the best for our people and make them proud.

Right from the start I found it really difficult to fit in. There were a few Labour MPs who I really liked and continue to like. I did feel, however, overall that philosophically we were probably poles apart. I never felt that I fitted. I was a bit of a round peg in a square hole, or a square peg in a round hole. I always had really strong views about things. You had to pledge allegiance to the party, but my first allegiance was always to our people.

Looking back I think I was probably typecast from the beginning as being one of Helen's chosen ones.

In this respect, former Labour MP Tim Barnett says:

> She was someone that Helen identified and had decided to promote, and there were a number of people like that: some succeeded and some didn't. They were always interesting souls: Georgina Beyer was one of them; I think Parekura was one of them; J. T. [John Tamihere] was one of them. Helen had amazing networks. Helen had identified people who would enrich the caucus. There were a number of people clearly there because Helen thought they added something to the caucus. And I think, probably a little bit like myself, she [Tariana] came from an NGO background; she was probably a bit of an outsider to the kind of mainstream of politics.

I remember my first Labour conference, and Maryan Street and Carol Gosche[2] were so good to me and made me feel welcome when no one else really did. I was always on the fringe. I have always been a bit direct and outspoken, and meant that I didn't always find favour or friends, either in the Māori caucus or the wider caucus.

I never drank or went out with them socially. I think it made me seem like I was not a team player. I remember Rick Barker saying to me that I was too intense and too serious about things; I needed to be a bit like a butterfly. And I remember saying to him, 'Well, I expect this place to be a really serious place because of the issues that are confronting our people, so I don't make any apology for taking it all so seriously'.

Jonathan Hunt was great. He was like a wise old owl, always giving me advice. I had no friends there. I thought I did. I had known Paul Swain from my days with the Employment Network with Robert Reid and all the others. When I first saw him I said, 'hi Paul', and he said, 'oh hello' and just walked past me. For the first ten days he never came near me, and I was gutted. And I thought, 'is this what it's going to be like?' I couldn't believe it.

And then right after I got in he comes to my office. He came and said, 'Tariana, let's have a cup of coffee'. His office was right next door. Then he started lobbying me; it was at the time they were choosing the whips. I felt so sad then. I thought, 'he doesn't really care about me at all'.

I had been there about eight months when Paul Swain asked me the question, 'where did my loyalty lie?' At that stage I was on the list, and when you're on the list you have to follow the party line. My answer to him was, 'Don't ever test it, because I think you know the answer to the question. The Party asked me to come to Parliament to be with them; I did not approach them.'

The other funny thing was they had put me in this little wee cubbyhole of an office, which didn't worry me because I'd hardly even had an office at home where I worked. It was in the old building on the ground level of Parliament House: a very little room at the end. I didn't care, but they kept on coming in and saying, 'we're going to move you'. Eventually they put me into this big office that was Richard Northey's, and Taito Phillip Field comes down the passage and says, 'look, sorry, I want that office; is that ok?' And I went, 'no, not really'. And he goes, 'but I've been here longer, and that's how it works'. And I said, 'yes, but I'm tangata whenua'. He didn't know what to say! I said, 'look, I'm only joking'; I was only having him on.

It was incredible the whole way the place worked. The House just floored me – how they treated one another. I couldn't believe the way they talked to each other; the racism was horrific.

I developed a really good relationship with Helen Clark. I found that I could really talk to her honestly, and I respected her leadership. I always felt that she genuinely wanted what was best for us as a people. I think she had huge trust in me, and I did in her too.

Tariana said in an interview in 2004:

> I've always found Helen really respectful and she works really hard to understand the issues. I've got huge regard for her. We don't always

> agree, but I think that's ok. I know in the end she's got a constituency which is the whole country that she has to serve, and my constituency is our people.[3]

But I always used to think to myself, 'how could people do things and say things that they didn't believe in?' I never did. I never felt she expected me to, but others would. Others in the caucus used to get pissed off with me.

I was in caucus one day and something came up. It's funny: you're never allowed to contradict the leader; well, in Labour you're not. Helen said something, and I said, 'I don't agree with that'. Nanaia was sitting next to me, and she got up and moved. And then Jill Pettis, something came up about the river, and I said something, and so she had a big go at me. Jill came up to me afterwards and she said, 'God, you're embarrassing'. And I said, 'but I don't agree with her'. I totally accept people not knowing, but I will never accept when you don't know, and yet you talk against.

I realised really early on in the piece that I was on my own, and I thought, 'the only thing that will get me through are the things that I hold fast to; the things that I know are important for our people'. And that's all I've ever done in there; stick with that – I haven't tried to be Einstein.

If there was one person whom I got along with in those early years, it was Tim Barnett.

Tim says:

> We got to know each other really well when we shared the same corridor in Parliament in the area that Labour is in now; the opposition area. There was a real sense of hierarchy of people, and there were factions. Generally the more progressive MPs and then the less progressive – and she and I were part of the more progressive bunch. I can't remember an epiphany when we first met, but we just sort of gravitated towards each other as people who came from that community activism background and were on a bit of a journey. I was an electorate MP; she was a list MP. I was urban; she was from a provincial centre.
>
> She was about five offices along from me. Tari has always been at home with people of differing sexualities in a very natural way – not many people manage that without any effort at all. We formed a

bond – that meant we would have meals together and share things together. She got into trouble a lot more than I did with the whips. I remember this one day I heard they were clearly mentioning her name, and they were off to see her. I think it was about leave – that would be what the conflicts were about – and not understanding the kind of cultural imperatives. They came back within about ten minutes looking very pissed off – Mark Burton and Rick Barker – two big men – and two minutes later Tari is in my office complaining about them. There was a lot of conflict around cultural matters.

Tim was very good to me. I'd put things up to the caucus, and I could never get them through. And then he came and offered to help me with the papers so I could get buy-in. It was really amazing – just by rewording them in a particular way. He was great. It's actually what drew me closer to him. He was pretty clear about the need for me to get my message across.

Tim explains:

> People didn't get her – a lot of caucus members never really got her – they were frustrated by her. Labour colleagues accepted that I had a different view towards her than many of them. It was a friendship; a political friendship across divides.

One time Tim invited me down to his electorate, to provide me with a chance to practise talking to a group that would not usually be part of my network.

Tim says of the occasion:

> She spoke to some of our older members about the two-house model[4] or her world view, and there was a bunch of older Pākehā, a lot of them migrants from a Labour background in Britain, who were part of the older part of my electorate organisation. For that moment they were completely supportive of her, because they understood. She didn't often open herself to different parts of the Party – I guess it was true of both sides.

If, with the help of Tim, Labour's caucus was beginning to listen to Tariana, she was under no illusion about how ready the rest of the country were to respond to her views. Less than four months after her maiden address, Anthony Hubbard reported in the *Sunday Star-Times* on the range of ideas that Tariana had expressed in her first days as an MP:

> Her tauiwi speech brought an extraordinary outpouring of nastiness against her: Hate mail, death threats, the lot. But then she just piled fuel on the fire. She said the Treaty was more important than the Ten Commandments; fellow MP Mike Moore's stand on race issues was 'evil'; she refused to condemn the activist who smashed the America's Cup; she said all the stolen Maori land should be given back though it will cost billions and billions and billions. She does not agree with the Crown's insistence that privately owned land be left out of any Treaty settlements. If private land is found to have been stolen she says, the Crown should buy it back and then pass it on to its rightful Maori owners.[5]

The America's Cup issue seemed to cause particular distress for some. On 14 March 1997 a young Māori man, Benjamin Nathan, attacked the America's Cup with a sledgehammer, denting the cup. He received a three-year jail sentence as a result. He took responsibility for the action on behalf of the Tino Rangatiratanga Liberation Organisation, stating the motive was to establish an independent Māori state. When asked her opinion, Tariana said that it would have been hypocritical of her to speak out against Nathan when her own son had served three months in jail for an action that had also been politically motivated. She told the press, 'I don't condone the smashing of anything but I can't speak against him'. Tariana's view was that we should listen to the messages from our young people, rather than dismissing them as defiant.

The *Dominion* reported:

> She said she would be keen to organise a hui to hear the different concerns and to take the ideas back to Parliament. 'Those of us in Parliament should be looking at our response to what is happening. Not focusing on one particular action, but looking at the future of these young people'.[6]

I honestly believe that we should never be afraid to talk about anything that we know to be true. I used to look around when I was in the debating chamber and think, 'who have we got to fear in here?' Nobody. No one here is above anybody else who is not here. Better to stick with what you know than to pretend any different.

Tariana maintained this view throughout her political career. In 2004, Tariana stated:

> I'd like to think politics is about people wanting to act in the interests of others and I don't feel it is: politics is about politicking. Someone will stand up and make a passionate speech about an issue and then the research library will come up with a speech the same person made five years before that said the opposite. That's why I think it's better to say what you really mean.[7]

There is one thing that I have never been afraid of. I've never looked at people and thought they were better than me. I would come out of the Labour caucus room and the media would be there and I would be terrified. It just scared me to death. The questions would be coming at me, and I had had no experience or training on any of that. But I've never been afraid to say what I think: not before I came into Parliament or at any time over the last eighteen years. My only concern has been how it impacts on my whānau.

The *Dominion* commented in 1997:

> Her outspokenness has prompted a stream of death threats. She fears for her children and grandchildren, but refuses to be frightened for herself. 'If people are weak enough to write letters like that without signing them, well, I'm not easily intimidated. There are risks, but the risks we face as a people are far greater than those I face personally'.[8]

In regard to the 'outspokenness', the *Evening Post* revealed that Labour had set up a committee, 'rather than allow a corrosive public slanging match to continue between Mike Moore and Tariana Turia'. The committee was to be 'a forum for debate, with ideas then heading back to leadership and caucus'. A programme of talks to the Labour caucus on the Treaty and other constitutional questions was also arranged. Activists Annette Sykes and Mike Smith were even rumoured to be on the speaker list. MP Jim Sutton would convene the committee, the purpose of which, most media were reporting, was more about damage control. There were also some who said it was a means of placating 'the catalyst of Tariana Turia'.

Sarah Boyd's article in the *Evening Post* on the subject stated:

> Quietly spoken but articulate and determined, she represents a brand of Maori radicalism not seen within the Labour caucus before. Moore said she could become the Pauline Hanson of New Zealand in dividing people. She labelled his approach to customary fishing rights 'evil' before Labour leader Helen Clark stepped in to dampen down the public row.[9]

Yet Tariana, when the paper asked her, was optimistic about the collective will of the caucus to take on new ideas:

> We're seeing a caucus that's trying to grapple with these things and starting to put in place a process as to how in fact they can be educated or inform themselves about the issues. If everyone is well-informed they can still have diverse views but not in conflict.

During her first term of Parliament, then, in many respects Tariana Turia laid down her own political agenda: issues that she believed the nation should debate. Just as the seventy-nine nights at Pākaitore had enabled the iwi to set an agenda, there was any number of contentious topics that could stir her to take a stand.

There was the vexed issue of Māori unemployment, which by 1997 had risen to 'an outrageous 16.6%'. In a press release of 5 August, Tariana stated:

> Government policy or lack of Government policy to not specifically deal with the needs of the Māori community is taking its toll and the fallout is becoming blatantly clear. Māori people want real work with real wages. They are absolutely sick of being on-the-training go round. Much of this training is absolutely irrelevant to the job market and worse still does not meet iwi development plans.[10]

Three days later, the Minister of Māori Affairs, Hon Tau Henare, and his newly established Māori Development Commissions became the target of Tariana's attack:

> Accountability and transparency is extremely important in a process such as this, the process the Minister chose to adopt was inappropriate and arrogant. This has created yet another layer that blocks iwi access to the Crown, a right guaranteed in the Treaty of Waitangi.[11]

She went on to describe Vote Māori Affairs as being 'distorted by creative book-keeping', inflating the Vote and twisting the true picture:

The money would be better spent if it was used for the delivery of programmes that actually reached the grassroots people, instead of being swallowed by yet another talkshop.[12]

A month later, that same theme was addressed in a House debate on Vote Māori Affairs. There, Tariana said:

> We see the launching of four Māori development commissions, another group of talkshop people who will sit around and then go out and talk to our people and find out what their problems are, even though we have known for thirty odd years, or probably 157 years, what our real problem is. At the end of the day it is our loss of self-determination … We have a right to be self-determining and we need a budget that will assist us to do that.[13]

The kōrero was nothing new. It was the same kōrero that had featured at the Hui Taumata in 1984; the same kōrero that Tariana had given at Hīrangi; the same kōrero laid down at Pākaitore. For Sister Makareta back at home, hearing these debates validated Tariana's decision to go into politics despite her initial reservations:

> It was contrary to everything we had been saying and practising at Pākaitore; we didn't recognise the court, the City Council and therefore Parliament. Having said that though, I knew that Tari would make her presence felt wherever she was, and she certainly has done that. Her kōrero is no different to what she has always said: Māori in control of their own

affairs … Māori self-determination, Te Tiriti. She is as vocal within the
system about the things that impact on our people as she was outside of it.

In the allocation of portfolios among the Labour caucus, Tariana had been given responsibility for youth affairs, for health and for social services; all areas that saw her standing for slots in debate to bring out the issues.

She asked the Minister of Education, Hon Wyatt Creech, whether he was 'satisfied with the system for the allocation of grades in sixth form certificate?' following this with a supplementary question as to whether students who performed well in School Certificate Māori had those grades discounted, and if so, whether he would 'subject that practice to a cultural audit to ascertain the reasons'.

The question stemmed from the controversial practice of scaling down marks earned in te reo Māori examinations. For the first time, Māori students were seen to be succeeding in higher numbers than ever before; a situation that the education bureaucracy was failing to register.

In regard to this issue, in a paper presented to the 'Now is the Future' conference held by the George Parkyn Centre Charitable Trust for Gifted Education in 2000, researcher Jill Bevan-Brown reported:

> One mother tells the story of her son's marks in Bursary Māori being scaled down from 94 to 67. This mother is a well-educated, assertive Māori woman who challenged the system on her son's behalf. She was told that the Government simply could not afford the cost of the large number of A Bursaries earned in the Māori Bursary exam. The drastic level of scaling her son's mark was required for financial reasons. The same degree of scaling was not applied to other languages such as Russian and French as the smaller number of A Bursaries earned in these subjects was economically manageable.[14]

The bureaucracy's shortcomings were a frequent theme of Tariana's speeches. Speaking to the Social Welfare Reform Bill, she asked why beneficiaries – 'the most vulnerable people in our society' – were being discriminated against:

> Is the department really that inept that it is unable to scrutinise breaches of the Human Rights Act despite the fact that it has been

in since 1993 … Is it because the department is short of staff, is it because it cannot be bothered, or is it that it has been discriminating against this particular group of people, which would probably be in line with National Government policy?[15]

The same speech raised questions about another department's failings:

It would appear that Te Puni Kōkiri has now taken the place of Maoridom, has taken the place of iwi, has taken the place of whānau and hapū, and in fact has become the main consultation process that the Crown is using. That must cause us concern.

Tariana's challenges were not only levelled at the hand of the state; she focused her attentions on many other issues that year that in her opinion called for a wider discussion. Her speech to the Adoption (Intercountry) Bill was typical of her approach:

As a country we need to debate and discuss all the issues regarding the adoption of children. Too often what we are hearing are the needs of adults who then use children to meet their adult needs … Throughout the world corporate entities, regardless of their sphere of activity, are most disrespectful of indigenous peoples and their lands. The relationship is one of exploitation. As Māori we stand alongside all other indigenous peoples and their right to have their children raised in their own country. We do not see the need to take other people's children to show our concern for them. We can and should help them where they already are.[16]

Tariana's contribution to the debate concluded by recognising:

… the uneasy feeling that taonga, which children are, could now be seen as commodities to be traded with and to be bought and sold by private enterprise organisations.

Occasionally her questions triggered a surprising consensus from the Government, as evidenced in this exchange with the Minister of Health:

TARIANA TURIA: Given the failure of mainstream mental health providers to deliver appropriate services to Māori and the fact that

> the national health strategy Looking Forward fails to commit the Government to contract with Māori providers for mental health services, what assurances can [the Minister of Health] give that the Government, without commitment or vision, will meet the needs of those Māori who are mentally ill?
>
> HON BILL ENGLISH: The member raises a very relevant point – that is the willingness of the Government to contract with Māori providers … as fast as those providers are willing and able to take up the work we will be keen to contract with them.[17]

The relationship Tariana had developed with Bill English predated her time in Parliament:

> I was a bit surprised that she joined the Labour Party, because that is not the place you go if you are looking for support for self-determination for Māori. They don't think like that about Māori. It was a fundamental difference, which more Māori understand now. So I had a little bit to do with her before Parliament, but it was mostly through admiration for that organisation that she was running.

Development of a respectful relationship with the Opposition was not something that Parliament actively encouraged. However, the concept was not new to Tariana. It was, after all, inbuilt in her whakapapa.

In 2010, Tariana told *Mana* magazine:

> I remember when Aunty Iriaka was with Labour the relationship wasn't always that rosy. For her to get houses in Ratana pā she had to go to National. Labour wouldn't do it. I remember as a kid that being talked about. It gave me an understanding when I went into politics how important it was to have alliances across the house. Of course it was frowned upon to build alliances, me being in Labour – with National. I often used to talk to Bill English who was the Minister of Health because I'd come from a health background.[18]

In her fledgling career as a politician, Tariana was warned by fellow colleagues that she should avoid relying on her own experiences to make political capital.

Discussion of mental illness and institutional violence that emerged in debate on the Mental Health Commission Bill was a good case in point.

Tariana had been appalled by the alleged mistreatment associated with the Child and Adolescent Unit at Lake Alice Hospital between 1972 and 1977. Abuse claims had included use of unmodified electroconvulsive therapy (ECT). Former patients had described the feeling as a sledge-hammer hitting the side of the head, causing them to pass out. There had been claims of ECT threatment on genitals and other body parts. Painful injections of an anti-epileptic, paraldehyde, had apparently been used for sedation, leaving patients unable to walk for hours. And there had been numerous claims of sexual abuse associated with the hospital.

As the *Sunday Star-Times* reported in 1997:

> It was [Tariana's] foster children, in fact, who got her into public politics. Some of the youngsters she took in from a local social welfare home complained they had been sent to Lake Alice Hospital for shock treatment as a punishment. Ms Turia called the press and got herself into a boiling row. The welfare home surely qualified as the kind of tauiwi institution she was later to accuse of causing damage to Maori people.[19]

Despite the warnings, Tariana was always one to pave her own way, to speak her truth, fully aware of the consequences. During the debate around the Mental Health Commission Bill, Tariana referred to her own family's experience before launching into an attack on the instigators of historic abuse within mental health institutions:

> As a tangata whenua I want to say that I have had personal experience of mental health illness. I had a brother and relatives who were mentally ill. Mental illness occurs when the balance is lost for us.[20]

Her speech referred to the institutional violence experienced in mental institutions in the 1970s, targeting the former head of the Child and Adolescent Unit of Lake Alice, Dr Leeks, who headed the unit until 1978. Complainants had wanted Dr Leeks to be charged as the one in control:

> I refer in particular to the aversion therapy practiced on children in the Lake Alice Hospital by Dr Selwyn Leeks who at present is still practising in Melbourne and the impact that therapy had on those young children who were as young as eight years old and who have continued to be mentally ill right through to today. I refer to that because two months ago one of our nephews, who was treated with this aversion therapy, committed suicide. He had spent the majority of his life in prison accessing mental health care through the justice system, as do many of the young Māori people who unfortunately have become ill over the years.[21]

Eventually the Government granted compensation to more than 180 former Lake Alice child patients. An excess of $10 million was paid out, following a report by retired High Court judge Sir Rodney Gallen, who described the behavior modification programme as a regime of terror.[22]

Tariana continued to speak about the inability of mental health services to respond to young people; particularly those impaired by drug- and alcohol-induced psychoses. What was needed was not more institutions but a Māori mental health workforce and an overhaul of mental health services, she maintained:

> I do not agree that it is necessary for people to be cared for within institutions … these people should be cared for either within their own family environment or by those best able to provide those services to them.[23]

There was very little Tariana was saying then that she would not say today. At the centre of her kōrero was a focus on cultural competency; a concept that would prove to be fundamental to her thinking when she eventually became a minister.

> When I took my mokopuna Piata to our little kōhanga reo at Whangaehu I remember reaching a certain part of the road past Rātana, and she would

point out to us Koro Ruapehu and Matua Te Maunga Taranaki, and then sing a waiata that connected her to them both. The connections she could make so simply, and yet so profoundly, to our awa, maunga and marae, the tikanga and kawa of her ancestors, was all about who she was; who we are. That confidence to be in touch with the essence of who you are – that is all that I have ever wanted for my kids. That's cultural competency.

Because of my nursing background I've always taken a huge interest in the way in which cultural safety emerged and influenced our nation. I had another special reason – Irihapeti Ramsden, an astute thinker, a philosopher, a Treaty educator and a very dear friend. During times of great pressure Irihapeti would appear out of nowhere. I would be under attack in the House and I would look up to the public gallery and there she was, quietly supporting me, her strength a source of great comfort.

I remember during the Holocaust debate[24], when the levels of hostility were at such a peak, Irihapeti came out publicly and defended me, explaining that the description of the mass annihilation of a population resonated in Aotearoa. She calmly explained that between 1846 and 1896 'over half the Māori population disappeared. That is genocide. It's a reality'.[25]

Irihapeti was able to say difficult things that needed to be said with such dignity and grace that you couldn't really take offence. I think of her still as one of our leading influences in the process of nation-building.

In a poroporoaki to Irihapeti in 2003, Tariana said:

> Irihapeti worked very hard, and very effectively, to build a nation based on inclusion. As an anthropologist, a nurse, a publisher and an educator, she strived to help people understand how their own culture impacted on others. Irihapeti was an outstanding educator on cultural issues and Treaty relationships. The cultural safety programme she helped to establish as part of nursing training is still bringing about significant changes.[26]

Irihapeti persevered with a heroic strength in completing her PhD thesis on cultural safety and nursing practice in Aotearoa. I remember all the fuss that happened when cultural safety was first made a requirement for nursing and midwifery education by the Nursing Council in 1992. The basic premise was that cultural safety training would assist nurses to be effective by encouraging them to reflect on their own cultural identity and understand the impact of differing cultures in nursing practice and patient care.

A major issue erupted in Christchurch around the cultural safety programme in 1993. Nursing student Anna Penn issued a letter to the *Press* laying a number of complaints about the teaching of cultural safety at the nursing school. All hell erupted, with papers, television and talkback salivating over the opportunity to talk about 'social engineering' and political correctness.

I remember that whole saga clearly. The media laid blame on the Polytechnic's kaumātua, the late Hohua Tutengaehe, for assessing Ms Penn as unfit to pass the culture and society component of the nursing diploma. Hohua was a very gentle, respectful man. Others in the nursing school had been angry with her, but he had met with her and treated her with dignity. Contrary to a view that cultural competency was an 'add-on' frill, I believe treating people with respect is a basic foundation of being a nurse, and as such, any student who fails to grasp the value of competency in this area is not living up to the nursing ideal.

It was perhaps as a result of all of these various experiences that when Tariana was appointed Associate Minister of Health she was determined to make cultural competency a priority. Cultural competency as a concept was also brought home to Tariana through her experience caring for her Aunty Wai when she broke her hip.

Aunty Wai was spending time in hospital, accessing care from the physiotherapists to help her get mobile. They would come into her room and they would put her food tray on the seat. So Aunty wouldn't eat her kai. I'd go up later on and the senior staff would say to me, 'she's not eating; we're worried about her'. So I asked her, 'why aren't you eating?' And she replied, 'I'm starving, but they put my kai where your kumu (bottom) goes.' Simple stuff that can have a huge impact on you.

They moved her into a room on her own, they tried hard, and then she wouldn't eat because they brought the bedpan into where she was to eat her kai. I felt quite sorry for them, but I sat them down and said, 'look, this is really difficult, but I have to tell you she's more important to me than any of you are, so I am going to say to you that there are certain things that we are going to have to ask you to not do, even if that means she has to suffer a bit more. She needs to be taken out to the toilet in a chair; that's what she wants to do. She is not to be fed in the same room as she is toileted.' It's quite amazing the impact on their hinengaro – their whole mental wellbeing – when those things happen.

A speech Tariana later gave at a conference reinforced the concept of cultural competency as a core requirement for health professionals:

> Cultural safety was publicly attacked as a form of racial privilege or Māori cultural imperialism. In reality, the programme simply pointed out that mono-cultural nursing in a multi-cultural society created risks to health. It never aimed to teach nurses about other cultures, but helped them to see that standard practice in nursing was in fact culturally defined. I am very pleased to see that aspects of this approach are being taken up by the National Health Committee. In their final report on Health Care Quality Improvement, they have identified cultural competency as an overarching theme of the quality framework. I would agree with that, provided that, for our people, their cultural needs as individuals are understood within a whānau context.[27]

A direct outcome of Tariana's advocacy for cultural competency is seen in section 118 of the Health Practitioners Competence Assurance Act 2003. That section made setting standards of clinical competence, cultural competence and ethical conduct one of the functions of health professional registration authorities. It was passed into law on 12 September 2003.

Ties that bind

Whakapuputia te kakaho e kore e whati; Binding together, we will not break.[28]

The whare karakia at Kaiwhaiki, Te Rongo o te Poi, is one of the few remaining whare that is made of kākaho. The kākaho flourishes in swampland; it is a tall, slender, reed-like plant that grows to four to six feet high. Its stems are three to six inches in diameter, and it is strong and tough. It was harvested in the summer months, picked when it was green and laid flat on the ground to dry out and harden in the sun. As a building material it was used for the interior of a whare – heke, amo, maihi – giving warmth and comfort. Individual kākaho had little usefulness but when bunches of the plant were placed sided by side, either vertically or horizontally, they made a building strong, durable and warm.

Just as the kākaho flourishes in the wetlands of the Whanganui hills, we must rebuild the right conditions and environments, lay strong foundations, so that our mokopuna can exercise the right to determine our own destiny. Our call must be to bind together, so that we will be strong in every aspect of our lives.

> When I look at the other wahine Māori in the House today – Georgina te Heuheu, Metiria Turei, Nanaia Mahuta, Jill Pettis, Moana Mackey, Georgina Beyer, Paula Bennett – I know, intuitively, that there is more that connects us, than divides us. I know too, when I think of the first Māori woman in this house, my aunty Iriaka Ratana; the first Māori woman to win a seat in a general electorate, Sandra Lee, of Poutini Ngai Tahu Waitaha; the first Maori woman cabinet Minister, Whetu Tirikatene-Sullivan – and all of the other Māori women who have occupied seats in the House, that the connections we have transcend party boundaries.[29]

Coming into Parliament as a Māori MP, I thought there would be ties that bind across the House by shared whakapapa (genealogy) and a commonly held respect for kaupapa (values). It was a difficult first year of trial and error before I realised those connections did not always work.

Tariana told *Mana* magazine in 2010:

> When I was with Labour you were dominated by the whole Party thing. It was like a machine that kind of rolled over the top of you. It was demoralising at times because you had a stoush and then you voted and most times you lost but every now and then they'd throw you a few crumbs just to keep you in the tent. The Party was more important than the people. I think probably that was the worst thing about it.[30]

But early on I recognised a kindred spirit in other wāhine Māori.

Similarly, Donna Awatere-Huata says:

> Māori women were able to cross the political separations in a way that the men never ever could, because our motivations, the reason for why we were there, was identical.

Long before I met her, Donna Awatere-Huata had been well known to me through her book *Maori Sovereignty*. I often wonder, if Donna hadn't brought up the issues of sovereignty back in the seventies, would all of us have been as politically active as we have been since then? We realised that despite becoming part of different political vehicles, we shared a burning passion for education that transcended political party divides.

Donna says:

> I was totally with them (Act Party) on education. That was my passion, and so I stayed there because I had that belief in that thing. But where I was drawn to Tari was in her total identification with my situation. I empathised with her; she empathised with me. We understood that we were both, almost, like one being if you like – we had the same thoughts; a passion for Māori development. A total commitment; and at all costs we just knew it – we really were kindred spirits.

Donna showed courage at a time when no one talked about it really, and so I've always had huge regard for her because of that. She raised the consciousness in government agencies through all her consultancy work in a way that I don't think many of us could have. We formed a strong friendship.

Donna says:

> We connected almost from the minute we were in Parliament. We connected straight away. It wasn't long before I started visiting her during question-time.

During this time, out of left field, I received a letter from Eva Rickard that issued a challenge that we needed to come together as Māori:

> Your track record tells me you are capable of anything and it is good for us on the outside to know that some of our people have got it in their Manawa to act in the best interests of our people. Although the road will be hard at times, there is nothing more sure than the fact that in the end truth will win in any debate. Because you are there for our people you will succeed in whatever you choose to do. I am concerned however by the posturing and mahi of our males that are in the house with you. More than ever, we need to unite and work together, whether we are men or women. But watching their performance I have serious doubts about their credibility and at how useful they are going to be.[31]

There was an important message in her words; a challenge to keep focused on the people, to unite and work together, in the interests of our own: Whakapūpūtia te kākaho e kore e whati – Binding together, we will not break.

The Ngai Tahu (Pounamu Vesting) Bill proved to be a clear point of such a connection for three of us as wahine Māori – Donna, myself and Sandra Lee. I was opposed to it, because I saw the Government settling with an iwi corporate structure as a breach of Treaty rights for hapū.

In the House, Tariana said:

> This significant bill is the legacy of colonisation with its resultant loss of mana, rangatiratanga, over land, all resources and people. The legacy still being lived today is the redefining of treaty rights from hapū to iwi … This bill pits that hapū against their own whanaunga because the Crown prefers to deal with one legal iwi corporate structure instead of recognising the treaty rights of the hapu. What is it that gives rise to iwi? It is the whānau and hapū who collectively belong to iwi.[32]

But I was a lone voice in my own caucus, and no matter how strongly I felt, the caucus wasn't going to oppose the Bill. My objections could only be aired in the debate:

> This bill is the creation by this Government of further grievances, which successive Governments will be expected to resolve. I am not a descendant of these lands, rivers and mountains but

The Realities of Parliament

> I take this opportunity humbly to acknowledge the mana, the rangatiratanga and the rights to kawanatanga over all that is theirs as tangata whenua.

The Ngai Tahu (Pounamu Vesting) Bill would prove to be a useful precursor to the Ngai Tahu Settlement Bill that came in the following year, in 1998.

Donna Awatere-Huata says of that Bill:

> One of the first bills that came up was the Ngai Tahu Bill – it was early on as I recall in my time in Parliament, and I was under real pressure to vote for the Ngai Tahu Bill. I wanted Ngāi Tahu to get their settlement – no doubt about it – but I didn't want it to be at the expense of small hapū, and I knew two who didn't want to be part of Ngāi Tahu, and I thought that was their right. To be their own masters. It was during that time that I felt pressure that I turned to Tari as someone who would understand my dilemma. I think she might have voted for the Bill, but they didn't have the opportunity to not vote. The good thing with ACT was that in ACT we were never whipped – you voted as your own conscience dictated.

In 1999 *Mana* magazine featured me on its cover, perched in between Donna Awatere-Huata and Sandra Lee. The cover question was 'Our women MPs ... united they stand?' For a moment in time, even if I was unable to vote in accord with Donna and Sandra, our kōrero was aligned. I agreed with the intent of Sandra's objection to the Bill.

Sandra Lee had told the House:

> I am Ngai Tahu. I say to members of this House that our children and our grandchildren will be back and we will engage theirs. This Parliament has a long history of imposing unjust laws on my people. At the time when they were passed the politicians of the day always thought that they could get away with it. They have not and they will not. What we see here today is history repeating itself. But we will

remain and we will stand. Our people here will be back, our children will be back, and our grandchildren will be back, because this does not represent a treaty settlement. In fact, regrettably it creates more grievances than it seeks to settle.[33]

Fighting a war not of our making

There was another, more positive opportunity for a relationship across party lines in the autumn of 1998, when I took part in a parliamentary delegation tour to Hungary, Poland, France and the United Kingdom.

I'd never put my hand up to go anywhere, partly philosophically: I wasn't sure whether it was the right thing that you should be doing, travelling overseas. I didn't feel right about it. It was Helen Clark who rang me and told me that I was to stand up. You had to self-promote; it was so horrible. I said, 'I'm not going to do that. They won't vote for me. They don't even like me'. She said 'you stand up'. There was only one other person who stood up in the caucus; it was Geoff Braybrooke. You had to say how many trips you'd had. I'd had none. And Helen of course had rung around. That was democracy at work. What she said went.

On the delegation were Hon Doug Kidd, the Speaker, and MPs Sandra Lee, Jenny Bloxham and David Carter, with our secretary, Cheryl Ferguson, and Reece Moors, the visits officer from Internal Affairs.

One of the most memorable aspects of the trip was the visit we made to northern France, where we paid our respects at Longueval to commemorate the Battle of the Somme, and Le Quesnoy. When we got to the ceremony, Sandra did this amazing karanga. I felt really proud because she hadn't done the karanga before, and it was powerful. It was very emotive. It really stirred something inside of me, seeing so many of our people buried there. Not only Māori; Pākehā people too, buried in foreign lands – fighting a war that wasn't even ours. There were just so many of them. They weren't only buried in the military war graves; they were buried in the urupā of those churches there too.

I don't think I understood war until I went to France. I used to go to every Anzac Day service as a child, but it didn't seem real. It wasn't until I went there and saw all these graves and listened to these people in the French villages talking about the New Zealand soldiers that had basically saved their lives. Our soldiers who had gone over the wall at Le Quesnoy and saved the people in that village. Le Quesnoy was the site where New

Zealand soldiers acquired a ladder from a nearby farm and climbed over the town wall to surprise and overpower the enemy. The hospitality and the warmth of the French people in these villages was overwhelming. They sang waiata about our soldiers, French waiata. After all those years, these old people would honour New Zealand's soldiers. When we got to that village it was so amazing, because we marched through the village and they had a band. Six or seven MPs, plus mayors, people who were with us, and a brass band. It just felt like the Rātana band; it really was comforting.

The Māori caucus

Tariana reached the end of her first term in Parliament with a clearer sense of where and with whom she could find common ground.

Despite the rumours prior to the 1999 general election that she would be given a low placing on the list, her placing improved, from twentieth to sixteenth. The Māori electorates had increased from five to six, and, much to the relief of Labour, the election ultimately returned all the Māori electorates from New Zealand First to Labour.[34]

In 1993, under the first-past-the-post system, representation of Māori MPs had languished at 8 percent, but in the first mixed-member-proportional election in 1996 it had risen sharply, to 17 percent. This should have been a good thing.

As Tariana said in 1997:

> There are after all only 16 people in there of Māori descent. If those 16 people can't be cooperative that's going to create enormous difficulties anyway and there are 104 others who can vote against anything Māori that they choose to and we are already seeing that with this debacle over Aotearoa Television. People hone in on every single little issue that they can and make it extremely difficult for anything Māori to survive and that's been the way of politics since the last century.[35]

Three years on, in 1999, a view was building that with increased numbers of Māori MPs in Labour, surely Labour could be influential in Māori affairs. Tariana's own influence was increasing. She was rewarded with ministerial roles in 1999, despite one of her Labour colleagues suggesting she only got them because she was Māori.

I never asked for it. I never tried to be in the 'in' team. I just did my job. I worked hard. I worked hard for our people and the Labour movement, and I think Helen recognised that, and that's how I became a minister.

Politics is always about making a difference; that's always been at the forefront of my thinking. Actually I remember when I was given the ministerial position, I was sick to the stomach. After they got in in 1999, Helen Clark rang me up at home and asked me to come down to Wellington on a Sunday because she wanted to talk to me. And she said, 'I want to offer you a ministerial'.

The first thing I thought was 'ME! Far out; I wouldn't have a bloody clue about it'. And to be honest with you, when I was first given the ministerial I didn't have a clue, because you don't; you've never done any of those things before. I think of myself as having really strong values and beliefs, and I don't care what we're talking about; I only think about those things. I don't get in to things that I know nothing about. And I try to listen really carefully to the people, so that everything I say and do is essentially coming from them, from the people.

I don't think you have to be a lawyer. But what you need is to have strong self-belief. To know that those things that are important to you, that what you would be prepared to fight for in here will translate into your work.

And so in 1999 we met together, the largest Māori caucus in Labour's history.

Georgina Beyer recalls:

> I remember the first time we had the Māori caucus after that election – eight of us: John Tamihere, Parekura Horomia, Mahara Okeroa, Mita Ririnui, Tariana Turia, Nanaia Mahuta, Dover Samuels and myself. We met in this little room in old Parliament House. I was a bit bemused as to why I'd been invited to a Māori caucus. I didn't have a Māori seat or anything – but apparently the more Māori the merrier. Anyway we meet; it's all good, the Māori caucus establishing

all of that. And J. T. and Dover and Tariana almost have this friggin' stand-up bloody argument. I can't remember what the hell it was about; some difference of opinion about something.

The writing was probably on the wall from that first day. At times it would seem that unity within the party faithful would prove to be more elusive than unity across party lines. Our division within the Māori caucus came to a head over the best way to support Māori aspirations, for those who described themselves best as 'Māori' – as in a Māori organisation or as a generic identifier – compared to those who work within the specific framework of whānau, hapū and iwi. I was clearly in the whānau, hapū, iwi camp. John Tamihere came from the other end of the spectrum, although essentially agreeing that we both wanted the best for our people.

Indeed, John Tamihere said in 2004:

> The end results Tariana and I want for our people are the same: an ability to be positive, progressive, participating citizens, where my people are proud of themselves but also Pākehā are proud of their contribution. Very simple, nothing huge. Our processes are at variance. Hers is quite an exclusive model, because you either sit within the mould of close kinfolk based society or you don't. Now the diaspora of Maoridom leave 86% of us not able to participate in that wonderful elite.[36]

I've always struggled to understand the false dichotomy created between iwi and urban Maori. The network of relationships which define us as tangata whenua cannot be separated and should not be redefined.

You cannot separate whānau, the act of giving birth, from hapū, the state of being pregnant. You cannot separate hapū from the common bones of ancestors. Therefore you can't isolate an individual whānau from the hapū which gave birth to it and from the iwi which it is a part of. We are bound together. Inseparable in our identity and our right to belong.

Self-determination for me means iwi managing our own affairs according to our own tikanga. Urban-based Māori are part of that. If they don't know their iwi, if they don't know their whakapapa, how do they know they are Maori? What we should be doing is restoring themselves to who they are.

NOTES

1. Tariana Turia, maiden address: *Hansard*, 26 February 1997.
2. Carol is the wife of Vui Mark Gosche, who was elected on to the Labour list in 1996 and served four terms, retiring from politics in 2008.
3. N. Shepheard, 'Fierce Kuia: profile of New Zealand Member of Parliament Tariana Turia', *North and South*, February 2004, p. 70.
4. A model of engagement between tangata whenua and tangata tiriti.
5. Anthony Hubbard, 'Foreign tag also fits Maori radical', *Sunday Star-Times*, 22 June 1997.
6. 'Labour MP won't condemn activist', *Dominion*, 31 March 1997, p. 2.
7. Shepheard, 'Fierce Kuia', p. 76.
8. Helen Bain, 'Tariana's will', *Dominion Post*, 14 June 1997.
9. Sarah Boyd, 'Confronting the Treaty', *The Evening Post*, 7 July 1997.
10. Tariana Turia, press release, 'Māori unemployment heading sky high', 5 August 1997.
11. Tariana Turia, press release, 'Maori Development Commissioners found, but will they find any new information', 8 August 1997.
12. Tariana Turia, press release, 'Maori Development Commissioners found, but will they find any new information', 8 August 1997.
13. *Hansard*, 4 September 1997.
14. Jill Bevan-Brown, 'Running the Gauntlet: A Gifted Māori Learner's Journey Through Secondary School' paper presented to the 'Now is the Future' conference, Auckland, October 2000.
15. *Hansard*, 6 August 1997.
16. *Hansard*, 25 November 1997.
17. *Hansard*, 23 October 1997.
18. Katherine Findlay, 'Grandmother of the nation', *Mana* no. 94, 2010, p. 14.
19. Anthony Hubbard, 'Foreign tag also fits Maori radical', *Sunday Star-Times*, 22 June 1997.
20. *Hansard*, 24 July 1997, Mental Health Commission Bill, second reading.
21. *Hansard*, 24 July 1997.
22. In 2012, the United Nations Committee Against Torture advised the New Zealand Government of its concerns over the police decision to end the investigation in 2009 without any prosecutions of staff, including Dr Leeks.
23. *Hansard*, 24 July 1997.

24 On 29 August 2000, Tariana Turia gave an address to the Psychological Society conference in which she referred to the use of the word 'holocaust' in the Waitangi Tribunal's Taranaki Report to describe the trauma of colonisation.

25 B. Ansley, 'Tariana Turia does not talk to Bruce Ansley', *New Zealand Listener*, 16–22 September 2000, p. 13.

26 Tariana Turia, 'Poroporoaki to Irihapeti Merenia Ramsden', 7 April 2003. http://beehive.govt.nz/release/poroporoaki-irihapeti-merenia-ramsden (accessed 12 February 2015).

27 Tariana Turia, 'Taranaki Gates and Rabbit-Proof Fences: Identity, culture and mental well-being', speech to the 29th International Conference Australian and New Zealand College of Mental Health Nurses, 'Earth, Sky and Number 8 wire'; Rotorua Convention Centre, 10 September 2003.

28 Tariana Turia, speech to Māori Women's Welfare League, 13 July 1997.

29 Tariana Turia, 'Being a Maori Woman in Politics', speech to Mana Wahine course, School of Māori Business Studies, Canterbury University, Christchurch, 23 September 2006. *Scoop Independent News*. http://www.scoop.co.nz/stories/PA0609/S00509.htm (accessed 11/2/ February 2015).

30 Findlay, 'Grandmother of the nation', p. 14.

31 Personal letter of 28 March 1997, Eva Rickard to Tariana Turia.

32 *Hansard*, 17 September 1997.

33 *Hansard*, 26 August 1998.

34 The Māori MPs in the Māori seats after the 1999 election were John Tamihere (Hauraki), Parekura Horomia (Ikaroa Rāwhiti), Nanaia Mahuta (Te Tai Hauāuru), Dover Samuels (Te Tai Tokerau), Mahara Okerau (Te Tai Tonga) and Mita Ririnui (Waiariki).

35 Tariana Turia, interview with Carol Archie, 'Mana News', Radio New Zealand, 4 February 1997.

36 Shepheard, 'Fierce Kuia', p. 60.

-CHAPTER FIFTEEN-
INSTITUTIONAL RACISM

We recommend that the following social policy objective be endorsed by the Government for the development of Social Welfare policy in New Zealand. Objective: 'To attack all forms of cultural racism in New Zealand that result in the values and lifestyle of the dominant group being regarded as superior to those of other groups, especially Maori'.[1]

Turia is the best ever Maori MP on institutional racism – that most repellent of subjects for Pakeha. Her malefic critics say she will leave in shame. But, when Tariana walks into the sunset of her career she can do so with her head held high.[2]

In her earliest days in the House, Tariana was horrified at the way people spoke to each other, characterised by personalised attacks, and words that served to belittle and humiliate their political colleagues. The tirades became especially offensive when racist slurs entered the mix, being liberally applied to pepper up the debate.

In a speech she gave in the House over a decade later, on 28 June 2007, she referred to the long-held association between politics, politicians and racism:

> We only need to cast our memories back to 1975, when television cameras gave extensive coverage to a billboard campaign erected by property investor, Bob Jones, attacking the Rowling Labour Government. The billboard that achieved national prominence however, was one of the former Minister of Māori Affairs, Matiu Rata, which said 'Matt Rata reads comics'.
>
> That a man of such mana, a leader of his people, was put up as a figure of fun, tormented by the popular press of his day, reflects badly on all those involved in such a shameful incident. Mr Speaker, these incidents, of so-called ridicule or denigration, could also be described as institutional racism.[3]

The categorisation of racism was something that Tariana had placed considerable emphasis on since 1988. At that time, a working group on a Maori Perspective for the Department of Social Welfare, headed by John Rangihau, travelled the country, holding a total of sixty-five meetings on marae, in institutions and with departmental officers. The expressions of frustration, of anger, of powerlessness the group found were profound, and were captured in a report entitled *Puao-te-ata-tu*. Tariana believed that the report should be on the essential reading list for every trainee doctor, teacher, social worker and nurse. Would-be policy advisors should analyse it, she said. University academics should deconstruct it. New Zealanders should understand it.

One of the most critical papers in the report is in Appendix III: The faces of racism. It states:

> While personal and cultural racism may be described in their own right, institutional racism is observed from its effects. It is a bias in our social and administrative institutions that automatically benefits the dominant race or culture while penalizing minority and subordinate groups.[4]

Tariana's life story has provided many examples of racism: experienced as a schoolgirl, a newlywed hunting for a house and as a young parent feeling judged by neighbours about the upbringing of her children. In Parliament, it distressed Tariana that the racism she had fought against for so long appeared to continue unabated.

Her son, Pahia, remembers in graphic detail the racism he experienced when he made the transition from Whangaehu School to Whanganui Boys College:

> Mum always believed us; it didn't matter what. If we got in trouble at school, she always took our side; we were never wrong. I was in the third form; we'd gone from a country school – sixty kids, you knew everyone intimately – to a school of 1300 boys – a major culture shock. We grew up in a valley, and I didn't know about racism. All my Pākehā mates were my bros. We stayed at each other's houses; their mums were my mum, we floated in and out of each other's houses. Then I go to college and all of a sudden they're 'honky white trash' and we're 'niggers'.

I always worried about my children. I remember my son coming home from school one day and asking me what a Māori was, because there was a boy at his school who they called a black Māori. When he told me who the boy was I told him that boy was a cousin of his; that the boy's mother and I were first cousins. I told my son that he should love that boy and support him and not allow other people to talk like that about him. I explained to him that that's called racism – and that we should not tolerate it.

Later, my boys were at boarding school, and they would come home in the school holidays. I was really interested that they liked this hostel manager who was quite a hard nut – all I'd heard about him was that he was quite hard on the kids. I asked my son, 'why do you like him?' And he said it was because he always pronounces our names correctly. He liked him because he felt he had respect.

I think that respect matters to Māori kids. So often there's no understanding for those kids themselves about the history of this country, and often when teachers raise things about history and the other kids laugh about it or denigrate it the kids get shy about their own history. Their history is not given to them in a way that makes them feel proud; proud of where they've come from, what their people may have contributed to the overall well-being of a community. You got taught about the Māori Wars, and there was no context. So our kids were always left feeling that we were the ones in the wrong. They didn't understand what our people were fighting for, or what the issues were.

Our kids haven't been taught to understand what their history is; to make them feel really proud of the role that their iwi played in all that. So they don't have that strong sense of pride in the essence of who they are and what their people contributed to the nation. They don't know any of that.

In Whanganui we only had to look at our name to see the intimate connection between history, identity, culture. The name Whanganui has a meaning and a history that is unique to the Whanganui river, the rohe and the iwi. It always was and always will be a Māori word. This is about te reo Māori.

Despite public views to the contrary, there is a significant amount of historical documentation that supports the spelling of Whanganui with an 'h'. Even in the Crown Purchase Deed of 1848, when the Crown purchased the land from Māori, W(h)anganui is spelt both with and without the 'h'. In his submission to the New Zealand Geographic Board, Che Wilson described the correct meaning for the name 'Whanganui' as 'the long wait': 'whanga' meaning to wait, and 'nui' meaning large or long. He explained how this name originated from the time of Kupe the great navigator. He talked about the extended name Te Whanga-nui-a-Kupe, referring to the extended wait for the return of Kupe from his exploration.

Surely that's a history of some meaning and relevance. And yet, as our most recent history would show, ignorance can still overrule reason.

On 17 September 2009, the New Zealand Geographic Board made their recommendation that the letter 'h' should be added to the name 'Wanganui'. Two months later, the Minister for Land Information, Maurice Williamson, announced that the spelling of Whanganui would be alternative – either with or without an 'h'. Tariana described the decisions as 'uplifting', as the *Dominion Post* reported:

> The spelling of place names and the correct use of te reo Māori was part of the ongoing negotiation and reconciliation between Maori, Government and communities, Mrs Turia said.
>
> 'I like the approach, which encourages Crown agencies to respect the special relationship that mana whenua have with this area, while also allowing time for the practical changes to occur – the letterhead to change, new signs to be erected'.[5]

And yet five years later, the District Council was no further ahead in actioning the decision, voting seven–six against a motion to have the Geographic Board consider adding the 'h' to the spelling of the Wanganui district name. (The urban area of the district can use either spelling, but not the district). Tariana, who had led a spirited campaign in public media, attended meetings, written to Ministers, asked questions in the House and spoken consistently about the issue, was most unhappy:

> That's about being not prepared to show leadership. Don't patronise us and don't tell us 'I would have done this' or 'I would have done that', because they never do, and they never showed the leadership our community actually needs. This is a massive issue in terms of our identity, and people have to get it right.[6]

Rotary and racism

The leadership that the Whanganui community needed in terms of cultural identity was never more evident than in two different meetings Tariana had with the local Rotary club. In 2004, the week before Tariana re-entered Parliament as the first Māori Party MP, she was asked to speak at the Whanganui Rotary Club. Looking back, it felt like a watershed moment; a pivotal turning point between the days before and her future in bringing a strong and independent voice for Māori to Parliament.

Tariana hadn't spoken to Rotary for years; the last time had been the mid-1980s, when Judge Bill Unwin had invited her to speak about racism at a time when she had been actively involved in attending the court, picking up rangatahi, guiding them through the court process and taking them home for a break on the farm. 'We took some very serious offenders, not only Māori. It was critical to save those kids lives. We didn't want them ending up on the heap.'[7]

At that time, she definitely had views about how well the justice system was serving Māori.

The focus for my speech in the mid-eighties, 'Racism', went down like a lead balloon among the Rotarians who had asked me to speak.

Unbeknown to me there had been a journalist at that meeting taking down every word. The *Chronicle* next day gave very full coverage, and so my phone was ringing hot for days. There were people there from our valley who had grown up with my mother, and others that knew my aunt really well who felt they needed to let me know how enraged they were, and that they didn't know where I'd got my ideas from. In fact they told me that my mother and extended family would never have thought like I did.

My family was very upset with me, and as a consequence I was isolated for quite a long period of time. Not because they didn't know it to be true, but because of the backlash that everybody from home got with it. My ever-devoted George had come with me that night, and was distressed that I could be so honest about the things that had happened in our community. Mum was annoyed, and Aunty Wai was livid, yet both agreed with me that what I had said was true. They just wished I hadn't said it. Aunty Wai rang me and she said to me, 'Some things are best left unsaid'. I said to her, 'Since when did you leave something unsaid?'

There was a long pause. 'Well, there are places for us to say these things. Saying it to the Rotary Club was not one of those places. I think many, many people are going to be offended.' I said, 'yes, you can expect a visit from Dr Schmidt'. He was a really good friend of hers, and he had stood up at the meeting and been clearly distressed by my contribution.

One of the more reflective calls at that time had come from our accountant, a wonderful old man who quietly said to me, 'It may well all be true, but I don't know whether you were wise enough to talk about it as you did. I think you need to be more guarded about how you feel about things.'

Moving forward then, to 19 July 2004. When I returned to Rotary, I could sense a different mood in the air. Normally their lunch meeting finishes at 1 – we were still there at 1.45. They were asking a lot of questions; they too were looking for a way forward – more unity. My view has always been that we can have unity with diversity – it's about respecting other people.

Of course I couldn't resist the opportunity to raise a few challenges. They asked me why we couldn't be just one people. My son was with me and he said to me, 'what shall we be? Māori? Asian? Pākehā? Which one?'

If Tariana had ever had any doubt about how the impact of racist ideas translated into practice, ironically it was while she was serving as Associate Minister of Social Services and Employment, early in her parliamentary career, that she came across one of the most startling examples of it, right under her nose. It was to do with the bed-nights issue.

When children and young people are in the custody of the Chief Executive of the Ministry of Social Development, or in the custody of another party, the state formalises that arrangement through contracted bed-nights, in a system that officially records care provided for a particular child for a particular night. Any third-party care provider has to meet specific recording requirements and comply with the specifications laid out in contract arrangements for occupancy rates per individual.

When I was Associate Minister, I asked to see the price rates that providers were receiving. It stunned me to find they were paying Māori providers less than Pākehā providers for bed-nights – now surely a bed is a bed.

I had come across blistering inequities in the allocation of funding. Organisations like the Youth Horizons Trust in Auckland were receiving up to $300,000 a year to employ a squad of clinical psychologists who would eventually return a child to families struggling on $120 a week. It didn't add up. I knew there were disparities, and I asked officials to front up. And what was so staggering was that it appeared that the practices had been going on forever, without anyone thinking to question it.

A 2000 press release stated:

> Racial prejudice remains rife among senior officials in government departments especially Child, Youth and Family Services, Associate Māori Affairs Minister Tariana Turia says. The service's 'absolute mistrust' of Māori families and iwi networks was the reason it was often unable to find foster placements for Māori children within their whanau, hapū or iwi.[8]

The Chief Executive of the Department of Child, Youth and Family Services at the time, Jacqui Pivac, was a very good person, and she moved quickly to address it. Many months after this event, a damning review of Child, Youth and Family carried out by the Treasury, the State Services Commission and the Social Development Ministry identified that the organisation was punctured by 'critical information gaps'. The review painted a damning picture of an agency culture that was resistant to change. It seemed to me then – and now – that there had been far too little attention paid to the *Puao-te-ata-tu* report of 1988 and the massive rethink it required.

'Us and them'

> The fact is though, that New Zealand institutions manifest a monocultural bias and the culture which shapes and directs that bias is Pakehatanga. The bias can be observed operating in law, government,

the processions, healthcare, land ownership, welfare practices, education, town planning, the police, finance, business and spoken language. It permeates the media and our national economic life. If one is outside, one sees it as 'the system'. If one is cocooned within it, one sees it as the normal condition of experience.[9]

The monocultural bias that Tariana refers to as institutional racism has all too often been excused in Parliament as 'robust debate'. To identify debate as 'racist' is considered unparliamentary. During his term as Speaker, Doug Kidd clarified what his predecessor, Sir Roy Jack, had intended when declaring 'racist' an unparliamentary word in 1977: 'An allegation that a member is racist clearly imputes what most members would regard as an improper motive and is out of order.'

The expression of racism in the House has frequently been unearthed in the context of the Treaty Settlement debates. A typical example was heard in the first reading of the Ngati Tuwharetoa, Raukawa, and Te Arawa River Iwi Waikato River Bill (28 July 2010).

Tariana was leading the debate that day: a privilege accorded her by Chris Finlayson, Minister of Treaty Negotiations. The Minister has established a convention during his reign in which almost without exception he offers the Māori Party the opportunity to head off the debate when Treaty Settlements are read in the House. It is a sign of the humility of the man that he graciously steps aside in order to enable tangata whenua to be the first speaker. According to the protocols of the House, the presiding Minister must take up the first slot of the allocated debate – if he or she is in the Chamber. Inevitably, then, Minister Finlayson, who has spent years negotiating, researching, arbitrating and advocating for the settlements, would have to wait in the lobby until Tariana's speech had concluded before he could take up his seat and thereafter take his slot.

On this day, the settlement had a special significance for Tariana, who said:

> I am proud to stand today as a direct descendent of Ngāti Hikairo, through whakapapa that connects me through my great-grandmother's line. I connect as I do with all river tribes to the

significance we place upon our tupuna awa as the central bloodline of our tribal heart. Ko au ko te awa; ko te awa ko au.[10]

Tariana went on to describe the Bill as respecting the mana of each of the iwi, reflecting the fact that each iwi has its own distinct relationship with the river and with the Crown. Five speakers later, David Garrett from the ACT Party rose to explain why his party would continue to oppose the Bill as part of 'these pathetic, misguided attempts at settlement', saying:

> This bill will further enshrine in law the concept of 'us and them', which is a far cry from the 'one people' vision that the Treaty intended … It is naive, however, not to think that there are those who look at the river and see dollar signs. Let us not pretend otherwise.

While iwi members looked on in amazement from the public gallery, Mr Garrett spouted forth his peculiar view about Māori:

> Many of their so-called leaders continue to play the 'we were here first' card.

In the course of one ten-minute diatribe, Mr Garrett had made an implicit reference to tangata whenua as exploitative, as elitist, and as deceptive or dishonest. Yet all hell broke loose when the Māori Party dared to point out the obvious. Hone Harawira stood to deliver the rebuke:

> Tēnā koutou, e ngā iwi kua tae mai nei i tēnei hāora o te pō kia rongohia i te tautoko o te Pāremata nei ki tā koutou nei pire. Hākoa, kua tū kē te pokokōhua nei te whakatakoto i ōna kōrero kaikiri, e tika ana kia mōhio, ko rātou anake e kore e whakaae ki tēnei pire. [To the tribes who have arrived here at this hour tonight to listen to this Parliament speaking in support of your Bill, I acknowledge your presence. Even though this boiled head stood and expressed his racist views, it should be noted that they are the only ones opposing this bill.]

Hone had no sooner spoken than Mr Garrett rose to his feet: 'I raise a point of order, Mr Speaker. I find the accusation of racism deeply offensive and I object to it. I believe it is unparliamentary, and it is inaccurate.'

Assistant Speaker Rick Barker ignored the remarks of Mr Garrett and instead moved to censure Hone:

> I think he is sailing very close to the wind referring to a person's views as racist; by implication he is saying that the person is. I caution the member and I ask him to speak to the bill.

The debate that ensued around the Waikato Tainui Raupatu claims (Waikato River) Settlement Bill was another example in which racist rhetoric was given free reign. Tariana was leading the debate again that day: a debate charged with feeling, following the recent passing of Lady Raiha Mahuta, a key Waikato River claim co-negotiator. Tariana said:

> Kei te rere iho a roimata ki te awa o Whanganui, kei te rere iho a wai kamo ki te awa o Waikato. E iri te rau kawakawa, e iri ki te whare aituā. Moe mai rā e kui e, moe mai rā. [Tears flow down upon the Whanganui River, as they do from the eyes upon the river of Waikato. Hang up the leaves of the kawakawa, hang them upon the house of calamity. Slumber there, ancient one, rest there.][11]

In her opening address, Tariana spoke about the special significance of river legislation to those who whakapapa so closely to their awa:

> As someone from one river tribe to those of another, I want to acknowledge the unique and distinctive role that our awa play in every aspect of our lives. As river people we share a special bond with our awa tupuna, recognising that it is our collective responsibility to protect the mana of the river.

She shared with the House the reflections of the kuia Iti Rangihinemutu Rāwiri, explaining the intimate connections between the people and their river:

> The Waikato River is our tupuna and looks over us throughout our lives. The river feeds us, nurtures us, and takes care of us, healing our hurts and protecting us from harm. The river is our lifeline from which we take our name, our identity and our mana.

One by one other members rose to acknowledge the legacy of Lady Raiha: Parekura Horomia, Chris Finlayson, Kevin Hague and, finally, Nanaia Mahuta, Lady Raiha's daughter, who said:

> I acknowledge the many tributes that have been put forward in this House, specifically to my mother, and, indeed, to the many people who have passed and have been involved with both the Waikato River settlement and the Waikato raupatu settlement. Many people have exhausted their effort, determination, talent, expertise, and wisdom to see the return of Waikato lands and our awa to our people so that we can look forward and so that there is a future for the next generation.

It was a deeply moving moment in time: a daughter and politician, reflecting on the history that was being made in the chamber that day. When Nanaia resumed her seat, up jumped Rodney Hide to take a call. He capped off his following speech with an analysis about the value of the river:

> So the whole lot, the whole catchment, is an indivisible living thing that is the ancestor of a people. The only people who can interpret whether that ancestor is upset or hurt, or being annoyed, disrupted, or affected are the people who believe that. Now, I do not happen to believe it. I think it is hocus-pocus. But what we are doing is legislating this hocus-pocus, and the Waikato River Authority, the Waikato Regional Council, and the people of the Waikato will have to live by that.

It would take Tariana a long time to forgive Rodney for those comments. Whether it was just attributable to a giant boost of testerone or a mistake that wasn't meant to happen, Tariana was distressed by the way in which Rodney had mocked a Māori world view with such careless disregard. To his credit, he realised he had gone too far, and tried to make amends. He asked to meet with her and apologise. Years later, he was still remorseful.

Rodney says:

> I realised that I had deeply hurt her feelings and it upset me terribly. It upset me not just because it was her, but I just don't think you

> should mock a person because of their deeply held beliefs. And I had trivialised it, so I was doubly upset. I went to see her and she was so gracious and I felt pathetic – you know how you feel when you fall well short of a decent standard, and she was so magnanimous. It was sort of like meeting Nelson Mandela and feeling shit because you've locked him up for all those years. I just felt terrible. She was very, very good about it and I thought, 'well, you know, it's a lesson in life'.

In one of her last interviews as a Member of Parliament, Tariana returned to the subject of institutional racism as one of the most fundamental challenges of our time:

> We don't have equity in our lives. The whole way this place works, the way the system works, never acts in the interests of everybody even though they pretend it does. If I was coming in now, my focus would be on looking at the institutions, the organs of government and looking at how they operate and whose interests they serve. I think that would be where my focus would be because they have such a huge impact on people's daily lives. Whether it's health, education, the Ministry of Social Development, employment, tertiary education. If you look right across the board, the statistics tell us that we are not treated equitably. We fill all the worst statistics in the country. And I think that's appalling in 2014. By the year 2050 this country is going to be decidedly browner. We have to prepare for that. And if we don't prepare for that what do we think as a country that we are going to leave as a legacy?[12]

NOTES

1 Ministerial Advisory Committee on a Maori Perspective for the Department of Social Welfare. *Puao-te-ata-tu (Day Break)*, 1988, p. 9.

2 Rawiri Taonui, 'Sharples key to Maori Party's run', *The New Zealand Herald*, 30 January 2013.

3 *Hansard*, 28 June 2007.

4 Ministerial Advisory Committee on a Maori Perspective for the Department of Social Welfare. *Puao-te-ata-tu*, p. 79.

5 Tracy Watkins and Simon Wood, 'Compromise over "h" in Wanganui', *Dominion Post*, 18 December 2009.

6 John Maslin, 'We have not seen end of "H" issue', *Wanganui Chronicle*, 4 December 2014.

7 Laurel Stowell, 'A life of service to Maori', *Wanganui Chronicle*, 31 August 2005.

8 Tariana Turia, press release, 'Officials race views sickening – Minister', 25 March 2000.

9 Ministerial Advisory Committee on a Maori Perspective for the Department of Social Welfare, *Puao-te-ata-tu*, p. 78.

10 *Hansard*, 28 July 2010.

11 *Hansard*, 20 April 2010.

12 Tariana Turia, interview with Eru Rerekura and Chris Bramwell, *Te Waonui a te Manu Korihi*, Radio New Zealand, 10 August 2014.

CHAPTER SIXTEEN
MĀORI PRIORITIES IN POLICY

Mauria ko ōku painga, waiho ko ōku wherū

Highlight my strengths, ignore my weaknesses

An old Cherokee chief was teaching his grandson about life. 'A fight is going on inside me', he said to the boy. 'It is a terrible fight and it is between two wolves. One is evil – he is anger, envy, sorrow, regret, greed, arrogance, self-pity, guilt, resentment, inferiority, lies, false pride, superiority, self-doubt, and ego. The other is good – he is joy, peace, love, hope, serenity, humility, kindness, benevolence, empathy, generosity, truth, compassion, and faith. This same fight is going on inside you – and inside every other person, too.'

The grandson thought about it for a minute and then asked his grandfather, 'Which wolf will win?' The old chief simply replied, 'The one you feed.'[1]

In December 1999, as part of the Labour Government, Tariana was made a Minister outside Cabinet with associate responsibilities for Māori Affairs, Corrections, Health, Housing and Social Services and Employment.

Nancy Tuaine says:

> Anyone who knows or has ever worked with Aunty Tariana knows that her work ethics and her work throughput are enormous, and her expectations of you if you work for her are enormous.

Bill English, an Opposition MP at that time, probably has the best insight into Tariana's work ethic, attributing it to her rural background:

> One way that I would see it is also that she is a rural woman – because they get a certain amount of independence because of the way of life. She reminded me a lot of women of my mother's generation, although she is a bit younger. A bit feisty, quite intelligent – because they didn't have a whole lot of choices in how their life turned out. Quite intelligent and easily underestimated. You know you're dealing with someone who has got her hands dirty in the non-government world, in her own whānau, in her own community, and who has a realistic grip on the kind of longer-term regeneration that it takes which ultimately can only come from the people themselves.

True to form, Tariana eagerly took up the ministerial responsibilities, driven by the priorities and the people and the potential of these roles to benefit them.

One of my first speeches as a brand new minister was at a conference in Waitangi to celebrate Māori social work paradigms. My message to that conference was around whānau safety:

> It is my wish that as you pursue your education in whanau, hapū and iwi work the focus of the education is not on the deficits or pathology of our people. We do internalise the negative views others have of whānau, hapū and iwi and as a result too many of us in the social work field think negatively of our people. This is despite the fact the vast majority of Māori families function successfully without any intervention on our part. I do hope that the focus is on nga tikanga mau painga or a strengths focus.[2]

Closing the gaps

A strengths-based approach to public policy has defined Tariana's ministerial character from her first days in Parliament. In a 2001 article she explained that approach:

> I just believe passionately that we have to see our people's potential. We can't focus on our deficits or else we'll never lift ourselves up. It really does impact on them. It impacts on me, you do this wrong, and that wrong, all those negative statistics. I read all these things and I go home and I think, 'Oh God it feels insurmountable'. But we can't think that. There is a way forward. It lies within our ability to actually look at our own tikanga and the disciplines of it and to live our lives by it.[3]

At first glance, however, the signature policy that the Māori Affairs Ministers introduced in the forty-sixth Parliament seemed to take the opposite tack.

On 9 December 1999 Dover Samuels was appointed Minister of Māori Affairs, with two associate ministers, Tariana and Parekura Horomia. A month after the 1999 general election, Minister Samuels made a bold promise to disestablish Te Puni Kōkiri 'in line with Labour's pre-election pledge to close the gaps between Māori and non-Māori'.[4]

Te Puni Kōkiri would be replaced by a new Ministry of Māori Economic and Social Development, and the new Ministry would have a broader mandate, through two new directorates. The new Minister was optimistic about what was required to achieve the vision outlined in Labour's 1999 Māori Policy Manifesto, *He Putahitanga Hou*. 'If we don't approach it with courage and determination as a nation then we will be second-class citizens forever', he said.

However, less than a month after Samuels made this statement, he was implicated in allegations of sexual misconduct that led to his eventual sacking from the ministerial portfolio in July 2000. It was a very dramatic six months, as journalistic innuendo and Opposition questioning brought the scandal to the forefront of parliamentary debate. Prime Minister Helen Clark concluded that Dover could not be effective while allegations, controversy and pulic debate were swirling around him. She told the *Herald*:

> Māori are looking for leadership to combat high rates of teenage pregnancy, domestic violence, assault, and crime generally. It was obvious to me that Mr Samuels could not give that leadership, not only because of his past, but because of his refusal to be direct with his party about it.[5]

As each new allegation erupted in the media, frequent allusion was made to the perceived role that Tariana had held in the course of events. Richard Harman even went as far as to suggest she had been directly influential in his eventual demise:

> Ms Clark's relationship with Ms Turia is obviously a complex one. A minister with Ms Turia's intellect is bound to get a good hearing on the ninth floor. Apparently, her support for sending a message to Māori men about their behaviour toward Māori women played a big role in Ms Clark's decisions on how to handle the Samuels affair.[6]

Ruth Laugesen in the *Sunday Star-Times* had much the same view:

> Within the government, Turia is known as vehement, articulate and constructive, drawing on her experience in Maori social service agencies to contribute to the framing of the government's Closing the Gaps policies. Clark trusts her and uses her as a sounding board to reassure herself that the government is on the right track with its Maori policies. There are not many people Clark trusts in this way. Turia is said to have been a tower of strength to the prime minister during the Samuels debacle, acting as a conduit for feedback from the Māori community.[7]

Others put a broader spin on the matter, describing the caucus factionalism, noting that the Goff camp was resentful of Clark's sacking of Samuels, and that it was a reflection of 'what former prime Minister Sir Geoffrey Palmer has called Miss Clark's muscular leadership and what some see as the politically correct flavour of her ministry'.[8]

Tariana had other things on her mind; the views of the press gallery did not concern her. She was strongly motivated by the challenge of driving a policy programme on the back of the 'Closing the Gaps' strategy.

'Closing the Gaps' had been branded by Labour as a 'flagship' policy. The Prime Minister, in her annual pilgrimage to Rātana Pā on 24 January 2000, had announced that she was not only setting up a special Cabinet committee to implement the policy, but she would personally chair it to ensure the full weight of her office would be behind the drive to close the social and economic gaps between Māori and Pasifika peoples and other New Zealanders. The 'Closing the Gaps' report issued in June 2000 profiled the social and economic disparities between Māori and non-Māori. It revealed that Māori experienced poorer education, higher unemployment, lower incomes, lower home ownership rates and poorer health. Disparities were shown to exist in all age groups.

Tariana was a member of the Cabinet committee and actively involved in the process of creating policies to respond to the disparities identified in the report.

She said at the time:

> The closing the gaps policy provides the Government with further impetus to focus its attention on its own departments, strategies and systems, to produce positive results for Māori. The Government expects its departments to improve their contributions to make a positive difference to the health, housing, education, employment, justice, welfare and business and enterprise outcomes for Māori. In my view, this suggests departments will need to be responsive to the needs, interests and priorities of Māori. …
>
> Closing the Gaps means there is even more reason for departments to engage with whānau, hapū, iwi and Māori organisations to deliver specified services to Māori communities. However, it is a 'needs-focused' policy through which Māori are treated as clients.[9]

Of the seventy-two policies grouped under 'Closing the Gaps' in the June 2000 Budget, thirty-nine were aimed specifically at Māori and Pasifika peoples and thirty-three were more broadly targeted at the disadvantaged. $114 million was dedicated over four years for 'Closing the Gaps', and another $50 million budgeted for further projects to be developed between Budgets. On Budget Day

2000 Tariana, with Steve Maharey, Minister of Social Services and Employment, announced over $72 million in new funding for programmes that would have a direct impact for Māori and Pasifika peoples. There was $20 million for capacity- and capability-building; $14 million for Māori women's development; $7 million for Pasifika community organisations; $3 million for investing in Māori communities; $10 million for a Māori Youth Contestable Fund; $3 million for Pacific provider development; and $14 million for iwi Māori provider and workforce development.

A shift in language signalled that the focus was moving from needs to development (representing a more proactive approach). Tariana said:

> I am especially heartened by the opportunity to focus on development and, therefore, capability rather than deficiencies. …
>
> In recent times, we have become obsessive about the needs our people have, all too often at the expense of their dreams and aspirations. Yet, for me, development is about finding ways to fulfil dreams. It is not about deciding whether to dream or not. However, when people are deprived, alienated and disaffected to the extent that our people have been, they tend not to have dreams.[10]

She further suggested that the emphasis should never be on a disparity analysis alone:

> The main point of the closing the gaps policy is to ensure Māori are not prevented from having the best possible chance to lead, manage and control their own development. Until now, the disparities between Māori and non-Māori have had the potential to be seen as a record of the failings of Māori people. This is neither sustainable nor appropriate.

In essence, this speech laid down all the fundamental tenets for an approach the country would later know as Whānau Ora. The 'Closing the Gaps' approach promoted the need for an improved system of government delivery; accountability; transparency; and value for money:

> Under-resourcing and inappropriate contracting processes have lead to ad hoc development with the priorities of government agencies taking centre stage. This type of scenario must be avoided at all costs if the Government is sincere in wanting to advance self-determination for whānau, hapū and iwi. Centralised control will not lead to this. The alternative is for taxpayers to continue to fork out massive amounts of money in crisis-point interventions, dealing with Māori who fell through the cracks in existing government programmes and services.[11]

A week later, Hon Dr Michael Cullen, Minister of Finance, echoed those sentiments in his Budget speech announcement:

> We need to know whether that effort is achieving the intended results. We are making a significant investment in improving the information base and our monitoring capability. Te Puni Kōkiri will receive an extra $12 million over the next four years to monitor the effectiveness of social policy programmes for Māori.
>
> We are also making government departments more accountable for their delivery to Māori and Pacific peoples. From this year, departmental chief executives will be required to disclose in their annual reports what steps they are taking to close the gaps, and will be held accountable for their effectiveness. …
>
> The Government will not stand back on this question. We are determined to close the gaps. Our very foundations as a country demand it.[12]

But it wasn't just about creating stronger mechanisms for monitoring results. In Tariana's mind the most powerful aspect of Closing the Gaps was the focus on capacity-building; on building and supporting the potential of the people. She upheld two key priorities for Closing the Gaps:

1. People are the most significant resource we have, and the socio-economic gaps between Māori and non-Māori are unsustainable. Therefore, we need to address the socio-economic disparities they endure. Hence the 'Closing the Gaps' policy.

2. Māori want to manage and control their own development, and they should be supported by the Government to do so. Hence the capacity-building policy.

Within six months of becoming a minister, Tariana had effectively championed an approach that enabled whanau, hapū and iwi to be involved in developing solutions for their individual issues. She was delivering on the aspirations outlined in Labour's Māori Policy Manifesto, *He Putahitanga Hou*, to be 'committed to fulfilling its obligations as a Treaty partner to support self-determination for whanau, hapū and iwi'.

But the initiative was also powerfully aligned with statements of faith in the people that Tariana had constantly reiterated through a wide range of public statements leading up to that first 2000 Budget.

She had reminded the nation that the right to speak on Waitangi marae was a Ngāpuhi issue; that 'as with rules, regulations and laws, the tikanga or protocol of an iwi is developed for a reason'.[13] She had confirmed that she would be at Waitangi on Waitangi Day because for government to 'make swift progress we must be accessible and accountable to Māori people'.[14]

She had voiced her concern that Wellington bureaucrats were driving policy, rather than the Minister they were supposed to serve:

> Our whānau, hapū, iwi and Māori have bared the brunt of exclusive policy decision-making processes which have become the norm for Government departments and the evidence is blatantly obvious. There is evidence both in New Zealand and internationally that the indigenous people are the most capable of directing their own development however they are too often excluded from sitting at the decision-making table.[15]

In March 2000, Tariana had been questioned in the House by Winston Peters after a release she had issued stated that prejudice against Māori families by senior officials made her sick. In her response Tariana told Parliament that it was clear that the Department of Social Welfare had shelved plans for implementing *Puao-te-ata-tu*, the 1988 report on developing a Māori Perspective for the Department of Social Welfare, including allocation of an equitable share of resources.[16]

And then in May, Tariana announced that:

> ... the strengthening of our whānau is the most critical development issue we are facing today ... Instead of reprimanding or dictating to families we need to assist them with the causes of their problems. This will better equip them to deal with problems they will face in the future. Individual problems cannot be addressed in isolation, there must be a whole family and whole community approach if we are to resolve violence issues within families.[17]

Of all of these statements, it was this last that would prove to be controversial: not so much for its substance, but because of the philosophical difference in its approach from one of the key organisations in the family violence network, Women's Refuge.

Merepeka Raukawa-Tait, in her role as Chief Executive of Women's Refuge, presented a bid to the Closing the Gaps Committee seeking an increase in funding for Women's Refuge from $4.2 million a year to $9.6 million. After the meeting Ms Raukawa-Tait and Roger McClay, the Children's Commissioner, met with Ministers Turia and Horomia in their office.

Parekura and I talked about promoting a more positive message. There was no argument that family violence was unacceptable. The difference we talked about, however, was in how we presented the strategies and solutions to address family violence. Our preference was to assist families to find long-term solutions that worked for them, rather than regurgitating the negative statistics and hoping that change would come.

We had hardly finished the meeting before all hell broke loose. Parekura and I were accused of 'gagging' them from telling the truth about the horrific domestic violence statistics. Meanwhile Merepeka was given the right of reply on every channel in town.

"'It is whanau members and wider whanau members who kill their children, not usually strangers," she said. "There are Maori members of Parliament that don't want to hear that and have certainly not appreciated the focus that I have put on to that," she said yesterday."I have been asked if I would highlight the positive things. "My job is to highlight the issues around domestic violence. The members of Parliament can highlight the other issues"[18].

The media had a field day. Talkback was raging, and every media outlet in town was competing with each other for increasingly sensational headlines. The papers became crowded with reports of 'horror, outrage and demands for action'.

I want to be absolutely clear now, as I was then. It was never about failing to face up to this reality. I know what it is to live with the horror of violence in your every waking moment. As an aunty, a sister, a daughter, a cousin, I have seen and felt the terror of men who haunt the lives of their alleged loved ones. I have seen far too many times the sunglasses that are meant to disguise the marks of violence left behind. I have known of far too many incidents; reoccurring violence which leaves scars of all description. Sexual assault. Physical wounds. Psychological terror. Emotional manipulation. Intimidation. The fear that younger siblings may be harmed.

I have heard the excuses, been sickened by the lies, experienced the contempt for acts of abuse that leave innocent children forever traumatised. I don't forget. This was nothing to do with the face of torture that is far too prevalent in our lives. It's all about the approach we take to dealing to it.

And I absolutely believe that we should challenge violence wherever and whenever it is played out. Pahia recently reminded me of the reaction I had the first time he got the cane at school:

> I told Mum and she said, 'what do you mean you got the cane?' I said, 'I had to bend over and touch my toes and this teacher whacked me'. Well, she just erupted. She said to me, 'you will never ever bend over for anybody'. She said, 'if we don't hit you, like hell is anybody else going to hit you', and from that day onwards I refused to bend over. She was down the school every time I'd get in trouble because I refused to get the cane and – I always remember this – she said to me, 'son, violence breeds violence'.

Yet report after report has failed to adequately represent why it might not be in the best interests of any child to keep a menu of brutality on instant replay.

The *Dominion* led with a strongly worded message:

> The women's refuge head challenges Maori leaders to face up to the crisis. Her words are too tough for some people. But it would be a monstrous injustice if her message were dashed against a brick wall of bureaucratic waffle and political correctness.[19]

While a war of words was being played out in the media, a moment of promise occurred when Parekura and I called a meeting of our Māori colleagues across the House to come together around the tragedies that were occurring in some of our whānau. Years later I spoke about the potential of the cross-party approach we took:

> I was reflecting back on a time some six years ago, after another similar child tragedy had gripped the nation. Māori members of Parliament from Labour, National, New Zealand First, the Alliance, and ACT met together in a wonderful demonstration of kotahitanga, the principle of unity of purpose and direction. We were all sickened by the very thought of losing another child, and shared together our various histories and strategies that could be useful in making a difference. As it turned out, the political power-game prevented the good ideas of that cross-party parliamentary team from ever taking life, but the very experience of working together for a common goal showed to me that it was definitely possible. It happened then; it could happen again.[20]

Back in 2000, the media speculated that because the Prime Minister was not coming out publicly and reprimanding us that we were clearly being given preferential treatment.

Victoria Main in the *Daily News* was one such speculator, saying of the Prime Minister:

> She came across as protective of her own two ministers. They are both her proteges. In Opposition, she backed Ms Turia, formerly a Moutoa Gardens protest leader, in rows with then caucus colleague Mike Moore over the status of the treaty. She wants to accommodate Ms Turia's radical voice within the Government. The media-wary Mr Horomia, formerly a bureaucrat, was Miss Clark's pick for the Maori affairs job after Mr Samuels' dismissal in June.[21]

It wasn't as if my ability to be influential in the Labour caucus had miraculously improved, or that I was suddenly able to achieve all the priorities I had advocated for. I still found it hard to get Māori views accommodated. Usually Bills and legislation were complete before you had an opportunity to comment. It was only about changing a word here or a sentence there.

Audrey Young got it right when she reported in August 2000 that tweaking with a word or two was never going to be enough for me:

> She is entrenching her reputation as someone who will take on anyone and who has a will as strong as Helen Clark's. Mrs Turia walked out of caucus several weeks ago after it had signed off the health restructuring legislation requiring new health boards to form partnerships with local iwi. She was upset she hadn't got a more strongly worded commitment to give effect to the Treaty of Waitangi. In fact what Labour has agreed upon is already hugely controversial.[22]

We had been working hard on getting a strong statement about mana whenua representation in health right from the start of the parliamentary term. I was part of an ad hoc ministerial committee, which also included Annette King, Ruth Dyson, Trevor Mallard and Margaret Wilson. The committee had formed at the end of January 2000 to look at options for appropriate partnership arrangements with Māori at the District Health Board level in funding and provision of services. In March 2000 I issued a media statement to outline what I believed the minimum threshold could be:

> Treaty relationships already established in the health sector must be built on and improved by mana whenua and these Hospital and Health Services boards until the District Health Boards are established, and trust must exist at all levels of the decision-making process.[23]

The Ministry of Health came back with a partnership model that emphasised both capacity-building and developing mainstream responsiveness.

A 2002 thesis by Louise Humpage analysing this model reflected:

> It appears that the partnership model was chosen for two main reasons. First, it was expected to give 'practical effect to the Government's commitment to the principles of the Treaty of Waitangi' and to 'accelerate improvement in Māori health and development'. The issue of 'closing the gaps' was consequently placed within a Treaty framework.[24]

The passage of policy and perception, however, never runs smooth.

My intention, as signalled in my March release, was that the new health legislation would formalise separate Māori seats on the new elected health boards, which in turn must form partnerships with 'mana whenua'. The new legislation would also contain a provision requiring it to be interpreted in accordance with the Treaty. According to Louise Humpage, this was a means to appease Māori constituencies, and reportedly upon my insistence.[25] If this was true, it did not take into account the opposition within my own caucus, spearheaded by my Labour colleague and chair of the Māori Affairs Select Committee John Tamihere.

At the time, Peter Luke in the *Press* reported:

> There are splits within the Government's Maori caucus. The most obvious is between traditional iwi backers such as Tariana Turia and urban Maori authority advocates such as John Tamihere. Ms Turia, for example, strongly supports the present treaty clause in health legislation. Mr Tamihere insists that the use of the term 'mana whenua' in the bill simply perpetuates an historic and feudal anachronism. The correct term would simply be Maori regardless of any iwi affiliation.[26]

Tamihere had an unlikely ally in the form of Race Relations Concilitator Rajen Prasad. Prasad told the Select Committee on 25 October 2000 that he wanted the Treaty of Waitangi clause in the health restructuring Bill removed because it was open to interpretation and could be seen as giving privileges to Māori. In his view, the provisions in question could be interpreted as 'racist' because they appeared to give Māori preferential treatment in the health system.

Tariana responded immediately to the comments:

> I've had a number of iwi groups ring me, saying how concerned they were to hear that the Race Relations Conciliator himself had made comment seeing the Treaty clause as one that would then give people preferential treatment which of course is simply not correct at all … The Treaty is about nation building. It is about inclusion. It is about a document that was between tangata whenua and the Crown and by

> putting the treaty into legislation it is acknowledging that significant relationship that existed at the time that government was formed in this country.[27]

Earlier that morning, the Prime Minister had also defended the mention of the Treaty, explaining that the Treaty was already mentioned in thirty pieces of legislation without the Race Relations Office ever having objected.

Yet in response to Prasad's submission and the media reaction, the Health Select Committee folded under pressure and replaced the Treaty provision with a general statement to the effect that the legislation aimed to reduce health disparities for Māori and other population groups. Recognition of the status of Māori as Treaty partners was omitted from the Bill, and a new clause added that nothing in the Act 'entitles a person to preferential access to services on the basis of race or limits section 73 of the Human Rights Act'.

The separate mention of the Treaty in section 4 was retained, but amended in such a way as to to limit its application to enabling Māori to 'contribute to decision-making on, and to participate in the delivery of, health and disability services'.

Despite the weakened intent, the introduction of the New Zealand Public Health and Disability Act 2000 was still ground-breaking in that it was the first tranche of social policy legislation to include a Treaty clause.

However, that issue wasn't the end of the perceived compromises and policy changes broadly associated with Closing the Gaps.

A couple of months into the next year, a new list of Cabinet committees was distributed that revealed that the Closing the Gaps committee chaired by the Prime Minister had disappeared. In its place a new 'Cabinet Social Equity Committee' had been established. The new committee would be chaired by Social Services and Employment Minister, Steve Maharey. Helen Clark subsequently admitted that the term 'Closing the Gaps' had carried too much baggage. Tariana also admitted it was not a concept she had liked, as she told the *Dominion Post*:

> Mrs Turia said closing the gaps was a term she had always preferred not to use.

"I think it's got quite negative connotations. Maori people themselves don't like the term," she said.

"Closing the gaps is, as far as I'm concerned, quite a negative term and focuses on deficiencies instead of on development opportunities, which I think Maori people prefer to concentrate in[28]."

Tariana's concern was not only that 'Closing the Gaps' was deficit-driven, but also that it pitted Māori against non-Māori, rather than judging each on their own merits.

It would not be long, however before New Zealanders became pitted against each other in a way that no one would ever have predicted.

One more controversy featured in Tariana's experience of the forty-sixth Parliament, and it was related to her role as Associate Minister of Corrections.

When Tariana had first been appointed in the Corrections role, the Department chose not to provide her with any staff. It was a portfolio that Tariana found extremely challenging, as she tried to reconcile the Department's rhetoric about rehabilitation and responsiveness to Māori with the reality of the prison experience as inmates portrayed it to her. Such stories were already familiar to her through her engagement with the many foster children she and George had taken into their home over the years.

The emphasis in the briefings that came across her desk was on 'strategies', 'memorandums of understanding' and 'cultural frameworks'. The Department accorded considerable priority to an analytical tool developed by neuropsychologist Garry McFarlane-Nathan: the Framework for Reducing Māori Offending (FReMO). The Framework was intended to encourage corrections staff and providers to focus on reducing Māori reoffending in the policy, interventions and research they commissioned.

To bring some life to the paperwork and see how the policy translated into practice, Tariana was always keen to see progress on the shop floor. Improving responsiveness to Māori became the mandate by which she reviewed outcomes from Te Piriti Special Treatment Unit in Auckland, the Montgomery House violence prevention programme in Hamilton, the 'bicultural therapy' model operating throughout correctional facilities, Te Ihi Tu (a community residential centre) in New Plymouth or the five Māori Focus Units (rehabilitative intervention units within certain prisons).

At Tariana's instigation, the Department of Corrections introduced Tikanga Māori programmes with the aim of encouraging offenders to develop a sense of awareness and responsibility for their behaviour and its impact on themselves and their whānau, hapū and iwi. On Tariana's initiative, it formalised the Kaiwhakamana Visitor Policy to give kaumātua greater access to Māori prisoners; these kaumātua assisted prisoners with whānau relationships, helped prisoners return to the community with the support of their iwi/hapū/whānau and advised the Minister and Department.

In the midst of all this activity and the piles of correspondence it involved, Tariana faced some ongoing criticism. One particular case related to intervention in the case of a maximum-security prisoner who had been one of the many foster children who had spent time in her home over the years.

In a press release, National MP Tony Ryall proclaimed 'the case for Turia to go builds' following one particular intervention:

> A 'pattern of behaviour' is continuing to emerge about Associate Corrections Minister Tariana Turia, National MP Tony Ryall said today. Information obtained by National under the Official Information Act shows Tariana Turia requested to review the file of 'Inmate C' who wanted her help to 'review/drop [his] charges to manslaughter'. An email sent by Tariana Turia's Senior Policy Advisor says 'Minister Turia has received a letter from [Inmate C] who is in Kaitoke Prison in Whanganui. The letter ... requests opportunity to review/drop charges to manslaughter. Minister has asked if she can look at his file'.

Ryall was convinced that the actions Tariana had taken in relation to this correspondence received breached conventions outlined in the Cabinet manual:

> 'Tariana Turia's misuse of her ministerial position was for far more serious purposes. We are looking at security classifications for inmates, transfers between prisons and now the charges brought against inmates. This cannot be swept under the carpet. Her judgement is not good and she should resign or be sacked'.[29]

The next day *Herald* reporter Francesca Mold honed in on the issue, referring to other instances where Tariana had allegedly been systematically misusing her position to try to influence prison authorities, and suggesting that the Government was trying to 'cocoon Mrs Turia from attacks in Parliament' by deflecting the questions to Corrections Minister Matt Robson.

Mold claimed that not only was Mr Robson protecting Tariana, but the Prime Minister had also been brought in on the defence team:

> Helen Clark went on the offensive yesterday, labelling the National Party accusations 'malicious' and aimed at 'Maori'. She said Mrs Turia's behaviour was 'entirely innocent'. The Prime Minister expressed admiration for Mrs Turia's 'good-hearted' nature, saying she deserved a medal, not criticism, for her willingness to take social welfare children into her home. This reference was to the inmate who was placed in her home for a year by the state.[30]

While Tariana appreciated the Prime Minister's support, she was quick to react to any suggestion that the Prime Minister's intervention reflected badly on her. Further analysis appeared in the *Herald*, which quoted Tariana as saying of Helen Clark's statements:

> 'I took it more as her attempting to provide me with some sort of protection.'
>
> Does she think she needs protection? 'Who me?' A big throaty laugh in response.

> 'I'm a big girl. I have a relationship with her and I don't think it's beyond either of us to give each other advice, and support ...'[31]

Tariana had recently bought the inmate of particular interest to Mr Ryall a ghetto blaster. She could only presume that the matter had been leaked by someone in the Department.

The young man had lived with Tariana for a year as a teenager, and had retained close communication with her and George ever since. The sound system had been a personal gift from their family, and had no connection to her role as a Minister. There was no evidence to suggest inappropriate behaviour on Tariana's behalf; all appropriate documentation had been provided to the authorities, and there was no reason why the gift should have been disclosed to the public.

Mold's *Herald* article had stated:

> Mr Robson told Parliament a conflict of interest did not exist because Mrs Turia had declared her personal connection with the inmate. She also did not exercise any executive decision-making powers, he said.
>
> But National questioned the closeness of the relationship, saying Mrs Turia had purchased an expensive stereo for the inmate and allowed him to use her private home telephone number.

The public outrage at this incident even made it into the pages of the *Women's Weekly*. Tariana told the magazine:

> Our office is inundated with letters from people from all around the country, not just Maori and not just from people who are in jail ... They raise their concerns on many issues and at different levels and some have tried everything else. I would never turn anybody down ... I feel very sorry for people who have written to you in good faith and then find their letter flashed on TV, it's appalling.[32]

The article showed a rare glimpse into the impact that the constant media surveillance was having upon Tariana:

> It's her husband Tariana looks to for support. 'I am very lucky I have George with me in Wellington', she says. 'It was a big sacrifice for him to make the move and I am very thankful.'

It also revealed how vital the support of whānau were in enabling Tariana to keep a sense of perspective when times were tough:

> 'Of course you question how effective you are being but my youngest boy summed it all up one day when I was feeling a little down', says Tariana. 'He said, why are you down, Mum? This is not about you. When you start thinking it's about you, then you should come home.'

The *Sunday Star-Times* featured an exclusive 'exposé' into the issue of Tariana's ministerial interventions, claiming she had personally sought help for eleven inmates, and that between November 2001 and February 2002 she had referred seventeen more cases to Corrections Minister Matt Robson and one to Justice Minister Phil Goff.

Tariana's defence was simple, as she told the *Women's Weekly*:

> A core part of an MP's work is to make representations on behalf of individuals, no matter who they are and where they come from … Frankly, if I'm the only one doing it, then it's a disgrace.[33]

The *Sunday Star-Times* didn't see it quite the same way:

> Of most concern in the early example of Turia's involvement was the case of Matthew Thompson. His relationship to Turia – he lived with her as a ward of the state – fuelled claims of a conflict of interest when she tried to have him transferred from Paremoremore Prison's maximum security wing to Wanganui to be closer to his family.[34]

While claims of nepotism and ministerial inteference loomed large in the press, the policy context was being conveniently overlooked. It was during this period that the Department was promoting 'whānau involvement plans' as a key focus in efforts to rehabilitate inmates back into their communities. Alongside Tikanga Māori programmes and a more cultural approach in general, the Department was actively supporting strategies to facilitate family involvement throughout the Corrections system, and relocation of inmates to be closer to their family members was becoming standard practice.

Tariana's actions had been entirely consistent with her philosophy, her approach to life: the view that the most effective policy solutions come from actively involving the whānau at every stage.

However, by the end of the forty-sixth parliamentary term, a perception that Tariana's performance as a Minister was heavily reliant on the respect and protection of the Prime Minister was firmly entrenched.

It would not be long, however, before that crucial relationship between Prime Minister and Minister would be tested beyond recovery.

The H word

In August 2000 Tariana addressed the New Zealand Psychological Society annual hui in Hamilton on how well psychologists were able to nurture the Māori psyche; the 'wounded spirit':

> Do you consider for example the effects of the trauma of colonisation? I know that psychology has accepted the relevance of PTSD (Post Traumatic Stress Disorder).
>
> I understand that much of the research done in this area has focussed on the trauma suffered by the Jewish survivors of the holocaust of World War Two. I also understand the same has been done with the Vietnam veterans.
>
> What seems to not have received similar attention is the holocaust suffered by indigenous people including Maori as a result of colonial contact and behaviour.
>
> The Waitangi Tribunal made such a reference in its Taranaki Report of 1996 and I recollect what appeared to be a 'but our holocaust was worse than your holocaust' debate. A debate, I must add, I do not wish to enter.[35]

Despite Tariana's words of caution, it was only a matter of hours before that same debate exploded.

As it turned out, one of my aunties had died in Taupō, and so I rang George and asked if he could pick me up from Hamilton. George said to me, 'Whatever possessed you to say what you did?' I said, 'It's the truth.' He said to me, 'You know you've always been drawn to saying things in a particular way and they end up being highly offensive'. I replied, 'oh, so you're offended too are you?'

We started to drive home and my daughter Lisa rang and told me not to go back to our house. The media were camped out in our garden, among the trees. My son then rings; it was like the hunga wairua with us, and he told me that Nanny Ada, my mother-in-law's sister, was in hospital and it didn't look good. This was another aunty, one of our very fit aunties, so it was a huge shock. We decided that instead of going home we'd go straight to the hospital. We'd just come out of the Parapara Road and we learned that she had died. I went to the hospital and we talked to the family about bringing her to my marae. Lisa by this stage has gone to my house to pack a bag; the media were still all staked out.

In the meantime, through all this, Helen Clark is overseas climbing a mountain. George and I are in the car; the telephone in the car rings. It's Helen.

She asked me, 'what in the hell possessed you to say what you did?' I said, 'because it's the truth'. She said to me, 'Look here, you can't say things like that when you are a Minister of the Crown. You've turned the country on its head.'

And I said, 'that's more their problem than mine'. She grunted, 'I'll be back in two days' time and I need to talk to you'. I told her, 'ok, but in the meantime I'm at a tangi so I'm not available for the next two days'.

Well, the media all turn up at our marae. My nephew goes out – he's quite a big boy – and tells them to go away because we have a tangi. 'I'll only offer once more for you to go away,' he tells them, 'because if you don't go away, someone is likely to smash your cameras.' They went.

In the meantime it gave me a couple of days to think about what I had said.

Ani Mikaere, in the Bruce Jesson Memorial Lecture for 2004, described the speech that had supposedly shaken the nation as appropriate for the context in which it was given:

> When in 2000 Tariana Turia spoke about the phenomenon of Post Colonial Traumatic Stress Disorder many leading politicians scaled new heights of sheer absurdity in their reactions, such was their horror at being reminded of a past they wanted so desperately to forget. As a result of the madness that erupted in the wake of her speech to the New Zealand Psychological Society Conference (and it is pertinent to note the head of the Psychological Society's public statement that her speech had been entirely appropriate in the context of the occasion) a whole new vocabulary of words that should not be mentioned in public emerged. We now know that, in relation to the Aotearoa context at least, the 'g' word (genocide) is considered impolite, the 'h' word (holocaust), simply unmentionable.
>
> Regrettably, amidst all the stupidity the message that was being conveyed was completely lost. Turia referred to Native American Psychologist Eduardo Duran who suggests that the colonial oppression suffered by indigenous people inevitably wounds the soul. There is no doubt in my mind that Māori continue to bear the scars of colonisation.[36]

Even at the time, not all of Tariana's colleagues reacted to the speech with anger. Simon Upton, a retiring member of the National Party, issued his own dignified challenge: 'New Zealanders who react with horror to her description of that as a "holocaust" are being a bit precious, or indulging in collective amnesia'.[37]

And Labour Party President Bob Harvey defended Tariana's right to speak out:

> A political party should have courage and it should have guts. You can't live in fear. I support anybody that has the courage of their convictions. You have got to fight if you believe things. Politics is about beliefs.[38]

But in early September 2000, those few voices of support were drowned out by the cacophony of rage that erupted when Tariana returned to

Wellington. There was palpable anger in the debating chamber from all sides of the House.

Professor Margaret Mutu summed up the reaction of the media:

> Overnight the media declared that the word holocaust was the sole preserve of Jewish people, misquoted Turia, and launched an attack on her that in its viciousness surpassed even the attacks on Tuku Morgan in 1997[39].

Sadly for Tariana, little support was forthcoming from her Labour colleagues. Mita Ririnui, the chair of Labour's Māori caucus, told the media that the speech had created unnecessary debate that could distract attention from the Government's programme: 'I do not agree that there is a similarity with the Holocaust[40]'. Parekura, in his new role as Minister of Māori Affairs, stated that 'holocaust' was too strong a description of the effects of colonisation[41], while Dover Samuels called Tariana's allusion to the Holocaust 'outrageous'.

The talkback raged; over 700 letters spilled into Parliament; and a typhoon of letters landed in editors' intrays right throughout the country.

One such example read on Radio New Zealand's *Insight* programme stated:

> Sir. Before colonisation Maoris were assaulting, raping, pillaging and murdering people. They kept slaves and ate their captives. Post colonisation some Maoris are assaulting, raping and murdering people. There has been some improvement. Come on Tariana Turia, wake up and face the issues. You are a disgrace to your American heritage, not to mention your Maori background.[42]

Tariana's office received an apple-box full of letters of protest. Tariana took the time to respond to every one. Her view has always been that if anybody takes the time to put pen to paper, then the very least she can do is to honour that effort by responding. It was an approach that distinguished her from other ministers. In other offices, staff routinely open mail and send auto-replies stating 'your letter has been placed before the Minister' without a second thought. Tariana's labour-intensive approach created long-standing relationships of respect with correspondents who realised her response was genuine. The approach is one aspect of a principle Tariana also demanded that her staff uphold: a standard based on kaupapa Māori; a benchmark of decency, respect and basic courtesy. Staff had to make the time to listen to phone calls, no matter how one-sided the kōrero. It was always about being open to dialogue; making space for conversation.

In the wake of the heat generated by the holocaust comments, the Prime Minister was not so interested in participating in conversation. On *Morning Report* on 4 September, speaking from New York, the Prime Minister shared her full wrath with the nation:

> ... that word must never be used again in a New Zealand context. I know the Tribunal used it with respect to Taranaki; I do not agree with that and I do not want to see Ministers using the term and causing offence again.

Eventually Helen returned to New Zealand, and I was called to her office.

I said to her, 'before you say anything to me, you read that report – I was only quoting the report. And she said, 'I know, but honestly, you and I could read the same book, and you would always find the bits that are going to get everybody going'.

After the meeting, my friend Gregory Fortuin came to see me. Gregory was a South African who had been appointed by Nelson Mandela as Honorary Consul to New Zealand in 1998. I first met Gregory in 1995 when he brought his family to support our whānau in the reclamation of Pākaitore. Gregory was a trusted advisor to Helen Clark; she was sufficiently impressed by him to invite him to speak to the Labour caucus on race relations issues.

He asked me, 'Are you prepared to say sorry?' I said, 'well, the issue is bigger than I am. If I have to say sorry because people are so upset about what I said, than I will say sorry.' Gregory said, 'Yes, but you have to say it as if you mean it'. I told him, 'I won't say it unless I do'.

The next day I duly sought permission to take a point of order and make a personal statement in the House, to apologise to those who had felt offended by my comments while also attempting to clarify the context to my comments:

> I am saddened at how my speech has been misreported and misconstrued and as a result caused distress to a number of

people including colleagues in this House and my own staff. I did not in my speech mean to belittle survivors of the World War Two holocaust or those whose houses have been invaded, nor do I intend to. As a member of a group that has been marginalised, I would never deliberately belittle the horrific experiences suffered by other people. I sincerely apologise to all those whom I have offended by these comments.

I was simply stating what I am sure that many New Zealanders, Māori and Pākehā agree, that Māori have been marginalised from the economic and mainstream of New Zealand life since the mid-19th century and that experience has been depressing for our people.[43]

Later that day Tariana's press secretary, Keri Iti, was advised to 'encourage' her to issue another statement of explanation, and Tariana did so: 'Lest there be any misunderstanding, I accept the Prime Minister's edict that ministers should not use this term [holocaust]'.[44]

The handling of the fallout was widely seen by the press gallery as a lack of political management by Clark's senior ministers. The *Daily News* reported:

> No fewer than three senior ministers worked late to extract yet another statement from their junior colleague. Acting Labour leader Michael Cullen, Cabinet trouble-shooter Trevor Mallard and Mrs Turia's official minder, Steve Maharey, oversaw the drafting of the statement without the knowledge of the prime minister's chief press aide, Mike Munro. Given that it came out so late as to miss most media deadlines, the ministers achieved little beyond creating an air of panic. The incident firmed up the impression that the minute Miss Clark leaves town, even her stronger ministers flounder.[45]

That whole day was amazing. The media hounded me. I couldn't get home until two in the morning because I couldn't get out of Parliament. They blocked every door of every floor. It was terrible.

A great deal was made of my decision to use the H word. A week later, when a poll revealed that Labour had fallen from 50 percent of the vote in March to 36 percent of the vote in September, one columnist summised that it was because 'list MP Tariana Turia's ill-disciplined self-indulgence [has alienated] a chunk of voters and [jeopardised] the Clark Government's prospects of a second term in office'.[46]

While I was under the microscope in Wellington, my real distress came from the fact that at home my whānau were also being attacked. People painted a swastika on my son's letterbox, threw food and eggs at our garage, shoved a bullet through our window, smashed my back door in, insulted my children. It was as a result of all of these incidents that my husband came down to Wellington to protect me, uprooting himself from our Whanganui home.

My colleagues in Labour attempted to paint a picture that my 'slip-up' was merely evidence of my inexperience as a first time minister. But Audrey Young had another view on that, citing the 'fine form' I had demonstrated earlier in same question time on 5 September:

> Without even drawing breath, she delivered a blow to the National leader, Jenny Shipley, who was rather careless with the high ground she chose.
>
> Mrs Shipley: Has the minister seen the statement made by Nelson Mandela at a Sydney conference this week, and I quote: 'During the times of tension, it is not the talented people who excel, who come to the top. It is the extremists who shout slogans'? And does she accept that Mr Mandela has accurately described her position?
>
> Mrs Turia: Perhaps I should remind the Opposition leader that it's not that long ago that that particular party called Nelson Mandela a terrorist.[47]

It was not usual form for me to take on Jenny Shipley. There is no doubt that when I first came in to Parliament, I looked up to her. In lots of ways she reminded me of my Aunty Wai – so strong, clear, determined. I thought she was a great politician, and deep down I thought I wanted to be like that – bold and fearless. But I couldn't let her get away with her line of question that day.

When all was said and done, was it worth it to use the H word? There is no question that it placed strain on the relationship I had with the Prime

Minister, placing her in the awkward position of having to defend me over the various incidents.

As the *Herald* said of Tariana:

> If she has fallen spectacularly (the H-word row, the accusations of abuse of her ministerial position over attempts to influence criminals' terms of imprisonment, the sniping at media), she has been caught by a safety net in the form of a prime minister. Helen Clark has publicly supported Turia, mildly chastising her lack of judgment but referring to her kind-heartedness, to the importance of hearing diverse voices.[48]

In a Radio New Zealand *Insight* programme that aired later, I told Chris Wikaira why I had thought it appropriate to use that term with the psychologists:

> I was asking them to research and understand what it is that has created all these things that are happening with the Māori people that they deal with, and do they understand the Māori psyche? I was focusing I guess on asking them to look at what has caused our people to change from what it is that we understand our people to have been pre-colonisation, what has been the impact of colonisation on them, and what has brought them to the situation today where we make up so much of the negative statistics. I regret the hurt that it has caused the Jewish people; ... I definitely regret that they were hurt by my use of the word[49].

Professor Mason Durie later suggested that although the term 'holocaust' might grate on the New Zealand psyche, 'when you think the population of 200,000 Maori in 1840 was reduced to 42,000 by 1900, that's pretty close to a holocaust.'[50]

I stand by the comment I made in the original speech, which I stated again in that first question time following it: 'I really do believe that mature, intelligent New Zealanders of all races are capable of the analysis of the trauma of one group of people suffering from the behaviour of another.'

Much to the concern of the security staff, there were public supporters in the gallery who applauded when I made that statement. But I also acknowledge that the whole incident incited a great deal of anger and heat among New Zealanders that I remain shocked by.

It taught me a valuable lesson. I think it's ok to tell the truth about things, but you have to think about what that truth means for a lot of other people. There are some things that are better left unsaid.

But more importantly, the incident taught me that your role in Government is not to be offensive to people. It is to be understanding of the reasons why people behave in particular ways. I've learnt to accept the things that I simply can't do anything about, and that's not been easy for me: to have been in Government, and not be able to make the changes that I would dearly loved to have made.

I remember we went out to dinner at an Indian place at America's Cup Village in Auckland, on the wharf, a month or two later. I was trying to encourage Helen Clark to meet with these young Māori who had business ideas that they wanted to promote for the America's Cup; they couldn't seem to get an in, and so I said 'I'll invite her to dinner'.

This very thin, drunk Pākehā woman – very aggressive – ran up to me. She said to me, hands on her hips, very loud, in front of our table, 'Listen here, you fucking fat so and so. You wouldn't even fit in an oven'. I didn't know what she was talking about. It was awful. I was so stunned. Fortunately for us the manager of the place overheard the fracas and quickly escorted the woman out the door.

Writer and historian Pat Snedden, my advisor and friend, places the whole H word affair into a context that has helped me to make sense of those hot-headed days in the autumn of 2000:

> One of the most important debates that she launched – and it made her hugely unpopular for a period, until people got what she was talking about – was the equivalence of Māori with colonisation and the Holocaust. Now there's an example of somebody deciding to provoke in a context where she has the ability to speak, and speak regally, to refine and define what she's talking about. And people were outraged. And then the outrage receded as she started, more and more, in that calm grandmotherly way, to just talk about what she means: when you are absolutely separated from all that gives you your sense of wairua and your sense of self.

It started to break through: she started to move from a very antagonistic conversation to a very intuitive conversation, where people were saying, 'actually, I think I understand now what she's talking about. I don't like to hear it, but I think I know what she means'.

If I was to characterise Tariana's value to New Zealand in the parliamentary process, I would say it has been in bridging the process where people do not like what they hear, to the point where they say, 'I think I understand what it means'. It may still irritate them, but they go beyond the defensiveness and into the conversation in a way that I think few New Zealanders have been able to manage.

NOTES

1 http://technotox.com/tag/joy/. Published by Technotox; a wellness centre for the mind.
2 Tariana Turia, 'Te Puawaitanga o te tohu, Māori social work paradigms', speech presented to Te Kaiawhina Ahumahi, 23 March 2000.
3 Elinore Wellwood, 20 August 2001, 'Closing the gaps in a different guise', *The Press*, 20 August 2001.
4 Vanessa Bidois, 'Maori Affairs brief aims for breadth', *New Zealand Herald*, 29 December 1999.
5 Alison Horwood, 'Dover Samuels down but not out', *New Zealand Herald*, 15 August 2000.
6 Richard Harman, 'Clark stuck with Rowling and Lange problem: Maori MPs', *National Business Review*, 25 August 2000.
7 Ruth Laugesen, 'Outburst raises voters' suspicions', *Sunday Star-Times*, 3 September 2000.
8 Victoria Main, 'Weak ministers make easy targets for Nats', *Daily News*, 11 September 2000.
9 Tariana Turia, 'Closing the Gaps', speech to Masters Class in Development Studies, Te Puawai Wānanga ki te Ao, 7 June 2000.
10 Ibid.
11 Ibid.
12 *Hansard*, 15 June 2000.
13 Tariana Turia, Press Release. 'Women's speaking rights', 17 January 2000.
14 Tariana Turia, Press release. 'Waitangi Day', 20 January 2000.

15 Tariana Turia, press release, 'Shifting attitudes, changing ways', 16 February 2000. www.beehive.govt.nz/node/6869 (accessed 12 February 2015).

16 'Turia's foster plan prejudiced – Peters', *Evening Post*, 31 March 2000, p. 15.

17 Tariana Turia, 'Family violence', 19 May 2000. www.beehive.govt.nz/node/7481 (accessed 6 May 2015).

18 Nick Venter, 'Pull your head in, refuge boss told', *Dominion*, 19 August 2000.

19 'Don't Shoot the messenger', *Dominion*, 23 August 2000.

20 *Hansard*, 21 June 2006.

21 Victoria Main, 'PM rides eternal tightrope on improving lot of Maori'; *Daily News*, 28 August 2000.

22 Audrey Young, 'Radical Minister Turia has space to beat her drum', *New Zealand Herald*, 26 August 2000.

23 Tariana Turia, press release, 'Maori nominations for HHS Boards', 10 March 2000.

24 Louise Humpage, 'Closing the Gaps: The Politics of Māori Affairs policy', PhD thesis, Massey University, 2002, p. 140.

25 Ibid, p. 156.

26 Peter Luke, 'Race issue haunts Govt', *The Press*, 28 October 2000.

27 Tariana Turia, *Morning Report*, Radio New Zealand, 26 October 2000.

28 *Dominion*, 'Maori didn't like Gaps term anyway – Turia', 12 December 2000.

29 National Party press release, 'The case for Turia to go builds', 7 November 2001.

30 Francesca Mold, 'Turia facing fresh meddling accusations', *New Zealand Herald*, 8 November 2001.

31 Michele Hewitson, 'Turia talking on a tightrope', *New Zealand Herald*, 16 March 2002.

32 Mere Mulu, 'Tariana Turia, Reluctant politician', *New Zealand Women's Weekly*, 3 December 2001.

33 Mulu, 'Tariana Turia, Reluctant politician'.

34 'Turia intervenes in more inmate cases', *Sunday Star-Times*, 3 February 2002.

35 'What Tariana Turia said – in full', *New Zealand Herald*, 31 August 2000.

36 Ani Mikaere, 'Are we all New Zealanders now? A Māori response to the Pākehā quest for indigeneity', Bruce Jesson Memorial Lecture, 2004.

37 *Hansard*, 12 December 2001.

38 'Turia stands by Holocaust remarks', *Dominion*, 31 August 2000.

39 Mutu, Margaret. 'Maori Issues'. The contemporary Pacific. Spring 2002. Polynesia in Review; Issues and Events, 1 July 2000 to 30 June 2001, p220.

40 'Turia stands by Holocaust remarks', *Dominion*, 31 August 2000.

41 Graeme Peters, 'Bridging the most difficult gap of all', *Evening Post*, 2 September 2000.

42 'A Taranaki Holocaust?', *Insight*, Radio New Zealand, produced by Sue Ingram and presented by Chris Wikaira, 27 April 2006.

43 *Hansard*, 5 September 2000.

44 Tariana Turia, press release, 'Turia – when I made my speech', 5 September 2000.

45 Victoria Main, 'Weak ministers make easy targets for Nats', *Daily News*, 11 September 2000.

46 'Maori Separatism', *The Press*, 18 September 2000.

47 Audrey Young, 'Holocaust apology puts minister in hot water', *New Zealand Herald*, 6 September 2000.

48 Hewitson, 'Turia talking on a tightrope'.

49 'A Taranaki Holocaust?', *Insight*, Radio New Zealand, produced by Sue Ingram and presented by Chris Wikaira, 27 April 2006.

50 Cited in A. Gifford (ed.) *Ngā Kōrero o te wā: A monthly summary of Maori news and views from throughout Aotearoa*, 31 August 2000, vol. 10, no. 12.

-CHAPTER SEVENTEEN-
NATION-BUILDING AND LOCAL SOLUTIONS

She says she believes the public perception of her is as 'non-normal'. She thinks of herself as 'a duck swimming in the wrong river'.

'If you think about what people perceive the norm to be, then I don't fit into what the norm is.

'And I think that people quite often interpret what I say to be outrageous, to lack truth, to lack substance. And yet usually I'm pretty careful about what I say.'[1]

When the forty-seventh Parliament was formed, it included a new Māori electorate, Tāmaki Makaurau, formed after the 2001 Māori Electoral Option resulted in an increased number of voters on the Māori electoral roll.

The 2002 elections were the first in which Tariana had run on the electorate ticket. With the choice now of seven electorates, Nanaia Mahuta opted to campaign in Tainui, while Tariana sought the mandate for Te Tai Hauāuru.

Tariana's choice of the electorate as her basis to represent was a well-calculated risk. She received 10,002 votes – 71 percent of all votes cast in the electorate – and a margin of 8657 over the runner-up, her long-time friend Ken Mair under the Mana Māori banner. Ken received 1345 votes; Greg White for National received 991. There were also candidates from United Future, the Alliance and the Christian Heritage Party.

In 2002, Tariana was appointed Minister for the Community and Voluntary Sector, as well as retaining associate ministerials in Māori Affairs, Health, Housing and Social Services. No doubt as a result of the negative publicity surrounding her interactions with inmates, she no longer had the challenge of the Corrections portfolio to deal with. But less than a month after the 2002 election, Tariana signalled she would continue to stand up for the rights of prisoners, whether or not she had the ministerial warrant. She told the Prisoners Aid and Rehabilitation Society:

> I hope I am not here on false pretences. When you invited me, I was Associate Minister of Corrections but not any longer. I gave up that role, so no-one can accuse me of conflicts of interest with my advocacy for prisoners. Advocacy is something I will continue to do.[2]

In her first public address as the new Minister for the Community and Voluntary Sector, Tariana described the basis for communities in Aotearoa as being a fluid relationship between hosts and guests.

In an address and reply speech in the House, she extended upon the hosting and guesting metaphor to emphasise the necessity of all citizens of Aotearoa learning about the Treaty of Waitangi:

> We cannot continue to pay lip service to this necessity. We must act, or this country will never develop a sense of nationhood. The Treaty

establishes the principles of unity, within which we can celebrate our diversity. It can help us to sing in harmony, to dance without trampling on each other's toes, and to compete internationally as a team with a game plan. Treaty education is essential to the smooth running of our society. The benefits of a proper programme of Treaty education are long overdue.

The Community and Voluntary Sector Working Party consulted widely on this matter over several years. They heard two recurring messages: iwi and the Crown need to develop an agreed understanding of the Treaty of Waitangi; and institutional racism in the public sector needs to be addressed urgently.

The denial of tangata whenua world views in policies, systems and practices is the essence of institutional racism. The flagship document Puao-te-ata-tu, which was the voice of tangata whenua people, represented the new dawn. Little did our people know that the sunset would come very quickly.[3]

Tariana began swiftly establishing an infrastructure for community development. On 5 December 2002 she announced a formal policy on volunteering, to recognise and value voluntary work, and to help increase understanding of volunteering. The policy contained a pledge to reduce barriers associated with volunteering in legislation, policy and practice. There was a commitment to assist public servants to contribute to voluntary work, as well as a statement covering a general duty of care for all volunteers.

Six months later, in the context of Budget 2003, Tariana announced that she had secured $3.59 million of new funding to establish the first Community and Voluntary Sector office in New Zealand, located in the Ministry for Social Development. The office was intended to strengthen community, voluntary and tangata whenua organisations and their relationships with the Government, to enable a strong voice for the sector in government decision-making. The policy and the office having been established, Tariana challenged the sector to focus on community outcomes, community well-being becoming the driving force for the sector:

> This takes us back to the principles of community development, or whānau development, or whānau ora – it is the community with the most at stake, so they should define the outcomes they seek. It is a contradiction in terms for the government to define what community development is, and how you do it.[4]

While Tariana was clear that a focus on outcomes and trust in the relationship underpinned sustainable community development, she also consistently emphasised the importance of building nationhood based on the Treaty of Waitangi. As she said in a speech to the national conference of the Community Organisations Grants Scheme and Department of Internal Affairs staff:

> A lack of agreement and trust between the Treaty partners is an impediment to political unity, and local and national development. The parties view many issues from different perspectives, and customary rights to the seabed and foreshore is just the most recent example. The voice of tangata whenua, their reo, is not being heard properly. Conflict can easily be avoided, if both sides make a real effort to engage with each other and understand the issues, instead of shouting slogans. This is a critical task of nation-building.[5]

While she was establishing the ground work for the community and voluntary sector, Tariana was also championing change in the areas of health, social services and Māori affairs.

It was during the term of the 2002–2005 Parliament that Tariana's reputation for transformative policy first emerged, through her work as Associate Minister of Māori Affairs in whānau development; her direct resourcing and local-level solutions; her initiatives in health through He Korowai Oranga; and an initiative in family violence, Project Mauriora.

Tariana appointed a ministerial Māori taskforce on family violence to develop a Māori conceptual framework for working with victims of family violence, perpetrators, whānau and their communities. The Taskforce was chaired by Tamati Kruger, and included Mereana Pitman, Di Grennell, Alva Pomare, Dennis Mariu, Tahuaroa McDonald, Teina Mita, Matehaere Maihi and Keri Lawson-Te Aho.

The Taskforce produced a report in September 2002 entitled *Transforming Whānau* Violence: A *Conceptual Framework* that presented responses to whānau violence prevention and intervention from a Māori world view.

Mauri ora (well-being) for whānau, hapū and iwi was the overall goal of the framework. The term refers to well-being created by the maintenance of balance between wairua (spiritual well-being), hinengaro (intellectual well-being), ngakau (emotional well-being) and tinana (physical well-being).

The challenge of achieving transformation in the area of whānau violence was close to Tariana's heart. She was excited by the practical approach developed by the Taskforce, which focused on whānau transformation. She loved the Mauri Ora model promoting a zero tolerance of violence, dispelling the illusion at a community and an individual level that violence is normal or acceptable and removing opportunities for violence to occur through transformative practice.

Project Mauri Ora was to work within whānau to restore whānau wellness and to eliminate whānau violence.[6] While the Taskforce was actively involved in consultation from August to December 2003, Tariana was also discussing with officials practical ways to support Project Mauri Ora through direct resourcing funding. Te Korowai Aroha was the group responsible for leading the project, by building the capacity of Māori practitioners and service providers; providing culturally appropriate interventions to victims, perpetrators and their whānau; and championing the message that violence is unacceptable to Māori communities. Ten pilots were funded over a two-year period, covering urban, provincial and rural communities, including Mātaatua, Tai Rāwhiti, Ngāti Whātua and Te Tai Tokerau, Te Āti Awa, Raukawa and Toa Rangatira.

The work that Tariana was leading in the family violence space, alongside the local-level solutions and direct resourcing options she was exploring in Māori Affairs, came together in a stream of work she described as whānau development. In a speech to the Women's Refuge movement at a hui in Taranaki, she described how all these strands might work together:

> Whānau development is the central idea. The challenge for the government is to help create a liberating environment that enables whānau to shape and direct their own lives to meet their own priorities. Many whānau will need support as they work through this process.

> As tangata whenua do this for ourselves, we expect government agencies to support us. They, too, must change ingrained behaviours and cultural patterns. Government agencies must work together with each other, and with the whānau – to support the whānau, not to direct them. Public servants need to learn and practise skills in inter-agency co-operation, recognising our people as members of whānau rather than as individual patients or clients, listening and responding rather than initiating and controlling.
>
> Of course, situations arise where urgent intervention by outside agencies is absolutely necessary for the safety of vulnerable members of the whānau. But, from a whānau development perspective, violating the integrity of whānau is not a long-term solution to violence. Whānau can learn ways to promote their own strength and well-being, instead of accepting violence as a normal way of dealing with problems. Every whānau has someone, somewhere, with something to offer, to start the process off.[7]

Two other key frameworks were introduced in this parliamentary term that reflected the bold spirit of innovation that came to characterise Tariana's influence on social policy.

On 8 September 2003, International Literacy Day, Tariana launched: Te Kāwai Ora, an initiative that proposed a new national definition of literacy.

Tariana had appointed a Māori adult literacy working party including Dr Kathie Irwin, an educational consultant, Bronwyn Yates of Literacy Aotearoa, Susan Reid of Workbase, Te Ripowai Higgins of Te Ataarangi, Wally Penetito of He Pārekereke at Victoria University, Mereana Selby of Te Wānanga o Raukawa, Bubs Taipana of the Whaia te Ara Tika Literacy Programme, and Rachel Wikaira of the Correspondence School.

A press release of the time stated:

> 'Te Kawai Ora: Reading the Word, Reading the World, Being the World' is a thought-provoking report on tangata whenua approaches to literacy,' said Mrs Turia. 'For tangata whenua, literacy means bi-literacy – being able to function in both iwi and Pākehā worlds. Otherwise, the

reality and worldviews of tangata whenua are doomed to wither away, and our people are doomed to live forever in someone else's reality.[8]

Tariana said that the report outlined that being able to 'read' the world Māori lived in required understanding 'the geography of the land, the meaning of whakapapa, of carvings and tukutuku in a meeting house, and the politics of life of tangata whenua'. Tariana was also able to articulate how a fuller understanding of literacy could, in itself, contribute to nation-building, by enabling greater participation in conversations that matter:

> Another example is the debate we are having over the seabed and foreshore. The core of the debate is the meaning of words like title, ownership, custom, rights, whakapapa, tupuna, rangatiratanga, mana, and tangata whenua. How do you 'read' these words without understanding the world-views, tikanga, reo or cultures of Pākehā and tangata whenua?[9]

The other key framework for transformation introduced at this time was *He Korowai Oranga: Māori Health Strategy*. Literally translated, the term 'he korowai oranga' means 'the cloak of wellness'. The new Māori Health Strategy symbolised the protective cloak and mana of the people – the cloak that embraces, develops and nurtures the people physically and spiritually.

At this time, there were about 200 Māori health and disability providers actively involved in the health sector. As Associate Minister of Health, Tariana negotiated $10 million a year for the Māori Provider Development Scheme, to focus on Māori workforce and provider development. The investment was critical to ensure Maori health providers had the infrastructure and management capacity to be sustainable.

On 13 November 2002, alongside then Health Minister Hon Annette King, Tariana launched the Māori Health Strategy at Te Papa in Wellington, saying:

> He Korowai Oranga: Māori Health Strategy recognises and builds on the considerable strengths and assets of whanau, hapu, and iwi Maori. 'Whanau ora' (family health and wellbeing) is at the heart of this strategy, because it is the whanau that is the foundation of Māori society.[10]

He Korowai Oranga was driven by three key themes: Māori aspirations for rangatiratanga (control) over their own lives, maintaining and building on gains already made in Māori health, and reducing health inequalities between Māori and non-Māori:

> 'If Maori are to have healthier lives and fulfil their potential, then all the factors that affect health need to be addressed. We can do this by providing integrated health and social services, with multi-disciplinary teams assisting individuals and their whanau to make their choices,' Mrs Turia said. 'He Korowai Oranga challenges us to create environments where whanau can shape and direct their own lives.'[11]

NOTES

[1] Michele Hewitson, 'Turia talking on a tightrope', *New Zealand Herald*, 16 March 2002.

[2] Tariana Turia, 'Whānau Aid and Rehabilitation', speech to the Prisoners Aid and Rehabilitation Society, Christchurch Branch, 26 August 2002.

[3] *Hansard*, 4 September 2002.

[4] Tariana Turia, 'Building communities', speech to national conference of Community Organisations Grants Scheme and Department of Internal Affairs staff, 29 July 2003.

[5] Ibid.

[6] An updated report was produced in September 2004, but the foreword was signed out by Hon Parekura Horomia, as by that stage Tariana had resigned from Parliament following the Foreshore and Seabed Bill.

[7] Tariana Turia, 'Whānau Violence and Whānau Development', speech to Women's Refuge hui, 13 January 2004.

[8] Tariana Turia, press release, 'Turia launches Māori literacy report', 8 September 2003.

[9] Ibid.

[10] Annette King, press release, 'He Korowai Oranga: Maori Health Strategy Launch', 13 November 2002.

[11] Ibid.

-CHAPTER EIGHTEEN-
THE FORESHORE AND SEABED DEBATE

I told my cousin Archie (Taiaroa) about the dream that I had after I went to Rātana. I had had this amazing dream about our tūpuna from the river, with a wave coming up at the mouth of our river and our tūpuna on that wave. Within the swell of a wave all the faces of our old people from the awa showed themselves to me. And I just knew that I would be ok. Archie said, 'No, you have to finish; you have to go'.

On 19 June 2003 the Court of Appeal delivered its judgment in the Marlborough Sounds foreshore and seabed case. It ruled that the Māori Land Court had jurisdiction to determine whether or not the foreshore and seabed of New Zealand had the status of Māori customary land.

Eight iwi of Te Tau Ihu, Ngāti Apa, Ngāi Kōata, Ngāti Kuia, Ngāti Rārua, Ngāti Tama, Ngāti Toa and Rangitāne, along with Te Ātiawa Manawhenua Ki Te Tau Ihu Trust, had applied to the Māori Land Court in 1997 requesting that the 'foreshore and seabed of the Marlborough Sounds, extending to the limits of New Zealand's territorial sea' be defined, under Te Ture Whenua Maori Act 1993, as 'Māori customary land'. The application had emerged out of the failure of the iwi to be awarded rights for mussel farming, and their concern at the issuing of marine farm permits by the Marlborough District Council in areas of special significance to them.

The Māori Land Court determined that it could consider the issue, but was overruled by the High Court via the Māori Appellate Court. The High Court ruled that Māori did not have customary interest in the foreshore, while the seabed below the low-water mark was owned by the Crown in common law. The case progressed to the Court Appeal.

The Court of Appeal's 19 June 2003 decision *Attorney-General v Ngati Apa*, overturning the decision of the High Court, was to have grave consequences for the stability of government and for the self-identity of tangata whenua, and lead to a dramatic turn of events for Tariana in her relationship with the Labour Party.

In *Attorney-General v Ngati Apa*, Chief Justice Sian Elias stated:

> It may well be that any customary property will be insufficient to permit a vesting order with the consequence of fee simple title. But that does not seem to me to be a reason to prevent the applicants proceeding to establish whether any foreshore or seabed has the status of customary land. I consider that the Maori Land Court has jurisdiction to entertain the application.[1]

The Court of Appeal ruled that the Crown did not own the foreshore and seabed, concluding that:

> … it cannot be too solemnly asserted that native property over land is entitled to be respected and cannot be extinguished ('at least in times of peace') otherwise than by consent of the owners.

The detail is important. Other elements of the ruling were that the definition of 'land' in Te Ture Whenua Maori Act 1993 did not necessarily exclude foreshore and seabed; that the title vested in the Crown was radical title, which was not inconsistent with native title; and that various Acts had influence over but did not extinguish property rights.

The Prime Minister and Attorney-General immediately responded with a press release that framed the decision as 'narrow and technical' with no 'immediate practical effect':

> Prime Minister Helen Clark and Attorney-General Margaret Wilson said today that the Court of Appeal decision pertaining to the legal status of New Zealand's foreshore and seabed has no immediate practical effect on either the current use or the regulation of the foreshore and seabed. 'The decision is a narrow and technical one relating to the jurisdiction within which claims to the foreshore and seabed may be considered. Ownership of the foreshore and seabed has long been considered to lie with the Crown, and the Crown has made provision for regulation of its use in the national interest.'[2]

The release concluded that: 'The government respects attempts to explore legal rights through the courts, but also acknowledges that issues of ownership and use affect all New Zealanders'.

That was Friday. By Monday it was a different story.

On 23 June 2003, the Government announced that it would legislate to reassert the Crown's ownership of the foreshore and seabed. Attorney-General Margaret Wilson said that the Cabinet had decided to clarify the law so that it said what everyone had assumed it said: that the Crown owns the seabed and foreshore for all New Zealanders. The next day in the House, Mrs Wilson, in her capacity as Associate Minister of Justice, reiterated this view:

> The intention of the proposed legislation is to give clear expression to the Crown's ownership of foreshore and seabed for the benefit of all New Zealanders ... It is the Government's intention to balance the interests of all parties in this matter.[3]

Following an interjection by Winston Peters, Bill English asked:

> Has the Associate Minister seen the following comments: 'This is a due process of law; there is no need for anxiety. If the claims of the tangata whenua are upheld there will no doubt be negotiations with the Crown', which are statements made by Tariana Turia on Saturday; and did the Government consult her and the members of the Māori caucus before making its statements that appeared in public yesterday?

Hon Margaret Wilson replied:

> No, I had not seen those specific comments, and, no, there was no formal negotiation with the Māori caucus on the point of principle. However, there will be extensive negotiation with the Māori caucus and with other members of the caucus in working out the detail of the policy.

The issue of negotiation with the Māori caucus is particularly important in Tariana's story. Later that same day, the Labour Māori Caucus released their own statement:

New ministers in Helen Clark's Labour Government, Parekura Horomia and Tariana, after the 1999 election.
Source: Newspix.co.nz

Tariana with (Robert) Boy Cribb (Chair of Tamahaki Developments), Chas Poynter (Whanganui mayor 1986–2004) and Sir Archie Taiaroa in November 2002, remembering the occupation of Pākaitore.
Source: Fairfax NZ

Tariana and George with their daughter Lisa at home in Broadmeadows, Wellington in 2005.
Source: Newspix.co.nz

Decision time: Tariana walks with friends and family toward her date with destiny at Rātana Pā on 30 April 2004 to announce she will quit the Labour Government after refusing to support Labour's foreshore and seabed legislation.
Source: Shane Bennett

'I was just so proud of her taking a stand – the hīkoi – that was a really defining moment in Mum's life.' Son Pahia, in left foreground of photo, with whānau from Whanganui marching down Lambton Quay to Parliament, 5 May 2004.
Source: Ngāti Kahungunu Iwi Incorporated

Customary rights to seabed and foreshore

Following the Labour Party caucus this morning the Prime Minister has agreed that she, Attorney-General Margaret Wilson and Deputy Prime Minister Michael Cullen will lead a committee engaging with the Māori caucus to explore the definition, application and implementation of Māori customary rights to seabed and foreshore.

The government has said it would prefer to resolve these issues through public policy processes, rather than through litigation. The Māori caucus will be involved in the design of those policy processes, to ensure that the views of tangata whenua are considered. Under no circumstances is the government extinguishing Māori customary rights. It is merely setting out a process in light of the circumstances where those rights can be recognised. The Appeal Court decision (para 16), quoting extracts from the Privy Council, says: ... 'it cannot be too solemnly asserted' that native property over land is entitled to be respected and cannot be extinguished ('at least in times of peace') otherwise than by consent of the owners.

The land wars are over, so the consent of tangata whenua is required before customary title can be extinguished. Otherwise it is a confiscation, and is likely to breach international law. The Māori caucus is clear that customary use flows from customary title, and if the title is lost, the rights of tangata whenua become privileges granted by the Crown.

The Māori MPs noted that tangata whenua have never excluded others from their customary lands, provided wahi tapu are respected and natural resources are not damaged or depleted.[4]

It appeared that the MPs of the Labour Māori Caucus were united in their opposition to anything that might suggest confiscation, speaking with one voice about the importance of working together to protect and preserve Māori customary rights.

Their statement was also consistent with many others being made by whānau, academics, lawyers and politicians alike. Constitutional lawyer Moana Jackson suggested that in denying Māori the right to a fair trial, the Government was in effect creating a festering sore.[5] Iwi spokesman for Te Tau Ihu iwi John Mitchell immediately announced that top of the south Māori would be getting advice after Government's move to 'stomp all over' their foreshore and seabed claims.[6] And Victoria University's dean of law Matthew Palmer advised that the tone of the Government's statement gave Māori legitimate cause to believe the Government was setting out to confiscate a property right and that the Government really had an obligation to consult with Māori and take account of their views.[7]

Two months later, it appeared that the unity of the Labour Māori Caucus was still intact. On 18 August 2003 the Caucus met with a group of stakeholders to report to them on progress from discussions with ministers on customary rights to foreshore and seabed. In an official statement the Caucus said:

> The outcome of our discussions with colleagues is to be seen in the government's discussion paper. In our view, custom involves the mana and rangatiratanga of tangata whenua, and issues must be resolved between tangata whenua and the Crown. We understand consultations and negotiations are about to commence. …
>
> From this morning's discussion, it is clear that any attempt to extinguish customary ownership of the foreshore and seabed will create huge conflict for tangata whenua. Our people have expressed that their interests are always compromised in the so-called public interest. Tangata whenua cannot relinquish customary rights because they are part of a whakapapa relationship with ancestors which cannot be denied. This is the nub of the issue expressed in the meeting. Any attempts by the Crown to define customary title and rights that flow from that will be contested.[8]

To reinforce the caucus position, Tariana released a statement on that same day, indicating clearly that if customary rights were compromised then there would be conflict:

'Our people expressed their views in the meeting this morning that their bottom line is the issue of ownership, and they did not want to compromise on that,' said Tariana Turia.

'The issue of tangata whenua ownership is not addressed in the government's proposals, so there must be a question of whether the process outlined will resolve the issues that our people want to address.

'Customary rights is clearly a defining issue for tangata whenua. Many of our people have voted us in here to uphold a particular position. Our role is to advocate that position, and the Māori caucus has been united on that.

If we, as the Government, take a different position then our people will no doubt believe they have been compromised. This will put all the Māori MPs in a difficult position.'[9]

As the days went by, tension started to build on all sides. In debate in Parliament, Dr Cullen was challenged for his use of the term 'racist' in reference to the Marlborough Mayor, having clashed with him the previous week when he said the District Council did not consult iwi properly over marine farm planning, which was the source of the friction leading to the foreshore row.

Tariana was very aware of the growing mood of discontent. In a Beehive Chat in July she predicted the backlash around the corner:

Tangata whenua around the country are bracing themselves for a wave of righteous anger to come crashing down on any Māori initiative while any pro-Māori person who dares to speak out will automatically become a target ... Allegations of racial privilege and separatism are just the softening up phase, to create a climate of opinion where personal attacks seem to be justified and obsessive nit-picking criticism of Māori undertakings has its own strange logic. The real campaign is just getting under way now.[10]

In mid-August 2003, the Government released a discussion document identifying four principles for consultation: access, regulation, protection and certainty. In doing so, it was by default framing the *Ngati Apa* decision as causing problems of uncertainty, creating unclear rights to regulation, establishing a lack of protection of Māori rights, and most of all jeopardising public access to the foreshore and seabed.

The Government then set out on the process of consultation hui. In her Beehive Chat that week, Tariana emphasised the importance of the hui:

> Tangata whenua insist this dispute is a matter of ownership because they feel 'ownership' is the only term they can use to make clear to the Crown and the legal system how important this issue is. They have told the Māori MPs they see it as a question of mana and authority — of justice not race.[11]

At this time, Tariana, in her associate Māori Affairs role, had also arranged a series of hui to discuss whānau development. In her mind she saw no conflict between the two:

> When we talk about mana whenua and customary title, ownership and rights, settlement and compemsation we must keep the people in focus. To tangata whenua recognising our rights means recognising our people. It is our whānau and hapū who must be prepared to assert and defend their rights and to fulfill their duties and obligations, to each other and to other people.[12]

The next few months were packed with activity. In her regular Beehive Chat column Tariana sometimes chronicled the events of her ministerial diary. On 22 September 2003, she reported that the last fortnight had included speaking at a whānau development hui in Kaitāia attended by 130 people: one of twelve regional hui that would contribute to a national whānau development strategy. She had also briefed the Minister of Women's Affairs on her recent trip to an indigenous women's conference in Australia; and given a keynote address to a conference in Rotorua on indigenous issues in mental health nursing and another keynote speech to the Problem Gambling Foundation Conference in Auckland. Back in Wellington she had met with Grandparents raising Grandchildren; launched her Office for the Community and Voluntary Sector and spoken to the AGM of the Credit Union Association in Hamilton.

She had been in Auckland to speak at an international conference on evaluating indigenous projects; and had returned to Parliament to present Dr John McLeod scholarships in Māori health. In between, she had met with a rural GP, met with women in her electorate to discuss family violence issues, hosted some social service students from Minginui, attended a performance of black South African school students and then wound up the fortnight accompanying the Prime Minister to the AGM of the Māori Women's Welfare League in Palmerston North.

In the midst of all the business, the controversy around the foreshore and seabed was never far from Tariana's mind. In her Beehive Chat she described the evolving kōrero:

> Bishop Max Mariu raised the seabed and foreshore issue there and how we must protect our tikanga and not allow legislation to override in. A young woman, Hinurewa Poutu, told the hui that the rangatahi speaking in the Nga Manu kōrero competitions also opposed the government's proposals.[13]

At the end of the year the Government released a new framework proposing a 'public domain' title: full and beneficial ownership of the foreshore and seabed would be vested in the Crown in perpetuity for the people of New Zealand.

Tariana's response was swift and left no doubt as to her opinion. In a speech to Te Ngawari Hauora, a Māori health provider, at the Island Bay Surf Club in Wellington she issued her response:

> Because tikanga involves questions of mana and identity, atua, ancestors and future generations, there is no way that tangata whenua will ever give up our rights voluntarily, or allow them to be subject to anyone else's authority. We will never agree that the Crown or anyone else should hold them on our behalf. Our tupuna who signed the Treaty of Waitangi in 1840 saw no conflict between exercising their rights in accordance with tikanga, and sharing their lands and resources with others. Neither do we today. But what our ancestors required, what the Crown guaranteed in writing, and what we expect from our fellow New Zealanders, is that our customary rights be respected and protected.[14]

The speech immediately raised the attention of an eager press gallery. *North and South* reporter Nicola Shepheard challenged Tariana to respond to the 'widespread sense in middle New Zealand that this is just one demand too far'. Tariana told her:

> This is a defining issue. It's actually about the last area which our people held kaitiakitanga (guardianship) over for over 1000 years. While the [Appeal] Court didn't find we still had property rights today, it found they hadn't been extinguished and said we had to go to court to prove we had a continuing relationship with those areas. Our response is, yes we never gave that up. Just because somebody has sovereignty over our land it doesn't mean they have the right to take it from you. In compensation (for historic land grabs) we've only got one percent back of what was stolen from us. How much more do people want to take from us? I'm sick of people saying we're greedy, that we're chequebook Maori, when in reality all we want is justice – justice for us and our grandchildren into the future. And any self-respecting New Zealander would want that for themselves. I wouldn't want to be living on someone else's land that had been ripped out from them and their family. We had children in our tribe who were murdered by the military over land[15]. It runs deep. And no matter how many generations, if it's today or in a 100 years time, we won't forget what's happened to us.[16]

Tariana's response was a blend of frustration at being misunderstood and a sadness that her genuine intent for nation-building was not recognised:

> The thrust of my speech was one of uniting. I get sick of people who choose to take one line completely out of context. I'm sorry people were offended but I don't think they needed to be. I've been called an immigrant, I've been called an American, I've been called heaps of things. This is about trying to show some leadership on a critical issue.[17]

The Island Bay speech provoked a new line of questioning from the Opposition in the form of Gerry Brownlee, Winston Peters, Don Brash, Heather Roy, Richard Prebble and Wayne Mapp in debate in the House on 16 December.

There were inferences that the Prime Minister had lost confidence in Tariana (Helen Clark responded that she had confidence in Tariana, because she was a hard-working and conscientious minister). Scrutiny was applied as to whether Clark had known about the substance of the speech, or whether she had received a 'heads up' as to its content. Wayne Mapp asked Tariana why she had said what she did. Her response expressed her clear alignment to the views of tangata whenua: 'That was a clear view that was expressed by tangata whenua at the eleven consultative hui held to discuss the Government's earlier proposals'.[18]

The parting shot in the debate was Don Brash's question to Helen Clark as to whether two rules were being played:

> Noting her press release saying she will be the sole judge of whether Tariana Turia has breached the Cabinet Manual in respect of collective Cabinet responsibility, is it that there are to be two standards of citizenship and two sets of rules depending on whether a Minister is Māori, in the same way that she intends to create two standards of citizenship on the foreshore?

The Prime Minister replied, 'There is one rule, and that is that the Prime Minister makes a judgment'.[19]

After an explosive six months at the end of 2003, Tariana began the new year clear about what she should do. In an article published in the *Sunday Star-Times* on 25 January 2004, she indicated the action she might end up taking:

> The foreshore and seabed is a very defining issue and it is one that has got significant meaning for me, bigger than anything. On this issue I will be strongly led by what our people say to me. Because it's about tikanga, it's about whakapapa, it's about our people's genealogical connection to those bits of land. That's not something that I could view lightly being taken from them.[20]

Tariana was laying the foundation for her actions over the next few months. Her next revelation came in a local column a week later:

> At the hui in Putiki last week, where iwi from within Te Tai Hauauru met to discuss the government's proposal for the seabed and foreshore I signalled my intention to abstain from voting on the planned legislation. I did not enter Parliament expecting to abstain on issues of importance. I have decided to abstain because I want to send a signal that I know tangata whenua do not support the government's proposals without supporting the opposition parties of National, Act and New Zealand First. This decision is not about what Tariana Turia wants to do. I have always said that as an iwi, we need to be disciplined in what we do.[21]

The decision she referred to was not an easy one. Tariana knew that in some quarters abstaining would look like a backdown, a Clayton's protest; letting the Government off the hook. She noted this, saying, 'I hope this is not so. I have consulted my conscience and tried my best to act with integrity.'[22]

That year at Waitangi the reaction to the Government's presence was hostile. Some opposed the Government being welcomed on to Te Tii. The messages were blunt, and left Labour in no doubt that people thought the policy breached the Treaty of Waitangi. Don Brash attended at Waitangi, but was splashed with mud by protesters, in a dramatic expression of the people's disgust for his views on 'getting rid of the Treaty'. Tariana was always safe, protected by her own WPS (Whanganui Protection Squad): Piripi Haami, Hapi Lomax, Ken Mair and others. However, an ever-present thread in Tariana's Beehive Chats indicated escalating tension associated with the Government's proposals alongside the Opposition campaign against alleged separatism or 'race-based policies'.

Fuel was added to the fire by the now infamous address given at the Orewa Rotary Club by Don Brash in his role as leader of the National Party. The speech attempted to create a new definition of Māori as a 'distinct South Seas race of New Zealanders', and set about designing the shape of Brash's utopian state:

> The 'principles of the Treaty' — never clearly defined yet ever expanding — are the thin end of a wedge leading to a racially divided state and we want no part of that. There can be no

basis for special privileges for any race, no basis for government funding based on race, no basis for introducing Māori wards in local authority elections, and no obligation for local governments to consult Māori in preference to other New Zealanders. We will remove the anachronism of the Māori seats in Parliament. Having done all that, we really will be one people – as Hobson declared us to be in 1840.[23]

In a series of articles, Tariana challenged Dr Brash to identify what these so-called special privileges for Māori were:

By virtually every statistical indicator, tangata whenua are disadvantaged, under-represented, not achieving our full potential … But we must be careful. There is racism in our society – at a personal, cultural and institutional level. Unleashing racial division will have dire consequences.[24]

A fortnight later, she continued the theme:

The race-based political campaign led by the National Party has breached a fragile consensus, that debate on race and Treaty issues should be based firmly on facts and supported by reasoned arguments. … Everywhere I go our elders and leaders are really worried about their ability to restrain their younger people. How can they convince their young to show discipline and good faith when the treaty partner is behaving so badly? I appeal to our people to remain dignified in the face of provocation, to remember the lessons of Parihaka and to take a longterm view of the current troubles.[25]

Ten years later, the fury that Tariana felt about Dr Brash's statements of that time is just as palpable:

I was outraged with Don Brash for taking that moment to try and turn New Zealanders against one another. I found his racism absolutely appalling. … The worst thing about all that behaviour is that it is all about votes.[26]

What hit Tariana even harder was the impact that the 'one New Zealand' campaign seemed to make with the general public. In Hinewehi Mohi's documentary *Lines in the Sand*, she said, 'I can remember the *Dominion* printing these pages and pages of letters to the editor. I wept. I wept to think that's what other New Zealanders thought of us as a people.'[27]

In March 2004 the Waitangi Tribunal released their report, finding that the seabed and foreshore policy clearly breached the principles of the Treaty of Waitangi. But beyond the Treaty, the Tribunal held that the policy also failed in terms of wider norms of domestic and international law. These included the principles of fairness and non-discrimination. The Tribunal was painstakingly clear, that the policy took legal rights away, and with them opportunities to affirm ancestral mana, to exercise kaitiakitanga and manaakitanga, to develop traditional uses and to derive commercial benefits as resource holders. It concluded that the Crown's policy response to the Court of Appeal decision not only abolished the rights of tangata whenua, it also violated the rule of law by denying them access to court.

In her Beehive Chat of 15 March 2004, Tariana asked the question, 'who is ready to seize a last chance to turn conflict into positive dialogue?'

The day before, she had addressed the Labour Party regional conference, telling delegates that she had considered resigning because of widespread opposition among tangata whenua to the Government's proposals to override due legal process:

> I spoke frankly to my party colleagues because they need to know the strength of our peoples' opposition to the current proposals. I told them that not a single iwi in my electorate is not opposed, and that the national hui on Saturday called for all of Labour's Māori MPs to cross the floor and vote against the introduction of the Bill. The people at the hui were literally horrified, not just at the loss of rights, but because the proposals for legislation deny them the fundamental democratic right of access to the courts to settle disputes. I told my colleagues this policy could cost them the Māori vote.[28]

Tariana reiterated that she might 'have to consider other options at some future time' and that she would make her decision on the legislation when it was in its final form.

It was around this time that the Labour Māori Caucus meetings started heating up. Georgina Beyer remembers that time:

> Helen could see that there was pushback from the Māori Caucus and this was dangerous. And so started the weeks of meetings – toings and froings of the Māori Caucus, going to Michael Cullen's office and having these meetings, all eight involved. He had all the relevant ministers sitting in the room – you had Dover, Tari, J. T., Parekura. J. T. was Land Information. We would go to Michael's office to have these meetings with him – he'd never come to our Māori Caucus meeting.

From all accounts it was a long, painful process of proposal and counter-proposal, the draft legislation at the centre of the debate. Georgina tells of the nights of conflict and contradiction:

> Usually they were evening meetings to find out what progress was on the Bill. Once we saw the draft of what it was Tari and others would take it away and start working on it and going through it and propose something else to go into the draft legislation that fitted the concerns of the Māori Caucus, and take it back. The only time I ever saw Michael Cullen being brought to tears of anger was one day when Dover pushed back real hard about something and he got very angry at the table, and Michael just exploded. 'No, you're not getting it, Dover; it can't be like that.' It was hugely frustrating. It got very heated and it was very very tense. It was horrible. And then we'd have to walk out of those meetings and walk straight into a doorstop in the bloody lift-well of the Beehive. 'What do you want to do, bring this government down?' – all of that kind of stuff.

At the end of this process, Tariana told TVNZ's *One News* in 2014, there was a key night when it seemed the Labour Māori Caucus had reached the point of no return:

> We had agreed that all of us would put a proposition to Helen Clark which would mean that all of us in fact could leave and be in coalition with Labour at that time. We would operate as a bloc. Parekura, Mita and I went up to meet with Helen, and she wept. When that happened Parekura gave me the eye, which meant I had to do all the talking. My biggest regret was that by 12 o'clock the next day the others had all decided to stay with Labour. Every single one of them had been talked around. And as I realised later, they had already been offered junior ministerials.[29]

Tariana's former colleagues, other than Georgina, contest her account of that night. Dover Samuels laughed it off: 'for me she had a dream, she had a dream'.[30] Mita Ririnui suggested that rather than walk away, the other Labour Māori MPs at that time were actually working with ministers to turn a bad Bill into something they could live with. Meanwhile, for Parekura, by the end of that month, he had confirmed his support for the legislation, despite acknowledging Tariana was opposed. 'Certainly there is real support for it,' he told the *Dominion Post*. 'You know as well as I do that there have been tensions but we are very clear on the benefit it can do for Maori.'[31]

The passage of the legislation was rapidly gathering pace. In the Prime Minister's press release of 4 May, she retraced the time line:

> On 5 April with the legislation being tabled in the House later that week on 8 April I phoned Ms Turia and I advised her that I had said at the press conference that I expected Caucus would give permission for her not to support the Bill but that she would not be able to hold her ministerial job if she crossed the floor. That evening on the phone she advised me that if that was my intention she would be leaving Parliament and causing a by-election and there was then a short discussion about what would happen to the house and car at that point.[32]

It was obvious at this stage that a rift was developing between Tariana and the rest of her Caucus. Her long-time colleague and friend Tim Barnett realised just how far apart they'd become when Tariana turned sixty and no one from Labour acknowledged it:

> Helen rang to say that she was concerned about Tari and Tari's feeling about the hīkoi, and just generally about the Caucus, and she felt that there was distance there, and she wanted somebody to just go and have a conversation. And then she said, 'I think Tari had a big birthday recently'. And I just thought, 'wow we had all moved so far from her' – not that Tari would be somebody who was deeply bothered about birthdays, but it was just that sense of something not right. So we drove over that day and had the day with her. She was living down by the beach. I stayed with her a couple of times; she was clearly talking about leaving Labour at that stage.

Everything collided in the last week of April 2004. The political pressure cooker reached boiling point. The calls from the people were growing in intensity. Restless nights over many months were sharpening my focus. The messages of our tūpuna were resonating with the submissions I was hearing at hui throughout the electorate; it was one and the same.

Just over three weeks had passed since the Foreshore and Seabed Bill had been introduced on 7 April 2004. We had been on the road ever since seeking the opinion of the people. Hui were called rapidly in Tokoroa, Mangakino, Whanganui, Foxton, Levin, Otaki, Waitara, New Plymouth and Palmerston North. The marae were packed, the grief of the mana whenua palpable as they described the impact the legislation would have for them. Mobile coverage was patchy; frequently the reaction from Wellington was relayed to us by the ever-eager media pack who were travelling these same roads with us. In the weekly column I published online, I rehashed the questions put to me by the people of Te Tai Hauāuru:

> How can we be tangata whenua when the last piece of customary land that we have left is being removed? What hope is there for tangata whenua when only a small number of Māori MPs uphold tikanga? What does this Bill mean for our ongoing relationship with the Crown? Am I prepared to make a mark in the sand, to be on the public record?[33]

My last line in that Monday column – in what was to be my last column as a member of the Labour Party – crystallised the messages I had received in those months when sleep had failed to come: 'I believe my role in this debate is to show leadership in the decisions for generations to come'.

In the last week of April, the Prime Minister called me and asked me to give consideration to not voting against the Bill. She wanted me to go back to my constituency. She invited me to discuss the matters, and gave me an undertaking that our conversation was confidential. I took my daughter with me that night. We headed up to her house at 11pm.

Tim Barnett also remembers being part of that discussion:

> I never knew how far Tari had made her mind up and we were going through the motions and how far there was still doubt. It must have been a Monday night when we went to the house in Wadestown. I went to see her and I rang Helen and said it might be worth us coming in. Michael Cullen had gone to bed, reading some obscure wonderful book, and he got out of bed and came in. We met about half past ten on Monday night, had a conversation. There was myself and Tari, Lisa, Michael and Helen. There was some purpose to the conversation. It was all about to what extent Tari could engage with the hīkoi. I always thought that it was possible; we would come out with something in the middle. I think it was one of the mistakes of Helen's premiership [that in the end we didn't]. I think there were other people who have to share the criticism – I'm thinking of the Māori Caucus, and I would probably include Tari in that – to my mind she carried some responsibility. Tari was in her own world by then – there had been this drift which had happened largely out of sight. The Monday night conversation was about whether it was possible to come up with a deal whereby Tari could be seen to engage with the hīkoi and retain the ministerial role or whether she resigned now; stepped down as a Minister in order to do that and then be reinstated. There were all these different possibilities we were looking at.

The next day (Tuesday, 27 April 2004), Tariana attended a special Caucus meeting at Premier House. In a media statement released later that day, she outlined the agreement that had been reached behind closed doors:

> The caucus has today given me and Nanaia Mahuta leave not to support the legislation. I appreciate the respect the Prime

Minister has shown us, and the sincere efforts she and senior Ministers have made to accommodate the diverse opinions within the caucus.[34]

But it was obvious that the divergent paths being traversed by the Labour hierarchy and the constituency were struggling to meet on middle ground. Tariana's statement revealed the bargaining position that was being negotiated by senior Labour ministers:

> I have been asked to consider another option in the last 24 hours, which I will send out to key leaders and others within the electorate.
>
> I remain open to hearing the views of people within Te Tai Hauauru, including those who may support the government's proposals. I have had no contact with anyone who might have expressed their support for the government's proposal to other MPs, and I look forward to hearing from them.[35]

The subtext of the negotiations was being powerfully orchestrated by the ninth floor of the Beehive. Tariana's cousin Archie was brought into the inner circle by either the Prime Minister or her Chief of Staff, Heather Simpson. As he was someone whose advice Tariana placed great value on, Tariana always believed he had been deliberately approached by seniors within the Labour Party to influence her into making a decision they approved of. Nancy Tuaine explains:

> Uncle Archie had great respect for her and pride in what she had achieved. He was definitely one of those people that she regarded closely because she could have those conversations in confidence with him, and his particular guidance she respected and she valued.

Archie was an adored mentor of Tariana; his wise counsel had guided her through many turbulent waters, and she was devastated that he had even been approached.

Archie and I shared the same heartline: ko au te awa ko te awa ko au; our ancestral connections would never be frayed by the political realm. But it was still shattering to learn that he had been rendered useful by the powers that be as part of the negotiating collateral.

Others appeared – one by one offering me beads and blankets to stay. Policy deals were proposed – how about writing off the tax bill for a controversial project on the East Coast, or investing more into local solutions? Labour confidantes turned up late at night. Gregory Fortuin offered to broker a conversation. Other offers were less subtle. I was told I could simply stay away when the crucial vote was taken. Would I like to stay in the ministerial house while being quarantined on the backbench for a decent period of time?

One night, Labour Party President Mike Williams and General Secretary Mike Smith came to my home in Whanganui to talk about my options.

Pahia remembers:

> They had dinner at Mum and Dad's, and this was their last-ditch attempt to convince her. We all had to be there. That kōrero that she gave to them that night was just brilliant – asking them to understand that this was more than her allegiance to a political party, because what they were doing was wrong – as a whānau we sat there and heard exactly why she was leaving.

Six months after I'd left, I reflected on how that time had been for me:

> I don't think I've ever realised the huge stress I was under and how depressed I got and during that whole nine months before I left I hadn't slept properly. I was having all these vivid dreams, you know, sort of tupuna dreams, as if I suppose they were trying to help me to make the right decision. It was a really hard time but once I came to that point I knew I had to resign.[36]

If the words being uttered behind closed doors were characterised by diplomacy and respect, the picture being painted by the media was far less flattering. On Tuesday 27 April, when the Caucus met at Premier House, a visual image was constructed that I will always regret. As I left the meeting and boarded the executive car, the Prime Minister turned to me and said, 'why don't you duck down on the back seat'; a piece of advice I took that would eventually humiliate me beyond compare.

The *Herald* reported:

> Damaging images of Mrs Turia lying across the seat were broadcast in slow motion, leaving her furious. Mrs Turia said the Prime Minister had made her look like a fool. She felt the image of her lying in the backseat of the car, hands covering her face, had been manipulated by Helen Clark. That was rejected by Helen Clark through her spokesman yesterday, who said Mrs Turia's claims were exaggerated. He said Helen Clark had suggested Mrs Turia might want to 'duck' her head when the car slipped out of the gates at Premier House, because she knew television crew were waiting. 'No one told her to lie down on the seat,' said Helen Clark's spokesman. 'She's a grown-up; she can make up her own mind.'[37]

I was extremely embarrassed, and to this day regret taking her advice.

Many others were also watching and forming their own opinions, including Opposition MP Bill English:

> Like many others I can still remember the TV shots of her being required to leave in the back of the car. When that happened I knew she'd leave because it sort of summed up the ability of the Labour political machine to humiliate people; to humiliate someone whose self-determination was too difficult for them. Instead of accommodating it they humiliated it, instead of respecting it they humiliated it.

I truly believed there was a campaign in force, creating a deliberate portrayal of me as some kind of idiot; someone who didn't know her mind. The media told me it was all coming out of Helen's floor.

But if I thought the backseat-of-the-car incident was difficult, it paled in comparison to the wānanga I was having in my head in the waking dawn, when the ancestors came to visit. Their words gradually comforted me into a quiet resolve. I know that I was driven to take the action I did, by those who spoke to and with me, during restless hours of sleep.

In the end it wasn't hard for me to leave. I told cousin Archie that I felt really good because I was able to say to him that being here (in Parliament) wasn't the be-all and the end-all for me. If I didn't get back in it didn't matter, but I had to live with myself in the end and to know that I had honoured our tūpuna and everything that they stood for. So it wasn't hard to leave, knowing that there was a possibility that I might not get re-elected.

It had taken some months, so obviously I felt that I owed it to Helen to try to resolve the issues with them. But on that Monday night meeting, Helen offered me various options – I could stay away from Parliament for a month and then return ostensibly to a ministerial role, the ministerial house and chauffeur-driven cars. They also offered for me to be away from Parliament so that I wouldn't have to vote.

It really hurt me that she thought I went to Parliament for a house, a car, the money. I was disgusted actually, and if anything it helped me to be more decisive about leaving. Our people had wanted me to move; my electorate supported me to leave. I think in that whole time I only had one email that asked me to stay with Labour. To find that within twenty-four hours the media had all that information was very distressing. I knew then that I would have to go. I couldn't stay. I had lost confidence in her – my colleagues – and I knew that I wouldn't be able to get back that trust; it would be too difficult.

I had always known it was going to be difficult in Parliament, but I naively thought with the MMP environment you had the opportunity to have a diverse voice, and the devastating thing for me was that it wasn't allowed. When it came to making the decision, in the end there was no room for doubt.

After that last Caucus meeting on 27 April, I released a statement indicating my view:

> I have heard the consistent call in my electorate from Tirau to Tawa to oppose the Bill and put forward their views to my colleagues ...
> I believe my role in this debate is to show leadership for future generations of New Zealanders. I see my decision to express opposition to the Bill as another marker of our need, as a nation, to work to build a healthy and respectful relationship between tangata whenua and the Crown.[38]

Originally I didn't intend to resign straight away; I intended to wait until the legislation had gone through, but it was too difficult in the end, so I went home; talked with our whānau from home; called a hui. About 300 turned up, just within a day, and I sought their guidance again. People came from right around the electorate and helped me make my decision, and I guess that it was then that I realised, when I felt so liberated from making the decision, I realised how oppressed I had been. The control that is exerted on you – being required to vote on things that went entirely against all the values and beliefs that you had been brought up in – made it really hard.

A key person who stood by Tariana throughout this whole experience was the late Sir Atawhai (Archie) Taiaroa. On the day of her announcement at Rātana, Archie sat with her on the stage: strong, quiet support that steadied her as she gave her decision. Hone Harawira reflects on the role that Archie had played:

> Back in those days, Archie Taiaroa had talked to me about it. Just quietly he was proud of her; he was proud of her. He said that she just did the sorts of things that he thought were the right things to do by her people. That it wasn't even a case of politics. It was a case of she felt that way. She went through a lot of angst about it, but she came out of it with her decision. It's not even a case of it was the right decision or the wrong decision. It was the right decision for her.

The role Tariana's whānau played in supporting her decision was also critical to helping pave the pathway forward. Tariana's son Pahia told *Tū Mai* magazine how optimistic they were about the change that lay ahead:

> I was so excited and so proud. I knew it was the only dignified thing Mum could do. We've seen the toll that working in a mainstream party has had upon Mum. Change and challenge always brings about some type of friction … it is our duty as her whānau to support her and educate others about the issues.[39]

Ten years later, that sense of pride remains for Pahia:

> Other than my mokopuna being born and my kids being born, the proudest day of my life was the day that she left – this overwhelming feeling of pride. You know, when she made that speech out at Rātana, I just thought, 'at last'. I was just so proud of her taking a stand – like,

as a family we were. It was the first time in her political career that I was one hundred percent there – honestly. And then the hīkoi – that was a really defining moment in Mum's life.

Curiously, the press quickly jumped to interpret Tariana's decision as being influenced by matters she saw as completely irrelevant. In an interview with Ruth Berry, Tariana summed up what she knew the media were saying about her: 'I won't be anything next week. My pay stops, everything stops. I'll be Miss Nobody next week.'[40]

But she was leaving with her integrity intact; her ideals still in place. It sat right. At last, there was sleep.

After months of conflict and controversy, consultation and parliamentary debate, the actual announcement was rapid. On 30 April 2004 from Rātana Pā, Tariana announced her resignation, effective from May 17. She confirmed she would resign and seek a fresh mandate through a by-election.

In various statements Tariana said that she had never wavered in her opposition, but that the Prime Minister had placed options before her and asked her to consider these after consulting her electorate. However, this was not the way the Prime Minister saw it. In her press release on 4 May, she categorised Tariana's decision as emerging out of a 'series of three outright acts of duplicity which have occurred since February'.[41] It was a view that the Prime Minister repeated often in the week leading up to the hīkoi, for example telling the *Herald*, 'I think she has had it in her mind to do this for some time. But when push came to shove she couldn't look me in the eye and say that.'[42]

Tariana had never considered not voting on the legislation, believing that if she had chosen that path her constituents would lose confidence in her:

> It didn't feel right to me ... to go away and not vote at all. I felt my electorate would lose confidence in me. It is my constituents who have put me into Parliament to be their voice. I believed I would be able to speak on those issues that affected our people and not be forced to have to vote against our own people. I'm not prepared to do that.[43]

In a stand-up press conference announcing her resignation, Tariana outlined why she had come to Rātana Pā:

> I see this as a positive opportunity for us to consider what our political future may be. Really that's what I'm going to be talking about to my whānau today – that if we are to consider a by-election, what does that mean to us as a people.[44]

Approximately an hour later, a brief statement was released from Helen Clark's office:

Tariana Turia relieved of ministerial responsibilities

> Prime Minister Helen Clark has advised the Administrator of the Government, who is acting in place of the Governor-General, to dismiss Tariana Turia from her ministerial responsibilities as Minister for the Community and Voluntary Sector and her associate portfolios, and from the Executive Council.

If the statement issued by the ninth floor was coolly neutral, the Prime Minister's immediate reaction to the Rātana announcement was anything but. The *Herald* reported that Helen Clark had said:

> Mrs Turia's naivety in wanting to vote against the Government and stay in the Executive was of astonishing proportions. 'It is an astonishing lack of perspective to throw your job and the work you do for your people up in the air over this issue.'[45]

From that day, then, a new journey began for Tariana. At that time, she was most concerned for how her decision would impact on others around her.

I had concerns about my staff, but I had always said to them from the very beginning that I felt passionately about things for our people and their jobs would be always be difficult in my office but I would expect their loyalty. I had asked that they always listen to what our people said, and that there may come a time when things had to change.

It was hard because I felt that I had gone to the people to vote for me and support Labour and now I had to go back to them and say, 'I'm sorry but we've all let you down'. I felt that I had let people down because I'd encouraged them into Labour. That was hard at a personal level.

I thought with Parekura Horomia that I would always have a relationship. He and I had known each other for over twenty years, so that wouldn't change. I'd worked with both Mahara Okeroa and Mita Ririnui in the past, and Mahara was also a whanaunga to me. To be frank, I'd hardly mixed socially since I had been in Parliament. Probably the person who had been the closest to me was Tim Barnett. I knew that I would miss Tim, but I was sure we would retain a friendship.

Tariana told *Tū Mai*:

> In politics it seems huge bitterness grows out of division. Relationships you viewed with considerable respect don't exist anymore and I do feel sad about that. There are still people within the Labour Party that I hold in high respect and regard for all the other things that they stood for.[46]

The saddest thing for me in leaving was to know the inner turmoil each of the Maori caucus MPs had borne, as they colluded with a catastrophe not of their making.

In his valedictory speech in 2011, Mita Ririnui expressed the impact of the foreshore and seabed legislation, speaking of the lasting wounds of that time as filling him with a 'deep sense of regret'. In 2004, Brian Dickson, chief executive of the Ngāi Te Rangi iwi, had described Mita's support for the Bill as 'a total betrayal of Tauranga Moana iwi', and Ngāti Pūkenga iwi chairman Rehua Smallman had said that, 'If he has any integrity he should cross the floor or resign'.

Yet Mita had chosen to support the Bill, gritting his teeth as thousands of protesters marched against it, knowing all the time that 'the law remained discriminatory'. He used his last speech as an MP to admit there had been a price to pay for the position he took: 'Having my children abused by their own cousins about their father selling Māori rights down the drain, being a sell-out and a kūpapa'.

Georgina Beyer also used the occasion of her Valentine's Day valedictory in 2007 to describe the turmoil she had been thrown into in being forced to vote in support for the Bill: 'My electorate wanted me to support the Government, but I was listening to my tūpuna, and I was listening to my whānau, who were not in support'. Her story bears retelling:

> When people ask me, 'oh, why did you leave Parliament?' I say it started with the foreshore and seabed. I can definitely pinpoint that issue as the end of my political career 'cos it made me do something really against my will. I vowed from that day on that I would never never allow that to happen again; nothing was worth that kind of compromise. Which makes what Tariana did just … I don't think there's any honour in the world that you can bestow on someone like that for the sacrifice, but by God, was it worth the injuries, the scars?
>
> The Māori Caucus was never the same after the foreshore and seabed. It was a hugely destructive thing, and every single member of that Māori Caucus I reckon quietly wished they had the balls that Tariana had to stand by her integrity and principles. I think quietly that each of us probably thought, 'I wish we'd done the same thing'. I always regretted having to support the foreshore and seabed – and although the dynamics for me were different politically, I never recovered from it. To this day it will always be a great day of shame to me. I think Tari did what we really should have done … Tari's the one that can stand proud on that one. God, when Michael Cullen left Parliament and he said we went wrong, I yahooed that day.

Dr Cullen, in his valedictory statement on 29 April 2009, almost five years to the day since Tariana had left Labour, expressed regret that the Labour Government had failed to create a consensus over the seabed and foreshore issue; regret he had articulated the year after the hīkoi came to town:

> No other issue in recent times has so deeply revealed the divisions between the world views of New Zealanders. No other issue has so clearly demonstrated the difficulty of providing an ongoing framework for the relationship between a rejuvenated tangata whenua and the enormously disparate groups of people that comprise the rest of us.[47]

Of course, not everyone in Labour saw it this way. Dover Samuels attempted to defend the Labour Māori Caucus' actions by implying those who marched in the hīkoi wanted them 'to cross the floor and jump over the cliff and become insignificant'. Minister of Māori Affairs of the day, Parekura Horomia, also dismissed the significance of the hīkoi, saying, 'Most of the people don't even know what crossing the floor means out here'.[48]

On 5 July 2004, Helen Clark moved to reward the four Māori MPs who had stayed loyal to Labour. Mahara Okeroa became Under-Secretary; Mita Ririnui added health to his portfolios; John Tamihere picked up responsibility for the new Department of Building and Housing; and Dover Samuels became Associate Minister of Housing.

In a speech Tariana gave days later to the people of Ngāruahine Rangi and Ngāti Ruanui, she mentioned the irony that this same group of MPs:

> … went out to consult, confront and eventually concur with the very position that they once stood united against … I do not blame them either, for accepting the promotions handed out to them yesterday. Ultimately they must decide what is right for them.[49]

Later that year, she reflected on another reward her former colleagues had received: a standing ovation at the Labour Party conference:

> The unprecedented outpouring of appreciation for the Māori MPs was not to commend the vigour of the politicians in representing the views of their constituency – the appreciation was for preserving the party position.[50]

The Foreshore and Seabed Debate

A lot has been said about how the foreshore and seabed issue galvanised and mobilised support among those who might otherwise have appeared to be somewhat strange bedfellows. The focus of ACT, and in particular Rodney Hide, was the issue of due access to the courts. Rodney recalls:

> I thought the foreshore and seabed issue was shocking. The idea that anyone in our country could go through the courts and, when they looked like winning, [face the possibility that they would] change the rules. ... We didn't probably make enough noise about it, but we were very clear where we stood on it. I was shocked by it. It was the cavalier way that you would treat the court process, and so I ended up watching it quite closely.

> I was very impressed when Tariana walked out – I thought that was just electrifying and magnificent – irrespective of the fact that I agreed with her position. But for a member of Parliament and a minister to walk out on a matter of principle – I can remember thinking that I hoped that I would have the same courage and guts.

There is no question that the way in which Tariana responded to the foreshore and seabed drew admiration from many quarters. Māori historian and political expert Danny Keenan was one who predicted her influence would be significant. He discussed her actions in an interview with Alister Browne:

> [Keenan] said the sacked junior minister was a tough operator with a charismatic presence who was well-respected within Maoridom. ...

> He expected the 'politically astute and very sharp' Mrs Turia to succeed in ... organising a new Māori political movement.

> 'The groundswell is out there now and I think she will have the flaxroots support'.[51]

Bill English credits Tariana as being brave enough to solve 'the worst kind of New Zealand problem':

She doesn't think about issues or politics in a normal way, and that was evident through the whole foreshore and seabed issue, which was quite a cathartic experience, certainly for her but for a lot of Māori and then for the new Government negotiating their way through it. And there is no doubt that she was one of the few people who would be able to manoeuvre that issue to where it ended up. I think she deserved a great deal more credit for the kind of nation-building impact of it.

Because we all found out we could solve what looked like the worst kind of New Zealand problem – and that is the one which provides the opportunity for division and potentially violence and resentment. And that's pretty brave stuff in the political world – to then pick solutions and then see them through – so we did end up with new foreshore and seabed legislation – a major achievement for New Zealand – driven by her – because it could have easily been put to one side.

In the final analysis, the view of the foreshore and seabed issue as a 'New Zealand problem' will perhaps apply for generations to come. Pat Snedden sums up the national relevance of that time:

The Government [on the one hand] asserting its right of rule of law and to be able to govern and import legislation, and Māori [on the other] asserting their complete right which they've never surrendered, which is customary ownership of the foreshore and seabed and the ability to exercise kaitiaki in that space. How is one to reconcile these two things?

You can reconcile these two things, but you have to have a bigger conversation to do it, because the bigger conversation recognises that when Māori talk about mana moana and mana whenua and kaitiaki they are not talking about fee-simple processes as understood by English law. They recognise through the Treaty process there's a role for kāwanatanga and rangatiratanga. What they are saying is that in New Zealand we are so ill-practised at managing those roles interfacing with each other that the majority culture get seriously spooked when a big issue comes which requires this level of intelligent engagement.

> As the community moves into a much more mature understanding of relationships between people, so the legislation changes. As the offshore mining becomes more of a New Zealand process so too will Māori interests. When commerce starts to alter its behaviour in anticipation of something, you know the argument's won.

On the Monday following Tariana's announcement at Rātana, Helen Clark alleged on breakfast television that the hīkoi making its way from Northland to Wellington to protest against the proposed Foreshore and Seabed Bill was comprised of:

> … the same old faces. The Ken Mairs, the Harawira family, the Annette Sykes, the haters and wreckers, the people who destroy Waitangi every year, now wanting to do a Waitangi in every town in New Zealand on the way to Wellington, where they will do a Waitangi on the steps of Parliament. Is this now what New Zealand has got absolutely sick and tired of?

Helen Clark told MPs she 'personally regretted' the 'pathway' Tariana had chosen, and that she should have stayed with Labour.[52]

But it was always bigger than the personal relationship of us as individuals. To think that she would belittle our people and denigrate them in that way really made me think here was someone who wanted power at all costs, even if it meant stepping on our people. It was always about more than two people. It was, at its core, about the relationship of the partners to the Treaty, between tangata whenua and the Crown.

Tariana told Radio New Zealand:

> All our lives we have had to live with others making the rules for us; determining what was in our interests, never ever honouring the Treaty relationship that we had had. I think that during that time it really made me think about the Kawenata that Tahupotiki Wiremu Ratana, my tupuna, had signed with Michael Joseph Savage. And I thought, 'how dare you!' How dare you sign up to this agreement, this compact and then think you can do this to our people. Our

people have been incredibly loyal to Labour and given them their vote. I was outraged during that time. I think Labour made the biggest mistake, because they were trying to appeal to mainstream New Zealand.[53]

The problem with Labour is that they always want us in to be in a position where others feel sorry for us. I didn't want to be in that state any more.

While Tariana has strenuously, consistently denied that the friction between her and Helen Clark was personal, political analysts have suggested that Helen Clark didn't see it that way. Former Māori Party campaign manager Matt McCarten believed the Prime Minister would have felt keenly a sense of betrayal. The *Herald* reported in October 2005:

'Clark would see in her own mind that she went out on a limb to handpick Tariana Turia for Parliament,' said McCarten. 'Clark's a self-confessed control freak – she'd feel very miffed that Tariana Turia didn't do what she was told. And then she not only didn't do what she was told, she actually went out, left, survived, and came back with numbers … Clark would find that very hard to stomach'.[54]

That sense of being let down by Tariana was shared by Tariana's Labour colleagues, the *Herald* reported:

Labour sources described the Maori MP's behaviour in caucus as 'septic' and said Clark was repeatedly forced to act as an intermediary in clashes with colleagues.

'Clark tried to accommodate her every step of the way,' one source has said.[55]

The true extent of Helen's feelings on the relationship breakdown remain unknown. Tariana, however, is clear that she feels no personal animosity. 'I've never spoken against her publicly, I haven't made disparaging comments about them – but I don't think we've been accorded the same respect', she told the *Herald*.⁵⁶

Tariana's irritation was validated at the time by Māori politics lecturer, Dr Maria Bargh, also quoted in the *Herald*:

> 'I think Tariana's been around long enough to be a bit more pragmatic and compromising,' she said. 'Presumably Tariana still has really strong feelings … about the Foreshore and Seabed Act but that's not specifically about Helen Clark'.⁵⁷

The issue as to whether or not the relationship between Tariana and Helen Clark was repairable would be deferred until talks following the 2005 election. The political environment was becoming increasingly intense. It was time for a new movement to emerge – the Māori Party.

NOTES

1. *Attorney-General v Ngati Apa* [2003] 3 NZLR 643.
2. Helen Clark, press release, 'Ministers comment on Court of Appeal decision', 20 June 2003.
3. *Hansard*, 24 June 2003.
4. Statement from the Labour Māori Caucus, 24 June 2003.
5. 'Government denies Māori fair trial – Jackson', *NZ City News*, 24 June 2003.
6. 'Iwi considers legal action on seabed decision', 24 June 2003, *stuff.co.nz*, http://homepages.ihug.co.nz/~sai/maorisea.html (accessed 17 June 2015).
7. 'Academic criticises lack of foreshore consultation', 30 June 2003, *stuff.co.nz*, http://homepages.ihug.co.nz/~sai/maorisea.html (accessed 17 June 2015).
8. Statement from the Labour Māori Caucus; 18 August 2003.
9. Tariana Turia, press release, 18 August 2003.
10. 'Nit-pickers are sharpening their knives again', *Wanganui Chronicle*, 21 July 2003, p. 6.
11. Tariana Turia, Beehive Chat, 25 August 2003.
12. Tariana Turia, Beehive Chat, 25 August 2003.
13. Tariana Turia, Beehive Chat, 22 September 2003.

14 Tariana Turia, 'Sharing and partnership: the value of Māori custom', speech to Te Ngawari Hauora, 15 December 2003.

15 Ngaa Rauru Kiitahi suffered loss of life during the wars, including the lives of unarmed children killed by government militia at Handley's Woolshed in an unprovoked attack. Ngaa Rauru Kiitahi Claims Settlement Act 2005, http://www.legislation.govt.nz/act/public/2005/0084/latest/whole.html (accessed 17 June 2015).

16 N. Shepheard, 'Fierce Kuia: profile of New Zealand Member of Parliament Tariana Turia', *North and South*, February 2004, p. 78.

17 Ibid.

18 *Hansard*, 16 December 2003.

19 Ibid.

20 Jonathan Milne, 'Turia still throwing stones', *Sunday Star-Times*, 25 January 2004.

21 Tariana Turia, Beehive Chat, 2 February 2004.

22 Tariana Turia, Beehive Chat, 2 February 2004.

23 Don Brash, 'Nationhood', speech to the Orewa Rotary Club, 27 January 2004.

24 Tariana Turia, Beehive Chat, 16 February 2004.

25 Tariana Turia, Beehive Chat, 1 March 2004.

26 Tariana Turia, interview with Eru Rerekura and Chris Bramwell, *Te Waonui a te Manu Korihi*, Radio New Zealand, 10 August 2014.

27 Hinewehi Mohi, *Lines in the Sand*, documentary, 30 July 2013.

28 Tariana Turia, press release, 'Tariana Turia not intending to resign', 14 March 2004.

29 'Turia reveals plan for MPs to desert Labour', *One News*, 2 March 2014.

30 Ibid.

31 Tracy Watkins, 'Horomia gives nod to seabed plan', *Dominion Post*, 31 March 2004.

32 Kevin List, 'PM's Presser: Of Hikois, Tariana Turia and Nukes', 4 May 2004, *Scoop Independent News*: www.scoop.co.nz/stories/HL0405/S00026/pms-presser-of-hikois-tariana-turia-and-nukes.htm (accessed 13 February 2015).

33 Tariana Turia, Beehive Chat, 26 April 2004.

34 Tariana Turia, press release, 27 April 2004.

35 Ibid.

36 Tariana Turia, oral history interview between Tariana Turia and Taina Tangaere McGregor, 10 November 2004, Oral History Political Diary project, Oral History Collection, Alexander Turnbull Library.

37 Helen Tunnah, 'Turia blames PM for humiliating car ride', *New Zealand Herald*, 3 May 2004.

38   Tariana Turia, press release, 27 April 2004.

39   K. Paki, 'Tilting the Tables', *Tū Mai*, July 2004, p. 19.

40   Ruth Berry, 'Turia taking time out in political limbo', *New Zealand Herald*, 14 May 2004.

41   Kevin List, 'PM's Presser', 4 May 2004.

42   Ruth Berry and Helen Tunnah, 'Turia quits Labour, stripped of portfolios', *New Zealand Herald*, 1 May 2004.

43   'Tariana Turia to resign and force byelection', *New Zealand Herald*, 30 April 2004.

44   Ibid.

45   Berry and Tunnah, 'Turia quits Labour, stripped of portfolios'.

46   Paki, 'Tilting the tables', p. 19.

47   Michael Cullen, 'Two Ticks for Clio: Reflections on NZ Politics and History', Michael King Memorial Lecture, 12 October 2005.

48   Tracy Watkins, 'Clark stands firm', *The Press*, 6 May 2004.

49   Tariana Turia, speech at Kanihi Pā, Okaiawa, 8 July 2004.

50   Tariana Turia, 'Nga Hau o te Ao Hurihuri: Winds of change in the political scene, confronting perceptions and harnessing potential', speech to Te Waka Āwhina o Aotearoa national conference, 25 November 2004.

51   Tino Rangatiratanga eMail Roopu, 'Politics expert says Turia could succeed where others failed', 4 May 2004. https://groups.yahoo.com/neo/groups/tino-rangatiratanga/conversations/messages/19057 (accessed 13 February 2015).

52   'Government survives confidence vote as pressure mounts', *New Zealand Herald*, 4 May 2004

53   Tariana Turia, interview, *Te Waonui a te Manu Korihi*, Radio New Zealand, 10 August 2014.

54   Patrick Crewdson, 'Clark and Turia still on a rocky road', *New Zealand Herald*, 16 October 2005.

55   Ibid.

56   Ibid.

57   Ibid.

-CHAPTER NINETEEN-
THE EMERGENCE OF THE MĀORI PARTY

Mai i te urunga o Ngai Taua te iwi Māori ki roto i ngā kāwai mātauranga o Tauiwi, inā, honotia te peka Māori ki te rākau rāwaho, he rerekē tona hua me te rongo o tōna kiko, he kawa. Kāti, tēnei te whakahoki ki ngā paiaka a kui mā, a koro mā.

Let us return to our origins. Since the time we as Maori were immersed in the knowledge streams of tauiwi we have become like a branch, grafted to a foreign tree, producing fruit of a different quality and somewhat unpalatable. It is time we returned to the rootstock of our ancestors.[1]

For Tariana it was about coming home. All the teachings of Aunty Wai and Aunty Pae, the expectations of her old people from Pūtiki and the challenge to do what was right came together in the creation of a new movement of change.

Tariana saw in that movement a powerful opportunity to promote and advance the survival of all that it meant to be tangata whenua. She was motivated by the demonstration of belief in all that marched in the initial hīkoi to dream of a better future, and to connect that future with the legacy left by her ancestors. She believed passionately that 'our future will be assured when we can map a pathway forward that fits within our values, our beliefs, our cultural practices'. She told people gathered at Te Raukura – Te Wharewaka o Pōneke in Wellington:

> We have lived a similar history, of people thinking they know what is best for us, and we have similar aspirations that we want to do for ourselves, and to have healthy, happy whānau. My cousin Tahu talked about the concept of the rākau, or the tree – and it is meaningful to me, because it fits within my understanding of the world.
>
> The point is, however, that we cannot continue to allow others to graft their ideas on to us. The fruit will never be as sweet as it once was, unless we rid ourselves of the many layers and layers of grafted ideas, and return to our roots, the roots that our ancestors left for us to flourish in.[2]

It was time to do whatever it would take to guarantee the survival of the people. Out of the hīkoi the Māori Party was born.

In her Beehive Chat on 17 May 2004, Tariana said:

> The hīkoi was a demonstration of how far our people have developed politically. This time we had tribal and marae groups marching under their own flags, led by toa [warriors] in traditional dress, accompanied by the thrilling sound of pūtatara [traditional trumpet]. As one Pākehā man said, the hīkoi was about ten percent protest, and 90 percent tangata whenua pride and power! There seems to be a real opportunity to build a national representative organisation

from the bottom up, starting with strong hapū, iwi and community organisations who see the advantages of working together.[3]

Hundreds had gathered at Te Rerenga Wairua in Northland in the dawn of 22 April 2004 to commence a two-week journey to Wellington in protest at the proposed foreshore and seabed legislation. The hīkoi had quickly taken on a life of its own, swelling to more than ten thousand marchers when it crossed the Auckland Harbour Bridge.

The momentum of the hīkoi was not fully appreciated until the people started arriving in the capital city.

On 4 May 2004, the day before the hīkoi landed in Wellington, it entered Paraparaumu. State Highway One traffic was crawling by midday. Hundreds of cars moved slowly down the hill into town. Marchers waving flags regularly appeared alongside the traffic that was ambling along, bumper to bumper along the highway, supervised by plenty of police: more than 200 from Wellington and the central districts had been called in. People were marching ahead as far in as Porirua.

The scale and the extent to which the masses had been mobilised will be a lifelong memory for many. Tariana told Radio New Zealand in 2014:

> I was just blown away. I can remember getting up that morning and saying to myself, 'oh, please let there be more than 2000 people there'. And when I went to the window – I was in 'Coventry' by then – Labour had moved me out of my ministerial office over on to the mezzanine floor in the old building. Someone came rushing past my door and they said to me, 'have you looked outside the window?' I was proud of our people; proud that they were prepared to stand up for what they knew to be right … I hope that they will always continue to stand up, no matter what the issue.[4]

For Tariana, the very fact that the people had to march was painful:

> To see our people at the hīkoi trying to hold fast to our tikanga, walking once more for justice, for recognition. I found all that intensely painful. Leaving Labour was easy in the context of their grief.[5]

The hīkoi represented a pivotal junction in New Zealand history; a point of uprising. In the *Herald*, Shane Jones noted:

> Parliament was festooned with flags of all description; there was theatre, pageantry, passion. A whole lot of incredible things about Maori identity were on show for just a few hours. The march encompassed the band from the Ratana Chuch, the poi group from Parihaka, the haka teams from many tribes, a host of conservative people, people from every tribe and rangatahi. It was a very powerful statement about Maori pride.[6]

Kōhanga and kura in their collective force sang waiata after waiata demonstrating the power of the next generation. They joined in on the chants: 'hīkoi (hīkoi) hīkoi ki Pāremata'. Other chants were blunter: 'tahi, rua, toru, whā, Helen Clark's a hōhā'. Loud hailers were used to good effect; lines of kapa haka groups performed rousing haka. Flags were flying high. Over in London, Tariana's nephew, Che, was watching on, when he suddenly caught sight of a special flag from home:

> I was living in England when the hīkoi happened, and I just wanted to be home because I saw this wave. I saw some footage, and in all of these flags I saw E te iwi kia ora. I didn't know that Dad was the one that was carrying it. It hit me because of the message that King Tawhiao gave to Mere Rikiriki when he gave that flag. Kia ora ai te iwi. Through all our despair, through all our taking, that we live on, and more than that, that we live in a well state of being. That's always been one of my karakia for her (Tariana) – E te iwi kia ora – knowing her connections to Mere Rikiriki as well as ours.

There were babies in backpacks and prams, peoples in wheelchairs, kuia and koroua walking alongside men in suits, ordinary New Zealanders together with leaders of every ilk. Banners flew with statements of defiance: 'this legislation is theft – again', 'No Raupatu in our Time' and 'Hands off our foreshore'. People wore stickers: 'Maori seabed ForShore'. In the midst of the crowd were about a dozen huge billboards of Tariana – a touch of hero worship rarely seen in New Zealand. It was a day like no other. Tariana said at the time:

> The hīkoi was an opportunity to celebrate our actions in standing up for our rights, in believing in ourselves. It was about a call to create our own destiny. A call to embrace our right to be self-determining. A call to operate within our own cultural framework rather than someone else's. It was a call that we have responded to in the drive to establish a Māori political movement.[7]

The Māori Party didn't just emerge overnight. Tariana explained this in her last Beehive Chat before her resignation took effect:

> Even before I announced my resignation many people asked if I would stand for a Māori party or if I would lead such a party. Obviously many people are discussing this idea and many feel the time may have come. It is very exciting that such discussions are taking place. I think a Māori party would help our Parliament to represent better the full range of public opinion. It could have helped to lift the veil of ignorance surrounding the seabed and foreshore issue. I know Pākehā who want to support a Māori party. But even more important for our people is what happens outside Parliament to give us a stronger national voice. The seabed and foreshore issue has united diverse groups all round the country.[8]

The pressure for change was also being brought to bear on the Māori MPs who had chosen to support the foreshore and seabed legislation. Tainui MP Nanaia Mahuta had refused to pledge her long-term support for the Government, despite being given the ability to vote against the Bill when it came before the House on 6 May. The *Herald* noted:

> Other Maori MPs also face mounting pressure with the foreshore hikoi arriving at Parliament tomorrow and major tribes such as Ngai Tahu expressing interest in forming a new Maori party ... Maori MPs and ministers were in a series of talks today about Ms Mahuta, the pressure on other Māori MPs and practical arrangements to meet the hikoi.[9]

And so the grounds of Parliament become the backdrop for one of the most dramatic acts of political theatre this country has ever witnessed, and at the same time the campaign court for a massive membership drive. Donna Awatere-Huata remembers the excitement of that day:

> I can remember when the march came through; Donna Hall and I had Xeroxed off all these membership forms and we had all these buckets. We were trying to get the 500 members on that day. We had volunteers; and we had buckets to collect membership fees of $2. We had hundreds of $2 coins – I don't know what ever happened to them! Donna knew the process – you need 500 people – and 500 of $2 coins is what we had to get.

The following day, around 3pm, the first reading of the Foreshore and Seabed Bill took place. The Bill was introduced by Dr Michael Cullen, and followed by speeches from Dr Don Brash, Winston Peters, Parekura Horomia, Jeanette Fitzsimons, Metiria Turei and Richard Prebble. At the point Tariana rose to seek leave to take a call in the debate,[10] the call was immediately blocked by Richard Prebble and others.

But finally, on that historic day, Mita Ririnui offered his speaking slot to Tariana, ensuring her speech was part of the *Hansard* record for that day. It was duly recorded:

> TARIANA TURIA (Labour – Te Tai Hauāuru): E ngā mana, e ngā reo, tēnā koutou katoa. E ngā tangata whenua o Aotearoa kua maranga ake i te karanga o te takutai moana, maranga mai, maranga mai.
>
> [To the authorities and the languages, greetings to you all. To the people of the land of New Zealand who have risen to the call of the coastal shores, rise up, rise up.]
>
> First of all I want to thank the Hon Mita Ririnui for giving over his time to me to speak in this debate. Tēnā koe, Mita. I will not go over all the other comments that have been made by others in this House today, given that I have only five minutes to speak. But I want to say that it is a fundamental principle of democracy that citizens have rights against the Crown. They are property rights, and we have the right to defend those rights in the courts of this land. This legislation

overturns the rule of law and it extinguishes the property rights of our people.

I want to commend those who were involved in the march yesterday on their discipline, solidarity, and courage in standing up for what we believe in. I have said on many occasions that this issue is the most significant issue facing our nation, and, indeed, yesterday was a day in our history that will be etched in our memories for years to come.

It could well have been different. I believe that a solution that would have pleased all New Zealanders could have been simple. All it would have taken to protect access to the foreshore and seabed was for the Government to amend the Resource Management Act. To ensure the land was inalienable and could never be sold, we could have changed Te Ture Whenua Māori Act. Instead, our relationship has been tested to its most extreme point by a foreshore and seabed package written in the interests of middle New Zealand. Our response to this insult has been to rise up, to stand up for our rights. We remain confident in our knowledge that tangata whenua rights are recognised in common law. Te Tiriti o Waitangi confirmed those rights, the Māori Land Act enshrines those rights in legislation, and the Court of Appeal has upheld those rights.

The bill impacts only on Māori. Our people have asked the Government to explain why no action has been planned against private landowners or foreign investors who own areas of the foreshore. Why are those privileged groups not targeted in this policy? Is it that they are specially privileged and can escape the scrutiny of the policy makers? The legislation is infused with racist overtones in that it is specifically targeted at ensuring Māori are prevented from claiming their inherent rights to the foreshore.

What has been taken away is not just tupuna rights, which Māori may have been able to establish. What is also under compromise is the right to justice in the hands of the court. We will not sit down and accept a compromise of basic rights, a denial of our tikanga, a belittling of our status as indigenous peoples. What we have heard over the months of discussion on this bill, and resoundingly through yesterday's hīkoi, is the powerful call to stand up and be counted. We are mana whenua. Our authority comes from our relationship and our access to our lands and the rights of guardianship and protection. We will not be relegated to second-class citizens in our own land. We are tangata whenua, and we are proud of it. It is that pride and determination that will drive us in the next hīkoi to the ballot box. We can determine our own future, and we will.

I have been inspired by the commitment and support shared across this nation for us to take control of our own political destiny. The hīkoi has represented a great coming together of our peoples, united in their strength of commitment to ensure that the last part of customary land is not removed from our hands. We owe this to our mokopuna. We owe them a chance to address their potential secure in the knowledge of who they are. Ultimately, it is because of our mokopuna that I have decided unequivocally to vote against the Foreshore and Seabed Bill. I do not want to be recorded in history as part of a Government that attacked the very nature of customary rights – the rights we have held according to our tikanga, for our children and our grandchildren. Kia ora.[11]

Once the Bill had been sent away to select committee, the security fences had been put back in Parliament stores and the last buses and vans had left Wellington for home, it was time to get to work. Tariana remembered in 2010:

It wasn't until I sat down with a group of people who I trusted [that I] talked about what's the best way forward for us. What I didn't take into account was the strength of feeling right throughout the country. When I got a sense of that I knew that it was the time for a political movement.[12]

Over the next fortnight Tariana worked feverishly to meet with groups right across the country about the prospect of setting up a new political party. Early on, she made a quick visit to her old friend Fernando Yusingco, who was now living in Auckland.

When the Māori Party started I went to Auckland to talk to him for advice, about how to organise people. I had great respect for him as a grass-roots organiser. He said to me 'only when you capture the hearts and minds of your people in their own space on the marae will you ever do well'. He was right, because where we have our biggest support is where those marae people support us.

A bucket of shining $2 coins was one thing; it was quite another to establish a constitution, a policy platform, and the framework for a movement. It was at this stage that Professor Whatarangi Winiata emerged as a key figure in Tariana's story.

> I had gone and spoken to Matua Whatarangi because he is whanaunga to me – he's my dad's first cousin. So I went to speak to him as whānau but also because I had a high regard for him. He thought the idea of starting a party was great, so I asked him if he would help. I asked if he would take an interim role until the Party could get going, and he agreed.[13]

Whatarangi was immediately enthusiastic about the transformation that he envisaged. He recalls:

> I was really interested in her idea and was willing to help. She asked me to come to join her at a meeting in Auckland to talk about planning. She led the discussion – she was the one who had done the thinking about it, and June Jackson was willing to have us meet at her place. Matt McCarten was there, because he had all the ideas – 'you can organise this and organise that' – and they developed quite a number of pathways to consider. Somehow it came up that there was the need to find a president. I hadn't been inclined to say, 'I better go home and ask' – I came back to Ōtaki as President of the Māori Party.

It appeared to Tariana that there was no one more suited to the role. She had the greatest respect for Whatarangi. He reminded her of the need for balance: to have humility, to adhere to kaupapa and tikanga. The respect was mutual.

Whatarangi valued highly the way in which Tariana expressed such firm belief in tikanga me ōna kaupapa.

He told *Te Karaka* magazine at the time:

> We are on a mission to make our contribution to the long-term survival of Māori as a people. Tariana Turia showed the ability to proceed according to kaupapa; she knows where she is from; she goes back there to get their advice.[14]

Whatarangi identified early on that the leadership provided by Tariana would be instrumental in securing nationwide support for the Māori Party:

> We are planning to compete for each of the seven Māori seats and we are hopeful that our people will see sufficient merit in our plans to support the Māori Party. We will be competitive in our ability to present a face that has integrity and commitment. Tariana is our model, she will be our teacher.[15]

Tariana's respect for Whatarangi was strengthened by his close connection to the only man she ever knew as her dad, Tariuha (Charlie) Manawaroa Te Aweawe. She said in 2004:

> That's been great for me to have his guidance, to have his support. To be able to call him and check myself. My mothers and fathers from home have all gone, so it has been really great for me because my adopted dad and Matua Whatarangi are first cousins, and so in his voice I hear my dad. It's been a very special relationship for me and very nurturing, always feeling that the concept of manaakitanga is always there. And it's been good for me too, because you know at times in this job you get mad with people and feel drawn to say things that you wish you could take back. In lots of ways just thinking about him ensures that I sort of keep faith with the kaupapa.[16]

Tariana's understanding of the connection between Charlie, Whatarangi Winiata and another man who was to come one of Tariana's mentors, Iwi Nicholson, had been relatively recent. Tariuha's mother Rangingangana had been one of the fourteen children of Pātaka Winiata and Ema (Nicholson).

Whatarangi Winiata's father, Tamihana, was the youngest of the fourteen. Uncle Iwi Nicholson came from the daughter of Howard, Ema's brother. These two men would play a key role in influencing Tariana in understanding leadership on a wider scale.

During a Māori Party hui at Wehiwehi Marae in Manakau, Iwi Nicholson referenced their shared links:

> There was a hui at Hongoeka about fisheries; Tariana was in the Labour Party at the time. I had mihi'd to her, referring to her as my tamāhine. We were standing on the marae after it was all over, and someone behind me said to her, 'why did Uncle Iwi refer to you as his niece?' I could tell Tariana had no idea why I had referred to her as my niece. I never said anything more; I don't impose myself on people. So I gave Tariana a piece of paper, and I said because of the connection Whatarangi and I have a responsibility to our tuakana that was responsible for part of her upbringing, to support her.

Whatarangi having accepted the mantle of presidency, Tariana's attention turned to the party leadership role. As early as 14 May 2004, less than ten days after the hīkoi, she had highlighted a suitable nominee. As the *Herald* reported:

> She hoped Dr Pita Sharples, a key supporter, would stand as a candidate and also believed he would make an 'ideal leader'. If she was asked to take a leadership role she hoped it could be as a co-leader, she said.[17]

Pita vividly recalls the first meeting he had with her on the subject, at June Jackson's house:

> In the back of my mind it was for me to get together with Tari and see what we could work together. Well, that was the first time I had really talked across the table with her. My first impression was, 'what a short lady – but one who's in charge, who's definitely in charge of her life, and if I'm not careful of mine as well too'. It was very, very clear to me that there was a bit of power in the house that night. She obviously had a lot of respect for me at that meeting, and I was very pleased about that because it meant we could possibly do things. And so some

sort of leadership arrangement between the two of us was mooted at that meeting, and so we just let it leak out before any major hui.

There was another reason that Tariana was keen to work alongside Pita: a recognition of the contribution that his skill in the Māori language would make to the success of the party:

> I do not have te reo. I just felt that to be a leader of a Māori party you should have te reo.[18]

In my childhood at Pūtiki, I learned the waiata of the awa; I heard the karanga of the kuia and the whaikōrero of the koroua. I learned to work in the dining room and the kitchen. I treasure that period of my life. Yet I've always felt inadequate because I don't have the reo, and because I think people have certain expectations of leaders which I am unable to fulfil.

I try not to focus on my inadequacies – even though there's many – because I know my whānau who have passed on always had expectations of me and I owe it to them to uphold the mana of our family. I've gone into hui in Tūhoe looking at housing issues or something else where they've conducted the whole hui in te reo. I'm sitting there and I might understand half of what they're saying to me. I've always been really lucky to have somebody with me to make sure that I'm not getting the kōrero wrong.

But in settings like that, that's when I feel the most inadequate. My inadequacy with the reo really distresses me, but my role in the parliamentary environment has been to be the most powerful advocate that I can be. I know that I can do that because while I don't have the reo, Aunty Wai used to always say to me 'you may not have the reo, i roto i tō waha, but you've got it i roto i tō ngākau' (you may not speak the language, but you have it in your heart). While I may not be able to speak, I certainly feel the spirit of the reo and understand its meaning. I try to articulate and say things that are all about the reo in whatever opportunity I can.

I just felt it was inappropriate to have the leader of an indigenous movement who couldn't speak te reo. I felt that our people had to hear their reo. Because I don't use the reo much, sometimes people may judge me as not being familiar with our taonga, our reo, our marae, our whakapapa. Actually, that was precisely what Pita Sharples thought at the beginning.

Pita says:

> When I first met her, I thought she was not a marae person, you know. And that was basically because she doesn't talk much Māori. But now I see, getting to know her and her family and stuff, I see she really is a marae person through and through.
>
> It's important to me that people have marae and culture, because it really embodies all our culture. The marae culture is like Māori culture. It has so many arms; it reaches in to families; it reaches into te reo Maori; it reaches into our customs; it reaches into whakapapa and all those things which are the basis of being Māori.
>
> So I identified her as a Māori woman initially with a great deal of mana and a big work ethic, and one who speaks her mind. It wasn't until a year or two in that I realised that this is a marae lady and I really was happy. I have no right to even say that, but that is how I seem to judge people.

We had a president, we had a co-leader, and most important of all we had a kaupapa.

Tariana said at the time:

> During that period when I was out [of Parliament] I had been working closely with Matua Whatarangi Winiata and looking at a way forward for us as a political movement where our kaupapa and our tikanga were the guiding principles by which we would operate, and I loved it. It was everything that I had dreamed about. To be able to bring those things into this environment; to be able to express those things and make them as much a part of your everyday life as they should be.[19]

For Whatarangi, the expression of kaupapa tuku iho was intimately associated with every aspect of his life. He has always talked about the expression of kaupapa as a pathway to the survival of the people, for example saying in 2008:

> Māori will commit to doing those things that contribute to the survival of Māori as a people and this will be happening when a substantial and growing number of people of Māori ancestry are living according to kaupapa tuku iho and tikanga tuku iho (those policies, practices and organisational arrangements that express the values).
>
> There are many kaupapa tuku iho, inherited values. Prominent among these and widely accepted among Māori are the following (with the English approximations in brackets): manaakitanga (generosity); rangatiratanga (chiefliness); whanaungatanga (familiness); kotahitanga (unity); wairuatanga (spirituality); ukaipotanga (nurturing); pukengatanga (scholarship); kaitiakitanga (guardianship), whakapapa (genealogy) and te reo (Māori language). These are values, the expression of which Māori find uplifting.[20]

The foundation that the kaupapa would provide for the Māori Party was crucial in encouraging me to stand as co-leader.

After the hīkoi I went home and talked to my family and asked them what they thought about forming a party. We did consider me running as an independent, but different ones had been suggesting there was a need for a Māori party. My family didn't want me to stand as an independent because they felt that would be like focusing on me rather than focusing on our people. Who would I be accountable to if I was an independent?

We had nothing to lose. I was terrified though because it seemed like a huge undertaking. The more Matt McCarten and others talked to us about starting a new party, the more scared I got. It all seemed too much. I always thought that my job was winning people's hearts and minds. It was something that we could do for ourselves. It wasn't about a political party coming in and doing it for us. We had to get out of that thinking.

Tariana told *Te Karanga* at the time:

> We are a proud, noble race of people. We can be self-determining, we can look after ourselves, and that is our message to our people. Do they (Māori) want to continue to be underneath tauiwi structures? Is that how they want to live their lives? If they do, I feel incredibly sad. … We have never been able to assert our mana in our own country, and this is our opportunity to do that and embrace all others.[21]

The combination of the kaupapa; the drive for self-determination and the mood of a people for change came together, uniquely, in the establishment of the Māori Party. Towards the end of 2004, Tariana shared the story with the Māori membership of Local Government New Zealand:

> We will no longer be satisfied to be marching to someone else's tune. This is our time, our renaissance, an opportunity to harness our potential and grow. Our first steps have been carefully, steadily planned. We have not wanted to take off running and risk falling over. Our intention has been to develop a secure footing from which to consciously, deliberately, purposefully walk forward. That secure footing has come with our kaupapa. Kaupapa based on our essential values, manaakitanga, rangatiratanga, whanaungatanga, kotahitanga, wairuatanga, mana whenua, kaitiakitanga, mana tupuna and te reo rangatira. The Māori Party does not intend to operate like any other political party. The tikanga Māori nature of the party is an essential part of the justification for its existence.

> The Māori Party will validate our knowledge, language and customs and such knowledge will underpin all policies and practices of the party. We believe this will be beneficial to Māori and to the nation.[22]

The stage was set for the party to take shape. The next step in its evolution took place on Sunday 23 May 2004 at a hui attended by 200 people called at Hoani Waititi marae in Auckland. The hui had started off well, following the results of a Marae DigiPoll survey of 1005 Māori voters carried out from 8 to 21 May 2004. Fifty-five percent of voters had said they were not satisfied with the Prime Minister's performance, and 58 percent were similarly dissatisfied with the Government's performance. The majority (65 percent) believed Tariana had made the right decision to resign, and 83 percent believed she had made the right decision to oppose the foreshore and seabed Bill. Fifty-five percent of voters (60 percent on the Māori roll) supported the creation of another Māori political party; 62 percent of Maori voters said they would vote for it.

As for the most effective Māori MP to represent their views, there appeared to be little room for doubt. Thirty-five percent of voters on the Māori roll named Tariana Turia in their answer to this question, followed by Winston Peters (11.9 percent) John Tamihere (9.2 percent) and Parekura Horomia (7.5 percent).[23]

At that Auckland hui were representatives from Te Tai Tokerau, Ngāti Whātua, Tāmaki Makaurau, Tainui/Raukawa, Waiariki, Te Arawa, Mātaatua, Ngāti Porou, Ngāti Kahungunu, Te Āti Awa, Ngāti Apa, Whanganui, Raukawa ki te Tonga and Ngāi Tahu, as well as the New Zealand District Māori Council. The hui was chaired by Dr Toby Curtis, with Dr Pita Sharples, Professor Whatarangi Winiata, Titewhai Harawira and Tariana part of the panel. The hui canvassed ideas from the floor about the need to establish an independent Māori political voice, to build on the momentum gained from the hīkoi while recognising and supporting the mana of each hapū and iwi that might seek to be involved.

The kōrero was far-ranging, encompassing a call to learn from the mistakes of the past, to act collectively and to promote the fact that Māori interests are of value to all New Zealanders. It was declared that the people were ready to act and the party should mobilise around the forthcoming July by-election. To do this required quality planning, principles, policies, processes and people. It would also be necessary to educate the people as to how to vote.

The hui determined that the new movement should contest at least the seven Māori seats. The following resolutions were then passed.

1. That this hui commits itself to forming a party to contest the upcoming by-election on 10 July 2004 and the next General Election.
2. That the name of the party shall be the Māori Party.
3. That this party shall be an incorporated society operating as a political party for the purposes of the Electoral Act 1993.
4. The founding conference of this party shall be held on the weekend of 10 July 2004 at Otaki.
5. That an organising committee will be authorised to act in the name of the party until the founding conference and make such decisions that they believe necessary to advance the interests of the party.
6. The organising committee will develop an electoral strategy for the Māori party and communicate that widely.
7. The organising committee will be responsible for the development of key policy principles that can be added to the founding conference for decision.
8. The General Secretary and Auditor that are already in place for the purposes of registering the party be accepted until the national hui.

The identity of the Party's first general secretary – prominent Māori lawyer Donna Hall – had already been considered newsworthy. The *Sunday Star-Times* reported:

> Turia said Hall's office was providing the secretarial and administrative support to deal with demand to join and support the Maori party.
>
> 'There has been widespread interest in the party,' she said.
>
> 'My understanding is that it's at the instigation of the Maori Council and its chairman Sir Graham Latimer, to ask her if she could provide a person to receive the party enrolments.

I understand that's all she's doing.'

It is understood Hall has provided the party's secretary, Naomi Waitai, who is co-ordinating membership and donations.[24]

The Hoani Waititi hui itemised the tasks expected of the organising committee, including registering the party with the Electoral Commission, appointing a Secretariat and staff to administer the party, appointing a media/communications person/committee, establishing a national office; raising funding and opening up party accounts. The committee was also required to recruit members and administer a membership database, to approve publications and recruitment materials and to report all party activity to the founding conference. It was charged with drafting up an interim constitution for the founding conference.

Another key objective of the Hoani Waititi hui was to designate the key personnel responsible for the Māori Party. Hon Tariana Turia was endorsed by the hui as the candidate for the Māori Party at the upcoming by-election. Tariana and Pita Sharples were asked to fill the positions of co-leaders, and Professor Whatarangi Winiata was asked to fill the position of president 'until they are endorsed or replaced at the founding conference'.

The following day, the recommendations put to the hui at Hoani Waititi were shared with a much wider audience. The *Herald* reported:

> Momentum for a new Maori political party continued yesterday with more than 1000 people who turned out for a hui in Ngaruawahia supporting its formation. The hui at Turangawaewae Marae, called by Tainui to get an update on the foreshore and seabed proposal and to discuss the new Maori Party, overwhelmingly endorsed resolutions supporting the creation of the party and the appointment of interim leaders.[25]

The hui at Ngaruawāhia was chaired by Tukoroirangi Morgan, and included representatives from every major iwi. Former Alliance leader Matt McCarten was formally introduced at the hui as Tariana's campaign manager for the Te Tai Hauāuru by-election.

Between 24 May and 10 July, a series of regional hui were held in Auckland, Te Arawa, Nelson, Christchurch, the East Coast and Kaikōura, focusing on policy ideas, the formation of the party constitution and the strategy for the 10 July by-election. Throughout those two months, over 3000 people attended hui, and 800 volunteers came forward to express their support for the formation of the Party.

On 9 June 2004, barely a month after the foreshore and seabed hīkoi, a registration application was submitted to the Electoral Commission, and on 9 July 2004, twenty-four hours before the by-election, the Commission resolved to register the Māori Party as a political party. The 500 current memberships had been validated, and all systems were go. Unfortunately, however, the logo registration for the Māori Party was not processed in time for the by-election. The Electoral Act specifically prevented the processing of a logo registration application while a by-election was under way.

Tariana campaigned door-to-door, bringing her message to the people. She said at the time:

> I was amazed at the number of people who didn't know it was a by-election because they don't get the paper and there was very little about it on TV. So we began using whānau networks and people who were involved in our campaign – there were 400 – we told them to concentrate on their own whānau. There were a couple of meetings in which only fifteen or so people came, but it didn't bother me because behind fifteen people usually sits around thirty relatives for each person sitting there. That was where you got questioned the closest at those meetings.[26]

While Tariana was out knocking on doors, attending small 'cottage hui' and covering thousands of miles driving the boundaries of the electorate, various strategies were being concocted back at home base. One issue that drew the party's attention concerned turnout and Māori electoral participation: there was a reduced number of polling booths available for the by-election. The exact location of the booths was not announced until the last week of the campaign.

Tariana said at the time:

> The excitement was still there with our people which was really heartening but we were worried, as we discovered that some people

would have to travel fifty kilometres one way just to get to a booth. There were 311 less booths than the general election, so we knew that that was going to have a significant effect on the ability of our people to get out and vote.[27]

Never one to resist a challenge, Professor Winiata took the issue to the Waitangi Tribunal, formally recording:

> I make this claim on behalf of registered Māori voters in the electorate of Te Taihauāuru that we are likely to be prejudicially affected by certain decisions of the Chief Electoral Officer in regard to the polling booth arrangements for the by-election this Saturday, 10 July 2004.[28]

Whereas the 2002 general election had allocated 406 polling booths for Māori voters to place their vote in the Te Tai Hauāuru electorate, the 2004 by-election had allocated only 95. In effect that meant that forty-seven towns and locations used in 2002 had been sliced off. In his statement of claim, Whatarangi described the abandonment of these booths as placing additional pressures on voters in terms of their travel to the nearest polling booth: 'This is in breach of Article One that provides for respectable kawanatanga and not one accepting of inconsistency.'

The second claim made to the Tribunal concerned the relative disparity between the substantially reduced services offered to Māori voters in Te Tai Hauāuru compared to those in the Taranaki-King Country electorate 1998 by-election: 'This is in breach of Article Three of the Treaty. The maintenance of booth services for one partner to the Treaty; but not so for Māori.'

Given the imminence of the by-election, the Waitangi Tribunal agreed to hear the claimants and the Crown on 7–8 July, noting: 'The claimant emphasised continually that the allocation of resources to Māori voting in this by-election was not reasonable, honourable or in good faith.'

In response to the claim, the Chief Electoral Office, through David Henry, explained that it had adopted a formula by which polling places that took twenty or fewer Māori votes at the 2002 general election were not to be used unless they could not be readily amalgamated with another polling place close by.

Māori Party tactician, of that time, Gerard Hehir assessed the polling booth record against Mr Henry's formula and found another nineteen booths that should have been retained.

The Tribunal's interim report recalled the 'distressingly low turnout in Te Tai Hauauru in 2002', and suggested that a suitable compromise might be relatively inexpensive, namely that the nineteen additional polling booths identified by the Party would cost the Crown $20,000. The Tribunal remained concerned about the distance some voters would still have to travel and the difficulty that posed 'given that the number of Māori without access to a vehicle is on average twice that for non-Māori'. It stated:

> It is unarguable in light of these facts that the Crown should take special steps to encourage Māori participation in the electoral system, including providing sufficient polling places for Māori electors to vote with reasonable convenience.[29]

The interim report of the Tribunal concluded that although it was not able to make a formal recommendation on the basis of the evidence, it suggested the Chief Electoral Officer might wish to reconsider his stance in respect of the nineteen polling booths referred to during the hearing. In the event, he did so.

The reduction in the number of polling booths was not the only issue Tariana confronted in her campaign to take back Te Tai Hauāuru. She also faced challenges from her by-election competitors.

Standing along with Tariana were independents David Bolton, Rusty Kane, Peter Wakeman and Tahu Nepia, as well as Aotearoa Legalise Cannabis Party candidate Dun Mihaka.

They were an interesting bunch, to say the least. Rusty Kane's campaign focus was that the Māori seats should be abolished. Tahu Nepia's aspiration was to establish an independent Rātana Party to contest the next general election. And Dun Mihaka, often described as a veteran Māori activist, was now fighting a different campaign; one which Tariana had little sympathy for, although Dun Mihaka presumed that others in her whānau might – as he proclaimed in a press release:

> If Tariana Turia's own mokopuna were to be given the choice between the regulated availability of cannabis or voting for the Māori Party, there is no doubt in my mind they would vote for cannabis.[30]

Wakeman, a Labour Party member standing as an independent, alleged biased television coverage of the by-election. He laid a complaint with the police because TVNZ's *Te Karere* programme had shown an 0800 number for the Māori Party, the *Herald* reported:

> Mr Wakeman said the Te Karere coverage amounted to a free election broadcast for Mrs Turia.
>
> If Mrs Turia had paid for it, she would have exceeded the $40,000 advertising budget permitted for the by-election, he said.[31]

The Party was registered; the booths were finalised; the campaign was wound up. All that was left was for people to turn up and vote. And turn up and vote they did. Tariana received a massive 92.74 percent of the vote (7256 votes), with a majority of 7059 over the next highest-polling candidate, Dun Mihaka, who received 197 votes.

Tariana had earnt herself another distinctive place in history. The only parliamentary candidate in New Zealand history to have received a higher share of the valid vote was Premier Richard Seddon in 1905, when he took 93.45 percent.

Media commentary was extremely positive, calling the result variously 'a dream result',[32] a 'commanding by-election win'[33] and a worry for Labour:

> For all Labour's efforts to belittle Tariana Turia's victory in last week's by-election it must have come as a rude shock to the Government. The surprise was in the scale of her victory – to be more precise, the number of Maori bothering to cast a vote for her when they knew she would retain her Te Tai Hauauru seat regardless. Turia has bolstered her mana as a shrewd, tough-minded political operator and given her new Maori Party a definite psychological edge over Labour. Because she will hold her constituency, Maori voters now know a vote for her party will not be a wasted vote.[34]

Tariana's ambition in contesting the by-election was always to seek a fresh mandate from the constituency; the legitimacy to stand. But in the process she had attracted widespread support for a far wider cause. In her victory speech to over 1500 supporters gathered at the Whanganui Memorial Hall, Tariana started off by sharing her aspirations for the Māori Party:

> What I will talk about is hope, the hope for a better future: where all peoples will have access to due process; where people can celebrate racial and cultural diversity; where the horizons to achieve are extended, where we will have the confidence to say we do not know and are prepared to learn and relearn ways of being which have been forgotten or unknown; where there is investment in the young and all who want to learn; where every child is loved and nurtured, where success is the model and failure is merely the creation of an opportunity to try again.
>
> Our political movement will assert its position of us: thinking for ourselves, speaking for ourselves, writing for ourselves, and of us doing for ourselves. We will not be seeking the permission of any other group or political party to express what it is that we aspire to, or to determine what action we need to take to achieve those aspirations. The permission we will seek will be from ourselves.[35]

That night then, the Māori Party was launched and a new beginning took shape. In the midpoint of her speech Tariana made a reference to travelling on someone else's bus; a reference that some commentators picked up on as an indirect allusion to the bus her former colleague, Parekura, had spoken about in his maiden speech:

> I relate that story because it is often said to Māori that 'we've missed the bus', but in many cases Māori have not even had the opportunity to get on the bus.[36]

For Tariana, the bus became a metaphor for a broader understanding of self-determination – tino rangatiratanga. Her speech continued:

> We are saying we will no longer travel as passengers on someone else's bus, unhappy with the songs being sung, unhappy with the direction

and the road on which the bus is travelling, but afraid to get off because we believe if we did, another bus will come along and leave us by the roadside.

Tariana rounded off her first speech as the co-leader of the Māori Party by referring to the kōrero of the late Waho Tibble, which had been shared with her on that day by her much-loved friend, colleague and confidant Harry Walker. This kōrero connected her directly to statements that had been expressed at the Hui Taumata in Parliament some twenty years earlier, in 1984:

Nā te ngutukura ko te hinengaro, nā te hinengaro ko te mahara, nā te mahara ko te whakaaro, nā te whakaaro ko te kōrero, mā te kōrero ka tū he tikanga, he taonga nui te wareware. I haere mai tātou i roto i ō tātou mātua, kai roto tātou i te ao kē, kai mua i a tātou ko te mate ara te tuturutanga o te ora.

Engaging the senses stirs the emotions, engaging the emotions stimulates the intellect, stimulating the intellect commissions the memory, from the memory comes the thoughts, from thoughts comes the words, from the words we construct customs, forgetfulness is to be treasured. We are of our parents, we exist in another world, before us lies death, the ultimate of life. Yes Waho, the thoughts of another confiscation stirred the emotions of anger. When we connected with the anger we began to think and the memories of our minds reflected on the confiscations that litter our history. We thought about what we should do, talked of and embarked on a hīkoi. We have now created a movement, the Māori Party. We will never forget.

And while we are of a different generation and time to that of our parents and while ours is a different world to theirs, they live on in us, as we will live on in our children and grandchildren. While we move to achieve the ultimate in life and join our ancestors in the future that lies behind us.

And with those words I now officially launch the Māori Party.

The next day, at the inaugural general meeting of the Māori Party, all of the establishment roles were allocated and confirmed as interim. The constitution was accepted, pending a review in six months. All of the rohe – each one being defined on the basis of the Māori electorate boundaries – were given until 1 January 2005 to finalise their positions and policies.

The emergence of the new party attracted unprecedented attention, both at home and abroad. A week after the by-election, the party president of Australia's Aboriginal Your Voice Party, Richard J. Frankland, wrote to 'the warrior, Hon Tariana Turia':

> Your stand is an inspiration to all indigenous peoples, indeed to all good thinking peoples. As indigenous peoples we have fought for our lands, our seas, our rivers, our rights, our past present and future. We have fought for recognition of our culture and our very voice. The formation of the party means simply this, we will not be silent, we will not go away, we will ascertain our rights and our voice will be heard throughout time forevermore. We will be heard in the halls of parliament as we have been heard around campfires since time began. Our voice is sacred and will not be silenced.[37]

Just two weeks after the by-election the first Māori Party member took her seat in Parliament. As a leader, Tariana was allocated a seat at the front bench, sitting to the left of United Future leader, Peter Dunne. She was now entitled to one five-minute speech every two months in the general debate on Wednesdays, and one question in the House every nine sitting days.

Her first day back, 27 July 2004, was always going to be eventful. *New Zealand Herald* columnist John Armstrong reported on it with great gusto:

> Nothing was going to upstage Tariana Turia's triumphant re-entry into Parliament yesterday, not even the freshly bleached locks of Labour's David Cunliffe ... Flanked by three Maori women MPs – Labour's Georgina Beyer, the Green's Metiria Turei and the independent Donna Awatere-Huata, Mrs Turia was out to show MPs dismissive of her by-election victory that her party had well and truly arrived as she entered the chamber to be sworn in as an MP

once more. On cue she was greeted by a rousing, raucous haka from her supporters packing the public galleries, probably bewildering delegations from the Vietnamese Parliament and British House of Commons sitting nearby.[38]

Tariana became the first MP in New Zealand history to take her oath of affirmation in te reo Māori without a translation.

Before 2004, if MPs wanted to swear the oath in te reo they had to also swear an English oath. The limitations around the oath had always irked Tariana; she had been pushing for a change since she first entered Parliament in 1996. At the opening of the forty-fifth Parliament on 12 December 1996, Tariana had added words to her Māori oath, pledging allegiance to the Māori Queen, Queen Elizabeth II and the Treaty of Waitangi. She had sought permission from Clerk of the House, David McGee, to make the oath in Māori, but he had turned her down. She had said at the time, 'I was really surprised and I made up my mind that I would do both anyway – I would speak in Maori and I would add to it'.[39]

At the opening of the forty-sixth Parliament on 20 December 1999, Tariana had again added allegiance to the Treaty to her oath. This time the Clerk of the House told her it was not acceptable, and that she needed to repeat her oath without the Treaty reference. Tariana told the *Herald*:

> There is a failure by this parliament to acknowledge the Treaty which in effect gave the Crown the right to govern. I think it is time that we started examining what the treaty means and don't just pull it out of the drawer when it suits us.[40]

Three years later, in the first speech Tariana made in the 2002–2005 Parliament, she wasted no time revisiting the fact that the oath had to be sworn in English and failed to reflect Te Tiriti o Waitangi:

> Last week Mr Speaker I swore allegiance to the Queen and Her descendants, as indeed I should as a member of this Parliament. I am, however, uncomfortable that the oath of allegiance makes no reference of the Treaty of Waitangi – the founding document that is the basis of constitutional government in this country; and, that the

oath must be taken in the English language to be valid. There is no inherent conflict between my role as a Member of Parliament and an agent of the Crown, and my role as part of a community of tangata whenua, which is a Treaty partner of the Crown. Our constitutional procedures should not create conflict.[41]

By the time Tariana re-entered Parliament as a Māori Party MP, there was therefore little doubt about her desire to make the oath she made meaningful – not just for Māori but for all New Zealanders. On 1 July 2004 the Oaths and Declarations (Māori Language) Regulations 2004 had been passed, effectively authorising a te reo Māori equivalent for certain oaths.

The new Regulations did not allow for capacity to swear allegiance to the Treaty, however, and this continued to be an issue that Tariana raised at every subsequent opening of Parliament, and that the Māori Party will continue to raise.[42] When she was joined by Dr Pita Sharples, Te Ururoa Flavell and Hone Harawira in Parliament following the 2005 election, Tariana led the charge as all four Māori Party MPs stood to swear allegiance to the Treaty. Even though they were each asked to stand and repeat their vows without the Treaty oath, the point was well made.

It was sort of exciting in a way to come back with an opportunity to remain true to all the things that you absolutely hold fast to. It felt to me like here for a long, long time we had wanted that opportunity to have our own voice, not one that is hindered by someone else. I was excited to come back, even though the media were saying we would be a five-minute wonder; we'd be lucky if we were able to maintain the movement.

When I came back in, our whānau came from home and then unexpectedly people came from around the country. It just blew me away that there were kuia and koroheke that had come from the North and they'd gone by cars to Auckland and then got in buses and trains to come down to Wellington.

A lot of them were really old. It just blew me away to think that this was such an important thing for them. And that was when I began to realise the importance of this movement. Some of them were people that had come down to the launch of the Party – just that ongoing support, that faith, that trust, was absolute. I felt very humbled by it and their presence here on that day. They were saying that for the first time ever in their lifetime – and some of them were in their late seventies, early eighties – they began to believe that a way forward for our people could happen.

I was excited but I was nervous as well about the huge expectations of our people. I was just in my heart of hearts praying that I would never let them down. I guess renewing my commitment as well to behave honourably here.[43]

After she had been formally sworn in, Tariana moved into the atrium area of the Beehive to deliver her first speech in Parliament as a Māori Party MP.[44] Her message was a consistent one: we can do this, and we can do it now:

> Ko tēnei te wā o te Ao Maori. It is time to look to ourselves. The best form of leadership for Māori is Māori. We need to seek leadership from within, to find the inspiration that exists in our people. That is how we are different to other political parties. We are a political movement, creating change from the people up and our politicians will reflect that. Our politicians will not be telling you what's good for you. Our politicians will be listening to you for that. We're better off with whānau whose wairua is strong and vibrant, with whānau who have fully developed their spiritual, intellectual, emotional and physical wellbeing.[45]

The speech ended with a call for the Māori Party to bring together a strong and independent Māori voice; a voice comprised of many different strands that, together, could create a more diverse nation:

> There is no conflict between unity and diversity. We can truly celebrate the bringing together of Mana Māori, Mana Motuhake and learn from all our views from one end of the spectrum to the other. We need to focus on what unites us rather than what divides us. Our key platform as the Māori Party is kotahitanga, rangatiratanga, Te Tiriti o Waitangi. We have shown we can stand up and be counted, together.

We will introduce a new language to this House. It is called Truth. We will introduce new ways of acting in this House. It is called Respect. And we will introduce a new movement to guide and advise Parliament about the aspirations or our people. It is called the Māori Party. E te iwi Māori, maranga! E ngā iwi katoa o Aotearoa, maranga! Maranga mai rā tātau ki tū tahi tātau i runga i te tika, i te pono. Tēnā koutou, tēnā koutou, tēnā koutou katoa.

NOTES

1 Rangitihi Rangiwaiata Tahuparae, quoted in Tariana Turia, speech to Te Piringa Hui Taumata, 26 April 2012.

2 Tariana Turia, 'Pūao te Atatū: A New Dawn Breaks', speech to Whānau Ora Planning Workshop, 22 November 2012. http://www.beehive.govt.nz/speech/p%C5%ABao-te-atat%C5%AB-new-dawn-breaks-%E2%80%94-wh%C4%81nau-ora-planning-workshop

3 Tariana Turia, Beehive Chat, 17 May 2004.

4 *Te Waonui a te Manu Korihi*, Radio New Zealand, 10 August 2014.

5 K. Paki, 'Tilting the Tables', *Tū Mai*, July 2004, p. 19.

6 Shane Jones, 'Theatre, drama and a warning', *New Zealand Herald*, 10 May 2004.

7 Tariana Turia, 'Leadership is more than anatomy', speech to the Te Tau Ihu Māori Women's Leadership Awards, 30 June 2004.

8 Tariana Turia, Beehive Chat, 17 May 2014.

9 'Government survives confidence vote as pressure mounts', *New Zealand Herald*, 4 May 2004.

10 Parliamentary Standing Orders stipulate that in any reading of a Government bill there is a prescribed arrangement of twelve speaking slots, based on the proportionality of parties represented in the House. Speaking order is generally organised by party whips in advance of the session that day.

11 *Hansard*, 6 May 2004.

12 Tariana Turia, oral history interview between Tariana Turia and Taina Tangaere McGregor, 21 July 2010, Oral History Political Diary project, Oral History Collection, Alexander Turnbull Library.

13 Tariana Turia, 'Now we've got to stand up for ourselves', personal interview, 22 September 2004.

14 R. Nuri, 'Arrival of the New Māori Party', *Te Karaka*, Koanga 2004, p. 15.

15 Paki, 'Tilting the Tables', p. 19.

16 Oral history interview between Tariana Turia and Taina Tangaere McGregor, 10 November 2004, Oral History Political Diary project, Oral History Collection, Alexander Turnbull Library.

17 Ruth Berry, 'Turia taking time out in political limbo', *New Zealand Herald*, 14 May 2004.

18 Tariana Turia, 'Now we've got to stand up for ourselves', personal interview 22 September 2004.

19 Oral history interview between Tariana Turia and Taina Tangaere McGregor, 10 November 2004, Oral History Political Diary project, Oral History Collection, Alexander Turnbull Library.

20 Whatarangi Winiata, 'Māori Innovation and Reconciliation', paper presented to the Ngā Pae o te Māramatanga Conference 2008, 8–11 June 2008.

21 Nuri, 'Arrival of the new Māori Party', p. 39.

22 Tariana Turia, 'Nga Hau o te Ao Hurihuri'.

23 Other MPs received under 1 percent (Dover Samuels, Georgina Beyer, Mita Ririnui, Metiria Turei, Jim Peters and Donna Awatere-Huata).

24 Jonathan Milne, 'Maori Party plays down Hall's role', *Sunday Star-Times*, 16 May 2004.

25 Jon Stokes, 'Maori Party gathering steam', *New Zealand Herald*, 25 May 2004.

26 Oral history interview between Tariana Turia and Taina Tangaere McGregor, 20 July 2004, Oral History Political Diary project, Oral History Collection, Alexander Turnbull Library.

27 Ibid.

28 Whatarangi Winiata, Claim of Professor Whatarangi Winiata to the Registrar, Waitangi Tribunal, 6 July 2004, WAI 1177.

29 Chief Judge Joe Williams, Chairperson on behalf of the Tribunal, *Interim Report of Waitangi Tribunal on the Te Tai Hauauru By-election*, 8 July 2004.

30 Dun Mihaka, press release, 'Pot issue bigger than Māori Party', 8 July 2004.

31 Kevin Norquay, 'Maori Party complains to Waitangi Tribunal over polling booths', *New Zealand Herald*, 8 July 2004.

32 'First victory for NZ's Maori Party', *ABC News*, 10 July 2004.

33 Ruth Berry, ' Maori Party victors turn their fire on Labour', *New Zealand Herald*, 12 July 2004.

34 John Armstrong, 'Turia assures party future, *New Zealand Herald*, 17 July 2004.

35 Tariana Turia, speech to launch Māori Party, 10 July 2004.

36 *Hansard*, 15 February 2000.

37 Personal letter of 17 July 2004, Richard J. Frankland to Tariana Turia.

38 John Armstrong, 'Turia the Queen of the Castle', *New Zealand Herald*, 28 July 2004.

39 'Maori oath requires law change', *Dominion*, 17 December 1996.

40 Audrey Young, 'Maori MP calls for oath to the treaty', *New Zealand Herald*, 21 December 1999.

41 *Hansard*, 4 September 2002.

42 On 7 November 2012 Te Ururoa Flavell championed the first reading of the Oaths and Declarations (Upholding the Treaty of Waitangi) Amendment Bill, the intention of which was simple. The Bill inserted the optional additional words: 'I will uphold the Treaty of Waitangi' or 'Ka whakaūngia e au te Tiriti o Waitangi' across a range of oaths and affirmations. Although Labour, the Greens and Mana supported the first reading, this was not enough to get the Bill across the line, and so the opportunity to swear allegiance to the Treaty is an issue that will live on for another day.

43 Oral history interview between Tariana Turia and Taina Tangaere McGregor, 10 November 2004, Oral History Political Diary project, Oral History Collection, Alexander Turnbull Library.

44 A Member of Parliament is given only one opportunity for their maiden address – Tariana's official maiden address was 26 February 1997. She chose, however, in her first days as a Māori Party MP to give a maiden address as leader of the new party. This had to be delivered in the atrium – the reception area for the Executive Wing.

45 Tariana Turia, 'E Te Iwi Māori, Maranga – Tariana Turia Maiden speech 2004', 27 July 2004.

-CHAPTER TWENTY-
BUILDING THE MĀORI PARTY

Victory in a great cause is measured not only by reaching the final goal. It is also a triumph to live up to expectations in your lifetime.[1]

From the triumphant day of her re-entry into Parliament, 27 July 2004, until her valedictory speech almost ten years later, on 24 July 2014, Tariana worked at a furious pace to establish the Party and consolidate its future direction.

Tariana said in 2004:

> People round the country started making contact. There was a coordinator appointed in each area, and then each rohe was broken up. In our rohe, Te Tai Hauāuru, there were ten regions, with a coordinator in each region to whom the branches were accountable. Then all the coordinators came together every two months. That group was the eyes and ears of the electorate. They were in touch by email. We had a lot of conference calls.
>
> People fed ideas in right from the start. We had a group of people drawing out the strands of the policies. Early papers were drafted – health, children and whānau, constitution, justice, education. The papers were sent out to the branches, and they fed back their ideas. Everywhere we've gone and discussed this process people have been really excited by it. They have never been asked what they thought before. So it is really important that we keep faith with that group and do what we say we will do.
>
> Our constitutional paper was the first to go out to branches. The family policy focuses on children, and it's about our responsibilities and obligations and sets it out really clearly. It's all culturally focused, because I believe that all the answers lie in who we are. If we start to reassert those things anything is possible.
>
> Even though we've got this policy framework which will go with us into Parliament, it's a story to tell ourselves; it's not about what politicians will do for us. I look to ourselves to do this. That's going to be the big difference for me. Everything in Labour was about what the Government will do for you. I don't want our people to want the Government to do things for them. We need to restore our mana to ourselves. I just know that we can do it, but we've got to believe it. We can change the whole way that our families relate to each other and others.[2]

By the time that the Party's annual general meeting was held on 27 November at Hoani Waititi marae in Auckland, considerable progress had been made in laying the groundwork for the Party. A working party was established to develop the proposal of establishing a Kāhui Kaumātua; Tariana and Pita were elected as co-leaders; Whatarangi Winiata was elected as president; and each electorate was asked to choose an executive – chairperson, secretary, treasurer and delegates, and to advise the secretary of the Party's National Council of these appointments by 12 December 2004.

At the AGM, Matt McCarten was appointed campaign manager for the 2005 general election, and a series of planning meetings were set up for between 4 and 11 December to bring Matt to each of the seven electorates.

The constitution was endorsed and carried by consensus, with a vote of thanks moved to Te Ururoa Flavell and his team for putting it together.

At the inaugural hui in Whanganui in July 2004, a set of interim rules for the Party had been approved, prefaced with nine broad objectives. Those objectives set in place goals as follows:

- to promote Māori self-determination, te tino rangatiratanga, within the framework of a unified nation state;
- to create a clean, safe and healthy environment;
- to promote a just and equitable society without poverty or discrimination; and
- to ensure all New Zealanders have an understanding of, and respect for the Treaty of Waitangi.

Four months later, at the AGM, the constitution looked very different. The objectives had been replaced by the articulation of kaupapa Māori as a platform for the future.[3] For founding president Winiata, these kaupapa – and the capacity to live by them – would be critical to the success of the Party. He told *Te Karaka*:

> The nation will want to entrench the Māori presence. It will bring value to the nation that is unique to this place. The nation will see that this Party is able to work together, that they are guided

by values and that they will make statements with a single voice. We want people to vote for the Māori Party because they believe that this collection of people will make a substantial difference to the country.[4]

Of course, it was not just a vision for the successful future for the Party that inspired Whatarangi to promote the importance of kaupapa as a basis for going forward. He always saw the kaupapa as fundamental to the long-term survival of Māori. His long-term plan for the future, as *Anglican Taonga* explains it, is that:

> We are more Māori than we are now. More Māori than the current generation … because that is what survival will mean. That more Māoriness will only come, Whatarangi believes, if Māori stick to the kaupapa, the inherited values which he believes are the keystones of Maoridom.[5]

For Tariana, the fact that kaupapa formed a founding basis of the Māori Party was something that she greatly valued.

I have grown up being very much involved with my old people back on my marae – they have guided me and been very strict with us about kaupapa and tikanga; you either believe this or you don't. It's either part of the core being of you, or what are you, who are you? So when Matua Whatarangi laid those foundation kaupapa down they resonated with me. And they haven't been easy to practise, to be honest, because you do get caught up in the hype of this place. And sometimes you will put something aside.

When he was president, Matua came to our caucus every week. And if he heard us talking about things that didn't fit, he would very quietly say to us, 'and what kaupapa is operating here? Can you tell me?' It was wonderful because it was quite controlling of you. The moment he would say that, I would know what I had said; I didn't need anybody to spell it out to me.

Once the constitution was in place, the next task ahead for the Party was candidate selection. The influence of the hīkoi, the inspiration provided by Tariana and the foreshore and seabed legislation were common factors in attracting likely candidates to the cause.

Dr Pita Sharples had been closely associated with early discussions planning the hīkoi. He remembers:

> I was at the meeting when we decided, Ngāti Kahungunu, to march on Parliament. The original idea was to take a kete full of sand, to take it on to the steps, to let it drop through the kete on to the floor on the steps, in protest of the fact they stole our foreshore and seabed. And then we called up a march and people responded.
>
> Tariana crossed the floor after that, and we were so impressed, and angry with the others who did not cross the floor. It just seemed so damn obvious. You have to stand up for something. Surely what more than your land? And that we had been abused by not even being consulted, and they were going ahead with it. So I thought, 'why haven't the others crossed the floor?' I was expecting them to follow. No one followed, and it just made it seem all the more miraculous what Tariana did. I remember ringing her and saying, 'are you going to stand again for Parliament? Whatever you do, we will support you'. I was really talking for Kahungunu I suppose at that time. We sent people down there for her campaign.

For Te Ururoa Flavell, there was no question of not stepping up. He told Eru Potaka Dewes in 2007:

> The Seabed and Foreshore issue was the catalyst for involving myself firstly in active protest against a Government that took away a right. I was inspired by Tariana Turia's actions of acting on principle and leaving her party and I was determined to assist her in whatever actions she was to take from developing the party to securing her seat.[6]

Te Ururoa, like Pita, hadn't had any real association with Tariana up until the hīkoi:

> I've always talked about arriving the night before the hīkoi and being on the forecourt of parliament looking at what the hell's going to happen here because I'd never been here too much. Seeing all the gates up and Hone and Ken had told me that I would be the MC for the following day. I had just come down from Patea. I had organised the Rotorua league of the hīkoi, I got down here the night before, the wind was blowing and I just remember you two (Tariana and the author) coming out of the rubber door, walking down in front of the statue and out. I still hadn't met her per se. So that was it.

For Hone Harawira, the hīkoi was a big factor in his decision to join the Party. He told Dewes:

> When somebody first tried to get me involved, it was some months before the hīkoi and I had other things on my mind. So I ignored the request and the Māori Party seemed to die a death. The next time I saw anything about the Māori Party was when someone tried to sign me up at parliament on the day the hīkoi arrived. I told them to get lost 'cause I was busy. When it became clear that the Māori Party was a goer, I decided to join because I saw the opportunity to help Māori break free from the shackles of Labour Party dependency, once and for all. I knew that as a result of the Hīkoi, my name would be at the top of the list, should the Māori Party decide to contest the 2005 elections.[7]

Once he had made his mind up, for Hone the action started immediately after the hīkoi as he and his wife, Hilda, headed back home to the North:

> We just slow-cruised it home for a couple of days, and by halfway home Hilda was saying to me, 'don't even think about it mate, it's not going to happen'. But by the time we got back to Auckland, and made a number of stops along the way, it was clear that there was going to be a Māori Party in the North and I was going to be the MP. Without the approval of anybody and before the hui at Hoani Waititi – I did a tour of Te Tai Tokerau and I established ten branches before the Whanganui hui.

While individual candidates were coming forward, the Party was enjoying an unprecedented media spotlight. Magazines like *Tū Mai* and *Mana* featured extensive coverage of the Māori Party during its first year; and Ngāi Tahu's *Te Karaka* in the Kōanga 2004 issue dedicated its cover and thirteen pages to answering the question, 'The new Māori Party: Can it deliver?'

Political commentators were excited about the possibility that lay ahead for a new political player in the market, *Tū Mai*, for example, speculating:

> This Māori Party, perhaps more so than any of its predecessors, has a strong platform of political gain to build from. The once-favoured Labour party's handling of the foreshore and seabed issue has soured relationships with most of its loyal Māori voters. Don Brash and the National Party's ignominious attacks on Māori issues have also, unsurprisingly, left many Māori feeling angry, infuriated and disillusioned. It is this disillusionment that has prompted Māori voters to look elsewhere for political affirmation and galvanized them into seeking a new direction for New Zealand politics.[8]

Then in September 2004 a Marae DigiPoll of Māori voters suggested the Māori Party could hold most or all of the seven Māori seats after the 2005 election, and possibly even the balance of power. The poll also showed strong support for Tariana as the most favoured Māori MP: 19.9 percent of voters selected Tariana in this regard, ahead of Winston Peters on 11.1 percent, John Tamihere on 6.7 percent and Parekura Horomia on 5.4 percent.

At this time Tariana was spending considerable time travelling around New Zealand, talking at hui. For two days at the end of September she was in Northland, sharing her vision with the crowds that gathered, telling them, 'we have huge potential, huge untapped potential'. It was time to discard the 'mad, bad and sad' stereotype, she said; for the people to believe in themselves and not rely on others to make decisions for them.[9]

The message was firmly couched in the context of an independent voice. In *Te Karaka*, Tariana talked about the party building on the momentum of previous Māori political vehicles, to bring about a clear sense of purpose. The magazine reported:

> Many Māori political parties have unsuccessfully attempted to change the political landscape of Aotearoa – Mauri Pacific, Mana Maāori Motuhake, Mana Māori Movement, Te Tawharau and Advance Aotearoa, to name a few. So why should the Māori Party succeed? According to Tariana Turia, 'The difference is we have brought about a unity of purpose. All of those Māori parties have come together, and what the foreshore and seabed has done is to galvanise our people into action.
>
> 'It is too difficult to work in a mainstream political party trying to achieve change for your people, when at every turn you're stopped. Why do people think we have our own kura, kōhanga, health and social services? Because we don't fit in the mainstream environment; it is ineffective and an inefficient spend of public money.'[10]

Meanwhile the 'mainstream political party' that Tariana had left was desperately trying to regain ground following months of polls damaged by the foreshore and seabed legislative process and Don Brash's attack of the 'race-based' policies of Labour. In February 2004, Clark had appointed Trevor Mallard Coordinating Minister, Race Relations, to review policies with racial preferences. New Zealand First Leader Winston Peters surmised the real reason for the new role:

> The appointment of Education Minister Trevor Mallard as Coordinating Minister For Race Relations, whatever that means, is a sign of panic among Labour's politically correct upper echelons. This is another response to New Zealand First's Treaty policies, but unfortunately, Mr Mallard has all the tact of a bull in a china shop and there is no doubt race relations are in for a rocky ride.[11]

Mr Mallard was charged with reviewing the policy and programmes formely covered under 'Closing the Gaps'. The review's objective was to give ministers, and the public, assurance that the policy was being developed on the basis of need, not race. The State Services Commission would coordinate the review, and a work plan would be sent to ministers in mid-May 2004.

It was some months, however, before Mallard made his first speech in his new role. That speech, entitled 'We are all New Zealanders now', contained a curious mix of generalisations and myths. It stated: 'It is simply irresponsible to make assertions about Māori constantly skiving off to tangi or Māori doctors being less able than their non-Maori counterparts.'

Mallard went on to explain that the indigenous peoples of Aotearoa, tangata whenua, had no particular significance in Te Tiriti o Waitangi. ('There is a myth that the Treaty gave Māori extra rights over and above those of other New Zealanders'). But perhaps most bizarre of all was Mallard's view of the county's new identity: 'Māori and Pākehā are both indigenous people to New Zealand now. I regard myself as an indigenous New Zealander – I come from Wainuiomata.'[12]

Tariana responded immediately to the speech, clarifying that 'indigenous' was a concept respected and protected by original peoples throughout the world:

> New Zealanders who have been here for some time could call themselves native New Zealanders, but I would think the 300 million indigenous people around the world would be surprised.[13]

In many respects, there were many similarities between what Brash was projecting as Opposition leader and what Mallard was projecting in his new role in race relations. Ani Mikaere noted:

> Yet, just as Brash continues to cultivate a coalition of the fearful, it is equally plain that Mallard is intent on forging a coalition of the forgetful: Māori must forgive and forget, and Pākeha must be allowed to forget, so that we can all live together as one big, happy, amnesic family.[14]

There were other areas of conflict between Tariana and Mallard, the next being aired four months later, around the topic of teenage pregnancy. Tariana had spoken out about fertility control at the first Māori Sexual and Reproductive Health Conference in Wainuiomata, on 1 November 2004:

> I am intolerant of the excessive focus on controlling our fertility. When I used to sit around the Cabinet table with colleagues, one of the many hot topics I got into strife about was discussion around the 'problem' of teenage pregnancy. My objection was the problematisation of conception. So when Cabinet Ministers sat around tut-tutting the fact that the fertility rate for Māori females aged 13–17 years was 26.2 per 1,000, more than five times that of non-Māori (4.9% per 1,000), I objected to their analysis of our fertility as a problem.[15]

It wasn't long before Mallard responded, issuing a press release calling her comments 'irresponsible':

> Co-ordinating Minister, Race Relations and Education Minister Trevor Mallard said today that comments by the Māori Party that appear to condone and not discourage young Māori teenagers from getting pregnant are simply irresponsible. Ms Turia has previously espoused a view that she thinks it is important to increase the Māori population and that early fertility and a shortening of the generation cycle is an appropriate way of doing this. We need to give them advice to minimise – not increase – teen birth rates. It is grossly irresponsible to argue otherwise.[16]

Tariana's former colleague John Tamihere had also commenced a sustained series of attacks on both Tariana and the Māori Party that appeared to be gaining traction:

> 'The rise of the Maori Party is unfortunate and frustrating for politicians like myself', he said. Frustrating because the party is led by very well off, very senior and very articulate Maori educationalists, academics and the new elite around the Treaty of Waitangi – chequebooks. I am pleased all the separatists now have a party to join, but we now must see it for what it is: the biggest duping exercise carried out on Maori by Maori this century.[17]

Tamihere described the 'elitism' he referred to as emerging from a sense of 'victimhood':

When I say 'elitist', they come from a small grouping who have done very well both personally but also in terms of making a name for themselves out of expressing our differences and our grievances and our sense of victimhood.[18]

As if the attacks from Mallard and Tamihere weren't enough to contend with in November 2004, a headline on *Scoop Independent News* held that 'Intel Sources say SIS Investigating Maori Party'. The story suggested that three people associated with the Party were being singled out for investigation: Brian Dickson (Ngāi Te Rangi), Whititera Kaihau (Ngāi Te Ata) and Tariana Turia:

> Intelligence sources have revealed the New Zealand Security Intelligence Service (SIS) has launched a major covert operation investigating the Maori Party, co-leader Tariana Turia, its members, networks and associates.[19]

It was also reported that the Prime Minister had suggested the concerns were 'laughable'. Yet ten days later the *Sunday Star-Times* reported that the SIS had been spying on Māori organisations and individuals over several years, according to documents acquired by journalists Nicky Hager and Anthony Hubbard. Tariana's response to the allegations was swift and deliberate:

> I have today, written to the Inspector-General of Intelligence and Security, Retired Judge, Hon. Paul Neazor, to ask him to initiate an immediate inquiry into the allegations made about the activities of the Security Intelligence Service', co-leader of the Māori Party, Tariana Turia, said today. 'There are too many serious questions left unanswered. New Zealanders take for granted that our freedom to live in an open democracy is a basic standard of living for our nation' said Mrs Turia. 'These latest allegations suggest that ordinary New Zealanders, Māori New Zealanders, are having their basic human rights infringed upon.
>
> The Prime Minister's response that the allegations are a 'work of fiction', or 'laughable', is not sufficient to allay the concerns of every-day, decent law-abiding citizens, that they too, will not run the risk of coming under

SIS surveillance if they join the Māori Party, or happen to belong to an iwi that opposes a Government that legitimises theft' said Mrs Turia.[20]

Tariana highlighted that the SIS, under the terms of the New Zealand Security Intelligence Service Amendment Act 1999 'must not take any action for the purpose of furthering or harming the interests of any political party'. She confirmed that when she had left the Labour Party in May, she had contracted independent security specialists to sweep her home because she believed her home telephone had been bugged.[21]

Tariana refused to be derailed by either the threat of SIS surveillance or the criticisms from her former colleagues. The public statements that Tariana and other members of the Māori Party were making directly spoke to 'middle New Zealand', through a call for the nation to be inclusive in shaping a new future:

> We'll definitely have policies and strategies that mainstream New Zealand will want to hold to. It's our intention to build a bicultural nation, a vision we have the capacity to achieve. In the end if people understand the nature of politics they will understand why I have said that we will work with whoever is in government. We want the best outcome for our people and so it is important to work with the party in the government benches, important to be cooperative and we will work to enhance opportunities for our people.[22]

The list of sixty-two candidates standing to represent the Māori Party at the 2005 elections actively demonstrated this commitment to build a bicultural nation. At a National Council meeting in March 2005, a somewhat blunt set of criteria had been proposed as part of the 'General Seat Strategy': 'Must be quality candidates, good cultural fit, ability to be self-sustaining and don't drain or dissipate the energy of our focus on the Māori seats'.[23]

Heading the list were the candidates who would contest the Māori electorate seats, dubbed the 'magnificent seven': Tariana Turia, Dr Pita Sharples, Te Ururoa Flavell, Angeline Greensill, Monte Ohia, Hone Harawira and Atareta Poananga. A press release explained:

> 'Included in our list are tangata whenua, pakeha, pasifika peoples, Chinese. Other ethnic communities have also expressed a desire to

work closely with us on further policy development' stated Professor Winiata. 'It also demonstrates the commitment our candidates have given to enacting Te Tiriti o Waitangi, particularly renown Treaty practitioner and author, Robert Consedine, and former Waitangi Tribunal director Morrie Love'.

'We are delighted with the inclusion of rangatahi at all levels of the party, and are thrilled that in our top forty, we have five outstanding candidates under the age of forty', stated Tariana Turia, co-leader of the Māori Party. 'We are particularly excited to have top Olympic ski champion Simon Wi Rutene, and environmentalist Glenis Philip-Barbara in our top five. Our youngest candidate is only 19 years old (Tell Kuka).[24]

Other candidates named included former Chief Advisor of Māori Health Dr Tony Ruakere, former President of the Māori Women's Welfare League Aroha Reriti-Crofts, Literacy Aotearoa Chief Executive Bronwyn Yates, tertiary education advisor Dr John Harre (father of Laila), Ngāti Kahungunu leader Ngahiwi Tomoana, peak oil advocate Anne Fitzsimon and forensic psychiatrist Charles Joe. The list also included union delegates; business mentors; social service workers; expert practitioners in health, organic horticulture, peace and social justice; teachers at kōhanga, kura, wānanga and mainstream schools, writers, performers, a music producer and audio engineer and a national champion of tae kwon do.

Tariana explained her views about the involvement of tauiwi on the list:

I have a firm view on this and I hope I can be influential. I want our people to show the generosity of spirit that I know they have and be inclusive. You can't just say the words, you have to mean it and you have to believe this is the new way forward. We used to have a huge māra (garden). Our families used to come together; my nan did most of the work. When the time came to gather the kai, my grandmother used to put it into three grades. The best kai was for the manuhiri, the second best for the rest of our families, and what was left was for us. I believe that's a philosophy we can continue just in the way we are.[25]

At number six on the list was author and Treaty educator, Irish Catholic fourth generation New Zealander Robert Consedine. His decision to stand for the Party represented his belief that Pākehā support and involvement was necessary for the Party to get the numbers and broaden the base. He told *Tū Mai*:

> A vote for the Māori Party at this moment in history would represent a conscious decision to support Māori aspirations and a relationship built on Te Tiriti. I will be challenging voters to vote for the future of the country, their children and grandchildren, not just for their personal benefit.[26]

To garner support for the Party, Tariana was meeting with the Muslim community, with Pasifika groups, with any other culture that embraced the philosophy of the Party. As she explained in 2006:

> Our goal is to have those communities operating autonomously, to be able to have control over the developments that they want for themselves. The great thing when we met with Pacific peoples was that they felt it was really important for tangata whenua to uphold their mana.[27]

One of the things that seemed to draw people to the Party was the call to kotahitanga: the promise of unity between many peoples.

> One of the exciting things about the establishment of the party is that we've had young people, old people, urban, rural, the radical, the conservative all wanting to unite. The hikoi has been an inspiration to many of our people not only to be involved in the hikoi but also to take control of our political destiny.[28]

Political commentator Kaapua Smith later suggested that the use of grassroots support underpinned and shaped the structure, values and policies of the Party:

> As well as providing the opportunity for supporters to express their opinions on the party's structure, policies and strategies, the hui process enabled the communities to meet the party leaders who

would be representing their interests during forthcoming election campaigns and in parliament. Many such hui were held off the beaten track in small towns that no other political party had ever visited. This process both empowered the communities and the grassroots party membership. In its first year, party membership mushroomed from 4000 in July 2004 to 20,000 by the time of the election.[29]

Alongside all of the campaigning that was taking place, the Māori Party National Council was meeting monthly, bringing people together to form the workforce. Minutes of the hui held in March 2005 at Tapu Te Ranga Marae, in Island Bay, Wellington, reported on twenty-two working parties around the country that were helping with the formulation of policy. At the AGM twenty-nine workshops had been held to debate various policy issues; and a mailout went out to 13,000 members. A schedule of subsequent hui was approved: Raglan in April; Whāngārei in June; and a victory rally scheduled for Tūranganui-a-kiwa in September, following the election. The March 2005 minutes described the need for a fighting fund to support the Party. They also recorded a proposal for a national art auction; and raised for discussion the ideas of corporate sponsorship and a card system for donations: a 'pounamu' card for $1000 donations, a 'pāua card' for $100 donations and a 'kōwhai' card for $1 donations.

The reality was, however, that even the best laid plans at National Council failed to result in the financial support that the campaign needed. A month out from the election, Tariana admitted she was hoping the people would be persuaded more by principle than pūtea (funding):

> We don't have the money Labour has so of course it is going to be difficult but I am hoping people are more interested in affirming and preserving their mana rather than thinking about money.[30]

The campaign involved action at every level. In Tokoroa, Māori Party candidate Billy Maea walked across the Taupo electorate, bringing attention to the cause. All around the country, Robert Consedine gathered crowds around his bus, distinguished by its Māori Party branding. In Tāmaki the Party hosted mayoral functions in Auckland, Manukau and Waitakere, Titewhai Harawira opening up debate on the Party's behalf. In Gisborne the Tūranga branch campaigned at the markets, while in Manurewa and Porirua their Auckland and Wellington counterparts followed suit. On the North Shore, three candidates staged a protest outside a meeting organised by Grey Power that the Party had been excluded from because the Grey Power branch president had 'no interest in racial separatism'.

Party members attended hui with Muslim women, with Pasifika communities, and with the Tamil community. They appeared on Niu FM and on TVNZ's *Tagata Pasifika*, and contributed articles to Chinese newspapers and Jewish chronicles. The message was one of diversity. The Māori Party song came out on CD, and a range of haka, waiata, rap songs and poems were composed to celebrate the growth of the movement. Tariana later reflected on the message of the Māori Party waiata, 'E Te Iwi', which had been composed by IWI[31]:

> This song really is about calling on our people to come together and to stand strongly together. It talks about the takutai moana – the importance of our land, our moana. But more importantly it talks about our people having kaupapa and tikanga that we should live by. It's telling us to rise up and to see those kaupapa as those things that should drive all our thinking and everything that we do. If we want rangatiratanga we have to see it as a belief that we can be that; we can be a strong and independent people. And that's what I love most about the waiata, because it is what Whānau Ora is about too.[32]

Whatarangi Winiata was in no doubt about the significance of the opportunity afforded the nation by the presence of the Māori Party, as he explained to the Māori Legal Forum:

> Article Three is about rights and privileges that Māori enjoy and for this land, the right and privilege to choose Members of Parliament is fundamental. More is required and in particular the opportunity for the Māori signatory to sit as a collective in parliament. And here I have a personal and political declaration to make: the Māori Party with its kaupapa-driven constitution and policy statements could be this collective. This is the reason for my involvement with Te Pāti

> Māori after nearly three decades of discussion, teaching, research and administration towards the shaping of tikanga Māori institutions and elucidation of the potential of kaupapa tuku iho to advance the interests of this land including its tangata whenua and those who are here under the protection of the Treaty of Waitangi.[33]

As election day grew closer, political pundits started predicting the outlook for the Māori Party. Marae DigiPolls suggested the Party would be likely to win four or five of the seven Māori seats. Tariana was predicting it would take all seven. The *Sunday Star-Times* reported:

> Maori broadcaster Willie Jackson is picking the Maori Party to win three seats at worst but no more than five. Labour's fear campaign that a vote for the Maori Party is a vote for National has been effective he says. … Political reality is starting to set in and some Maori are thinking maybe it is better the devil you know.[34]

Throughout the whole gestation of the Party, an ongoing focus on the seabed and foreshore law had kept issues of injustice to the fore. In March 2005, the United Nations' Committee on the Elimination of Racial Discrimination had released a report stating that Labour's new legislation discriminated against Māori, by extinguishing the possibility of establishing Māori customary title over the foreshore and seabed. The report had been in response to a submission from Te Rūnanga o Ngāi Tahu to the Permanent Forum on Indigenous Issues. Ngāi Tahu had taken the claim alongside Ngāti Kahungunu, Ngāi Tāmanuhiri and Hauraki iwi.

Ngāi Tahu Chair Mark Solomon had been vocally opposed to the foreshore and seabed law from early on, stating that he thought it undermined the rule of law, interfered with judicial independence and breached human rights. In May 2004 he published an open letter in major newspapers, after weeks of calls from Ngāi Tahu members, he explained, 'telling me to represent the views of Ngai Tahu families' who were aggrieved by Labour's position.[35] At around the same time that the United Nations condemned the legislation, Whakatōhea claimed a customary rights order under the new Act, 'to allow guardianship to be recognised'. The *Sunday Star-Times* reported:

Whakatohea elder Claude Edwards, who lodged the claim with the support of others, including neighbouring iwi, said the Crown had opened a can of worms when it implemented the law.[36]

The United Nations Special Rapporteur on the rights of indigenous people, Professor Rodolfo Stavenhagen, indicated his intention to visit New Zealand on a fact-finding mission as a result of enactment of the Foreshore and Seabed Act, and thereafter to report back to the United Nations on the status of indigenous human rights in Aotearoa.

After all that had taken place, it was inevitable that Tariana would raise the repeal of the Foreshore and Seabed Act as a 2005 election issue. A month before voters went to the polls, in an interview with Audrey Young and Ruth Berry for the *Herald*, she declared her intention:

> We have got a number of things we are putting on the table. [Repeal of the Act] would be one of them and we are asking for it to be repealed so that due process can be followed, that our people can go to court as they have a right to.[37]

That interview traversed a lot of ground, including Tariana's vision for New Zealand; a vision of the world she wanted her grandchildren to grow up in:

> So what I want for them is that they are healthy, they are well-educated, they are able to participate fully in a society that respects all cultures who live here in this land, that Maori people as the tangata whenua be acknowledged as such and their status as the treaty partners would be upheld.

However, by far the most airspace in the interview was given to the divide between National and Labour, and the question of which would be the better party for the Māori Party to form a relationship with. Tariana, as always, said that the Māori Party was a 'people-driven party and they will make the decision':

> If you look at the very significant developments that have happened – you look at kohanga reo, kura kaupapa, wananga, all the Maori

health services, the social services, they've all come out of the National Party. The difference is National never talks about what it does for us because basically they've got a red-neck voting population. And because Labour has always wanted our vote and needed our vote they have always gone and told our people what they do for us.

Tariana concluded that there was little to distinguish between the two parties:

For many people today they can't really see a lot of difference. If you go to hui our people say you've got National stabbing you in the front. You know where they stand on absolutely everything. You've got Labour stabbing you in the back.

Tariana also responded to the standard Labour Party slogan, 'a vote for the Māori Party is a vote for National': 'A vote for the Maori Party is a vote for Maori political power in the parliamentary environment. That's what it is.'

Young and Berry asked Tariana why the Party had opposed the motion to ask New Zealand Cricket to call off the Zimbabwe Tour ('the government should be consistent in its approach to human rights issues around the world and not single out Zimbabwe'); to explain the Māori Party policy on superannuation (Maori should receive superannuation from 60 years of age because of reduced life expectancy); to describe tikanga and kaupapa (tikanga is about living your life; 'the restoration of values and practices'); to discuss her vote on gay marriage (people can have a legal relationship with one another without necessarily being married); and to respond to the National Party branding of 'kiwi vs iwi' ('I don't know what that argument is about'). In the interview, Tariana articulated how the Māori Party could be culturally inclusive:

We see the Maori Party as an opportunity to basically put in place what we think the Treaty wanted. … in bringing other people along with us, we're trying to see the Treaty in action … We are here to be inclusive but we are unashamedly Maori-led.

The interview also elicited a rare insight into Tariana's views about the role she had now been occupying for the last nine years, member of Parliament:

> It's not my favourite occupation. I do it because I was asked to by our people and I try to do it the best way I can. But I wouldn't say that I enjoy this environment. I find the House incredibly difficult and I find the behaviour incredibly racist.

In line with these views, Tariana also revealed that she was hoping that the next term would be her last:

> I'd always intended to leave Parliament at the end of this term. It was never my intention to stay any longer, I believe you can stay too long and you begin to think you are all powerful and someone else owes you, but they don't and I'm really proud of the numbers of our young Maori people who are coming through and I want to move over and make way for them.
>
> I'd always decided in my mind that I came in here to do particular things. I've done the best that I can while I've been here. But I've got some other priorities. I've got a granddaughter (Piata) that we're raising who I don't see enough of and who I feel that I owe a lot more to in my twilight years.

In saying as much, Tariana was expressing a yearning that she would often repeat over the coming years. As it transpired, it would take another nine years before the call could be realised.

NOTES

1 Personal letter of 21 August 1989, Nelson Mandela to Rev. Frank Chikane, from Victor Verster Prison.

2 Tariana Turia, 'Now we've got to stand up for ourselves', personal interview 22 September 2004.

3 Kotahitanga, manaakitanga, rangatiratanga, wairuatanga, te reo Māori, whanaungatanga, kaitiakitanga, mana tupuna/whakapapa and mana whenua.

4 R. Nuri, 'Arrival of the new Māori Party', *Te Karaka*, Koanga 2004, p. 9

5 Lloyd Ashton, 'What is it that we want?', *Anglican Taonga*, Easter 2012, no. 39, p. 15.

6 Eru Potaka Dewes, 'The Birth of the Māori Party', *Mai i Rangiātea*, January 2007.
7 Ibid.
8 'Will Labour loyalty be lost to new player?', *Tū Mai*, June 2004.
9 'Maori should believe in themselves, says Turia', *New Zealand Herald*, 1 October 2004.
10 Nuri, 'Arrival of the new Māori Party', p. 8.
11 New Zealand First Party, press release, 'New cabinet – can't dance, can't sing', 24 February 2004.
12 Trevor Mallard, 'We are all New Zealanders now', speech to Stout Research Centre for New Zealand Studies, 29 July 2004.
13 Audrey Young, 'Mallard fuels race debate', *New Zealand Herald*, 30 July 2004.
14 Ani Mikaere, 'Are we all New Zealanders now? A Māori response to the Pākehā quest for indigineity', Bruce Jesson Memorial Lecture, 2004.
15 Tariana Turia, 1st National Sexual and Reproductive Health Conference, Wainuiomata Marae, Wellington, 1 November 2004.
16 Trevor Mallard, press release, 'Turia's comments irresponsible', 5 November 2004.
17 Jon Stokes, 'Tamihere rounds on Maori Party and "separatists"', *New Zealand Herald*, 20 January 2005.
18 Nuri, 'Arrival of the new Māori Party'.
19 Selwn Manning, 'Intel Sources Say SIS Investigating Maori Party', 11 November 2004, *Scoop Independent News*: www.scoop.co.nz/stories/HL0411/S00144.htm (accessed 11 May 2015).
20 Māori Party press release, 'Māori Party calls on Inspector General to investigate SIS activities', 22 November 2004.
21 Merania Karauria and Derek Cheng, 'Bugging raises serious questions, says Turia', *Wanganui Chronicle*, 23 November 2004.
22 *Tū Mai*, July 2004, p. 19.
23 Māori Party National Council, minutes of meeting, 11–13 March 2005.
24 Māori Party press release, 'Māori Party announces list', 26 June 2005, http://maoriparty.org/panui/maori-party-announces-list (accessed 19 May 2015).
25 Turia, 'Now we've got to stand up for ourselves'.
26 K. Paki, 'The Pākehā within the Māori Party', *Tū Mai*, August 2005, p. 24.
27 Oral history interview between Tariana Turia and Taina Tangaere McGregor, 25 May 2006, Oral History Political Diary project, Oral History Collection, Alexander Turnbull Library.
28 Ruth Berry, 'Turia taking time out in political limbo', *New Zealand Herald*, 14 May 2004.
29 Kaapua Smith, 'Māori Party', in Raymond Milller (ed.), *New Zealand Government and Politics*, 2010.

30 Helen Bain, 'Mana will prevail over money – Turia', *Sunday Star-Times*, 28 August 2005, p. 4.
31 'E Te Iwi', written by Kimo Winiata, Keelan Ransfield, Moses Ketu and Liam Ogden and performed by IWI, was later to become a finalist for the 2013 APRA Maioha Awards for Maori songwriters.
32 'Tariana Turia on the Soundtrack to Your Life', Radiolive, 3 February 2013.
33 Whatarangi Winiata, 'Understanding the implications of Article Three of the Treaty of Waitangi', speech to the Māori Legal Forum, 14–15 July 2005.
34 Helen Bain, 'Mana will prevail over Money', *Sunday Star-Times*, 28 August 2005.
35 Mark Solomon, 'Ngai Tahu head writes open letter against foreshore bill', *stuff.co.nz*, 5 May 2004.
36 'Claim to test seabed and foreshore law', *Sunday Star-Times*, 27 March 2005.
37 Audrey Young and Ruth Berry, 'Interview: Tariana Turia, Maori Party co-leader', *New Zealand Herald*, 6 August 2005.

CHAPTER TWENTY-ONE
LAST CAB OFF THE RANK: 2005–2008

We cannot continue to rely on the state to do for us, to act for us, to tell us how to be. We have to stand on our own two feet and no one else can do it for us. It means that whānau in its widest sense have to come together to support one another. Our job is to see the resources are available to help them do it.[1]

SAINSBURY: If you had to, could you deal with the Māori Party in terms of forming a coalition? Yes or no.

BRASH: I think it would be very hard indeed, given our differences.

SAINSBURY: Helen Clark?

CLARK: They would be the last cab off the rank, because I've got other options.[2]

On 17 September, 2005, Māori Party voters elected into Parliament Tariana Turia, Dr Pita Sharples, Hone Harawira and Te Ururoa Flavell. Māori voted in record numbers; many polling stations ran out of voting papers. The mood for change was electrifying. Captured by the campaign slogan, 'tēnei te wā', meaning 'this is the time', supporters gave strong support to Tariana with 61 percent of the vote in Te Tai Hauāuru (10,922); Te Ururoa with 53 percent of the vote in Waiariki, and Pita and Hone with 51 percent of the vote in Tāmaki Makaurau and Te Tai Tokerau respectively.

By the morning after, the political pundits were already predicting the Māori Party would be in a decisive position in the formation of the 2005 Parliament. The *Sunday Star-Times* trumpeted its success, reporting 'parliament's newest entrant, the Maori Party, is easily the election's biggest winner'. The paper reported that the Party had 'stormed in'; even with a party vote of only about 1.98 percent, it 'could muster significant heft in Parliament'.[3]

There was also significant mention of the fact that due to its low party vote, the Māori Party had in effect created the first overhang (Parliament now had 121 seats). But the question that got people talking was how would the Māori Party make use of the power it had won – what was its preferred political positioning?

On the night, the party vote in the Māori electorates had swung in favour of the Labour Party, which captured between 49 percent (in Te Tai Tokerau) and 57 percent (in Te Tai Tonga and Ikaroa Rāwhiti). The most that the Māori Party was able to achieve in the party vote was 31 percent in both Te Tai Tokerau and Te Tai Hauāuru, closely followed by 30 percent in Waiariki. Although Labour lost four Māori seats, its overall party vote share in the seven Māori seats was 54 percent: twice that of the Māori Party's 27 percent. The National Party vote in the Māori electorates never reached double figures, hovering between 2.7 percent (in Tainui) and 7.3 percent (in Te Tai Tonga). In Tariana's electorate of Te Tai Hauāuru, 3.5 percent of the party vote went to National.

Given the historic gulf between National and Labour in the Māori electorate seats, analysts were greatly surprised that on the night before election day, the Māori Party seemed to be throwing opening the possibility of coalition talks with National. On election night, Whatarangi Winiata confirmed the Party would meet with both major parties on the same day – 18 September – to discuss coalition. In a frank evaluation of the 2005 election, Hone Harawira referred to the 'clear public perception that a relationship with National was still a possibility' as a major issue in the Party's failing to combat the Labour threat to their vote:

> For all that perception may have been incorrect it was there. And it burned me horribly. People actually came up to me on election day to say that while they gave me their vote, they had given their party vote to Labour because they had heard we might still be going with National. I was bloody furious.[4]

For Tariana, the focus was on determining what party was the appropriate vehicle to achieve change.

> The return of co-leader Tariana Turia was never in doubt. She said having four MPs in Parliament gave the party enough power to make a difference, especially in tempering National's divisive racial policies. It was a dangerous precedent for National to say it would wipe out the Maori seats, marginalise the Treaty of Waitangi, and 'basically try to turn us into white folk'. Already, the party had made other Maori politicians accountable and more proactive.[5]

The paper noted that Dr Pita Sharples was singing the same tune about the perils of the white backlash that Brash had engineered throughout National's campaign:

> The Maori Party has virtually ruled out doing a deal with National, although co-leader Pita Sharples has not ruled out discussions if National was 'desperate'. As Sharples points out, it would be suicidal to do a deal with a party that wants to abolish the Maori seats – the basis of the Maori Party's representation in parliament.[6]

Dr Brash was publicly musing that a deal between National and the Māori Party was not beyond the realms of possibility, but it would be conditional, 'Any agreement would require the Maori Party to relinquish its bid to entrench the Maori seats.'[7]

Initial activity after the election was fast and frenzied. Within forty-eight hours, 'exploratory talks' had been held between the Māori Party and Labour. Attending for Labour were Helen Clark, Michael Cullen, Parekura Horomia and chief of staff Heather Simpson. The Māori Party was represented by its co-leaders and their negotiator Ken Mair, ironically one of the so-called 'haters and wreckers' Helen Clark had named a few months prior.

The fact that there was even an opportunity for a meeting to take place had undoubtedly been assisted by a quiet phone call the day after the election between Helen Clark and Tariana. 'She said she wanted to put it all behind her,' Tariana told the *Herald*; 'I accepted that and I presume that's what she's doing.'[8]

There had also been a phone conversation between Sharples and Brash. The *Dominion Post* reported:

> 'I said (to Dr Brash) we're so poles apart that maybe we should meet and discuss our extreme differences,' Dr Sharples told reporters. National would have to make 'a very big bend' backward on its policies for Maori to consider a deal.[9]

In the Māori Party's first meeting with Labour, the talks had canvassed a number of options for the Party: remaining in opposition, a formal coalition, agreements to give support or abstention on confidence and supply, a cooperation arrangement and 'an indigenous model of relationships'. During this process, Helen Clark was giving little away to the media. Her only comments related to the possibility of revisiting the foreshore and seabed legislation: 'I hope that is not a track that people will want to go down.'[10]

There were of course glaring differences in the parties' philosophies, not just between the Māori Party and Labour or National but between the minor parties as well. New Zealand First wanted to restructure the Waitangi Tribunal into a standing Commission of Inquiry and scrap all references to Treaty principles in legislation, while the Māori Party wanted to retain these same references, entrench the Māori seats and repeal the foreshore and seabed legislation.

The day after the Māori Party met with Labour, it was the National Party's turn. This time Tariana, Ken Mair and Whatarangi Winiata attended the meeting, with a strong turnout from National, including leader Don Brash, president Judy Kirk, deputy leader Gerry Brownlee, former Māori affairs spokeswoman Georgina te Heuheu, campaign manager Steven Joyce and strategist Murray McCully. Speaking to the *Dominion Post*, Tariana described the hour-long meeting that took place in Dr Brash's office as:

> … a meet-and-greet, just establishing the relationship. You do have long meet-and-greets when you're getting to know one another … and we've had a very good discussion.[11]

The emphasis the Party placed on the importance of relationships in this first week of negotiations was a theme that the Party would return to in every subsequent election. So, too, was the focus on consultation with the Party's members, enabling them to determine the next steps. The Party had made a commitment to its members before the election that whatever governing arrangements it discussed with other parties, it would fully consult members before making any decisions. *Herald* columnist John Roughan was interested in the process the Party used to advance its aspirations:

> Whatever happens, the Maori Party is the most interesting new element in national politics. Its next important move is not the decision to join or not join a governing arrangement, but rather the procedures it has for making the decision. Co-leaders Tariana Turia and Pita Sharples promise to take any offers back to meetings of their people. That is what they could do with every bill of any consequence that comes before the next Parliament. By setting up tribal or regional forums to feed Maori opinion into a national Maori representative body, constituted on Maori traditions, the party could achieve much more than it has done by winning four of the seven Maori seats. It could begin to establish distinct political institutions capable of attracting national attention because their decisions would have the force of independent votes in Parliament.
>
> At the very least the Maori Party promises not to be a conventional partisan organisation. It has demonstrated by its willingness to deal

with National – at least until Don Brash declared abolition of its seats non-negotiable – that it is not sitting neatly on the left-right axis. It is a third dimension.[12]

By the end of the first week after the election it was conceivable that no compromise would be reached between the Māori Party and Labour or National. As talks progressed, the Party indicated it might choose to stay out of government to preserve bottom lines such as the protection of the Māori seats and repeal of the foreshore law. Pita Sharples spoke candidly to the *Dominion Post* about a focus on creating relationships rather than agreement against all odds:

> … the reality is we need to be able to champion Maori wishes without being compromised, which is what we are saying happened to the other Maori MPs in Labour over the foreshore (and seabed issue). It would be ridiculous to put ourselves in the same situation.[13]

Ten days after election day, columnists were devoting considerable space to a 'formidable' party. Peter Luke in the *Press* suggested:

> … the party's four seats could be crucial, one way or another, in determining the shape of the next government. Go back just two decades and today's Maori political scene would have seemed incomprehensible. Then, partly courtesy of the historic Labour-Ratana alliance, the four Maori seats – and the number had not changed since their inception in 1867 – were Labour sinecures.[14]

Luke went on to suggest that the Māori Party had established itself as a voice for Māori, independent of the other parties. But it would be 'fanciful to the extreme' to believe that a potential agreement with National was anything other than 'rhetoric' and 'political posturing', he said. Why would the Māori Party think it had anything in common with National, when they had sought to 'abolish the Maori seats that proved to be the Maori Party's lifeblood this election'? In turn, Luke suggested that Labour viewed the Māori Party as unreliable (given Tariana's defection) and dangerous (based on the Party's support for Donna Awatere-Huata, and the presence in the Party of the long-time face of Waitangi protest Hone Harawira and 'protest stalwart' Ken Mair).

The media often referred to the relationship between Helen Clark and Tariana as a stumbling block:

> Clark is not willing to rely on Tariana Turia, not least because she fears the Maori Party could implode.[15]

> Clark was reluctant to rely only on the Maori Party for a majority because it had not proved its stability. There is also still some bad blood between co-leader Tariana Turia and Labour over the foreshore and seabed issue.[16]

> Clark regards the Maori Party as inherently unstable, unreliable or both.[17]

Indeed, the issue presented such a block, it appeared, that when the special votes were counted and were found to give Labour a crucial advantage, the possibilities of a relationship with the Māori Party were still a step too far. The *Herald* reported:

> With Jim Anderton and the Greens in tow, [Helen Clark] now just needs the backing of the Maori Party. If push came to shove, she would get that at least on an interim basis. But Helen Clark will not take up that option. It remains a fall-back position that strengthens her hand in dealings with NZ First and United Future.[18]

The coalition chess game was reaching its final stages. Rather than end in defeat, Tariana made a definitive next move. Following a forty-minute meeting with Helen Clark and Michael Cullen, Tariana and Pita revealed the talks had gone well, and that they would share progress at the series of twenty-one nationwide hui the Party planned to hold with its members (three hui in each electorate). Tariana openly reported her feelings about the viability of a coalition deal with Labour:

> 'I don't think the Maori Party will be going into coalition,' Turia said. 'That's a decision for our members to make but it's not a want. It's about maintaining our integrity, our identity, our credibility with our people. We don't think that when you are in coalition you are necessarily able to maintain that.'[19]

And so the four Māori Party MPs went out on the road. On Wednesday 5 October 2005, they embarked on a whistle-stop tour of Aotearoa, travelling to New Plymouth, Invercargill, Gisborne, Whāngārei, Kaitāia, Dunedin, Taumarunui, Kaikohe, Christchurch, Hastings, West Auckland, Whanganui, Hamilton, Ōtaki, Nelson, Porirua, South Auckland, Ōtorohanga/Te Kūiti, Wellington and Waiariki.

The first stop for Tariana was Taranaki. A 150-strong crowd turned up to the Quality Hotel Plymouth International to discuss a pathway forward. 'There was a resolution passed about maintaining a strong, independent voice for Maori', the *Taranaki Daily News* reported, 'and it was unanimously passed'.[20]

In the midst of the hui, however, it was revealed that National had made another overture to seek the Māori Party's interest in a coalition. Tariana urged New Plymouth supporters to reconsider perceptions that National was the 'bogey'.[21] Kōrero was had; options were discussed. It appeared from Tariana's reported comments that bottom lines were being softened by the willingness of National to compromise on its positions. Among the greatest of the reported compromises was an agreement to consider axing the Foreshore and Seabed Act as part of a possible support deal. Tariana explained the value of such a measure:

> It's the number one issue why this party started. If a political party was prepared to repeal and we were able to get through some of the other discussions that we're having, then we will go with whoever repeals.[22]

Tariana also revealed that the 'softening' of bottom lines included National reviewing its position on axing the Māori seats and scrapping all race-based funding. Tariana was of the view that the hard line position on the Māori seats was not, in fact, a shared bottom line amongst National Party members.

> It's not a feeling that I've ever had about National per se. I know a lot of them. I've been in contact with a couple of them and I know that the line that was run was not necessarily the line of the whole caucus.

When asked whether the backlash of partnering with National would be worth it, Tariana responded that she was 'solely interested in getting the best deal for Maori, no matter who she had to work with'.

It could be argued that the 2005 post-election consultation process revealed all the key philosophical arguments that would be rerun in 2008, 2011 and 2014. In this first election, however, strong alarm bells were being sounded within the Māori Party membership about the risk of ignoring the extremely low party vote that National had earned in the Māori electorate seats. As John Armstrong explained in the *Herald*:

> Any wheeling and dealing between the two parties can be justified only if circumstances force them into co-habitation. Otherwise rapprochement will be viewed by both parties' supporters with a mixture of horror and foreboding. Forget the Maori Party's current round of hui. By casting their party votes overwhelmingly for Labour, Maori have made it absolutely clear they do not want to see Turia and Sharples getting into bed with National. That is not to say the Maori Party should never back National. The last thing it wants to be is Labour's poodle. That is not a recipe for longevity either. But for now the Maori Party should bide its time.[23]

By 10 October media reports were revealing that Tariana was considering the possibilities of forming a government with either National or Labour:

> Mrs Turia said that although many Maori Party supporters had given their party vote to Labour, the hui had revealed this was because many had been driven by fear of what National would do. Some voters now realised they may have been misled, she said. 'In the end the message that has come through for me is that they trust us. They trusted the four of us [MPs] to have listened to us and basically in the end to make the best decision in their interests.'[24]

On Tuesday 11 October, the Māori Party met with National, New Zealand First and United Future to discuss the possibility of a governing arrangement. But just when it appeared that they were making progress, a raft of unusual events occurred. Firstly, Winston Peters criticised Green co-leaders Rod Donald and Jeanette Fitzsimons as undesirable coalition partners claiming he would not allow extremists to hold sway[25]. Not long after, the Greens conceded that it was unlikely that they would acquire seats at the Cabinet table.[26]

It was then revealed that a Christian sect, the Exclusive Brethren, had approached New Zealand First in an attempt to broker a deal against Labour. At the same time, unlikely bedfellows ACT, National and the Māori Party came together on Parliament's forecourt in support of Te Wānanga o Aotearoa's protest in response to Government claims alleging misappropriation, fraud and nepotism.

As coalition talks stumbled along, the possibility of any relationship between the Māori Party and National was challenged by Atareta Poananga, an unsuccessful candidate ranked third on the Māori Party list, who declared that any alliance between the Party and National would be political suicide:

> Any sort of move towards going to National will … kill this party dead. We've got to say that our best position is to be independent, because that way we're not going to be contaminated by either party.[27]

A couple of days later, Labour sympathiser Chris Trotter picked up on Poananga's theme, describing 'Turia's revenge drama' as political murder:

> Driven by the tauntings of her private demons, Turia seems absolutely determined to heap ruin upon the head of her enemy, Helen Clark. Such reckless hate can have only one outcome – the destruction of everything the 21,000 members of the Maori Party have built. Is this utu – the Maori quest for reciprocity – at its most terrifying?

It appeared to Trotter that what looked like a soap opera was fast approaching a tragic end; he predicted a bittersweet final act:

> Tragically, Tariana Turia's highly equivocal attitude towards Helen Clark has come to be seen by Labour's negotiators as an insuperable obstacle to the formation of a progressive and innovative Centre-Left government.[28]

The pace of negotiations was now speeding up. On the night of Thursday 13 October, Labour presented a written offer to the Māori Party: a draft

Tom Scott's take on the Māori Party's choice after the 2005 election.
Source: 'Things are getting hot and heavy with Helen here. I'm thinking we should go with Labour ' 13 October, 2005. Scott, Thomas, 1947- :[Digital cartoons published from 2003 onward in the *Dominion Post*]. Ref: DCDL-0000280. Alexander Turnbull Library, Wellington, New Zealand. http://natlib.govt.nz/rec ords/22342957

Pita Sharples, Tariana Turia and Tariana's cousin Bessie Paki at Rēhua Marae, Christchurch, on their first visit to promote the Māori Party, in June 2004.
Source: Personal collection (Author)

Dr Pita Sharples, Te Ururoa Flavell, Hone Harawira, the late Monte Ohia, Atareta Poananga, Tariana Turia and Angeline Greensill at a candidate training workshop held at Parliament, August 2005.
Source: Personal collection (Author)

Tariana with Whanganui iwi leader John Maihi and Te Manawanui Pauro of Kaiwhaiki (Nanny Nui) on election night, 17 September 2005. Tariana said, 'She gave us the kōrero: "Korowaitia te puna waiora hei oranga motuhake mō te iwi". It translates into our vision of "Absolute wellness crossing generations".'
Source: Gail Imhoff

The five Māori Party MPs in Parliament after the 2008 election, Hone Harawira (L), Rahui Katene, Pita Sharples, Tariana and Te Ururoa Flavell, moments after the group appeared on the *Marae* post-election television special on 9 November 2008.
Source: Newspix.co.nz

Dressed for the occasion: Tariana and George attend the launch of the *Howard Morrison Show* on Māori Television on 5 December 2008.
Source: Newspix.co.nz

Tariana and John Key seal the Relationship Accord between their parties of 16 November 2008. The Agreement stated that 'The National Party and the Māori Party recognise the importance of mana maintenance and enhancement for both parties to this agreement'.
Source: Aaron Smale/IKON

Tariana and Pita Sharples at their swearing-in as ministers in the 2008 Key Government on 19 November 2008.
Source: Fairfax NZ

Tariana and Pita look on as Prime Minister John Key in 2010 announces the scrapping of Labour's Foreshore and Seabed Act and the introduction of the Marine and Coastal Area (Takutai Moana) Bill.
Source: Newspix.co.nz

A strained Tariana and Pita Sharples hold a news conference to announce the Māori Party's parting of the ways, after Hone Harawira's decision on 23 February 2011 to become an independent MP.
Source: Newspix.co.nz

agreement that included a few concessions, but not on the Maori Party's key foreshore and seabed policy.

The next day, a 'clandestine' meeting was held between National, ACT, the Māori Party and United Future leader Peter Dunne at which it was noted that together the grouping held fifty-seven seats. On the other side of the gridlock, Labour had fifty seats, and with Progressive leader Jim Anderton and the six Green MPs could also line up fifty-seven seats. Sitting on the fence was New Zealand First, with seven seats. Leader Winston Peters gleefully described it as a 57–57 Mexican standoff; once again he found himself to be the kingmaker. Reporter Tracy Watkins labelled the coalition chaos as akin to the Madhatter's Tea Party[29].

While speculation was rife, the Māori Party co-leaders were quick to assure the public that they were still open to negotiation:

> Maori Party co-leader Tariana Turia strenuously denied any arrangement had been brokered with National. And co-leader Pita Sharples insisted last Thursday that the party was still open to supporting Labour on confidence and supply in return for policy concessions.[30]

However, it was generally considered to be extraordinary that centre-right parties would meet together as a collective, and that within that grouping the Māori Party was obviously prepared to play ball. Former parliamentarian Richard Prebble commented in the *Herald*:

> The first development was the realisation that the Maori Party's priority was not electing a Labour government but getting a pledge to review the foreshore and seabed legislation – something Helen Clark cannot do, and National can. It was Rodney Hide who said 'as the right has not got the votes in parliament to abolish the Maori seats, let us park the issue'. So the biggest obstacle was overcome.[31]

By Monday 17 October, the Māori Party had returned Labour's offer, with amendments … and then, all of a sudden, it was all over.

The new government was to be a Labour–Progressive coalition; the Greens were locked out of the deal. New Zealand First and United Future entered into agreements of support on confidence and supply motions. Winston Peters became Foreign Minister, Peter Dunne picked up Revenue.

New Zealand First Party president Doug Woolerton resigned before the ink on the agreement had time to dry.

And the Māori Party was now free to be a strong and independent voice, unencumbered by any agreements, and able to find its own feet. Its four MPs were pleased that their offices were allocated alongside Mātangireia, a special room that had been dedicated to the former Native Affairs Committee in 1922. The name 'Mātangireia' refers to the thirteenth and uppermost heaven, and thus represented a space where all iwi could meet in peace, harmony and tranquillity. It was a constant reminder to the Māori Party to keep its vision fixed on distant horizons, while dealing with the here and now. The room features a large reproduction of Te Tiriti o Waitangi, with all its signatories. Along the walls of the corridor are portraits of all the former Māori parliamentarians. Tariana was proud that her office was located by the portraits of her relations: Iriaka, Matiu and Tokouru Rātana.

Less than a month after the opening of Parliament, Tariana stood to speak in the Address in Reply debate for the forty-eighth Parliament, in a speech that touched on themes that would become vintage Māori Party. She pointed out the irony of a nation in which one law for all is said to apply, when the Treaty as our founding document was not able to be honoured in the oaths and allegiances every MP swore. She forewarned the Parliament of two private member's bills the Māori Party would introduce : one to repeal the Foreshore and Seabed Act; the other to entrench the Māori seats.

She noted that in two days' time Professor Rodolfo Stavenhagen, Special Rapporteur for the United Nations, would be visiting Aotearoa to review the impact of discriminatory laws. She lamented that New Zealand had criticised the Draft Declaration on Indigenous Peoples' Rights as being 'unworkable and unacceptable'. She touched on the need for Māori economic independence and financial autonomy, the importance of maintaining the integrity of the natural environment and the necessity to reduce our reliance on non-renewable energy sources. She described it as a national disgrace that the Education Review Office Annual Report had described 'a group at the bottom, perhaps as large as 20%, who are currently not succeeding in our education system'. She concluded her speech by seeking to restore a decent income to all New Zealanders:

We must set tangible goals, if we are to achieve one law for all – the right to a decent standard of life. Central to this is agreement on a specific target-date to reduce child poverty … If [the Working for Families] package is meant to be about supporting children, why exclude our most vulnerable? If it is meant to be about eliminating poverty, why exclude the poorest?[32]

A statistical breakdown of the contribution of the Māori Party to debate over the course of the forty-eighth Parliament is staggering. Between 7 November 2005 and 24 September 2008, Tariana herself delivered 101 speeches in the House, including seventy-one contributions to bills; thirteen to general debates, five to urgent debates, two poroporoaki and two responses to statements by the Prime Minister. In total, the Māori Party stood to deliver 544 speeches in that three-year term. By way of contrast, during that same period, Parekura Horomia delivered forty-six speeches, Nanaia Mahuta forty-one and Dover Samuels seventeen.

In the President's Report to the 2007 annual general meeting of the Māori Party, Whatarangi Winiata described the Party as having succeeded in representing the independent Māori voice in Parliament. He noted that each of the Māori Party MPs had occupied the speaking stage three times as often as the other four most active Māori speakers in the Parliament. But it wasn't just about quantity, he said:

> We can say not only has there been wide diversity in the topics covered in our speeches, not only has the content been compelling for the reason, history and evidence presented in our speeches, not only has the flow of language and the oratory been of the highest parliamentary performance in delivering our speeches but in addition they have been imbued with kaupapa tuku iho that underpin the Party's Constitution and our many activities that make us distinctive and that contribute to our survival as a people.[33]

Whatarangi concluded that after twenty-five months of activity, 'the nation expects that our MPs will express a view on every matter of importance that reaches the floor of this chamber'.

In the same address, the President explained the operating procedures that the Party had developed over its first term. He reported on the activities of its Caucus, held every Tuesday morning when Parliament is in session. At these meetings, the four MPs, three senior staff members (Harry Walker, Helen Leahy and Helen Potter) and the President would meet to analyse Bills, allocate responsibilities and discuss the issues of the week.

The Party followed a standard methodology. When analysing any Bill, the Caucus had to be satisfied that the legislation was assessed in terms of how it would contribute to the survival of Māori. Would the proposal defend Māori rights? How would it benefit Māori interests for the benefit of the nation? What contribution would the Bill make to improving outcomes for te pani me te rawakore, the marginalised and dispossessed? In the analysis, could Caucus identify any potential for brokering relationships with other parties, ko te nohotahi i te pāremata? Was the Bill reflective of tribal history? What consultation needed to be undertaken to consolidate the Party's position? Was the Bill consistent with tikanga Māori? Would there be any opportunities for the Bill to influence the position of the Party at the next election?

The Caucus would apply the methodology consistently to every issue, particularly relying on the influence of kaupapa in guiding the MPs towards consensus. Professor Winiata further described this process in a paper entitled 'Māori innovation and reconciliation' presented to the Ngā Pae o te Māramatanga Conference:

> In caucus, when the Māori Party MPs are giving consideration to legislative proposals the first question asked is 'will this proposed legislation contribute to the survival of Māori as a people? Or will it do the reverse?' The answers to these questions reside in the extent to which the proposed legislation gives expression to one or more of the kaupapa tuku iho in the Constitution of the Māori Party. Such is the centrality of kaupapa tuku iho in the affairs of the Māori Party.[34]

The Māori Party focused on the centrality of the kaupapa through ten broad approaches:

1. We see every issue as a Māori issue. We speak of indigeneity as the strength of the many people who live in this land.
2. Despite a desire by some to relegate Te Tiriti o Waitangi to the annals of history we consider it the foundation document for the nation.
3. We seek to eradicate poverty. The poor did not create poverty nor do they have an investment in it.
4. We seek genuine progress in our nation through a Genuine Progress Index which measures benefits against deficits.
5. We believe whānau are best able to determine their own solutions.
6. We demonstrate our belief in the potential of people to achieve the impossible.
7. We look to our tikanga and kaupapa to guide us in our responses. We desist from belittling others.
8. We promote a system based more on justice that heals than justice that hurts.
9. We encourage an opportunity for people to participate.
10. We exist to defend Māori rights and advance Māori interests for the benefit of all who live in Aotearoa.[35]

The Party's desire to truly be the independent voice of Māori in Parliament was also demonstrated by their voting practice on all Bills in the forty-eighth Parliament. The Party did not consistently align its votes with any single party. It did, however, collaborate with the Greens more than with any other party, by two to one. The Māori Party voted the same as the Greens 108 times, compared to 89 for Labour and 55 for National.

The Party's contributions were multiple and varied. It issued releases about research into kūmara; its MPs spoke out about the proposed prohibition on the docking of dogs' tails; the Party had a view on flat tax, fat tax, fart tax – nothing was outside its realm of investigation.

And while the Māori Party MPs were speaking, someone out there was quietly standing by, watching their every move. Throughout that first term, the Māori Party received anonymous analysis from someone describing themselves as 'Thinking Māori'. The emails would appear out of the blue with the subject line: 'Watching, listening, reading, thinking'.

The emails detailed 'not so good bits', 'good bits', 'questions' and 'cautions'. In the 'not so good bits' recorded in an email received on 30 January 2007, for example, 'Thinking Maori' mentioned the Mapp Bill, which introduced a ninety-day probationary period for new employees after which he or she could be sacked:

> Not convinced with Turia, think she still believes in the Mapp bill, watch out, a weakness there to be exploited, she sounds anti-union, probably influenced by conservative provincial town background. Do not become the Maori experts, the tribes will become annoyed. Be clear about whose tikanga members are talking about.

In September 2006, a controversy emerged concerning the practice of koha, in the context of allegations that Labour MP Taito Philip Field had accepted cash from fellow Samoans for immigration assistance. Hone Harawira and Pita Sharples admitted they had accepted koha; Tariana said she directed gifts to party funds or schools in her electorate; and Te Ururoa Flavell said no one had ever offered him anything. Thinking Maori observed: 'Koha, bit confused there, fed prejudice … Turia showed good leadership. Did not have to happen.'

The 'good bits' portion of Thinking Maori's email remarked:

> Speeches well written and researched, good history lessons, believe people (Maori and Pakeha) have learnt a lot about the country they live in. Some clever ones. Very smart to say every issue is a Maori issue and speak on them with a particular tangata whenua flavour.

The questions asked by Thinking Maori were often open-ended and somewhat confrontational:

> How politically savvy is this lot? What is the long term political strategy? Is open debate welcome? Who challenges them? Do they really walk the talk? Are they really driven by principle? Who gives them advice? Do they take it?

Thinking Maori handed out a good portion of well-intended advice, encouraging MPs to be careful, not to attack the media, and to watch for members who kept changing their mind. The advice didn't just focus on parliamentary debate – it was also about being consistent in attitudes and behaviour: for example, on 30 January 2007, Thinking Maori expressed the hope that 'If [MPs] attended the Xmas parties hope they did not get drunk and the guys did not chase women or let the women catch them'.

On 13 March 2007, Thinking Maori eerily revealed insights into the way the Party worked, noting with surprise the lack of strategy exhibited by Hone Harawira: 'are his skills being ignored like the President's?' (an earlier email had commented on the wasted opportunity entailed in the Party's not using Professor Winiata as party spokeperson on the economy). There were observations about work output: 'Your team has been busy. Lots of media activity following that two day meeting. Bit confused with some of the messages.' Nothing seemed to escape the attention of Thinking Maori:

> Mrs Turia also revealed the contents of a private conversation with Luamanuvao Winnie Laban about 'brownies sticking together' – not good. Must be a Labour 'hang-over habit'.

However, as suddenly as they had started, the emails finished, leaving the MPs with an uneasy sense that they never knew when next their innermost secrets would be revealed.

A significant event occurred around the time of the Māori Party's first birthday in Parliament, on 12 October 2006: the Party's first private member's bill was pulled out of the ballot. That particular day was also ten years to the day after Tariana entered Parliament for the first time, in the general election for the forty-fifth New Zealand Parliament. In her Beehive Chat, Tariana referred to that auspicious occasion:

> Last Thursday I celebrated ten years in Parliament. As an incredible anniversary present, my first ever Member's Bill, the Repeal of the Foreshore and Seabed Act was drawn from the ballot. Our old people always call on te hunga wairua, to guide us, to heal us, to lift our spirits. It is that unshakeable faith that there is a greater power watching over us that made me know, without doubt, that it was right for the Bill to be drawn on that day. It was the right time for a revolution.[36]

NOTES

1. Audrey Young and Ruth Berry, 'Interview: Tariana Turia, Maori Party co-leader', *New Zealand Herald*, 6 August 2005.

2. 'Leader's debate', TV One, 22 August 2005.

3. Tara Ross, 'Four-seat sweep sets up Maori Party to make a difference', *Sunday Star-Times*, 18 September 2005, p. 2.

4. Hone Harawira, 'Looking back on the 2005 Election Campaign', internal paper to Māori Party National Council, pp. 7–8.

5. Ross, 'Four-seat sweep sets up Maori Party'.

6. Anthony Hubbard, 'Minority parties key to power', *Sunday Star-Times*, 18 September 2005, p. 3.

7. Colin Espiner, 'PM clears timetable for talks with minor party leaders', *The Press*, 19 September 2005, p. 1.

8. Patrick Crewdson, 'Clark and Turia still on a rocky road', *New Zealand Herald*, 16 October 2005.

9. Haydon Dewes, 'Suitors court Maori Party', *Dominion Post*, 20 September 2005, p. 2.

10. Haydon Dewes, 'Maori to talk to Nats', *The Press*, 20 September 2005, p. 3.

11. Martin Kay, 'Brash and Turia get to grips', *Dominion Post*, 21 September 2005, p. 1.

12. John Roughan, 'Dunne just may be key to the healing', *New Zealand Herald*, 24 September 2005.

13. Haydon Dewes, 'No compromise says Sharples', *Dominion Post*, 26 September 2005, p. 2.

14. Peter Luke, 'Will problematic alliances spawn odd bedfellows?' *The Press*, 1 October 2005, p. 17.

15. John Armstrong, 'One-seat change a huge difference', *New Zealand Herald*, 2 October 2005.

16. Vernon Small, 'Labour set to govern by itself', *The Press*, 10 October 2005, p. 3.

17. 'Winston's game', *The Press*, 15 October 2005, p. 10.

18. John Armstrong, 'Brash's hopes were gone by lunchtime', *New Zealand Herald*, 3 October 2005.

19. Colin Espiner, 'Maori Party unlikely to join coalition', *The Press*, 4 October 2005, p. 5.

20. Rochelle West, 'Taranaki Maori Party backers seek strong, independent voice', *Taranaki Daily News*, 6 October 2005.

21. Tony Gee, Audrey Young and Ruth Berry, 'National Courts the Maori Party', *New Zealand Herald*, 7 October 2005.

22. Martin Kay, 'Nats willing to dilute pledges says Turia', *Dominion Post*, 8 October 2005, p. 2.

23. John Armstrong, 'Danger lurks in minor party courting rituals', *New Zealand Herald*, 8 October 2005.

24 Ruth Berry, 'Turia takes carte blanche from hui', *New Zealand Herald*, 10 October 2005.

25 "During the election campaign Peters stressed that neither National nor Labour would need to rely on what he termed 'extreme parties like the Greens' to form a minority government". 'Departing MP wants Greens in Cabinet'. *Radio New Zealand/One News*. 27 September 2005.

26 Colin Espiner, 'Green Cabinet hopes fade', *The Press*, 11 October 2005.

27 Ruth Berry, 'Maori Party gets suicide warning', *New Zealand Herald*, 11 October 2005.

28 Chris Trotter, 'Turia should add a third grave', *Taranaki Daily News*, 14 October 2005, p. 8.

29 Tracy Watkins, 'Seating arrangements at Mad Hatter's tea party', *Dominion Post*, 17 October 2005, edition 2, p. 7.

30 Patrick Crewdson, **'**Coalition talks in chaos as Nats accuse Clark of failure', *New Zealand Herald*, 16 October 2005.

31 'Richard Prebble: It's looking good for Brash', *New Zealand Herald*, 16 October 2005.

32 *Hansard*, 16 November 2005. The Working for Families package had little impact on poverty rates for children in beneficiary families (close to 75% in both 2004 and 2007), but halved child poverty rates for those in working families (22% in 2004 to 12% in 2007, and close to the same since then). See: Bryan Perry, *Household Incomes in New Zealand: trends in indicators of inequality and hardship 1982 to 2013*, Ministry of Social Development, Wellington, 2014.]

33 Whatarangi Winiata, 'The Tikanga Māori House: The influential independent Māori voice', speech to Māori Party AGM, 2007.

34 Whatarangi Winiata, 'Māori Innovation and Reconciliation', paper presented to the Ngā Pae o te Māramatanga Conference, 8–11 June 2008.

35 Tariana Turia, speech to the ACT Party Conference, Wellington, 13 April 2006.

36 Tariana Turia, Beehive Chat, 13 October 2006.

CHAPTER TWENTY-TWO

REVOLUTION DEPENDS ON WHAT IS DONE:
2008–2014

Revolution is a serious thing, the most serious thing about a revolutionary's life. When one commits oneself to the struggle, it must be for a lifetime.[1]

When our tupuna and the Crown agreed on Te Tiriti o Waitangi both signatories knew that they were creating a situation in which a natural tension between Kawanatanga and Tino Rangatiratanga would exist. This has been the reality and it will continue. Both partners must be vigilant in monitoring the tension and searching for reconciliation of the two forces. Kawanatanga has dictated the outcomes of the tension. Reconciliation of Kawanatanga and Tino Rangatiratanga has been elusive.[2]

There is nothing more difficult to take in hand, more perilous to conduct or more uncertain in its success than to take the lead in the introduction of a new order of things. For the reformer has enemies in all those who profit by the old order, and only lukewarm defenders in all those who would profit by the new order, this lukewarmness arising partly from fear of their adversaries … and partly from the incredulity of mankind, who do not truly believe in anything new until they have had actual experience of it.[3]

In Tariana's maiden address, she had drawn upon a statement from Professor Jock Brookfield, 'Revolution rests upon what is done – not what is legal, or necessarily moral or just'. Going into the 49th Parliament, Tariana resolved to make as much progress as she could; the revolution would take place through undoing the injustices, in doing what was right.

In the lead-up to the 2008 election, the Māori Party campaigned on taking action: action inspired by and on behalf of the people. The Party's 2008 manifesto was entitled *Taking it to the people*:

> This election, the Māori Party is asking an important question. He aha te mea nui o te Ao? What is the most important thing in the world? Many of you have told us, he tangata, he tangata, he tangata: it is people, it is people, it is people. But such is the rich and creative tapestry of the people who inhabit Aotearoa, that we have received many other answers. Real wages for real work; being respected; a clean environment; my kids; seeing the Treaty honoured; thriving whānau and communities; having hope.

The manifesto introduced three broad areas of focus for the Party's long-term plan 'to achieve what we as a people know is right for this nation': Te Tiriti o Waitangi, the economy and Whānau Ora. The Party entered nineteen candidates in the election, the first seven places going to the seven Māori electorate candidates. Co-leaders Tariana Turia and Pita Sharples topped the rankings, and MPs Hone Harawira and Te Ururoa Flavell were at places three and four respectively. Hauraki Waikato candidate Angeline Greensill was at number five, ahead of broadcaster Derek Fox, who would challenge Parekura Horomia in Ikaroa Rāwhiti. Te Tai Tonga candidate Rahui Katene was number seven.

The remaining twelve places were occupied by Naida Glavish, Iritana Tawhiwhirangi, Hector Matthews, Te Orohi Paul, Amokura Panoho, Grant Hawke, Bronwyn Yates, Josie Peita, Richard Orzecki, Mereana Pitman, Awanuiarangi Black and Georgina Haremate-Crawford.

Before the party had finalised this list, they had suffered a tragedy in the sudden loss of 'gentle giant' Rereamoamo Monte Ohia, who had stood for Te Tai Tonga in 2005 and had been intending to stand again in 2008.

On 11 June 2008, the *Otago Daily Times* had featured an article covering a four-day southern campaign tour being undertaken by the Māori Party, encompassing visits to Dunedin, Invercargill, Christchurch, Kaikōura and Picton, where the Party was 'rallying support, listening to concerns and encouraging enrolment'. The article featured a photograph of Monte Ohia with the four Māori Party MPs at a hui in Dunedin.[4] That night, the team travelled to Christchurch to attend a hui at Rehua marae. Monte, as the last speaker, was in full flight. He gazed upon the photos of those who had passed on: the faces of Nanny Ruku Arahanga, Hohua Tutengaere, Wahawaha Stirling and Meikura Taiaroa-Briggs. He said that the candidates owed it to them to win their seats: 'we have never been this way before'. Monte's passionate call to the hui was 'this is our time'. It was the proud cry of a true champion for the people in what turned out to be his last campaign; he died the next morning.

Tariana felt a deep sense of grief at the loss of someone she held in such high regard:

> Monte's collapse at home in Christchurch, as he prepared to travel to Wairau for the final day of the tour, has shattered his family, his friends, and those who shared his dreams. 'Monte was a man of great integrity, unstinting dedication and enormous strength,' said Tariana Turia. 'We are broken-hearted at this huge loss for us all'.[5]

It was the cruellest blow to the Party: to have to pick itself up and, with an election less than five months away, immediately commence a rapid selection process to appoint a new candidate. Te Tai Tonga was by far the largest electorate geographically. Voting hui were held in Lower Hutt, Nelson, Picton, Blenheim, Kaikōura, Christchurch, Arowhenua, Dunedin, Invercargill and Arahura.

And so, one brief month after the Party had farewelled Monte, Rahui Katene, a lawyer of Ngāti Kōata, Ngāti Kuia, Ngāti Toa, Ngāti Tama, Te Āti Awa and Kai Tahu whakapapa, was announced as the Māori Party candidate for Te Tai Tonga.

The national campaign and policy manifesto was launched in the hustle and bustle of the Frankton Markets in Hamilton, with the theme of 'taking it to the streets'. Whānau Ora and economic policies were launched in the heart of Flaxmere, and the Treaty policy was launched in Victoria Park in Christchurch, reflecting the Party's view that the Treaty belonged to everyone.

The 2008 election campaign featured extensive use of 'kaakoi' – cars of supporters travelling in convoy with Māori Party flags flying high. Derek Fox, a skilled aviator, organised for a Māori Party banner to be flown overhead at Warriors and All Blacks games in Mount Smart and Eden Park stadiums. There was extensive use of merchandise emblazoned with the Māori Party logo – beanies, jackets, vests, visors, teeshirts, flags.

The Party's television advertising campaign featured heroes and champions – Rob Hewitt, Amster Reedy, Iritana Tawhiwhirangi and Robyn Kahukiwa – alongside everyday stars – a young mum and three little girls.

Throughout the campaign, the most frequent question asked was, 'who would the Māori Party go with?' The standard response was that the question should actually be, 'who will go with us?' Therese Arseneau answered that question when she outlined the detail of the mana-enhancing partnership the Māori Party eventually entered into with National after the 2008 election:

> The Maori-National Party pact seems to be based primarily on good personal relationships rather than on the written agreement. Being 'wanted' was a potent draw for the Maori Party especially after being disparagingly dismissed by Helen Clark in 2005 as the 'last cab off the rank'.[6]

Yet polling throughout the 2008 campaign had consistently reflected the desire of Māori voters for the Māori Party to work with Labour, not National. How, then, did the Māori Party come to consider forming a relationship with National?

Before the election in 2008 they had talked to us – Bill and John – about whether, if they got in, we would consider a relationship with them. Labour had basically turned us down flat – we were the 'last cab off the rank'. It was really clear that they weren't interested in any of the ideas that we had or weren't prepared to do anything. So we had to sit those first three years in the cross benches.

Whatarangi was President at that time. He laid it on the line to us that if we weren't prepared to go into government with whoever the government was, there was no point in us having a Māori movement, because we would never be able to make a difference in the lives of people. And on the night of the election, after National had won, they rang us. At that point they didn't really need us, but they rang us and offered us an opportunity to talk to them.

What we have tried to focus on really strongly with them, and in working with anybody, is the relationship: working with people, being respectful of one another, accepting that there will be a difference of views and basically respecting the position that people took. Agreeing to disagree without making it a bottom line, because otherwise it is destabilising – and so we decided we could work like that. It fitted with our kaupapa and the tikanga that we believe we should be practising in here, and that is about being respectful. You don't have to agree. That is probably what National have found – that we have been able to work with them constructively because we are disciplined.

I am really proud of the work we have done in the last six years. One of the things that I learned from leaving Labour ten years ago is that when you are in a mainstream caucus it is very difficult to advance the issues that are important for your people, because you have all the competing interests within that caucus, and whether you like it or not those things for Māori are not at the top of their agenda.

So when I left and we began negotiating across the table with Prime Minister John Key and Deputy Prime Minister Bill English, I discovered how much easier it was to convince two people on the importance of particular initiatives for our people. In the last six years I have only had to convince two people – the Prime Minister and the Deputy. That's been the great thing about being in coalition – you don't have to convince a whole caucus.

I have enjoyed that opportunity, and it hasn't mattered to me who the government is. I believe, as Matua Whatarangi expected of us, that we're not here to be in opposition, not being able to make a difference in any way at all. No matter how difficult it will be to work with whoever is the government, that's the responsibility that we have to our people. I have really appreciated the opportunity that the Māori Party has had to work alongside the government of the day.

I have had a really good relationship with Bill English – even when I was with Labour and I first came up, he rang me on a number of occasions about Māori health issues. He was the Minister of Health then. He is someone that I have always looked up to, mainly because I know he genuinely wants to make a difference. In the Whānau Ora space he has been huge. I don't think that without him we would have got the buy-in from the National Government that we did get, and he has been committed to it all the way through, encouraging other ministers to see the value of it.

The respect that Tariana has for Bill English is matched by his admiration for her; an admiration that has grown considerably over the years:

> I don't think that it was just about the foreshore and seabed and the way she was treated, which was disgraceful. But it was a fundamental difference which more Māori understand now. So I had a little bit to do with her before Parliament, but it was mostly through admiration for that organisation she was running. She came into Parliament and I wasn't surprised when it all blew up, but then she had the courage to follow through and found the Māori Party.
>
> When they formed up I was struck by the dignity of the way they behaved. For a brand new party it was taken seriously quite quickly – they did simple things with dignity, particularly in the House. They used the House extremely well, not by the usual method of being loud and extravagant and getting on TV, but by pursuing their kaupapa consistently. By doing their homework, delivering their messages with dignity. They were taken seriously from fairly early on, and of course a big element of that was Tariana. It was unexpected, because the Labour Party tried to portray her as some kind of reckless firebrand. The sponsor of the 'haters and wreckers'.

I thought that there was a possibility of coalition or support arrangements, because the Māori Party was about people taking control of their own lives, which was fundamentally a philosophy, a view of the world, we could connect with.

Yet few would have thought the alliance was possible.

The Māori Party had made some inroads in the seven Māori electorates, its share of the party vote in those electorates rising from 27.7 percent in 2005 to 28.9 percent in 2008, and had captured a fifth seat with the election of Rahui Katene in Te Tai Tonga. But because it still had only 2.39 percent of the party vote in total, the electoral strength of the Māori Party was not significant enough on its own to warrant inclusion in a governing arrangement. The infamous Orewa speech of Dr Brash and National's campaigning promises to abolish the Māori seats had hardly endeared National to the Māori Party membership. Indeed, Jonathan Boston had hypothesised that 'there was an electoral risk: having hitherto drawn most of its votes from the centre-left of the political spectrum, the Māori Party stood to lose support by aligning with National'[7]. So why do it?

It all came down to the value that each side placed on forming a relationship. It was clear to the Māori Party from the outset that establishing a relationship with another political party would come with risks. The most critical of these, in Tariana's view, was the threat that the major party would dominate the smaller party. She told Gordon Campbell at the time:

> That's something we have to discuss with our constituency. All those arguments have been put to us, about being in the tent and part of decision making and therefore having more influence and then of losing your identity, through being forced to keep your trap shut and not speak out on issues. Those are really important matters because we can't give away, we cannot lose, the independence of our voice.
>
> We have to be incredibly careful. It's not for me to say what decision the Maori Party will make. We've always said we go back to our constituency. We owe it to our people once elected to go back and put all the options before them. They will be the ones who will decide what we put on the table for the negotiables.[8]

And so, following the election on 8 November 2008, the Māori Party went out on the road again. By the Friday following the election, the mood of the consultation was remarkably buoyant. And all the more remarkable was the positive support being expressed by Hone Harawira about the opportunity for an agreement with National. On 14 November it was reported that:

> Maori Party MPs had last night completed 18 of 40 hui to seek approval from party members and supporters for a draft agreement that will exchange ministerial positions outside cabinet for five confidence votes. Te Tai Tokerau MP Hone Harawira told NZPA after attending hui at Waipu and Wellesford yesterday that the consultation process was 'bloody fabulous'. He rated support for the agreement at about 98%. 'People are wanting us to have a shot, they're cautious but they are saying go for it anyway'.[9]

A mere eight days after the 2008 election, the Māori Party announced it had negotiated an unprecedented and unexpected accord with National. The day before the agreement was signed, its historic significance was noted in the *Herald*:

> This week's deal is historic both in its potential long-term impact on the electoral landscape and in bringing together two strands of New Zealand society which have little contact, rural and provincial conservatism and Maori radicalism. It is a volatile mixture. But if it can be made to work, National will be laughing all the way to the Beehive.[10]

The first three lines of the Relationship Accord signed on 16 November 2008 spelt out its unique approach:

> The National Party and the Māori Party recognise the importance of mana maintenance and enhancement for both parties to this agreement. The relationship between the Māori Party and the National Party will be one of good faith and no surprises. Both the National Party and the Māori Party will act in accordance with te Tiriti o Waitangi, the Treaty of Waitangi.

One of the interesting differences about the Agreement between National and the Māori Party compared to the confidence and supply agreements National had signed with ACT and United Future was in the area of policy gains. The Agreement with the Māori Party contained a recognition that:

> The two parties both have policy priorities and there are areas of commonality and other areas of difference. The National Party and the Māori Party will work together to progress these priorities as and where agreement can be found.

For both ACT and United Future the requirement was more stark – both parties had to promise to support legislation emerging out of National's post-election Action Plan and key commitments. Not so the Māori Party. Therese Arseneau described the relationship as more arm's-length. Again, initiation of the relationship could be attributed to the unique leadership of Tariana, as Bill English notes:

> This is someone who had the insight and the courage to sign up to a coalition agreement with a centre-right government. Something which is now regarded as so normal that no one takes any notice, but as recently as seven years ago was almost unthinkable. She had the courage to sign on with a group of people [about] whom her supporters would say 'these are the worst kind of people to solve this sort of problem with'; she was brave enough, she followed her instinct.

> She just followed her intuition about John Key, about National: that she could do business with them and be respected for the way in which she did it. And that's exactly how it's turned out. I always thought it was vital to this whole thing – it was based on a respectful agreement. The way in which she acted had already earnt respect. And we've all learned how to deal with disagreement.

> She's a conviction politician – and those are rare these days. She's not driven by the normal political considerations. She's driven by a pretty profound sense of what she's trying to achieve.

Tariana reflects on the ultimate success of the 2008 Relationship Agreement.

> We never ever wanted to be at the Cabinet table, because if you are at the Cabinet table you have to be disciplined; you have to vote with the Government. When you are not at the table, you can be as we have been. We are very disciplined but we are also very clear about the things we will vote for and the things we won't. In a way my associate roles all dovetailed very neatly into the Whānau Ora space. I basically need to focus on what is in the best interests of families. I have found it very constructive and respectful – difficult at times, when we do disagree – but never, ever disrespectful. I have really valued the relationship.

Tariana's colleagues were just as positive about the relationship, including, in those early days, Hone Harawira, as Peter Wilson reported:

> Key's really important achievement has been to mould an unprecedented alliance with the Maori Party. In doing so he has significantly lessened Labour's chances of winning the next election. If this new accommodation works, the Maori Party's support for National will be locked in through to 2011 and beyond. As much as anything, and perhaps more than anything, it is based on respect. The Maori Party feels it is being treated like an equal in a co-operative and trusting relationship. 'In three days, National offered us more than Labour did in three years,' said one of its MPs, Hone Harawira.[11]

In an interview with Tariana a couple of months before the 2008 elections, she shared her vision for the future, not just politically but as an overarching aspiration:

> I think that if we do nothing else while we are here, if we can bring about a sense of respect – between people – for difference, and for the different ways that people may view the world, and if that can be encapsulated in the way we put together legislation then I'll be a happy person. I don't want anything more than that. It's that families be able to take care of themselves, to take care of the ones they love, and that they have sufficient income to be able to live. And that

people just learn to get on with one another. That's really important for this country, as we go forward.

Going in to the Agreement with National, Tariana believed that the fundamental premise for effective relationships was respect for one another; unity through diversity. It definitely wasn't about one homogenous entity – nationhood through one lens, as she told Gordon Campbell:

> I don't believe that we've got one waka, and one nation. If you look at the way the systems in this country have been organised – and Parliament is one of them – then everything is seen through a particular set of eyes. And they're not Maori eyes. Maori people don't have any say how these things are organised, how the state operates, how state departments operate. So I'm not sure about the one waka or the one nation. The bottom line is that the Maori people are the first people of this land. The Treaty of Waitangi established that status and they signed the Treaty of Waitangi allowing others to come. They allowed a government to be established to take care of those people. What they didn't anticipate is being taken over. When you open your house to somebody, you don't expect to be relegated to the toilet.[12]

The Agreement between the two parties, while essentially only five pages long, set out some pivotal gains for the Māori Party. First and foremost, the question of the Māori seats was resolved by a compromise: an agreement that National would not remove the Māori seats 'without the consent of the Māori people' and that, accordingly, the Māori Party would not pursue entrenchment of the seats in that parliamentary term. There was also an agreement that there would no question about the future of the Māori seats in the proposed referendum on MMP, in implicit acknowledgement of the fact that referenda never work in the interests of minority populations.

The constitutional status of the Treaty was provided for in the Agreement's announcement that a group would be established no later than early 2010 to consider constitutional issues including Māori representation. A second major pledge was the promise to review the Foreshore and Seabed Act by the end of 2009:

> The National Party and the Māori Party will, in this term of Parliament, initiate as a priority a review of the application of the Foreshore and Seabed Act 2004 to ascertain whether it adequately maintains and enhances mana whenua.

A third pledge established ministerials for Pita Sharples in Māori Affairs, Corrections and Education, and for Tariana in the Community and Voluntary Sector. Tariana also became Associate Minister of Health and Social Development and Employment.

The Agreement ended with a recognition of the demands of the large geographical boundaries of the Māori electorates. It promised that all Māori MPs and MPs with an electorate larger than 20,000 square kilometres would receive a third out-of-parliament staff member. This was a significant acknowledgement of the additional pressures placed on Māori MPs of serving Māori electorates:

> The challenges of servicing the disproportionately large size of the Māori electorates will be addressed through immediate implementation of the recommendation from the March 2007 report of the Committee of the Third Triennial Review (Goulter report). There is inequity in respect of the support that Parliament provides the very large electorates compared to the very small ones. One comparison is between Te Tai Tonga (147,000 sq km) and Epsom (22 sq km).

This last commitment was one that Tariana had been requesting for some time, through her membership on the Parliamentary Services Commission, and reflected her knowledge of the challenge of trying to be an effective constituent MP in a large electorate, where even the amount of travel required to make regular visits was formidable.

Thus the stage was set for a new approach to government. And for Tariana, it was quickly off to work. The Community and Voluntary Sector portfolio was familiar territory. She quickly picked up the challenge, and started planning how best to achieve change for the sector. It was obvious that the impacts of economic recession were being felt in increased demand for services, as a press release from her office noted:

It has taken just one week into the job for new Minister of the Community and Voluntary Sector, Tariana Turia, to identify direct repercussions happening at home in response to the global capital crisis. 'This morning, the Bay Trust announced it was temporarily suspending the bulk of its grant programme as a result of the effects of "unprecedented worldwide financial difficulties"' said Mrs Turia.[13]

Within three months, Tariana had turned the rhetoric from downturn and despair towards practical solutions that could inspire change. She worked with the New Zealand Federation of Voluntary Welfare Organisations, Philanthropy New Zealand and the Office of the Community and Voluntary Sector to bring people together from across the community, voluntary, philanthropic and government sectors, to develop practical solutions to combat the economic downturn. In another press release, she stated:

What we know, is that even while the impact of the economic recession on the philanthropic sector funding is uncertain, there is likely to be less funding available for distribution in the immediate three to five years. Teri Williams, an American author, had some insights into the nature of despair. She said: 'Despair shows us the limit of our imagination. Imaginations shared create collaboration. Collaboration creates community and community inspires social change'. A vivid example of such inspiration was on the front page of the *Dominion Post* when a young woman who had lost the use of both of her legs, enlisted the help of Weta Studios to become transformed into a mermaid. I thought that was just wonderful.[14]

Tariana worked on all fronts, bringing interested parties together, focusing on solutions and changing attitudes all at the same time. Her emphasis was consistently centred on the power of communities to solve issues. Reflecting on *Counting for More*, a report produced by PricewaterhouseCoopers on the 'Value Added by Voluntary Agencies' project that had been initiated in 2002 to provide economically valid measures of the work of voluntary organisations, she told the House:

> Counting for More proved without doubt, that the outcomes for people who use services provided by voluntary welfare organisations are often significantly understated and undervalued. It demonstrated that across justice, health, social wellness, and education investment in the community can actually achieve significant cost savings across agencies, government and families and communities. The greatest challenge in these times must be to trust in communities to find solutions rather than topping up a contracting regime that is taking us nowhere. We need to be firm in our resolve that some of our most intractable problems will be best managed through encouraging ownership and innovation from local communities to find their own solutions.[15]

In no time at all, the Beehive website was being inundated with Tariana's accounts of the measurable change taking place in communities around the country. She opened the Wellington Housing Trust, which sought to invest in a 'community that enables access to appropriate and affordable housing for all'. She praised seventy-four-year-old Pakura Ahuriri of Maraenui, for providing a community garden for all to share. She commended Henare O'Keefe for wheeling out his mobile kitchen, 'Tunutunu', late at night to give street kids in Flaxmere a sausage in bread, while at the same time looking out for their well-being. She congratulated Sanitarium for the leadership it was showing in the Department of Labour's Pautaunofo Manukau Project, focusing on well-being and workplace safety for Pasifika workers. She spoke up for the voluntary ambulance drivers of the St John's ambulance service in Franz Josef Glacier, one of the most isolated ambulance services in the country.

In Budget 2009, she secured $1.2 million to strengthen local networks and give a voice to community groups that are often not heard.

She launched a book called *Trust: A True Story of Women and Gangs* by Pip Desmond, which told of the extraordinary lives of a group of women who challenged the gang movement over their attitude to rape. She championed the need to promote generosity: to grow giving in all its forms – money, time, in kind and acts of kindness. She introduced taxation changes to enable payroll giving as a way of supporting the community and voluntary sector.

She announced $420,000 for community organisations to employ skilled interns from the government, private and community sectors.

And she launched *A Guide for Carers: He Aratohu mā ngā Kaitiaki*, the Ministry of Social Development's manual for carers on government-funded services and supports available for family carers. In the launch, Tariana acknowledged the vital role that carers play in the well-being of others. She made a particular reference to her brother Kawana, Uncle Ted and Aunty Wai's son. He was just three years older than Tariana: he was born in 1941 and died in 1997. Kawana left home at seventeen and toured the world, playing keyboards in a band. Four years before he died he was in a car accident, leaving him a tetraplegic. The family organised a roster for care of Kawana throughout the weekend, to feed him, sit with him and support him the best way they knew how. Tariana said at the launch:

> When I think about my own whanau, I know that many of us have experienced real challenges in our lives, when we take on the care of our loved ones. I remember the experience we all had in the care of our brother, who was tetraplegic. It was our greatest wish that our brother could enjoy the pleasures of life, to be able to participate in the way he determined, and to feel that nothing was beyond him.
>
> And yet we often felt overwhelmed, or simply didn't have the time or access to the information that would help us find out about the range of support and resources available. It is a response I have heard echoed by many carers – they are frustrated by the maze of agencies who each appear to play a different part in the puzzle.[16]

Interestingly, some five years later, in her new capacity as Minister of Disability Issues, Tariana came to realise that her own response to Kawana's circumstances had been somewhat wanting. She has never been afraid to open herself up to scrutiny; to show leadership by her capacity to reflect and reconsider her own actions. She told documentary filmmaker Tanya Black:

> I don't think I ever thought of him in a disability context. He was my brother and I just don't think that I ever thought about the difficulties for him. I realised in fact after I got the [disability]

portfolio that in fact we were probably quite disempowering of him. We didn't have accessible marae so we lifted him over the top of things. He had an electric chair but we always pushed him – we couldn't help ourselves. It was a big learning curve for me. I did feel very sad afterwards when I realised that we hadn't given him the autonomy that he deserved.[17]

One of Tariana's biggest sources of satisfaction in the 2008 term was the progress she was able to make in bringing the world of information, computers and technology to people who were 'digitally disadvantaged'. In the 2009 Budget Tariana announced that $5.99 million would be distributed to twenty-eight information and communication technology projects, with the aim of building skills and capabilities in New Zealand communities where access was limited.

The difference that being digitally connected can make in the lives of communities became extremely important to her, as she told Tui Glen School in 2011 when reflecting on the Computers in Homes project:

> The really powerful thing about Computers in Homes is that through this programme, you get your licence to drive – along with a computer, ongoing ICT support and a free internet connection for six months. Over 5000 New Zealand families have already benefited from this programme and the results have been really exciting – leading to increased participation in the economy, improved educational outcomes, more resilient communities, and better access to online services and support.

> Recently I announced that I have managed to secure additional funding of another $3.3 million dollars over three years for community-based initiatives to increase digital literacy and connection. The funding will contribute towards further families participating in Computers in Homes and the development of a further Computer Clubhouse – another fantastic community initiative like this one. This new funding builds on the $8.345 million I announced at last year's budget – the funding which I understand has been responsible for establishing your programme here.

This announcement sat alongside a recent announcement by my colleague Dr Pita Sharples, in introducing Nga Pu Waea – the national Māori Broadband Group – to ensure Māori can maximize the opportunities, and that Māori views are represented as the rollout progresses.[18]

While Tariana was using every minute of the day to attend hui, visit with non-government organisations and celebrate the achievements of volunteers, she was always thinking of the big picture: the ability for communities to be self-serving and self-sustainable. It was from this basis that she began to develop a relationship agreement between the community, voluntary sector and the Government.

The name 'Kia Tūtahi – Standing Together' was deliberately chosen to represent the importance of engagement. The name had arisen during the unveiling of a foundation stone marking 115 years since the ancestor Tutange Waionui started building the whare tupuna, Taiporohenui, at Pariroa Pā, Kakaramea. As a surprise gift for the anniversary, the Prime Minister, John Key, presented a framed copy of a letter sent in 1895 by the pā's founder, Tutange Waionui. The letter had been a special project that Tariana had been working on with Lewis Moeau, the Prime Minister's advisor, and demonstrated the dedication of Tutange in advancing land negotiations for Ngāti Ruanui.

At the unveiling, the people gave the Prime Minister a pounamu patu to symbolise standing together – and called it Tūtahi. Key had been the first prime minister to ever visit the marae. In the *Taranaki Daily News*, South Taranaki deputy mayor Debbie Ngarewa-Packer reflected on the significance of the letter:

'The letter has brought our rangatira back to life. We're overwhelmed at the thoughtfulness of the Government giving us this. This is representative of John Key's reign which we think complements Tariana Turia's leadership. It's a relationship that is respected and highly regarded here and needs to be as one,' she said.[19]

Two years later, at Parliament on 1 August 2011, Tariana and the Prime Minister hosted a signing ceremony, and together on behalf of the

Government signed the Kia Tūtahi Relationship Accord, signifying commitment between government and communities to engage effectively to achieve social, economic and environmental outcomes. The Accord was also signed by community representatives, and endorsed by the government chief executives present. The Kia Tūtahi vision is for the communities of Aotearoa and Government to be working together for a fair, inclusive and flourishing society.

During the 2008–2011 Parliament the Māori Party made progress in putting forward private member's bills. Te Ururoa Flavell achieved the greatest momentum, firstly putting forward the Local Electoral (Māori Representation) Amendment Bill, requiring all territorial authorities and regional councils to establish Māori wards and constituencies to provide for Māori representation, and then a month later putting forward the Public Works (Offer Back of and Compensation for Acquired Land) Bill. Rahui Katene put forward the Te Rā o Matariki Bill/Matariki Day Bill proposing to formalise a day every year on which to celebrate the Māori New Year. A year later, she submitted a Bill to debate the exemption of GST from healthy food.

At the same time, Tariana was fast-tracking legislation to advance tobacco reform. Her first attack was the Excise and Excise-equivalent Duties Table (Tobacco Products) Amendment Bill, which proposed three cumulative increases to duties on all tobacco products. The following year, also at Tariana's instigation, the Smokefree Environments (Controls and Enforcement) Amendment Bill was passed, prohibiting the display of tobacco products in retail and other sales.

Pita Sharples oversaw the Whakarewarewa and Roto-a-Tamaheke Vesting Bill, which enabled the transfer of the Whakarewarewa Thermal Springs Reserve, Roto-a-Tamaheke Reserve and Southern Arikikapakapa Reserve to the Whakarewarewa Joint Trust.

And of course the most significant advance of all for the Māori Party was the Marine and Coastal Area (Takutai Moana) Bill, which was passed into law on 24 March 2011.

On the day it passed into law, as she had been at every stage, Tariana was the first speaker in the debate. She dealt with the challenges that the Bill had presented, while encouraging people to lift their sights higher, on the 'politics of possibility':

> There was more at stake in this bill than simply repealing the 2004 Act, notwithstanding how fundamental that is. It is about honouring the Treaty in principle and in practice. There are those who are unable to accept the legitimacy of Parliament and it is their right to do so. But the path for the Māori Party is a different one. We have chosen the vehicle of Parliament to advance our aspirations in a modern context. We have chosen to participate in kāwanatanga and to uphold the mana of our tūpuna. We can do both.
>
> New Zealanders do not expect the critical business of the State to be delayed for questions that amount to little more than wasting Parliament's time and taxpayers' money. The people deserve better. The Māori Party came to Parliament because we want the very best for our people. We want their aspirations heard. We want tangata w'enua to be a strong voice and to be leading the future of Aotearoa. It is a mission that I know others have carried before us. Nevertheless, it is the most critical reason for our existence as a political movement. It is, after all, about our struggle for survival; the reconciliation of kāwanatanga with rangatiratanga; and the long-term plan 100 years from now, and onwards.
>
> One of the saddest aspects of this time has been the way in which some have chosen to use this legislation as a tool to create division both within Parliament and, indeed, within our own party. To act in such a way is an anathema to me, and it operates against all of our kaupapa. I have always been someone who has sought to foster unity and to celebrate diversity rather than to promote divisiveness. As members of whānau, hapū, and iwi we are already divided along so many lines: by religion, politics, income, and education. What I genuinely hoped was that we could look, as a nation, at this issue with new eyes, understand the differences, and work together to make change, as small as they may be. …

…We have chosen not to participate in the politics of attack but to invest in the politics of possibilities.

We have honoured our word – we have removed the Foreshore and Seabed Act from the statue book of this House. The challenge now is to test this new law. The message we have been getting from some iwi leaders is that now that the right of access to the courts has been restored, case law and customary rights may be politically achievable. …

This bill is another step in our collective pursuit of Treaty justice. We have absolutely no doubt that there will come a day when this bill, like every single piece of legislation debated in this House, is reviewed and improvements are made, and we will move on together.

Finally, we pay our utmost respect to the champion of the Marine and Coastal Area (Takutai Moana) Bill, the Attorney-General, Chris Finlayson. From the onset he has demonstrated remarkable resilience, insight, and personal integrity to do what is right. I will never forget the depths to which he has gone in order to treat this take with the respect it deserves. Nā reira, tēnā koutou katoa.[20]

NOTES

[1] Professor Angela Davis cited in a speech by Tariana Turia, 'Revolution of Cancer Care for Maori, Whanau', 12 August 2009, *Scoop Independent News*: http://www.scoop.co.nz/stories/PA0908/S00179/turia-revolution-of-cancer-care-for-maori-whanau.htm (accessed 17 June 2015). The Māori Party hosted Professor Davis at Parliament on 26 June 2007. Professor Davis was Presidential Chairperson for African American and Feminist Studies at the University of California in Santa Cruz.

[2] Whatarangi Winiata, 'The Tikanga Māori House: The influential independent Māori voice', speech to the Māori Party AGM, 2007.

[3] Nicolo Machiavelli, *The Prince*, Chapter vi, Concerninig New Principalities which Are Acquired by One's Own Arms and Ability, 1532.

4   Elspeth McLean, 'Maori Party heads tour south', *Otago Daily Times*, 11 June 2008.

5   Māori Party, 'Poroporoaki: Rereamoamo Monte Ohia', 12 June 2008: http://maoriparty.org/panui/poroporoaki-rereamoamo-monte-ohia (accessed 16 February 2015)

6   Therese Arseneau, '2008: National's winning strategy', in Stephen Levine and Nigel S. Roberts (eds.), *Key to Victory: The New Zealand General Election 2008*, 2010, p. 291.

7   Jonathan Boston, 'Innovative Political Management: Multi-party Governance in New Zealand', *Policy Quarterly*, vol. 5, issue 2, May 2009, p. 55. http://ndhadeliver.natlib.govt.nz/delivery/DeliveryManagerServlet?dps_pid=IE1251681 (accessed 17 June 2015).

8   'Gordon Campbell interviews Tariana Turia', 21 April 2008, *Scoop Independent News*: http://gordoncampbell.scoop.co.nz/2008/04/21/gordon-campbell-interviews-tariana-turia/ (accessed 16 February 2015).

9   'Maori Party Heading for a deal with National', NZPA, 14 November 2008.

10 John Armstrong, 'Protecting the Maori Party is in National's interest', *New Zealand Herald*, 15 November 2008.

11 Peter Wilson, 'John Key's Brave New World', 16 November 2008: http://www.guide2.co.nz/politics/blogs/john-keys-brave-new-world/75/3921 (accessed 16 February 2015).

12 'Gordon Campbell interviews Tariana Turia'.

13 Tariana Turia, press release, 'Tariana Turia sees early impacts of global capital crisis', 27 November 2008.

14 Tariana Turia, press release, 'Impact on Communities: Managing the Downturn together', 25 February 2009.

15 *Hansard*, 11 February 2009.

16 Tariana Turia, 'Tomorrow's care today', speech to the National Carers' Conference, 24 September 2009.

17 Tanya Black, *Tariana Turia's Legacy*, video for AttitudeLive website: http://attitudelive.com/blog/tanya-black/film-tariana-turias-legacy (accessed 20 May 2015).

18 Tariana Turia, 'Computers in Homes Graduation', speech to Tui Glen School, 29 June 2011.

19 'Leaders' presence "healing"', *Taranaki Daily News*, 8 October 2009.

20 *Hansard*, 24 March 2011.

-CHAPTER TWENTY-THREE-
THE PERSONAL IS POLITICAL

RT HON WINSTON PETERS: Why is the Minister making allegations of racism in respect of the longevity of the Māori people and Māori health, when she knows full well that housing and a sound diet would be the most important things for Māori, and what racist element in our society is forcing people to go down to Kentucky Fried Chicken, or Pizza Hut, or McDonald's, and have Fanta and Coca-Cola by way of refreshments? Why does she not stick to the facts?

HON TARIANA TURIA: As usual, that member has a lot of rhetoric but no evidence.

RT HON WINSTON PETERS: When the Minister said that my question was all rhetoric without evidence, would she accept that my evidence is herself?

HON TARIANA TURIA: I do not think I need to account to Mr Peters for my eating habits; nor do I expect him to account to me for his drinking behaviour.[1]

A year into her new ministerial roles in the forty-ninth Parliament, Tariana took on a personal transformation which had nothing and everything to do with the work she was doing in Parliament. Tariana was now well used to the relentless scrutiny that comes with being a public figure. Four days after the 2008 Relationship Accord had been signed, she featured in a two-page special in the *Listener* focusing on the diabetes epidemic. The article reported:

> In August Turia was diagnosed with diabetes. The devastating news couldn't have come at a worse time. With just three months of campaigning left before the election, she knew how challenging it would be to make her health a priority. 'Eating healthily is incredibly difficult with this kind of job, especially when you're on the road all the time. I've found it really, really difficult'.[2]

Soon after her diagnosis with type two diabetes, Tariana attempted to change her lifestyle – drinking more water and trying to give up fatty foods. 'I've always loved pūhā', she says, 'and pūhā isn't that great without meat that has a bit of fat on it.'

The whānau were very supportive. George, who does most of the cooking, tried to adapt the meals to make them healthier. Even Piata, the couple's granddaughter, got in on the act. The *Listener* recounted:

> The couple have continued to buy ice cream on the pretext that it's for their seven year old granddaughter who lives with them. 'Actually she's been great. Whenever I reach for a lolly, she asks me whether I'm allowed sugar, which makes me feel quite ashamed'.[3]

The *Listener* article finished with a statement from Tariana that would become prophetic: 'We never imagine ourselves reaching the stage where we become a burden on our families, on society and on ourselves'.[4] Barely six weeks later, she was in hospital, fighting to be well.

Fear. It's not an emotion I willingly invite into my life. I simply can't see the point. I don't read thrillers; I've never found any reason why I would want to watch a horror movie. Sitting on the edge of my seat, too frightened to leave the light, listening out to every creak of the floorboards as danger approaches, simply doesn't do it for me. But I have smelt fear and known what it is like to be paralysed by that sense of shrinking hope. I have experienced that churning deep in my puku, as if my inner organs are being squeezed through the wringer, leaving me gasping for air, suffocating in my own panic.

I will never forget the day my baby thought my days were numbered. It was the summer of 2009. I'd been looking forward to the break for so long.

The election campaign had been exhilarating and all-consuming, the coalition negotiations had been both terrifying and thrilling; I'd been flat tack setting up the ministerial office and I'd got to the end of that year with very little in reserves. I had been desperate for some days at home; to be with the whānau and bask in the post-Christmas luxury of days without a schedule.

But freedom came at a price. As the relentless chaos of my diary eased off, my body gave me a timely reminder that I wasn't beyond being human. And so eventually I found myself once more taking up bed space in Good Health Whanganui, fighting off a particularly nasty kidney infection.

I hate the indignity of being sick; that helplessness in which your will becomes secondary to the physical. Up until the time I was fourteen and at boarding school, I'd never been to a doctor. We kept well within the whānau – we relied on our own remedies, no outside professionals were required. But as my life went on, and stress accumulated, periods of ill health became more and more frequent. No matter how much I want to rise above it, the body takes over. I have a stubborn streak and I'm not the best patient – my nursing training probably gives me that false belief that most times I can heal myself. But this time it was a bit different.

Because our mokopuna, Piata, was at stake. I can remember the moment she walked into the room as clearly as if it was yesterday. She was seven at the time, and George had kept her away when I'd first been admitted. She'd been with my niece, Karen, who's always there when we need her, and I knew would keep her calm and fully occupied. But there was no doubt that our bright little button still knew something was up, and she'd been begging her aunty to bring her to me.

She had that unmistakable imprint of terror written right across her face. Her eyes darting uncontrollably around the room, her visible alarm at my condition out there for all to see. And then she just fell onto my bed in a crumpled heap, her little shoulders heaving up and down, sobbing as if her heart was breaking. When the tears subsided and finally she could take a breath, she looked up at me and said, 'Mama, I don't want you to die'.

Those words pierced far into my soul; I couldn't ignore them. That plea from Piata became the genesis for the surgery that was literally life-changing; life-saving. Once I'd made the decision, I never looked back. In fact, it was surprisingly easy. All it took was to open the cheque book and, with the help of Mr Stubbs, rewrite the future for my mokopuna.

Professor Richard Stubbs, the gastrointestinal surgeon, is the most unassuming of men. His quiet sense of self-assurance, his humble manner meant so much to me as our family prepared for the procedure they describe as a Fobi gastric bypass. Others call it stomach stapling; I call it the day my life took a different direction. We'd had a big red ring circling 24 November for months; we'd all heard the kōrero, watched the DVD, mentally prepared ourselves for the lifestyle change ahead. So by the time I was finally on the operating table I was well and truly ready.

The operation stunned me in its simplicity. The Fobi pouch operation divides the stomach, and places a band around your new stomach. It involves open surgery, and of course all the risks that come with a general anaesthetic. But I was amazed how painless it seemed; I was blessed with a rapid recovery and in under a week I was home, ready to watch the weight slip away. The first four days all I had was ice to suck on, and they bring you out these ridiculous little bowls – a miniature meal – to acclimatise you into a new menu. Thing is, I wasn't hungry – my first spoonful of soup, as bland as it was, filled me up. It was a completely new phenomenon.

It's the head that needs readjusting. When your first meal arrives, you think to yourself, 'am I going to have to sneak another couple of bowls?' You virtually have to re-educate yourself about food.

Of course, once the euphoria of the surgery was over, it wasn't quite so easy in reality. The key to success with the Fobi pouch is that it limits the amount of food you can eat at one time, and it also slows the passage of the food. It took me a long time to learn the lesson about how much and how fast the food can be absorbed. It would be a tortured journey of trial and error.

Rushing from the table when that extra mouthful tipped the balance. Encountering the sensation of dumping – the state of being uncomfortable. Basically, you feel lousy. There's nothing you can do about it other than to accept your fate and lie down, waiting for balance to be restored as you reflect on whether you had really needed that scallop. Once you've survived dumping you really don't want to feel like that again, so, believe me, you do think about what you eat far more carefully.

I have a terrible tendency to eat one piece more than I should. My favourite meal of all time is macaroni cheese. I remember early on after the op and George served me up maybe half a cup. I gobbled it up with huge gusto – and sure enough, I was sick. There are other foods that you just can't touch – I'm not good with rice, fresh bread, pasta, steak. But I can still manage a lamb chop! About a month after surgery, I had the delirious luxury of eating an entire lamb chop in one sitting. It took me about an hour to eat just half of it, but oh my goodness it was worth it.

There are always times when I think, 'perhaps I could just eat what I like without it going down the wrong way'. And yet there have been more car trips than I like to recall in which everyone has diplomatically looked the other way while I lose the lunch we've just devoured. My poor, loyal staff, consigning themselves to silence; taking up the code of amnesia as they consciously delete the memory of their Minister in various stages of distress.

Yet all these episodes pale into insignificance when I reflect on the transformation I have enjoyed post-op. I have climbed a small hill; even entered the Real Women's Duathlon and clocked up an incredible 10 kilometres walking – something I'd never have thought possible. We did it as a team – all the women at the office, supporting each other to walk or bike the event.

What's best, I walked it with Piata. She was delighted as our registration tags were emblazoned with our entry number – number one – and she'd worked out that even with the wonders of bariatric surgery her grandmother was never going to be the front-runner in this race without outside intervention. Number one is number one – it doesn't matter how we came by it.

More than anything else, what I love is the amazing energy I've acquired once the pounds were shed. My motivation was always about our whānau. I wasn't doing it for the weight loss, and how I looked wasn't so important to me; mirrors are fairly irrelevant in our home. I wanted to rid myself of the diabetes, the asthma, the high blood pressure – and in all of those areas the change has been incredible. But as I started to lose weight, I did like the feeling. I felt good. I can do more. And there's so much to do. It is dramatic the change in how you feel about yourself, how you feel about your ability to do things.

The funny thing is that psychologically I struggled with adjusting to the new me. I'd buy clothes a bigger size than I needed and then look ridiculous, like some old frumpy granny in clothes that don't fit. My daughter took over the wardrobe, priding herself on outfitting me in the way that I should look, rather than put up with the mess that clearly I was making of it. Lisa loves nothing better than to be armed with my credit card, equipping me into a style to which I have become accustomed. And if by chance the style doesn't suit me, she's more than happy to take it off my hands and earn herself a new outfit as due compensation for all that I put her through. As she says, it's a tough job dressing Miss Daisy, but someone has to do it.

First and foremost it was always about my baby: being there for her teenage years and beyond; being healthy and fit enough to keep up with her mischief. She's a really out-there kid; some will say it's because of the way George and I have spoiled her. I say it's nothing of the sort – it's because she has an exceptional intellect and nobody else appreciates quite how bright she is.

Deborah Coddington summed it up for me in an article in which she referred to Piata, ten at the time, as being 'as tricky as a truckful of monkeys'. 'She's an outrageously lovable child in a non-precocious, unaffected manner. In another decade, I can see her striding the political stage'.[5]

But beyond Piata, the responsibilities go far wider – to all those who have suffered the embarrassment, the frustration, the despair of feeling fat, of being over-burdened with excess weight that try as they may they can't seem to lose. I am tired of the stigma attached to obesity. There is an attitude out there that if you've got diabetes it's because it's your fault. That's not true.

Of course we know the statistics; the pandemic of plumpness that is hampering our children and depriving our adults of a healthy, functioning life. But force-feeding a population on seven easy steps to diet or yet another miracle weight-loss service will not achieve the change we all need to see.

I know too many people who think that they've failed when they can't do anything about their weight. They beat themselves up, thinking that it's all their fault that they are sick; that it's all about willpower and clearly they're lacking. We need to be able to be open and talk about these things and give people the opportunity to be well so they can be contributing citizens.

At home, they still call me Tubs. I'm poto (short) – all my cousins are too. We weren't blessed with Rachel Hunter legs – and we all enjoy our kai probably more than we should. But I never bought into the happy fatty myth – my weight slowed me down, and increasingly brought with it health complications that I could do without. Most of all, this was never about me, myself, I. I am a great-grandmother, grandmother, mother, wife, sister, aunty, cousin. I have a responsibility and an obligation to be there; to support my whānau to be the best that they can be; to help them travel life's journey in their own unique way.

And quite frankly, I can not do that if my health holds me back. Well-being is all about experiencing the richness of life, the awesomeness, the spine-tingling wonder of being in love with life and one another. We have a right to be well; our families have to demand the best for us. The downstream costs of diabetes – amputations, blindness, liver failure, paralysis – are not part of anyone's grand plan. We pay billions of dollars to care for diabetics; it affects every organ in our body. I also accept that diabetes is a genetic disease affecting indigenous people.

People often ask me, given the costs of the operation and the fact that it is perceived as fairly invasive, would I do it all again? I take a snap second to respond, 'without a doubt'. I have too many reasons to live for; not the least being that little girl who made me make the choice to stay alive.

On 28 October 2010, a year after her own operation, Tariana announced in her capacity as Associate Minister of Health that she had secured $8 million for 300 operations for bariatric surgery. The funding would provide for bariatric operations for approximately 75 people per year. A press release noted:

> Mrs Turia says as Associate Minister with responsibility for diabetes, she is gravely concerned about the dire effects of the prevalence of obesity amongst New Zealanders. This surgery can improve quality of life and reduce the costs and harm from preventable disease that severe obesity causes.[6]

In May 2014, the Budget statement extended the initial funding to provide for at least 480 bariatric surgery operations over four years, with additional funding set aside within the elective surgery allocation. In that same year, Tariana was appointed Patron of New Zealand's Weightloss Surgery Trust.

Parekura passes

The difference that the surgery made to Tariana's life and that of her whānau gave her a new lease of life. People would stop her in the street, email her and write long letters sharing their personal journeys, and to every one Tariana would respond with a genuine desire to help. She would ask her Ministry of Health advisor to contact the taxi-driver from Auckland or the woman at the airport who wanted to know what process to follow.

More than anything, she wanted to help her beloved friend Parekura Horomia. Tariana had had great respect for the late Dr Pat Ngata, who had made it a personal mission of his to help Parekura to do something about his weight. Tariana gave Parekura the contact details for Mr Stubbs, and lent him the DVD to watch himself, and all the time, as Tariana describes it, Parekura said only 'yes mate, that's what I'll do, when I've got the time'. The tragedy was that time ran out. On 29 April 2013, at the age of sixty-two, Parekura Tureia Horomia passed away. Tariana was devastated. The Māori Party's poroporoaki stated:

> 'Words cannot express the sadness that we feel. He was such an open and warm person, he was always there to support each and every one of us when we needed it.
>
> 'I have loved Parekura as a great friend – not just since his early days in Parliament, but before that. We both worked on employment, when he was stamping his mark on CEGS', said Co-leader Tariana Turia. 'He was a confidante; my special mate through thick and thin, and I am heartbroken to lose him'.[7]

Tariana travelled to Hauiti Marae in Tolaga Bay to grieve for her mate, a man who had been her friend no matter what the political circumstances of the day.

The *Herald* reported:

> An emotional Tariana Turia, Maori Party co-leader, said she had known Mr Horomia for about thirty years. He was a strong man who had supported her during her split from the Labour Party. 'He'd been unwell for a little while, and he just kept going because that's

the kind of person he was. It was the people who always came first and no matter what, that was the kind of leader he was. He always gave 100 per cent of himself to the people.'[8]

During this period of personal transformation and loss, a third event occurred that greatly affected Tariana: the resignation of Hone Harawira as a Māori Party member.

Resignation of Hone

The breakdown of relationships between the rest of the Māori Party and Hone Harawira, and the subsequent disciplinary hearings and Hone's resignation, never sat easily with Tariana. But at the same time, it was difficult for her to stand by and watch the influence of ill-disciplined behaviour impact on the reputation of the Party.

The relationship that Hone and Tariana had developed had begun long before either went to Parliament. It evolved at Pākaitore, in the days of the work co-ops and employment trusts. When Tariana entered Parliament, Hone had watched on:

> I watched her a couple of times speak on TV on different occasions, and I just thought, 'very, very strong', eh. The fact that she could have been Labour, she could have been National. But in those days it didn't matter; she was just going to be herself. And that gave me confidence, knowing that if we were going to come in here, that we had that kind of person who was already here, who had gone through those kinds of ropes. I know that was what endeared her to a lot of people – that she just carried on being Tariana. I know that was what endeared her to a lot of people when the hīkoi was on the road – they knew that when they got down here, regardless of how many Māori that were or weren't down here, there would be one on our side.

One of my biggest regrets was when we parted company with Hone. Up until then, I truly believe that for the first time in the history of this country our people could grow really strong for having a proud and independent Māori voice. I believe that had we been able to hold it all together, today we would have had the seven seats, or maybe even more, because we would have encouraged our people to understand and know what is right in this place.

We have always been clear that to make progress for our people, we needed to operate in a relationship with the governing party and Hone knows this because he was party to the discussion with Whatarangi Winiata when we first began the Party. He was clear with us that if we were going to come into Parliament and take the easy road and just go left or right that we were going to be of no value to our people. No matter how hard it was to sit at the table of government, that's what we had to do for our people. We genuinely wanted to make a difference; if you only want to come in here to be in Parliament in opposition then you are no benefit to our people. He laid that down for us, so we knew from day dot that it didn't matter who the government was; that we would have to be there at the table.

There are lots of things about Hone that I value, but I don't believe that this environment was good for him in terms of the causes that he believes in.

That whole thing of being respectful all the time, not losing it and talking against other people was difficult for him. It is hard when you have got somebody like that in the caucus. Trust and respect are the two things that you have to work through first. If you have no trust in one another that means you have no respect for one another, and unfortunately your relationship will fall apart. I can relate that back to our relationship with Hone – once trust and respect went, there was no relationship. Because Hone was one of the people that really wanted us to go with National. He pointed to things up in the North that had happened under a National government. He knew that all the health and social services, kura, kōhanga reo, wānanga, all grew out of a National government, and so he wanted to go with them.

I think the real issue for Hone wasn't anything to do with National. It was that he has never been in a team when he hasn't been the leader. I think that was the difficulty. There were friends of his who spoke to us and said, 'could we give him more responsibility?' But there was no way that National was going to give us another ministerial. Pete tried to give Hone responsibilities, but in the end, if I am being really honest, he wasn't disciplined, he wasn't reliable and he didn't keep to the kaupapa that was laid out by Matua Whatarangi when we started; he couldn't keep to it, and you have to have discipline.

Quite often he wouldn't even be disagreeing with the reason for what we were doing – he was just disagreeing. I am someone who has always had a lot of time for him but, boy, when he was in that frame of mind there was nothing that you could say or do that would get him over the line. And he would often just leave and get out of here. So we would have to alter all our schedules because he would be gone. You have to be disciplined in here. If you get someone in here who on the spur of the moment goes walkabout in Australia or goes to another country and goes to Paris instead of the meetings he was supposed to, well, it's hard.

In Hone's defence, it would be fair to say he wasn't the only one to ever disagree with Tariana and lose the argument. He recalls:

> It wasn't until I came to Parliament that I realised that beneath the calm was a lot more calm. There was never any raging with Tariana; it was just a steely kind of a thing. Me and Pete used to sit around talking; and me and Te Ururoa would sit round talking; and me and Rahui would sit round talking; and then we'd have a caucus meeting and Tari would say, 'we're going left', and we'd all go left. Regardless of how rational our debates might have sounded and how correct they might have sounded. That's just the force of her personality; she's a very strong individual. I don't know necessarily that she always had things thought through, but she had things that she felt comfortable in leading, and once she had made her decision, that was it.

According to Hone, so persuasive was Tariana that even if the majority of caucus were opposed, inevitably she would exert her influence to create change. He describes the process at one hui at which there was a stalemate:

> We went around the whole hui and there was six to one. All of us wanted to go right and Tari wanted to go left. There was a big pause, and then I said to Whata, 'Mr President, can you tell us what we are going to do?' Whata looked at me and then he looked at Tariana and then he said, as he does, really quietly, 'I wonder if it's possible to come up with a way in which we can get the other six to come on board with what Tariana is saying'. I remember at the time thinking,

'for fuck's sake'. I think even Whata believed in the line of the six. But then that was his way. Because once Tari has set her mind on something … I think Whata knew that it would take heaven and earth to change her.

Hone frequently refers to Tariana's steely determination and consistency:

Tari was never a bunch of laughs, but her demeanour never changed; you know what I mean. You took comfort in that she was like that. I have no doubt Pete had views too, but it was always going to be difficult for Pete. You know Pete, nice guy, always wanting to be liked by all sides. That's one thing Tari never had an issue with. She never was particularly fussed about being liked by any particular side. Just being comfortable in her own skin about the decisions she made and that she could stand by them. I guess that's why Tari pretty much ran things, because she was strong enough in her personality to say, 'no, we're going left' or 'no, we're going right' or 'no, we're going over here'.

It was hugely challenging, but actually it never ever changed my respect for her steel. Even now I can chuckle about it. John Key might disagree with her, and he might say no to her, but he doesn't muck around with her. Nobody does in the Māori Party and nobody in any other party. You could see that in other ministers higher up in the loop. They might say no to Tari, but nobody ever gave her the run-around. I think that was just a carry-on when she was in Labour. That same steely determination to achieve things. We had huge disagreements, often, but it never ever changed the personal stuff in terms of my respect for her.

The other day I was asked how was life after Hone.

I replied – the same as it was before Hone. Babies have been born; rents need to be paid; whānau cope with bad news; rangatahi wonder what their future will be like; we bid farewell to loved ones.

The Māori Party has always been bigger than any one individual. It is a movement founded, proudly and passionately, on aspirations for a better life for all our whānau. That determination revolves around whānau at the core. It is a vision for all of us and it will remain our vision whatever government is in power; whatever MPs fill our seats. It is a big task that relies on all of us to create the difference we need but it is not an impossible task.

When Hone chose to leave, I saw no value in defending our party against the various claims he and others were placing in the public arena. Ever since Ranginui and Papatuanuku were separated, so that we can stand fully human in a world of enlightenment, differences of opinion have emerged. The greatest role for us all, at times of such intense scrutiny, is not to add to the noise by reciprocating with personal attack or denigrating comments – but instead to simply accept that Hone has a different road to travel, and that's his right to do so.

Importantly, we need to believe and keep faith, that we are doing the best we can do at any given time in a very difficult environment. I know our people generally understand this though they may not be aware of the parliamentary processes. What they do know is we would never betray them.

At this point of our lives the Māori Party have consciously chosen to enter Parliament to see what pressure can be applied to achieve the outcomes we seek for our people. Our four MPs know it is not the only approach to make change. But being in government, we know we can achieve gains and we would rather do that, we would rather feed our future with hope, than to be in opposition and watch the moment pass. In the end it makes no difference whether the government is Red, Blue, Green, Yellow or Mauve. They all represent the majority constituency who vote them in or out each election. Every decision they all make is carefully considered and expressed based on the politics and votes. Sadly no decision is based on what is moral, right, fair or just.

When you have only five votes, your choice is to maximise your opportunities as part of government, or be forever in the wilderness as others have been, saying everything you want to say and never being part of government to be held to account.

And we are absolutely committed to empowering and enabling whānau to maximise their capabilities to the fullest extent. We believe that a whānau ora approach is an essential part of the framework of change. We need an all-of-government commitment so that we can focus on the big picture – not just the issue of the day. We also believe lessons can be learnt from this approach for all communities – including the people of the Pacific, migrant and refugee communities, and other vulnerable groups.

What will it take? It will take what it has always taken – passion; political will; people prepared to make a difference and the commitment to our kaupapa and tikanga to ensure we always stay true to the vision our tupuna set for us.[9]

NOTES

[1] *Hansard*, 20 November 2003.

[2] Linley Boniface, 'Hitting home', *Listener*, 22 November 2008, p. 50.

[3] Ibid.

[4] Ibid, p. 51.

[5] Deborah Coddington, 'Dining with the leaders: Whanau focus fuels final charge', *New Zealand Herald*, 20 November 2011.

[6] Tariana Turia, press release, 'Turia delighted with funding for life-saving weight-loss operations', 28 October 2010.

[7] Māori Party press release, 'Poroporoaki ki a Parekura Horomia', 29 April 2013, *Scoop Independent News*: www.scoop.co.nz/stories/PA1304/S00552/poroporoaki-ki-a-parekura-horomia.htm (accessed 20 May 2015).

[8] 'Parekura's last promise: "I'll rest now"', *New Zealand Herald*, 30 April 2013.

[9] Tariana Turia, 'Life after Hone' *Tū Mai*, no. 117, April 2011; pp. 22–3.

-CHAPTER TWENTY-FOUR-
MOVING FORWARD

I don't want to sit in opposition, moaning about everything that's wrong and never ever being able to do anything that's right. I like being part of the decision-making.[1]

As the heat of the forty-ninth Parliament raged on, inevitably some in the party hierarchy were thinking about the need for change. It was a view that Professor Whatarangi Winiata was considering carefully, and it led him to table his resignation at the Hui-a-Tau (AGM) held in Auckland on 17 October 2009. In a press release, the co-leaders revealed that his intention to resign had not been accepted by the loyal membership who had attended the hui:

> 'Everyone who stood to speak on Whatarangi's resignation appealed for him not to go,' co-leaders Pita Sharples and Tariana Turia said. 'The influence of the president of the Māori Party has been fundamental to our success as a political party. It was Matua Whatarangi who inspired the membership to consider the value of a Party constitution based on kaupapa Māori, the inherited values of our tupuna. His vision, his strategic leadership and his political analysis have enabled us to flourish as a movement, and we could well understand why there was such reluctance to let him go,' the leaders said.

The love and sacrifice that Whatarangi committed to the development of the Party had ventured well outside the call of duty. As an accountant, Whatarangi was aware of the importance of valuing the vital contribution that volunteers make in establishing change. He refused to accept any payment from the Party for travel or accommodation. He, his wife Francie (Maata Te Taiawatea) and one of his children as a loyal driver for their dad had travelled the width and breadth of the country, taking the Māori Party to the people. He had given and given and given:

> 'The experience he has brought to the table has been critical in enabling us to present an independent, Māori voice in Parliament. Our party has thrived under Whatarangi's guidance, wisdom, knowledge and love for the Māori people.

Having declined the resignation, the AGM then concentrated on the Party's ambitions for moving forward. There was kōrero about the desire to have eighteen seats in Parliament by 2017, including all the Māori seats. The Party wanted to increase its membership to have more influence in legislation, *3 News* reported:

Mrs Turia said and for this to be done, more people needed to 'cough up' more funds, particularly those who were well heeled.[2]

There was also passionate discussion about climate change and the Emissions Trading Scheme (ETS): issues that had been foremost in the public arena in the preceding weeks, leading up to the introduction of the new law (Climate Change Response (Moderated Emissions Trading) Amendment Act 2009).

It took less than a month for the action-orientated energy of the 2009 AGM to bear fruit. On 12 November Matua Whatarangi attended a hui in Kaitaia at which he suggested the possibility of Hone Harawira taking on an 'independent status', and noted that he could stay with the Party 'so long as he doesn't destroy the party in the process'.

While Matua Whatarangi was still in the North, Tariana and Pita held a press conference at Parliament where it was clear 'that their tolerance for Mr Harawira is at an end'.

The *Otago Daily Times* reported:

> The leadership see him as an increasing liability, whose divisiveness goes against the kaupapa – underlying ethos – of the party and who threatens to damage the party's ability to pursue its policy agenda in the coming year.
>
> Next year will be a crucial year for the Maori Party, with the groundbreaking whanau ora social policy set to be a feature of the 2010 Budget, the sensitive repeal of the Foreshore and Seabed Act due to be enacted and a constitutional review considering the place of the Treaty of Waitangi to be set up. …
>
> There can be no mistaking the message: Mr Harawira is not a team player and is not suited to the disciplines of a political party. The hope is that he recognises that himself. But Harawiras don't do humiliation, and the default position would have to be one in which he fought expulsion – which in itself could be damaging to the party. It is a battle the leadership has calculated is worth risking.[3]

Life moved on, and before the end of the month, the Māori Party had announced a major deal with National involving the Party's support for the ETS. As part of the negotiated package, around 35,000 hectares of Department of Conservation land would be set aside for some iwi to plant for carbon credits – and the door would be open for other iwi to be involved in similar indigenous planting. The costs of petrol and power would be halved,[4] and an additional $24 million was negotiated to insulate the homes of low-income families. Other concessions from the Government included inserting a Treaty clause into the ETS legislation, reserving positions for iwi representatives on a range of advisory boards, and continuing to fund enviroschools and other mechanisms.

It was clear that iwi leadership and Māori business, through the Māori Party, had been pivotal in influencing the ultimate form of the ETS. In an interview on the television programme *Q+A*, Tariana was forced to explain the complexity surrounding the Party's stance:

> Look, the Māori Party is in quite a difficult position. The Māori economy is made up of fishing, farming, and forestry; we've had huge lobbying from that sector because they are major employers of Māori people. In fact they've been making their own representations to the government with us sitting alongside them. On the other hand they've also given us assurances that they're prepared to look at the way they farm sustainably into the future and that's really important for us; we were not a party that supported ETS.

Tariana stressed:

> I think in the end it's not so much particularly what the Māori Party want; it is what the iwi leadership want, and they are the ones who have been leading the dialogue, they have been asking us to definitely sign up to it.[5]

Notwithstanding the concessions it had achieved, the Party's position on the ETS was never a comfortable fit, and it was not altogether surprising that in the next Parliament it reversed its the vote of support, stating in 2012:

> The Māori Party has confirmed that they will vote against the Climate Change Response (Emissions Trading and Other Matters) Amendment Bill when it comes up for its second reading in the house.
>
> Co-Leader Tariana Turia said 'the emissions trading scheme was initially established to incentivise changes in behaviour for the sake of protecting the mauri of our environment. As the scheme has rolled out we have been gravely disappointed that not only have the environmental outcomes not been achieved, but that it has created another commercial market for speculators which has resulted in increasing the cost of living for our people.'
>
> 'The flood of cheap carbon credits from overseas has distorted the local market and slashed the value of forestry holdings, where Māori are major stakeholders.'
>
> 'Instead of taking bold measures to address the failings of this scheme, the legislation simply maintains the status quo for immediate respite of the few.'[6]

At the start of 2011, it was obvious that the ETS and the Takutai Moana Bill were causing concern for some Māori Party members, including Hone. Before long he spoke out, in a column that condemned the Māori Party's relationship with National:

> For the party to maintain its credibility, MPs must speak out against National's anti-social initiatives, no more of the polite press releases that say nothing. If we can't stop them at party or Cabinet level, then we need to signal that we will oppose them vigorously in the House, at select committee, at public meetings and on the streets if necessary.[7]

A train wreck was suddenly in the making. Within days of the column's publication, Te Ururoa Flavell had laid an official complaint, constitutional lawyer Mai Chen had been brought in to provide advice, and it was evident the Party was in for a rough few months leading into 2011.

The Party now had a new president, Pem Bird, who had been elected at the AGM at Ōmāhu Marae in Hastings on 31 October 2010. A press release stated:

> The new Māori Party President, Pem Bird, says the party is in for the long haul, even if at times members have strong differences of opinion. ...
>
> He says the party has never been more relevant.
>
> 'In terms of article three of the treaty, equality of citizenship, we're nowhere near there. We want to create solutions for ourselves and be responsible for taking charge of our own destinies and to the richness of this country's heritage, our heritage, our political heritage, and doing a heck of a lot better than we've done before,' Mr Bird says.[8]

Despite the turbulent times, the Party leadership never blinked. On 25 June 2011 it put forward Solomon Tipene to stand in the Te Tai Tokerau by-election that had resulted from Hone's resignation from the Party. However, fate was against Solomon. Only 41 percent of the population turned out to vote; of those, just 1087 people gave their vote to Solomon. Hone Harawira reclaimed the seat with 6065 votes.

Three days later, Tariana reflected on what the Māori Party needed to do as it prepared for the general election, now mere months away:

> Complacency can be our own worst enemy. None of us can afford to sit and watch the pot boil. We must liberate ourselves from conversations which do not serve to advance the wellbeing of our people and remobilize the movement forward that I know whānau seek. Like our whānau today, our tupuna had clear aspirations for our iwi. They wanted us to have Influence With Integrity (IWI). I am proud that this is what the Māori Party stands for unashamedly. We are at a vital juncture in our political history. I have no energy for talk that portrays Māori as the victims of ill-doing: of being continually described as the poor and dispossessed. We have a responsibility to move forward, to take our people with us, and

to restore a sense of wonder that each of us has the potential for transformation.

During the campaign Solomon shared an intimate story of a man he'd met in hospital who overheard him giving a radio interview. When Solomon finished his kōrero the man followed him out of the room, cried on his shoulder and thanked him for giving him hope. That man had been suicidal. In just that brief time listening to Solomon he found a sense of optimism through the ideas he talked about. It is moments like that which remind me that even if we improve the situation of one person our journey has been worth it. Noam Chomsky once said 'Optimism is a strategy for making a better future. Because unless you believe that the future can be better, you are unlikely to step up and take responsibility for making it so'. We need to move on from the negativity that has characterised this campaign and work to achieve the sense of optimism that we can do for ourselves, that we are the architects and designers of our own destiny. We owe it to ourselves, we owe it to the next generation to pave a positive pathway ahead.[9]

Despite the call to optimism, at the general election on Saturday 26 November 2011 the Māori Party earned 1.43 percent of the party vote, representing only 31,982 New Zealanders. Tariana, Te Ururoa and Pita were re-elected. But the loss of Te Tai Tonga MP, Rahui Katene shocked everyone. The *Herald* reported:

Maori Party leader Tariana Turia said it appeared the electorate was sending the Maori Party a message. 'And it may well be ... that they haven't liked the relationship with National,' she told TV3. 'I think the really disappointing thing for me is that Rahui Katene has worked harder than any Te Tai Tonga member that I can think of'.[10]

The Party had submitted a list of seventeen, with only the first ranking going to a Māori electorate candidate (Waihoroi Shortland). The next four places went to candidates described as 'the faces of the future' – Kaapua Smith, Wheturangi Walsh-Tapiata, Tina Porou and Awanuiarangi Black. Three of the Māori electorate candidates had stayed off the list (Rahui Katene, Na Raihania and Tau Bruce Mataki), opting to place all their faith in the electorate.

The brand was fresh, the messaging clear: Our Whānau our Future. The 2011 policy platform was grounded in three broad approaches:

Whānau Ora: restoring the essence of who we are – putting the vibrant traditions of our people at the heart of our whānau

Te Tiriti o Waitangi: we want to face our past with courage, so we can build our future together

Kāwanatanga: We want a government that values accountability and serving the people; we want a public service that understands the aspirations of whānau, hapū and iwi.[11]

The incentive for change was a bold one. The 2011 Policy Manifesto began:

Whānau Ora begins with you. Whānau is the heart of our people, it is the foundation on which our country thrives. It is about reaffirming a sense of self-belief.

Tariana was absolutely clear that Whānau Ora must play a critical part in establishing the pathway forward. It was a message that she shared willingly across New Zealand, with marae, rūnanga, iwi, non-government agencies, social service providers, business, private sector organisations and whānau. In a speech to Chapman Tripp in March 2011, she said:

We are at the starting point of major transformation in the way services are designed and delivered, contracts arranged and the way providers work together. But most of all we are at the starting point of our cultural transformation; celebrating the power and potential of a whanau-centred approach which will enable our people to flourish.

Whanau Ora is about maximising our survival through a model of transformation which will impact on all our futures.

It is the means by which we take up our collective responsibility for each other; it is possibly the first time in which Government has been able to measure value for money against a cultural construct.

And most of all – it forms the basis for a conversation that we can all enjoy within this land of ours, Aotearoa New Zealand.[12]

My love for the people: Whānau Ora

> I have one thing that counts and that is my heart. It burns in my soul. It aches in my flesh and it ignites my nerve. That is my love for the people.[13]

If there is one thing that most New Zealanders would now associate Tariana Turia with, it would be the transformation we recognise as Whānau Ora.

Some of the key concepts of Whānau Ora are encapsulated in a waiata written and composed by Morvin Simon and Chelsea Edmonds in 2010:

Mai i te kākano iti rawa ko te rākau whakaruruhau

Me ōna pūkenga ōna hua ātaahua.

Ehara i te kupu noa nā ngā karaipiture kē

E tipu e rea mai te whānau ora e.

Ruruia mai tō rangatiratanga tō aroha whakapono tūmanako

Hoea ngātahi nei tātou te marea nui tonu kia puāwaitia te whānau ora e

E tipu e rea te taonga whānau ora.

From the smallest seed grows the greatest tree with its benefits, its fruits and beauty.

These are not just ramblings, they are drawn from the scriptures so we encourage whānau ora to grow and burgeon.

Disseminate your sovereignty, your love, faith and encourage ambition and hope so that together we can propel our waka forward to bring about the fruition of whānau ora.

Go and flourish this gift that is whānau ora.

When I was in Te Oranganui, the Iwi Health Authority, we began that whole thing of developing policy for Whānau Ora. Because it has been how we have all lived – all of us know what it is to live Whānau Ora. It seemed to me such a simple thing to put in place a practice to restore our rights, our responsibilities, our obligations to care for one another. I can't think of anything more simple.

And yet it's been made complex, because people want it to be complex. They don't want family to be empowered or to be given resources to actually lift themselves up. They want others: they want service providers; they want the state and all its agencies to be the solution, and they're not. It's very simple.

I know, I see it, and I practise it myself: when families are collective, when they come together in the best interests of each other, they can solve the majority of problems themselves. The Government needs to give families a hand up so that they can maintain the essence of who they are, but more importantly be proud and independent people.

As Associate Minister of Health I introduced *He Korowai Oranga: the Māori Health Strategy*. We began to run whānau development hui back in 2002, so the whole concept of whānau ora began that long ago. I've always been whānau-focused – that's the whole nature of me – and trying to keep that focus in everything that I do has been quite important to me.

A lot of my work with the Pasifika nations has been about coming together to address significant issues impacting on them. Helping them to get resources so that they could develop frameworks that were within their own nations. Part of the problem is that everyone calls them Pacific Islanders, so that they treat them as if they are all the same. And they have different languages, different cultures – so it was important to get this framework established for them, and to enable them to take back responsibility and control over their lives living here in Aotearoa at this time.

What we want to do is build confidence in the Pasifika community on the backs of them determining it themselves. While we see it as a right for ourselves, we also believe that they are our closest relatives here, and we should be supporting them to do more for themselves. And to get the Government to acknowledge that they can, because they don't secure much budget from the system – from health, social, education – they lose budget hand over fist through not reporting in the way in which a government department might require them to. That feels like a really negative approach. We should see government agencies working alongside these service providers, who generally work beyond the call of duty.

My work in the disability sector, as the Minister for Disability Issues, has also paved the way to Whānau Ora. Disabled people are an amazing group of people – they inspire me constantly, because they never talk about what they can't do; they only talk about what they can do. I think the biggest disabling factor for them is the attitudes of our community towards them, and I think that's sad. I've taken their lead – they have wanted a project, the Enabling Good Lives project – which really has been about the families and the disabled people themselves determining what their life should be like, rather than having others – a provider – define it for them.

We must restore to our families, our whānau, our hapū, the resources and the right to uphold kaupapa and tikanga and not subject ourselves to state control or the influences of others. We must first look to ourselves.

I want our people to heal and restore themselves, be independent and interdependent, be healthy and well educated, so we can achieve our full potential to care for ourselves, for each other and our environment.

Whānau Ora is not something that only belongs to Māori people. I have heaps of Pākehā people who say to me, 'how can we implement this into the work we do?' They're working with people with mental illness. Many Pākehā organisations are working with our families, and they are at a loss because they work with individuals, and that's how the Government contracts them. Only families can change their own situation. Nobody from outside changes what happens within your family. Other people can come in and they can provide you with support, they can provide you with guidance, but in the end your family generally are a lot firmer about why these things need to happen, and they are lot more honest with us, I believe.

Since I've been in Parliament I go home and I've got aunties – I'm seventy now – and they still call me 'kōtiro' – how's that for putting you in your place and making you know that in the scheme of things you are just a member of the whānau? I've loved that. I love the way they interact with one another.

I went and visited an aunty one day, to listen to her daughter saying to her, 'oh Mum, the health service provider is coming to take you to the specialist'. And I looked at her and thought, 'why's someone else taking your mum to the specialist?' We sat and had a talk about that. None of them had even thought about the implications of that – of the daughter not going with her mum so that the daughter would know what's wrong with mum, and how she could provide the ongoing support. When I said that to her, she said, 'Oh god, I didn't even think of that.' When I talked to my aunty she said, 'Oh well, you know, dear, I did want to ask them to take me, but I didn't want to be a hōhā. And the service provider is there.' That's not good thinking: making us dependent on the state; transferring that to our organisations when we don't need to.

I think it is going to take time.

I have seen some amazing transformation for some families, and I have seen some families struggle with the whole concept. It requires ensuring that all the whānau know what's going on. We have learnt to be secretive: there is all this confidentiality – things that are not ours; they don't come from our history; they don't come from our culture. Our people learn to be secretive – that whole thing of 'you don't tell so and so'. If you have a family group conference you choose who can come – it's nonsense. It is nonsense. When we have issues that impact on whānau, even if we are the problem, even if the issues are about us as a whānau, we should still come together and talk it through and provide support. Because quite often with those who are creating the issues, there's been issues for them too. All of us need support.[14]

In many respects, Whānau Ora is the culmination of Tariana's life work.

It came from her nan making plans for her, plotting out her life path. It was cultivated by Aunty Wai, teaching her to do what was right; her dad throwing her on his shoulders and nurturing in her a love and sense of belonging to the land, knowing the places she could be home.

It came through being raised by many; the thousand pairs of eyes at the pā watching over her; Aunty Pae and Uncle Frosty gently teaching her the skills and strategies she would need along the way. Aunty Rita fixing her up after Alan was born; Aunty Julie turning up when she was needed most, taking her to the water to heal.

Whānau Ora was reinforced by the love of the sisters, brothers and cousins who surrounded Tariana; those who lived with her in the big house; those who lived across the paddock at Pūtiki; and those who lived apart but always resided within her.

It evolved from the lessons she learnt with the love of her life, George: the shoulder to lean on; the ever-present rock of strength that has been with her every step of the way. Their experiences in trying to heal the hurt of the many children who found their way into their home. Seeing the impact of violence – the grief, the anger, the frustration – tear people apart. Realising, too, at the point of losing Francie, that the most important work is always to bring our children home, to return them to the places and people that gave them life.

Whānau Ora grew out of seeing the change in fortunes of the rangatahi who flocked to Te Awa Marae Youth Trust; seeing how a bit of belief can make the world of difference. Seeing beyond the impossible to the possible. To believe in the can do and can be. It was refined through the teachings of a Filipino priest, Father John Curnow, and the Sisters of St Joseph. It was given force through the powerful assertion of Whanganuitanga at Pākaitore: the staunch determination of the people of te awa tupua.

And it was practised in the fledging movement of kura kaupapa Māori, the establishment of Te Oranganui and the momentum of the Māori Party.

It has also been powerfully demonstrated in the homes and lives of those closest to her, who learnt from Tariana the full expression of collective responsibility.

Alan talks about the many times his mother would ring and ask him to help over the years:

> She has a real strong sense of whānau and caring for people. She will ring up, 'I need you to go round to your brothers' and sisters' houses, collect up a whole lot of groceries, and drop them off at such and such address'. We won't even know them. Mum used to ring morning, night, whenever: 'I need you to do such and such; can you go and drop some firewood off to your nan?'

Alan sees her generosity demonstrated in many different ways:

> She's never been materialistic, Mum. She'd give you her last dollar; that's the type of person she is – she'll give somebody our last dollar too. With all the tangi she went to she must have just about given all her money away now as koha.

Inevitably the dreams that Tariana had became aspirations shared by the next generations. Alan, particularly, loves the concept of living collectively:

> If Mum had her way all us kids and our kids would be living together. At one part there she talked to us about combining our incomes and living collectively. We didn't like that idea, but as you get older, that's exactly how I'd like to live – just like a village, looking after one another. It's an idea that Mum's always held close to her heart. The marae was a huge part of Mum's life, and she made sure it was a huge part of ours too, which has been awesome.

Whānau Ora was indeed Tariana's greatest dream, the dream to be. As an opposition MP she had often given voice to the concept that underpinned Whānau Ora – that the well-being of whānau is crucial. For example, in 2006 she had told the House:

> It is time to stop the useless hand-wringing, the desperate blaming game, and the knee-jerk judgments that being Māori, being a teen parent, or being a single parent is the cause of this nation's woeful record. The Māori Party has consistently spoken of our desire to ensure that all people realise their potential, that the gifts and special qualities of every New Zealander are supported, and that our families are treasured as the collective cultural capital of Aotearoa. Gasping in horror or pointing the finger of blame will not achieve anything. We need to commit, as a nation, to protecting all our vulnerable, innocent tamariki through building a strong family network around them. And we can start that new beginning here, today, in this Parliament.[15]

For all of her working life, Tariana had been speaking about the need to focus at the level of whānau. She told Gordon Campbell in 2008:

> We are worried when we look at our families. Iwi development is important for the overall wellbeing of an iwi, for collective strength. However, we have to get resources as close as possible to where the greatest need is. And it's not at the iwi level. It is at the whanau and

hapu level, which is the collectives of whanau. That is where we want to see the greater focus in future.[16]

It needs to be said that long before Whānau Ora was established as an official government priority, Tariana had experienced frustration that the State would rather waste money than take a risk and place its faith in the people:

> People are learning how to establish themselves and be collective. There is marae. All marae have an administration group. There is no reason why we can't use marae to reach hapu and iwi. There is no reason why we can't use particular Maori organisations in urban settings to try and get the services, or the opportunities or even the money as close as possible to that level. The Government operates programmes that are based on need, they don't trust people to find their own solutions. What you've got is a lot of money being wasted because you have bureaucracy prescribing how to combat the issues that are confronting various communities, Maori communities, Pacific communities. Other people determine what the solutions will be, and how they will be achieved. You will never achieve them.[17]

When the Māori Party entered into a relationship with National, therefore, it was only a matter of when, rather than if, Whānau Ora would eventually emerge. Sir Wira Gardiner retraces some of the steps in the journey:

> It was not until 2008 that she was able finally to give expression for her cornerstone ideals now deeply enshrined in the policy of Whānau Ora. This policy was given political expression in 2010, and saw Tariana assert a hands-on leadership role in what was to become her legacy project. And our paths crossed again.

> Our relationship developed a little further in 2011 during the coalition talks when for some reason I got involved with negotiations with the National Party and the Māori Party, especially around the issue of Whānau Ora. Tariana was sitting four square at the table. She gave the impression she knew what she wanted and she was

determined to get it. I understood that Tariana did have difficulties with some National Party ministers, who were probably not used to her absolute determination and at times bloody-minded approach to the things she believed in. She has not only lived the principles which drive her but she has succeeded in bringing those principles to bear in what one might arguably suggest will be a huge legacy, and that is the Whānau Ora policy.

When Deborah Coddington interviewed Tariana during the 2011 election campaign, she asked her what would be her biggest drive in the next Parliament. Tariana replied:

> Delivery of Whanau Ora across every state agency and to all aspects of our lives, to Pakeha, Pasifika, migrant communities. While we can give a hand up we can also achieve vision, a focus of the future for famlies. If family is the problem then I firmly believe that family is also the solution.[18]

The 2008 Relationship Accord between the National and Māori Parties signalled a commitment to 'significant outcomes in Whānau Ora, through eliminating poverty, advocating for social justice and advancing Māori social, cultural, economic and community development in the best interests of the nation'.

In June 2009 the Whānau-Centred Taskforce was announced to find 'a better way for the government to deal with Māori whānau', as a press release of the time explained:

> 'Whānau Ora is the way forward to achieving a future where whānau determine what is in their best interests. How Whānau Ora will be applied to government policy will be the job of the taskforce and I'm extremely excited by the possibilities,' Mrs Turia said. The specific job of the taskforce will be to develop a policy framework for a new method of government interaction with Māori service providers to meet the social service needs of whānau.[19]

It was always going to be an ambitious mission. In the end, six people were appointed to the Taskforce. Each had 'expertise in whānau health, education, cultural transmission, social innovation, economics, justice, housing and service delivery'. Professor Sir Mason Durie was appointed the first chairperson of the Taskforce of Whānau-Centred Initiatives.

> I want to acknowledge the intellectual power, the formidable knowledge, the flax-roots experience, and above all the cultural competency of these five champions who comprise the Taskforce: Professor Durie; Rob Cooper; Suzanne Snively; Di Grennell and Nancy Tuaine. I want to make a special mention too, of Linda Grennell of Ngāi Tahu who would have dearly loved to have contributed had her health enabled that to happen, and I mihi to her today. Kia piki te ora ki a koe, Linda[20].

The Taskforce reported to Tariana on two-monthly intervals, releasing a consultation document in October 2009 and formally reporting back in January 2010. Between 7 October and 25 November 2009, hui were held in Gisborne, Ruatōria, Whakatāne, Rotorua, Hamilton/Hauraki, Invercargill, Dunedin, Whāngārei, Christchurch, Waitākere, Kaitāia, Kaikohe, Wellington, Wairarapa, Whanganui, Hāwera, Blenheim, Napier, Hastings, Auckland and Manukau. Twenty-two hui were held: sometimes two on one day. Over 600 attended and shared their views, and another hundred written submissions were received.

At many of the hui a waiata composed by the kuia Te Inupo Farrar, was sung:

Whānau Ora karanga
Karanga rā te kaupapa
I roto i te aroha
Whānau Ora kia kaha

The people responded to that call. They talked about the need for Whānau Ora to demonstrate a 'Māori heart', and about how to ensure local representation in decision-making. There was a cry for minimal bureaucracy, for sustainability and for adequate resourcing. The people spoke about the importance of research and evaluation, and shared their aspirations about how to create quality relationships between whānau, providers and iwi.

Tariana spent an enormous amount of time at hui, travelling, speaking and sharing the excitement of the approach. Yet she also maintained a fierce workload, delivering the third-highest number of ministerial speeches in the 2008–2011 Parliament (506 speeches), behind Minister of Justice, Hon Simon Power (564), and the Prime Minister (638).

Tariana has always said that Whānau Ora as an approach didn't start solely with her initiative. She explained on *Q+A* in 2010:

> The decisions must be made by the family; the family must themselves be aware that these are issues for them, and therein really lies the solution, re-empowering the family to take back control over their own situation, to determine the solutions that impact on them. This is something that has been around for a long time; it's not new. Sir Mason has been working on research in this area for some 25, 30 years, so you know we're not reinventing the wheel. What we're trying to do is to bring to fruition the aspirations of our people to take back responsibility and obligation.[21]

On 11 February 2010, the momentum of Whānau Ora took on a new energy, with a formal handing over of the Taskforce's report in the sacred space of Mātangareia, where the Māori Party had first had its offices in the early days of 2005.

On that occasion, Tariana was enthusiastic in her praise for the work of the Taskforce:

> I want to thank Professor Sir Mason Durie for his words of inspiration; his outstanding leadership of the Taskforce on Whānau-Centred Initiatives and the hope he gives us all, that Whānau Ora is the pathway towards the transformation of our people.
>
> We placed in their hands an awesome responsibility to test the waters for a new approach; an approach based on ways of old. We asked them to be challenged by hundreds of New Zealanders, to go out on the road to hear the stories, and then to return to Wellington with a whānau-centred framework which would lift outcomes in a meaningful and sustainable way.

Tariana attends a Whānau Ora hui at Kimiora Marae, Hamilton in November 2010.
Source: Fairfax NZ

Tariana with one of the architects of Whānau Ora, Professor Sir Mason Durie, on 8 March 2002, at the opening of Te Rau Matatini, a body established to provide Māori health and disability workforce solutions.
Source: Courtesy of Wanganui District Council

Tariana on 21 February 2013 announcing the Government's decision to bring in legislation to put tobacco products into plain packaging.
Source: Newspix.co.nz

Tariana attending the Waitangi Tribunal hearing into the ownership of water at Waiwhetū Marae, Lower Hutt in July 2013, wearing her trademark beret.
Source: Fairfax NZ

Tariana signing the Deed of Settlement for Te Āti Awa's settlement at Owae Marae, Waitara, on 9 August 2014 – one of her last official engagements as the MP for Te Tai Hauāuru.
Source: Fairfax NZ

Tariana and Marama Fox, old and new co-leaders, in front of Rangatāhuahua, following the Māori Party AGM of 1 November 2014.
Source: Chris Bramwell

Tariana with her ministerial office staff – Kat Paton (L), Tariana's daughter Lisa, Te Atarangi Whiu, Tariana, Helen Leahy, Ana Bidois and Shelly Rangihuna-Vlietstra – on the occasion of the Real Women's Duathlon on 10 April 2011 in Wellington.
Source: Jane Patterson, The Patter Ltd owner of the REAL Women's Duathlon Series

Te Ururoa, Tariana and Pita (with Te Rata Hikairo and Elijah Pue in the background) at an event following Tariana's valedictory speech at Wharewaka in Wellington on 24 July 2014.
Source: Gail Imhoff

Foundation members of the Māori Party Te Ururoa Flavell, Hon Dr Pita Sharples, Aunty Kiwa Hutchens and Tariana, marking the tenth anniversary of the Party at Te Papaiouru Marae, Ōhinemutu, Rotorua, on 12 July 2014.
Source: Cinzia Jonathan

Nancy Tuaine at the 20 Year Celebration of Pākaitore, 28 February 2015. Nancy says, 'Anyone who knows or has ever worked with Aunty Tariana knows that her work ethics and her work throughput is enormous, and her expectations of you if you work for her are enormous'.
Source: Gail Imhoff

Whatarangi Winiata, of whom Tariana says: 'I love the way Matua views the world. I love his gentleness. I think he is an absolute role model for our men. I love the notion of the use of kaupapa and tikanga and I've tried to live my life by that'.
Source: Gail Imhoff

You have been advocates, guardians, historians, campaigners, academics, entrepreneurs, writers, and policy analysts – all the while staying firmly fixed on multiple goals of how to demonstrate results, provide accountability for public funds and develop a brave new approach for the integration of funding and delivery of services. But more importantly you have been focused on the re-empowerment of whānau to be decision-makers; enabling them to be self-determining.[22]

The speech reinforced the focus on outcomes, as the NZPA reported:

In speech notes from the handover of the report today, which media were not invited to, Mrs Turia said the report called for integrated and coherent delivery systems.

The policy would require government agencies to be innovative and more flexible, she said.

'And perhaps for the first time, accountability for public spending will be for outcomes, rather than activity. This is about people being accountable for the difference they make.'[23]

Indeed, Whānau Ora is distinguished by its focus on outcomes. Tariana described the development of the approach as sequential:

The important first step in this process is integrating all of those contracts, so that the provider doesn't have to spend considerable time on compliance and transactional costs. The agencies have to reach an agreement around that and then those providers will then start preparing for a different approach, not doing to and for, but working in a much more transformational way with the family to accept that the responsibilities and the obligations for the issues that are confronting them lie with themselves. There'll be research running alongside: it's an outcomes approach, not an activity approach, so it will be considerably different to what we've got now.[24]

Sir Mason Durie also described the benefits of an outcomes-driven approach:

You'll be wanting to measure people by the outcomes they produce, not by the amount of work they do, and that's a very different sort of accountability. You'd expect that a Whānau Ora practitioner, if they're dealing with a whānau, they should be able to demonstrate that the whānau is better off financially, better off socially, more social cohesion, and better off culturally. They're broad areas I know, but they're indicators within all of those areas that will be useful in measuring the outcome: the accountability will be greater not less.[25]

And from then, it was all on. For Tariana's sixty-sixth birthday, she was given a distinctive present by the Prime Minister:

Prime Minister John Key has today appointed Hon. Tariana Turia as Minister Responsible for Whānau Ora. Mr Key says Mrs Turia's passion for Whānau Ora, coupled with her strong foundation work to date on the policy, will make her an effective and valuable leader of the initiative. 'Mrs Turia has worked tirelessly to make the Whānau Ora concept a reality, and she has a clear vision for how Whānau Ora will help New Zealand families. Mrs Turia will work closely with other relevant Government Ministers and the Whānau Ora Governance Group to oversee the roll-out and progress of Whānau Ora.'[26]

To cap her birthday off, Tariana joined with the Deputy Prime Minister in releasing the Taskforce's report, and announcing the appointment of a governance group to manage Whānau Ora. The group would be chaired by Rob Cooper, and include Professor Durie, Nancy Tuaine and three chief executives: Leith Comer (from Te Puni Kōkiri), Peter Hughes (from the Ministry of Social Development) and Stephen McKernan (from the Ministry of Health).

In announcing the basic framework, both Ministers English and Turia were careful to emphasise the value of the approach for all New Zealanders:

'Rather than having different agencies working with individual family members, Whānau Ora will work with whānau and families as a whole,' Mrs Turia says.

> 'It will empower them to take control by meeting their obligations and taking responsibility.
>
> 'By building on the strengths of the entire whānau, it will require agencies to work together in better and smarter ways to support whānau and families. I am confident that Whānau Ora has the potential to help all families, right across New Zealand'.[27]

Barely a month later, the Prime Minister announced that Whānau Ora would receive $134.3 million in funding over the next four years, and that the first wave of twenty Whānau Ora providers would be selected through an expressions of interest process to be initiated the following month. A press release stated:

> 'Mr Key says Whanau Ora contracts will be focused on results – meaning the providers will be held accountable for what they achieve with Government funding. Whanau Ora represents a significant change in how New Zealand delivers assistance to families. I believe this is a change for the better,' Mr Key says. This approach demands that families have their own plan. They have to be ambitious themselves – it's a higher trust model and it has the potential to deliver better results not only for families, but also for taxpayers who are not currently getting the value for money they should be.[28]

Whānau Ora received an additional $30 million in Budget 2011, and $15 million was appropriated in Budget 2014 to ensure whānau are able to access whānau navigators during the next phase.

As the approach evolved, Tariana grew frustrated with the operations of the three government agencies charged with its overview: the Ministry of Health, the Ministry of Social Development and Te Puni Kōkiri. She told Radio New Zealand:

> I guess my determination and it will still be my determination, I don't need to be a politician or to be in Parliament, to see that those agencies do not get focused on organisations but that they do get focused on making the changes for families and that the resources

should get as close to family as possible if we want to make the difference. Whānau Ora does not need to be delivered by a service provider – there are other organisations, family collectives, family trusts and marae who already deal with people in family settings who could be doing really important jobs.[29]

By June 2013, Tariana had established a new commissioning approach which involved three commissioning agencies: Te Pou Matakana in the North Island, Te Pūtahitanga o Te Wai Pounamu in the South and Pasifika Futures, charged with commissioning for Pacific families.

Tariana recommended that the Māori Housing Fund she had fought for and established as Associate Minister of Housing be assigned to Te Pou Matakana for administration and distribution. The concept of applying Whānau Ora more widely across the social policy sector was dear to her heart.

She also laid the groundwork for a payment-by-results regime to be overseen by Treasury and the Productivity Commission, in what the Māori Party 2011 Policy Manifesto described as 'Iwi Investment in Ourselves':

> Iwi investors implement a programme of actions on a payment-by-results basis in a model based on Social Impact Investment. If they meet their targets, the iwi investors will receive a financial return from Government. If they do not, investors will not get all their funding back. The model can be used for early intervention e.g. literacy skills; preschool readiness; recidivism, or employment for our most vulnerable.[30]

This demonstrates another important aspect of the Relationship Accord between the Māori Party and National: the increasing significance of the dialogue between iwi leaders and the Crown.

I have really valued the relationship. I have also valued the open door we have had, in that we have been able to get iwi leaders in and others – it is good to meet with them and meet with other ministers. That's never happened before. Political parties operate in a particular way; their power lies definitely in their leadership. We have had quite a different arrangement ourselves, because our party in representing our people ensures they have a greater say about things. We do go back to them, regularly, about significant issues that we are discussing with National to get some guidance from them.

We always hope that the platforms that we have laid down will continue and be seen as really important. I think that there will continue to be a role for the Māori Party. There will be some ministers who have not had that relationship with iwi leaders to discuss issues, and it is about the ministers also getting into respectful relationships with our people at the coalface.

Bill English reflects on the relationships brokered by the Māori Party and maintained by National Party ministers:

> One of the challenges for them was the growth of the iwi leaders process. It took us a wee while to figure it out: the combination of the democratic relationship and the Treaty relationship. I think she found that pretty uneasy, because she's not really an iwi person – she's a whānau person. But I think they showed respect and flexibility through what particularly early on was a pretty tense time.
>
> There had been a bit of an assumption in the Māori Party that they would be the gateway between Government and Māoridom in the way that some people we had dealt with had exploited that in the past. But actually when tested there was a kind of generosity there, which again is not that typical of politicians who are normally quite jealous of their constituency and their access.
>
> They ended up being the instigators and the incubators of what has been a pretty effective constitutional innovation in the way Government deals with the iwi leaders group. We've learned a lot from her about how Māori leadership works, because we were dealing with her every day, her and Pita, and learning about how we could successfully deal with this wider group. While there's certainly been tension, the coalition agreement and the iwi leaders group have

added up to something greater than the sum of the parts, which is now sufficiently successful that people take it for granted.

I think she can be confident that she has achieved certainly what I believe is one of the aims of the Māori Party, and that is a change in the nature of the relationship between Government and Māori in the practice of decision-making. It has changed that. That relationship has been turned from what was essentially a rhetorical one – people talked about it – like the relationship between Australia and New Zealand – to a now-tested practical one.

Some of the fruits of the relationship were easily visible in a raft of legislation that the Māori Party championed in the 2011–2014 Parliament.

There was the historic agreement between the Crown and Te whānau a Mokomoko relating to statutory recognition of the free pardon granted to Mokomoko by the Governor-General. Mokomoko was tried and executed in 1866 for his alleged role in the murder of Rev. Carl Sylvius Völkner, a crime that Mokomoko consistently denied. The Mokomoko (Restoration of Character, Mana, and Reputation) Bill was passed to address the shame and stigma the whānau had carried for so long. Te Ururoa pushed through the Mount Maunganui Borough Reclamation and Empowering Act Repeal Bill in 2012, which repealed prior legislation that had authorised the council to undertake reclamation of the harbour for sewerage; trampling over the mana of the ancestral landscape of Ngā Pōtiki. In the following year Te Ururoa led the New Zealand Mission Trust Board (Otamataha) Empowering Bill, which transferred certain assets of the Mission Trust for the benefit of the hapū of Ngāti Tapu and Ngaitamarāwaho. Tariana led legislation to give effect to the deed of settlement entered into by the Crown and the descendants of the original owners of the Maraeroa A and B blocks, as a local bill in her electorate.

There were other tangible gains, such as the $5-million-dollar fund, Te Mana o Te Wai, announced in Budget 2014 to specifically build on the leadership of iwi in maintaining the health of fresh water. Iwi leadership was actively involved in providing advice to guide the National Policy Statement on Freshwater Management. Specific budget provision for their ongoing involvement in protecting and promoting water quality was a negotiated gain that could ensure action on that strategy. The Policy Statement says:

> The Treaty of Waitangi (Te Tiriti o Waitangi) is the underlying foundation of the Crown–iwi/hapū relationship with regard to freshwater resources. Addressing tāngata whenua values and interests across all of the well-beings, and including the involvement of iwi and hapū in the overall management of fresh water, are key to meeting obligations under the Treaty of Waitangi.[31]

Right up until the day before the National Policy Statement was released, Tariana kept the pressure on about the need for iwi leaders to be kept closely informed about developments related to freshwater reform.

Similarly, when it came to the Resource Management Act, Tariana was always very clear that the legislation had to be consistent with the aspirations of hapū and iwi. In 2013, in relation to proposed changes to the Act, TVNZ's *One News* reported:

> Maori Party Co-leaders Tariana Turia and Te Ururoa Flavell have made it clear they will not support legislation that breaches the rights and responsibilities of hapu and iwi.
>
> Co-leaders Tariana Turia and Te Ururoa Flavell said it was only through the advocacy of their party that they retained the Treaty of Waitangi clause in the Act.
>
> Ms Turia said they are pleased the clause has been retained in the latest reform but are disappointed the reform proposals are 'a missed opportunity to advance the concept of co-governance with iwi in freshwater planning'.
>
> 'The Land and Water Forum recommended a national body with 50:50 co-governance – instead this appears to have been reduced to iwi having "a seat" on collaborative stakeholder groups'.[32]

As the term progressed, mutual opposition to the proposed changes by the Māori Party and United Future in effect blocked the Government from being able to proceed. The influence of the Māori Party's relationships with iwi were pivotal. A party press release stated in May 2014:

> The Māori Party is pleased that its refusal to compromise on environmental values has defeated plans to fundamentally rewrite the Resource Management Act in favour of commercial interests. 'Our priority was always about maintaining environmental protections in the context of kaitiakitanga/guardianship,' said Co-leader Tariana Turia. 'Environment management issues are tangata whenua issues, so we gave considerable priority to consulting amongst whānau, hapū and iwi, to read the lay of the land as they saw it. The RMA is a framework that all hapū and iwi would need to work within so it was important that we got the balance right. Tangata whenua take seriously their role as stewards of the natural environment, and in this light the Māori Party were supportive of the move to make consenting procedures more efficient as long as the quality of the environment retained central importance,' said Mrs Turia.[33]

If opposition to changes to the Resource Management Act was one of the distinguishing features of the National–Māori Party relationship in 2011–2014, it was the political impact of measures associated with goods and services tax (GST) that had stood out in the previous term and the associated focus on poverty that arose out of the GST debacle that would dominate the next term, the 2014-2017 parliament.

In 2010 Rahui Katene had put forward a Bill to exempt healthy foods from GST, but the Bill had failed at its first reading on 8 September. While Rahui's Bill had attracted a certain amount of interest, it was overshadowed by National's decision to increase GST in the 2010 Budget: the same Budget that had invested $134 million in Whānau Ora.

> I remember the most difficult period with National was when they increased GST. That came out of left field – we were not expecting it. They hadn't told us that they were going to increase GST as part of confidence and supply. I was devastated. If I had had my way I would have voted against them, but of course we had signed up, and so we had to be disciplined. We were very much opposed to it.

I was beside myself. I knew it would hugely impact on our families, because all of their income was disposable, so I knew that it would affect them just because of purchasing their food. They would have been struggling just with paying their food, their power, their rent. That took up almost all of their income, let alone to add another 2.5 percent on to it. Our people don't have extra money sitting there to adjust their budget. Most of them wouldn't have had that sort of money, and we were extremely worried.

There was a meeting with John Key and Bill English. If I recall, I think I walked out and said that we needed to talk about it ourselves. We weren't going to talk about it in front of them. We had a very testy discussion about it. It was really difficult. I felt resentful that we hadn't been told right at the initial stage of our relationship that they were going to do that.

It really showed me how little they knew about people who were poor. But you know poverty isn't a new experience for us. I do get fed up with the way that Labour and the Greens talk about poverty, because they talk about it as if it's a new phenomenon and it's only just happened in the last six years.

As a direct result of the GST fiasco, when it came time to form a new relationship accord after the 2011 election, Tariana was adamant about the need to target support for vulnerable families. In announcing the focus of the new relationship, Tariana highlighted the continuation of Whānau Ora and the call to address poverty as the two key features:

> The Māori Party has today signed a Relationship Accord with the National Party, to enable progress to be made in advancing Whānau Ora while at the same day placing poverty on the Government's agenda.

> 'We are very pleased to have secured a commitment to extend the reach, coverage and capability of Whānau Ora', said Mrs Turia. 'The establishment of a stand-alone commissioning entity is an important step in advancing opportunities for our whānau to be self-determining.'

> 'The cost of living was also a significant concern for us in heading into negotiations. We are very conscious that over the last decade

power prices have risen by 87% and so our negotiators argued to target an additional 20,000 warm homes, recognising also the obvious connection to health outcomes.'

'We welcome the Government's agreement with the Māori Party to establish a Ministerial Committee on Poverty. The initiatives in environment, housing, employment and training and education are significant gains in helping to alleviate poverty.'[34]

Tariana spent the final term of her ministerial life doing everything she could in her capacity as Deputy Chair of the Ministerial Committee on Poverty to lift the quality of people's lives.

As the first budget approached in 2012, Tariana reflected on the gains that had been made.

The Māori Party was very keen to look at the state of housing, and we have been able to achieve some progress in that area, given the high levels of rheumatic fever and the poor quality of too much housing.

A lot of it has come through our negotiations with the Government. We have had an external group providing advice to the ministerial committee. We have listened to the advisory panel headed by the Children's Commissioner and then in our negotiations, the Māori Party with the Government, these are the initiatives that we think will make the biggest difference in families' lives.

It is addressing a range of needs within families. We have heard there is extra money going into budgeting services, but there are other things that families have great difficulty with in terms of meeting the costs that will come through in this budget. One of the big issues we have been very worried about ever since we have been in Parliament has been the role of loan sharks, so the budget enabled us to really investigate and pilot partnerships looking at that issue.

The work Tariana led in the prevention, treatment and management of rheumatic fever brought her international attention. In May 2014, she was invited to be a guest speaker at the World Heart Foundation's congress in Melbourne. She shared with the conference the fact that the New Zealand Government, under her watch, had invested more than $65 million to tackle rheumatic fever in vulnerable communities, with the aim of reducing rates by two-thirds by 2017. *NZ Doctor* reported her rationale:

> I pushed to get it placed high on the Government's health agenda, so we could start a campaign to stamp out this preventable, avoidable, unnecessary Third-World disease.[35]

Tariana told the congress that no one could be proud of the inequality in New Zealand evidenced by the fact that about 550 hospitalisations and 140 deaths occurred for rheumatic heart disease each year:

> At least 90% of rheumatic fever cases are in Māori and Pasifika children … This profile is totally unacceptable to me. No ethnic groups or geographical communities should be disadvantaged by higher rates of rheumatic fever.

In addressing the congress Tariana referred to her invitation from the World Heart Federation, in which New Zealand had been described as a 'shining star in a wasteland of neglect'. In her classic, hard-hitting style, she played down any suggestion that New Zealand's efforts stood out as worthy of praise:

> I want to say, first and foremost, that the wasteland metaphor is as apt a description of our setting as any other jurisdiction. I have frequently said to audiences at home that no-one can be proud of the inequities that we have witnessed. We should be ashamed that we are still seeing the impact of a preventable third world disease upon different groups across New Zealand.[36]

The ability to say what she thinks is right, even if it creates backlash, is a quality that distinguishes Tariana from many other politicians. In her last two terms as a minister, as she had done in her first two terms, Tariana again scrutinised the delivery of family violence services for their effectiveness. On 1 April 2011, she announced an initiative to channel funding to services at the front line 'so that families in crisis are kept safe and are supported to be resilient and strong so the whole family can return to a state of wellbeing'. While the overall level of funding for family violence remained the same, it would now be more tightly focused on supporting vulnerable families: the place where it would have the greatest impact. Of the $11 million invested in family violence, the great bulk ($8.5 million) would now be channelled into:

> … the Family-Centred Services Fund for direct services to families and whānau where family violence has occurred, to restore their safety and wellbeing and help to create longer-term changes to prevent family violence from reoccurring.[37]

There was a rapid reaction from the sector. Headlines revealed the extent of the backlash: 'Fears family violence will rise if funding recedes'; 'Taking from Te Rito [New Zealand Famly Violence Prevention Strategy] a questionable move'; 'Cuts to family violence funding no good says Waves [Waitakere Anti-violence Essential Services]'. In response to the negative reaction, Tariana submitted an opinion piece to the *Dominion* that explained that, in making the decision, she had reviewed the funding spent on perpetrators, victims, advocates and agencies; she had talked to providers dealing with family violence, the judiciary, reference groups and agency advisers; she had read countless reports; she had visited front-line services; and she had sat in the family court on the days that family violence cases featured, to find solutions:

> Though the 'It's not OK' campaign has achieved a significant increase in awareness of the key message, it would be irresponsible to raise awareness without having the services to respond to the heightened demand. I have made the call to shift our emphasis into frontline services, to directly respond to the call from families for help. When I was a child, we had no such thing as social workers in schools, family violence advocates, victim support. In fact I didn't even go to a doctor until I was 15. But we did have plenty of aunts and uncles, nannies

and koros who kept their watchful gaze on us all. My concern, today, is that we too often forget those natural supports.

Providers have become de facto family, managing a seemingly bottomless pit of resources that can be sought for those who manage to master the system.

I want us to reinvigorate our families into taking up their full responsibility for their own. As a society we have become accustomed to branding families as dysfunctional – certain families become 'code' for all that is wrong in our communities. It is time to place more faith back in our families. My intentions in reallocating the funding to frontline services is that we invest in our families by equipping them with tools to transform their homes into sites of safety; where their liberation is based in their own self-education and empowerment. Helping agencies will always be a vital backstop for community change. But we must not allow ourselves to lose sight of the most vital platform for transformation – and that will always be frontline with our families.[38]

There were other aspects of the April 2011 announcement that received scant media attention: a commitment of $500,000 funding for the E Tū Whānau campaign, building on whānau strengths within the context of Te Ao Maori, and $500,000 to address violence within Pasifika families. Another $1 million was designated to implement a training programme for Pacific providers to provide culturally appropriate interventions to victims of family violence and their families.

The investment in Pasifika solutions to family violence was one of Tariana's most exciting initiatives in her latter days as a minister. The development and publication of the Pacific Family Violence Framework, Nga Vaka o Kāiga Tapu, wove together strands of knowledge and culture from seven different Pacific nations (the Cook Islands, Fiji, Niue, Sāmoa, Tokelau, Tonga and Tuvalu). Each strand was treated as a culture-specific model; cumulatively, the strands came together within the Pacific Conceptual Framework to address family violence. Nga Vaka o Kāiga Tapu was inspired and managed by the

Pacific Advisory Group on family violence. The group established a series of regional fono, leading to a national gathering called the Champions of Change fono. The conclusion that emerged unchallenged was that culture must be the basis for constructing solutions to family violence.

Tariana was profoundly moved by the initiative, the visions and the culturally specific insights that resulted. She genuinely believes that we are our ancestors: that our ancestors have left us many gifts with which to protect their visions, and honour them in today's world. In her mind, Nga Vaka o Kāiga Tapu was a fantastic expression of cultural strength as a means of achieving well-being. It was the same approach that underpins Whānau Ora as a model for collective development.

The respect was mutual. The love shared between Pasifika peoples and Tariana was a genuine love that drew her to them and them to her; a connection of hearts and minds. In introducing the Framework, Fa'amatuainu Tino Pereira, chair of the Pacific Advisory Group, said:

> PAG owes a debt of gratitude to a true friend of the Pacific, Hon Tariana Turia, for her invaluable commitment to our journey and making funding available to help kickstart our search and implementation of our solutions to family violence.
>
> Tariana, *ia manuia ou faiva ma ia fa'afualoa e le Matai Sili lou soifua* – may your endeavours continue to be blessed, and may the Almighty Matai give you long life.[39]

As Tariana approached her last years as a minister, her output was prodigious; her appetite for challenge all the more extraordinary. She travelled many times to the Chatham Islands, treasuring the rugged terrain and the remote landscape, ever conscious of the need to provide tangible support there to those who needed it most. In January 2014 she attended a community hui in the Chathams, signalling her commitment to support the people:

> I have to admit, coming from a smaller rural community outside of Whanganui, I certainly appreciate the gritty determination and fierce independence that defines the way in which you live. But the fact that you have nerves of steel should not disqualify you from receiving

the very best support and care in improving the quality of your lives. And I say that because sometimes, when we say communities are resilient, we then mean we'll leave them alone – and this is not what this is about![40]

Six months later she announced new funding of $16 million over four years to support the improvement of housing on the Chatham Islands. At the same time, she announced investment in the repair and rebuild of rural housing, and the development of Māori social housing providers.

Another of Tariana's initiatives – one no doubt influenced by her rich memories of Te Awa Youth Trust – was the employment and skills project known as Community Max, and the Māori and Pasifika Trades Training scheme that followed.

Community Max was an example of the Māori Party and National joining together for mutual goals with different purposes. When it was announced in August 2009, the concept was that unemployed youth living in rural areas would directly benefit from some 3000 employment opportunities involving local projects of up to six months' duration, through a $40.3 million government investment. National's motivation was to reduce the numbers of young people aged sixteen to twenty-four on the unemployment or independent youth benefit, whereas Tariana was optimistic about the opportunity the scheme offered communities to work together with young people. The young people would receive at least the minimum wage, while strengthening their relationships with iwi, marae, Māori trust boards, Māori land incorporations and councils. In introducing the project, Tariana said: 'I've always been a great believer in communities knowing what's best for them and this initiative aims to support them in doing that.'[41]

Ten months later, an extension of the scheme was announced, investing an additional $17.4 million into high-unemployment areas, and providing opportunities for another 1500 young people. In the press release announcing the extension, the difference between the two political philosophies involved was obvious:

> 'It is really pleasing to know that 82% who've completed it have so far remained off a benefit, with 43% of those currently in work or training and gaining real life skills,' says Ms Bennett.

> 'Most importantly, disconnected young people are engaging with their communities and in turn, communities are taking responsibility for nurturing and encouraging their young people to develop their potential,' says Mrs Turia.[42]

Three years down the track, Tariana teamed up with a different National Party minister, Steven Joyce, to create employment opportunities, strengthen communities and ensure sustainable outcomes. The two announced an investment of $43 million to extend the number of Māori and Pasifika Trades Training places to 3000:

> 'We have seen some great results emerge from the new approaches trialled in the He Toki ki te Rika and Pasifika Trades schemes to improve opportunities in education and employment for young Māori and Pasifika; and this initiative builds on that success.'

> 'The extra training places will come from innovative partnerships between Māori and Pasifika organisations, tertiary training providers, and employers. Government agencies, complemented by social support organisations, will provide support and funding,' Mrs Turia says. 'This partnership model is flexible and responsive to meet the needs of Māori and Pasifika communities as well as delivering outcomes which are useful and relevant for employers.'[43]

The hallmarks of all these initiatives – strengthening communities, encouraging the spirit of self-reliance, promoting collaboration and focusing on outcomes – are pure Tariana. In her work throughout her final years in Parliament, there was one area of focus in which these strands were intricately and intimately linked, and that was the area of disabilities.

When Tariana become Minister for Disability Issues in 2009, she said she wanted to help create a more inclusive New Zealand, change attitudes and address a disabling society. But she had also come to the disability portfolio with a certain amount of trepidation. In a free and frank interview with Tanya Black for the AttitudeLive website (which produces short documentaries pertaining to disability and chronic health) she revealed:

> I was incredibly nervous. I felt that it was such an important portfolio for a very marginalised group of people and so I was a little bit scared that I wouldn't do it justice. I don't think you are allowed to say no when you are being asked to do certain things. I wasn't as confident.[44]

In the interview, Tariana shared her views about how the Māori culture responded to issues around disability:

> One of the things that struck me and something I had never realised was that with blind people there were some marae that wouldn't allow them to take their dogs in with them into the wharepuni. It stunned me because I thought we would be flexible enough with our tikanga. Tikanga means doing the right thing. It doesn't mean having something that is imposed for no reason. I was also really saddened to hear that in some cases, people in wheelchairs were told that they couldn't speak on the marae because they couldn't stand. Oh my god. We have got to work out what is the right thing to do because that's what tikanga tells us. It made me look at home. I'm very much a marae person and it did make me think about all the things on the marae that we could change to accommodate. We have a lot of work to do.[45]

Tariana shared how much she had learnt, and how much she valued the approach that people with disabilities had demonstrated in working with her:

> I was worried about how I would work with the disability community. I realised that as they came to my office they never came about things that they could not do. They came to tell me what they could do. I loved the proactive nature of the sector and I realised that all I had to do was to listen really carefully and then to use my role as an advocate to be the most powerful advocate that I could be on their behalf.[46]

Tariana used her influence to introduce a range of initiatives to improve the lives of those living with disabilities. Budget 2013 invested $6 million in extending the Think Differently campaign, to increase the participation of disabled people in all aspects of community life and change social attitudes and behaviours. The campaign aimed to develop inclusive environments and build the capacity of both disabled and non-disabled people to lead change.

There was funding to increase the number of houses built to universal design standards to accommodate the needs of people of all ages and life stages, so that New Zealand homes are more usable and safer for all.

The 2013 Budget also invested more than $2.5 million in the Enabling Good Lives project. The Enabling Good Lives approach is about changing disability support and services so that disabled people spend less time at providers' facilities and more time in their own communities.

> I think through Enabling Good Lives people are having much more control over their decision-making, being able to determine what's in their best interests, I like that. I know that there were some providers who were nervous about it because the more autonomy that you give to a family and a disabled person to make decisions for themselves the less likely they are to choose some of the things that are being offered through service providers. But in the end our job really is to do what is in their best interests, to give them back their autonomy to decide.

Many other initiatives that Tariana introduced in the five years she was Minister for Disability Issues bear mentioning. An important step in consolidating sector gains was the creation of the Convention Coalition, comprised of seven disabled people's organisations. The Coalition is one of three partners recognised by the Government as responsible for the independent monitoring of the United Nations Convention on the rights of Persons with Disabilities. (The others are the Human Rights Commission and the Office of the Ombudsman.) Tariana saw the Coalition as a critical means of enabling disabled people to monitor their rights, as well as giving them access to relevant ministers and agencies. She told Tanya Black:

> I would like to think that the legacy would be that we have a ministerial group and group of CEOS from across the agencies who are prepared to have the disability sector come in to tell them how it could be. Because then everyone can learn from it.

Disability comes across every agency. It's not a portfolio that you can just put into health and leave it there. To keep bringing those ministers and the agency CEOs together is to understand the change that they need to make is really critical. I think if you go into the portfolio realising and understanding that others know more than you do; that the disability community in fact are very clear about what should be happening in the sector. We should be able to listen to them clearly.[47]

Suddenly, before she had even realised it, the 2014 election campaign had begun. Tariana Turia's parliamentary career was rapidly coming to an end.

We look now to the next generation of Māori Party MPs: Te Ururoa Flavell, the new Minister for Māori Development, Minister for Whānau Ora, and Associate Minister of Economic Development; and Marama Fox, a member of the Justice and Electoral and Māori Affairs Select Committees, over-brimming with energy and enthusiasm to carry on the example set by Tariana. The candidates who stood to represent the Party in the 2014 elections were of an impressive calibre. New president Naida Glavish has an awesome responsibility to nurture the leaders of tomorrow, as they bravely carry the kaupapa forward.

We turn also, to all the champions Tariana has helped to nurture. The defenders of Whānau Ora: Pati Umaga, Charmeyne Te Nana-Williams, Piri Rurawhe, Brendon Pongia, Nancy Tuaine. The hero of the disability sector: Minnie Baragwanath, who encourages us to simply Be Amazing. The architects and designers of Nga Vaka o Kāiga Tapu, and of E Tū Whānau (family violence), who are doing what they love best to create homes of safety, where all whānau can thrive.

We will watch, with eager anticipation, Tariana's children and mokopuna, as they proudly bear the flame of her magic in their own whānau and wider society too.

Tariana has been the leader of a lifetime – a champion for whānau, a crusader for our babies, a vigilante for doing what is right. She has led a transformation in thinking; a revolution in our homes. Her sheer determination to seek justice is legendary; her irrepressible energy left us all awestruck.

The greatest hope we can hold on to is that her consistent courage, her innate determination to do what is right, and her ways of knowing and being will be protected, preserved and upheld by all who follow. She has challenged us to look beyond the barriers; to dig deep and find that mettle that we need to demand better, to live happier, to share, to believe, to have faith.

NOTES

1 'Turia reveals plan for MPs to desert labour', 2 March 2014, *tvnz.co.nz*: http://tvnz.co.nz/politics-news/turia-reveals-plan-mps-desert-labour-5855565 (accessed 11 May 2015).

2 'Maori Party President continues in role', *3 News*, 17 October 2009.

3 Audrey Young, 'Call for Harawira to quit will cause Maori Party chaos', *Otago Daily Times*, 14 November 2009.

4 The main impact of emissions trading for households would be a rise in transport fuel and electricity prices. Costs for householders would be halved through amendments to legislation.

5 *Q+A*, 18 October 2009.

6 Māori Party press release, 'Māori Party to vote against ETS Bill', 24 October 2012.

7 Hone Harawira, 'Crunch time for Maori grumbles', *Sunday Star-Times*, 16 January 2011.

8 'Pem Bird new Māori Party President', 1 November 2010, *tangatawhenua.com*: http://news.tangatawhenua.com/2010/11/pem-bird-new-maori-party-president-waatea-news (accessed 20 May 2015).

9 Tariana Turia, Beehive Chat, 28 June 2011.

10 'Election 2011: Labour holds on in Dunedin South stronghold', *New Zealand Herald*, 27 November 2011.

11 Māori Party, *Our Whānau; Our Future*, Policy Manifesto, 2011, p. 1.

12 Tariana Turia, 'Whānau Ora', address to Chapman Tripp Breakfast Series, 29 March 2011.

13 Eva Peron, cited in Tejvan Pettinger, 'Biography of Eva Peron', Oxford, www.biographyonline.net, 1 January 2008 (accessed 17 June 2015).

14 Tariana Turia, interview with Eru Rerekura and Chris Bramwell, *Te Waonui a te Manu Korihi*, Radio New Zealand, 10 August 2014.

15 *Hansard*, 21 June 2006.

16 'Gordon Campbell interviews Tariana Turia', 21 April 2008, *Scoop Independent News*: http://gordoncampbell.scoop.co.nz/2008/04/21/gordon-campbell-interviews-tariana-turia/ (accessed 16 February 2015).

17 Ibid.

18 Deborah Coddington, 'Dining with the leaders: Whanau focus fuels final charge', *New Zealand Herald*, 20 November 2011.

19 Tariana Turia, press release, 'Whānau Ora Taskforce announced', 14 June 2009.

20 Tariana Turia, 'Handover of Report from the Taskforce on Whānau-Centred Initiatives', 11 February 2010: www.beehive.govt.nz/speech/handover-report-taskforce-whanau-centred-initiatives (accessed 11 February 2015).

21 *Q+A*, 4 April 2010.

22 Tariana Turia, 'Handover of Report from the Taskforce on Whānau-Centred Initiatives, 11 February 2010: www.beehive.govt.nz/speech/handover-report-taskforce-whanau-centred-initiatives (accessed 11 February 2015).

23 NZPA, 'Whanau Ora Taskforce Report Goes To Government', 11 February 2015.

24 *Q+A*, 4 April 2010.

25 *Q+A*, 4 April 2010.

26 John Key, press release, 'PM appoints Whanau Ora Minister', 8 April 2010: www.beehive.govt.nz/release/pm-appoints-whanau-ora-minister (accessed 17 February 2015).

27 Bill English, press release, 'Government welcomes Whanau Ora report', 8 April 2010: www.tpk.govt.nz/_documents/press-release-govt-welcomes-whanau-ora-report.pdf (accessed 17 February 2015).

28 John Key, press release, 'Budget 2010 – Whanau Ora launches with $134.3m', 6 May 2010: www.beehive.govt.nz/release/budget-2010-whanau-ora-launches-1343m (accessed 17 February 2015).

29 *Te Waonui a te Manu Korihi*, Radio New Zealand 15 October 2014.

30 Māori Party *Our Whānau; Our Future*, Policy Manifesto 2011 p. 6.

31 National Policy Statement for Freshwater Management, 4 July 2014, p. 3.

32 Widespread opposition to RMA changes, 10 August 2013, *One News*.

33 Māori Party press release, 'Māori Party Holds the Line on RMA', 20 May 2014.

34 Māori Party press release, 'Transformation and Poverty at the Heart of Relationship', 11 December 2011: www.scoop.co.nz/stories/PA1112/S00070/transformation-and-poverty-at-the-heart-of-relationship.htm (accessed 17 February 2015).

35 Denise Piper, 'Health inequalities unacceptable, says Turia', *NZ Doctor*, 9 May 2014.

36 Tariana Turia, press release, 'All about equity: Building political will for rheumatic fever prevention in New Zealand', speech to the World Congress of Cardiology, 6 May 2014.

37 Tariana Turia, press release, 'Funding for family violence focuses on frontline services', 1 April 2011: www.scoop.co.nz/stories/PA1104/S00057/funding-for-family-violence-focuses-on-frontline-services.htm (accessed 17 February 2015).

38 Tariana Turia, 'Focus must be on helping the families', *Dominion Post*, 6 April 2011.

39 *Nga Vaka o Kāiga Tapu: A Pacific Conceptual Framework to address family violence in New Zealand*, 2012, p. iv.

40 Tariana Turia, 'Wharekauri, Rēkohu, Chatham Islands Health and Social Needs', speech, 14 January 2014.

41 Tariana Turia, press release, 'Rural Youth to benefit from full wage subsidy', 2 August 2009: www.beehive.govt.nz/release/rural-youth-benefit-full-wage-subsidy (accessed 17 February 2015).

42 National Party, press release, 'Community Max programme expanded', 24 June 2010: www.national.org.nz/news/news/media-releases/detail/2010/06/24/community-max-programme-expanded (accessed 17 February 2015).

43 Steven Joyce, Tariana Turia, press release, 'Budget 2013: Expansion of Māori and Pasifika trades training', 9 May 2013. *Scoop Independent News*: www.scoop.co.nz/stories/PA1305/S00157/budget-2013-expansion-of-maori-and-pasifika-trades-training.htm (accessed 17/2/ February 2015).

44 Tanya Black, *Tariana Turia's Legacy*. Video for AttitudeLive website: http://attitudelive.com/blog/tanya-black/film-tariana-turias-legacy (accessed 20 May 2015).

45 Ibid.

46 Ibid.

47 Ibid.

-CHAPTER TWENTY-FIVE-
A MOTHER'S LEGACY

'There have been times when I have wept with rage. It's very rare for you to put up a proposal and have all of your colleagues say "what a great idea". No, they think about how many votes will we lose if they go with this idea.' It has been enough for her to question her time in Parliament. 'I look back and I think to myself, "was there a purpose?"' Tariana Turia turns 70 soon and after a career she describes as draining and tiresome, she says it's time for whānau.[1]

Throughout every stage of Tariana's life story, a central theme has been the determination to make a positive difference in the lives of her children. One anecdote shared by her brother demonstrates the extent she would go to in order to protect her children and keep them warm within the love of whānau.

Wilson was a prison officer, and in light of his role as a public servant, unable to be politically involved. Inevitably his sister's influence, particularly as Associate Minister of Corrections, would impact on his work. He says: 'I used to hear all the Pākehās at work running her down. I used to say, "excuse me, but you're talking about my sister", and that would shut them up.'

What really got Wilson's colleagues talking one day was when Tariana's son Mark was in Kaitoke Prison and the authorities sought to transfer him to another prison. Wilson says:

> She stood in front of the prison bus to try and stop his transfer when they transferred him out of here. Staff out there were running her down and what, and one of the bosses said, 'if every mother was like that we wouldn't have anybody in here'.

Tariana's youngest son, Pahia, also speaks of the incredible commitment his mother gave to supporting her children to be the best that they can be:

> Mum always invested a lot of time in us. She wanted nothing but the very best. Right from when I was really young Mum used to always say to me, 'you're going to be the Prime Minister'. She always expected that we were going to be something great; we weren't just going to be anything, we were going to be something great.

A pivotal factor in Tariana's decision to leave Parliament emerged when she least expected it.

1 July 2013. The phone rang. It was a blocked call. I'd take pot luck – I'm not one for playing cautious.
   It was Pita. 'I wanted to tell you before the media got to you', he said. ('Too late', I thought; I'd already been given the tip-off and asked for comment.) 'I told my electorate tonight that I won't be standing again next year, and that I intend to stand down at the AGM'.

A Mother's Legacy

Awkward silence. And then it came. A flash flood of tears; I was sobbing, breathless, unable to speak. It was all too much, too hard. Waves of grief were plunging me into a dark hole from which I was struggling to see a way out.

'I'll have to go, Pita', I said, and ended the call abruptly, fiercely trying to compose myself.

Get a grip. In usual circumstances I'd be right into action mode. Arrange an urgent conference call with the National Council: our members need to know first. Get all our staff on a call and start planning out the steps for the next twenty-four hours. Better craft up a statement. Ring John and give him a heads-up. Make contact with Pem. Think about our lines – it was more important than ever to be singing off the same song sheet.

But this wasn't 'usual circumstances'.

Moments before I'd answered that call, there had been another. My son Micky (Pahia), reporting on the verdict for his brother Alan after the doctor's round. He told me that it had been determined that my first-born, the boy born with a halo in place, had suffered a stroke two days earlier. So here I sat in the ministerial car, my plans for the night suddenly disrupted, my sense of reality shattered by the winds of misfortune that we were all reeling from. We made our way to the hospital.

It had been only two months ago that we'd celebrated Alan's fiftieth birthday at home, at Whangaehu. It had been an amazing night. The marae was transformed into a barnyard, everyone dressed on theme, with plenty of Alan's trademark Red Band gumboots in force. It had been a carnival of love, of laughter and of the sheer joy of being with each other.

We'd had almost 200 of us there: just close whānau. In our immediate Turia whānau we count six children, twenty-six mokopuna and twenty-eight mokopuna tuarua, and still counting. They are our living legacy; everything I do is with their future in mind. My love has known no boundaries from this union George and I started out on over five decades ago. I have been so lucky.

I was trying to remember that as I sat in the organised chaos of Ward 7 South: an artificial time zone in which the world stands still. Hushed conversations occur, set against the incessantly shrill distraction of the machines that keep people alive. Our lights are dimmed, but the cubicle next door has all beams on high alert. The air is dry with a stifling heat; the pace is set by erratic movements from family or nursing staff. There is no pattern to the activity – every human heartbeat demands a different line of attack.

I've had my cry. Alan had cried too; he's so vulnerable, so scared. He'd always hated the thought of a stroke. Before he'd gone under he'd told me point-blank: he'd rather be gone than to have a stroke and end up changed beyond recognition. I'd told him not to think like that; that so many of our loved ones had come back from situations of despair and still managed to recover, rebuild and restore a good quality of life. But Alan wouldn't listen then, and I knew it would be all he would be thinking about now.

I kept talking the faith talk, to remind myself of hope, but my heart broke to see him so sick. On a drip because he wasn't eating or drinking enough. All of us having to accept it will be a long slow journey ahead.

Ultimately perhaps Tariana's greatest legacy will live on through the influence and inspiration she has been for those closest to her – her children, her mokopuna, her mokopuna tuarua. But while the children all wear her influence in their lives as a badge of honour, they also know, better than anyone else, the toll her job as a parliamentarian took. Before her retirement, Alan said:

> It's been hard for her. She'd ring back here crying: just wanted to talk, saying how much she hates the place. I hate the hours that she works – she works far too long. It annoys me when I hear people talking about lazy politicians. I know some of the hours that she works. Dad's the same – he doesn't know when to stop. I notice that when you travel with her you can go to three or four different hui during the day – each one's totally different – and she's able to just shift from this mindset to that one, and be so in touch and on target.

Pahia notes:

> It was hard for Dad too – I think amongst all of this, through Mum's journey, Dad's been her rock. I don't think people really appreciate what Dad's given up to have Mum doing what she's done – he's pretty much said farewell to his wife. I suppose as a family we have all had to share her with so many others, but out of anybody Dad's probably the one who's born the brunt of that.

As Tariana's retirement approached, Pahia also shared his concerns that the impact of a caustic political chamber was impacting negatively on his mother's attitude to life:

> I think more recently Mum's become very cynical about everything. It's worried me a little bit. Her and I have had a couple of humdingers. She'll question me about things that fundamentally hurt me – I think to myself, 'why would you need to question me on those things, Mum?' I can assure you that our iwi are very focused on the fact that our success is only going to be as great as those of our most vulnerable families. I say to her, 'Mum, I expect you to have my back and have faith in me, just like I have in you.' I really think it's time for her to leave – I thought it was time for her to leave at the last election. There's never going to be a good time, and the point is that if the Māori Party has got to a point where someone becomes indispensable, then we're screwed. It's time for her to hang up her boots and just call it a day.

It takes a certain type of person to withstand constant challenge, and still go back for more. Alan says:

> She's a really strong woman. I've seen her come out of some really ugly situations, whether with family or with politics; she's always stood strong and still loves that family, doesn't matter how big the raru was. I've been at marae hui where they've had the biggest, ugliest arguments. She might be hurt for a week, but she still loves them and cares for them. When she first went to stand for Labour we went up to Taupō; it was against Nanaia. A busload from the pā came through and all went against her. When she got home, where did she go? Straight back to the Pā, to the people.

If there has been one connecting theme over the years in all the conversations I have had with the children and mokopuna, it is the absolute love and admiration they have for their mum and nan; for the example she has modelled in her life. Alan says:

When Whānau Ora came in, I looked at it and I thought it was everything that Mum believed in for us. As a recipient of that life I believed in it, because I know that it was Mum: it was her and what she lived and what she preached and what she practised with us as a whānau.

She's become a mother to all of our cousins, because of all of her cousins dying young (many from lung cancer), and I suppose with that key message around instilling in us our obligations and responsibilities to ahi kā and our obligations and responsibilities to our whakapapa in terms of our family and what we should do to be able to support them. In a way it's been a huge burden, because we have all these extra responsibilities that no one else seems to have, but on reflection, would we change anything? Nah, definitely not, because it's right, it's the right thing to do.

NOTES

[1] 'Turia reveals plan for MPs to desert Labour', *One News*, 2 March 2014.

-CHAPTER TWENTY-SIX-
LAST WORDS

When Mother Teresa was asked how do you achieve world peace, she said, go home and love your family.[1]

We all reach a time when we become conscious of how old we are. I was fifty-two when I went into Parliament. All these critics started calling us the kaumātua party – it was kind of true, because I was already a grandmother when I went in there. I wanted to go home because I'm seventy, and very few of my family have got past sixty. My mokopuna is a little bit out there, a bit of a challenge. She often talks to me about dying. She says to me, 'you know Mama, you're getting real old. You should come home before you die'. I say to George, 'oh my god, she's just about got me stitched up and in a coffin already'. My little one is getting to the challenging stage, and I know I need to invest time in her.

I am so lucky that my darling has been with her all this time. She is definitely a major focus going into the future, and my other grandchildren.

I remember one day going to leave home and it was her inter-country sports, and she said to me, 'you're not coming?' I said I had to go to such and such. The tears welled up in her eyes. I went to the phone and said that I needed to spend this day with her. And I turned up at the day, and her little face just lit up like a neon light. I have missed out on all of that with her. Her school things, her sports ... she's quite good at sport. I have to pick up on my responsibilities. George has done it all, and it has been hard on him; it has been very hard on him.

I'm lucky that all of my kids act and operate very much at a whānau level – so when she is playing up, it would be nothing for my oldest son, or my youngest boy, to come and talk to her; or if they're there, my other grandchildren tell her off. But I need to pick up my responsibility and be there for her.

Tariana's decision to go home is also about treasuring time with the person with whom she has shared every moment of her life for over five decades: her husband Hori. George has been her benchmark, her hero, her helpmate, the source of her greatest frustration. He has been everything to her and her mokopuna. A 2012 feature on Tariana told a relevant story in this regard:

> Once aged around 5, Piata asked Mrs Turia who her real mother was. Her answer was to list all the things mothers do for their children and ask Piata who did them for her. She was hoping the little girl would choose her. Instead she said 'my koro' which Mrs Turia said was a true reflection of her husband's role.[2]

In her first official speech since handing back her ministerial warrants, Tariana reflected on her remarkable career and the highlights of her life:

> Over the last eighteen years I have had the most incredible privilege of looking into people's lives at home and abroad, travelling to far off places like Russia, Canada or Hawai'i, spending time in the rugged isolation of Wharekauri or the lush depth of the Ureweras, being hosted on marae, in boardrooms, in hotels all across the world. I have seen so much; I have learnt so much.
>
> And yet, when my mind wanders over the years, I'd have to say some of the happiest days in my life date back to that time [when our children were small]. In those years we were dairy farming at Whangaehu; our marae was literally next door; we were raising our tamariki on tupuna lands. Our children had access to the richest archives of oral history; they knew who they were; we belonged to the land; our awa tupua was our place to heal, to swim, to be as one.
>
> In those times before iphones, ipads, ipods, tablets and on-demand tv, our whānau were all we needed. And in the ultimate act of defiance for my days post the beehive, I restore to myself, that nirvana – the state of bliss in which whānau fulfill all my needs. We can be, and we will be, the leaders of our own destiny.[3]

Through thick and thin, George has been consistent to a fault; his reactions are predictable and a strong gauge on how a particular constituency might react. I love his blunt analysis of my performance – if I was terrible, he'd be the first to tell me. There's never any flowery flattery coming from his direction; he says what he thinks and never tries to dress it up.

I have grandchildren who struggle. My husband is quite firm with them. If they want money they have to come and work for it. They have to go out and dig the garden, do jobs. He will not just give them money. I'm probably quite liberal. If they need ten bucks I'll just give it. George, he's trying to teach them about life. And that's good. And they know too that what I am doing is probably not right.

George is the quiet one in the background with daily routines that he sticks to like clockwork: dinner by 6pm, laundry washed and dried every day. There's even a distinctive routine for the way in which strawberries are planted, as I've found out by trial and error. He's the chief cook and bottle washer. After I chopped the end of my finger off at the marae they all think I'm a bit hopeless.

In one of her more recent interviews, Tariana was asked what was next. She said:

> Number one: I have to learn to be a good nanny. I have got out of the habit. Probably have to learn to be a good wife again. George and I have to renegotiate our relationship after eighteen years of passing each other as ships in the night. We have to learn how to live together again. It's going to be huge, actually. I don't think it's going to happen readily or easily, but after fifty-one years I hope it's not going to be too hard.[4]

I'd been thinking about leaving (Parliament) before the previous election, so I have been talking that through with my family and relatives and people who have supported me all the way through since I have been in Parliament. You can't base your decision on people thinking that you are the one who needs to make things happen.

I am really privileged that I have been able to have been of service. As an MP you should be the ultimate public servant: if you keep telling yourself that, don't get ideas beyond your station, you will do alright. I have been privileged to serve, because that is what we grew up being told – to be of service to your whānau, to be of service to others. It's about whether you're doing the work and whether you're advocating well for your people – that's the main thing.

I believe it has been a privilege to walk in greater footsteps and to serve our whānau, hapū and iwi, plus the various sectors I have had the pleasure of working with. To the Pasifika nations, the disability community, Pasifika Pride, E Tū Whānau, the community and voluntary sector, the health and social services sector, Whānau Ora collectives and commissioning agencies, educational organisations, housing groups, tangata whenua organisations, and suicide prevention organisations: me ērā atu rōpū, ka nui te mihi.

I want to leave people with a message of hope in our future. That we will not build a society that builds organisations out of the misery of people, but will strive to build capacity and capability in people to be the best they can be, and inspire themselves to transform their lives.

There have been times when I have been away and I have had a mokopuna be born, and I've tried to get out of whatever I'm doing and to get home, to karanga my mokopuna into this world. I have had three occasions when I have lost mokopuna – two of them at birth and one a bit older – and I was so thankful that I got home for those moments. I was down here in Wellington, and I just felt compelled to go home, to leave, and I did; and I got into a bit of trouble for walking out without asking for permission.

I am looking forward to going home, to do more, because there is so much more to do. There's lots of things I'm quite keen to look at. Our hapū is planning our future right now, so I'm very keen to work with them on the plans and put them into practice. To see beyond the impossible to the possible. To believe in the can do and can be. We are planning a papakāinga settlement in nearby Marangai. We are looking at building a little ecovillage up on the land block, because we so often get flooded on our marae, close to the valley.

I love the fact that we live collectively. My son, Alan, milks a cow every day; Mark is raising pigs, chickens and sheep, and of course George grows a magnificent vegetable garden. We have everything we need.

I am intending to be at home every weekend at least, even if it is just for a day – I am planning on making more time to be home. All of my children still live in Whanganui. I have only got one grandson who lives over in Australia, and we are hoping that he will come back. We are very, very lucky, George and I, because we have our children around us and our grandchildren and our great-grandchildren: we are very fortunate as a family. There are moments in our life, really significant moments in our life – there are times that mean the most to us.

It doesn't matter what work we do; it doesn't matter where we are; it doesn't matter how high we think we rise; it doesn't matter how important we think we are. At the end of the day, those who count the most are your family and your whānau, hapū and iwi.

Kia Kaha, Kia Māia, Kia ū ki ngā kaupapa me ngā tikanga a ō tātou mātua tūpuna.

As Tariana started to pack up office, and begin the transition to a new life, many people were moved to share their impressions and memories of the impact that she had made on the political scene. One particularly moving tribute was presented by Rt Hon Dame Jenny Shipley, Former Prime Minister of New Zealand.

> In my experience this world is made up of builders and wreckers! Tariana Turia is a builder. She is a person who came to Parliament as a leader, not to be defined by what she stood against, but what she stood for.
>
> Her contribution has been remarkable, her impact game-changing and her legacy far greater than many of her peers. I have had the privilege of observing Tariana since she arrived in Parliament. In her early years she was a feisty, courageous and spirited individual pursuing a cause. She had the foresight and ability to make serious change for the people she came to Parliament to represent. She has been a voice of reason, and a firm and insistent voice for those who have not otherwise been heard. She has been enormously successful because her voice has resonated not only in the Parliament, but also in front of the people whose lives she sought to improve.
>
> Tariana always had a vision for the future, but MMP has allowed her to bring this to life through her leadership, her people skills and her political acumen. Her leadership of ideas have been game-changers, for not only the people she sought to represent, but for New Zealand.
>
> While I have not always agreed with Tariana, there have been very few times that I haven't found myself experiencing a deep respect for the passion and earnest belief that was reflected in the cause she was putting forward, always well researched, always considered and when necessary direct.
>
> As a Minister of the Crown she has clearly demanded things from officials that others would not dare to argue. In doing so she has been able to, through her leadership, make enormous change to the smoking rates in New Zealand, in particular to the smoking rates

among Maori, the improvements of public health facilitated through marae programmes and now more recently her focus on sweet drinks and the detrimental impact they are having on the status of health of not only Maori, but other New Zealanders. She has been highly effective as a Minister and has delivered.

Whānau Ora I hope will be her enduring legacy. It is one of the most inspired public policy programmes I've seen come to life in New Zealand. It has not come out of a university or a think tank, but the heart of a leader committed to changing the prospects for her people in a meaningful way. It is my great hope that the initiative and the potential of Whānau Ora, which is a new process of self-discovery, self-realisation and self-determination through personal action, family action, and taking and sharing that responsibility within the whanau, will endure long after Tariana leaves. It is a gift to New Zealand that must be allowed to blossom.

Despite these achievements perhaps her greatest contribution to New Zealand is to show voters what is possible under MMP. Her capacity as a leader to bring MMP to life will, in my opinion, go down in New Zealand history. In the post-MMP environment she stands ahead of others in her ability to put forward the programmes she believes are critical to her people and her cause and then to collaborate with major parties to achieve a win-win outcome resulting in a rich and diverse policy agenda for us all. As in the European MMP parliamentary models, Tariana has demonstrated that to be successful small parties which have a clear vision and determination, the foresight and understanding to collaborate and negotiate and the confidence to take a position can shape the future.

I pay my respects to Tariana for all she has achieved and the sacrifices she has made. I pay my respects to her for her foresight in establishing the Māori Party and its enormous effectiveness in the MMP context. I am grateful to her for her leadership of ideas which challenged the status quo and in many ways bought the Treaty of Waitangi to life.

How lucky we are to have a Treaty and how lucky we have been to have a leader like Tariana who has given it meaning.

Finally Tariana, I pay my respects to you as you now retire from parliamentary life and return to your beloved whānau. As you do so it is my hope that you will take enormous satisfaction from the fact that you have made a profound difference for those you sought to represent and in doing so has helped shape a much better future for New Zealand and for us all.[5]

Tariana's Valedictory Speech was delivered in Parliament in the late afternoon of 24 July 2014.

Tēnā koe, te kaiwhakawā o tēnei whare.

E rere kau mai te awa nui mai i te kāhui maunga ki Tangaroa, ko au te awa, ko te awa ko au. [*The great river flows from the mountains to the sea, I am the river and the river is me.*]

There is nowhere that I feel more at peace than in the still tranquillity of the Whanganui River, te awa tupua, our lifeblood, our tribal heartbeat, the sacred umbilical cord that unites us from the mountain to the sea. Every year our iwi come together to connect as one through the journey that we call the Tira Hoe Waka. In many ways the last 18 years in this place have been like that same journey that we take: a journey of hope, hope for a better future for our mokopuna. Our hīkoi always starts in the spirit of those who watch over us.

Today I remember those who paved the way before me, to restore our right to see Te Tiriti o Waitangi as the first relationship agreement between tangata whenua and with the Government representing the Crown. I am proud to have upheld the Treaty of Waitangi, the kaupapa and tikanga of our people, in all that I have done in this environment.

My tūpuna have walked before me. They have walked beside me, and my mokopuna will carry those philosophies on as we build nationhood in this country that we all love. I am genealogically linked to Ngā Wairiki/Ngāti Apa, Te Awa Tupua o Whanganui, Ngā Rauru Kītahi, and Ngāti Tūwharetoa. It is to these people whom I will return when I leave here at the end of my parliamentary term – those who have grounded me, those who have reminded me of my place, and yet have loved me despite.

I was raised by my grandmother Hoki Waewae, my aunt Mihiterina and Tariuha Manawaroa Te Aweawe, my precious dad, who was my dad although he was not my father. When I was eight, I became a whāngai to my wonderful aunts at Pūtiki. My Auntie Wai and Auntie Paeroa had huge expectations of me. I was brought up to believe that doing what was right was more important than doing what was popular. They instilled discipline and strong whānau values in me – to love unconditionally and to be the best at whatever I did.

When I came to Parliament with Labour in 1996 I followed in the footsteps of whānau: Tokouru Rātana, Matiu Rātana, and Iriaka Rātana. They came here to honour the kawenata their papa had with Michael Joseph Savage of the Labour Party. Today I ask as an uri of their iwi: what happened to that kawenata? When will the mōrehu and the iwi of our country see the outcomes that Tahupōtiki Wīremu Ratana sought for us all yet has never been honoured?

To Chester, Nathan, Jonathan, and Ian, those of you who are part of my electorate too, I want to mihi to you all and to say to you how proud I have been to walk alongside you, and for your friendship, and I have so appreciated that. There are others who have watched over me too and I will forever cherish the memories that I carry with me.

My cousin the late Sir Archie Taiaroa supported me all the way through my political career, and I would call him for his wise counsel. Archie stood with me when I resigned from the Labour Government at Rātana, and I will never forget that. When I was thinking of leaving, he talked to me about the experience of Matiu Rata, whom he himself had encouraged to leave, not realising at the time that our people would forget his sacrifice and not vote for him.

Archie worried that the same thing would happen to me – that our people would forget. I was able to reassure him that I would always be political whether I was here or outside of Parliament, that in the end I had to live with myself, and there is no greater challenge than to be true to one's own self.

I think about my cousin Rangitihi Tahupārae, who worked for many years here at Parliament, the most distinguished and eloquent orator in either language. He taught me to love all that we are and to walk with pride in the knowledge of our whakapapa.

The late Dr Irihāpeti Ramsden, a wonderful friend and whanaunga, was another one who when I found myself in trouble here, which seemed to happen a bit, would always appear in the public gallery – so beautiful, so gracious, and so principled.

And my beloved friend-in-arms Parekura – I miss him so much. Whenever I think of Parekura, I think of how important he has been to my family. My baby, my mokopuna whom I have raised, Piata, who would have given anything to be Ngāti Porou, used to come home from school and say to me 'Māmā, can I just say that I am?' because she wanted Parekura to be her real pāpā.

I have carried those people who have shaped me into the person have become, and I will love them and my extended whānau forever. Because of them our tira has a strong foundation.

Today is my chance to acknowledge all those who helped to keep our waka afloat to ensure that our tira moves forward. So I stand to honour so many amazing people in this complex, who give so much and so freely. The security teams, the VIP drivers, the messengers, the library staff, and the travel team – all of these people constantly go out of their way to make our lives easier. The cleaners who restore order in our offices and on our floor, the Bellamy's team, the Clerk of the House, our interpreters, the conscientious team in the Cabinet Office, Parliamentary Service, and Ministerial Services, your sacrifices were many and your dedication has been appreciated. On the many sides of this whare are those whom I have served alongside of, whether at the Cabinet table or in a select committee, or being held to account at question time or in political panels – all of you who work so hard for what you believe in.

I would not have come to Parliament if it was not for the endorsement of the Rt Hon Helen Clark and the Hon Maryan Street, and I will never forget that it was your trust in me and your advocacy that got me here. I will always remember that. There were other people in Labour whom I value working with, many of you. I will not name you all, but there were some whom I learnt so much from. I think of Tim Barnett and that when I used to go to caucus, I could never get a paper through until Tim took it off me and worked on it for me. Annette King was an amazing Minister and taught me so much. I want to mihi to you today, Annette. And Darren Hughes – that amazing young man Darren Hughes – who I thought would one day be the leader of the Labour Party and who, in fact, would end up being the Prime Minister of New Zealand. I miss him so much; he was a great young man, a beautiful young man.

I mihi to my colleagues who were foundation members of the Māori Party, because you have shaped a new horizon for this country. You have imbued this chamber with the beauty and force of te reo Māori, you have established cultural competency as a norm, and you have ensured that nobody gets left behind. We are stronger because of your influence, bolder because of your integrity.

Dr Pita Sharples – I hate following him in speeches! I said 'Mr Nice Guy', but I should have said 'Mr Funny Guy'. He is always 'Mr Nice Guy'. He is never one to look for the problems. He is always positively focused. Te Ururoa, the steady hand on the rudder steering us on the right course, the general manager of everything, the ideal member of Parliament who understands process so well, a great leader.

Hone Harawira, my great friend who has also been my great foe. How do you really love the essence of someone and yet be so frustrated by them at the same time?

Rahui Katene, the hardest-working paddler in our waka – always willing, always there. I was so sad because you deserved to win. You put in the hard yards. You were just so great.

I have an all-encompassing love for our founding president, Matua Whatarangi Winiata. When we were having arguments in the caucus – not only with Pete would I argue, but often get into stoushes with Hone. Matua would look at us and I would say to him: 'Matua, what do you think?' He would say: 'Yes, I am just trying to work out which kaupapa is operating here today.' I want to thank Pem Bird and Naida Glavish, who have been two incredible leaders, for the vital role that you have played not only in our first ten years but in getting us to where we are today. I want to say thank you to Heta Hingston for gifting us our very first constitution. As much as we have often struggled to keep to the rules, we have tried so hard.

I am indebted to the people of Te Tai Hauāuru for your generosity and support to both me and my whānau. You have worked tirelessly. I mihi to you all because you believed in the kaupapa of our tūpuna and saw the vision of the Māori Party. There are many others who have helped along the way of our journey.

I mihi to Rob Cooper and Sister Makareta Tawaroa, who politicised me – probably much to everybody else's dismay. I mihi to Professor Sir Mason Durie for your exceptional leadership, to Nancy, to Doug, to Merepeka, to Suzanne, the various departmental heads who comprised the original governance group that set out Whānau Ora and set us on the right path.

I have valued the enormous support that I have received as a Minister from officials of various agencies who have provided me with support and advice. I know that I have not been an easy Minister for you to serve. I can acknowledge that, as I am sure officials and others across this House will say so also. How can I ever put into words the love that I have for our parliamentary staff, who have been exceptional, working always beyond the call of duty, with one of two of them working almost through the night? I have expected you all to put the people you serve before your agencies and your careers. I know that that has been a huge sacrifice.

And, of course, my whānau. A wall plaque was given to me by Pati Umaga, somebody whom I just so love. He gave it to me, and it read: 'Whānau: we may not have it all together, but together we have it all'. I believe this implicitly.

Every journey along our river inevitably faces the churning waters of the rapids, the turmoil and the chaos of the riporipo that we find ourselves swirling within. In this place I have felt profoundly the pain of the entrenched inequities too many Māori and Pasifika families face in terms of the lack of equitable access to health, education, housing, employment, and economic opportunity. I have at times been devastated by the institutional racism that continues to limit our potential as a people. We should never be silent on the things that matter – the barriers that block our ability to be the best that we can be – and we must never be afraid to talk about anything that we know to be true and that we know to be right. It is only when we let fear take over and when we do not speak up that we let people down.

I recall being really nervous when I accepted the role of Minister for Disability Issues. I felt so inadequate to fulfil this position and I realised very quickly that my job was to listen carefully to the many voices and to translate that into actions with support from the excellent officials and people in the sector. The disability sector has had an enormous influence on me, with their brave audacity to tell their own tale: 'Nothing about us without us'. They asked me to have the confidence and the trust to believe that we can do whatever it takes, to believe in our abilities, not our disabilities, and the words continue to reverberate in my heart and mind. I will always be indebted to the disability communities for their ability to lead with so much dignity and inspiration.

In my time here I have challenged officials that we must not be fixated by a focus on deficits, looking at everything that is wrong. It is so much better to look for the potential in people to change. It is in our attitudes, our ability to think differently, that the key to transformation lies. In this regard I mihi to those peoples of the Pacific who let me share their journey, Nga Vaka o Kāiga Tapu – one of the most revolutionary frameworks that I have ever known. I thank the people of Te Moana-nui-a-Kiwa, who have been so generous in sharing their vision with me – people like Peseta Betty Sio, Tino Pereira, Judge Ida Malosi, Yvonne Crichton-Hill, and many others.

I acknowledge, too, the leadership of the Pacific Advisory Group and the Māori Reference Group for your proactive work on family violence. I mihi to Judge Peter Boshier and to Judge Paul von Dadelszen for your leadership and trust in people-led solutions.

If ever it is possible to form a really strong relationship with a community, it must be the one that has been established for me in the Chathams. Their resilience, their absolute belief in themselves, probably to the detriment of their own growth as they were overlooked by funders, has been totally inspiring, and I thank them for their manaakitanga towards me and towards Chris also.

Even the steadiest waka can be overturned, and it was that way for me in the early months of 2004 as we reeled to the decisions made in haste around the foreshore and seabed. In those moments of despair I have always gone to our river, to our awa, to reclaim a sense of being – the blessing of the water that heals – and in that quiet space I find the answers that lie within me. And so it was for our whanau, hapū, and iwi as we considered how we would respond to the denial of due process and access to justice, the belittling of our status as tangata whenua, which will always be forever recorded as a modern-day Treaty breach. The advent of the foreshore and seabed legislation created the tensions that led to me leaving Labour and in the same breath gave birth to our indigenous political movement, the Māori Party. I am not sorry today that that happened and that I left.

I have the utmost respect for Georgina Beyer, who sacrificed her political aspirations to stand alongside of me at Rātana. Ten years on, those days are still vividly written in my mind as a milestone moment in the story of our nation. Through the anguish and the pain as the people came together in solidarity, we knew that we were part of an incredible juncture in our history as we witnessed a powerful uprising of the spirit. It was the most evocative moment of my life – to feel the will of the people, the calling of our tūpuna to reclaim the essence of who we are, and to stand up for what we knew was right. It was self-determination in action.

As I think of that sea of flags and placards that filled the foreground of Parliament, I am reminded of the image that we see at home every summer when our collective fleet of waka glide into Pūtiki, an amazing expression of pride, of strength, of power, and of peace. The Tira Hoe Waka is a journey of rediscovery, in which we literally fall in love with ourselves again.

In many ways, for me so too is the Māori Party. Put simply, this is the dream of Whānau Ora – to know ourselves, our strengths, and our challenges, and to plot our futures. We cannot talk rangatiratanga and not be self-determining. We know the call from Pūao-te-ata-tū, Matua Whāngai, kōhanga reo, kura kaupapa, kura-ā-iwi, whare wānanga, local level solutions, direct resourcing, even closing the gaps, *He Korowai Oranga*, and Māori and Pasifika health and social services. They are all models where the people have put forward a framework for tomorrow. We stand on the shoulders of the past to look forward to a greater future.

I want to take this opportunity to mihi to somebody in the House for whom I have huge respect and regard, and that is Hekia. Tēnā koe ki te Minita. I have absolutely loved your passionate belief that all of our children have a right to succeed in education. Second-best is not part of your vocabulary, and only excellence will do. You know that we are preparing the next leaders of this nation. I believe totally in what you are doing and I want to say that today in this House.

One of the most exhilarating experiences of my life was to travel throughout the country, meeting with Māori and Pasifika communities about a whānau way forward. Often the halls were crowded to full capacity – 600 people crammed together, standing room only. It was a buzz and I will always remember it. Whānau Ora resonated with them because they understood completely what collective responsibility and obligation was and how it needed to be restored to those who had been affected by the many losses that they had suffered. They did not ask what the Government could do for them. They asked instead that we trust them to develop their own solutions, to take them forward, and to trust that they knew better than anyone in the huge bureaucracies that we have here in Wellington.

This hīkoi that we have been on, then, is a hīkoi for all time. What we have represented with the growth of the Māori Party is the possibility of a strong and independent Māori voice, forever able to sit in Parliament. We were not content to sit on the sidelines and to watch from afar as the lives of our people waited in the queue for the time to be right. We have never been about the rhetoric of the right or the left, and I am so grateful to those members of the press gallery who actually got that, who have asked searching questions and been prepared to reflect our philosophies, rather than regurgitating their own. We are driven by kaupapa and what unites us rather than what divides us.

Being in the Māori Party has been the greatest opportunity to sing our songs and to tell our stories. We have had the freedom to focus on what is right for tangata whenua and to know that it would also be right for our brothers and sisters from Te Moana-nui-a-Kiwa, and we knew it would be right for this country. It is the first time in our history and of the world that an indigenous political party has been truly part of Government in a coalition arrangement. It has been exciting, liberating, invigorating, inspiring, and occasionally challenging.

I have so enjoyed the respectful, honest, and upfront relationship with John Key and Bill English, a relationship that has allowed both of us to be direct, acknowledging our different constituencies and agreeing to disagree. It has been a relationship that is based on mutual cooperation, and we are pleased with what we have achieved. We are also proud of what we have managed to change or stop, and we are not going to talk about the disappointments. I have been driven by a determination, passion, and desire, and, as Bill English would say, a stubborn resolve to make a difference. I always wanted to be in relationship where what we had to say mattered, to be part of the solution, and not limited to picking the problems apart. Although we were unable to achieve all the aspirations of our people, I know that we have made a difference in the lives of whānau, whatever their circumstances, and in that respect I leave with a feeling of peace, that we have always tried to do our best and to do what it is that is right for them.

I cannot leave this House without recognising a real friend, Chris Finlayson. Chris is the greatest Treaty settlements Minister that we have ever had in this country. In our iwi we have had the longest litigation in the history of this country over our river. It is just around the corner, and I want to say thank you to you so much for working so hard alongside our whānau, hapū, and iwi of Whanganui.

I have tried to live up to the legacy and the expectation from so many of our iwi leaders who have sacrificed so much to let the stories of our whānau, hapū, and iwi resound, not just in books of history but in the throbbing heartbeat of a nation that knows.

I come then to a turning point in my journey, as I prepare to steer our waka homewards. I say to you all to be led by the people you serve. It is the greatest opportunity that anyone could ever have hoped for. I have been humbled by the trust that has been placed in me, and there are so many people who have helped me throughout my lifetime – too many to name individually – but I want you all to know that I can be for ever thankful for the influence that you have had on my thinking.

Your lessons will continue to inspire me, and your advice and your challenges will no doubt occupy my mind.

But now it is time to return home, to give back to those who placed their trust in me, to rest awhile, to be with my darling George, who has put up with me for 51 years – it has got to be a record – and with my great children, and my 26 grandchildren and 26 great-grandchildren. (I had to say that, Pete, because you only have one! I was trying to work out how I could beat him at something). And then on Saturday I will start thinking about my next project for transformation.

To everyone who has given me the strength and the support to promote possibility and belief for every whānau to grow, I thank you. Your vision, our vision, will be evident in the nation that we create together tomorrow. To the three Whānau Ora commissioning agencies, I want to mihi to you all for the great opportunity and the great direction that I know you will take us in.

E te iwi, kia piri, kia tata whakamaua kia tīna (tīna), hui e (tāiki e)! Nō reira, tēnā koutou, tēnā koutou, tēnā tātou katoa.

[*Oh people close up, fasten on to it firmly (it is) gather together (it is done)! So accolades and acknowledgements to you collectively and to us all.*]

Waiata

Haka

NOTES

1 Tariana Turia, 'Maori Wellbeing – Defying the Oxymoron', speech to 'Our People, Our Future, Our Way': Te Aho Summit, 14 October 2014.

2 Laurel Stowell, 'Crusader leaves a lesson in respect', *Whanganui Chronicle*, 22 December 2012.

3 Turia, 'Maori Wellbeing – Defying the Oxymoron.'

4 Tanya Black, *Tariana Turia's Legacy*. Video for AttitudeLive website: http://attitudelive.com/blog/tanya-black/film-tariana-turias-legacy (accessed 20 May 2015).

5 Rt Hon Dame Jenny Shipley, written statement provided on 25 June 2014.

Song composed and sung by Sharon Thorburn QSM for Dame Tariana Turia to commemorate her retirement

You've left footprints...
Blazed a trail across our nation for our Moko to walk hand in hand
A living legacy...
Written on the faces of our children given safe passage home
No one can count what it cost you to give our nation your all
What can we give you in return?
We can answer the call
Aotearoa...
First place to see the sun, we can become two people standing as one
It starts with whanau...
We've such a long, long way to go, but we must look at how far we have come
You need our footprints...
Walking boldly through the doors that only open when our hearts beat as one
A living legacy...
Written on the faces of our children and our children to come
We'll be the candle for our family. We'll be the voice you've never heard
We'll be the difference that you've longed for
We'll lift our feet, become the prayer
No one can count what it cost you to give our nation your all
What can we give you in return?
We can answer the call. We can give it our all

Song design and graphics: Janet Balcombe

©Sharon Thorburn, August 2014

-POSTSCRIPT-

THE STILL SMALL VOICE OF COURAGE: THE HONOURABLE DAME

The only tyrant I accept in this world is the 'still small voice' within me. And even though I have to face the prospect of being a minority of one, I humbly believe I have the courage to be in such a hopeless minority.[1]

On 1 January 2015, as the nation greeted a new year, it woke to the announcement of a new Dame, the Hon Dame Tariana Turia; Dame Companion of the New Zealand Order of Merit, for her services as a Member of Parliament.

For some, the honour reflected the policy gains she had achieved as a minister:

> The Whanau Ora policy, which devolves social policy delivery to communities and whanau and aims to support families rather than individuals, is seen as her proudest legacy.[2]
>
> The Whanau Ora approach across government, and the Enabling Good Lives approach in the disability sector are hallmarks of her leadership, in which strategies for change are considered to be most enduring when whanau/families and people with disabilities have responsibility for determining their own solutions.[3]

For others, it reflected the political changes she had been instrumental in forging:

> History will show she has cemented a relationship between National and the Maori Party that many believe was the best deal on the table and she took it.[4]

> Some would argue that the party's close relationship with the Government has been a factor in its current downturn. … But that does not lessen the contribution made by those who so bravely stared down the Government and forged their own path. And in particular, one Tariana Turia.[5]

But for the Dame herself, the reason for the honour was succinctly put in the *Herald*'s own headline: 'This is for whanau, hapu and iwi'.

'I don't think any individual can say, I did all this, and I did it on my own. Because that's not true', she told *One News*.[6]

In fact it was only because Dame Tariana had seen the award as a collective acknowledgement of the journey the people had taken that she even conceded to accepting it:

'In the first instance I thought I might not take it but they [her whanau] said it's not really for me, it's for our whanau, hapu and iwi – for all the people I have worked alongside,' said Dame Tariana from her Wanganui home.

'It's a shared thing so I guess when you look at it in that context it does make it easier to give consideration to accepting it'.[7]

Tariana has routinely been reluctant to stand in the limelight and bask in the glory of praise. She was always an unconventional politician. While some would be happy to be pushed to the front, accepting recognition as a right of office, Tariana was always most comfortable among the people, easily sacrificing the podium for others who sought it more.

There is a whakataukī that encapsulates the quality of humility that Tariana lives by: Waiho mā te tangata e mihi – Let someone else sing your praises.

She resisted the opportunity to monopolise the microphone and demand attention, just because she could. She often voiced a feeling of inadequacy in 'doing the spin'; in talking the Party up. She would recall the words of Aunty Wai: 'let your reputation be known by your good deeds rather than by telling the people how good you are'. If your actions are not consistent with your kōrero, then the people will judge you as wanting.

On the marae ātea, sometimes the people would seek to bestow honour upon Tariana by placing her in such a way to elevate her prestige. They might ask her to sit in the front row of the manuhiri, or in a single chair slightly in front of the others. On every occasion Tariana would graciously decline the invitation to be seated up front and away from those who had come on with her. Her first thought was always that the kuia who accompanied her were the ones who should be acknowledged ahead of herself. She would walk behind them, her hand on the small of their back, gently letting them know they had her support, and then quietly retreat, leaving the focus for these distinguished elders, whom she held in such regard.

Tariana was uncomfortable about the risk of politicians breaching sacrosanct cultural protocols, whether it was at marae or in Parliament itself. During her tenure as a Labour Party minister, Tariana was frequently on the alert for situations that might place the Rt Hon Helen Clark at risk of causing cultural offence. In part, this was due to her determination to never again see the Prime Minister become vulnerable, as she had been in 1998 at a hui at Te Tii marae in Waitangi. At that hui Ngāpuhi activist Titewhai Harawira had reduced Helen Clark to tears, loudly challenging her right to speak on the marae as a Pākehā woman. Titewhai told Clark in no uncertain terms that protocol forbade her to speak, and that, most certainly, a Pākehā woman would not be allowed to speak before Māori women. Tariana had sat behind Helen during the altercation, comforting her and demonstrating support for her leader – while at the same time understanding the point that Titewhai was making. Tariana did not forget that incident. She would often say to others that every time there was a risk of the protocols being breached, she would think about her aunts from Pūtiki – what would they think? how should she act? The exercise immediately restored a sense of what was right.

She came to rely on this guidance from her aunts on the numerous occasions when speaking rights for women became fodder for the press. In July 2013, during the Youth Parliament, two of Tariana's former Labour Party colleagues drew the attention of the press when they arrived late at the pōwhiri, and then sought seats on the front row. One, Annette King, later approached the Speaker about her concerns. *Voxy.co.nz* reported:

> Labour MP Annette King said she was not comfortable with the 'segregated nature' of the welcoming.
>
> 'In no way would this have happened during Helen Clark's day,' she said.
>
> Ms King said she would strive for gender equality for future Powhiri's so that they could 'accurately reflect' the House of Representatives.[8]

In response to the concerns, Speaker David Carter immediately called for a review of the tikanga and kawa laid down by Te Āti Awa, the iwi of that region. Tariana recalled the efforts her late cousin, Rangitihi Tahuparae, had put into developing these protocols with Te Āti Awa when he was first appointed Kaumātua O Te Whare Pāremata[9]. She questioned whether the review was necessary, telling the *Dominion Post*:

> ... the Parliament has no place whatsoever in trying to alter the kawa and tikanga of tangata whenua, who are the sole authorities and guardians of their own cultural heritage.

'Parliament should recognise and respect the culture and customs of tangata whenua alongside Westminster parliamentary traditions without compromising the integrity of either.'[10]

Labour MP Louisa Wall agreed with Tariana that the protocols around pōwhiri were not a matter for 'melding (or moulding) cultures and philosophies':

'It is for Maori and Maori alone to determine the appropriateness and nature of tikanga and the kawa that emanates from that,' Ms Wall says.[11]

Tariana consistently acted in ways that reflected and respected the cultures and traditions of the home people, whether those people were mana whenua, Muslim, local community groups or others. It was about doing what was right, being attune to our differences and celebrating the distinctive traditions, protocols and ways of being that are at the essence of who we are. She had once told the Federation of Islamic Associations of New Zealand:

If we were all born the same, how would we know my brother from my sister, my mother from my father? Our gods deliberately created us different so that we would not bring confusion into the world.

Ramadhan symbolises understanding, tolerance and togetherness as catalysts for peace and harmony. …

Whatever political party, or religion, or belief system may be represented here tonight, we would hope that the struggle against the oppressive forces who want us to be like them, to think like them, to speak like them, to dress like them, to believe in their Gods, and to reject all that we are must be resisted.

We need to be able to celebrate our differences together. As tangata whenua and as members of the Maori Party, we welcome you and we implore that you continue to believe in your Gods, that you continue to celebrate who you are, that you continue to speak your language. Do not forsake the essence of your souls.[12]

When the time came then for the nation to award Tariana its highest honour, it was no surprise that in accepting her damehood, it was singularly important to her to acknowledge the voice of the people. Tariana's most fervent wish was to heed the call of the karanga, He aha te mea nui o te ao? He tangata, he tangata he tangata. What is the most important thing of all? It is the people, the people, the people. The *Herald* reported:

> Dame Tariana said she felt the greatest thing for her was 'to earn the trust and respect of people throughout the country. I have always believed in the people and will continue to do so'.[13]

A decade prior, in 2005, a collection of Tariana's speeches presented between 2000 and 2005 had been published, entitled *Walking the Talk*.[14] In her introduction to the book, Rachael Selby summarised the speeches as representing a woman who 'truly represents her whanau': a politician who had made 'a principled decision' to resign over the failure of the 2004 Government to adequately respond to Māori:

> The Government was afraid and Tariana walked. Now she is walking the talk as she has always done, promoting values of caring for ourselves, caring for each other and caring for our world.[15]

Walking the talk was very much Tariana's approach to upholding the tikanga and the kawa that her elders had passed on to her. She defines tikanga as doing what is right; the right thing at the right time in the right way. When a death rattle was first heard, Tariana's instincts were always to go – to travel to be with those who mourned, to share in the grief for the deceased. Ko te tinana, he waka tuku kōrero – it was important to express the sadness and the love in person; to comfort the bereaved by being there with them.

This was a tikanga that did not always endear her to the whips when she was in the Labour Party, but was never questioned during her years with the Māori Party. It did not matter how far away the destination, how many hours were taken out of her frantic schedule in Parliament; her first obligation at the time of tangihanga was to express her respects to the whānau pani, the bereaved.

At a tribute dinner to outgoing ministers Tariana and Pita Sharples on 20 August 2014, former colleague Hon Simon Power referred to Tariana as possessing a 'stillness': 'nerves of steel' that enabled her to never cave in when decisions were being made. Those same nerves of steel empowered her to put up with intense physical pain or distress, to be a voice for the people, to support and comfort those who needed it, to advocate and to do what it takes to make the difference.

Tariana might have been on the brink of exhaustion, but if her whānau needed her she would go; it was difficult, bordering on impossible, to persuade her not to. Too many times, the sacrifices she made to support others exacerbated her own health issues.

Asthma, psoriasis, chest infections, skin inflammations and a range of other health conditions occasionally overtook Tariana, and against her will she would be forced to slow down and take a rest. But it would never be long before Madam would be sending emails or texts from her hospital bed or home, issuing instructions until she could be there in person. And even in her sickest state, she would never forget what she had asked you to do. Woe betide those who hoped an absence from the office might mean a temporary let-up in the workload.

In a speech she gave to the National Māori Asthma conference in Whanganui, Tariana revealed that she had been diagnosed as an asthmatic while working in a stressful job in Māori Affairs. The *Herald*'s account stated:

> 'Within the space of a weekend my life and my future changed dramatically.' For the following twelve years 'I never went anywhere without my blue, orange, brown inhalers in my bag ...' Mrs Turia said she was 'pathologically focused on removing the triggers and would always blame the cat hair on the couch, heavily perfumed guests, the air-conditioning in the office, for aggravating my asthma'.
>
> It all changed one day when she saw an advertisement for the Buteyko method. It taught her how to breathe slowly but shallowly and to adopt routines and exercises to manage asthma without drugs and 'completely changed my attitude'.
>
> 'Then 18 months later I left Labour. I tell you – I can thoroughly recommend it! The rest is history. ...'
>
> '... One day I woke up and realised that without even knowing I hadn't had asthma for three months.'[16]

The knowledge that Tariana would always act out of her great love for the people saw many whānau ring her late at night or early in the morning, from the mortuary or the deathbed of their loved ones, asking for her guidance. They would ring from Australia, or whānau from home would ring on their behalf. There would be requests from prison for a son wanting to pay his last respects to his mother. There would be so many calls from family members anxious and not knowing what to do, but knowing that Tariana would.

In each and every case, Tariana understood the nature of duty; the privilege of office that enabled her to fulfil responsibilities to the people whom she represented. She would contact the Chief Coroner personally; ring up the local iwi liaison office in the police, or email the Minister of Foreign Affairs for his advice on expired passports and access to embassy staff – and if she couldn't help a family in person, she would send one of her staff in support. She would respond to requests for her assistance immediately with helpful information, with guidance, and without judgment. Tariana had learnt a very clear message from Aunty Wai when one day she had passed a comment about her mother's drinking. Aunty Wai had swung around with a swift retort: 'How dare you judge your mother in that way? You have no idea what she's been through'. It was a salutary lesson that Tariana held fast to in her later life.

Tariana's passion to honour the people, to respect their achievements and do what she could to support them made her an exceptional minister of her many constituencies. Tariana frequently urged her staff to focus on the positives; to be strengths-based rather than deficit-driven. She wanted us to always acknowledge the amazing work of committed people throughout New Zealand who did so much to make a difference.

She made decisions about invitations not on the basis of the numbers who would attend or media that might be represented, but according to matters of the heart – if the people wanted her, she had no hesitation in creating diary upheaval in order to attend. There are people everywhere who recall the day Tariana came to their services, their marae, their community hall to launch a building or a document as a vital moment in their history. To them all Tariana would say that the very least she could do was to acknowledge their many sacrifices and thank them for the impact they had achieved.

The importance Tariana placed on responding to invitations to join people at important occasions was not always understood by members of the press gallery. Ministers Sharples and Turia were frequently castigated by the press for racking up high expenses as they travelled to remote parts of the country to meet with communities face to face, kanohi ki te kanohi. Every quarter, when the expenses were published, Tariana would be questioned as to why she travelled more than most ministers. She would oblige with the same response every time; that meeting with the people was important: 'There are huge expectations on Maori members of Parliament and especially Maori ministers. I'm a hard worker: I take my job very seriously'.[17]

Eventually Tariana lost her patience with the incessant line of questioning, and the implication that the travel that saw her leave home at 5am and return at 11pm every day of the week was clearly a 'perk' that misused taxpayer funding. She lost her usual characteristic cool:

> You make me sick. All you are looking for is to get a story that shows ministers in a bad light. You have questioned me about the use of ministerial expenses. You were looking for a story and you've got one – I'm a big spender.[18]

The sensational headlines that resulted never acknowledged the heavy personal costs that came with being a politician of the people. However, in 2007 the *Dominion Post* did report:

> That's probably been my hardest thing about being in Parliament, being away from my family. You miss out on so many things. I've missed some of the birthdays being down here, I've missed a couple of births of grandchildren.[19]

Whatever the press made of it, Tariana was always resolutely clear that the people came first: before policy, politics and Parliament. Her annual pilgrimages to key events in the Māori year – to places such as Rātana Pā, Tūrangawaewae, Waitangi or Pākaitore – were dominated by the need to listen to the views of the people, to be present, rather than to find a political soapbox.

In 2007, the *Dominion Post* reported:

> Tariana Turia won the first important event on the Maori calendar at Ratana Pa hands down with National and Labour a distant second and third. The Maori Party decision to forego a party powhiri at Ratana was perspicacious. They are on home ground with Maori; Maori are at home with them; as the strong independent voice that's always won the respect of Pakeha politicians. They comment on all Maori issues and at an astonishing rate for a small party.[20]

As time went on, it became evident that the respect in which the Māori Party in general and Tariana in particular was held was increasing, including among a significant Pākehā following. Early on in her political life, Tariana had admitted to some nervousness about working with Pākehā:

> It's going to be a long road to hoe, building bridges, tearing down walls. I suppose I am suspicious of Pākehā processes and motives too. It's been a time of caution, settling in and sounding out allies.[21]

Conversely, when Tariana first arrived in Parliament she encountered a fair amount of distrust from Pākehā about the person they had only seen on their television screens. As the editor of the *Manawatu Standard* recalled upon the occasion of her damehood:

> It's probably fair to say the former co-leader of the Maori Party was one of the most hated women in New Zealand for a time, her name spat out in shrill, angry bites with the likes of controversial cohorts Corkery, Huata, Bradford and Clark. Such vitriol was unfair at the time and seems, with the clearer vision that history and perspective provide, at best ignorant and at worst, downright racist.
>
> That Turia was able to face such anger and return it with a steely stare and largely dignified determination emphasises her special place in New Zealand political history and worthiness as a recipient of this royal acknowledgment.[22]

Perhaps, when all is said and done, that dignified, determined response in the face of discord may be the frame through which the life of Tariana Turia may be examined. Hers is a story of 'an ordinary person' doing extraordinary things.

When she was asked what would change after she had been awarded New Zealand's top honour, her reply was classic Tariana:

> It's highly unlikely anything would change for me because essentially all my life I've been a pretty ordinary person who lives a very ordinary life and I don't anticipate any of this will change'.[23]

It was that 'pretty ordinary person' who was recently awarded one of six global awards presented throughout the Western Pacific Region on World No Tobacco Day.[24]

And in January 2015, not long after the New Year honours list was made public, it was announced that Tariana was to receive an international tobacco control award for outstanding leadership and accomplishment: the 2015 Luther L. Terry Award, named for the late United States Surgeon General who laid the groundwork for public health scrutiny of the dangers of tobacco use.

Tariana had been nominated by the Smokefree Coalition, the National Heart Foundation and Hāpai te Hauora, a provider of Māori health services in the greater Auckland region. Programme notes for the conference at which the award was presented stated:

> Dame Tariana Turia (New Zealand) has been a powerful champion of tobacco control in New Zealand, executing multiple reforms to reduce tobacco consumption in all types of tobacco products and across all population groups. Her endgame strategy against tobacco has been a comprehensive campaign in all spheres of influence – health education, legislation, removal of tobacco displays, plain packaging, smoking cessation, and successive tobacco taxation. Her unwavering commitment to tobacco control has been an inspiration in the movement to achieve a Smokefree New Zealand by 2025.
>
> During her time in government, she was an instrumental supporter of a number of legislative efforts, including: cumulative increases in tobacco excise taxes, banning tobacco retail displays, a lowering of the duty free allowance for cigarettes, implementing plain packaging for tobacco products, promoting smoke-free environments in cars, and the establishment of a NZ$20 million 'Innovation Fund' for projects that will increase effective cessation among the country's priority populations.[25]

Tariana's many successes in the area of tobacco control are all the more remarkable for being passed by a National Government not previously known for its liquor and cigarette reform.

In nominating Tariana for the award, Smokefree Coalition director Dr Prudence Stone acknowledged Tariana's 'tremendous, tireless and courageous' work championing a smokefree New Zealand. The concept of courage was reiterated by another tobacco reform advocate, Pacific Heartbeat Manager and Smokefree Coalition Board member Louisa Ryan, who said that:

> ... in addition to her massive Parliamentary output, Hon Ms Turia should also be recognised for both her courage and her compassion.
>
> 'The Minister's fearlessness in the face of constant criticism and opposition – both from within Parliament and from the tobacco industry – has been pivotal'.[26]

The adjectives used here to describe Tariana are typical: tireless, fearless, courageous, powerful, pivotal. And yet Tariana always felt she was simply doing what she was born to do, saying what needed to be said.

In her political life, as in her personal life, she honoured the message of her tupuna Mere Rikiriki, 'He ringa kaha, he ringa poto, kāore e whakahoa' – hold true to yourself; be self-controlled without friend or favour. Tariana sets the highest expectations upon herself of the values she should live by. In 1997, she described these values as:

> ... no different to what I have aspired to for most of my adult life and certainly what I would expect of any Maori person irrespective of what position they hold in the community. To be accountable, ethical, have integrity and be true to our people.[27]

Tariana has always placed a high premium on being in control of herself, drawing on the lessons of her Uncle Hop to keep calm while others are agitated. However, her life has not been without its severe challenges.

Tariana's eldest son Alan recalls the regularity of nightmares that his mother used to suffer from when he was a young child:

> Mum might have been in bed for half an hour. Next thing she would come tearing through the passage, screaming. Next thing, we're all crying, wondering what on earth is going on, and Dad is shouting, 'Tari, you're scaring the kids'. She would have had a bad dream, and then she'd wake up and settle down and go back to bed. She said she even used to scare herself.

Throughout Tariana's life, there have been many periods of intense loss and sadness; the impact of violence across so many levels, and lived experiences of racism and prejudice. She has battled post-natal depression. She has smelt fear and looked it in the eye. Tariana understands the stirring unease of unresolved questions around identity; she knows the pain of isolation and alienation, of feeling cut off from those you love.

And so when she left the Labour Party and she was relegated to the office politicians nicknamed 'Siberia' – the 'isolation unit' squashed between the photocopiers and the toilets on the second floor of Parliament Buildings, it was not the first time that she had felt out in the cold. At such times, she felt on her own, but never alone.

And that is the greatest honour in Tariana's life – to be of whānau. She considers that her primary purpose, her most important role in life is to recreate the sense of whānau that she inherited from her own. Speaking with her children, there is no question that she has done that work well. Alan says:

> We have been the luckiest kids on earth. And I know Mum and Dad have done a really good job because we're all living here; we're a really close family. We constantly talk about staying close together. We have seen just in one generation how you can lose contact with your cousins, and we don't want that for our kids. Mum's always been strong on that.

On Waitangi Day 2015, Tariana was awarded the ultimate compliment from the *Marae* television programme: 'Māori of the Year'. But for her, there had never been a time when she contemplated living by any benchmark other than kaupapa Māori, upholding the aspirations that her tūpuna had left for her. As she had told the *Listener* in 2006:

> You have to have faith in the essence of who you are and do what you know will work. I think you have to cling to those dreams that you know are true and work for you as a people. I just know it works, so why would I not continue to believe in it.[28]

At times, when Tariana's faith was most put to the test, it was whānau who always restored her; who reminded her of her greater purpose. Following an ugly spate of media attention on the dispute concerning the use of family violence data between Merepeka Raukawa-Tait, Parekura Horomia and Tariana, a simple one-page fax from home lifted her spirits as only a message from home could:

> Kia kaha Tariana. Don't lose sight of the fact that the motive for your actions is to make life easier for whanau, hapu and iwi. We can't control how uninformed people will react especially when they are out to score points. Maybe the harvest from the seeds that are being sown down there will be a real Maori Party. As Niko (Tangaroa) used to say never give up hope for without hope there is no future. Hang in there taku hoa. Remember all of your whanau back here are on your side (especially when someone else is picking on you). You are precious to us all and it's only at times like this that we bother to let you know.[29]

The importance of hope is central in Tariana's life. During the course of her parliamentary life, she came across many organisations of people whose experiences moved her to tears. One such group that she fell in love with was the Kotuku Choir, a choir founded to offer troubled youth a voice. As Tariana's parliamentary days came to an end, the founder of Kōtuku, Sharon Thorburn, specifically composed a song to honour Tariana. In seeking the opportunity to sing it for her, Sharon shared her reason for doing so:

> It was Tariana who lit the hope torch in the Wellington stadium. It was Tariana who cried when she shared for a moment the transparent and vulnerable hope in the Kotuku choir youth faces as they sang the hope song ... It was Tariana, who by her life, is an inspiration for all of us and the children of Kotuku are part of her legacy to New Zealand.[30]

In this auspicious year, the 175th anniversary of the signing of Te Tiriti o Waitangi, there are many aspects of Tariana that exemplify the promises of nationhood made by our ancestors so long ago.

There is her pioneering energy and dogged determination to create the best possibilities out of difficult circumstances. Tariana and George have demonstrated their entrepreneurial flair as champions for local and regional business; founders of the Te Awa Marae Youth Trust; investors in development in health, education and employment; and a vital core of the brains trust that would establish Te Oranganui Iwi Health Authority and other related organisations.

There is the spirit of self-determination and iwi resilience that shines through the stories of Tariana's experience at Pākaitore, her role in restoring the h to Whanganui, her role in rescuing the Whanganui Iwi Law Centre, and most profoundly her involvement in the pathway to settlement of the Whanganui River Claim, the longest history of litigation in the land. On her retirement from Parliament, political blogger David Farrar commented:

> There is that vital negotiating power between iwi and the Crown which she was able to sanctify, holding true to her belief in tino rangatiratanga while operating as a distinguished and respected Minister of the Crown.
>
> Attorney General Chris Finlayson has described her as his favourite politician – 'utterly principled and a very decent woman. The Foreshore and Seabed Act is Helen Clark's legacy to New Zealand; its repeal is Tariana Turia's and I have to say that Mrs Turia is by far the greater politician'.[31]

Most of all, the passion of Dame Tariana is at its most powerful when it expresses her hopes for whānau, hapū and iwi; for people of all ethnicities and backgrounds; for our mokopuna to come. Her courage, her integrity and her relentless pursuit of social justice are the hallmark qualities of her work; they come together beautifully in the Whānau Ora approach.

Retirement is a foreign concept to someone so driven by the challenges of the every day. Announcing her damehood, the *Dominion Post* quoted Tariana:

> 'You always feel you wish you could do more,' she said. 'We never do enough, if you understand what I mean, in politics and I always felt it would be great if we could make decisions based on what was right rather than what was political'.[32]

Dame Tariana, thank you for lighting the torch of hope, for listening to your conscience, for holding true to the small still voice of courage. Yours is a legacy of passion, principles and politics. We are stronger because of your story: a story of transformation; a story that it is now time to share.

NOTES

1. Gandhi quoted in Louis Fishcer (ed.), *The Essential Gandhi: An Anthology of His Writings on His Life, Work, and Ideas*, 2002.
2. Vernon Small, 'Tariana Turia made Dame in New Year Honours', *Dominion Post*, 31 December 2014.
3. James Ihaka, 'This is for whanau, hapu and iwi, says Dame Tariana', *New Zealand Herald*, 31 December 2014.
4. Tommy Wilson, 'A new year and another new era', *Bay of Plenty Times*, 5 January 2015.
5. Rob Mitchell, 'Turia's legacy proof of honour richly deserved', *Manawatu Standard*, 31 December 2014.
6. 'Tariana Turia made a Dame in New Year Honours', *One News*, 31 December 2014.
7. Ihaka, 'This is for whanau, hapu and iwi'.
8. Sasha Borissenko, 'Outrage at "segregated nature" of powhiri', *Voxy.co.nz*, 16 July 2013: www.voxy.co.nz/politics/outrage-segregated-nature-powhiri/5/161537 (accessed 27 May 2015).
9. The Kaumātua manages the Māori component of all formal and important occasions, ceremonies and events for the Speaker and his departments, the Office of the Clerk and the Parliamentary Service.
10. 'Maori protocol warning', *Dominion Post*, 8 January 2014.
11. 'Tradition at risk in powhiri review', *Waatea News*, 10 January 2014.
12. Tariana Turia, speech to the Silver Jubilee of the Federation of Islamic Associations of New Zealand, 16 November 2005.
13. Ihaka, 'This is for whanau, hapu and iwi'.
14. Rachael Selby (ed.), *Walking the Talk: A collection of Tariana's papers*, 2005.
15. Selby, *Walking the Talk*, p. 5.
16. Ruth Berry, 'Turia's technique for beating asthma: Leave Labour', *New Zealand Herald*, 11 October 2005.
17. 'I'm a big spender, Turia says', *New Zealand Herald*, 7 August 2011.
18. Ibid.
19. 'What makes women happy?' *Dominion Post*, 2 June 2007.
20. Rawiri Taonui, 'The Power to decide', *Dominion Post*, 2 February 2007.
21. *Kōkiri Paetae* (Te Puni Kōkiri publication), 4 June 1997.
22. Mitchell, 'Turia's legacy proof of honour richly deserved'.
23. Ihaka, 'This is for whanau, hapu and iwi'.

24 Māori Party press release, 'Māori Party congratulates Tariana Turia – recipient of the 2014 WHO 'World No Tobacco Day' award', 1 June 2014. http://maoriparty.org/panui/maori-party-congratulates-tariana-turia-recipient-of-the-2014-who-world-no-tobacco-day-award/ (accessed 27 May 2015).

25 World Conference on Tobacco or Health, programme notes, 17–21 March 2015.

26 Heart Foundation press release, 'Congratulations Dame Tariana Turia', 28 January 2015: *LiveNews*: http://livenews.co.nz/2015/01/28/congratulations-dame-tariana-turia (accessed 17 February 2015).

27 *Kōkiri Paetae*, 4 June 1997.

28 Joanne Black, 'Upping the Auntie', *New Zealand Listener*, 29 July 2006, p. 26.

29 Personal fax of 24 August 2000, Rii Templeton and Ken Mair to Tariana Turia. Note that this was four years prior to the 'real' Māori Party being launched!

30 Personal email of 25 May 2014, Sharon Thorburn to Lisa Turia.

31 David Farrar, 'Farewelling Tariana', *Kiwiblog*, 30 September 2014: www.kiwiblog.co.nz/2014/09/farewelling_tariana.html (accessed 27 May 2015).

32 Small, 'This is for whanau, hapu and iwi'.

THE AUTHOR'S STORY

When I first approached George and Tariana about taking on this book, they were characteristically humble: successes were understated, achievements hurried over. I realised that writing Tariana's story was not going to be as easy as I had thought. As the tape played on and my questions became more feeble, we stumbled upon a different tack, and in essence that is how this book has evolved. Tariana and George thought it might be best to ask others what they thought; to let their stories be her story too. They suggested a dozen or so names of people that might be prepared to talk with me.

And so it came to be that I shared stories with close to forty amazing people. Whānau have always occupied the space at the core of Tariana's being. I had the privilege of talking with Aunty Julie Ranginui at her home, and Kui Piki Waretini, taking a moment to talk during the Hui Aranga. I sat in the cool serenity of Pākaitore as Uncle John Maihi transformed the empty grounds into a bustling marae through the vivid memories he shared. The beautiful Matua Whatarangi Winiata honoured me with his stories of Tariana's dad, as we talked in his office studio at Te Wananga o Raukawa.

I laughed with Tariana's brothers, Johnny Tihema, Joe and Wilson Huwyler, as we ate pikelets in the old homestead at Pūtiki. I caught up with three of her children, Pahia, Carmelle and Lisa, at our offices in Parliament, spent time with Alan and Andy at home, interviewed Ilona on the phone.

I visited Aunty Jo Maniapoto at home; she then set up a time for me to have coffee with Tariana's netball buddy, Aroha Henry. That was how it was – on another occasion, breakfast at the Jet Inn with Tariana's cousin, Linda Thompson, brought up the opportunity to share some stories from Doreen Bennett, who was in transit. One story would lead to another. Pahia told me I had to talk with Te Reo Hemi from Rātana Pā, and the brothers urged me to ring Tariana's best friend Helen Drew in Whāngārei; those two interviews gave wonderful perspectives that added so much to the story.

The river runs through this story as a key connecting thread. The river spoke through the kōrero of Che Wilson, as we sat together at Tirorangi Marae in the heartland of Ngāti Rangi. It was heard in the silences of my time with Nancy Tuaine, as we talked in the offices of Te Oranganui, and as I sat perched on a high stool in the kitchen of Ken Mair. Its influence was never far away as Aunt Reti Cribb and I chatted in the classrooms of Te Kura o Kokohuia.

The machinations of the Beehive of course were also ever-present. During the course of writing, I visited the Executive Wing to talk with Hon Bill English, and various offices in Bowen House to talk with Hon Dr Pita Sharples, Te Ururoa Flavell and Hone Harawira. I travelled to Hastings to talk with Donna Awatere-Huata and her husband, Wi; was hosted in the recently renovated villa of Rodney Hide and the inner-city apartment of Tim Barnett; and sat sipping coffee on Courtenay Place with Georgina Beyer.

The history of Tariana's contributions to health, employment and community development took me to Auckland to talk with Robert Reid in the offices of First Union and to a Ponsonby cafe to listen a while to the wise insights of Pat Snedden. I caught up with vivian Hutchinson in the library cafe in New Plymouth and with Pati Umaga at his home in Naenae, and finished up my research into that chapter of Tariana's life by talking with Peter Glensor and Don Matheson in Wellington.

The influence of Tariana Turia is felt in the lives of so many fabulous people, who all have rich stories of their own to share. I was treated to strong Danish coffee and pastries in the garden of paradise of Jens and Karen Bukholt. Marilyn and Michael Payne shared stories in the beautiful tranquillity of the Quaker Settlement in Whanganui. Dame Iritana Tawhiwhirangi had me in hysterics as she held court in her lounge, letting me in to her version of the history of the world.

Others shared their reflections through the written word. I am indebted to Rt Hon Dame Jenny Shipley, Lieutenant-Colonel Sir Harawira (Wira) Tiri Gardiner, Professor Sir Mason Durie and Hon Maryan Street for their generosity in responding without hesitation to my calls to them to be part of this project. I offered that same opportunity to Rt Hon Helen Clark, but as with Tariana's son Mark, obviously now is not the right time for that story to unfold.

But there is another story that has crept into this book, shaping the way the memories are gathered, the truths assembled, the comments selected or edited out. My own story. The story of my relationship with Tariana had its genesis in Lambton Quay, but from the outset was always about so much more. I have had the privilege of being in the company of someone who has inspired me to be a better person from the moment we first met. It has been a tale of extremes — years of sleep-deprived commitment set alongside the excitement and the passion of being part of something visionary, vibrant; a journey of transformation.

My first meeting with Tariana told me everything about a woman who would without a doubt change the lives of my own whānau in immeasurable ways. I had been on maternity leave, falling in love with my firstborn, Te Puawai. I was in no hurry to return to Te Puni Kōkiri, where I had been managing a policy team. The chief executive at that time, Dr Ngatata Love, rang and asked me if I would be interested in going into the Minister's office as her advisor.

To say I was surprised is an understatement. I was terrified. This was 1999, and the impact Tariana had made on the national scene through her involvement in Pākaitore was still uppermost in many minds. I was amused that Ngatata could even contemplate that she would want a Pākehā woman advising her on Māori Affairs matters. Things must be desperate if they had had to call me in.

I dreaded the first meeting, my anxiety levels at an all-time high. I had to bring baby with me, snuggled into her car seat, all wide-eyed and ready for the world. As with all offspring of political junkies, Parliament has had to be their playground; party politics their game.

As I held my breath, waiting for the inevitable interrogation, Tariana held baby close and asked me about her connections. Te Puawai's father, David

Kopeke, is connected to Tariana on the Mareikura line, through his father Turama Kopeke (Akapita). David's paternal grandmother, Nanny Maggie, was a sister to Koro Keru Mareikura; the maternal grandfather to my partner, Deana Wilson. Nanny Maggie and Koru Keru are the children of Kui Pare – and that is where the connection to Tariana comes in.

Writing whakapapa into words always makes connections sound cumbersome. Yet when you sit in the company of master orators, hearing the way in which they weave together generations, tracing back genealogy over centuries, it is like the most intricate tāniko patterns are being created anew, breathing life into the sense that relationships matter. That is always how it is with Tariana.

The families of Rānana and Maungārongo Marae in Ohakune are a special part of Tariana's life and have been a defining landscape for me over the last twenty years through association with Deana. It was this connection that would become the platform for my relationship with Tariana. The aunties in Ohakune were always keen to know whether I was caring for their cousin Tari. I have felt a sense of huge obligation to do right by them; to honour the faith they placed in me to protect and support their beloved relation.

At our first meeting, then, there was much to talk about, but very little of it related to my skills in policy analysis. We finished up with an agreement for a three-month trial. If it worked out, all good; if not, I would return to Te Puni Kōkiri when the time was up.

Te Puawai is now sixteen years old, and her entire life has been punctuated by the milestones of the political journey we have travelled. Our family grew with the arrival of our daughter Pisivalu in 2000 and our son, Rangipunehu, in 2009. They have all been Māori Party mascots; attending hui with me up and down the country, wearing the teeshirts and delivering pamphlets. The girls featured in the 2008 television ads; Rangipunehu starred on a billboard in the 2011 campaign. They have waved flags on street corners, and at the same time hated the fact that I have been so obsessive-compulsive about whatever it is I do.

Deana has driven miles, cooked and cared for me, provided constructive criticism on the latest headlines, irrespective of whether I wanted to hear it, and growled me for spending every waking moment on Māori Party business. My decision to work for Tariana has involved massive sacrifice from them all, not the least being the last eighteen months as I have retreated into the burrows of my study to write this book. I could never have done what I needed to do without the most amazing support from our wider family, and I will be forever grateful for just how wide and all-encompassing their love has been for me and for Aunty/Nanny Tari.

In 2015 I continue to be inspired by the vision and the challenge that I associate with Tariana. Her nephew Te Ringa Te Awhe has kept us connected; he has become a vital lifeline when our schedules are both still so crazy. Her presence in my life is constant; her opinions matter; her feedback is crucial. I am invariably challenged by her response to an email; amazed at her attention to detail, her insatiable quest for solutions. I have never met anyone who can remember the finer points of an issue in such meticulous clarity. Despite my best attempts at obfuscation, she always knows when I have taken longer than she expected to get on to it.

I have also experienced more than my fair share of withering looks as Tariana responded to advice or ideas I have presented her with. She is, after all, human. Yet she has a superhuman capacity to work. In her parliamentary career, days off were few; after a break, 'the Minister' invariably returned to work far earlier than her staff anticipated. Deadlines were tight; expectations to deliver high. It was an unyielding work ethic that my interviews uncovered had been evident in every sphere in which Tariana worked. She demands nothing less than your total commitment.

All of this may make it seem like Tariana Turia is a fierce taskmaster – the toughest boss in town – and she is. But she is also the most compassionate of women; her love for people bears no boundaries. She simply loves. She has provided a touchstone in my adult life in the way in which she expresses that love. She cares that people are looked after; manaakitanga is her middle name. Her generosity is unconditional; her largesse knows no limits. She is always prepared to go on to pōwhiri, carrying koha, or food for the table should we just drop in unexpected. She places great emphasis on knowing our place, as hosts or as guests; following the protocols no matter what culture or what setting she finds herself in.

When you travel with her, to hui after hui, you see a remarkable constancy in her behaviour. She respects the role of the mana whenua, the host of the hui. Unlike some dignitaries, she never expects a speaking slot. And if by chance she is asked to speak, her focus is on what the people of that area are doing, rather than her own achievements. Her consistency of message is something I have loved as a speech-writer. She doesn't do statistics, and is never comfortable trumpeting government gains. Her focus is invariably on how to support all our peoples to be the best that they can be.

I have been her departmental advisor, press secretary, speech-writer and, more recently, chief of staff. I have written articles for her approval; drafted correspondence; spoken up on her behalf at meetings she had to miss. At times, I would meet with groups when she was otherwise predisposed, when another meeting was taking too long, or when she had been called to an emergency on the ninth floor, or at home. There was never any uncertainty when home called – births, tangihanga, situations when whānau were in trouble, sickness, or when times were grim – Tariana would always go.

We travelled together to Rarotonga and Australia, the Chathams and Abu Dhabi, but more often than not, Aotearoa was our chosen destination. We came to rely on the expertise of VIP drivers who always knew the best routes to get us to hui on time; we went to places that don't feature on the map.

I have also been national secretary for the Māori Party, supporting Tariana in her role as co-leader. That job, unpaid and all-consuming, required me to drive her across the country, occasionally earning tickets on the way. We bunked in together at motels of all description; stopped for a sneaky dozen oysters just because we could; debated between ourselves whether we needed chocolate to pick up the energy levels. I have sung her waiata, carried her bags, tried to hustle her out of hui in order to get her to the next appointment.

And through every minute of this time, I have felt profoundly blessed to learn from her example.

Thank you for opening the doors for so many; for being prepared to walk bravely into the unknown; and for always looking around to see who else can come with you. Crossing the floor, standing up for what is right, has become a powerful metaphor for action in our story as a nation, and for that, we thank you, Tariana Turia.

REFERENCES

3 News. 2009. 'Maori Party President continues in role'. 17 October 2009.

ABC News. 2004. 'First victory for NZ's Maori Party'. 10 July 2004.

Ansley, B. 2000. 'Tariana Turia does not talk to Bruce Ansley'. *New Zealand Listener*, 16–22 September 2000, p. 12.

Armstrong, J. 2004. 'Turia the Queen of the Castle'. *New Zealand Herald*, 28 July 2004.

Armstrong, J. 2005. 'Brash's hopes were gone by lunchtime'. *New Zealand Herald*, 3 October 2005.

Armstrong, J. 2005. 'Danger lurks in minor party courting rituals'. *New Zealand Herald*, 8 October 2005.

Armstrong, J. 2005. 'One-seat change a huge difference'. *New Zealand Herald*, 2 October 2005.

Armstrong, J. 2008. 'Protecting the Maori Party is in National's interest'. *New Zealand Herald*, 15 November 2008.

Arseneau, T. 2010. '2008: National's winning strategy' in S. Levine and N. S. Roberts (eds.). *Key to Victory: The New Zealand General Election of 2008*. Wellington: Victoria University Press.

Ashton, L. 2012. 'What is it that we want?' *Anglican Taonga* Easter 2012, no. 39, pp. 10–16.

Bain, H. 1997. 'Tariana's will'. *Dominion*, 14 June 1997.

Bain, H. 2005. 'Mana will prevail over money – Turia'. *Sunday Star-Times*, 28 August 2005.

Barber, D. 1995. 'Maoris appeal to the Crown'. *Sydney Morning Herald*, 12 April 1995.

Bates, A. 1980. 'Raina Pine in conversation with Arthur Bates'. *Whanganui River Annual*, November 1980.

Berry, R. 2004. 'Maori Party victors turn their fire on Labour'. *New Zealand Herald*, 12 July 2004.

Berry, R. 2004. 'Turia taking time out in political limbo'. *New Zealand Herald*, 14 May 2004.

Berry, R. 2005 'Maori Party gets suicide warning'. *New Zealand Herald*, 11 October 2005.

Berry, R. 2005. 'Turia takes carte blanche from hui'. *New Zealand Herald*, 10 October 2005.

Berry, R. 2005. 'Turia's technique for beating asthma: Leave Labour'. *New Zealand Herald*, 11 October 2005.

Berry, R. and Tunnah, H. 2004. 'Turia quits Labour, stripped of portfolios'. *New Zealand Herald*, 1 May 2004.

Bevan-Brown, J. 2000. 'Running the Gauntlet: A Gifted Māori Learner's Journey Through Secondary School'. Paper presented to the 'Now is the Future' conference, October 2000.

Bidois, V. 1999. 'Maori Affairs brief aims for breadth'. *New Zealand Herald*, 29 December 1999.

Black, J. 2006. 'Upping the Auntie'. *New Zealand Listener*, 29 July 2006, p. 26.

Black, T. 2014. *Tariana Turia's Legacy*. Video for AttitudeLive website. http://attitudelive.com/blog/tanya-black/film-tariana-turias-legacy (accessed 20 May 2015).

Boniface, L. 2008. 'Hitting Home'. *New Zealand Listener*, 22 November 2008, pp. 50–1.

Borissenko, S. 2013. 'Outrage at "segregated nature" of powhiri'. *Voxy.co.nz*, 16 July 2013. www.voxy.co.nz/politics/outrage-segregated-nature-powhiri/5/161537 (accessed 27 May 2015).

Boston, J. 2009. 'Innovative Political Management: Multi-party Governance in New Zealand'. *Policy Quarterly*, vol. 5, issue 2, May 2009, p. 55. http://ndhadeliver.natlib.govt.nz/delivery/DeliveryManagerServlet?dps_pid=IE1251681 (accessed 17 June 2015).

Boyd, S. 'Confronting the Treaty'. *Evening Post*, 7 July 1997.

Brash, D. 2004. 'Nationhood'. Speech to the Orewa Rotary Club, 27 January 2004.

Campbell, G. 2008. 'Gordon Campbell interviews Tariana Turia'. *Scoop Independent News*, 21 April 2008. http://gordoncampbell.scoop.co.nz/2008/04/21/gordon-campbell-interviews-tariana-turia (accessed 16 February 2015).

Clark, L. 2000. 'Mother Courage'. *Grace*, September 2000, pp. 44–8.

Coddington, D. 2011. 'Dining with the leaders: Whanau focus fuels final charge'. *New Zealand Herald*, 20 November 2011.

Council for International Development. 2007. *Treaty Journeys: International Development Agencies Respond to the Treaty of Waitangi*. Auckland.

Crewdson, P. 2005. 'Clark and Turia still on a rocky road'. *New Zealand Herald*, 16 October 2005.

Crewdson, P. 2005. 'Coalition talks in chaos as Nats accuse Clark of failure'. *New Zealand Herald*, 16 October 2005.

Cullen, M. 2005. 'Two Ticks for Clio: Reflections on NZ Politics and History'. Michael King Memorial Lecture, 12 October 2005. http://beehive.govt.nz/speech/two-ticks-clio-reflections-nz-politics-and-history (accessed 13 February 2015).

Davis, A. 2009. Cited in a speech by Tariana Turia, 'Revolution of Cancer Care for Maori, Whanau', 12 August 2009, *Scoop Independent News*: http://www.scoop.co.nz/stories/PA0908/S00179/turia-revolution-of-cancer-care-for-maori-whanau.htm (accessed 17 June 2015).

Dewes, H. 2005. 'Maori to talk to Nats'. *The Press*, 20 September 2005.

Dewes, H. 2005. 'No compromise says Sharples'. *Dominion Post*, 26 September 2005.

Dewes, H. 2005. 'Suitors court Maori Party'. *Dominion Post*, 20 September 2005.

Dominion. 1995. 'Lawyer blames history for statue's beheading'. 29 July 1995.

Dominion. 1995. 'Moutoa helped in win, says Poynter'. 16 October 1995.

Dominion. 1995. 'Poynter Faces Six Challengers in Wanganui's Mayoralty Contest'. 14 September 1995.

Dominion. 1996. 'Maori oath requires law change'. 17 December 1996.

Dominion. 1997. 'Labour MP won't condemn activist'. 31 March 1997.

Dominion. 1998. 'Ngai Tahu bill ventures on with support from Labour'. 27 August 1998.

Dominion. 2000. 'Don't shoot the messenger'. 23 August 2000.

Dominion. 2000. 'Maori didn't like Gaps term anyway – Turia'. 12 December 2000.

Dominion. 2000. 'Turia stands by Holocaust remarks'. 31 August 2000.

Dominion Post. 2007. 'What makes women happy?' 2 June 2007.

Dominion Post. 2014. 'Maori protocol warning'. 8 January 2014.

Durie, M. 2000. Cited in A. Gifford (ed.) *Nga Korero o te wa: A monthly summary of Maori news and views from throughout Aotearoa*, vol. 10, no. 1231, August 2000.

Durie, M. H. 1995. 'Proceedings of a hui held at Hirangi Marae, Turangi' (1995) 25 VUWLR 109.

English, B. Press release. 2010. 'Government welcomes Whanau Ora report'. 8 April 2010. www.tpk.govt.nz/_documents/press-release-govt-welcomes-whanau-ora-report.pdf (accessed 17 February 2015).

Espiner, C. 2005. 'Green Cabinet hopes fade'. *The Press*, 11 October 2005.

Espiner, C. 2005. 'Maori Party unlikely to join coalition'. *The Press*, 4 October 2005.

Espiner, C. 2005. 'PM clears timetable for talks with minor party leaders'. *The Press*, 19 September 2005.

Evening Post. 2000. 'Turia's foster plan prejudiced – Peters'. 31 March 2000.

Evening Post. 2001. 'Closing gaps committee scrapped'. 10 February 2001.

Farrar, D. 2014. 'Farewelling Tariana'. *Kiwiblog*, 30 September 2014. www.kiwiblog.co.nz/2014/09/farewelling_tariana.html (accessed 27 May 2015).

Findlay, K. 2010. 'Grandmother of the nation'. *Mana* no. 94, pp. 12–16.

Fischer, L. (ed.) 2002. *The Essential Gandhi: An Anthology of His Writings on His Life, Work, and Ideas*. New York: Vintage Books.

Freire, P. 1970. *Pedagogy of the Oppressed*. New York: Seabury Press.

Gardiner, W. 1996. *Return to Sender: What Really Happened at the Fiscal Envelope Hui*. Auckland: Raupo.

Gee, T., Young, A. and Berry, R. 'National courts the Maori Party'. *New Zealand Herald*, 7 October 2005.

Gower, P. 2013. 'Opinion: Turia has absolutely smashed Big Tobacco'. *3news.co.nz*, 19 February 2013. www.3news.co.nz/opinion/patrick-gower/opinion-turia-has-absolutely-smashed-big-tobacco-2013021909#axzz3YmfH5ShK (accessed 30 April 2015).

Hansard. 1997. Mental Health Commission Bill, second reading, 24 July 1997.

Harawira, H. 2011. 'Crunch time for Maori grumbles'. *Sunday Star-Times*, 16 January 2011.

Harman, R. 2000. 'Clark stuck with Rowling and Lange problem: Maori MPs'. *National Business Review*, 25 August 2000.

Heart Foundation. 2014. 'Heartfelt Tributes for our Smokefree Champion'. 21 August 2014. www.heartfoundation.org.nz/news-blogs-stories/blogs/heartfelt-tributes-for-our-smokefree-champion (accessed 1 May 2015).

Heart Foundation press release. 2015. 'Congratulations Dame Tariana Turia'. 28 January 2015. http://livenews.co.nz/2015/01/28/congratulations-dame-tariana-turia/ (accessed 17 February 2015).

Hewitson, M. 2002. 'Turia talking on a tightrope'. *New Zealand Herald*, 16 March 2002.

Horwood, A. 2000. 'Dover Samuels down but not out'. *New Zealand Herald*, 15 August 2000.

Housing New Zealand. n.d. 'Kainga Whenua Loans for Individuals'. http://www.hnzc.co.nz/buying-a-house/kainga-whenua/kainga-whenua-loans-for-individuals (accessed 11 February 2015).

Hubbard, A. 1997. 'Foreign tag also fits Māori radical'. *Sunday Star-Times*, 22 June 1997.

Hubbard, A. 2005. 'Minority parties key to power'. *Sunday Star-Times*, 18 September 2005.

Humpage, L. 2002. 'Closing the Gaps: The Politics of Māori Affairs policy'. PhD thesis, Massey University.

Ihaka, J. 2014. 'This is for whanau, hapu and iwi, says Dame Tariana', *New Zealand Herald*, 31 December 2014.

Insight, Radio New Zealand, 17 September 2000.

Insight, Radio New Zealand. 2006. 'A Taranaki Holocaust?', produced by Sue Ingram and presented by Chris Wikaira, 27 April 2006.

Johnston, M. 2012. 'The women who shape New Zealand: Tariana Turia'. *New Zealand Women's Weekly*, 27 June 2012.

Jones, D. 1996. *Nga Whare Uku: the houses of earth and how to build them*. Wanganui: David Jones.

Jones, S. 2004. 'Theatre, drama and a warning'. *New Zealand Herald*, 10 May 2004.

Joyce, S. and Turia, T. Press release. 2013. 'Budget 2013: Expansion of Māori and Pasifika trades training'. 9 May 2013. *Scoop Independent News*: www.scoop.co.nz/stories/PA1305/S00157/budget-2013-expansion-of-maori-and-pasifika-trades-training.htm (accessed 17 February 2015).

Karauria, M. and Cheng, D. 2004. 'Bugging raises serious questions says Turia'. *Wanganui Chronicle*, 23 November 2004.

Kay, M. 2005. 'Brash and Turia get to grips'. *Dominion Post*, 21 September 2005.

Kay, M. 2005. 'Nats willing to dilute pledges says Turia'. *Dominion Post*, 8 October 2005.

Key, J. Press release. 2010. 'Budget 2010 – Whanau Ora launches with $134.3m'. 6 May 2010. www.beehive.govt.nz/release/budget-2010-whanau-ora-launches-1343m (accessed 17 February 2015).

Key, J. Press release. 2010. 'PM appoints Whanau Ora Minister'. 8 April 2010. www.beehive.govt.nz/release/pm-appoints-whanau-ora-minister (accessed 17 February 2015).

King, A. Press release. 2002. 'He Korowai Oranga: Maori Health Strategy Launch'. 13 November 2002. http://beehive.govt.nz/release/he-korowai-oranga-maori-health-strategy-launch (accessed 12 February 2015).

King, M. L. 1968. 'The Other America'. Speech to Grosse Point High School, 14 March 1968. www.gphistorical.org/mlk/mlkspeech/ (accessed 11 February 2015).

Kōkiri Paetae (Te Puni Kōkiri publication), 4 June 1997.

Labour Māori Caucus. Media statement. 2003. 'Customary rights to seabed and foreshore'. 24 June 2003. www.converge.org.nz/pma/title.htm (accessed 13 February 2015).

Labour Māori Caucus. Media statement. 18 August 2003. www.converge.org.nz/pma/infssub.htm (accessed 13 February 2015).

Laugesen, R. 2000. 'Outburst raises voters' suspicions'. *Sunday Star-Times*, 3 September 2000.

Leaders' debate, TV One, 22 August 2005.

List, K. 2004. 'PM's Presser: Of Hikois, Tariana Turia and Nukes'. *Scoop Independent News*, 4 May 2004. www.scoop.co.nz/stories/HL0405/S00026/pms-presser-of-hikois-tariana-turia-and-nukes.htm (accessed 13 February 2015).

Luke, P. 2000. 'Race issue haunts Govt'. *The Press*, 28 October 2000.

Luke, P. 2005. 'Will problematic alliances spawn odd bedfellows?' *The Press*, 1 October 2005.

Machiavelli, N. 1532. *The Prince*, Chapter vi, Concerninig New Principalities which Are Acquired by One's Own Arms and Ability.

MacKie, B. 1984. *An Evaluation of the Detached Youth Worker Funding Scheme*. Wellington: Department of Internal Affairs.

Main, V. 2000. 'PM rides eternal tightrope on improving lot of Maori. *Daily News*, 28 August 2000.

Main, V. 2000. 'Weak ministers make easy targets for Nats'. *Daily News*, 11 September 2000.

Mallard, T. 2004. 'We are all New Zealanders now'. Speech to the Stout Research Centre for New Zealand Studies, Victoria University of Wellington, 29 July 2004. *Scoop Independent News*: www.scoop.co.nz/stories/PA0407/S00504.htm (accessed 27 May 2015)

Mallard, T. Press release. 2004. 'Turia's comments irresponsible'. 5 November 2004. www.beehive.govt.nz/release/turia039s-comments-irresponsible (accessed 27 May 2015)

Mana. 1996/7. 'Māori political muscle at last'. Summer 1996/97, no. 14, pp. 38–39

Mana News, Radio New Zealand, 4 February 1997.

Mandela, N. 1989. Personal letter of 21 August 1989 to Rev. Frank Chikane.

Manning, S. 2004. 'Intel Sources Say SIS Investigating Maori Party'. *Scoop Independent News*, 11 November 2004. www.scoop.co.nz/stories/HL0411/S00144.htm (accessed 11 May 2015).

Māori Legal Forum. 2005. 'Understanding the implications of Article Three of the Treaty of Waitangi'. Seminar, 14–15 July 2005.

Māori Party. 2011. *Our Whānau; Our Future*, Policy Manifesto.

Māori Party media statement. 2011. 'Transformation and Poverty at the Heart of Relationship'. 11 December 2011. *Scoop Independent News*: www.scoop.co.nz/stories/PA1112/S00070/transformation-and-poverty-at-the-heart-of-relationship.htm (accessed 17 February 2015).

Māori Party press release. 2004. 'Maori Party calls on Inspector General to investigate SIS activities'. 22 November 2004. http://maoriparty.org/panui/maori-party-calls-on-inspector-general-to-investigate-sis-activities (accessed 13 February 2015).

Māori Party press release. 2005. 'Māori Party announces list'. 27 June 2005. http://maoriparty.org/panui/maori-party-announces-list (accessed 19 May 2015).

Māori Party press release. 2007. '"The Abusers have to be outed" says Turia'. 24 October 2007. http://maoriparty.org/panui/the-abusers-have-to-be-outed-says-turia/ (accessed 11 February 2015).

Māori Party press release. 2008. 'Poroporoaki: Rereamoamo Monte Ohia'. 12 June 2008. http://maoriparty.org/panui/poroporoaki-rereamoamo-monte-ohia/ (accessed 16 February 2015).

Māori Party press release. 2009. 'Co-leaders welcome wise decision from wise man'. 18 October 2009. *Scoop Independent News*: www.scoop.co.nz/stories/PA0910/S00232.htm (accessed 20 May 2015).

Māori Party press release. 2012. 'Māori Party to vote against ETS bill'. 24 October 2012.

Māori Party press release. 2013. 'Poroporoaki ki a Parekura Horomia'. 29 April 2013. *Scoop Independent News*: www.scoop.co.nz/stories/PA1304/S00552/poroporoaki-ki-a-parekura-horomia.htm (accessed 20 May 2015).

Māori Party press release. 2014. 'Māori Party Holds the Line on RMA'. 20 May 2014. http://maoriparty.org/panui/maori-party-holds-the-line-on-rma (accessed 17 February 2015).

Māori Party press release. 2014. 'Māori Party congratulates Tariana Turia – recipient of the 2014 WHO "World No Tobacco Day" award'. 1 June 2014. http://maoriparty.org/panui/maori-party-congratulates-tariana-turia-recipient-of-the-2014-who-world-no-tobacco-day-award/ (accessed 27 May 2015).

Māori Party press release. 2014. 'Poroporoaki – Morvin Te Anatipa Simon'. 14 May 2014. *Scoop Independent News*: www.scoop.co.nz/stories/PA1405/S00221/poroporoaki-morvin-te-anatipa-simon.htm (accessed 11 February 2015).

Maslin, J. 2014. 'We have not seen end of "H" issue'. *Wanganui Chronicle*, 4 December 2014.

McLean, E. 2008. 'Maori Party heads tour south'. *Otago Daily Times*, 11 June 2008.

Mihaka, D. Press release. 2004. 'Pot issue bigger than Māori Party'. 8 July 2004. *Scoop Independent News*: www.scoop.co.nz/stories/PO0407/S00078/pot-issue-bigger-than-maori-party-dun-mihaka.htm (accessed 27 May 2015)

Mikaere, A. 2004. 'Are we all New Zealanders now? A Māori response to the Pākehā quest for indigeneity'. Bruce Jesson Memorial Lecture.

Milne, J. 2004. 'Maori Party plays down Hall's role'. *Sunday Star-Times*, 16 May 2004.

Milne, J. 2004. 'Tariana still throwing stones'. *Sunday Star-Times*, 25 January 2004.

Ministerial Advisory Committee on a Maori Perspective for the Department of Social Welfare. 1988. *Puao-te-ata-tu (Day Break)*. Wellington.

Ministry of Social Development. 2006. Social Welfare Residential Care 1950–1994, Volume Two, National Institutions, Holdsworth Reports F000001599381.

Mitchell, R. 'Turia's legacy proof of honour richly deserved'. *Manawatu Standard*, 31 December 2014.

Mohi, H. *Lines in the Sand*. Documentary. 30 July 2013.

Mold, F. 'Turia facing fresh meddling accusations'. *New Zealand Herald*, 8 November 2001.

Moon, P. 1996. *The Occupation of the Moutoa Gardens*. Auckland: Auckland Institute of Technology.

Morning Report, Radio New Zealand, 26 October 2000.

Mulu, M. 2001. 'Tariana Turia, Reluctant politician'. *New Zealand Women's Weekly*, 3 December 2001.

Mutu, M. 2002. 'Maori Issues'. The contemporary Pacific. Spring 2002. Polynesia in Review; Issues and Events, 1 July to 30 June 2001.

National Party. 2014. National Policy Statement for Freshwater Management. 4 July 2014.

National Party press release. 2010. 'Community Max programme expanded'. 24 June 2010. www.beehive.govt.nz/release/community-max-programme-expanded (accessed 17 February 2015).

New Zealand First press release. 2004. 'New Cabinet – can't dance, can't sing'. 24 February 2004. *Scoop Independent News*: www.scoop.co.nz/stories/PA0402/S00412.htm (accessed 13 February 2015).

New Zealand Herald. 1995. 'MP critical of "pussy-footing" over Moutoa'. 28 March 1995.

New Zealand Herald. 1995. 'Occupiers say they will quit Moutoa'. 16 May 1995.

New Zealand Herald. 2000. 'What Tariana Turia said – in full'. 31 August 2000.

New Zealand Herald. 2004. 'Government survives confidence vote as pressure mounts'. 4 May 2004.

New Zealand Herald. 2004. 'Maōri should believe in themselves, says Turia'. 1 October 2004.

New Zealand Herald. 2004. 'Tariana Turia to resign and force byelection'. 30 April 2004.

New Zealand Herald. 2004. 'Turia assures party future'. 17 July 2004.

New Zealand Herald. 2011. 'Election 2011: Labour holds on in Dunedin South stronghold'. 27 November 2011.

New Zealand Herald. 2011. 'I'm a big spender, Turia says'. 7 August 2011.

New Zealand Herald. 2013. 'Parekura's last promise: "I'll rest now"'. 30 April 2013.

New Zealand Herald. 2014. 'Tariana Turia hits out at Labour'. 20 April 2014.

New Zealand Listener. 2011. 'The Best Advice I ever got'. 1 January 2011.

Ngā Kōrero o te wā: A monthly summary of Maori news and views from throughout Aotearoa, 31 August 2000, vol. 10, no. 12.

Norquay, K. 2004. 'Maori Party complains to Waitangi Tribunal over polling booths'. *New Zealand Herald*, 8 July 2004.

Northern Advocate. 2000. 'Whanau way worked for me'. 11 November 2000.

Nuri, R. 2004. 'Arrival of the new Māori Party'. *Te Karaka*, Kōanga 2004, pp. 4–15.

NZ City News. 2003. 'Government denies Māori fair trial – Jackson'. 24 June 2003.

NZPA. 2008. 'Maori Party Heading for a deal with National'. 14 November 2008.

NZPA. 2015. 'Whanau Ora Taskforce Report Goes To Government'. 11 February 2015.

Office of Treaty Settlements. 1994. *Crown Proposals for the Settlement of Treaty of Waitangi Claims*. Wellington.

One News. 2009. 'Wanganui's favourite son returns'. 29 October 2009.

One News. 2013. 'Widespread opposition to RMA changes'. 10 August 2013.

One News. 2014. 'Tariana Turia made a Dame in New Year Honours'. 31 December 2014.

One News. 2014. 'Turia reveals plan for MPs to desert Labour'. 2 March 2014.

Pacific Advisory Group. 2012. *Nga Vaka o Kāiga Tapu: A Pacific Conceptual Framework to address family violence in New Zealand*. Wellington.

Paki, K. 2004. 'Tilting the Tables'. *Tū Mai* no. 55, July 2004, pp. 18–20.

Paki, K. 2005. 'The Pākehā within the Māori Party'. *Tū Mai* no. 67, August 2005, pp. 24–5.

Pearson, J. Dr 2014. Personal tribute made on behalf of Cancer Society.

Perry, B. 2014. *Household Incomes in New Zealand: trends in indicators of inequality and hardship 1982 to 2013*. Wellington: Ministry of Social Development.

Peters, G. 2000. 'Bridging the most difficult gap of all'. *Evening Post*, 2 September 2000.

Pettinger, T. 2008. 'Biography of Eva Peron'. Oxford, www.biographyonline.net, 1 January 2008 (accessed 17 June 2015).

Piper, D. 2014. 'Health inequalities unacceptable says Turia'. *NZ Doctor*, 9 May 2014.

Pomare, E., Tutengaehe, H., Ramsden, I., Hight, M., Pearce, N. and Ormsby, V. 1991. *He mate huango: Maori asthma review: Report to the Minister of Maori Affairs from the review team to consider asthma among Maori people*. Wellington.

Potaka-Dewes, E. 2007. 'The Birth of the Māori Party'. *Mai i Rangiātea*, vol. 3, January 2007, pp. 5–18.

Prebble, R. 2005. 'Richard Prebble: It's looking good for Brash'. *New Zealand Herald*, 16 October 2005.

Q+A, 4 April 2010.

Q+A, 18 October 2009.

Radiolive. 2013. 'Tariana Turia on the Soundtrack to Your Life'. 3 February 2013.

Radio New Zealand. 2014. 'Tariana Turia – Walking in two worlds'. Interview with Colin Peacock, 6 February 2014.

Radio New Zealand/One News. 2005. 'Departing MP wants Greens in Cabinet'. 27 September 2005.

Rickard, T. E. 2013. Cited in Tariana Turia, speech to the International Council of Thirteen Indigenous Grandmothers Conference, Te Wānanga o Aotearoa, Gisborne, 5 December 2013.

Robertson, C. 1999. 'It's Been Hard'. *Mana* February–March 1999, pp. 42–3.

Ross, T. 2005. 'Four-seat sweep sets up Maori Party to make a difference'. *Sunday Star-Times*, 18 September 2005.

Roughan, J. 2005. 'Dunne just may be key to the healing'. *New Zealand Herald*, 24 September 2005.

Ryall, T. Press release. 2001. 'The case for Turia to go builds'. 7 November 2001.

Selby, R. A. 2005. *Walking the Talk: A collection of Tariana's papers*. Ōtaki: Te Wānanga o Raukawa.

Shepheard, N. 2004. 'Fierce Kuia: profile of New Zealand Member of Parliament Tariana Turia'. *North and South*, February 2004.

Sinclair, K. 2002. *Prophetic Histories: The People of the Māramatanga*. Wellington: Bridget Williams Books.

Small, V. 2005. 'Labour set to govern by itself'. *The Press*, 10 October 2005.

Small, V. 2014. 'Tariana Turia made Dame in New Year Honours'. *Dominion Post*, 31 December 2014.

Smart, M. J. G. and Bates, A. P. 1972. *The Wanganui Story*. Wanganui: Wanganui Newspapers Ltd.

Smith, K. 2010. 'Māori Party' in R. Miller (ed.), *New Zealand Government and Politics*. Melbourne: Oxford University Press, pp. 509–21.

Snedden, P. 2005. *Pakeha and the Treaty: Why it's our Treaty too*. Auckland: Random.

Solomon, M. 2004. 'Ngai Tahu head writes open letter against foreshore bill'. *Stuff.co.nz*, 5 May 2004.

Stokes, J. 2004. 'Maori Party gathering steam'. *New Zealand Herald*, 25 May 2004.

Stokes, J. 2005. 'Tamihere rounds on Maori Party and "separatists"'. *New Zealand Herald*, 20 January 2005.

Stowell, L. 2005. 'A life of service to Maori'. *Wanganui Chronicle*, 31 August 2005.

Stowell, L. 2012. 'Crusader leaves a lesson in respect'. *Wanganui Chronicle*, 22 December 2012.

Stuff.co.nz. 2003. 'Academic criticises lack of foreshore consultation'. 30 June 2003. http://homepages.ihug.co.nz/~sai/maorisea.html (accessed 17 June 2015).

Stuff.co.nz. 2003. 'Iwi considers legal action on seabed decision'. 24 June 2003. http://homepages.ihug.co.nz/~sai/maorisea.html (accessed 17 June 2015).

Sunday Star-Times. 2002. 'Turia intervenes in more inmate cases'. 3 February 2002.

Sunday Star-Times. 2005. 'Claim to test seabed and foreshore law'. 27 March 2005.

Tangatawhenua.com. 2010. 'Pem Bird new Māori Party President'. 1 November 2010. http://news.tangatawhenua.com/2010/11/pem-bird-new-maori-party-president-waatea-news (accessed 20 May 2015).

Taonui, R. 2007. 'The Power to decide'. *Dominion Post*, 2 February 2007.

Taonui, R. 2013. 'Sharples key to Maori Party's run'. *New Zealand Herald*, 30 January 2013.

Taranaki Daily News. 2009. 'Leaders' presence "healing"'. 8 October 2009

Te Ahi Kaa, Radio New Zealand, 28 September 2014.

Te Ao Hou. 1958. 'Taku Piki Amokura: My Beloved One, recorded by Matutaera'. *Te Ao Hou* no. 23, July 1958.

Te Ao Hou. 1959. 'Haere ki o Koutou Tipuna'. *Te Ao Hou* no. 28, September 1959.

Te Heuheu, H. 1995. Opening address to Hīrangi Hui, 29 January 1995.

Te Tapikitanga o Apa. 2014. 'Pitopito Korero. A tribute to Aunty Tari'. Te Rūnanga o Ngāti Apa. Hōngongoi, no. 17, pp. 17–18.

Te Waonui a te Manu Korihi, Radio New Zealand, 10 August 2014.

Te Waonui a te Manu Korihi, Radio New Zealand, 15 October 2014.

Templeton, R. and Mair, K. 2000. Personal facsimile of 24 August 2000 to Tariana Turia.

The Press. 2000. 'Maori Separatism'. 18 September 2000.

The Press. 2005. 'Winston's game'. 15 October 2005.

Tino Rangatiratanga eMail Rōpū. 2004. 'Politics expert says Turia could succeed where others failed'. 4 May 2004. https://groups.yahoo.com/neo/groups/tino-rangatiratanga/conversations/messages/19057 (accessed 13 February 2015).

Trotter, C. 2005. 'Turia should add a third grave'. *Taranaki Daily News*, 14 October 2005.

Tuaiwa Hautai Kereopa whānau. 1998. 'Tuaiwa Hautai Kereopa Rickard 1925–1997' in *Nga Puna Roimata; He maumaharatanga ki a Tuaiwa*. Independent State of Whāingaroa, Aotearoa: Tuaiwa Hautai Kereopa whānau and Moko Productions.

Tū Mai. 2004. 'Will Labour loyalty be lost to new player?' *Tū Mai* no. 54, June 2004, p. 31.

Tunnah, H. 2004. 'Turia blames PM for "humiliating" car ride'. *New Zealand Herald*, 3 May 2004.

Turia, T. 1995. Submission to WAI 167; A055 Waitangi Tribunal.

Turia, T. 1997. Press release. 'Maori Development Commissioners found, but will they find any new information'. 8 August 1997.

Turia, T. 1997. Press release. 'Maori unemployment heading sky high'. 5 August 1997.

Turia, T. 1997. Speech to Māori Women's Welfare League, 13 July 1997.

Turia, T. 2000. 'Closing the Gaps'. Speech to Masters Class in Development Studies, Te Pua Wānanga ki te Ao, 7 June 2000.

Turia, T. 2000. Press release. 'Family violence'. 19 May 2000. www.beehive.govt.nz/node/7481 (accessed 6 May 2015).

Turia, T. 2000. Press release. 'Maori nominations for HHS Boards'. 10 March 2000. *Scoop Independent News*: www.scoop.co.nz/stories/PA0003/S00166/maori-nominations-for-hhs-boards.htm (accessed 12 February 2015).

Turia, T. 2000. Press release. 'Officials race views sickening – Minister'. 25 March 2000.

Turia, T. 2000. Press release. 'Shifting attitudes, changing ways'. 16 February 2000. www.beehive.govt.nz/node/6869 (accessed 12 February 2015).

Turia, T. 2000. Press release. 'Turia – when I made my speech', 5 September 2000.

Turia, T. 2000. 'Te Puawaitanga o te tohu, Māori social work paradigms'. Speech to Te Kaiāwhina Ahumahi, 23 March 2000.

Turia, T. 2000. Waitangi Day. Press release.

Turia, T. 2000. 'Women's speaking rights'. 17 January 2000. Press release.

Turia, T. 2002. 'Whānau Aid and Rehabilitation'. Speech to the Prisoners Aid and Rehabilitation Society, Christchurch Branch, 26 August 2002.

Turia, T. 2003. Beehive Chat. 25 August 2003.

Turia, T. 2003. Beehive Chat. 22 September 2003.

Turia, T. 2003. 'Building Communities'. Speech to national conference of Community Organisations Grants Scheme and Department of Internal Affairs staff, 29 July 2003.

Turia, T. 2003. Press release. 'Poroporoaki to Irihapeti Merenia Ramsden'. 7 April 2003. http://beehive.govt.nz/release/poroporoaki-irihapeti-merenia-ramsden (accessed 12 February 2015).

Turia, T. 2003. Press release. 'Turia launches Māori literacy report'. 8 September 2003. www.beehive.govt.nz/node/17765 (accessed 12 February 2015).

Turia, T. 2003. 'Sharing and partnership: the value of Māori custom'. Speech to Te Ngawari Hauora, 15 December 2003.

Turia, T. 2003. 'Taranaki Gates and Rabbit-Proof Fences: Identity, culture and mental well-being'. Speech to Earth, Sky and Number 8 wire, the 29th international conference of Australian and New Zealand College of Mental Health Nurses, Rotorua Convention Centre, 10 September 2003.

Turia, T. 2004. 1st National Sexual and Reproductive Health Conference, Wainuiomata Marae, Wellington, 1 November 2004.

Turia, T. 2004. Beehive Chat. 2 February 2004.

Turia, T. 2004. Beehive Chat. 16 February 2004.

Turia, T. 2004. Beehive Chat. 1 March 2004.
Turia, T. 2004. Beehive Chat. 15 March 2004.
Turia, T. 2004. Beehive Chat. 26 April 2004.
Turia, T. 2004. Beehive Chat. 17 May 2004.
Turia, T. 2004. 'Leadership is more than anatomy'. Speech to the Te Tau Ihu Māori Women's Leadership Awards, 30 June 2004.
Turia, T. 2004. 'Letter to my Dad'. *New Zealand Listener*, 4 September 2004, p. 21.
Turia, T. 2004. 'Now we've got to stand up for ourselves'. Interview. 22 September 2004.
Turia, T. 2004. Press release. 'Statement'. 27 April 2004. www.beehive.govt.nz/release/statement (accessed 13 February 2015).
Turia, T. 2004. Press release. 'Tariana Turia not intending to resign'. 14 March 2004. http://beehive.govt.nz/release/tariana-turia-not-intending-resign (accessed 13 February 2015).
Turia, T. 2004. Speech at Kanihi Pā, Okaiawa, 8 July 2004.
Turia, T. 2004. Speech to launch Māori Party, 10 July 2004.
Turia, T. 2004. 'Nga Hau o te Ao Hurihuri: Winds of change in the political scene, confronting perceptions and harnessing potential'. Speech to Te Waka Āwhina o Aotearoa national conference, 25 November 2004.
Turia, T. 2004. 'Whānau violence and Whānau development'. Speech to the National Collective of Independent Women's Refuge Hui, Parihaka, Taranaki. 13 January 2004. http://beehive.govt.nz/speech/whanau-violence-and-whanau-development (accessed 19 March 2015).
Turia, T. 2005. Speech to the Silver Jubilee of the Federation of Islamic Associations of New Zealand, 16 November 2005.
Turia, T. 2006. Beehive Chat, 13 October 2006.
Turia, T. 2006. 'Being a Māori Woman in Politics'. Speech to Mana Wahine course, School of Māori Business Studies, Canterbury University, 22 September 2006. *Scoop Independent News*: www.scoop.co.nz/stories/PA0609/S00509.htm (accessed 11 February 2015).
Turia, T. 2006. Speech to ACT Party Conference, Wellington, 13 April 2006.
Turia, T. 2008. Press release. 'Tariana Turia sees early impacts of global capital crisis'. 27 November 2008. www.beehive.govt.nz/release/tariana-turia-sees-early-impacts-global-capital-crisis (accessed 16 February 2015).
Turia, T. 2009. 'Impact on Communities: Managing the Downturn together'. Speech to Community and Voluntary Sector Workshop, Ministry of Social Development, 25 February 2009. www.beehive.govt.nz/speech/impact-communities-managing-downturn-together (accessed 16 February 2015).

Turia, T. 2009. Press release. 'Rural youth to benefit from full wage subsidy'. 2 August 2009. www.beehive.govt.nz/release/rural-youth-benefit-full-wage-subsidy (accessed 17 February 2015).

Turia, T. 2009. Press release. 'Whānau Ora Taskforce announced'. 14 June 2009. www.beehive.govt.nz/release/whanau-ora-taskforce-announced (accessed 16 February 2015).

Turia, T. 2009. Speech to the Central Cancer Network Hui, 27 February 2009.

Turia, T. 2010. 'Handover of Report from the Taskforce on Whānau-Centred Initiatives'. Speech, 11 February 2010. www.beehive.govt.nz/speech/handover-report-taskforce-whanau-centred-initiatives (accessed 11 February 2015).

Turia, T. 2010. Press release. 'Turia delighted with funding for life-saving weight-loss operations'. 28 October 2010. www.beehive.govt.nz/release/turia-delighted-funding-life-saving-weight-loss-operations (accessed 27 May 2015).

Turia, T. 2010. Speech to the New Zealand Family and Foster Care Federation, 18 June 2010. *Scoop Independent News*: http://www.scoop.co.nz/stories/PA1006/S00297/family-and-foster-care-federations-conference.htm (accessed 27 May 2015).

Turia, T. 2010. Speech to Whakamīharo Lindauer Online Launch, 3 July 2010.

Turia, T. 2010. Speech to Māori Law Students Association, 29 September 2010.

Turia, T. 2011. Beehive Chat, 28 June 2011.

Turia, T. 2011. 'Computers in Homes Graduation'. Speech to Tui Glen School, 29 June 2011.

Turia, T. 2011. 'Focus must be on helping the families'. *Dominion Post*, 6 April 2011.

Turia, T. 2011. 'Life after Hone'. *Tū Mai* no. 117, April 2011, pp. 22–3.

Turia, T. 2011. Press release. 'Funding for family violence focuses on frontline services'. 1 April 2011. *Scoop Independent News*: www.scoop.co.nz/stories/PA1104/S00057/funding-for-family-violence-focuses-on-frontline-services.htm (accessed 17 February 2015).

Turia, T. 2011. Speech to the Community Economic Development Conference, 20 April 2011.

Turia, T. 2011. 'Whānau Ora'. Speech to Chapman Tripp Breakfast Series, 29 March 2011.

Turia, T. 2012. 'Pūao te Atatū: A New Dawn Breaks'. Speech to Whānau Ora Planning Workshop, Te Raukura – Te Wharewaka o Pōneke, Wellington 22 November 2012. www.beehive.govt.nz/speech/p%C5%ABao-te-atat%C5%AB-new-dawn-breaks-%E2%80%94-wh%C4%81nau-ora-planning-workshop (accessed 13 February 2015).

Turia, T. 2013. Beehive Chat, 3 September 2013.

Turia, T. 2014. 'All about equity: Building political will for rheumatic fever prevention in New Zealand'. Speech to the World Congress of Cardiology, 6 May 2014.

Turia, T. 2014. 'Maori Wellbeing – Defying the Oxymoron'. Speech to 'Our People, Our Future, Our Way': Te Aho Summit, 14 October 2014.

Turia, T. 2014. Speech to the Inaugural Māori and Indigenous Suicide Prevention Symposium, 10 February 2014. http://maoriparty.org/panui/speech-minister-turia-inaugural-maori-indigenous-suicide-prevention-symposium (accessed 11 February 2015).

Turia. T. 2014. Speech to the New Zealand Business and Parliament Trust, 18 June 2014.

Turia, T. 2014. 'Wharekauri, Rēkohu, Chatham Islands Health and Social Needs'. Speech to Chatham Islands community, Community Hall, 14 January 2014.

Tuwhare, H. 1994. *Deep River Talk: Collected Poems*. Hawaii: University of Hawaii Press.

Venter, N. 2000. 'Pull your head in, refuge boss told.' *Dominion*, 19 August 2000.

tvnz.co.nz. 2014. 'Turia reveals plan for MPs to desert Labour'. 2 March 2014. http://tvnz.co.nz/politics-news/turia-reveals-plan-mps-desert-labour-5855565 (accessed 11 May 2015).

Waatea News. 2014. 'Tradition at risk in powhiri review'. 10 January 2014.

Wanganui Chronicle. 1995. 'Poor Poll no surprise to Maori themselves'. *Wanganui Chronicle Extra*, a special election supplement, 16 October 1995, p. 2.

Wanganui Chronicle. 1997. 'Pushing on with project but under our terms'. 1 September 1997.

Wanganui Chronicle. 2003. 'Nit-pickers are sharpening their knives again'. 21 July 2003, p. 6.

'Wanganui woman had key role at hui'. September 1995.

Watkins, T. 2004. 'Clark stands firm'. *The Press*, 6 May 2004.

Watkins, T. 2004. 'Horomia gives nod to seabed plan'. *Dominion Post*, 31 March 2004.

Watkins, T. 2005. 'Seating arrangements at Mad Hatter's tea party'. *Dominion Post*, 17 October 2005, edition 2, p. 7.

Watkins, T. and Wood, S. 2009. 'Compromise over "h" in Wanganui'. *Dominion Post*, 18 December 2009.

Wellwood, E. 2001. 'Closing the gaps in a different guise', *The Press*, 20 August 2001.

West, R. 2005. 'Taranaki Maori Party backers seek strong, independent voice'. *Taranaki Daily News*, 6 October 2005.

Williams, J. (Chairperson on behalf of the Tribunal). 2004. *Interim Report of Waitangi Tribunal on the Te Tai Hauauru By-election*. 8 July 2004.

Wilson, P. 2008. 'John Key's Brave New World'. *Guide2*, 16 November 2008. www.guide2.co.nz/politics/blogs/john-keys-brave-new-world/75/3921 (accessed 16 February 2015).

Wilson, T. 2014. 'A new year and another new era'. *Bay of Plenty Times*, 5 January 2015.

Winiata, W. 2004. Claim of Professor Whatarangi Winiata to the Registrar, Waitangi Tribunal, 6 July 2004. WAI 1177.

Winiata, W. 2007. 'The Tikanga Māori House: The influential independent Māori voice'. Speech to Maōri Party AGM, 26 October 2007.

Winiata, W. 2008. 'Māori Innovation and Reconciliation'. Paper presented to Ngā Pae o te Māramatanga Conference, 8–11 June 2008.

World Conference on Tobacco or Health. 2015. Programme notes. 17–21 March 2015.

Young, A. 1999. 'Maori MP calls for oath to the treaty'. *New Zealand Herald*, 21 December 1999.

Young, A. 2000. 'Holocaust apology puts minister in hot water', *New Zealand Herald*, 6 September 2000.

Young, A. 2000. 'Radical Minister Turia has space to beat her drum'. *New Zealand Herald*, 26 August 2000.

Young, A. 2004. 'Mallard fuels race debate'. *New Zealand Herald*, 30 July 2004.

Young, A. 2005. 'Interview: Tariana Turia, Maori Party co-leader'. *New Zealand Herald*, 6 August 2005.

Young, A. 2009. 'Call for Harawira to quit will cause Maori Party chaos'. *Otago Daily Times*, 14 November 2009.

Young. A. 2014. ' Parliament loses "a decent woman" as Tariana Turia departs'. *New Zealand Herald*, 30 September 2014.

Young, D. 1998. *Woven by Water: Histories from the Whanganui River*. Wellington: Huia.

Other sources

New Zealand Parliamentary Debates (*Hansard*).

New Zealand Parliament Questions for Oral Answer (*Hansard*).

Oral history interviews between Tariana Turia and Taina Tangaere McGregor on 20 July 2004, 22 September 2004, 10 November 2004, 25 May 2006 and 21 July 2010, Oral History Political Diary project, Oral History Collection, Alexander Turnbull Library.

Personal interviews

Awatere-Huata, Donna. Interview 14 February 2014. Home, Bridge Pa.

Barnett, Tim. Interview 24 April 2014. Home, Wellington.

Beyer, Georgina. Interview 27 March 2014. St James Theatre, Wellington

Bukholt, Jens and Karen. Interview 27 February 2014. Home, Whanganui.

Cribb, Retihiamatikei. Interview 9 March 2014. Te Kura o Kokohuia, Whanganui.

Davis, Ilona. Telephone interview 30 June 2014.

Drew, Helen. Telephone interview 18 June 2014.
English, Hon Bill. Interview 8 May 2014. Parliament Buildings, Wellington.
Flavell, Hon Te Ururoa. Interview 26 June 2014. Parliament Buildings, Wellington.
Gardiner, Lieutenant Colonel Sir Harawira. Written statement provided on 26 April 2014.
Glensor, Peter. Interview 26 January 2014. Korokoro, Wellington.
Harawira, Hone. Interview 12 June 2014. Parliament Buildings, Wellington.
Hemi, Te Reo. Telephone interview 11 June 2014.
Henry, Aroha. Interview 27 February 2014. Cafe, Whanganui.
Hide, Hon Rodney. Interview 28 February 2014. Home, Wellington.
Hutchinson, vivian. Interview 23 March 2014. New Plymouth Library, Taranaki.
Huwyler, Joe. Interview 10 June 2014. Home, Pūtiki, Whanganui.
Huwyler, Wilson. Interview 10 June 2014. Home, Pūtiki, Whanganui.
Maihi, John. Interview 26 February 2014. Pākaitore, Whanganui.
Mair, Ken. Interview 10 June 2014. Home, Whanganui.
Maniapoto, Josephine. Interview 26 February 2014. Home, Whanganui.
Matheson, Don. Interview 26 January 2014. Parliament Buildings, Wellington.
Nicholson, Iwi. Interview 22 June 2014. Ngāti Wehiwehi Marae, Manakau.
Payne, Marilyn and Michael. Interview 26 February 2014. Quaker Settlement, Whanganui.
Ranginui, Julie. Interview 10 June 2014. Home, Whanganui.
Reid, Robert. Interview 22 January 2014. First Union Buildings, Auckland.
Sharples, Hon Sir Pita. Interview 1 July 2014. Parliament Buildings, Wellington.
Shipley, Rt Hon Dame Jenny. Written statement provided on 25 June 2014.
Snedden, Pat. Interview 22 January 2014. Ponsonby cafe, Auckland.
Tawaroa, Sister Makareta. Interview 27 February 2014. Kaiwhaiki, Whanganui.
Tawhiwhirangi, Dame Iritana. Interview 25 January 2014. Home, Porirua.
Thompson, Linda. Interview 9 March 2014. Jet Inn Hotel, Auckland.
Tihema, Johnny. Interview 10 June 2014. Home, Pūtiki, Whanganui.
Tuaine, Nancy. Interview 26 March 2014. Te Oranganui, Whanganui.
Turia, Alan. Interview 10 June 2014. Home, Kaitoke, Whanganui.
Turia, Lisa. Interview 24 April 2014. Bowen House, Parliament Buildings.
Turia, Pahia. Interview 28 June 2014. Parliament Buildings, Wellington.
Turia, Hon Dame Tariana. Interview 27 April 2014.
Umaga, Pati. Interview 26 March 2014. Home, Naenae.
Waretini, Piki. Interview 20 April 2014. St Patricks College, Silverstream, Wellington.
Wilson, Carmelle. Interview 14 July 2014. Leader's Unit office, Wellington.
Wilson, Che. Interview 16 May 2014. Tirorangi Marae, Karioi, Ohakune.
Winiata, Professor Whatarangi. Interview 5 February 2014. Te Wānanga o Raukawa, Ōtaki.

INDEX

Bold type indicates photographs between the numbered pages

A

ACT party 243, 245, 262, 335, 407
Akapita, Joan 9, 11, 19
Alliance Party 205–206, 210
America's Cup incident 230
Amohia, Hikaia 11, 167
Anderton, Jim 403, 407
Anglican Church 75
Aroha Ngāi Tatou 205
August, Dennis 168–169
Awatere-Huata, Donna 123, 208, 221, 243, 245, 348, 367, 402

B

Ballance, John 168–169, 173, 175, 191
Baragwanath, Minnie 489
Bargh, Dr Maria 339
Barker, Rick 229
Barnett, Tim 226, 228–230, 322–324, 332, 509

Bates, Bill Teupo 57
Bennett, Henry 189, 200
Bennett, Manu 16
Bennett, Paula 242, 485
Bennett, Rii 41
Bennett family 41
Beyer, Georgina 226, 242, 248–249, 321, 333, 367, 513
Bidois, Ana **470–471**
Bird, Pem 458, 510
Bishop, Tangiwai 22
Black, Awanuiarangi 418, 459
Bloxham, Jenny 246
Bolger, Jim 137, 166, 188
Boshier, Judge Peter 512
Bourke, Betty 151–152
Bowler, Michael 122, 140
Brash, Don 316–319, 348, 381–383, 397, 399–402
Braybrooke, Geoff 208, 246
Broughton, Ruka 95
Bukholt, Jens 68–69

563

Bukholt, Karen 68
Burton, Mark 229
by-election, 2004: 2, 360–365

C

Carr, Dr Julia 154
Carroll, Sir James 204
Carter, Chris 210
Carter, David 246, 524
Catholic Church 131
Chapman, Dickson 114
Chatham Islands 484–485, 512
Clark, Helen 191, 232, 269–271, 280, 523–524
   support for TT 207–210, 226–228, 246, 248, 270, 277, 283–284, 286–287, 509
   relationship fractures 290–294, 322–328, 330–331, 338–339, 403, 406
   in foreshore and seabed controversy 309, 317, 321–328, 330–331, 337–339, 400
   after 2005 election 400, 403, 406–407
Closing the Gaps policies 270–275, 278, 280–281, 382
Comer, Leith 472
Community Volunteers Programme 69
Computers in Homes project 432
Consedine, Robert 387–389
Cooper, Dame Whina 7
Cooper, Rob 131, 469, 472, 510
Corbett, Ernest 222
Cotterill, Joseph 30
Court of Appeal 308–309, 311, 349
Coutts, John 115

Creech, Wyatt 234
Cribb, Piri 155–156
Cribb, Retihiamatikei 17, 115, 136, 207
Cribb, Robert (Boy) **310–311**
Crichton-Hill, Yvonne 512
Cullen, Michael 208, 273, 291, 400
   in foreshore and seabed controversy 311, 313, 321, 324, 333–334, 348
cultural safety programme 239–241
Curnow, Father John 129–130, 135, 141, 172, 465
Curtis, Toby 358

D

Daahya, Randhir 199–200
Dalziel, Lianne **182–183**
Davis, Ilona 62, 70, 79–81
Declaration of Independence 215
decolonisation 179, 197, 217
Democratic Party 205
Department of Child, Youth and Family Services 260
Department of Corrections 281–286
Department of Internal Affairs 110
Department of Māori Affairs 115–118
Department of Social Welfare 69, 127–128, 274
Dickson, Brian 332, 385
disability issues 280, 305, 431–432, 463, 486–489, 511–512
domestic violence 82–85, 275–277, 302–304, 482–484
Drew, Helen 40, 47, 59–60
Dunne, Peter 407
Durie, Sir Mason 196, 293, 469–472, **470–471**, 510
Dyson, Ruth 278

E

Earp, Ria 116
Edmonds, Chelsea 461
Edwards, Claude 392
Elder, Jack 208
election 1996: 204, 210–211
election 1999: 247–248
election 2002: 300
election 2005: 386–394, 398
   post-election negotiations 397–408
election 2008: 418–423
election 2011: 459
Emissions Trading Scheme (ETS) 455–457
Employment Network 139–141
English, Bill 158, 162, 236, 268, 310, 327, 335–336, 420–423, 425, 472, 475–476, 515
Evans, Ripeka 116, 208

F

Field, Taito Phillip 227, 412
Finlayson, Chris 261, 264, 436, 515
Fitzsimon, Anne 387
Flavell, Dean 110
Flavell, Te Ururoa 2, 170–171, 369, 377, 379–380, 386, 398, 412, **406–407**, 418, 434, 457, 459, **470–471**, 476–477, 489, 509
foreshore and seabed legislation 2, 12, 308–341, 345–350, 379, 381, 391–392, 512–513
   revisited 400, 404, 407, **406–407**, 427–428; see also Marine and Coastal Area (Takutai Moana) Act

Fortuin, Gregory 290, 326
Fox, Derek 205, 418, 420
Fox, Marama **470–471**, 489
Fraser, Peter 29–30
Freire, Paulo 129, 132, 135

G

Gardiner, Wira 116–118, 177, 189–191, 467–468
Garrett, David 262–263
Genesis Energy 191
Glavish, Naida 418, 489, 510
Glensor, Peter 154–155, 159, 161–162, 184–185
Goff, Phil 270
goods and services tax (GST) 478–479
Gosche, Carol 226
Graham, Doug 215–216
Grant, John 128
Green, Ripeka 149, 155
Green Party 205, 403, 406–407, 411
Greensill, Angeline 206, 386, **406–407**, 418
Grennell, Di 469
Grennell, Linda 469
Grey, George 172
Grey Power 390

H

Haami, Piripi 175, 318
Hague, Kevin 264
Haitana, Makere 22
Halkyard-Harawira, Hilda 207–208
Hall, Donna 348, 359–360
Hapuka, Naomi 46
Harawira, Hilda 380

Harawira, Hone 2, 206, 220–221, 262–263, 329, 369, 380, 386, 398–399, 402, **406–407**, 412–413, 418, 510
  and 2008 pact with National 424, 426
  resignation 447–452, 455, 457–458
Harawira, Titewhai 358, 389, 524
Haremata-Crawford, Georgina 418
Harre, Dr John 387
Harre, Laila 210
Harvey, Bob 288
Haumihi kapa haka club 67–69
Hawea, Rua 43, 48, 51–52, 152
Hawea, Tom 48
Hawke, Grant 418
Hawke, Joe 221
Hawkins, George 208
He Korowai Oranga: Māori Health Strategy 302, 305–306
health (public) 147–163, 278–280, 302, 305–306, 445, 481, 505
  see also tobacco reform
Health Care Aotearoa 159–162, 184–185
Hehir, Gerard 363
Hemi, Te Oranga (Auntie Girlie) 112
Hemi, Te Reo 111, 114, 118–119
Hemi, Tracey 113
Henare, Manuka 131, 185
Henare, Tau 233
Henry, Aroha 65–66
Heron, Justice 189
Hewitt, Rob 420
Hide, Rodney 264–265, 335, 407
Higgins, Te Ripowai 304
Hight, Makere 148
hikoi, 2004: 2, **310–311**, 323–324, 334, 337, 344–348, 379–380

Hingston, Heta 510
Hipango, Harete 113, 116
Hipango, Hori 21
Hipango, Huia 132, 149, 155
Hirangi hui 196–198, 217
Hobson, William 170
Holdsworth School 69–70
Holland, Sid 30
'holocaust' controversy 239, 286–295
Holyoake, Sir Keith 20–21, 30–31
Horomia, Parekura 156, 226, 248, 269, 275, 277, 289, **310–311**, 358, 365, 381, 400, 409, 508
  death 446–447
  in foreshore and seabed controversy 321–322, 332, 334, 348
Hubbard, Norm 20
Hughes, Darren 509
Hughes, Peter 472
Hui Tamata 1984: 115–116, 122
Huirua, Matt 149–150
Hunia, Pahia (Uncle Frosty) 36, 48–49, 177, 213, 464
Hunia, Takimoana (Doug) Kawana 40, 48
Hunia-Hawea, Paeroa (Aunty Pae) 27, 39–40, 48, **54–55**, 94, 464, 507
Hunia-Waitere, Waiharakeke (Aunty Wai) 5–6, 20, 23, 27, 33–34, 39–54, **54–55**, 56–58, 67–68, 74–75, 91, 94, 123–124, 213, 240–241, 258–259, 354, 507, 523, 528
Hunt, Jonathan 227
Hutchens, Kiwa **470–471**
Hutchinson, vivian 137–139, 143–144
Huwyler, Horo Parapera (Dan) 48, 181
Huwyler, Joe 34, 48, 50, 181
Huwyler, Takimaana (Maana) 48, 56, 58
Huwyler, Wilson 34, 43, 48, 494

I

Ihaka, Kingi 52
Irwin, Kathie 304
Iti, Keri 291
Iti, Tame 206
Iwi Community Law Centre 144–145, **182–183**
iwi leadership 474–478

J

Jack, Sir Roy 261
Jackson, June 351
Jackson, Moana **182–183**, 197, 312
James, Bobby 111
James, Dave 102
James, Rewi 113
Joe, Charles 387
Jones, Bob 254
Jones, David 93
Jones, Shane 209, 346
Joyce, Stephen 401, 486

K

Kahukiwa, Robyn 420
Kaihau, Whititera 385
Kainga Whenua housing policy 6
Kaiwai, Maggie 113
Karetu, Timoti 217
Katene, Rahui **406–407**, 418–419, 434, 459, 510
Katene, Rangimotuhia 21
Kawana Mill 19–21
Keenan, Danny 335
Key, John **406–407**, 420–421, 426, 433–434, 450, 472–473, 515
Kidd, Doug 246, 261

King, Annette 278, 305, 509, 524
Kiriona, Hokiwaewae *see* Uru Te Angina, Hokiwaewae
Kiriona, Mere Te Ma/Mere Panitua (Mary-Anne Pestell) 16–17, 20, 22
Kiriona-Marsh, Roka 92
Kirk, Judy 401
kōhanga reo 111
Kopu, Alamein 205, 221
Kotuku Choir 534
Kuka, Tell 387
Kumeroa, Frances (Francie) 62, 81, 85–88, 465
kura kaupapa Māori 132–134

L

Laban, Luamanuvao Winnie 413
Labour Party
    caucus 226–232, 242, 244, 270, 277–279
    Māori caucus 226, 247–249, 279, 289, 310–312, 321–322, 324, 332–334, 347–348
    TT's entry to 206–210, 221
land, importance of 2, 5–8, 139, 166, 168–170, 316–317, 379
    customary land *see* foreshore and seabed legislation
Land March, 1975: 7, 12n1
Latimer, Sir Graham 359
law centre 144–145
Leahy, Helen 410, **470–471**
Lee, Sandra 31, 188, 204–206, 221, 242, 244–246
Leeks, Dr Selwyn 237–238
Lindauer portraits 98–100
literacy 110, 304–305, 474
Lomax, Hapi 318

Love, Morrie 387
Luxton, John 188

M

MACCESS 112, 115–119, 122
Mackey, Moana 242
Maea, Billy 389
Maharey, Steve 280, 291
Mahuta, Nanaia 208, 221, 228, 242, 248, 264, 300, 324, 347, 409
Mahuta, Lady Raiha 263–264
Maihi, John 130–131, 156–157, 158–159, 177–178, 187–188, 199, 209, **406–407**
Mair, Ken 127, 171–175, 178–181, **182–183**, 189, 191, 199–200, 206, 209, 300, 318, 337, 400, 402
Malcolm, Dr Laurence 154, 157
Mallard, Trevor 278, 291, 382–384
Malosi, Judge Ida 512
MANA 115–118, 122
Mana Māori 205–206, 300, 370, 382
Mana Motuhake 95, 188, 204–206, 209, 370
Mana Tangata 134
Mana Wahine 205
Maniapoto, Jo 60–61, 122–124, 129, 139–140
Māori Congress 196
Māori Land Court 308–309
Māori MPs 27–32, 204–205, 221–223, 247, 277, 358, 367–368, 381
    see also Labour Party/Māori caucus; Māori seats
Māori Party **406–407, 470–471**
    formation 2, 347–348, 350–373
    growth 375–382, 386–391

in negotiations after 2005 election 397–408
in 2005-2008 Parliament 408–413
in 2008 election 418–423
coalition with National 105–107, 420–436, 448, 456, 467–468, 475–480
Māori seats 29, 31–32, 247, 428
    abolition/entrenchment issues 319, 399, 402, 404, 427
    voting in 210–211, 300, 398, 423
Māori Women's Welfare League 196
Mapp, Wayne 316–317
Māramatanga 9–10
Mareikura, Roana (Biddy) 20–21
Mareikura, Hori Enoka 9–10
Mareikura, Koro Paul 19
Mareikura, Matiu Marino 11
Marine and Coastal Area (Takutai Moana) Act 434–436
Mariu, Geoff 156
Mariu, Bishop Max 315
Mark, Ron 221
Marlborough District Council 308, 313
Marshall, Russell 100, 134
Marumaru, Rangipouri 22
Matahiwi 19–21
Mataki, Tau Bruce 459
Matheson, Dr Don 154, 157, 161
Matthews, Gray 176
Matthews, Hector 418
Mauri Pacific 205, 382
McCarten, Matt 338, 351, 356, 360, 377
McClay, Roger 275
McKenzie, Sharon 207
McKernan, Stephen 472

McWilliam, Peter 19
mental health services 235–238
Metekingi-Mato, Dardanella **182–183**
Meurant, Ross 188
Mihaka, Dun 363–364
Mikaere, Ani 288, 383
Ministry of Māori Economic and Social Development 269
Mitchell, John 312
Mitchell, Paul 200
mixed member proportional (MMP) system 204, 247, 328, 504–505
Mokomoko pardon 476
Montijo, Robert 35–37, 49
Moore, Mike 230–232
Morgan, Tukoroirangi 360
Morison, D.L.B. 4
Moses, Marie 127, 129, **182–183**
Moutua Gardens *see* Pākaitore reoccupation
Mutu, Margaret 197, 289

N

Nathan, Benjamin 230
National Party 318–319, 381
 and Māori Party 392–393, 397–407, **406–407**, 467–468, 475–480
netball 65–67
New Labour Party 205
New Zealand Company 170
New Zealand First 210–211, 247, 382, 400, 405, 407–408
New Zealand Māori Council 196, 359
Ngā Iwi Morehu 205
Ngā Paerangi 131, 176
Ngā Poutama 19, 21
Ngā Wairiki 6, 90
Ngāi Tahu 391

Ngapaki, Te Urumanao 27
Ngata, Sir Apirana 204
Ngāti Apa 6, 18, 90, 176
Ngāti Poutama 18
Ngāti Tūwharetoa 18
Nicholson, Iwi 352–353
Nicholson, Rangingangana 33
Nikorima, Taika 21
Northey, Richard 210

O

Ohia, Monte 386, **406–407**, 418–419
Okeroa, Mahara 248, 332, 334
Omana, Tiaki 30
Ormsby, Vera 148
Orzecki, Richard 418

P

Pākaitore reoccupation 3, 165–166, 169–194, **182–183**, 216–217
Paki, Bessie **406–407**
Paki, Sam 110
Palmer, Matthew 312
Panitua, Te Ma 16–17, 18–20
Panoho, Amokura 418
Parata, Hekia 513–514
Parewanui 9–10
Parihaka 180
Paton, Kat **470–471**
Paul, Te Orohi 418
Pauro, Te Manawanui a Tohu Kakahi (Nanny Nui) 11, 157, **406–407**
Payne, Marilyn 45, 67–70, 179–180, 182–185
Payne, Michael 41, 67–68, 182–185
Pearse, Neil 148
Peeti, Te Kuia 129

Peita, Josie 418
Penetito, Bob 102
Penetito, Cathy 124
Penetito, Wally 304
Penn, Anna 240
Pereira, Tino 484, 512
Pestell, Mere Te Ma (Mary-Anne)
 see Kiriona, Mere Te Ma
Pestell, Richard 16–17, 18–21
Pestell, Richard (Billy) 20
Pestell, Te Po Moetu (Elizabeth)
 see Uru Te Angina, Te Po Moetu
Peters, Winston 221, 348, 358, 381, 382, 406, 407, 439
Pettis, Jill 31, **182–183**, 207, 210, 221, 228, 242
Philip-Barbara, Glenis 387
Phillips, Wiki 58
Pine, Raina 19–20
Piripi, Haami 191
Pitman, Mereana 206, 418
Pivac, Jacqui 260
Poananga, Atareta 386, 406, **406–407**
police 126, 128, 180–181
Pomare, Eru 148
Pomare, Sir Maui 204
Pongia, Brendon 489
Porou, Tina 459
Potter, Helen 410
Pouwhare, Robert 207
Power, Simon 526–527
Poynter, Chas 171–172, 174, 199–200, **310–311**
Prasad, Rajen 279–280
Prebble, Richard 116, 348, 407
Public Health and Disability Act 2000: 280

Puketapu, Brendon 190–191
Puohotaua, Kelly 49

Q

Quakers 182–184

R

racism 61–62, 113, 157, 168, 184, 253–265, 301, 318–319, 349
Raihania, Na 459
Ramsden, Irihapeti 148, 239, 508
Rangihau, John 254
Rangihuna-Vliestra, Shelly **470–471**
Ranginui, Julie 12, 61, 173, 464
Rangitāhuahua 90–100, 110
Rata, Matiu 95, 204–205, 215, 223, 254, 507
Rātana, Dennis 87, 126, 128, 152–153
Rātana, Ginny 113
Rātana, Haami Tokouru 22, 27–29, 215, 507
Rātana, Iriaka 22, 27, 29–31, 33, 34, 37, **54–55**, 215, 221–222, 236, 242, 507
Rātana, Matiu 27, 29–31, 215, 507
Rātana, Raniera Te Aohou 29
Rātana, Rosie **182–183**
Rātana, Tahupōtiki Wiremu 8–10, 17, 22, 26–28, 148, 215, 337, 507
Rātana Church 29, 42–43, 95
Rātana Pā 7, 10, 27, 37, 98, 148, 222, 271, 330–331, 529
Rauhina, Paringatai 101, 112
Raukawa 33
Raukawa-Tait, Merepeka 275
Raurangi, Kataraina (Bumpsy) 152–153
Reedy, Amster 420

Index

Reeves, Sir Paul 185
Reid, Robert 96, 135–136, 139–141
Reid, Susan 304
Renee, Hilda 129
Rennie, Hapeta (Uncle Hop) 100–101
Reriti-Crofts, Aroha 387
Resource Management Act 477–478
Rickard, Eva 168–169, 186, 205–206, 209, 243–244
Rikiriki, Mere 8–10, 532
Ririnui, Mita 248, 289, 322, 332, 334, 348
Roberts, Bob 35–36
Robinson, Miss (teacher) 46–47
Robson, Matt 210, 283–285
Rowan, John 168, 189
Ruakere, Tony 387
Rurawhe, Mihi 127, **182–183**
Rurawhe, Piri 489
Ruruku Whakatupua 192
Ryall, Tony 8, 282–284

S

Samuels, Dover 221, 248–249, 269–270, 289, 321–322, 334, 409
Savage, Michael Joseph 337, 507
Security Intelligence Service (SIS) 385–386
Selby, Mereana 304
Sharples, Dr Pita 2, 398–403, **406–407**, 407, 412, 418, 428, 434, 450, 459, **470–471**, 494–495, 509
  in formation of Māori Party 353, 358, 360, 369, 377, 386
  impressions of TT 354–355, 379
Shelford, Tapihana (Dobby) 102, 113, 221–222

Shipley, Jenny 292, 504–506
Shortland, Waihoroi 459
Simon, Morvin Te Anapita 50, 52, 176, 461
Simpson, Heather 325, 400
Sio, Peseta Betty 512
Sisters of St Joseph 131, 465
Smallman, Rehua 332
Smith, Kaapua 459
Smith, Lil 155
Smith, Mike 232, 326
Snedden, Pat 160, 174, 294–295, 336–337
Snively, Suzanne 469
Solomon, Mark 391
Spain, William 170
Springbok Tour 1981: 123–125
Stavenhagen, Rodolfo 392, 408
Street, Maryan 207–208, 226, 509
Stubbs, Richard 442
Sutton, Jim 232
Swain, Paul 139–140, 227
Sykes, Annette 197, 232, 337
Szazy, Mira 208

T

Tahuparae, Rangitihi Rangiwaiata 11, 176, 508
Taiaroa, Sir Archie 11, 156–157, 308, **310–311**, 325–329, 507–508
Taipana, Bubs 304
Takarangi, Rangi Tamou 46
Tamehana, Bessie 59
Tamehana, Harry 59
Tamehana, Raymond 59
Tamihere, John 226, 248–249, 279, 321, 334, 358, 381, 384–385

Tangaroa, Niko 159, 173, 179–180,
    182–183, 189
Tapiata, John 148
Tapsell, Peter 188, 198, 215, 222–223
Taumata Hauora 158
Tawaroa, Sister Makareta 43–44, 122,
    126, 129–131, 133–135, 139, 157,
    172, 233–234, 510
Tawhiri, Taitoko 150, 152
Tāwhiwhirangi, Dame Iritana 90,
    418, 420
Te Ahi Kaa 175
Te Ahura o te Rangi *see* Te Wunu
    Rangiwerohia
Te Awa Tupua 192
Te Awa Youth Trust 70, 110–119, 122,
    137, 465
Te Aweawe, Hunga 33
Te Aweawe Larkin, Manawaroa 33
Te Aweawe, Mihiterina (Lena) Larkin
    17, 22, 25–26, 33, 40, 215, 507
Te Aweawe, Rangingangana (Ngana) 33
Te Aweawe, Tariuha Manawaroa (Dad;
    Charlie) 6, 23, 25–26, 32–35, 37,
    54–55, 215, 352, 507
te Heuheu, Georgina 221, 242, 401
te Heuheu, Sir Hepi 196, 198
Te Hunga o Te Rangi *see* Te Wunu,
    Hamiora
Te Ira Tangata 205
Te Kāwai Ora 304–305
Te Korimako Māori Health Committee
    149, 157
Te Korowai Aroha 303
Te Moana, Whare 148
Te Nana-Williams, Charmeyne 489
Te Ora, Linda 78
Te Oranganui 148, 154–162, 185,
    182–183

Te Patu, Mana 56, 58
Te Patu, Melody 112
Te Patu, Moki 52, 94
Te Puea Herangi, Princess 31
Te Puni Kōkiri 98, 189–191, 269
te reo Māori 24, 30, 41, 98, 100–102,
    113, 132, 217, 234, 354–355
    in Parliament 368–369
Te Ringa Atawhai 149
Te Tai Hauāuru 300, 360–365, 376, 398
Te Tauri, Koro Wiremu 49
Te Tawharau 205, 382
Te Waipuna 155, 156
Te Waipuna o te Awa 157
Te Wana 162
Te Wānanga o Aotearoa 406
Te Whiti O Rongomai 180
Te Wunu, Hamiora (Te Hunga o Te
    Rangi) 16, 18
Te Wunu, Makere 16, 18
Te Wunu Rangiwerohia (Te Ahura o te
    Rangi) 18
teenage pregnancy controversy 383–384
Thompson, Linda 149–156, 162
Thompson, Matthew 285
Thompson, Mere Panitua 22
Thompson, Pip 86–87
Thorburn, Sharon 519, 534
Tibble, Waho 366
Tiehutia Te Waka Te Kōhanga Reo 111
Tihema, Johnny 34, 48
Tihu, Koro Titi 4–5, 11
tikanga 32, 41, 135, 161, 217, 282,
    315, 349–352, 393, 410–411, 487,
    524–526
Tipae, Aperahama 19
Tipene, Solomon 458–459
Tirakatene, Rino Senior 206–207
Tirikatene, Eruera 30–31

Index

Tirikatene-Sullivan, Whetu 31, 207, 210–211, 215, 222, 242
tobacco reform 77–78, 103–107, 434, **470–471**, 504–505, 531–532
Tohu Kakahi 180
Tomoana, Ngahiwi 387
Treaty of Waitangi/Tiriti o Waitangi 6, 26–27, 169, 204, 302, 383, 417–419, 427
  breaches of 320, 337
  changing views of 131–132, 136, 138, 505–506
  settlements and fiscal envelope 166–167, 175–178, 196, 230
  Treaty implementation 160–162, 278–280, 336, 424, 456, 477
  in TT's speeches and oath as MP 215–216, 220, 300–301, 349, 368–369
Tuaine, Nancy 111–112, 114, 155–156, 173, 179, 181–182, 186, 268, 325, 469, 472, **470–471**, 489
Tunua, Pikiora Girlie 113
Turei, Metiria 242, 348, 367
Turia, Alan George Kawana **54–55**, 58, 62, 75, 81, 85–87, 92, 101, 465–466, 494–498, 503, 532–533
Turia, George 51–52, **54–55**, 55–70, 78, 82, 140–141, **310–311**, **406–407**, 534–535
  exchanges with Tariana 123–125, 130, 258, 287
  in health care 154–155, 157
  marae restoration 90–93, 98
  support for Tariana 187, 192–193, 285, 440, 465, 496, 500–502
  in Te Awa Youth Trust 110, 112–113, 115, 118
  in Whanganui Regional Development Board 122–123, 153, 157
Turia, Lisa Te Aroha 36–37, **54–55**, 62, 76, 84, 86–87, **310–311**, 444, **470–471**
Turia, Mark Teina Charles **54–55**, 62, 75–79, 86, 92, 98, 168–169, 494, 503
Turia, Mere 60–61
Turia, Pahia Simon Anthony 51–52, 62, 85–87, 96, 101–102, **310–311**
  quoted 75–76, 79, 85–86, 97, 102, 124–125, 169, 178, 182, 192–193, 223, 255, 276, 326, 329–330, 494, 496–497
Turia, Piata **54-55,** 238–239, 394, 440–442, 444, 500, 508
Turia, Rita 62–63, 464
Turia, Tariana **54–55**, **182–183**, **310–311**, **406–407**, **470–471**
  childhood 2, 16, 23–35, 40–44
  whakapapa 16–22; birth father 17, 35–37
  teenage years 44–49, 56–58
  marriage **54–55 ,** 56–62
  as mother and grandmother **54–55**, 62–65, 73–88, 493–498
  character 47, 117, 126–127, 156, 231–232, 268, 278, 299, 449–450, 467–468, 526–527, 532, 543–544
  ill-health 440–446, 527
  influences 2–3, 8–12, 23, 26–32, 39–40, 45–47, 129–136, 141–143, 177, 351–353, 507
  leadership 173, 177–178, 185–186, 352–354, 425, 489–490, 504–506
  religion 74–75
  election to Parliament, 1996: 203–214

first term in Parliament 213–238, 245–247
as Associate Minister, 1999-2002: 103–107, 259–260, 268–295, **310–311**
as Minister, 2002-2004: 300–306
resignation from Labour and seat 327–332
in formation of Māori Party 350–358, 365–367, 376–377, **406–407**
in 2005-2008 Parliament 408–409
as Minister, 2008-14: 428–434, 445, 470, 472–474, 479–489, 504–505
relationship with National Party 236, 399–405, 467–468
valedictory speech in Parliament 506–516
awards 107, 522–523, 526, 530–531, 533
reflections 500–503
Tutengaehe, Hohua 148, 240

U

Umaga, Pati 114–115, 489, 511
Uncle Frosty *see* Hunia, Pahia (Uncle Frosty)
United Future 405, 407, 477–478
United Nations committee and rapporteur 391–392, 408
Unwin, Judge Bill 258
Upton, Simon 288
urban-based Māori 249, 279
Uru Te Angina, Hokiwaewae (Nan) 16–18, 22, 24–25, 27, 507
Uru Te Angina, Lizzie 22
Uru Te Angina, Mohi Toahiko 22
Uru Te Angina, Rangimatapu 22

Uru Te Angina, Ripeka 22, 26–27, 215
Uru Te Angina, Te Aroha (Dorsey) 2, 25, 27, 36, 37–38, 49, 91–92, 96–97, 103–105
see also Wilson, Te Aroha
Uru Te Angina, Te Po Moetu (Elizabeth) 16–17, 19, 22
Uru Te Angina Wunu, Hamiora Tukotahi (Sam Woon) 16, 18, 22, 26–27, 215

V

Vercoe, Bishop Whakahuihui 42
von Dadelszen, Judge Paul 512

W

Waaka, Te Kuru 198
Waitai, Naomi 360
Waitai, Rana 212
Waitangi Tribunal 204, 320, 362–363
Waitere, Kawana Hunia Piripi 40–41, 45, 51, 431–432
Waitere, Piripi (Uncle Ted) 33–34, 40, 50
Waitere, Waiharakeke (Aunty Wai) *see* Hunia-Waitere, Waiharakeke
Wakefield, E.J. 170
Wakeman, Peter 363–364
Walker, Harry 366, 410
Walsh-Tapiata, Wheturangi 459
Walters, Waireti 153
Waretini, Kui Piki 43–44
Wetere, Koro 148, 215, 222–223
Whai Oranga 127–128, 153–154, **182–183**
Whakarake, Kahukiwi 4
Whakatōhea 391–392

Whanaruru, Ina 176
Whānau Ora 3, 74, 82–83, 155–156, 418–419, 422, 426, 460–474, **470–471**, 479, 505, 522
Whangaehu 6, **54–55**, 59, 89–100
Whanganui Boys College 255
Whanganui City Council 170–172
Whanganui Community Foundation 98
Whanganui District Council 133, 188–189, 191, 199–200, 257
Whanganui District Health Board 149–152, 157
Whanganui Girls College 45–47
Whanganui Māori Women's Group 131
Whanganui Regional Development Board 122–123, 127, 132, 134–135, 137, 140–142, 144, 148, 153–154, 156–157
Whanganui River 11, 18–21, 191–192
   Treaty claim 4–5, 167–168, 175–176
Whanganui Rotary Club 258–259
Whanganui spelling issue 256–257
Whiu, Te Atarangi **470–471**
Wi Rutene, Simon 387
Wikaira, Rachel 304
Wilks, Angela **182–183**

Williams, Mike 326
Wilson, Anthony 49, 80
Wilson, Carmelle 62, 80–81, 86, 95–96
Wilson, Che 19, 75, 211–212, 346
Wilson, Margaret 278, 309–311
Wilson, Te Aroha (Dorsey) 22
   see also Uru Te Angina, Te Aroha
Winiata, Whatarangi 43, 74, 351–362 *passim*, 377–378, 387, 390–391, 398–400, 409–410, 413, 421, 448–450, 454–455 **470–471**, 510
Women's Refuge 275
Woon, Patu 22
Woon, Sam *see* Uru Te Angina Wunu, Hamiora Tukotahi
Woon, Tariana *see* Turia, Tariana

Y

Yates, Bronwyn 304, 387, 418
Young, Robert 98
Young Māori Party 204
Yusingco, Fernando 135, 141, 157, 350–351